MARTIN LUTHER
Selections From His Writings

JOHN DILLENBERGER, president of the Graduate Theological Union in Berkeley, taught at Princeton University, Columbia University (where he took his Ph.D. degree in 1948), Harvard University, and Drew University. His previous writing includes *God Hidden and Revealed*, *Protestant Christianity* (with Claude Welch), and *Protestant Thought and Natural Science*.

MARTIN LUTHER

Selections From His Writings

Edited and with an Introduction by

JOHN DILLENBERGER

ANCHOR BOOKS
A DIVISION OF RANDOM HOUSE, INC.
NEW YORK

All rights reserved under International and Pan-American Copyright Conventions. Published in the United States by Anchor Books, a division of Random House, Inc., New York, and simultaneously in Canada by Random House of Canada Limited, Toronto. Originally published in the United States by Anchor Books.

Anchor Books and colophon are registered trademarks of Random House, Inc.

ACKNOWLEDGMENTS

The editor is grateful to the officials of the Muhlenberg Press, Butterworth Press, Fleming Il, Revell Company, and James Clarke and Co., Ltd., for granting permission to use selections from their texts in this volume. The precise text and its location in each instance have been indicated in a footnote at the beginning of every selection.

This book is also available in a hardbound edition from Quadrangle Books, Inc.

Library of Congress Catalog Card Number 61-9503

ISBN 0-385-09876-6

www.anchorbooks.com

Printed in the United States of America

CONTENTS

IV

V

A NOTE
TO THE READER

The selections in this volume are intended for the general reader. They are meant for individuals interested in gaining a picture of the essential insights of Luther and of his enduring significance on the basis of a direct, even if limited, acquaintance with his writings. With this in mind, the selections have been made with a concern for variety in form and content. Hence, expository and polemical treatises, Biblical commentaries, sermons, and theses have been included. Moreover, an attempt has been made to cover the major subjects on which he wrote. At the same time, the general order of arrangement is such that his central, positive ideas are given in the early documents. In this way, the reader will have the core of Luther's thought before him as he examines its implications for specific problems or sees it in contrast to previous or subsequent developments in his thought.

The selections, as will be noted from the Table of Contents, have been arranged in general groupings of allied subject matter. In most instances, later works precede earlier ones. In sections I and II this order appeared to be the best path into the heart of Luther's central conceptions. In sections III and IV it was felt that it would be more advantageous to read the later and generally more positive and less polemical works first. Such an order can in fact help in the understanding of the more polemical writing. Section V is in the form of an Appendix. This is because this material does not directly or necessarily imply a Reformation conception of the Church. It is a debated question whether or not Luther had come to his new understanding of the Gospel at this time. It is incontrovertible that neither the new understanding nor its implications are explicitly present. For the reader who wishes to read the selections in chronological order, the dates have been provided in the Table of Contents.

Brief introductory notes have been provided for each selection. The footnotes and Biblical references are largely those of the translators and editors of the respective volumes from which the materials are taken. But they have frequently been condensed and, wherever possible, they have been eliminated entirely because of considerations of space. Brackets—[ ]—indicate editorial comments and additions throughout.

For the reader who wishes an account of the life of Luther in his context and a delineation of his Reformation ideas as a whole, either as a preface to reading or as a sequel, an Introduction has been provided.

It is of interest to note that, although Luther lived at the beginning of the sixteenth century, his writings have never been published in their entirety. The definitive Weimar edition, begun in Germany in 1883, will be completed by approximately 1970 and will include fifty-seven volumes of his writings, twelve volumes of his work on the German Bible, eleven volumes of letters, and six volumes of the Table-Talk, the latter being material taken down by students and others at Luther's table. The first extensive English edition is now in process of publication: a fifty-five-volume edition produced jointly by the Muhlenberg Press and the Concordia Publishing House. Each year at least a dozen major books appear on Luther, as well as approximately fifty articles and a not insignificant number of pamphlets. In addition, nearly all German Protestant theologians, and not infrequently their American colleagues, feel impelled to comment extensively upon Luther in the course of their own theological exposition.

J. D.

AN INTRODUCTION
TO MARTIN LUTHER

It would be as wrong to attribute the breakup of the medieval world and its consequent course to the genius of Luther as it would be to interpret Luther himself as just a product of the forces then bringing a new world into being. The corporate world of Christendom, once exhibited in church, state, and culture alike, was being undermined as the result of a variety of factors. Such divergent movements as mysticism, with its emphasis upon the direct encounter with the divine, and nominalism, with its stress upon the concrete and discrete, inadvertently challenged the hierarchical and corporate claims of the Church. Humanists, with the enthusiasm of their new discoveries in the field of classical learning, favored the culture of Greece and Rome rather than the studied subtleties of the scholastic theologians. The empire itself was beset with the self-consciousness of rising ethnic and national feelings. The consequence was that the demands of empire frequently had to be adjusted to the aggressive demands of such new groups, which, in German lands, were usually represented by princes and nobles. In the social context, the feudal system was challenged by the rise of a middle class interested in trade and commerce. Small towns became urban centers, and there was a new feeling of independence from the feudal lords. Peasants dissatisfied with their lot were ready to revolt, and did so in the period of the Reformation. The travels of Columbus and Magellan, the new ideas of Copernicus, and above all the spread of information through the printing press exposed new horizons of knowledge not heretofore available.

Surely, without those forces, Luther would only have been another martyr. Sometimes men supported him because they believed in the rightness of his cause and his convictions concerning the Gospel. Sometimes men supported him because he seemed to belong to the new age and helped to weld new patterns of social cohesion. Not infrequently Luther himself was bewildered by the new world he encountered, and his instincts in such moments were conservative.

While he helped to give form and direction to many of the new patterns, a good deal of the subsequent direction of the Reformation and its impact upon history were out of his hands.

Fundamentally, the significance of Luther must be seen in the religious understanding which he forged. That came not through the new cultural forces but through the insights which Luther won in the struggle to understand Scripture. These insights became decisive in forging an understanding of the Gospel which necessitated a break from the medieval church. That such a break could occur was made possible by the nonreligious developments previously mentioned. But these developments in no sense explain the faith which informed the Reformation development. Luther the man and the time were matched in a manner seldom seen in history. In the late Middle Ages, the Church had consolidated its power and defined the expression of its claims to power. But at the same time new currents of life and thought had risen, all of them potentially explosive. Many of these forces were given new form and power through Luther's reformation insights.

This has not always been clearly understood. We have at our disposal today a more adequate and extensive body of knowledge of Luther and his period than has ever existed since his lifetime. For the most part, too, we have been able to separate the man as he was from the legends which have grown up around him, and this has cleared the ground for a more realistic appreciation of his contribution to theological thought. This does not mean that Luther is now thought to be beyond criticism. Karl Barth has said, for example, that the German people suffered from "Martin Luther's error on the relation between Law and Gospel, between the temporal and the spiritual order and power," and that Hitlerism was the "evil dream of a German pagan who first became Christianized in a Lutheran form."[1] But Barth, like other interpreters, has seen in Luther a man who saw the nature and ramifications of faith with a clarity seldom witnessed in history.

Some current criticism of Luther is overly doctrinaire. The earlier Roman Catholic polemic has largely subsided as a result of the responsible work of scholars like Joseph Lortz.[2] Over-doctrinaire comment now comes from the psychological and psychiatric interpreters.[3] There is no question but that much about Luther, seen in isolation from the rest of the man, borders on the pathological. But many men who exhibit pathological traits nevertheless see depths and dimensions of existence and of faith which are denied to others. To see such men only in psychological terms is to misunderstand them.

Luther was a robust spirit who had many facets to his being. Sensitive to the complexity of issues and problems, he was yet impatient. Aware of the important differences made by nuances of thought, he nevertheless rejected the subtlety of the Scholastic theologians. He was given to zest and enthusiasm, and he had a healthy sense of the incongruous; but he was also merciless in his attacks on others and not seldom vulgar in his demeanor. Like many great men, he was pushed from issue to issue, and one wonders how he found the strength to carry through. Practically nothing which Luther did could be planned or anticipated. Once his direction was clear, he met problem after problem as they arose, resolutely making decisions profoundly affecting the developing new shape of Western history.

[1] Karl Barth, *This Christian Cause* (New York: Macmillan, 1941), no pagination.

[2] Joseph Lortz, *Die Reformation in Deutschland*, I and II (Freiburg, 1939–40).

[3] See, for instance, Erik H. Erikson, *Young Man Luther* (New York: W. W. Norton & Co., 1958). This is a well-meaning book, but there is too much of the "clinician's judgment" and not enough substance from Luther, hence the doctrinaire designation. More instructive, though not to be accepted uncritically with reference to the sources, is the chapter on Luther in Norman O. Brown, *Life Against Death* (Middletown, Conn.: Wesleyan University Press, 1959).

I. *The Making of the Reformer*

Luther's early development took place within the limitations of conventional medieval education and ecclesiastical life. Born in 1483 of Hans Luther, a peasant who had turned to the copper-mining industry and become prosperous, and Margarete Ziegler, daughter of a family of some social standing, Martin Luther spent his early years in the city of Mansfield, located in the heart of the mining district in Thuringia. But we know little for certain about these years. Luther's reflections in his old age indicate a rather oppressive and stern atmosphere pervading the early years at home and at school. In any case, from his fourteenth year on, Luther was mostly away from home. After a year in the Latin School of the Brethren of the Common Life in Magdeburg, and from three to four years at school in Eisenach—the ancestral area to which he had been sent by his parents—Luther matriculated at the University of Erfurt in 1501. In 1502 he received his bachelor's degree and in 1505 the Master of Arts. Although Luther had entered the university at the age of eighteen—several years older than the average age in those days—he completed these university degrees in the minimum time permitted and took his Master's at the earliest allowable age of twenty-two.

Soon thereafter Luther began his studies with the Faculty of Law at Erfurt, in preparation for the respected and prosperous legal career which his father so desired for him. Returning to Erfurt from a visit to his family in July of the same year, he encountered a violent thunderstorm. When a bolt of lightning knocked him to the ground and nearly took his life, Luther cried to the patron saint of the miners of his youth: "St. Anne, help! I will become a monk!" Approximately two weeks later, in obedience to his vow, he entered the Augustinian monastery in Erfurt.

Surely this dramatic event is not understandable by itself. There is too much evidence that Luther had long been exercised by religious questions. Moreover, his own education had accentuated rather than diminished his interest and concern. Extremely sensitive to the problem of how one could become worthy to receive the grace of God rather than the

damning consequences of His righteousness, Luther was prepared for the decision to take what was accepted as the higher
path of becoming a monk. Being a monk was a matter of special
status and safety as well as of responsibility in the mediation
of grace. While the thunderstorm precipitated the decision to
become a monk, the possibility of that course of action was
surely part and parcel of Luther's natural and educational
equipment. In the monastery, like others before him from the
University of Erfurt, Luther strove to acquire that holiness on
the basis of which he could stand before God and reflect His
purposes and will in the world.

The first two years in the monastery were apparently tradi-
tional enough. They were marked only by Luther's serious attempt to follow the prescribed way and to do even more than
was required. Two years later we find Luther saying his first
Mass, with the usual anxiety attendant upon those who for
the first time celebrated the holy mysteries. Luther's father
and a number of fellow townsmen were present for this event
and the subsequent celebration. Though Hans Luther had at
first opposed the entrance of his son into the monastery, in the
interim he had become reconciled to Martin's destiny. But
Luther, pressing for his father's full approval on this occasion,
only precipitated the latter's haunting declaration: "God grant
it was not an apparition of the Devil." Luther was, however,
more disappointed than troubled by his father's outburst. We
must look elsewhere for the source of Luther's developing
anxieties.

We must recall the problem which plagued Luther before
he entered the monastery, namely, how one could stand in
holiness before a righteous, demanding God. This problem tormented him no less when a monk—that is, when exercising the
very vocation which was the epitome of man's relation to God.
To understand Luther's difficulty, we must have before us a
picture of the thought and practices of the medieval Catholic
Church. Fundamental to its understanding was the belief in
grace as an objective reality given in the celebration of the
sacraments. Through the sacraments man was presented as
blameless and acceptable in the sight of God. From birth to
death, from baptism to extreme unction, there were sacraments
for all the occasions and problems of man's existence; God's

grace was freely available. In order to receive such riches, only one condition was to be met, namely, to confess one's sins, exhibiting thereby a minimal worthiness for the reception of grace. What could be more reasonable than that!

With an acute sensitivity hardly reasonable, Luther discerned a telling difficulty in trying to live in terms of this outlook. Could one be sure that one confessed all one's sins? In attempting to find that certainty, Luther frequently made confession of his sins. His fellow monks were not only annoyed by the frequency with which they were sought out as confessors without regard to time or place but also by the apparent triviality of the offenses he confessed. The counsel of the Superior of the monastery, Staupitz, that if Luther expected Christ to forgive him he should come with something really needing to be forgiven, such as murder or adultery, instead of the trivialities he enumerated, and that Luther should not be angry with God, because God was not angry with him, did not allay Luther's agony. For Luther, the declared views of the Church had to be taken seriously or consciously modified. They could not be subverted by fatherly advice.

Moreover, there was a further difficulty inherent in the accepted views. Even if one formally met the requirements, had the expected and demanded internal transformation of man really taken place? It was believed that man, anchored, to be sure, in God's grace, could effect a total contrition, that is, both confess his sins and maintain a proper relation to God. Difficult though it may be, it was believed that one could love God with a good deal of the spontaneity with which God loves us. Luther did not find himself so persuaded. Neither in his conduct nor in his attitude did Luther find ground for hope. Instead he saw despair, and God appeared as wrath, not as love.

In spite of such questionings, Luther's superiors apparently had confidence in him. He had been encouraged in the study of theology, loaned to the University of Wittenberg in the year 1508 to lecture on philosophy, and recalled to Erfurt to lecture on the *Sentences of Peter Lombard*, that topical collection of passages from Scripture, the Church Fathers, and occasional Scholastics which formed the basis of lectures in theology in the Middle Ages. In 1510 Luther was part of a delegation to Rome which pleaded the cause of the Augustinian monastery

in Erfurt in a jurisdictional dispute. In 1511 he was permanently transferred to the University of Wittenberg and, in the
following year, took his doctorate in theology. Behind these
last developments was the hand of his Superior, Johann
Staupitz, who had selected him to be his successor at Wittenberg in the chair of Bible. In addition to his university lectures, Luther had to undertake preaching assignments, and
he soon found himself assigned to administrative responsibilities in the university and to supervising monasteries in the
area. In the years 1513 to 1515 Luther gave his first series of
lectures on the Psalms, followed in 1515–16 by lectures on
Romans, and in 1516–17 by his first lectures on Galatians.

Luther came to a fresh understanding of the Gospel some-
time between 1513 and 1519. The most dramatic event in that
reconception is generally known as the "tower experience,"
because his new insight apparently came to him when in the
tower of the Augustinian monastery in Wittenberg. But exactly when this experience took place and what its precise
meaning was are not settled. In the *Preface to the Complete
Edition of Luther's Latin Writings* of 1545, Luther himself refers to the discovery as having taken place at a time when he
was engaged with the second series of lectures on Psalms in
1518. But until quite recently the prevailing interpretation of
Luther held this to be a mistaken recollection and, instead,
dated the "tower experience" as early as the first lectures on
Psalms in the years 1513–15. More recently still, scholars such
as Ernst Bizer have again placed it in the years 1518–19.[4]
Other interpreters have despaired of coming to an exact date.
The precise meaning of the event is as difficult to ascertain as
the date. In fact, its precise meaning may have some bearing
on the date. It makes a difference whether the "tower experience" represents a moment when Luther came to a fresh understanding of the Gospel, which later underwent extensive
transformation, or whether it represents the view of the mature

[4] Ernst Bizer, *Fides ex Auditu, Eine Untersuchung über die
Entdeckung des Gerechtigkeit Gottes durch Martin Luther* (Neukirchen Kreis Moers, 1958). See also F. Edward Cranz, *An Essay
on the Development of Luther's Thought on Justice, Law, and
Society* (Cambridge: Harvard University Press, 1959); Hans Pohl-
mann, *Hat Luther Paulus entdeckt?* (Berlin, 1959).

Luther, which is subsequently elaborated with reference to all other problems. We shall not tarry at this point. Since Luther, even if in retrospect, movingly indicates in the *Preface to the Complete Edition of Luther's Latin Writings* how his eyes were opened to the center of the Gospel, that work has been included in this volume. It conveys Luther's awareness of the focal point of his mature understanding, whether or not it represents the actual "tower experience."

Luther's great contribution centers in the recovery of the Biblical meaning of the righteousness of God. Generally the medieval church defined the righteousness of God as the demanding justice of God; for the mature Luther, by contrast, the righteousness of God was fundamentally the mercy of God. This transformation in understanding was made in three stages. In so far as the medieval view interpreted the righteousness of God as His demanding justice, the fundamental problem was how man could stand before such a God.

The medieval church did not believe that man could do this in terms of his own righteousness. Rather, in the prevailing medieval view, man hoped to stand before the righteousness of God by virtue of a combination of serious intentions, righteous works whose imperfections are met by grace, and the sacramental realities which covered all the situations of men. It was a combination of grace and of the best acts of men. We have already delineated this position and the difficulties Luther discovered in it.

The second stage in the transition is that found in Luther's first lectures on the Psalms and to some extent in his lectures on the letter to the Romans. Two significant shifts in the emphasis of Luther's thinking are apparent at this stage. In the first place, the righteousness of God is no longer seen as just a demanding justice before which a man may stand by virtue of his own good works and the forgiving grace of God. The righteousness of God is now primarily the grace which transforms and makes man righteous. The righteousness of God is no longer encountered in terms of a transaction in which satisfaction is made to God. In the second place, human activity no longer has any part in the ultimate determination of man's destiny. Grace alone enables man to stand before the righteousness of God. This general view was shared to some extent by figures who represent the Augustinian tradition in the Middle Ages. But Luther gave it a more classical and evangelical expression, and for this reason many have dated Luther's new insights from this period.

The third position is Luther's full-blown Reformation conception. Formally, it bears similarities to his earlier understanding. The righteousness of God and His grace are identified, though now more emphatically than before. Grace alone is decisive, though now in an entirely new way. The crucial difference is that the emphasis is no longer on God's grace in enabling man to be righteous. God's grace, which is His righteousness, is shown in His treating man as righteous whatever the state of his life. Still utilizing the medieval language in which a man needed to stand in righteousness before the demands of God, Luther declared that acceptability is imputed to man; righteousness is ascribed to him. A man now stands before God in the light of His grace alone, and that righteousness of life and man's activity, so important in other contexts, are irrelevant here.[5]

This understanding, on which we shall elaborate in its various ramifications in the next section, gave birth to the Reformation in its radical character. On its basis, the medieval sacramental understanding was challenged at its best. Gone was any idea that man's relation to a righteous God depended on works and the infusion of actual righteousness. In its place stood grace alone.

That conception was not yet fully developed in Luther's mind as he posted the *Ninety-five Theses* in Latin on the Castle church door in 1517, in the hope of precipitating a debate on the system of indulgences. The *Theses* clearly hinted what later became explicit. Already here, Luther maintained that the reference to repentance in Matthew 4:17 meant that the "entire life of believers is to be one of repentance" and had no reference to the sacrament of penance. Penitence, rather than being a single act, was a continuous mood and

---

[5] It is possible that Luther telescoped and thereby obscured the distinction between his earlier and later discoveries in the *Preface to the Complete Edition of Luther's Latin Writings*. Such a telescoping, even if unconscious, is different from a mistaken identification, which the older theories demanded.

determination of spirit in the presence of God who is both holy and gracious. It was precisely because Luther took repentance so seriously, as the mark of the believer before God, that he was moved to attack the practice and claims of the indulgence system through the *Theses*.

An indulgence was a way of drawing upon the merits of Christ to meet the inescapable punishment for sin and to make satisfaction to God even though one's sins were forgiven. In consideration of the payment of a sum of money to the Church or some other virtuous act, a great deal, if not all, of the punishment for one's sins was said to be remitted, and a written certification of this remission was provided by the Pope's agent. Such an indulgence, when proclaimed by the papacy, was considered of great worth for the welfare not only of oneself but of the departed dead. Indulgences had been declared for service in the Crusades. More recently, however, they had been offered for gifts to the Church when special financial goals had to be met.

The immediate occasion for the posting of the *Ninety-five Theses* was the indulgence preaching of the Dominican, Johann Tetzel. In the effort to raise money for the completion of St. Peter's in Rome, he apparently promised not only release from punishment but also the forgiveness of sins. In the *Theses*, Luther proposed that the indulgences had no reference either to purgatory or to the making of satisfaction to God. Indulgences had reference only to the possibility of the remission of penalties which the papacy had the right to impose upon believers as a sign of their seriousness. But to say this, was to make indulgences relevant to the discipline of the Church, not binding upon the Eternal. It was to attack a medieval development which long since had become standard and accepted practice. Thus, in the *Theses*, the Roman development is directly attacked, even though the evangelical Gospel is apparent only partly in this document.

The evangelical concern is more apparent in the *Theses* which Luther prepared for the disputation at Heidelberg in the spring of 1518. This is due to the fact that the *Ninety-five Theses* were addressed to the correction of an abuse, while the *Heidelberg Theses* were directly concerned with such central issues as sin, free will, and grace. Staupitz, who arranged the disputation at the Augustinian monastery in Heidelberg, had asked Luther to concentrate on those points in order that his more evangelical ideas might become apparent and open to examination. In these *Theses*, Luther gave classic expression to the theology of the cross in contrast to the theology of glory: that is, the apprehension of God in suffering and lowliness in contrast to the apprehension of Him on the basis of the visible things of creation. He also opposed the Scholastic theology in an outright attack upon Aristotle. Since the theology which informed the *Ninety-five Theses* is more apparent in the *Heidelberg Theses* than in the *Ninety-five Theses* themselves, the theological theses for the Heidelberg debate have also been included in these selections.

The events which followed the publication of the *Ninety-five Theses* had not been anticipated by Luther. Instead of instigating a scholar's debate, the *Theses* were surreptitiously translated into German and widely disseminated. That this happened testifies to the widespread unrest and dissatisfaction with the practices of the Roman Church in Germany. As an attempt to elaborate on what he meant and to avoid misunderstanding, Luther wrote and had published his *Explanation of the Ninety-five Theses*. A copy of the *Theses* had been forwarded to the Pope, and initially there was little reaction, apparently under the conviction that the matter was not too serious. But the popular interest in and support of Luther, and Luther's attacks on the power of the papacy, with reference to such crucial questions as the power to consign men to purgatory, drastically changed the picture. When Luther heard that he was under a papal ban, he proclaimed that the papacy had no ultimate power with respect to a man's relation to God. This made the matter worse. At that juncture, the Pope asked the Dominican, Sylvester Prierias, to answer Luther. Moreover, the Pope demanded that Luther appear in Rome to respond to the charge of heresy and of flouting constitutional authority. But the Elector Frederick (the ruler in whose territory Luther lived), partly from political motives, successfully brought pressure to have the issue joined in Germany rather than in Rome. It was arranged that Luther should be given a personal hearing by the papal legate, Cardinal Cajetan, prior to the Diet of Augsburg. But no agreement resulted and

Luther appealed from the Pope to a general council. In the meantime, the Vatican clarified its understanding of indulgences and purged some of the most offensive practices. Further, John Eck, a professor from the German University of Ingolstadt who was sympathetic to Rome, persuaded the University of Leipzig to sponsor a debate with Luther. And in 1519 the Leipzig debate was held, in the wake of which both the papal party and Luther's side claimed victory.

More important than who could claim victory was the fact that in the debate Luther was driven to see and to express more clearly the limits which must be put on the power of the papacy. Now the final conflict appeared inevitable, and the groundwork was complete for the stand he was to take when he was later summoned to appear before the Imperial Diet at Worms in 1521.

It would serve no purpose here to elaborate on the complex political events or on the threats and counterthreats during the period from the posting of the *Theses* through the Leipzig debate to the Diet of Worms. More significant for us is that this is the period in which Luther's Reformation faith—whether already present for many years or now newly emerged—was hammered out to its full consciousness and to an awareness of its implications. In the controversy with Rome, the initial abuses against which he protested were left far behind and a conception of Christianity emerged which rejected the very foundations of the medieval church. From that point on, nothing less than the total reformation of the Church would do. In the debates of this period, Luther kept coming back to certain definite and inescapable convictions. Fundamental to them all was that the norm of the Church's life could be taken only from Scripture. Hence he rejected the notion that the Roman pontiff cannot err in matters of faith and that he alone can interpret Scripture. Moreover, Luther was forced to the conclusion that councils could not be trusted entirely either, since the decisions of various councils contradicted one another. When Luther was finally summoned to the Imperial Diet meeting at Worms in 1521 and asked to repudiate his writings, he replied in terms of a conviction which had already become clear three years earlier: "Since then your serene Majesty and your Lordships seek a simple answer, I will give it in this manner, neither horned nor toothed. Unless I am convinced by the testimony of the Scriptures or by clear reason (for I do not trust either in the Pope or in councils alone, since it is well known that they have often erred and contradicted themselves), I am bound by the Scriptures I have quoted and my conscience is captive to the Word of God. I cannot and I will not retract anything, since it is neither safe nor right to go against conscience. . . . May God help me. Amen."[6]

In the previous year, 1520, a papal bull had been issued condemning all of Luther's writings and giving him sixty days within which to recant. But it was a productive year from a literary standpoint. There appeared such major writings as *The Treatises on Good Works, The Papacy at Rome, An Appeal to the Ruling Class of German Nationality, The Pagan Servitude of the Church*, and *The Freedom of a Christian*. With good merit, the latter three have frequently been called the Reformation Treatises. In *An Appeal to the Ruling Class of German Nationality*, Luther called upon the nobles to reform the Church and indicated the grounds upon which this was essential. In *The Pagan Servitude of the Church* he attacked the entire sacramental system of the Church, particularly the Mass, and delineated his own conception of the sacraments. *The Freedom of a Christian* is an eloquent account of the nature of Christian faith and life. Since these selections are included in this volume and since we shall delineate Luther's thought in another section, the contents of these writings will not be summarized here. But by the end of the year 1520, on the eve of the Imperial Diet of Worms, Luther's newly won theological views had been fully expressed and the implications drawn for the life of the Church. From here on, the emergence of a Reformation church was inevitable.

We have followed the main contours of Luther's life and development to the Diet of Worms. In the period immediately following the Diet, Luther was taken into protective custody at the Wartburg Castle in order to protect his life from attack by the papal proponents. In this enforced isolation, he began the translation of the Scriptures into German. Meanwhile, in Wittenberg, the Reformation reorganization of the liturgy and

[6] *Luther's Works* (Philadelphia: Muhlenberg Press, 1958), volume 32, pp. 112–13.

life of the local church was beginning to take place under the leadership of Luther's colleagues, Philip Melanchthon and Gabriel Zwilling. But from the neighboring town of Zwickau, self-styled prophets came to Wittenberg, claiming special revelations of the spirit over and above Scripture. When they appeared to succeed in winning some to a radical reorganization of the Church rather than its reformation, Luther cut short his exile and risked returning to Wittenberg (at first temporarily, then permanently) to take command of events.

For a general orientation, it is superfluous to chronicle the further events of Luther's career. In the ensuing years the reformer was engaged in preaching, teaching, writing, and dealing with innumerable problems and crises of church and state. His problems multiplied, as did his irascibility. There were protracted periods of illness, during which his literary productivity was prodigious. After the Diet of Worms and the stay at the Wartburg, Luther threw his energies not only into negating the pretensions and errors of the Roman See but also into the positive task of the reformation of the life and thought of the Church. From the preaching of the Word for the edification and education of the masses through the reformation of the liturgy and the organization of new patterns of church life, there would have been problems enough even in the normal course of things. One example will suffice. When Luther denied that monasticism was a higher calling than the other stations in men's lives, the foundation for monasticism collapsed in many sections of Germany, and the Reformation faced the problem of the rehabilitation of the lives of countless monks and nuns who were fleeing the monasteries, as well as the difficult task of reconceiving the whole understanding of Christian vocation. It is common knowledge that on one of these occasions, when several nuns had left the cloistered walls, Luther took to wife one of the nuns who apparently would settle for nothing less than Luther himself. Katharine von Bora, whom Luther came to love and cherish, was a woman of unusual ability, managing the large household and "hangers-on" who were always around her husband.

There were also problems occasioned by differences within the emerging Protestantism and by the close connection between religious and political aspirations. On the question of baptism, Luther found himself between the Roman Catholic sacramental views, on the one side, and the Anabaptist conception of believer's baptism. For the latter, baptism expressed the faith in which believers already stood, and they therefore rejected infant baptism. On the Lord's Supper, Luther found himself between the Roman Catholic concept of transubstantiation (that at a point in the Mass the elements were transformed into the actual body and blood of Christ) and the Zwinglian concept of remembrance (that the rite of the Lord's Supper was a dramatic recalling of the meaning of life, death, and the resurrection of Christ). And in spite of numerous attempts to come to agreement on the Lord's Supper, as we shall see later, no final agreement was reached.

When the peasants interpreted the new freedom of the Christian man as favoring their own plight, and revolted, Luther showed himself at his worst. While sympathetic to their situation, his own judgment on theological and social grounds was that their action would open the world to anarchy and that constituted authority must therefore be supported at every point. Some of his most vindictive writings came out of this period. An example of Luther's more balanced viewpoint on authority, even if one should judge it mistaken, is his writing on *Secular Authority,* which has been included in this volume. Whatever Luther may or may not have been in controversy, his unmistakable achievement was his singlehanded recovery of the Gospel and the spelling out of its implications for the life and thought of the Church.

II. Luther's Reformation Affirmations

It is not by accident that the slogans associated with the Reformation were "justification by faith" and "Scripture alone." The first points to the central Christian reality recovered by Luther, and the latter points to the source through which faith becomes a reality. In looking at the former we need to delineate more fully the meaning given by Luther to the words *righteousness, justification, grace,* and *faith.* The central meaning of the Reformation is usually expressed in the phrase "justification by grace through faith." That formula makes clear that the righteousness of God is seen most clearly in the

grace by which we are accounted right and justified before
God. It also points to, but inadequately expresses, the notion
of faith as the matrix of the appropriation of grace. Faith is
nothing else but the lively apprehension of grace made known
and received. It is the stance of the believer as a result of the
grace which he has known and in which he trusts. Therefore,
the phrase "through faith" is not to be understood as a means
for apprehending grace but as the mode of living by and in
the power of God's graciousness.[7]

It is particularly important to note the radical character of
Luther's central concept. It ruled out every attempt to justify
or acquit oneself before God. One was made acceptable or
justified before God in faith, that is, in the lively apprehension
of God's word of love and mercy. Before God, this alone was
the ground of trust.

One can hardly overemphasize the emancipation which this
discovery brought to Luther. He had not tried to justify himself before God simply on the basis of his deeds. He had tried
to do so by that combination of trusting and living in accord
with a sacramental system which allegedly guaranteed that a
man could be righteous before God. His new discovery ended
his religious attempt to justify himself before God in terms of
the prescribed combination of sacraments and works. For this
reason, Luther declared that even if the path of works were
possible, he would not want to have to depend upon works
before God, for that would be to depend on a broken reed,
namely oneself. That possibility could only introduce uncertainty and be oppressive. For Luther, the joy and freedom of a
Christian was that in faith he did not need to look to self but
only to God for his destiny. From this it followed logically
that the fundamental sin of man, that sin which is the foundation of all other sins, is man's attempt to justify himself, his
unwillingness to accept that his future rests alone in the gratui-

[7] The phrase "justification by grace through faith" (cf. Ephesians
2:8) or "justification by faith" (Romans 5:1) is a slogan which
points to the way in which Luther broke through the medieval
development at a central point through a recovery of a certain
Pauline understanding. In our day, it is better to speak of "grace"
and "freedom," defining them, than to continue to use the term
"justification." In that way, Luther's classical insight can more
readily become our own.

tous act of God. It is man's unwillingness to let God be God for him.

Two questions immediately arise in this context. First, what is the origin of faith? Second, if works are of no avail before God, what is their place? Reared in the tradition of the Church, Luther himself never faced the question of the origin of faith as a movement from unbelief to belief, that is, from disbelieving in God's existence to believing in it in a meaningful way. But the distinction which Luther knew, the difference between believing in the mere existence of God and the lively apprehension of His reality in Christ, corresponds in our day to the difference between denying His existence and affirming a genuine encounter with Him. For Luther, as for many others in his time, the belief that there was a God without knowing that He was a God for oneself was tantamount to atheism, that is, to acting as if His existence made no difference. The question of faith and un-faith is the same then as now. The decisive transition rests on apprehending the incomprehensible, gratuitous mercy of God.

The transition from un-faith to faith occurs through the Word—usually the proclaimed Word—which is given and received in the miracle of faith. There is a strong element of discontinuity between the "before" and the "after" of the inception of faith, irrespective of whether the change is traumatic or gradual. The conditioning factors do not account for the new situation. This point is clearly made in *The Bondage of the Will*, the forceful reply to Erasmus which Luther considered to be his best book. (A selection from this work has been included in this volume.) By "the bondage of the will," Luther did not mean that man is incapable of making significant and meaningful decisions. Nor did he mean that man as man is a stone, beast, or rascal. But he did mean that there is no act or capacity of will by which the self can successfully will itself into an adequate and proper relation to God. In more contemporary language, man cannot by his own resolution and effort overcome his estrangement from God. In theological terms, it is this incapacity which previous generations, not without giving cause for considerable misunderstanding, called "the total depravity of man." It is the incapacity of the best of men at the crucial point of their existence.

Luther developed this point through his concept of the "all-working" character of God and of the notion of predestination. Because of the context in which he worked, both concepts were developed in deterministic categories. It is as if the argument was that if God determines all things, no one has any ground for self-defense or merit. It is partly because of this deterministic frame of reference, which was historically developed as a powerful source of confidence against the dark powers of fate and fortune, that *The Bondage of the Will* has not received the attention which it deserves. Since the problem of freedom as we know it today is a development subsequent to the Reformation, it is hard for us to grasp the context within which Luther was working. But the crucial theological point, as distinguished from its elaboration, was that predestination was a comfort to the believer. It was an affirmation on the part of the believer that God could be trusted, trusted even at the point where one's faith was weak and wavering. It was the confession that God could be trusted, that He had a sure and safe destiny for us. Predestination was confessed by those who, by a miracle which they could ascribe only to God, discovered themselves delivered from the incapacity of their wills and now living by God's grace and promise.

It is important to stress that faith here means, basically, not the decision to assent to a proposition, but a fundamental reorientation and redirection of life. The life of faith is the mode of existence which finds its vital source and center in God's forgiving and renewing grace. This means further that faith includes a new possibility of decision. Decision itself is placed *within* the dynamics of a relationship of grace. It is not that grace is offered and then man decides whether or not to accept it. This would be man's last work, his last attempt to justify himself. Rather it is confessed that the mystery of God's act in all its priority incorporates and includes the redirection of man's capacity of decision. Another way of putting this is to say that faith includes infinitely more than the deciding capacity of man. Certainly without the inclusion of will and the voluntaristic aspects of man, faith is not fully faith for the mature man. But as a gift, faith cannot be reduced to rational and voluntaristic levels. Because Luther believed that the voluntaristic aspects were too prominent among those who in-

sisted upon believer's baptism, he continued to insist upon the
baptism of infants and suggested the notion of "infantile faith."
The latter term could hardly be elucidated; but it protected
the mystery of God's initiating gift and act against those for
whom voluntaristic and decisional aspects loomed prominent
in any description of faith.

In faith, man stands before God in the light of grace. For
him, even at his best, there is no other possibility. Hence, for
Luther, good works are not determinative of one's relation to
God; they follow from faith as day follows night, as good fruit
comes from a good tree. Where there are no works, there is
no faith; the seriousness and joy of belonging to God are not
known. But the temptation of the believer is to look at the
works which he does in faith and suddenly to reinstitute
works and merit as a new form of slavery in the very citadel
of the freedom of the Gospel. For Luther, the ethical rigor of
the New Testament teachings and of the law should convince
the Christian that he, too, is still sinner. Moreover, the very
looking at one's works spoils them. Genuine works point to
God, not to self. This is why Luther can declare that, apart
from faith, all works are nothing but "truly wicked and damnable sins."[8] On the external, moral level, they may be better than other courses of action. But in terms of their total
orientation, that is, in terms of one's status before God, they
are of no effect. On that level, everything is a matter of relationship, a relationship into which man enters by virtue of
God's unaccountable activity. Confronted by God, man cannot depend on a combination of works and faith, or faith and
works, but only on faith not without works, or of faith active
in love. The Christian is to live and to struggle, to be a Christ
to his neighbor, and above all to trust God. Luther's powerful
delineation of this motif is to be found in *The Freedom of a
Christian*, which is included in this volume.

In the light of God's imputation of righteousness to man,
he is totally a saint; aside from this, the actuality of his situation is that he is totally a sinner. He is at once saint and sinner.
The recognition that man is still sinner is a description of his
life before God. The sin in his position before God is reflected

[8] See p. 69.

in the sins of his life. But to look at the latter in isolation is to misunderstand the problem of sin. This would be an anthropological rather than a theological view and would obscure the fundamental issue, man's trust or lack of trust before God.

The Scriptural commandments and teachings disclose man's lack of an adequate relation to God, but also serve to give direction to his responsibilities. The negative and positive functions of the law, as well as the way in which faith transcends every aspect of law with respect to man's ultimate destiny, are most graphically delineated in Luther's 1531 lectures on Galatians, selections from which are included in this volume.

We have stated that the second slogan associated with the Reformation is "Scripture alone." It means that the sole source of authority for the Christian and for the Church is derived from Scripture. As a slogan, it is to be understood in the context of the medieval world, where, in spite of divergent interpretations, the Church was nevertheless considered the rightful interpreter of Scripture. In the more extreme forms of the medieval view, it was held that revelations were vouchsafed to the Church apart from Scripture. It is in this context that Luther insisted upon the sole authority of Scripture. But his position of insisting on Scripture is not to be understood in any literal or fundamentalist sense. While Luther, as a sixteenth-century figure, would not have challenged the literal accuracy of the Bible, the latter was not an item of concern. The Scripture was significant in the light of that to which it witnessed, namely Christ, and because by the power of the Spirit, Scripture became the agent through which faith was born and nourished. Scripture was the Word of God because through it the word of the living God became known to men in all its dimensions. So much, in fact, was this the case for Luther that he believed that Scripture itself was to be interpreted in the light of its center, Christ. This is why he did not consider all books of the Bible to be of equal value. As an indication of Luther's manner of interpreting Scripture, we have included several of his prefaces to Biblical books.

It was not easy for Luther to insist upon this particular interpretation of Scripture in face of the claims of both papacy and councils. Nevertheless, Luther's historical work showed him that there was merit in his interpretation and that it could be maintained that the Church had made the Scripture captive to its own concerns. Luther's use of the term "right reason," alongside of or in connection with Scripture—in controversy both at Augsburg and at Worms—was not so much a call upon reason as a source of faith (a view which he found obnoxious), as it was a demand for sensible interpretation of Scripture against the presumptuous claims of the Church. Luther too believed that the Scripture needed to be interpreted. This he did extensively in his own preaching and teaching. But he also believed that, in the community of the Church, Scripture was its own interpreter. Such interpretation involved being grasped by the Biblical Word and the Spirit conjoined in such a way that one was laid hold of by more than what the text said. It was being grasped in one's depth, being redirected in one's total being, including heart and mind, by the living Word.

Luther's understanding of the Gospel dictated a conception of the Church different from that held in the medieval period. The Church was no longer fundamentally a sacramental agent; instead, it was the community of believers. The true Church, that is, the elect of God, was hidden in the visible Church. When Luther delineates the marks and characteristics of the Church, he refers to the visible community. He maintained that the Church exists where the Word is preached and the sacraments are duly administered. The Word of God may be apprehended anywhere in creation; but it is to be sought where God has made Himself manifest, that is, in preaching and in the sacraments. The worshiping community confesses its faith, hears the Word of judgment and, above all, of grace. In content, the Word preached and the Word in the Sacrament are not to be distinguished. They are two instituted forms addressed to man in the diversity and totality of his being. Hence, they belong together. According to Luther, the preaching of the Word is to be followed by the sacrament of the Lord's Supper and there is to be no administration of the sacrament without the preaching of the Word. The sacraments are essential; but they do not imply a special grace not imparted in the preached Word. One is to come to the sacrament as one comes also to the hearing of the Word, in the expectation that the promise of God's presence in mercy will be fulfilled.

The sacrament of baptism implies incorporation into the Christian community, the dying unto self and the new life in Christ. It includes the gift and reality of faith unto life eternal. Luther frequently counseled distraught believers to remember the promises of God's presence made to them in the sacrament of baptism. In the midst of man's doubt and anxiety, his baptism, like predestination, was a comfort, a token, and a pledge of his safe destiny under God.

It is in the mode of Christ's presence in the Lord's Supper that Luther's views set him in marked contrast to both the Roman Catholic and other Protestant traditions. Luther rejected the notion that the elements at a particular point in the Mass were transformed into the actual body and blood of Christ. But he maintained the view that believer and unbeliever alike masticated the actual body and blood of Christ in partaking of the elements of bread and wine. For Luther, Christ is present in the Supper not because at some point the priest as the agent of God is responsible for the transformation of the elements. Christ is present because God has promised to be present. Moreover, such presence for Luther meant total presence. For this reason, he insisted upon the notion of the bodily presence of Christ in the elements. For Luther, the designation "spiritual presence" did not sufficiently imply the full and total presence. But his conception of bodily presence did not imply spatial characteristics. For Luther it was not enough to say that in the Lord's Supper one remembered the life, death, and resurrection of Christ. He insisted upon the substantive meaning of "This *is* my body"; but he refused to become involved in discussions on the metaphysics of the "is."

Such an understanding of the sacraments presupposes that one receives them in faith. The sacrament is neither pleasing to God nor efficacious apart from faith. But it is not faith which makes the sacrament. A sacrament is instituted of God as a visible sign to which a promise is connected for the one who comes in faith. The sacrament therefore is more than faith; yet it is not a sacrament without faith.

Luther wrote extensively on the sacraments. Moreover, he touched upon them throughout his writings, and for this reason no special separate work on the sacraments has been included. In the selections that follow, the sacraments are dealt with most extensively in *The Pagan Servitude of the Church*.

As the community of believers, Christians bear each other's burdens, and the burdens of the world, as Christ did before them. For Luther, that way of conceiving the Church included two fundamental assumptions. First, the ministry was no longer understood as a position of *necessary* mediatorship, that is, it no longer represented a special transaction between God and man. Rather, in the community of the Church all men were priests to each other, that is, occasions for and messengers of grace and support. This was expressed in the notion of the priesthood of all believers. It described the relationship of Christians to each other and their common direct relationship to God. But this did not mean that a special ministry was superfluous. While the proclamation of the Word and the administration of the sacraments did not depend on a separate ministry for their efficacy and nature, faithful proclamation of the Word required time, talent, and industry, and faithful administration of the sacrament required decorum and order. Hence, a special and educated ministry was essential.

At this point, the second assumption becomes explicit. The ministry is functionally, not ontologically, distinct. It implies no special status. The higher and lower callings, as in the prior distinctions between monks and the laity, are abolished. Luther does not mean that all possible callings are equally honorable. But ministers, cobblers, or magistrates may equally serve God in the exercise of their responsibilities. We may all, whatever our calling or station, face with confidence the conflicts and ambiguities of life and hope to be used of God as vessels to redeem the time. This is possible because through the gift of faith we have learned to trust not in our own virtue but in Him who rules over all and who alone can bring good out of evil.

I

Preface to the Complete Edition of Luther's Latin Writings[1]

Wittenberg, 1545

[While the 1545 preface to Luther's Latin writings is chronologically the latest item to appear in these selections, it has deliberately been chosen to be the first item. Luther, in the year before his death, here reviews his life, the context in which he lived and worked, and the discovery of the meaning of justification by faith. As such, it provides a picture of how Luther saw himself and his work. This is true in spite of the fact that there are historical problems occasioned by the fact that Luther undoubtedly did not correctly remember everything as it happened. The dating of the break-through in understanding justification, as was indicated in the Preface,[2] has continued to plague historians. But, in spite of this, the Preface is a good point of departure for understanding and reading Luther.]

Martin Luther wishes the sincere reader salvation!

For a long time I strenuously resisted those who wanted my books, or more correctly my confused lucubrations, published. I did not want the labors of the ancients to be buried by my new works and the reader kept from reading them. Then, too, by God's grace a great many systematic books now exist,

[1] Reprinted by permission of the publisher from *Luther's Works*, volume 34, *Career of the Reformer*: IV, edited and translated by Lewis W. Spitz (Philadelphia: Muhlenberg Press, 1960), pp. 327–38.
[2] See p. xvii.

among which the *Loci communes* of Philip excel,[8] with which a theologian and a bishop can be beautifully and abundantly prepared to be mighty in preaching the doctrine of piety, especially since the Holy Bible itself can now be had in nearly every language. But my books, as it happened, yes, as the lack of order in which the events transpired made it necessary, are accordingly crude and disordered chaos, which is now not easy to arrange even for me.

Persuaded by these reasons, I wished that all my books were buried in perpetual oblivion, so that there might be room for better ones. But the boldness and bothersome perseverance of others daily filled my ears with complaints that it would come to pass, that if I did not permit their publication in my lifetime, men wholly ignorant of the causes and the time of the events would nevertheless most certainly publish them, and so out of one confusion many would arise. Their boldness, I say, prevailed and so I permitted them to be published. At the same time the wish and command of our most illustrious Prince, Elector, etc., John Frederick[4] was added. He commanded, yes, compelled the printers not only to print, but to speed up the publication.

But above all else, I beg the sincere reader, and I beg for the sake of our Lord Jesus Christ himself, to read those things judiciously, yes, with great commiseration. May he be mindful of the fact that I was once a monk and a most enthusiastic papist when I began that cause. I was so drunk, yes, submerged in the pope's dogmas, that I would have been ready to murder all, if I could have, or to co-operate willingly with the murderers of all who would take but a syllable from obedience to the pope. So great a Saul was I, as are many to this day. I was not such a lump of frigid ice in defending the papacy as Eck[5] and his like were, who appeared to me actually to defend the pope more for their own belly's sake than to pursue the matter seriously. To me, indeed, they seem to laugh at the

---

[8] The reference is to Philip Melanchthon.

[4] Elector John Frederick of Saxony (d. 1554) was a man of strong evangelical convictions. He further consolidated the church in his territories, gave the University of Wittenberg renewed support, and encouraged Luther in his work as a reformer.

[5] *At the Leipzig Debate.*

pope to this day, like Epicureans! I pursued the matter with all seriousness, as one, who in dread of the last day, nevertheless from the depth of my heart wanted to be saved.

So you will find how much and what important matters I humbly conceded to the pope in my earlier writings, which I later and now hold and execrate as the worst blasphemies and abomination. You will, therefore, sincere reader, ascribe this error, or, as they slander, contradiction, to the time and my inexperience. At first I was all alone and certainly very inept and unskilled in conducting such great affairs. For I got into these turmoils by accident and not by will or intention. I call upon God himself as witness.

Hence, when in the year 1517 indulgences were sold (I wanted to say promoted) in these regions for most shameful gain—I was then a preacher, a young doctor of theology, so to speak—and I began to dissuade the people and to urge them not to listen to the clamors of the indulgence hawkers; they had better things to do. I certainly thought that in this case I should have a protector in the pope, on whose trustworthiness I then leaned strongly, for in his decrees he most clearly damned the immoderation of the quaestors, as he called the indulgence preachers.

Soon afterward I wrote two letters, one to Albrecht, the archbishop of Mainz, who got half of the money from the indulgences, the pope the other half—something I did not know at the time—the other to the ordinary (as they call them) Jerome, the bishop of Brandenburg. I begged them to stop the shameless blasphemy of the quaestors. But the poor little brother was despised. Despised, I published the *Theses* and at the same time a German *Sermon on Indulgences*,[6] shortly thereafter also the *Explanations*,[7] in which, to the pope's honor, I developed the idea that indulgences should indeed not be condemned, but that good works of love should be preferred to them.

This was demolishing heaven and consuming the earth with fire. I am accused by the pope, am cited to Rome, and the whole papacy rises up against me alone. All this happened in the year 1518, when Maximilian held the diet at Augsburg. In

[6] *The Sermon on Indulgences and Grace*, March, 1518.
[7] *The Explanations of the Ninety-five Theses*, August, 1518.

it, Cardinal Cajetan served as the pope's Lateran legate. The most illustrious Duke Frederick of Saxony, Elector Prince, approached him on my behalf and brought it about that I was not compelled to go to Rome, but that he himself should summon me to examine and compose the matter. Soon the diet adjourned.

The Germans in the meantime, all tired of suffering the pillagings, traffickings, and endless impostures of Roman rascals, awaited with bated breath the outcome of so great a matter, which no one before, neither bishop nor theologian, had dared to touch. In any case that popular breeze favored me, because those practices and "Romanations," with which they had filled and tired the whole earth, were already hateful to all.

So I came to Augsburg, afoot and poor, supplied with food and letters of commendation from Prince Frederick to the senate and to certain good men. I was there three days before I went to the cardinal, though he cited me day by day through a certain orator, for those excellent men forbade and dissuaded me most strenuously, not to go to the cardinal without a safe conduct from the emperor. The orator was rather troublesome to me, urging that if I should only revoke, everything would be all right! But as great as the wrong, so long is the detour to its correction.

Finally, on the third day he came demanding to know why I did not come to the cardinal, who expected me most benignly. I replied that I had to respect the advice of those very fine men to whom I had been commended by Prince Frederick, but it was their advice by no means to go to the cardinal without the emperor's protection or safe conduct. Having obtained this (but they took action on the part of the imperial senate to obtain it), I would come at once. At this point he blew up. "What?" he said, "Do you suppose Prince Frederick will take up arms for your sake?" I said, "This I do not at all desire." "And where will you stay?" I replied, "Under heaven." Then he, "If you had the pope and the cardinals in your power, what would you do?" "I would," said I, "show them all respect and honor." Thereupon he, wagging his finger with an Italian gesture, said, "Hem!" And so he left, nor did he return.

On that day the imperial senate informed the cardinal that

the emperor's protection or a safe conduct had been granted
me and admonished him that he should not design anything
too severe against me. He is said to have replied, "It is well.
I shall nevertheless do whatever my duty demands." These
things were the start of that tumult. The rest can be learned
from the accounts included later.

Master Philip Melanchthon had already been called here
that same year by Prince Frederick to teach Greek literature,
doubtless so that I should have an associate in the work of
theology. His works attest sufficiently what the Lord has performed through this instrument, not only in literature but also
in theology, though Satan is mad and all his adherents.

Maximilian died, in the following year, '19, in February, and
according to the law of the empire Duke Frederick was made
deputy. Thereupon the storm ceased to rage a bit, and gradually contempt of excommunication or papal thunderbolts arose.
For when Eck and Caraccioli brought a bull from Rome condemning Luther and revealed it, the former here, the latter
there to Duke Frederick, who was at Cologne at the time together with other princes in order to meet Charles who had
been recently elected, Frederick was most indignant. He reproved that papal rascal with great courage and constancy,
because in his absence he and Eck had disturbed his and his
brother John's dominion. He jarred them so magnificently that
they left him in shame and disgrace. The prince, endowed with
incredible insight, caught on to the devices of the Roman Curia
and knew how to deal with them in a becoming manner, for
he had a keen nose and smelled more and farther than the
Romanists could hope or fear.

Hence they refrained from putting him to a test. For he did
not dignify with the least respect the Rose, which they call
"golden," sent him that same year by Leo X, indeed ridiculed
it. So the Romanists were forced to despair of their attempts
to deceive so great a prince. The gospel advanced happily under the shadow of that prince and was widely propagated.
His authority influenced very many, for since he was a very
wise and most keen-sighted prince, he could incur the suspicion only among the hateful that he wanted to nourish and
protect heresy and heretics. This did the papacy great harm.

That same year the Leipzig debate was held, to which Eck

had challenged us two, Karlstadt[8] and me. But I could not, in spite of all my letters, get a safe conduct from Duke George.[9] Accordingly, I came to Leipzig not as a prospective debater, but as a spectator under the safe conduct granted to Karlstadt. Who stood in my way I do not know, for till then Duke George was not against me. This I know for certain.

Here Eck came to me in my lodging and said he had heard that I refused to debate. I replied, "How can I debate, since I cannot get a safe conduct from Duke George?" "If I cannot debate with you," he said, "neither do I want to with Karlstadt, for I have come here on your account. What if I obtain a safe conduct for you? Would you then debate with me?" "Obtain," said I, "and it shall be." He left and soon a safe conduct was given me too and the opportunity to debate.

Eck did this because he discerned the certain glory that was set before him on account of my proposition in which I denied that the pope is the head of the church by divine right. Here a wide field was open to him and a supreme occasion to flatter in praiseworthy manner the pope and to merit his favor, also to ruin me with hate and envy. He did this vigorously throughout the entire debate. But he neither proved his own position nor refuted mine, so that even Duke George said to Eck and me at the morning meal, "Whether he be pope by human or divine right, yet he is pope." He would in no case have said this had he not been influenced by the arguments, but would have approved of Eck only.

Here, in my case, you may also see how hard it is to struggle out of and emerge from errors which have been confirmed by the example of the whole world and have by long habit become a part of nature, as it were. How true is the proverb, "It is hard to give up the accustomed," and, "Custom is second nature." How truly Augustine says, "If one does not resist custom, it becomes a necessity." I had then already read and taught the sacred Scriptures most diligently privately and publicly for seven years, so that I knew them nearly all by memory.

[8] Andreas Bodenstein von Karlstadt (1480–1541), professor of theology at Wittenberg, 1513–1523.

[9] Duke George (1471–1539) of Albertine Saxony, which separated after 1485 from electoral Ernestine Saxony, remained an uncompromising foe of the Reformation.

I had also acquired the beginning of the knowledge of Christ and faith in him, i.e., not by works but by faith in Christ are we made righteous and saved. Finally, regarding that of which I speak, I had already defended the proposition publicly that the pope is not the head of the church by divine right. Nevertheless, I did not draw the conclusion, namely, that the pope must be of the devil. For what is not of God must of necessity be of the devil.

So absorbed was I, as I have said, by the example and the title of the holy church as well as my own habit, that I conceded human right to the pope, which nevertheless, unless it is founded on divine authority, is a diabolical lie. For we obey parents and magistrates not because they themselves command it, but because it is God's will, I Peter 3 [2:13]. For that reason I can bear with a less hateful spirit those who cling too pertinaciously to the papacy, particularly those who have not read the sacred Scriptures, or also the profane, since I, who read the sacred Scriptures most diligently so many years, still clung to it so tenaciously.

In the year 1519, Leo X, as I have said, sent the Rose with Karl von Miltitz, who urged me profusely to be reconciled with the pope. He had seventy apostolic briefs that if Prince Frederick would turn me over to him, as the pope requested by means of the Rose, he should tack one up in each city and so transfer me safely to Rome. But he betrayed the counsel of his heart toward me when he said, "O Martin, I believed you were some aged theologian who, sitting behind the stove, disputed thus with himself; now I see you are still young and strong. If I had twenty-five thousand armed men, I do not believe I could take you to Rome, for I have sounded out the people's mind all along the way to learn what they thought of you. Behold, where I found one standing for the pope, three stood for you against the pope." But that was ridiculous! He had also asked simple little women and girls in the hostelries, what they thought of the Roman chair.[10] Ignorant of this term and thinking of a domestic chair, they replied, "How can we know what kind of chairs you have in Rome, wood or stone?"

Therefore he begged me to seek the things which made for peace. He would put forth every effort to have the pope do

[10] The Roman See.

the same. I also promised everything abundantly. Whatever I
could do with a good conscience with respect to the truth,
I would do most promptly. I, too, desired and was eager for
peace. Having been drawn into these disturbances by force
and driven by necessity, I had done all I did: the guilt was
not mine.

But he had summoned Johann Tetzel of the preaching order,[11] the primary author of this tragedy, and had with ver-
bose threats from the pope so broken the man, till then so
terrible to all, a fearless crier, that from that time on he wasted
away and was finally consumed by illness of mind. When I
found this out before his death, I comforted him with a letter,
written benignly, asking him to be of good cheer and not to
fear my memory. But perhaps he succumbed a victim of his
conscience and of the pope's indignation.

Karl von Miltitz was regarded as vain and his advice as vain.
But, in my opinion, if the man at Mainz[12] had from the start,
when I admonished him, and, finally, if the pope, before he
condemned me unheard and raged with his bulls, had taken
this advice, which Karl took although too late, and had at
once quenched Tetzel's fury, the matter would not have come
to so great a tumult. The entire guilt belongs to the one at
Mainz, whose smartness and cleverness fooled him, with which
he wanted to suppress my doctrine and have his money, acquired by the indulgences, saved. Now counsels are sought in
vain; in vain efforts are made. The Lord has awakened and
stands to judge the people. Though they could kill us, they
still do not have what they want, yes, have less than they
have, while we live in safety. This some of them who are not
entirely of a dull nose smell quite enough.

Meanwhile, I had already during that year returned to interpret the Psalter anew. I had confidence in the fact that I
was more skilful, after I had lectured in the university on St.
Paul's epistles to the Romans, to the Galatians, and the one
to the Hebrews. I had indeed been captivated with an extraordinary ardor for understanding Paul in the Epistle to the
Romans. But up till then it was not the cold blood about the
heart, but a single word in Chapter 1 [:17], "In it the right-

11 The Dominican Order.
12 Albrecht of Brandenburg.

eousness of God is revealed," that had stood in my way. For I hated that word "righteousness of God," which, according to the use and custom of all the teachers, I had been taught to understand philosophically regarding the formal or active righteousness, as they called it, with which God is righteous and punishes the unrighteous sinner.

Though I lived as a monk without reproach, I felt that I was a sinner before God with an extremely disturbed conscience. I could not believe that he was placated by my satisfaction. I did not love, yes, I hated the righteous God who punishes sinners, and secretly, if not blasphemously, certainly murmuring greatly, I was angry with God, and said, "As if, indeed, it is not enough, that miserable sinners, eternally lost through original sin, are crushed by every kind of calamity by the law of the decalogue, without having God add pain to pain by the gospel and also by the gospel threatening us with his righteousness and wrath!" Thus I raged with a fierce and troubled conscience. Nevertheless, I beat importunately upon Paul at that place, most ardently desiring to know what St. Paul wanted.

At last, by the mercy of God, meditating day and night, I gave heed to the context of the words, namely, "In it the righteousness of God is revealed, as it is written, 'He who through faith is righteous shall live.'" There I began to understand that the righteousness of God is that by which the righteous lives by a gift of God, namely by faith. And this is the meaning: the righteousness of God is revealed by the gospel, namely, the passive righteousness with which merciful God justifies us by faith, as it is written, "He who through faith is righteous shall live." Here I felt that I was altogether born again and had entered paradise itself through open gates. There a totally other face of the entire Scripture showed itself to me. Thereupon I ran through the Scriptures from memory. I also found in other terms an analogy, as, the work of God, that is, what God does in us, the power of God, with which he makes us strong, the wisdom of God, with which he makes us wise, the strength of God, the salvation of God, the glory of God.

And I extolled my sweetest word with a love as great as the hatred with which I had before hated the word "righteousness of God." Thus that place in Paul was for me truly the gate to paradise. Later I read Augustine's *The Spirit and the Letter*, where contrary to hope I found that he, too, interpreted God's righteousness in a similar way, as the righteousness with which God clothes us when he justifies us.[13] Although this was heretofore said imperfectly and he did not explain all things concerning imputation clearly, it nevertheless was pleasing that God's righteousness with which we are justified was taught. Armed more fully with these thoughts, I began a second time to interpret the Psalter. And the work would have grown into a large commentary, if I had not again been compelled to leave the work begun, because Emperor Charles V in the following year convened the diet at Worms.

I relate these things, good reader, so that, if you are a reader of my puny works, you may keep in mind, that, as I said above, I was all alone and one of those who, as Augustine says of himself, have become proficient by writing and teaching. I was not one of those who from nothing suddenly become the topmost, though they are nothing, neither have labored, nor been tempted, nor become experienced, but have with one look at the Scriptures exhausted their entire spirit.

To this point, to the year 1520 and 21, the indulgence matter proceeded. Upon that followed the sacramentarian and the Anabaptist affairs. Regarding these a preface shall be written to other tomes, if I live.

Farewell in the Lord, reader, and pray for the growth of the Word against Satan. Strong and evil, now also very furious and savage, he knows his time is short and the kingdom of his pope is in danger. But may God confirm in us what he has accomplished and perfect his work which he began in us, to his glory, Amen. March 5, in the year 1545.

[13] Augustine *The Spirit and the Letter*, chapter xi.

Selected Biblical Prefaces

(New Testament, Romans, St. James and St. Jude, Psalms)

[*Luther began the translation of the New Testament into German at the Wartburg in 1521, and it was published in September 1522. From 1523 on, parts of the Old Testament began to appear, and the complete Bible appeared in 1534. Although the Scriptures were translated into German so that they might be read and made available generally, Luther provided introductions to many of the books as an aid to understanding them. Some of these prefaces are remarkable, not as summaries of the books, but as articulate expressions of the Gospel and as clues to understanding the way in which he interprets Scripture. With this in mind, the preface to the entire New Testament and the preface to Romans have been selected for inclusion because of the light they shed on Luther's understanding of the Gospel; the preface to St. James and St. Jude has been included to show Luther's freedom of judgment concerning Biblical books in the light of the Gospel. The preface to the Psalms has been included because the Psalms were a special favorite of Luther's. They have been put after the New Testament prefaces to show that Luther understood them in a Christological or Christian sense. The prefaces to the New Testament appeared in the 1522 German edition of the New Testament; the preface to the Psalms here included appeared in the 1528 edition of a separate booklet containing the Psalms, which first appeared in 1524.*]

PREFACE[1]

[Later editions added the words: to the New Testament]

It would only be right and proper if this volume were published without any preface, or without any name on the title page, but simply with its own name to speak for itself. However, many unscholarly expositions and introductions have perverted the understanding of Christian people till they have not an inkling of the meaning of the gospel as distinct from the law, the New Testament as distinct from the Old Testament. This distressing state of affairs calls for some sort of guidance by way of preface, to free the ordinary man from his false though familiar notions, to lead him into the straight road, and to give him some instruction. He must be shown what to expect in this volume, lest he search it for commandments and laws, when he should be looking for gospel and promises.

In the first place, then, we must grasp the importance of getting rid of the vain idea that there are four gospels, and only four evangelists; and we must dismiss once for all the view that some of the New Testament writings should be classed as books of law or history or prophecy or wisdom, as the case may be. The purpose of this classification is to make the New Testament similar to the Old (though I myself fail to see the similarity). Rather we must be clear and definite in our minds, on the one hand, that the Old Testament is a volume containing God's laws and commandments. It also preserves the records of men who kept them, and of others who did not. On the other hand, the New Testament is a volume containing God's promised evangel, as well as records of those who believed or disbelieved it. We can therefore take it for certain that there is only one gospel, just as the New Testament is only one book. So too, there is only one faith and only one God: the God who makes promises.

[1] Reprinted by permission of the publisher from *The Reformation Writings of Martin Luther*, volume II, *The Spirit of the Protestant Reformation*, translated and edited by Bertram Lee Woolf (London: Lutterworth Press, 1956), pp. 278–83.

Evangel is a Greek word meaning glad tidings, good news, welcome information, a shout, or something that makes one sing and talk and rejoice. When David defeated the giant, Goliath, there was a great shout, and an encouraging message was passed round among the Jews to say that their terrible enemy had been killed, and that they were free to enjoy liberty and peace; thereupon they sang and danced and made merry. Similarly, God's evangel, the New Testament, is a good piece of news, a war-cry. It was echoed throughout the world by the apostles. They proclaimed a true David who had done combat with, and gained the victory over, sin, death, and the devil. In so doing, He had taken all who were enchained by sin, threatened by death, and overpowered by the devil. Though they had merited no rewards, He redeemed them, justified them, gave them life and salvation, and so brought them peace and led them back home to God. For these reasons, they sing thanks and praises to God, and they will ever continue to be happy if they remain firm in faith.

This kind of war-cry, this heartening news, this evangelical, divine message, is called a new testament. It is also like a testament when a dying man decides how his property shall be divided among certain heirs, whom he names. In the same way, Christ, before His death, decided and commanded that this evangel was to be proclaimed to all the world after His death. He thereby gave all believers possession of all His goods: namely, His life, by which He had vanquished death; His righteousness, by which He had washed away sin; and His holiness, by which He had overcome eternal damnation. No poor fellow chained in sin, dead, and bound for hell can ever hear anything more comforting and encouraging than this precious and lovely message about Christ; the sinner cannot help exulting from the bottom of his heart and rejoicing over it when he accepts its truth.

Now God, in order to strengthen such faith, often promised this evangel, this testament of His, through the prophets in the Old Testament. Thus Paul says in Romans 1 [:1], I have been set apart for the gospel of God which He promised beforehand through the prophets in Holy Scriptures, concerning His son who was born to Him from the seed, etc. And, in order that we might apply certain of these words to our own selves,

God's first promise was spoken when He said, to the serpent, I will cause enmity between you and the woman, between your seed and her seed. He shall trample on your head, and you will trample on his heel [Gen. 3:15]. Christ is the seed of the woman, and He has trampled down the devil's head, meaning, sin, death, hell, and all its powers. Without this seed it is impossible for any man to escape sin, death, hell.

Moreover, in Genesis 22 [:18], His promise to Abraham was, In thy seed shall all the nations of the earth be blessed. Christ is the seed of Abraham according to St. Paul in Galatians 3 [:16], and has given a blessing to all the world through the gospel; for where Christ is not found, there remains the curse which was pronounced on Adam and his descendants, after his sin. The effect of this curse was that they too were guilty of sin, and that death and hell would be their lot. But, contrary to the curse, the gospel brought a blessing to all the world when it proclaimed, for all to hear, that whoever believed on the seed of Abraham should be blessed, i.e., delivered from sin, death, and hell. Thus made righteous, he would live in eternal bliss. This is what Christ Himself said in John 11 [:26], He who believes on me shall never die.

He gave a similar promise to David, II Kings 17, when He said, I will raise up your seed after you to build a house for me, and I will establish his kingdom for ever. I will be his father, and he shall be my son. That is the kingdom of Christ proclaimed by the gospel. It is an eternal kingdom of life, blessedness, and righteousness; all who believe enter it, and are loosed from the bonds of sin and death. Promises of this kind are made abundantly by the gospel in the other prophets, e.g., Micah 5 [:1], And you, Bethlehem, though small among the thousands of Judah, from you shall come one who shall be a leader of my people, Israel; and, again, Hosea 13 [:14], I will deliver them from the hand of death, from death will I rescue them.

This proves that there is only one gospel, just as there is only one Christ because the *euangelion*, the gospel, neither is, nor can be, anything other than the proclamation of Christ the son of God and of David, truly God and man. By His death and resurrection, He has conquered sin, death, and hell for us and all who believe in Him. The gospel may be proclaimed in few words or in many; one writer may describe it briefly and another at length. If at length, then many of the works and words of Christ will be set down, as in the case of the four evangelists. Those who write it briefly, like Peter or Paul, say nothing of Christ's works, but tell succinctly how He conquered sin, death, and hell by His own death and resurrection on behalf of those who believe in Him.

Therefore, beware lest you make Christ into a Moses, and the gospel into a book of law or doctrine, as has been done before now, including some of Jerome's prefaces. In fact, however, the gospel demands no works to make us holy and to redeem us. Indeed, it condemns such works, and demands only faith in Christ, because He has overcome sin, death, and hell for us. Thus it is not by our own works, but by His work, His passion and death, that He makes us righteous, and gives us life and salvation. This is in order that we might take to ourselves His death and victory as if they were our own.

Christ in the gospels, and Peter and Paul in their letters, set forth many doctrines and regulations, and expounded those regulations. That they should have done so must be regarded as another of the many beneficial works of Christ. To know His works and His life's story is not the same thing as to know the gospel, because it does not mean that you know that He conquered sin, death, and the devil. Similarly, it is not knowledge of the gospel if you just know doctrines and rules of this kind. But you will know the gospel when you hear the voice which tells you that Christ Himself is yours, together with His life, teaching, work, death, resurrection, and everything that He has, does, or can do.

A further point to note is that He does not constrain us, but gently draws us, as when He says, Blessed are the poor, etc. [Matt. 5:3]; and, similarly, the apostles use the words, I exhort, I beseech, I pray. On every count, it is evident that the *euangelion* does not form a book of laws, but a proclamation of the good things which Christ has offered us for our own, if only we believe. On the other hand, Moses, in his books, urges, drives, threatens, lashes out, and severely punishes; for he is a maker and administrator of law. That, moreover, is why laws are not prescribed for believers. It is as St. Paul says in I Timothy 1 [:9], Understand this, that a man is given righteousness, life, and salvation by faith; and nought is required of him to give proof of this faith.

If he have faith, the believer cannot be restrained. He betrays himself. He breaks out. He confesses and teaches this gospel to the people at the risk of life itself. His whole life and all his effort are directed towards the benefit of his neighbour, and this not just in order to help him to attain the same grace; but he employs his strength, uses his goods, and stakes his reputation, as he sees Christ did for him, and therefore follows His example. Christ never gave any other commandment than that of love, because He intended that commandment to be the test of His disciples and of true believers. For if (good) works and love do not blossom forth, it is not genuine faith, the gospel has not yet gained a foothold, and Christ is not yet rightly known. Watch that you apply yourself to the books of the New Testament so that you may learn to read them in this way.

The books which are the best and noblest in the New Testament.[2]

You are in a position now rightly to discriminate between all the books, and decide which are the best. The true kernel and marrow of all the books, those which should rightly be ranked first, are the gospel of John and St. Paul's epistles, especially that to the Romans, together with St. Peter's first epistle. Every Christian would do well to read them first and most often, and, by daily perusal, make them as familiar as his daily bread. You will not find in these books much said about the works and miracles of Christ, but you will find a masterly account of how faith in Christ conquers sin, death, and hell; and gives life, righteousness, and salvation. This is the true essence of the gospel, as you have learned.

If I were ever compelled to make a choice, and had to dispense with either the works or the preaching of Christ, I would rather do without the works than the preaching; for the works are of no avail to me, whereas His words give life, as He himself declared. John records but few of the works of Christ, but a

[2] This concluding section appeared only in the first edition, the "September Testament," of 1522.

great deal of His preaching, whereas the other three evangelists record many of His works, but few of His words. It follows
that the gospel of John is unique in loveliness, and of a truth
the principal gospel, far, far superior to the other three, and
much to be preferred. And in the same way, the epistles of
St. Paul and St. Peter are far in advance of the three gospels
of Matthew, Mark, and Luke.

In sum: the gospel and the first epistle of St. John, St. Paul's
epistles, especially those to the Romans, Galatians, and Ephesians; and St. Peter's first epistle, are the books which show
Christ to you. They teach everything you need to know for
your salvation, even if you were never to see or hear any other
book or hear any other teaching. In comparison with these,
the epistle of St. James is an epistle full of straw, because it
contains nothing evangelical. But more about this in the other
Prefaces.

PREFACE TO THE EPISTLE OF ST. PAUL
TO THE ROMANS[1]

This epistle is in truth the most important document in
the New Testament, the gospel in its purest expression. Not
only is it well worth a Christian's while to know it word for
word by heart, but also to meditate on it day by day. It is
the soul's daily bread, and can never be read too often, or
studied too much. The more you probe into it the more precious it becomes, and the better its flavour. God helping me,
I shall try my best to make this Preface serve as an introduction which will enable everyone to understand it in the best
possible way. Hitherto, this epistle has been smothered with
comments and all sorts of irrelevances; yet, in essence, it is a
brilliant light, almost enough to illumine the whole Bible.

[1] Reprinted by permission of the publisher from *The Reforma-
tion Writings of Martin Luther*, volume II, *The Spirit of the
Protestant Reformation*, translated and edited by Bertram Lee
Woolf (London: Lutterworth Press, 1956), pp. 284–300.

The first thing needed is to master the terminology. We must learn what St. Paul means by such words as law, sin, grace, faith, righteousness, flesh, spirit, and the like; otherwise we shall read and only waste our time. You must not understand the term "law" in its everyday sense as something which explains what acts are permitted or forbidden. This holds for ordinary laws, and you keep them by doing what they enjoin, although you may have no heart in it. But God judges according to your inmost convictions; His law must be fulfilled in your very heart, and cannot be obeyed if you merely perform certain acts. Its penalties do indeed apply to certain acts done apart from our inmost convictions, such as hypocrisy and lying. Psalm 117 [116:11] declares that all men are liars, because no one keeps God's law from his heart; nor can he do so; for to be averse to goodness and prone to evil are traits found in all men. If we do not choose goodness freely, we do not keep God's law from the heart. Then sin enters in, and divine wrath is incurred even though, to outward appearance, we are doing many virtuous works and living an honourable life.

In chapter 2, St. Paul therefore asserts that the Jews are all sinners. He says that only those who keep the law are righteous in God's eyes, his point being that no one keeps the law by "works". Rather, Paul says to the Jews, "You teach us not to commit adultery, but you commit adultery yourselves. Further, in judging others; you condemn yourselves, since you do the very things which you condemn" [Rom. 2:1, 22 f.]. It is as if he were to say, To outward appearance, you observe the law scrupulously, condemning those who do not observe it, and being quick to teach one and all. You see the splinter in the other man's eye, but are unaware of the timber in your own. Granted that, in appearance and conduct, you observe the law, owing to your fear of punishment or hope of reward, yet you do nothing from free choice and out of love for the law, but unwillingly and under compulsion; were there no law, you would rather do something else. The logical conclusion is that, in the depths of your heart, you hate the law. What is the use of teaching others not to steal if you are a thief at heart yourself and, if you dared, would be one in fact? Of course, the outer conduct of this kind is not continued for long by humbugs of this kind. It follows that, if you teach others, but not your own selves, you do not know what you teach, and have not rightly understood the nature of the law. Nay, the law increases your guilt, as Paul says in chapter 5 [:20]. A man only hates the law the more, the more it demands what he cannot perform.

That is why, in chapter 7 [:14], Paul calls the law spiritual; spiritual, because, if the law were corporeal, our works would meet its demands. Since it is spiritual, however, no one keeps it, unless everything you do springs from your inmost heart. Such a heart is given us only by God's spirit, and this spirit makes us equal to the demands of the law. Thus we gain a genuine desire for the law, and then everything is done with willing hearts, and not in fear, or under compulsion. Therefore, because that law is spiritual, when it is loved by hearts that are spiritual, and demands that sort of mind, if that spirit is not in our hearts, sin remains; a grudge abides together with hostility to the law, although the law itself is right and good and holy.

Therefore, familiarize yourself with the idea that it is one thing to do what the law enjoins, and quite another to fulfil the law. All that a man does or ever can do of his own free will and strength, is to perform the works required by the law. Nevertheless, all such works are vain and useless as long as we dislike the law, and feel it a constraint. That is Paul's meaning in chapter 3 [:28] when he says, "Through the works of the law shall no man be justified before God". It is obvious—is it not?—that the sophisticators wrangling in the schools are misleading when they teach us to prepare ourselves for grace by our works. How can anyone use works to prepare himself to be good when he never does a good work without a certain reluctance or unwillingness in his heart? How is it possible for God to take pleasure in works that spring from reluctant and hostile hearts?

To fulfil the law, we must meet its requirements gladly and lovingly; live virtuous and upright lives without the constraint of the law, and as if neither the law nor its penalties existed. But this joy, this unconstrained love, is put into our hearts by the Holy Spirit, as St. Paul says in chapter 5 [:5]. But the Holy Spirit is given only in, with, and through, faith in Jesus Christ, as Paul said in his opening paragraph. Similarly, faith itself comes only through the word of God, the gospel. This gospel proclaims Christ as the Son of God; that He was man; that He died and rose again for our sakes, as Paul says in chapters 3, 4, and 10.

We reach the conclusion that faith alone justifies us and fulfils the law; and this because faith brings us the spirit gained by the merits of Christ. The spirit, in turn, gives us the happiness and freedom at which the law aims; and this shows that good works really proceed from faith. That is Paul's meaning in chapter 3 [:31] when, after having condemned the works of the law, he sounds as if he had meant to abrogate the law by faith; but says that, on the contrary, we confirm the law through faith, i.e., we fulfil it by faith.

The word SIN in the Bible means something more than the external works done by our bodily action. It means all the circumstances that act together and excite or incite us to do what is done; in particular, the impulses operating in the depths of our hearts. This, again, means that the single term, "doing", includes the case where a man gives way completely, and falls into sin. Even where nothing is done outwardly, a man may still fall into complete destruction of body and soul. In particular, the Bible penetrates into our hearts, and looks at the root and the very source of all sin, i.e., unbelief in the depth of our heart. Just as faith alone gives us the spirit and the desire for doing works that are plainly good, so unbelief is the sole cause of sin; it exalts the flesh, and gives the desire to do works that are plainly wrong, as happened in the case of Adam and Eve in the garden of Eden, Genesis 3 [:6].

Christ therefore singled out unbelief and called it sin. In John 16 [:8 f.], He says, The spirit will convict the world of sin because they do not believe in me. Similarly, before good or evil works are performed, and before they appear as good or evil fruits, either faith or unbelief must be already in our hearts. Here are the roots, the sap, and the chief energy of all sin. This is what the Bible calls the head of the serpent and of the old dragon, which Christ, the seed of the woman, must crush, as was promised to Adam.

The words GRACE and GIFT differ inasmuch as the true meaning of grace is the kindness or favour which God bears towards us of His own choice, and through which He is will-

ing to give us Christ, and to pour the Holy Spirit and His
blessings upon us. Paul makes this clear in chapter 5 [:15 f.]
when he speaks of the grace and favour of Christ, and the
like. Nevertheless, both the gifts and the spirit must be received by us daily; although even then they will be incomplete; for the old desires and sins still linger in us, and strive
against the spirit, as Paul says in Romans 7 [:14–23] and
Galatians 5 [:17 f.]. Again, Genesis 3 [:15] speaks of the enmity between the woman's children and the serpent's brood.
Yet grace is sufficient to enable us to be accounted entirely
and completely righteous in God's sight, because His grace
does not come in portions and pieces, separately, like so many
gifts; rather, it takes us up completely into its embrace for the
sake of Christ our mediator and intercessor, and in order that
the gifts may take root in us.

This point of view will help you to understand chapter
7 [:9 f.], where Paul depicts himself as still a sinner; and yet,
in chapter 8 [:1], declares that no charge is held against
those who are "in Christ", because of the spirit and the (still
incomplete) gifts. Insofar as our flesh is not yet killed, we are
still sinners. Nevertheless insofar as we believe in Christ, and
begin to receive the spirit, God shows us favour and goodwill. He does this to the extent that He pays no regard to our
remaining sins, and does not judge them; rather He deals with
us according to the faith which we have in Christ until sin is
killed.

FAITH is not something dreamed, a human illusion, although this is what many people understand by the term.
Whenever they see that it is not followed either by an improvement in morals or by good works, while much is still being said about faith, they fall into the error of declaring that
faith is not enough, that we must do "works" if we are to become upright and attain salvation. The reason is that, when
they hear the gospel, they miss the point; in their hearts, and
out of their own resources, they conjure up an idea which they
call "belief", which they treat as genuine faith. All the same,
it is but a human fabrication, an idea without a corresponding
experience in the depths of the heart. It is therefore ineffective
and not followed by a better kind of life.

Faith, however, is something that God effects in us. It

changes us and we are reborn from God, John 1 [:13]. Faith puts the old Adam to death and makes us quite different men in heart, in mind, and in all our powers; and it is accompanied by the Holy Spirit. O, when it comes to faith, what a living, creative, active, powerful thing it is. It cannot do other than good at all times. It never waits to ask whether there is some good work to do, Rather, before the question is raised, it has done the deed, and keeps on doing it. A man not active in this way is a man without faith. He is groping about for faith and searching for good works, but knows neither what faith is nor what good works are. Nevertheless, he keeps on talking nonsense about faith and good works.

Faith is a living and unshakeable confidence, a belief in the grace of God so assured that a man would die a thousand deaths for its sake. This kind of confidence in God's grace, this sort of knowledge of it, makes us joyful, high-spirited, and eager in our relations with God and with all mankind. That is what the Holy Spirit effects through faith. Hence, the man of faith, without being driven, willingly and gladly seeks to do good to everyone, serve everyone, suffer all kinds of hardships, for the sake of the love and glory of the God who has shown him such grace. It is impossible, indeed, to separate works from faith, just as it is impossible to separate heat and light from fire. Beware, therefore, of wrong conceptions of your own, and of those who talk nonsense while thinking they are pronouncing shrewd judgments on faith and works whereas they are showing themselves the greatest of fools. Offer up your prayers to God, and ask Him to create faith in you; otherwise, you will always lack faith, no matter how you try to deceive yourself, or what your efforts and ability.

RIGHTEOUSNESS means precisely the kind of faith we have in mind, and should properly be called "divine righteousness", the righteousness which holds good in God's sight, because it is God's gift, and shapes a man's nature to do his duty to all. By his faith, he is set free from sin, and he finds delight in God's commandments. In this way, he pays God the honour that is due to Him, and renders Him what he owes. He serves his fellows willingly according to his ability, so discharging his obligations to all men. Righteousness of this kind cannot be brought about in the ordinary course of nature, by our own free will, or by our own powers. No one can give faith to himself, nor free himself from unbelief; how, then, can anyone do away with even his smallest sins? It follows that what is done in the absence of faith on the one hand, or in consequence of unbelief on the other, is naught but falsity, self-deception, and sin, Romans 14 [:23], no matter how well it is gilded over.

FLESH and SPIRIT must not be understood as if flesh had only to do with moral impurity, and spirit only with the state of our hearts. Rather, flesh, according to St. Paul, as also according to Christ in John 3 [:6 f.], means everything that is born from the flesh, i.e. the entire self, body and soul, including our reason and all our senses. This is because everything in us leans to the flesh. It is therefore appropriate to call a man "carnal" when, not having yet received grace, he gibbers and jabbers cheerfully about the high things of the spirit in the very way which Galatians 5 [:19 f.] depicts as the works of the flesh, and calls hypocrisy and hatred works of the flesh. Moreover, Romans 8 [:3] says that the law is weakened by the flesh. This is not said simply of moral impurity, but of all sins. In particular, it is said of lack of faith, which is a kind of wickedness more spiritual in character than anything else.

On the other hand, the term spiritual is often applied to one who is busied with the most outward of works, as when Christ washed His disciples' feet, and when Peter went sailing his boat and fishing. Hence, the term "flesh" applies to a person who, in thought and in fact, lives and labours in the service of the body and the temporal life. The term "spirit" applies to a person who, in thought and fact, lives and labours in the service of the spirit and of the life to come. Unless you give these terms this connotation, you will never comprehend Paul's epistle to the Romans, nor any other book of Holy Scripture. Beware then of all teachers who use these terms differently, no matter who they may be, whether Jerome, Augustine, Ambrose, Origen, or their like; or even persons more eminent than they. But let us now turn to the epistle itself.

The first duty of a preacher of the gospel is to declare God's law and describe the nature of sin. Everything is sinful that does not proceed from the spirit, or is not experienced as the

outcome of faith in Christ. The preacher's message must show
men their own selves and their lamentable state, so as to make
them humble and yearn for help. St. Paul follows this plan
and, in chapter 1, begins by condemning certain gross sins and
infidelities which are plain as the day. Such were the sins of
the pagans, and so remain, because they live apart from the
grace of God. Paul therefore says that through the gospel the
wrath of God is revealed, coming from heaven upon all mankind, on account of their godlessness and wickedness. For, although they know and daily recognize that there is a God,
yet human nature, in itself and apart from grace, is so evil
that it neither thanks nor worships Him. Rather, it blinds its
own eyes, and falls continually into wickedness; with the result that, in addition to worshipping false gods, it commits
disgraceful sins and all kinds of evil. It knows no shame and,
if unpunished, commits other sins.

In chapter 2, Paul extends these punishments and applies
them to persons who only appear to be godly, or commit secret sins. Such were the Jews, and such too are all hypocrites,
for they live without joy and love. In their hearts they hate
the divine law and, as is the way with all hypocrites, they
habitually condemn others. They regard themselves as spot-
less, although they are full of envy, hatred, pride, and all
kinds of impurity, Matthew 23 [:28]. These are precisely the
people who despise God's goodness, and heap up the divine
wrath by their hardness of heart. St. Paul therefore, as a true
preacher of the law, asserts that no one is without sin; rather,
he declares the wrath of God against all who try to live by
following their own nature or idle fancies. He does not regard
people of this kind as any better than open sinners. He even
says that they are obstinate and unrepentant.

In chapter 3, he treats of both kinds together, and says, of
one as of the other, all are sinners in God's sight. Moreover,
the Jews have been given God's word, although many have
not believed in it. This attitude has not made either God's
truth or faith of no effect. He cites in addition what Psalm 50[2]
says, namely, that God remains true to His word. Then Paul
returns to the fact that all men are sinners, and proves his

[2] Psalm 51:6 in the edition of 1546, which follows the Hebrew
and no longer the Vulgate enumeration.

case from Scripture. He declares that no one will be justified
by fulfilling the requirements of the law, because the law was
given only to show the nature of sin. He then elaborates his
teaching of the right way to become godly and sanctified.
He says that all men are sinners, and that none are approved
by God. Salvation can only come to them, unearned, by virtue
of faith in Christ. Christ has earned it for us through His
blood. For our sakes, He has become God's "mercy seat", and
so God forgives all the sins that we have committed in the
past. In this way, God shows that His own righteousness,
which He confers through the medium of faith, is our only
help. He revealed this righteousness when the gospel was
preached; but the law and the prophets had already testified
to it. Faith, then, lends its support to the law, although, at the
same time, it repudiates works done according to the law, and
denies the esteem in which they are held.

In chapter 4, having shown the nature of sin in the first
three chapters, and taught how faith leads to righteousness,
Paul begins to deal with certain objections and difficulties.
The first to be discussed is the common case of all those who,
hearing that faith justifies us apart from works, proceed to
ask, Is there any need to do good works? Paul thereupon
claims the support of Abraham and asks, What did Abraham
do in the matter of works? Were they all in vain? Were his
works valueless? He concludes that Abraham, apart from any
works, was justified simply by faith. Indeed, before he did the
"work" of circumcision, righteousness was attributed to him
by Scripture simply on account of his faith, Genesis 15 [:6].
Although the work of circumcision had not contributed to his
righteousness, yet God had commanded it, and, as an act of
obedience, it was a good work. Thus it is also certain that no
other good works contribute to making a man righteous. Like
Abraham's circumcision, they are only outward signs proving
that his righteousness is contained in his faith. Consequently,
we are to understand that good works are purely and simply
outward signs. They proceed from faith, and, like good fruits,
prove that the man himself is already righteous at heart in
God's sight.

In this way Paul adduces a cogent example from Scripture
in support of his doctrine of faith in chapter 3. He now calls

David as a further witness, and he says in Psalm 33 [32:1 f.] that we shall be justified apart from works, although, when justified, we shall not continue without works. Paul then gives this example a broader application, and extends it to all other observances of the law. He concludes that the Jews cannot be heirs of Abraham merely by virtue of their descent, and still less by observing the works of the law. Rather, if they be truly his heirs, they must inherit his faith, because, prior to the laws of Moses and prior to circumcision, Abraham was justified by faith and described as the father of all believers. Moreover, the law issues in wrath rather than in grace, for no one fulfils it willingly and with joy. Hence the works of the law produce reluctance rather than grace. It follows that only faith can obtain the grace promised to Abraham; and examples like this are written in Scripture for our sakes, so that we, too, may have faith.

In chapter 5, Paul comes to the fruits or works to which faith gives rise. These are peace, joy, love to God and all mankind; in addition, assurance, courage, confidence, and hopefulness in spite of sorrow and suffering. Where faith is at home, it is joined by all things of this kind because of the overflowing goodwill which God shows to us in Christ. For our sakes, God let Him suffer death, not only before we could intercede in prayer to Him, but even while we were still enemies. We therefore maintain that faith justifies us apart from any works, although we must not draw the conclusion that we have no need to do any good works. Nay, rather, works of the right kind must not be neglected, works of which the mere ceremonialists know nothing. They trump up their own kind of works, but these breathe neither peace, nor joy, nor assurance, nor love, nor hope, nor courage, nor certainty, nor anything that partakes of genuine Christian conduct or faith.

Paul now makes an interesting digression, and discusses the origin of both sin and righteousness, of death and life. He shows how Adam and Christ represent two contrary types, and says, in effect, that Christ had to come as a second Adam and to transmit His righteousness by virtue of a new, spiritual birth in faith. This is the counterpoise to what Adam did when he transmitted sin to us through our earlier, physical birth. That is how Paul proves his assertion that no one can deliver himself from sin, or attain righteousness, by means of works, any more than he can prevent his own physical birth. At the same time, Paul proves that the God-given law, which would have helped, if anything could help in attaining righteousness, not only gave no help when it did come, but only increased sin. Our evil nature becomes all the more hostile to it, and prefers to pursue its own devices, in proportion to the strictness of that law. Thus the law makes Christ more necessary to us, and increases the need for grace to help our nature.

In chapter 6, Paul discusses the special function of faith. The question at issue is that of the battle of the spirit struggling against the flesh, and finally killing outright the sins and passions that remain alive after our justification. He teaches that faith does not free us from sin to the extent that we can relax into laziness and self-assurance, as if sin no longer existed. Sin still exists; but, on account of the faith that battles with it, is not held against us to our condemnation. Throughout our whole lives, we shall be kept fully employed with our own selves, taming our body, killing its passions, controlling its members till they obey, not the passions, but the spirit. This self-discipline is needed in order that we might conform to the death and resurrection of Christ, and also that we might complete the meaning of our baptism; for baptism, too, signifies the death of sin and the new life of grace. The final goal is that we should be entirely liberated from sin, rise again in the body with Christ, and live for ever.

Paul declares that this is possible because we are not under the law, but under grace. He gives a clear explanation of what it means to live "not under the law". This is not the equivalent of saying that no laws bind us, and that we can all follow our own devices; but rather, to be "under the law" means to live apart from grace, and to be occupied with fulfilling the works of the law. In a case like this, it is certain that sin dominates us through the law, since none take a natural delight in the law; and our condition is then very sinful. But grace makes us take pleasure in the law; then sin no longer enters in, and the law is no longer against us, but on our side.

To have the law on our side is the very nature of freedom from sin and the law, and Paul continues his discussion of this state of affairs to the end of the present chapter. He says that this freedom consists of taking pleasure simply in doing good, or in living uprightly, without being constrained to do so by the law. This freedom is therefore a spiritual freedom; it does not abolish the law; rather it supplies and furnishes what the law lacks, namely, willingness and love. Thus the law is silenced and put out of action; it makes no further demands. It is as if you were in debt to a lender, and unable to pay; there would be two ways of settling the matter and setting you free. In the first, the lender would refuse to accept anything from you, but simply rule off the account in his ledger. Or, on the other hand, some kind person might give you enough to settle up and pay the account; and this is how Christ has set us free from the law. Our freedom is not a crude, physical freedom by virtue of which we can refuse to do anything at all; rather, it does much, in fact everything; it is freedom from the demands and obligations of the law.

In chapter 7, Paul consolidates his argument with an analogy drawn from married life. If the husband dies, the wife is exempt from the marriage bond. By the death of one, the other is made free and set at liberty. The woman is not obliged, nor even merely permitted, to take another husband; rather, the point is that she is now quite at liberty for the first time to please herself about taking another husband. She could not do this earlier, not before she was free from her former husband. Similarly, our conscience is bound to the law in its former state of the old sinful self. But when this self is put to death by the spirit, our conscience is set at liberty, and each is released from the other. This does not mean that our conscience has become inactive, but that now, for the first time, it can really cling to Christ as a second husband, and bring forth the fruit of life.

Paul then proceeds to give a broader description of the nature of sin and the law, explaining that only by virtue of the law does sin really come alive and grow strong. The old self becomes all the more hostile to the law when it can no longer render what the law requires. The nature of the old self is sinful, and cannot help being so. To that self, therefore, the law means death and all the pains of death, and this, not because the law is evil, but because our evil nature is averse to goodness, the very goodness which is demanded by the law. Similarly, it is impossible to ask a sick man to walk about and leap and do what a healthy man does.

St. Paul therefore asserts at this point that if the law is rightly understood, and if it is construed in the best way, it only reminds us of our sins, uses them to kill us, and makes us liable to everlasting wrath. All this our conscience learns perfectly by experience when it meets the law face to face. Hence, if we are to be upright and attain salvation, we shall require something different from, and better than, the law. Those people who fail to understand the law aright, are blind; in their presumptuous way, they think they can fulfil it with works. They are unaware how much the law demands; in particular, a heart that is free and eager and joyful. Hence they do not read Moses aright; the veil still covers and conceals his face.

Paul now explains how flesh and spirit contend with each other in our hearts. He cites himself as an example, in order that we may learn properly how to put our indwelling sin to death. But he applies the name of law to both the spirit and the flesh, because, just as it is the nature of the divine law to make requirements and demands, so does the flesh strive and struggle and rage against the spirit, and insist on its own way. Conversely, the spirit strives and struggles against the flesh, and insists on its own way. This wrangling continues within us as long as we live; more in some, less in others, according as the flesh or the spirit is the stronger. But we must understand that our complete self consists of both elements: spirit and flesh; we fight with ourselves until we become wholly spiritual.

In chapter 8, Paul gives comfort to those engaged in this warfare, and says that the flesh shall not condemn them. He also shows the nature of flesh and spirit, and explains that the spirit comes from Christ, who gives us His Holy Spirit. This makes us spiritual, constrains the flesh, and assures us that, no matter how violently sin rages within us, we are the children of God as long as we obey the spirit and strive to put sin to death. But, because nothing else is so effective in taming the flesh as are our cross and the sufferings we must bear, he comforts us in our sufferings by assuring us of the support of the spirit, of love, and of all created things. In particular, not only does the spirit sigh within us, but also every creature shares our longings to be free from the flesh and from sin. Thus we see how these three chapters discuss the real work of faith, namely, to put the old Adam to death, and to control the flesh.

In chapters 9, 10, and 11, Paul deals with the eternal providence of God. It is by this providence that it was first decided who should, and who should not, have faith; who should conquer sin, and who should not be able to do so. This is a matter which is taken out of our hands, and is solely at God's disposal —that so we might become truly righteous. And this is our greatest need. We are so weak and wavering that, if it were left to us, surely not a single person would be saved, and the devil would certainly overpower us all. On the other hand, God is constant, and His providence will not fail, nor can anyone prevent its fulfilment. We therefore have hope in spite of sin.

At this stage, we must put a stop to those impious and arrogant persons who use their reasoning powers here first, and in their high and mighty way begin to probe into the deeps of the divine providence, inquiring to no purpose whether they are among the elect; they cannot help bringing disaster on themselves, either by failure or by running needless risks. But you must study this epistle yourself, chapter by chapter. Concentrate first of all on Christ and His gospel, in order to learn how to recognize your sins and to know His grace. Next, wrestle with the problem of sin as discussed in chapters 1, 2, 3, 4, 5, 6, 7, and 8. Then, when you have arrived at chapter 8, dominated by the cross and passion of Christ, you will learn the right way of understanding the divine providence in chapters 9, 10, and 11, and the assurance that it gives. If we do not feel the weight of the passion, the cross, and the death, we cannot cope with the problem of providence without either hurt to ourselves or secret anger with God. That is why the Adam in us has to be quite dead before we can bear this doctrine, and drink this strong wine, without harm. So beware! Avoid drinking wine when you are still a suckling infant. Every doctrine requires us to be of the appropriate ability at the right age, and of the due maturity.

In chapter 12, Paul speaks of the true way of serving God.

He shows that all Christians are priests, and that the sacrifices they offer are not money or cattle, as prescribed by the law, but their own selves after their passions have been put to death. He then describes the outward conduct of Christians under the discipline of the spirit; how they must teach, preach, rule, serve, give, suffer, love, live, and act towards friend, foe, and fellow-man. These are the works which a Christian does, for, as I have said, faith is not an inert thing.

In chapter 13, he teaches us to respect and obey the secular authorities. This subject is introduced, not indeed because such conduct will make the people good in God's eyes, but because it ensures the public peace and the protection of those who are good citizens; whereas the wicked will not be able to do evil without fear, or with easy minds. Such authority must therefore be held in respect by good people, although they do not require its services. But Paul ends by showing that love includes everything else; and he clinches the whole with the example of Christ, who has done for us what we too must do in following Him.

In chapter 14, Paul teaches us how to deal with any who have an unstable conscience and to spare them. He teaches us not to use our Christian liberty to hurt the weak, but to help them. Where this is not done, dissension arises and the gospel comes into contempt, although all depends on it. It is therefore better to humour the weak in faith a little, till they grow stronger, rather than that the gospel should be lost altogether. Love alone can do a work like this, and it is particularly needed just now when the question of eating meat, and other matters of free choice, are being discussed intemperately and brusquely, disturbing to no purpose those of unstable conscience before they know the truth.

In chapter 15, Paul cites the example of Christ, and teaches that we should bear with others who are weak, even including open sinners and those who have disgusting habits. We must not cast them off, but be patient with them until they reform. That is what Christ did in our own case, and continues to do day by day; for He bears with many shortcomings and evil habits, as well as all sorts of imperfections on our part; yet He never fails to help us.

Then, in conclusion, Paul prays for them, praises them, and

commends them to God. He explains his own status and message, begs them earnestly to give gifts on behalf of the poor at Jerusalem, and avers that he speaks and acts entirely out of love. It may therefore be said that this epistle gives the richest possible account of what a Christian ought to know, namely, the meaning of law, gospel, sin, punishment, grace, faith, righteousness, Christ, God, good works, love, hope, and the cross. It tells what our attitude should be to our fellows, whether righteous or sinful, strong or weak, friend or foe; and to our own selves. Moreover, everything is cogently proved from Scripture, and illustrated by Paul's own case or that of the prophets; it leaves nothing to be desired. Therefore, it seems as if St. Paul had intended this epistle to set out, once for all, the whole of Christian doctrine in brief, and to be an introduction preparatory to the whole of the Old Testament. For there can be no doubt that if we had this epistle well and truly in our hearts, we should possess the light and power found in the Old Testament. Therefore, every Christian ought to study Romans regularly and continuously. May God grant His grace to this end. Amen.

The final chapter consists of greetings. It includes, too, a noble warning in regard to man-made doctrines which were being disseminated side by side with the gospel, and which were doing harm. It is exactly as if St. Paul had foreseen that, out of Rome and through the Romanists, would come the misleading and vexatious canons and decretals, together with all the crawling maggots of man-made laws and regulations, which by now have eaten into the entire world, and which have not only swallowed up this epistle and all Holy Scripture, but prevented the work of the spirit, and destroyed our faith; so that nothing else remains than their God, the belly. Paul here depicts them as its servants. God deliver us from them. Amen.

PREFACE TO THE EPISTLES
OF ST. JAMES AND ST. JUDE[1]

I think highly of the epistle of James, and regard it as valuable although it was rejected in early days. It does not expound human doctrines, but lays much emphasis on God's law. Yet, to give my own opinion without prejudice to that of anyone else, I do not hold it to be of apostolic authorship, for the following reasons:

Firstly, because, in direct opposition to St. Paul and all the rest of the Bible, it ascribes justification to works, and declares that Abraham was justified by his works when he offered up his son. St. Paul, on the contrary, in Romans 4 [:3], teaches that Abraham was justified without works, by his faith alone, the proof being in Genesis 15 [:6], which was before he sacrificed his son. Although it would be possible to "save" the epistle by a gloss giving a correct explanation of justification here ascribed to works, it is impossible to deny that it does refer Moses's word in Genesis 15 (which speaks not of Abraham's works but of his faith, just as Paul makes plain in Romans 4) to Abraham's works. This defect proves that the epistle is not of apostolic provenance.

Secondly, because, in the whole length of its teaching, not once does it give Christians any instruction or reminder of the passion, resurrection, or spirit of Christ. It mentions Christ once and again, but teaches nothing about Him; it speaks only of a commonplace faith in God. It is the office of a true apostle to preach the passion and resurrection and work of Christ, and to lay down the true ground for this faith, as Christ himself says in John 15 [:27], You shall be my witnesses. All genuinely sacred books are unanimous here, and all preach Christ emphatically. The true touchstone for testing every book is to

[1] Reprinted by permission of the publisher from *The Reformation Writings of Martin Luther*, volume II, *The Spirit of the Protestant Reformation*, translated and edited by Bertram Lee Woolf (London: Lutterworth Press, 1956), pp. 306-8.

discover whether it emphasizes the prominence of Christ or not. All Scripture sets forth Christ, Romans 3 [:24 f.] and Paul will know nothing but Christ, I Corinthians 2 [:2]. What does not teach Christ is not apostolic, not even if taught by Peter or Paul. On the other hand, what does preach Christ is apostolic, even if Judas, Annas, Pilate, or Herod does it.

The epistle of James, however, only drives you to the law and its works. He mixes one thing with another to such an extent that I suspect some good and pious man assembled a few things said by disciples of the apostles, and then put them down in black and white; or perhaps the epistle was written by someone else who made notes of a sermon of his. He calls the law a law of freedom, although St. Paul calls it a law of slavery, wrath, death, and sin.

Yet he quotes St. Peter's saying that "Love covers a multitude of sins", and again "Humble yourselves under the hand of God"; further, St. Paul's word in Galatians 5, The spirit lusteth against hate. But St. James was killed by Herod in Jerusalem before St. Peter's death, which shows the writer to have been far later than St. Peter or St. Paul.

In sum: he wished to guard against those who depended on faith without going on to works, but he had neither the spirit nor the thought nor the eloquence equal to the task. He does violence to Scripture, and so contradicts Paul and all Scripture. He tries to accomplish by emphasizing law what the apostles bring about by attracting men to love. I therefore refuse him a place among the writers of the true canon of my Bible; but I would not prevent anyone placing him or raising him where he likes, for the epistle contains many excellent passages. One man does not count as a man even in the eyes of the world; how then shall this single and isolated writer count against Paul and all the rest of the Bible?

The Epistle of St. Jude

No one can deny that this epistle is an excerpt from, or copy of, the second epistle of St. Peter, for all he says is nearly the same over again. Moreover, he speaks of the apostles as would a disciple of a much later date. He quotes words and events which are found nowhere in Scripture, and which moved the fathers to reject this epistle from the canon. Moreover, the apostle Jude did not go into Greek-speaking lands, but into Persia; and it is said that he could not write Greek. Hence, although I value the book, yet it is not essential to reckon it among the canonical books that lay the foundation of faith.

PREFACE TO THE PSALMS[1]

Text and Notes

Many of the fathers have loved and praised the Book of Psalms above all the other books of the Bible. Although the book itself is a sufficient monument to the writers, we ought to express our own praise and thanks for it. In years gone by, all our attention has been taken up by innumerable legends of saints, many Passionals,[2] books of edification, and moral stories, which have been in circulation while this book was put away on the top shelf, and so utterly neglected that scarcely a single psalm was properly understood. Yet the Book of Psalms continued to radiate such a sweet and lovely fragrance that every devout man was sustained and encouraged when he came upon its unfamiliar phrases, and so grew to love it. No books of moral tales and no legends of saints which have been written, or ever will be written, are to my mind as noble as the Book of Psalms; and if my purpose were to choose the best of all the edificatory books, legends of saints, or moral stories, and to have them assembled and presented in the best possible way, my choice would inevitably fall on our present Book.

In it we find, not what this or that saint did, but what the chief of all saints did, and what all saints still do. In it is shown

[1] Reprinted by permission from *The Reformation Writings of Martin Luther*, volume II, *The Spirit of the Protestant Reformation*, translated and edited by Bertram Lee Woolf (London: Lutterworth Press, 1956), pp. 267–71.

[2] Accounts of the lives and sufferings of the saints.

their attitude to God, to their friends, to their foes; and their manner of life and behaviour in face of manifold dangers and sufferings. Above all this, the book contains divine and helpful doctrines and commandments of every kind. It should be precious and dear to us if only because it most clearly promises the death and resurrection of Christ, and describes His kingdom, and the nature and standing of all Christian people. It could well be called a "little Bible" since it contains, set out in the briefest and most beautiful form, all that is to be found in the whole Bible, a book of good examples from among the whole of Christendom and from among the saints, in order that those who could not read the whole Bible through would have almost the whole of it in summary form, comprised in a single booklet.

The virtue of the Book of Psalms is unique, and is more finely exhibited than elsewhere when we compare it with the multitude of other books which continually babble about the saints and their doings, but seldom or never quote their words. Here the Book of Psalms is unique. It tastes good and sweet to those who read it, and it gives a faithful record of what the saints did and said: how they communed with God and prayed to Him in the old days, and how such men still commune with Him and pray to Him. In comparison with the Book of Psalms, the other books, those containing the legends of saints and other exemplary matter, depict holy men all with their tongues tied; whereas the Book of Psalms presents us with saints alive and in the round. It is like putting a dumb man side by side with one who can speak: the first is only half alive. Speech is the most powerful and exalted of human faculties. Man is distinguished from animals by the faculty of speech, much more than by shape or form or any other activity. A block of timber can be given a human shape by the art of the woodcarver; and an animal is a man's equal in seeing, hearing, smelling, singing, running, standing, eating, drinking, fasting, thirsting; or in bearing hunger, cold, and hardship.

The Book of Psalms has other excellencies: it preserves, not the trivial and ordinary things said by the saints, but their deepest and noblest utterances, those which they used when speaking in full earnest and all urgency to God. It not only tells what they say about their work and conduct, but also

lays bare their hearts and the deepest treasures hidden in
their souls: and this is done in a way which allows us to contemplate the causes and the sources of their words and works.
In other words, it enables us to see into their hearts and understand the nature of their thoughts; how at heart they took
their stand in varying circumstances of life, in danger, and in
distress. Legends and moral tales cannot, and do not, do this,
and so they make much of the miracles and works of the
saints. But it is impossible for me to tell the state of a man's
heart by only looking at or hearing about his many remarkable activities. And, just as I would rather hear a saint speak
than see his actions, so I would rather look into his heart and
the treasures of his soul than listen to his words. What the
Book of Psalms gives us in richest measure in regard to the
saints is the fullness of certainty as to what they felt in their
hearts, and what was the sound of the words which they used
in addressing God and their fellow-men.

The human heart is like a ship on a stormy sea driven about
by winds blowing from all four corners of heaven. In one man,
there is fear and anxiety about impending disaster; another
groans and moans at all the surrounding evil. One man min-
gles hope and presumption out of the good fortune to which he
is looking forward; and another is puffed up with a confidence
and pleasure in his present possessions. Such storms, however,
teach us to speak sincerely and frankly, and make a clean
breast. For a man who is in the grip of fear or distress speaks
of disaster in a quite different way from one who is filled with
happiness; and a man who is filled with joy speaks and sings
about happiness quite differently from one who is in the grip
of fear. They say that when a sorrowing man laughs or a
happy man weeps, his laughter and his weeping do not come
from the heart. In other words, these men do not lay bare, or
speak of things which lie in, the bottom of their hearts.

The Book of Psalms is full of heartfelt utterances made during storms of this kind. Where can one find nobler words to
express joy than in the Psalms of praise or gratitude? In them
you can see into the hearts of all the saints as if you were
looking at a lovely pleasure-garden, or were gazing into
heaven. How fair and charming and delightful are the flowers
you will find there which grow out of all kinds of beautiful

thoughts of God and His grace. Or where can one find more profound, more penitent, more sorrowful words in which to express grief than in the Psalms of lamentation? In these, you see into the hearts of all the saints as if you were looking at death or gazing into hell, so dark and obscure is the scene rendered by the changing shadows of the wrath of God. So, too, when the Psalms speak of fear or hope, they depict fear and hope more vividly than any painter could do, and with more eloquence than that possessed by Cicero or the greatest of the orators. And, as I have said, the best of all is that these words are used by the saints in addressing God; that they speak with God in a tone that doubles the force and earnestness of the words themselves. For when a man speaks to another man on subjects such as these, he does not speak from his deepest heart; his words neither burn nor throb nor press so urgently as they do here.

It is therefore easy to understand why the Book of Psalms is the favourite book of all the saints. For every man on every occasion can find in it Psalms which fit his needs, which he feels to be as appropriate as if they had been set there just for his sake. In no other book can he find words to equal them, nor better words. Nor does he wish it. And there follows from this a further excellence that when some such a word has come home and is felt to answer his need, he receives assurance that he is in the company of the saints, and that all that has happened to the saints is happening to him, because all of them join in singing a little song with him, since he can use their words to talk with God as they did. All this is reserved to faith, for an ungodly man has no idea what the words mean.

Finally, the Book of Psalms contains an assurance and a valid passport with which we can follow all the saints without danger. The moral stories and legends of the saints whose words are never given, advocate works that no man can imitate, works that are, in most cases, the beginnings of sects and factions, that lead and even drag one away from the fellowship of the saints. The Book of Psalms, on the other hand, preserves you from factions and leads you into the fellowship of the saints; for, whether in joy, fear, hope, or sorrow, it teaches you to be equable in mind and calm in word, as were all the saints. The sum of all is that, if you wish to see the holy Christian church depicted in living colours, and given a living form, in a painting in miniature, then place the Book of Psalms in front of you; you will have a beautiful, bright, polished mirror which will show you what Christianity is. Nay, You will see your own self in it, for here is the true γνῶθι σεαυτόν,[3] by which you can know yourself as well as the God Himself who created all things.

Let us therefore take care to thank God for these immeasurable benefits. Let us accept, use, and exercise them diligently and earnestly to the glory and honour of God, lest by our ingratitude we earn something worse. For of old, in the dark times, what a treasure it would have been held to be, if a man could have rightly understood one single Psalm, and could have read or heard it in simple German. To-day, however, blessed are the eyes that see what we see and the ears that hear what we hear. But beware (for unfortunately we witness it) lest it happen to us as to the Jews in the wilderness, who said of the heavenly manna, Our soul turns from this poor food. For we ought to understand what is also said, "that they suffered from plagues and died", lest it happen to us, too. To this end, may we be helped by the Father of all grace and mercy through Jesus Christ our Lord, to whom be praise and thanks, honour and glory, for the Book of Psalms in the common German tongue, and for all his innumerable and unutterable mercies for ever. Amen.

[3] Know thyself.

THE FREEDOM OF A CHRISTIAN[1]

[The Freedom of a Christian, *with its accompanying* Open Letter to Pope Leo X, *was among Luther's last attempts at conciliation with Rome. In the letter, Luther affirms that it is not the Pope's person he has attacked, but the ungodly doctrines and corruption which have surrounded the papacy.* The Freedom of a Christian *is a small treatise, dedicated to the Pope "as a token of peace and good hope." In Luther's own words, "it contains the whole of Christian life in a brief form. . . ." If one were to single out one short document representing the content and spirit of Luther's faith,* The Freedom of a Christian *would undoubtedly be at the top. It was published in November 1520, soon after* An Appeal to the Ruling Class of German Nationality as to the Amelioration of the State of Christendom (*usually called* The Address to the German Nobility) *and* The Pagan Servitude of the Church (*usually called* The Babylonian Captivity of the Church).]

LETTER OF DEDICATION TO MAYOR MÜHLPHORDT

To the learned and wise gentleman, Hieronymus Mühlphordt,[2] mayor of Zwickau, my exceptionally gracious friend

[1] Reprinted by permission of the publisher from *Luther's Works*, volume 31, *Career of the Reformer: I*, edited by Harold J. Grimm (Philadelphia: Muhlenberg Press, 1957), pp. 333–77. The translation is by W. A. Lambert and revised by Harold J. Grimm.
[2] The given name of Mühlphordt was actually Hermann.

and patron, I, Martin Luther, Augustinian, present my compliments and good wishes.

My learned and wise sir and gracious friend, the venerable Master Johann Egran, your praiseworthy preacher, spoke to me in terms of praise concerning your love for and pleasure in the Holy Scripture, which you also diligently confess and unceasingly praise before all men. For this reason he desired to make me acquainted with you. I yielded willingly and gladly to his persuasion, for it is a special pleasure to hear of someone who loves divine truth. Unfortunately there are many people, especially those who are proud of their titles, who oppose the truth with all their power and cunning. Admittedly it must be that Christ, set as a stumbling block and a sign that is spoken against, will be an offense and a cause for the fall and rising of many [I Cor. 1:23; Luke 2:34].

In order to make a good beginning of our acquaintance and friendship, I have wished to dedicate to you this treatise or discourse in German, which I have already dedicated to the people in Latin, in the hope that my teachings and writings concerning the papacy will not be considered objectionable by anybody.[8] I commend myself to you and to the grace of God. Amen. Wittenberg, 1520.

AN OPEN LETTER TO POPE LEO X

To Leo X, Pope at Rome, Martin Luther wishes salvation in Christ Jesus our Lord. Amen.

Living among the monsters of this age with whom I am now for the third year waging war, I am compelled occasionally to look up to you, Leo, most blessed father, and to think of you. Indeed, since you are occasionally regarded as the sole cause of my warfare, I cannot help thinking of you. To be sure, the undeserved raging of your godless flatterers against me has compelled me to appeal from your see to a future council, despite the decrees of your predecessors Pius and Julius, who with a foolish tyranny forbade such an appeal. Nevertheless,

[8] In place of the German version, the Latin version dedicated to the pope was used as the basis of the present English translation.

I have never alienated myself from Your Blessedness to such an extent that I should not with all my heart wish you and your see every blessing, for which I have besought God with earnest prayers to the best of my ability. It is true that I have been so bold as to despise and look down upon those who have tried to frighten me with the majesty of your name and authority. There is one thing, however, which I cannot ignore and which is the cause of my writing once more to Your Blessedness. It has come to my attention that I am accused of great indiscretion, said to be my great fault, in which, it is said, I have not spared even your person.

I freely vow that I have, to my knowledge, spoken only good and honorable words concerning you whenever I have thought of you. If I had ever done otherwise, I myself could by no means condone it, but should agree entirely with the judgment which others have formed of me; and I should do nothing more gladly than recant such indiscretion and impiety. I have called you a Daniel in Babylon; and everyone who reads what I have written knows how zealously I defended your innocence against your defamer Sylvester.[4] Indeed, your reputation and the fame of your blameless life, celebrated as they are throughout the world by the writings of many great men, are too well known and too honorable to be assailed by anyone, no matter how great he is. I am not so foolish as to attack one whom all people praise. As a matter of fact, I have always tried, and will always continue, not to attack even those whom the public dishonors, for I take no pleasure in the faults of any man, since I am conscious of the beam in my own eye. I could not, indeed, be the first one to cast a stone at the adulteress [John 8:1–11].

I have, to be sure, sharply attacked ungodly doctrines in general, and I have snapped at my opponents, not because of their bad morals, but because of their ungodliness. Rather than repent this in the least, I have determined to persist in that fervent zeal and to despise the judgment of men, following the example of Christ who in his zeal called his opponents "a brood of vipers," "blind fools," "hypocrites," "children of

---

[4] Sylvester Mazzolini (1456–1523), usually called Prierias, had exaggerated the authority of the papacy.

the devil" [Matt. 23:13, 17, 33; John 8:44]. Paul branded Magus [Elymas, the magician] as the "son of the devil, . . . full of all deceit and villainy" [Acts 13:10], and he calls others "dogs," "deceivers," and "adulterers" [Phil. 3:2; II Cor. 11:13; 2:17]. If you will allow people with sensitive feelings to judge, they would consider no person more stinging and unrestrained in his denunciations than Paul. Who is more stinging than the prophets? Nowadays, it is true, we are made so sensitive by the raving crowd of flatterers that we cry out that we are stung as soon as we meet with disapproval. When we cannot ward off the truth with any other pretext, we flee from it by ascribing it to a fierce temper, impatience, and immodesty. What is the good of salt if it does not bite? Of what use is the edge of a sword if it does not cut? "Cursed is he who does the work of the Lord deceitfully . . ." [Jer. 48:10].

Therefore, most excellent Leo, I beg you to give me a hearing after I have vindicated myself by this letter, and believe me when I say that I have never thought ill of you personally, that I am the kind of a person who would wish you all good things eternally, and that I have no quarrel with any man concerning his morals but only concerning the word of truth. In all other matters I will yield to any man whatsoever; but I have neither the power nor the will to deny the Word of God. If any man has a different opinion concerning me, he does not think straight or understand what I have actually said.

I have truly despised your see, the Roman Curia, which, however, neither you nor anyone else can deny is more corrupt than any Babylon or Sodom ever was, and which, as far as I can see, is characterized by a completely depraved, hopeless, and notorious godlessness. I have been thoroughly incensed over the fact that good Christians are mocked in your name and under the cloak of the Roman church. I have resisted and will continue to resist your see as long as the spirit of faith lives in me. Not that I shall strive for the impossible or hope that by my efforts alone anything will be accomplished in that most disordered Babylon, where the fury of so many flatterers is turned against me; but I acknowledge my indebtedness to my Christian brethren, whom I am duty-bound to warn so that fewer of them may be destroyed by the plagues of Rome, at least so that their destruction may be less cruel.

As you well know, there has been flowing from Rome these many years—like a flood covering the world—nothing but a devastation of men's bodies and souls and possessions, the worst examples of the worst of all things. All this is clearer than day to all, and the Roman church, once the holiest of all, has become the most licentious den of thieves [Matt. 21:13], the most shameless of all brothels, the kingdom of sin, death, and hell. It is so bad that even Antichrist himself, if he should come, could think of nothing to add to its wickedness.

Meanwhile you, Leo, sit as a lamb in the midst of wolves [Matt. 10:16] and like Daniel in the midst of lions [Dan. 6:16]. With Ezekiel you live among scorpions [Ezek. 2:6]. How can you alone oppose these monsters? Even if you would call to your aid three or four well learned and thoroughly reliable cardinals, what are these among so many? You would all be poisoned before you could begin to issue a decree for the purpose of remedying the situation. The Roman Curia is already lost, for God's wrath has relentlessly fallen upon it. It detests church councils, it fears a reformation, it cannot allay its own corruption; and what was said of its mother Babylon also applies to it: "We would have cured Babylon, but she was not healed. Let us forsake her" [Jer. 51:9].

It was your duty and that of your cardinals to remedy these evils, but the gout of these evils makes a mockery of the healing hand, and neither chariot nor horse responds to the rein [Virgil *Georgics* i. 514]. Moved by this affection for you, I have always been sorry, most excellent Leo, that you were made pope in these times, for you are worthy of being pope in better days. The Roman Curia does not deserve to have you or men like you, but it should have Satan himself as pope, for he now actually rules in that Babylon more than you do.

Would that you might discard that which your most profligate enemies boastfully claim to be your glory and might live on a small priestly income of your own or on your family inheritance! No persons are worthy of glorying in that honor except the Iscariots, the sons of perdition. What do you accomplish in the Roman Curia, my Leo? The more criminal and detestable a man is, the more gladly will he use your name to destroy men's possessions and souls, to increase crime, to suppress faith and truth and God's whole church. O most unhappy Leo, you are sitting on a most dangerous throne. I am telling you the truth because I wish you well.

If Bernard felt sorry for Eugenius[5] at a time when the Roman See, which, although even then very corrupt, was ruled with better prospects for improvement, why should not we complain who for three hundred years have had such a great increase of corruption and wickedness? Is it not true that under the vast expanse of heaven there is nothing more corrupt, more pestilential, more offensive than the Roman Curia? It surpasses beyond all comparison the godlessness of the Turks so that, indeed, although it was once a gate of heaven, it is now an open mouth of hell, such a mouth that it cannot be shut because of the wrath of God. Only one thing can we try to do, as I have said: we may be able to call back a few from that yawning chasm of Rome and save them.

Now you see, my Father Leo, how and why I have so violently attacked that pestilential see. So far have I been from raving against your person that I even hoped I might gain your favor and save you if I should make a strong and stinging assault upon that prison, that veritable hell of yours. For you and your salvation and the salvation of many others with you will be served by everything that men of ability can do against the confusion of this wicked Curia. They serve your office who do every harm to the Curia; they glorify Christ who in every way curse it. In short, they are Christians who are not Romans.

To enlarge upon this, I never intended to attack the Roman Curia or to raise any controversy concerning it. But when I saw all efforts to save it were hopeless, I despised it, gave it a bill of divorce [Deut. 24:1], and said, "Let the evildoer still do evil, and the filthy still be filthy" [Rev. 22:11]. Then I turned to the quiet and peaceful study of the Holy Scriptures so that I might be helpful to my brothers around me. When I had made some progress in these studies, Satan opened his eyes and then filled his servant Johann Eck, a notable enemy of Christ, with an insatiable lust for glory and thus aroused him to drag me unawares to a debate, seizing me by means of one little word which I had let slip concerning the primacy of the

---

[5] Bernard of Clairvaux had written a devotional book, *On Consideration*, to Pope Eugenius III (1145–53), in which he discussed the duties of the pope and the dangers connected with his office.

Roman church. Then that boastful braggart, frothing and gnashing his teeth, declared that he would risk everything for the glory of God and the honor of the Apostolic See. Puffed up with the prospect of abusing your authority, he looked forward with great confidence to a victory over me. He was concerned not so much with establishing the primacy of Peter as he was with demonstrating his own leadership among the theologians of our time. To that end he considered it no small advantage to triumph over Luther. When the debate ended badly for the sophist, an unbelievable madness overcame the man, for he believed that it was his fault alone which was responsible for my disclosing all the infamy of Rome.

Allow me, I pray, most excellent Leo, this once to plead my cause and to indict your real enemies. You know, I believe, what dealings your legate, cardinal of St. Sisto,[6] an unwise and unfortunate, or rather, an unreliable man, had with me. When out of reverence for your name I had placed myself and my cause in his hands, he did not try to establish peace. He could easily have done so with a single word, for at that time I promised to keep silent and to end the controversy, provided my opponents were ordered to do likewise. As he was a man who sought glory, however, and was not content with such an agreement, he began to defend my opponents, to give them full freedom, and to order me to recant, even though this was not included in his instructions. When matters went fairly well, he with his churlish arbitrariness made them far worse. Therefore Luther is not to blame for what followed. All the blame is Cajetan's, who did not permit me to keep silent, as I at that time most earnestly requested him to do. What more should I have done?

There followed Karl Miltitz, also a nuncio of Your Holiness, who exerted much effort and traveled back and forth, omitting nothing that might help restore the order which Cajetan had rashly and arrogantly disturbed. He finally, with the help of the most illustrious prince, the Elector Frederick, managed to arrange several private conferences with me. Again I yielded out of respect for your name, was prepared to keep silent, and even accepted as arbiter either the archbishop of Trier or the

---

[6] Cardinal Cajetan.

bishop of Naumburg. So matters were arranged. But while this arrangement was being followed with good prospects of success, behold, that other and greater enemy of yours, Eck, broke in with the Leipzig Debate which he had undertaken against Dr. Karlstadt. When the new question of the primacy of the pope was raised, he suddenly turned his weapons against me and completely upset our arrangement for maintaining peace. Meanwhile Karl Miltitz waited. The debate was held and judges were selected. But again no decision was reached, which is not surprising, for through Eck's lies, tricks, and wiles everything was stirred up, aggravated, and confused worse than ever. Regardless of the decision which might have been reached, a greater conflagration would have resulted, for he sought glory, not the truth. Again I left undone nothing that I ought to have done.

I admit that on this occasion no small amount of corrupt Roman practices came to light, but whatever wrong was done was Eck's fault, who undertook a task beyond his capacities. Striving insanely for his own glory, he revealed the shame of Rome to all the world. This man is your enemy, my dear Leo, or rather the enemy of your Curia. From his example alone we can learn that no enemy is more pernicious than a flatterer. What did he accomplish with his flattery but an evil which not even a king could have accomplished? The name of the Roman Curia is today a stench throughout the world, papal authority languishes, and Roman ignorance, once honored, is in ill repute. We should have heard nothing of all this if Eck had not upset the peace arrangements made by Karl [von Miltitz] and myself. Eck himself now clearly sees this and, although it is too late and to no avail, he is furious that my books were published. He should have thought of this when, like a whinnying horse, he was madly seeking his own glory and preferred his own advantage through you and at the greatest peril to you. The vain man thought that I would stop and keep silent out of fear for your name, for I do not believe that he entirely trusted his cleverness and learning. Now that he sees that I have more courage than that and have not been silenced, he repents of his rashness, but too late, and perceives—if indeed he does finally understand—that there is One in heaven who opposes the proud and humbles the haughty [I Pet. 5:5; Jth. 6:15].

Since we gained nothing from this debate except greater confusion to the Roman cause, Karl Miltitz, in a third attempt to bring about peace, came to the fathers of the Augustinian Order assembled in their chapter and sought their advice in settling the controversy which had now grown most disturbing and dangerous. Because, by God's favor, they had no hope of proceeding against me by violent means, some of their most famous men were sent to me. These men asked me at least to show honor to the person of Your Blessedness and in a humble letter to plead as my excuse your innocence and mine in the matter. They said that the affair was not yet in a hopeless state, provided Leo X out of his innate goodness would take a hand in it. As I have always both offered and desired peace so that I might devote myself to quieter and more useful studies, and have stormed with such great fury merely for the purpose of overwhelming my unequal opponents by the volume and violence of words no less than of intellect, I not only gladly ceased but also joyfully and thankfully considered this suggestion a very welcome kindness to me, provided our hope could be realized.

So I come, most blessed father, and, prostrate before you, pray that if possible you intervene and stop those flatterers, who are the enemies of peace while they pretend to keep peace. But let no person imagine that I will recant unless he prefer to involve the whole question in even greater turmoil. Furthermore, I acknowledge no fixed rules for the interpretation of the Word of God, since the Word of God, which teaches freedom in all other matters, must not be bound [II Tim. 2:9]. If these two points are granted, there is nothing that I could not or would not most willingly do or endure. I detest contentions. I will challenge no one. On the other hand, I do not want others to challenge me. If they do, as Christ is my teacher, I will not be speechless. When once this controversy has been cited before you and settled, Your Blessedness will be able with a brief and ready word to silence both parties and command them to keep the peace. That is what I have always wished to hear.

Therefore, my Father Leo, do not listen to those sirens who

pretend that you are no mere man but a demigod so that you may command and require whatever you wish. It will not be done in that manner and you will not have such remarkable power. You are a servant of servants, and more than all other men you are in a most miserable and dangerous position. Be not deceived by those who pretend that you are lord of the world, allow no one to be considered a Christian unless he accepts your authority, and prate that you have power over heaven, hell, and purgatory. These men are your enemies who seek to destroy your soul [I Kings 19:10], as Isaiah says: "O my people, they that call thee blessed, the same deceive thee" [Isa. 3:12]. They err who exalt you above a council and the church universal. They err who ascribe to you alone the right of interpreting Scripture. Under the protection of your name they seek to gain support for all their wicked deeds in the church. Alas! Through them Satan has already made much progress under your predecessors. In short, believe none who exalt you, believe those who humble you. This is the judgment of God, that ". . . he has put down the mighty from their thrones and exalted those of low degree" [Luke 1:52]. See how different Christ is from his successors, although they all would wish to be his vicars. I fear that most of them have been too literally his vicars. A man is a vicar only when his superior is absent. If the pope rules, while Christ is absent and does not dwell in his heart, what else is he but a vicar of Christ? What is the church under such a vicar but a mass of people without Christ? Indeed, what is such a vicar but an antichrist and an idol? How much more properly did the apostles call themselves servants of the present Christ and not vicars of an absent Christ?

Perhaps I am presumptuous in trying to instruct so exalted a personage from whom we all should learn and from whom the thrones of judges receive their decisions, as those pestilential fellows of yours boast. But I am following the example of St. Bernard in his book, *On Consideration*, to Pope Eugenius, a book every pope should know from memory. I follow him, not because I am eager to instruct you, but out of pure and loyal concern which compels us to be interested in all the affairs of our neighbors, even when they are protected, and which does not permit us to take into consideration either their dignity or lack of dignity since it is only concerned with the dangers they face or the advantages they may gain. I know that Your Blessedness is driven and buffeted about in Rome, that is, that far out at sea you are threatened on all sides by dangers and are working very hard in the miserable situation so that you are in need of even the slightest help of the least of your brothers. Therefore I do not consider it absurd if I now forget your exalted office and do what brotherly love demands. I have no desire to flatter you in so serious and dangerous a matter. If men do not perceive that I am your friend and your most humble subject in this matter, there is One who understands and judges [John 8:50].

Finally, that I may not approach you empty-handed, blessed father, I am sending you this little treatise dedicated to you as a token of peace and good hope. From this book you may judge with what studies I should prefer to be more profitably occupied, as I could be, provided your godless flatterers would permit me and had permitted me in the past. It is a small book if you regard its size. Unless I am mistaken, however, it contains the whole of Christian life in a brief form, provided you grasp its meaning. I am a poor man and have no other gift to offer, and you do not need to be enriched by any but a spiritual gift. May the Lord Jesus preserve you forever. Amen.

Wittenberg, September 6, 1520.

MARTIN LUTHER'S TREATISE ON CHRISTIAN LIBERTY

[THE FREEDOM OF A CHRISTIAN]

Many people have considered Christian faith an easy thing, and not a few have given it a place among the virtues. They do this because they have not experienced it and have never tasted the great strength there is in faith. It is impossible to write well about it or to understand what has been written about it unless one has at one time or another experienced the courage which faith gives a man when trials oppress him. But he who has had even a faint taste of it can never write, speak, meditate, or hear enough concerning it. It is a living "spring of water welling up to eternal life," as Christ calls it in John 4 [:14].

As for me, although I have no wealth of faith to boast of and know how scant my supply is, I nevertheless hope that I have attained to a little faith, even though I have been assailed by great and various temptations; and I hope that I can discuss it, if not more elegantly, certainly more to the point, than those literalists and subtile disputants have previously done, who have not even understood what they have written.

To make the way smoother for the unlearned—for only them do I serve—I shall set down the following two propositions concerning the freedom and the bondage of the spirit:

A Christian is a perfectly free lord of all, subject to none.

A Christian is a perfectly dutiful servant of all, subject to all.

These two theses seem to contradict each other. If, however, they should be found to fit together they would serve our purpose beautifully. Both are Paul's own statements, who says in I Cor. 9 [:19], "For though I am free from all men, I have made myself a slave to all," and in Rom. 13 [:8], "Owe no one anything, except to love one another." Love by its very nature is ready to serve and be subject to him who is loved. So Christ, although he was Lord of all, was "born of woman, born under the law" [Gal. 4:4], and therefore was at the same time a free man and a servant, "in the form of God" and "of a servant" [Phil. 2:6–7].

Let us start, however, with something more remote from our subject, but more obvious. Man has a twofold nature, a spiritual and a bodily one. According to the spiritual nature, which men refer to as the soul, he is called a spiritual, inner, or new man. According to the bodily nature, which men refer to as flesh, he is called a carnal, outward, or old man, of whom the Apostle writes in II Cor. 4 [:16], "Though our outer nature is wasting away, our inner nature is being renewed every day." Because of this diversity' of nature the Scriptures assert contradictory things concerning the same man, since these two men in the same man contradict each other, "for the desires of the flesh are against the Spirit, and the desires of the Spirit are against the flesh," according to Gal. 5 [:17].

First, let us consider the inner man to see how a righteous, free, and pious Christian, that is, a spiritual, new, and inner

man, becomes what he is. It is evident that no external thing
has any influence in producing Christian righteousness or freedom, or in producing unrighteousness or servitude. A simple
argument will furnish the proof of this statement. What can
it profit the soul if the body is well, free, and active, and eats,
drinks, and does as it pleases? For in these respects even the
most godless slaves of vice may prosper. On the other hand,
how will poor health or imprisonment or hunger or thirst or
any other external misfortune harm the soul? Even the most
godly men, and those who are free because of clear consciences, are afflicted with these things. None of these things
touch either the freedom or the servitude of the soul. It does
not help the soul if the body is adorned with the sacred robes
of priests or dwells in sacred places or is occupied with sacred
duties or prays, fasts, abstains from certain kinds of food, or
does any work that can be done by the body and in the body.
The righteousness and the freedom of the soul require something far different since the things which have been mentioned
could be done by any wicked person. Such works produce
nothing but hypocrites. On the other hand, it will not harm
the soul if the body is clothed in secular dress, dwells in un-
consecrated places, eats and drinks as others do, does not pray
aloud, and neglects to do all the above-mentioned things which
hypocrites can do.

Furthermore, to put aside all kinds of works, even contem-
plation, meditation, and all that the soul can do, does not help.
One thing, and only one thing, is necessary for Christian life,
righteousness, and freedom. That one thing is the most holy
Word of God, the gospel of Christ, as Christ says, John 11
[:25], "I am the resurrection and the life; he who believes in
me, though he die, yet shall he live"; and John 8 [:36], "So
if the Son makes you free, you will be free indeed"; and Matt.
4 [:4], "Man shall not live by bread alone, but by every
word that proceeds from the mouth of God." Let us then consider it certain and firmly established that the soul can do
without anything except the Word of God and that where the
Word of God is missing there is no help at all for the soul. If
it has the Word of God it is rich and lacks nothing since it is
the Word of life, truth, light, peace, righteousness, salvation,
joy, liberty, wisdom, power, grace, glory, and of every incal-

culable blessing. This is why the prophet in the entire Psalm [119] and in many other places yearns and sighs for the Word of God and uses so many names to describe it.

On the other hand, there is no more terrible disaster with which the wrath of God can afflict men than a famine of the hearing of his Word, as he says in Amos [8:11]. Likewise there is no greater mercy than when he sends forth his Word, as we read in Psalm 107 [:20]: "He sent forth his word, and healed them, and delivered them from destruction." Nor was Christ sent into the world for any other ministry except that of the Word. Moreover, the entire spiritual estate—all the apostles, bishops, and priests—has been called and instituted only for the ministry of the Word.

You may ask, "What then is the Word of God, and how shall it be used, since there are so many words of God?" I answer: The Apostle explains this in Romans 1. The Word is the gospel of God concerning his Son, who was made flesh, suffered, rose from the dead, and was glorified through the Spirit who sanctifies. To preach Christ means to feed the soul, make it righteous, set it free, and save it, provided it believes the preaching. Faith alone is the saving and efficacious use of the Word of God, according to Rom. 10 [:9]: "If you confess with your lips that Jesus is Lord and believe in your heart that God raised him from the dead, you will be saved." Furthermore, "Christ is the end of the law, that every one who has faith may be justified" [Rom. 10:4]. Again, in Rom. 1 [:17], "He who through faith is righteous shall live." The Word of God cannot be received and cherished by any works whatever but only by faith. Therefore it is clear that, as the soul needs only the Word of God for its life and righteousness, so it is justified by faith alone and not any works; for if it could be justified by anything else, it would not need the Word, and consequently it would not need faith.

This faith cannot exist in connection with works—that is to say, if you at the same time claim to be justified by works, whatever their character—for that would be the same as "limping with two different opinions" [I Kings 18:21], as worshiping Baal and kissing one's own hand [Job 31:27–28], which, as Job says, is a very great iniquity. Therefore the moment you begin to have faith you learn that all things in you are altogether blameworthy, sinful, and damnable, as the Apostle says in Rom. 3 [:23], "Since all have sinned and fall short of the glory of God," and, "None is righteous, no, not one; . . . all have turned aside, together they have gone wrong," Rom. 3 [:10–12]. When you have learned this you will know that you need Christ, who suffered and rose again for you so that, if you believe in him, you may through this faith become a new man in so far as your sins are forgiven and you are justified by the merits of another, namely, of Christ alone.

Since, therefore, this faith can rule only in the inner man, as Rom. 10 [:10] says, "For man believes with his heart and so is justified," and since faith alone justifies, it is clear that the inner man cannot be justified, freed, or saved by any outer work or action at all, and that these works, whatever their character, have nothing to do with this inner man. On the other hand, only ungodliness and unbelief of heart, and no outer work, make him guilty and a damnable servant of sin. Wherefore it ought to be the first concern of every Christian to lay aside all confidence in works and increasingly to strengthen faith alone and through faith to grow in the knowledge, not of works, but of Christ Jesus, who suffered and rose for him, as Peter teaches in the last chapter of his first Epistle, I Pet. [5:10]. No other work makes a Christian. Thus when the Jews asked Christ, as related in John 6 [:28], what they must do "to be doing the work of God," he brushed aside the multitude of works which he saw they did in great profusion and suggested one work, saying, "This is the work of God, that you believe in him whom he has sent" [John 6:29]; "for on him has God the Father set his seal" [John 6:27].

Therefore true faith in Christ is a treasure beyond comparison which brings with it complete salvation and saves man from every evil, as Christ says in the last chapter of Mark [16:16]: "He who believes and is baptized will be saved; but he who does not believe will be condemned." Isaiah contemplated this treasure and foretold it in chapter 10: "The Lord will make a small and consuming word upon the land, and it will overflow with righteousness" [Cf. Isa. 10:22]. This is as though he said, "Faith, which is a small and perfect fulfilment of the law, will fill believers with so great a righteousness that they will need nothing more to become righteous." So Paul says, Rom. 10 [:10], "For man believes with his heart and so is justified."

Should you ask how it happens that faith alone justifies and offers us such a treasure of great benefits without works in view of the fact that so many works, ceremonies, and laws are prescribed in the Scriptures, I answer: First of all, remember what has been said, namely, that faith alone, without works, justifies, frees, and saves; we shall make this clearer later on. Here we must point out that the entire Scripture of God is divided into two parts: commandments and promises. Although the commandments teach things that are good, the things taught are not done as soon as they are taught, for the commandments show us what we ought to do but do not give us the power to do it. They are intended to teach man to know himself, that through them he may recognize his inability to do good and may despair of his own ability. That is why they are called the Old Testament and constitute the Old Testament. For example, the commandment, "You shall not covet" [Exod. 20:17], is a command which proves us all to be sinners, for no one can avoid coveting no matter how much he may struggle against it. Therefore, in order not to covet and to fulfil the commandment, a man is compelled to despair of himself, to seek the help which he does not find in himself elsewhere and from someone else, as stated in Hosea [13:9]: "Destruction is your own, O Israel: your help is only in me." As we fare with respect to one commandment, so we fare with all, for it is equally impossible for us to keep any one of them.

Now when a man has learned through the commandments to recognize his helplessness and is distressed about how he might satisfy the law—since the law must be fulfilled so that not a jot or tittle shall be lost, otherwise man will be condemned without hope—then, being truly humbled and reduced to nothing in his own eyes, he finds in himself nothing whereby he may be justified and saved. Here the second part of Scripture comes to our aid, namely, the promises of God which declare the glory of God, saying, "If you wish to fulfil the law and not covet, as the law demands, come, believe in Christ in whom grace, righteousness, peace, liberty, and all things are promised you. If you believe, you shall have all things; if you do not believe, you shall lack all things." That which is impossible for you to accomplish by trying to fulfil all the works of the law—many and useless as they all are—you will accomplish quickly and easily through faith. God our Father has made all things depend on faith so that whoever has faith will have everything, and whoever does not have faith will have nothing. "For God has consigned all men to disobedience, that he may have mercy upon all," as it is stated in Rom. 11 [:32]. Thus the promises of God give what the commandments of God demand and fulfil what the law prescribes so that all things may be God's alone, both the commandments and the fulfilling of the commandments. He alone commands, he alone fulfils. Therefore the promises of God belong to the New Testament. Indeed, they are the New Testament.

Since these promises of God are holy, true, righteous, free, and peaceful words, full of goodness, the soul which clings to them with a firm faith will be so closely united with them and altogether absorbed by them that it not only will share in all their power but will be saturated and intoxicated by them. If a touch of Christ healed, how much more will this most tender spiritual touch, this absorbing of the Word, communicate to the soul all things that belong to the Word. This, then, is how through faith alone without works the soul is justified by the Word of God, sanctified, made true, peaceful, and free, filled with every blessing and truly made a child of God, as John 1 [:12] says: "But to all who . . . believed in his name, he gave power to become children of God."

From what has been said it is easy to see from what source faith derives such great power and why a good work or all good works together cannot equal it. No good work can rely upon the Word of God or live in the soul, for faith alone and the Word of God rule in the soul. Just as the heated iron glows like fire because of the union of fire with it, so the Word imparts its qualities to the soul. It is clear, then, that a Christian has all that he needs in faith and needs no works to justify him; and if he has no need of works, he has no need of the law; and if he has no need of the law, surely he is free from the law. It is true that "the law is not laid down for the just" [I Tim. 1:9]. This is that Christian liberty, our faith, which does not induce us to live in idleness or wickedness but makes the law and works unnecessary for any man's righteousness and salvation.

This is the first power of faith. Let us now examine also the second. It is a further function of faith that it honors him whom it trusts with the most reverent and highest regard since it considers him truthful and trustworthy. There is no other honor equal to the estimate of truthfulness and righteousness with which we honor him whom we trust. Could we ascribe to a man anything greater than truthfulness and righteousness and perfect goodness? On the other hand, there is no way in which we can show greater contempt for a man than to regard him as false and wicked and to be suspicious of him, as we do when we do not trust him. So when the soul firmly trusts God's promises, it regards him as truthful and righteous. Nothing more excellent than this can be ascribed to God. The very highest worship of God is this that we ascribe to him truthfulness, righteousness, and whatever else should be ascribed to one who is trusted. When this is done, the soul consents to his will. Then it hallows his name and allows itself to be treated according to God's good pleasure for, clinging to God's promises, it does not doubt that he who is true, just, and wise will do, dispose, and provide all things well.

Is not such a soul most obedient to God in all things by this faith? What commandment is there that such obedience has not completely fulfilled? What more complete fulfilment is there than obedience in all things? This obedience, however, is not rendered by works, but by faith alone. On the other hand, what greater rebellion against God, what greater wickedness, what greater contempt of God is there than not believing his promise? For what is this but to make God a liar or to doubt that he is truthful?—that is, to ascribe truthfulness to one's self but lying and vanity to God? Does not a man who does this deny God and set himself up as an idol in his heart? Then of what good are works done in such wickedness, even if they were the works of angels and apostles? Therefore God has rightly included all things, not under anger or lust, but under unbelief, so that they who imagine that they are fulfilling the law by doing the works of chastity and mercy required by the law (the civil and human virtues) might not be saved. They

are included under the sin of unbelief and must either seek
mercy or be justly condemned.

When, however, God sees that we consider him truthful
and by the faith of our heart pay him the great honor which
is due him, he does us that great honor of considering us truthful and righteous for the sake of our faith. Faith works truth
and righteousness by giving God what belongs to him. Therefore God in turn glorifies our righteousness. It is true and just
that God is truthful and just, and to consider and confess him
to be so is the same as being truthful and just. Accordingly he
says in I Sam. 2 [:30], "Those who honor me I will honor, and
those who despise me shall be lightly esteemed." So Paul says
in Rom. 4 [:3] that Abraham's faith "was reckoned to him as
righteousness" because by it he gave glory most perfectly to
God, and that for the same reason our faith shall be reckoned
to us as righteousness if we believe.

The third incomparable benefit of faith is that it unites the
soul with Christ as a bride is united with her bridegroom. By
this mystery, as the Apostle teaches, Christ and the soul become one flesh [Eph. 5:31-32]. And if they are one flesh and
there is between them a true marriage—indeed the most perfect of all marriages, since human marriages are but poor examples of this one true marriage—it follows that everything
they have they hold in common, the good as well as the evil.
Accordingly the believing soul can boast of and glory in whatever Christ has as though it were its own, and whatever the
soul has Christ claims as his own. Let us compare these and
we shall see inestimable benefits. Christ is full of grace, life,
and salvation. The soul is full of sins, death, and damnation.
Now let faith come between them and sins, death, and damnation will be Christ's, while grace, life, and salvation will be
the soul's; for if Christ is a bridegroom, he must take upon
himself the things which are his bride's and bestow upon her
the things that are his. If he gives her his body and very self,
how shall he not give her all that is his? And if he takes the
body of the bride, how shall he not take all that is hers?

Here we have a most pleasing vision not only of communion
but of a blessed struggle and victory and salvation and redemption. Christ is God and man in one person. He has neither
sinned nor died, and is not condemned, and he cannot sin, die,

or be condemned; his righteousness, life, and salvation are unconquerable, eternal, omnipotent. By the wedding ring of faith he shares in the sins, death, and pains of hell which are his bride's. As a matter of fact, he makes them his own and acts as if they were his own and as if he himself had sinned; he suffered, died, and descended into hell that he might overcome them all. Now since it was such a one who did all this, and death and hell could not swallow him up, these were necessarily swallowed up by him in a mighty duel; for his righteousness is greater than the sins of all men, his life stronger than death, his salvation more invincible than hell. Thus the believing soul by means of the pledge of its faith is free in Christ, its bridegroom, free from all sins, secure against death and hell, and is endowed with the eternal righteousness, life, and salvation of Christ its bridegroom. So he takes to himself a glorious bride, "without spot or wrinkle, cleansing her by the washing of water with the word" [Cf. Eph. 5:26–27] of life, that is, by faith in the Word of life, righteousness, and salvation. In this way he marries her in faith, steadfast love, and in mercies, righteousness, and justice, as Hos. 2 [:19–20] says.

Who then can fully appreciate what this royal marriage means? Who can understand the riches of the glory of this grace? Here this rich and divine bridegroom Christ marries this poor, wicked harlot, redeems her from all her evil, and adorns her with all his goodness. Her sins cannot now destroy her, since they are laid upon Christ and swallowed up by him. And she has that righteousness in Christ, her husband, of which she may boast as of her own and which she can confidently display alongside her sins in the face of death and hell and say, "If I have sinned, yet my Christ, in whom I believe, has not sinned, and all his is mine and all mine is his," as the bride in the Song of Solomon [2:16] says, "My beloved is mine and I am his." This is what Paul means when he says in I Cor. 15 [:57], "Thanks be to God, who gives us the victory through our Lord Jesus Christ," that is, the victory over sin and death, as he also says there, "The sting of death is sin, and the power of sin is the law" [I Cor. 15:56].

From this you once more see that much is ascribed to faith, namely, that it alone can fulfil the law and justify without works. You see that the First Commandment, which says, "You shall worship one God," is fulfilled by faith alone. Though you were nothing but good works from the soles of your feet to the crown of your head, you would still not be righteous or worship God or fulfil the First Commandment, since God cannot be worshiped unless you ascribe to him the glory of truthfulness and all goodness which is due him. This cannot be done by works but only by the faith of the heart. Not by the doing of works but by believing do we glorify God and acknowledge that he is truthful. Therefore faith alone is the righteousness of a Christian and the fulfilling of all the commandments, for he who fulfils the First Commandment has no difficulty in fulfilling all the rest.

But works, being inanimate things, cannot glorify God, although they can, if faith is present, be done to the glory of God. Here, however, we are not inquiring what works and what kind of works are done, but who it is that does them, who glorifies God and brings forth the works. This is done by faith which dwells in the heart and is the source and substance of all our righteousness. Therefore it is a blind and dangerous doctrine which teaches that the commandments must be fulfilled by works. The commandments must be fulfilled before any works can be done, and the works proceed from the fulfilment of the commandments [Rom. 13:10], as we shall hear.

That we may examine more profoundly that grace which our inner man has in Christ, we must realize that in the Old Testament God consecrated to himself all the first-born males. The birthright was highly prized for it involved a twofold honor, that of priesthood and that of kingship. The first-born brother was priest and lord over all the others and a type of Christ, the true and only first-born of God the Father and the Virgin Mary and true king and priest, but not after the fashion of the flesh and the world, for his kingdom is not of this world [John 18:36]. He reigns in heavenly and spiritual things and consecrates them—things such as righteousness, truth, wisdom, peace, salvation, etc. This does not mean that all things on earth and in hell are not also subject to him—otherwise how could he protect and save us from them?—but that his kingdom consists neither in them nor of them. Nor does his priesthood consist in the outer splendor of robes and postures like those of the human priesthood of Aaron and our present-day church; but it consists of spiritual things through which he by an invisible service intercedes for us in heaven before God, there offers himself as a sacrifice, and does all things a priest should do, as Paul describes him under the type of Melchizedek in the Epistle to the Hebrews [Heb. 6–7]. Nor does he only pray and intercede for us but he teaches us inwardly through the living instruction of his Spirit, thus performing the two real functions of a priest, of which the prayers and the preaching of human priests are visible types.

Now just as Christ by his birthright obtained these two prerogatives, so he imparts them to and shares them with everyone who believes in him according to the law of the above-mentioned marriage, according to which the wife owns whatever belongs to the husband. Hence all of us who believe in Christ are priests and kings in Christ, as I Pet. 2 [:9] says: "You are a chosen race, God's own people, a royal priesthood, a priestly kingdom, that you may declare the wonderful deeds of him who called you out of darkness into his marvelous light."

The nature of this priesthood and kingship is something like this: First, with respect to the kingship, every Christian is by faith so exalted above all things that, by virtue of a spiritual power, he is lord of all things without exception, so that nothing can do him any harm. As a matter of fact, all things are made subject to him and are compelled to serve him in obtaining salvation. Accordingly Paul says in Rom. 8 [:28], "All things work together for good for the elect," and in I Cor. 3 [:21–23], "All things are yours whether . . . life or death or the present or the future, all are yours; and you are Christ's. . . ." This is not to say that every Christian is placed over all things to have and control them by physical power—a madness with which some churchmen are afflicted—for such power belongs to kings, princes, and other men on earth. Our ordinary experience in life shows us that we are subjected to all, suffer many things, and even die. As a matter of fact, the more Christian a man is, the more evils, sufferings, and deaths he must endure, as we see in Christ the first-born prince himself, and in all his brethren, the saints. The power of which we speak is spiritual. It rules in the midst of enemies and is powerful in the midst of oppression. This means nothing else than that "power is made perfect in weakness" [II Cor. 12:9] and that in all things I can find profit toward salvation [Rom. 8:28], so that the cross and death itself are compelled to serve me and to work together with me for my salvation. This is a splendid privilege and hard to attain, a truly omnipotent power, a spiritual dominion in which there is nothing so good and nothing so evil but that it shall work together for good to me, if only I believe. Yes, since faith alone suffices for salvation, I need nothing except faith exercising the power and dominion of its own liberty. Lo, this is the inestimable power and liberty of Christians.

Not only are we the freest of kings, we are also priests forever, which is far more excellent than being kings, for as priests we are worthy to appear before God to pray for others and to teach one another divine things. These are the functions of priests, and they cannot be granted to any unbeliever. Thus Christ has made it possible for us, provided we believe in him, to be not only his brethren, co-heirs, and fellow-kings, but also his fellow-priests. Therefore we may boldly come into the presence of God in the spirit of faith [Heb. 10:19, 22] and cry "Abba, Father!" pray for one another, and do all things which we see done and foreshadowed in the outer and visible works of priests.

He, however, who does not believe is not served by anything. On the contrary, nothing works for his good, but he himself is a servant of all, and all things turn out badly for him because he wickedly uses them to his own advantage and not to the glory of God. So he is no priest but a wicked man whose prayer becomes sin and who never comes into the presence of God because God does not hear sinners [John 9:31]. Who then can comprehend the lofty dignity of the Christian? By virtue of his royal power he rules over all things, death, life, and sin, and through his priestly glory is omnipotent with God because he does the things which God asks and desires, as it is written, "He will fulfil the desire of those who fear him; he also will hear their cry and save them" [Cf. Phil. 4:13]. To this glory a man attains, certainly not by any works of his, but by faith alone.

From this anyone can clearly see how a Christian is free

from all things and over all things so that he needs no works to make him righteous and save him, since faith alone abundantly confers all these things. Should he grow so foolish, however, as to presume to become righteous, free, saved, and a Christian by means of some good work, he would instantly lose faith and all its benefits, a foolishness aptly illustrated in the fable of the dog who runs along a stream with a piece of meat in his mouth and, deceived by the reflection of the meat in the water, opens his mouth to snap at it and so loses both the meat and the reflection.

You will ask, "If all who are in the church are priests, how do these whom we now call priests differ from laymen?" I answer: Injustice is done those words "priest," "cleric," "spiritual," "ecclesiastic," when they are transferred from all Christians to those few who are now by a mischievous usage called "ecclesiastics." Holy Scripture makes no distinction between them, although it gives the name "ministers," "servants," "stewards" to those who are now proudly called popes, bishops, and lords and who should according to the ministry of the Word serve others and teach them the faith of Christ and the freedom of believers. Although we are all equally priests, we cannot all publicly minister and teach. We ought not do so even if we could. Paul writes accordingly in I Cor. 4 [:1], "This is how one should regard us, as servants of Christ and stewards of the mysteries of God."

That stewardship, however, has now been developed into so great a display of power and so terrible a tyranny that no heathen empire or other earthly power can be compared with it, just as if laymen were not also Christians. Through this perversion the knowledge of Christian grace, faith, liberty, and of Christ himself has altogether perished, and its place has been taken by an unbearable bondage of human works and laws until we have become, as the Lamentations of Jeremiah [1] say, servants of the vilest men on earth who abuse our misfortune to serve only their base and shameless will.

To return to our purpose, I believe that it has now become clear that it is not enough or in any sense Christian to preach the works, life, and words of Christ as historical facts, as if the knowledge of these would suffice for the conduct of life; yet this is the fashion among those who must today be regarded as our best preachers. Far less is it sufficient or Christian to say nothing at all about Christ and to teach instead the laws of men and the decrees of the fathers. Now there are not a few who preach Christ and read about him that they may move men's affections to sympathy with Christ, to anger against the Jews, and such childish and effeminate nonsense. Rather ought Christ to be preached to the end that faith in him may be established that he may not only be Christ, but be Christ for you and me, and that what is said of him and is denoted in his name may be effectual in us. Such faith is produced and preserved in us by preaching why Christ came, what he brought and bestowed, what benefit it is to us to accept him. This is done when that Christian liberty which he bestows is rightly taught and we are told in what way we Christians are all kings and priests and therefore lords of all and may firmly believe that whatever we have done is pleasing and acceptable in the sight of God, as I have already said.

What man is there whose heart, upon hearing these things, will not rejoice to its depth, and when receiving such comfort will not grow tender so that he will love Christ as he never could by means of any laws or works? Who would have the power to harm or frighten such a heart? If the knowledge of sin or the fear of death should break in upon it, it is ready to hope in the Lord. It does not grow afraid when it hears tidings of evil. It is not disturbed when it sees its enemies. This is so because it believes that the righteousness of Christ is its own and that its sin is not its own, but Christ's, and that all sin is swallowed up by the righteousness of Christ. This, as has been said above, is a necessary consequence on account of faith in Christ. So the heart learns to scoff at death and sin and to say with the Apostle. "O death, where is thy victory? O death, where is thy sting? The sting of death is sin, and the power of sin is the law. But thanks be to God, who gives us the victory through our Lord Jesus Christ" [I Cor. 15:55–57]. Death is swallowed up not only in the victory of Christ but also by our victory, because through faith his victory has become ours and in that faith we also are conquerors.

Let this suffice concerning the inner man, his liberty, and the source of his liberty, the righteousness of faith. He needs neither laws nor good works but, on the contrary, is injured by them if he believes that he is justified by them.

Now let us turn to the second part, the outer man. Here we shall answer all those who, offended by the word "faith" and by all that has been said, now ask, "If faith does all things and is alone sufficient unto righteousness, why then are good works commanded? We will take our ease and do no works and be content with faith." I answer: not so, you wicked men, not so. That would indeed be proper if we were wholly inner and perfectly spiritual men. But such we shall be only at the last day, the day of the resurrection of the dead. As long as we live in the flesh we only begin to make some progress in that which shall be perfected in the future life. For this reason the Apostle in Rom. 8 [:23] calls all that we attain in this life "the first fruits of the Spirit" because we shall indeed receive the greater portion, even the fulness of the Spirit, in the future. This is the place to assert that which was said above, namely, that a Christian is the servant of all and made subject to all. Insofar as he is free he does no works, but insofar as he is a servant he does all kinds of works. How this is possible we shall see.

Although, as I have said, a man is abundantly and sufficiently justified by faith inwardly, in his spirit, and so has all that he needs, except insofar as this faith and these riches must grow from day to day even to the future life; yet he remains in this mortal life on earth. In this life he must control his own body and have dealings with men. Here the works begin; here a man cannot enjoy leisure; here he must indeed take care to discipline his body by fastings, watchings, labors, and other reasonable discipline and to subject it to the Spirit so that it will obey and conform to the inner man and faith and not revolt against faith and hinder the inner man, as it is the nature of the body to do if it is not held in check. The inner man, who by faith is created in the image of God, is both joyful and happy because of Christ in whom so many benefits are conferred upon him; and therefore it is his one occupation to serve God joyfully and without thought of gain, in love that is not constrained.

While he is doing this, behold, he meets a contrary will in his own flesh which strives to serve the world and seeks its own advantage. This the spirit of faith cannot tolerate, but with joyful zeal it attempts to put the body under control and hold it in check, as Paul says in Rom. 7 [:22–23], "For I delight in the law of God, in my inmost self, but I see in my members another law at war with the law of my mind and making me captive to the law of sin," and in another place, "But I pommel my body and subdue it, lest after preaching to others I myself should be disqualified" [I Cor. 9:27], and in Galatians [5:24], "And those who belong to Christ Jesus have crucified the flesh with its passions and desires."

In doing these works, however, we must not think that a man is justified before God by them, for faith, which alone is righteousness before God, cannot endure that erroneous opinion. We must, however, realize that these works reduce the body to subjection and purify it of its evil lusts, and our whole purpose is to be directed only toward the driving out of lusts. Since by faith the soul is cleansed and made to love God, it desires that all things, and especially its own body, shall be purified so that all things may join with it in loving and praising God. Hence a man cannot be idle, for the need of his body drives him and he is compelled to do many good works to reduce it to subjection. Nevertheless the works themselves do not justify him before God, but he does the works out of spontaneous love in obedience to God and considers nothing except the approval of God, whom he would most scrupulously obey in all things.

In this way everyone will easily be able to learn for himself the limit and discretion, as they say, of his bodily castigations, for he will fast, watch, and labor as much as he finds sufficient to repress the lasciviousness and lust of his body. But those who presume to be justified by works do not regard the mortifying of the lusts, but only the works themselves, and think that if only they have done as many and as great works as are possible, they have done well and have become righteous. At times they even addle their brains and destroy, or at least render useless, their natural strength with their works. This is the height of folly and utter ignorance of Christian life and faith, that a man should seek to be justified and saved by works and without faith.

In order to make that which we have said more easily understood, we shall explain by analogies. We should think of the works of a Christian who is justified and saved by faith because of the pure and free mercy of God, just as we would think of the works which Adam and Eve did in Paradise, and all their children would have done if they had not sinned. We read in Gen. 2 [:15] that "The Lord God took the man and put him in the garden of Eden to till it and keep it." Now Adam was created righteous and upright and without sin by God so that he had no need of being justified and made upright through his tilling and keeping the garden; but, that he might not be idle, the Lord gave him a task to do, to cultivate and protect the garden. This task would truly have been the freest of works, done only to please God and not to obtain righteousness, which Adam already had in full measure and which would have been the birthright of us all.

The works of a believer are like this. Through his faith he has been restored to Paradise and created anew, has no need of works that he may become or be righteous; but that he may not be idle and may provide for and keep his body, he must do such works freely only to please God. Since, however, we are not wholly recreated, and our faith and love are not yet perfect, these are to be increased, not by external works, however, but of themselves.

A second example: A bishop, when he consecrates a church, confirms children, or performs some other duty belonging to his office, is not made a bishop by these works. Indeed, if he had not first been made a bishop, none of these works would be valid. They would be foolish, childish, and farcical. So the Christian who is consecrated by his faith does good works, but the works do not make him holier or more Christian, for that is the work of faith alone. And if a man were not first a believer and a Christian, all his works would amount to nothing and would be truly wicked and damnable sins.

The following statements are therefore true: "Good works do not make a good man, but a good man does good works; evil works do not make a wicked man, but a wicked man does evil works." Consequently it is always necessary that the substance or person himself be good before there can be any good works, and that good works follow and proceed from the good person, as Christ also says, "A good tree cannot bear evil fruit, nor can a bad tree bear good fruit" [Matt. 7:18]. It is clear that the fruits do not bear the tree and that the tree does not grow on the fruits, also that, on the contrary, the trees bear the fruits and the fruits grow on the trees. As it is necessary, therefore, that the trees exist before their fruits and the fruits do not make trees either good or bad, but rather as the trees are, so are the fruits they bear; so a man must first be good or wicked before he does a good or wicked work, and his works do not make him good or wicked, but he himself makes his works either good or wicked.

Illustrations of the same truth can be seen in all trades. A good or a bad house does not make a good or a bad builder; but a good or a bad builder makes a good or a bad house. And in general, the work never makes the workman like itself, but the workman makes the work like himself. So it is with the works of man. As the man is, whether believer or unbeliever, so also is his work—good if it was done in faith, wicked if it was done in unbelief. But the converse is not true, that the work makes the man either a believer or an unbeliever. As works do not make a man a believer, so also they do not make him righteous. But as faith makes a man a believer and righteous, so faith does good works. Since, then, works justify no one, and a man must be righteous before he does a good work, it is very evident that it is faith alone which, because of the pure mercy of God through Christ and in his Word, worthily and sufficiently justifies and saves the person. A Christian has no need of any work or law in order to be saved since through faith he is free from every law and does everything out of pure liberty and freely. He seeks neither benefit nor salvation since he already abounds in all things and is saved through the grace of God because in his faith he now seeks only to please God.

Furthermore, no good work helps justify or save an unbeliever. On the other hand, no evil work makes him wicked or damns him; but the unbelief which makes the person and the tree evil does the evil and damnable works. Hence when a man is good or evil, this is effected not by the works, but by faith or unbelief, as the Wise Man says, "This is the beginning of sin, that a man falls away from God" [Cf. Sirach 10:14–15], which happens when he does not believe. And Paul says in Heb. 11 [:6], "For whoever would draw near to God must believe. . . ." And Christ says the same: "Either make the tree good, and its fruit good; or make the tree bad, and its fruit bad" [Matt. 12:33], as if he would say, "Let him who wishes to have good fruit begin by planting a good tree." So let him who wishes to do good works begin not with the doing of works, but with believing, which makes the person good, for nothing makes a man good except faith, or evil except unbelief.

It is indeed true that in the sight of men a man is made good or evil by his works; but this being made good or evil only means that the man who is good or evil is pointed out and known as such, as Christ says in Matt. 7 [:20], "Thus you will know them by their fruits." All this remains on the surface, however, and very many have been deceived by this outward appearance and have presumed to write and teach concerning good works by which we may be justified without even mentioning faith. They go their way, always being deceived and deceiving [II Tim. 3:13], progressing, indeed, but into a worse state, blind leaders of the blind, wearying themselves with many works and still never attaining to true righteousness [Matt. 15:14]. Of such people Paul says in II Tim. 3 [:5, 7], "Holding the form of religion but denying the power of it . . . who will listen to anybody and can never arrive at a knowledge of the truth."

Whoever, therefore, does not wish to go astray with those blind men must look beyond works, and beyond laws and doctrines about works. Turning his eyes from works, he must look upon the person and ask how he is justified. For the person is justified and saved, not by works or laws, but by the Word of God, that is, by the promise of his grace, and by faith, that the glory may remain God's, who saved us not by works of righteousness which we have done [Titus 3:5], but by virtue of his mercy by the word of his grace when we believed [I Cor. 1:21].

From this it is easy to know how far good works are to be rejected or not, and by what standard all the teachings of men concerning works are to be interpreted. If works are sought after as a means to righteousness, are burdened with this perverse leviathan, and are done under the false impression that through them one is justified, they are made necessary and freedom and faith are destroyed; and this addition to them makes them no longer good but truly damnable works. They are not free, and they blaspheme the grace of God since to justify and to save by faith belongs to the grace of God alone. What the works have no power to do they nevertheless—by a godless presumption through this folly of ours—pretend to do and thus violently force themselves into the office and glory of grace. We do not, therefore, reject good works; on the contrary, we cherish and teach them as much as possible. We do not condemn them for their own sake but on account of this godless addition to them and the perverse idea that righteousness is to be sought through them; for that makes them appear good outwardly, when in truth they are not good. They deceive men and lead them to deceive one another like ravening wolves in sheep's clothing [Matt. 7:15].

But this leviathan, or perverse notion concerning works, is unconquerable where sincere faith is wanting. Those worksaints cannot get rid of it unless faith, its destroyer, comes and rules in their hearts. Nature of itself cannot drive it out or even recognize it, but rather regards it as a mark of the most holy will. If the influence of custom is added and confirms this perverseness of nature, as wicked teachers have caused it to do, it becomes an incurable evil and leads astray and destroys countless men beyond all hope of restoration. Therefore, although it is good to preach and write about penitence, confession, and satisfaction, our teaching is unquestionably deceitful and diabolical if we stop with that and do not go on to teach about faith.

Christ, like his forerunner John, not only said, "Repent" [Matt. 3:2; 4:17], but added the word of faith, saying, "The kingdom of heaven is at hand." We are not to preach only one of these words of God, but both; we are to bring forth out of our treasure things new and old, the voice of the law as well as the word of grace [Matt. 13:52]. We must bring forth the voice of the law that men may be made to fear and come to a knowledge of their sins and so be converted to repentance and a better life. But we must not stop with that, for that would only amount to wounding and not binding up, smiting and not healing, killing and not making alive, leading down into hell and not bringing back again, humbling and not exalting. Therefore we must also preach the word of grace and the promise of forgiveness by which faith is taught and aroused. Without this word of grace the works of the law, contrition, penitence, and all the rest are done and taught in vain.

Preachers of repentance and grace remain even to our day, but they do not explain God's law and promise that a man might learn from them the source of repentance and grace. Repentance proceeds from the law of God, but faith or grace from the promise of God, as Rom. 10 [:17] says: "So faith comes from what is heard, and what is heard comes by the preaching of Christ." Accordingly man is consoled and exalted by faith in the divine promise after he has been humbled and led to a knowledge of himself by the threats and the fear of the divine law. So we read in Psalm 30 [:5]: "Weeping may tarry for the night, but joy comes with the morning."

Let this suffice concerning works in general and at the same time concerning the works which a Christian does for himself. Lastly, we shall also speak of the things which he does toward his neighbor. A man does not live for himself alone in this mortal body to work for it alone, but he lives also for all men on earth; rather, he lives only for others and not for himself. To this end he brings his body into subjection that he may the more sincerely and freely serve others, as Paul says in Rom. 14 [:7–8], "None of us lives to himself, and none of us dies to himself. If we live, we live to the Lord, and if we die, we die to the Lord." He cannot ever in this life be idle and without works toward his neighbors, for he will necessarily speak, deal with, and exchange views with men, as Christ also, being made in the likeness of men [Phil. 2:7], was found in form as a man and conversed with men, as Baruch 3 [:38] says.

Man, however, needs none of these things for his righteousness and salvation. Therefore he should be guided in all his works by this thought and contemplate this one thing alone, that he may serve and benefit others in all that he does, considering nothing except the need and the advantage of his neighbor. Accordingly the Apostle commands us to work with our hands so that we may give to the needy, although he might have said that we should work to support ourselves. He says, however, "that he may be able to give to those in need" [Eph. 4:28]. This is what makes caring for the body a Christian work, that through its health and comfort we may be able to work, to acquire, and lay by funds with which to aid those who are in need, that in this way the strong member may serve the weaker, and we may be sons of God, each caring for and working for the other, bearing one another's burdens and so fulfilling the law of Christ [Gal. 6:2]. This is a truly Christian life. Here faith is truly active through love [Gal. 5:6], that is, it finds expression in works of the freest service, cheerfully and lovingly done, with which a man willingly serves another without hope of reward; and for himself he is satisfied with the fullness and wealth of his faith.

Accordingly Paul, after teaching the Philippians how rich they were made through faith in Christ, in which they obtained all things, thereafter teaches them, saying, "So if there is any encouragement in Christ, any incentive of love, any participation in the Spirit, any affection and sympathy, complete my joy by being of the same mind, having the same love, being in full accord and of one mind. Do nothing from selfishness or conceit, but in humility count others better than yourselves. Let each of you look not only to his own interests, but also to the interests of others" [Phil. 2:1–4]. Here we see clearly that the Apostle has prescribed this rule for the life of Christians, namely, that we should devote all our works to the welfare of others, since each has such abundant riches in his faith that all his other works and his whole life are a surplus with which he can by voluntary benevolence serve and do good to his neighbor.

As an example of such life the Apostle cites Christ, saying, "Have this mind among yourselves, which you have in Christ Jesus, who, though he was in the form of God, did not count equality with God a thing to be grasped, but emptied himself, taking the form of a servant, being born in the likeness of men. And being found in human form he humbled himself and became obedient unto death" [Phil. 2:5–8]. This salutary word of the Apostle has been obscured for us by those who have not at all understood his words, "form of God," "form of a servant," "human form," "likeness of men," and have applied them to the divine and the human nature. Paul means this: Although Christ was filled with the form of God and rich in all good things, so that he needed no work and no suffering to make him righteous and saved (for he had all this eternally), yet he was not puffed up by them and did not exalt himself above us and assume power over us, although he could rightly have done so; but, on the contrary, he so lived, labored, worked, suffered, and died that he might be like other men and in fashion and in actions be nothing else than a man, just as if he had need of all these things and had nothing of the form of God. But he did all this for our sake, that he might serve us and that all things which he accomplished in this form of a servant might become ours.

So a Christian, like Christ his head, is filled and made rich by faith and should be content with this form of God which he has obtained by faith; only, as I have said, he should increase this faith until it is made perfect. For this faith is his life, his righteousness, and his salvation: it saves him and makes him acceptable, and bestows upon him all things that are Christ's, as has been said above, and as Paul asserts in Gal. 2 [:20] when he says, "And the life I now live in the flesh I live by faith in the Son of God." Although the Christian is thus free from all works, he ought in this liberty to empty himself, take upon himself the form of a servant, be made in the likeness of men, be found in human form, and to serve, help, and in every way deal with his neighbor as he sees that God through Christ has dealt and still deals with him. This he should do freely, having regard for nothing but divine approval.

He ought to think: "Although I am an unworthy and condemned man, my God has given me in Christ all the riches of righteousness and salvation without any merit on my part, out of pure, free mercy, so that from now on I need nothing except faith which believes that this is true. Why should I not therefore freely, joyfully, with all my heart, and with an eager will do all things which I know are pleasing and acceptable to such a Father who has overwhelmed me with his inestimable riches? I will therefore give myself as a Christ to my neighbor, just as Christ offered himself to me; I will do nothing in this life except what I see is necessary, profitable, and salutary to my neighbor, since through faith I have an abundance of all good things in Christ."

Behold, from faith thus flow forth love and joy in the Lord, and from love a joyful, willing, and free mind that serves one's neighbor willingly and takes no account of gratitude or ingratitude, of praise or blame, of gain or loss. For a man does not serve that he may put men under obligations. He does not distinguish between friends and enemies or anticipate their thankfulness or unthankfulness, but he most freely and most willingly spends himself and all that he has, whether he wastes all on the thankless or whether he gains a reward. As his Father does, distributing all things to all men richly and freely, making "his sun rise on the evil and on the good" [Matt. 5:45], so also the son does all things and suffers all things with that freely bestowing joy which is his delight when through Christ he sees it in God, the dispenser of such great benefits.

Therefore, if we recognize the great and precious things which are given us, as Paul says [Rom. 5:5], our hearts will be filled by the Holy Spirit with the love which makes us free, joyful, almighty workers and conquerors over all tribulations, servants of our neighbors, and yet lords of all. For those who do not recognize the gifts bestowed upon them through Christ, however, Christ has been born in vain; they go their way with their works and shall never come to taste or feel those things. Just as our neighbor is in need and lacks that in which we abound, so we were in need before God and lacked his mercy. Hence, as our heavenly Father has in Christ freely come to our aid, we also ought freely to help our neighbor through our body and its works, and each one should become as it were a Christ to the other that we may be Christs to one another and Christ may be the same in all, that is, that we may be truly Christians.

Who then can comprehend the riches and the glory of the Christian life? It can do all things and has all things and lacks nothing. It is lord over sin, death, and hell, and yet at the same time it serves, ministers to, and benefits all men. But alas in our day this life is unknown throughout the world; it is neither preached about nor sought after; we are altogether ignorant of our own name and do not know why we are Christians or bear the name of Christians. Surely we are named after Christ, not because he is absent from us, but because he dwells in us, that is, because we believe in him and are Christs one to another and do to our neighbors as Christ does to us. But in our day we are taught by the doctrine of men to seek nothing but merits, rewards, and the things that are ours; of Christ we have made only a taskmaster far harsher than Moses.

We have a pre-eminent example of such a faith in the blessed Virgin. As is written in Luke 2 [:22], she was purified according to the law of Moses according to the custom of all women, although she was not bound by that law and did not need to be purified. Out of free and willing love, however, she submitted to the law like other women that she might not offend or despise them. She was not justified by this work, but being righteous she did it freely and willingly. So also our works should be done, not that we may be justified by them, since, being justified beforehand by faith, we ought to do all things freely and joyfully for the sake of others.

St. Paul also circumcised his disciple Timothy, not because circumcision was necessary for his righteousness, but that he might not offend or despise the Jews who were weak in the faith and could not yet grasp the liberty of faith. But, on the other hand, when they despised the liberty of faith and insisted that circumcision was necessary for righteousness, he resisted them and did not allow Titus to be circumcised, Gal. 2 [:3]. Just as he was unwilling to offend or despise any man's weak faith and yielded to their will for a time, so he was also unwilling that the liberty of faith should be offended against or despised by stubborn, work-righteous men. He chose a middle way, sparing the weak for a time, but always withstanding the stubborn, that he might convert all to the liberty of faith. What we do should be done with the same zeal to sustain the weak in faith, as in Rom. 14 [:1]; but we should firmly resist the stubborn teachers of works. Of this we shall say more later.

Christ also, in Matt. 17 [:24–27], when the tax money was demanded of his disciples, discussed with St. Peter whether the sons of the king were not free from the payment of tribute, and Peter affirmed that they were. Nonetheless, Christ commanded Peter to go to the sea and said, "Not to give offense to them, go to the sea and cast a hook, and take the first fish that comes up, and when you open its mouth you will find a shekel; take that and give it to them for me and for yourself." This incident fits our subject beautifully for Christ here calls himself and those who are his children sons of the king, who need nothing; and yet he freely submits and pays the tribute.

Just as necessary and helpful as this work was to Christ's righteousness or salvation, just so much do all other works of his or his followers avail for righteousness, since they all follow after righteousness and are free and are done only to serve others and to give them an example of good works.

Of the same nature are the precepts which Paul gives in Rom. 13 [:1–7], namely, that Christians should be subject to the governing authorities and be ready to do every good work, not that they shall in this way be justified, since they already are righteous through faith, but that in the liberty of the Spirit they shall by so doing serve others and the authorities themselves and obey their will freely and out of love. The works of all colleges,[7] monasteries, and priests should be of this nature. Each one should do the works of his profession and station, not that by them he may strive after righteousness, but that through them he may keep his body under control, be an example to others who also need to keep their bodies under control, and finally that by such works he may submit his will to that of others in the freedom of love. But very great care must always be exercised so that no man in a false confidence imagines that by such works he will be justified or acquire merit or be saved; for this is the work of faith alone, as I have repeatedly said.

Anyone knowing this could easily and without danger find his way through those numberless mandates and precepts of pope, bishops, monasteries, churches, princes, and magistrates upon which some ignorant pastors insist as if they were necessary to righteousness and salvation, calling them "precepts of the church," although they are nothing of the kind. For a Christian, as a free man, will say, "I will fast, pray, do this and that as men command, not because it is necessary to my righteousness or salvation; but that I may show due respect to the pope, the bishop, the community, a magistrate, or my neighbor, and give them an example. I will do and suffer all things, just as Christ did and suffered far more for me, although he needed nothing of it all for himself, and was made under the law for my sake, although he was not under the law." Although tyrants do violence or injustice in making their de-

---

[7] The word "college" here denotes a corporation of clergy.

mands, yet it will do no harm as long as they demand nothing contrary to God.

From what has been said, everyone can pass a safe judgment on all works and laws and make a trustworthy distinction between them and know who are the blind and ignorant pastors and who are the good and true. Any work that is not done solely for the purpose of keeping the body under control or of serving one's neighbor, as long as he asks nothing contrary to God, is not good or Christian. For this reason I greatly fear that few or no colleges, monasteries, altars, and offices of the church are really Christian in our day—nor the special fasts and prayers on certain saints' days. I fear, I say, that in all these we seek only our profit, thinking that through them our sins are purged away and that we find salvation in them. In this way Christian liberty perishes altogether. This is a consequence of our ignorance of Christian faith and liberty.

This ignorance and suppression of liberty very many blind pastors take pains to encourage. They stir up and urge on their people in these practices by praising such works, puffing them up with their indulgences, and never teaching faith. If, however, you wish to pray, fast, or establish a foundation in the church, I advise you to be careful not to do it in order to obtain some benefit, whether temporal or eternal, for you would do injury to your faith which alone offers you all things. Your one care should be that faith may grow, whether it is trained by works or sufferings. Make your gifts freely and for no consideration, so that others may profit by them and fare well because of you and your goodness. In this way you shall be truly good and Christian. Of what benefit to you are the good works which you do not need for keeping your body under control? Your faith is sufficient for you, through which God has given you all things.

See, according to this rule the good things we have from God should flow from one to the other and be common to all, so that everyone should "put on" his neighbor and so conduct himself toward him as if he himself were in the other's place. From Christ the good things have flowed and are flowing into us. He has so "put on" us and acted for us as if he had been what we are. From us they flow on to those who have need of them so that I should lay before God my faith and my righteousness that they may cover and intercede for the sins of my neighbor which I take upon myself and so labor and serve in them as if they were my very own. That is what Christ did for us. This is true love and the genuine rule of a Christian life. Love is true and genuine where there is true and genuine faith. Hence the Apostle says of love in I Cor. 13 [:5] that "it does not seek its own."

We conclude, therefore, that a Christian lives not in himself, but in Christ and in his neighbor. Otherwise he is not a Christian. He lives in Christ through faith, in his neighbor through love. By faith he is caught up beyond himself into God. By love he descends beneath himself into his neighbor. Yet he always remains in God and in his love, as Christ says in John 1 [:51], "Truly, truly, I say to you, you will see heaven opened, and the angels of God ascending and descending upon the Son of man."

Enough now of freedom. As you see, it is a spiritual and true freedom and makes our hearts free from all sins, laws and commands, as Paul says, I Tim. 1 [:9], "The law is not laid down for the just." It is more excellent than all other liberty, which is external, as heaven is more excellent than earth. May Christ give us this liberty both to understand and to preserve. Amen.

Finally, something must be added for the sake of those for whom nothing can be said so well that they will not spoil it by misunderstanding it. It is questionable whether they will understand even what will be said here. There are very many who, when they hear of this freedom of faith, immediately turn it into an occasion for the flesh and think that now all things are allowed them. They want to show that they are free men and Christians only by despising and finding fault with ceremonies, traditions, and human laws; as if they were Christians because on stated days they do not fast or eat meat when others fast, or because they do not use the accustomed prayers, and with upturned nose scoff at the precepts of men, although they utterly disregard all else that pertains to the Christian religion. The extreme opposite of these are those who rely for their salvation solely on their reverent observance of ceremonies, as if they would be saved because on certain days they fast or abstain from meats, or pray certain prayers; these make a boast of the precepts of the church and of the fathers, and do not care a fig for the things which are of the essence of our faith. Plainly, both are in error because they neglect the weightier things which are necessary to salvation, and quarrel so noisily about trifling and unnecessary matters.

How much better is the teaching of the Apostle Paul who bids us take a middle course and condemns both sides when he says, "Let not him who eats despise him who abstains, and let not him who abstains pass judgment on him who eats" [Rom. 14:3]. Here you see that they who neglect and disparage ceremonies, not out of piety, but out of mere contempt, are reproved, since the Apostle teaches us not to despise them. Such men are puffed up by knowledge. On the other hand, he teaches those who insist on the ceremonies not to judge the others, for neither party acts toward the other according to the love that edifies. Wherefore we ought to listen to Scripture which teaches that we should not go aside to the right or to the left [Deut. 28:14] but follow the statutes of the Lord which are right, "rejoicing the heart" [Ps. 19:8]. As a man is not righteous because he keeps and clings to the works and forms of the ceremonies, so also will a man not be counted righteous merely because he neglects and despises them.

Our faith in Christ does not free us from works but from false opinions concerning works, that is, from the foolish presumption that justification is acquired by works. Faith redeems, corrects, and preserves our consciences so that we know that righteousness does not consist in works, although works neither can nor ought to be wanting; just as we cannot be without food and drink and all the works of this mortal body, yet our righteousness is not in them, but in faith; and yet those works of the body are not to be despised or neglected on that account. In this world we are bound by the needs of our bodily life, but we are not righteous because of them. "My kingship is not of this world" [John 18:36], says Christ. He does not, however, say, "My kingship is not here, that is, in this world." And Paul says, "Though we live in the world we are not carrying on a worldly war" [II Cor. 10:3], and in Gal. 2 [:20], "The life I now live in the flesh I live by faith in the Son of God." Thus what we do, live, and are in works and ceremonies, we do because of the necessities of this life and of the effort to rule our body. Nevertheless we are righteous, not in these, but in the faith of the Son of God.

Hence the Christian must take a middle course and face those two classes of men. He will meet first the unyielding, stubborn ceremonialists who like deaf adders are not willing to hear the truth of liberty [Ps. 58:4] but, having no faith, boast of, prescribe, and insist upon their ceremonies as means of justification. Such were the Jews of old, who were unwilling to learn how to do good. These he must resist, do the very opposite, and offend them boldly lest by their impious views they drag many with them into error. In the presence of such men it is good to eat meat, break the fasts, and for the sake of the liberty of faith do other things which they regard as the greatest of sins. Of them we must say, "Let them alone; they are blind guides." According to this principle Paul would not circumcise Titus when the Jews insisted that he should [Gal. 2:3], and Christ excused the apostles when they plucked ears of grain on the sabbath [Matt. 12:1–8]. There are many similar instances. The other class of men whom a Christian will meet are the simple-minded, ignorant men, weak in the faith, as the Apostle calls them, who cannot yet grasp the liberty of faith, even if they were willing to do so [Rom. 14:1]. These he must take care not to offend. He must yield to their weakness until they are more fully instructed. Since they do and think as they do, not because they are stubbornly wicked, but only because their faith is weak, the fasts and other things which they consider necessary must be observed to avoid giving them offense. This is the command of love which would harm no one but would serve all men. It is not by their fault that they are weak, but by that of their pastors who have taken them captive with the snares of their traditions and have wickedly used these traditions as rods with which to beat them. They should have been delivered from these pastors by the teachings of faith and freedom. So the Apostle teaches us in Romans 14: "If food is a cause of my brother's falling, I will never eat meat" [Cf. Rom. 14:21 and I Cor. 8:13]; and again, "I know and am persuaded in the Lord Jesus that nothing is unclean in itself; but it is unclean for any one who thinks it unclean" [Rom. 14:14].

For this reason, although we should boldly resist those

teachers of traditions and sharply censure the laws of the popes by means of which they plunder the people of God, yet we must spare the timid multitude whom those impious tyrants hold captive by means of these laws until they are set free. Therefore fight strenuously against the wolves, but for the sheep and not also against the sheep. This you will do if you inveigh against the laws and the lawgivers and at the same time observe the laws with the weak so that they will not be offended, until they also recognize tyranny and understand their freedom. If you wish to use your freedom, do so in secret, as Paul says, Rom. 14 [:22], "The faith that you have, keep between yourself and God"; but take care not to use your freedom in the sight of the weak. On the other hand, use your freedom constantly and consistently in the sight of and despite the tyrants and the stubborn so that they also may learn that they are impious, that their laws are of no avail for righteousness, and that they had no right to set them up.

Since we cannot live our lives without ceremonies and works, and the perverse and untrained youth need to be restrained and saved from harm by such bonds; and since each one should keep his body under control by means of such works, there is need that the minister of Christ be far-seeing and faithful. He ought so to govern and teach Christians in all these matters that their conscience and faith will not be offended and that there will not spring up in them a suspicion and a root of bitterness and many will thereby be defiled, as Paul admonishes the Hebrews [Heb. 12:15]; that is, that they may not lose faith and become defiled by the false estimate of the value of works and think that they must be justified by works. Unless faith is at the same time constantly taught, this happens easily and defiles a great many, as has been done until now through the pestilent, impious, soul-destroying traditions of our popes and the opinions of our theologians. By these snares numberless souls have been dragged down to hell, so that you might see in this the work of Antichrist.

In brief, as wealth is the test of poverty, business the test of faithfulness, honors the test of humility, feasts the test of temperance, pleasures the test of chastity, so ceremonies are the test of the righteousness of faith. "Can a man," asks Solomon, "carry fire in his bosom and his clothes and not be burned?"

[Prov. 6:27]. Yet as a man must live in the midst of wealth, business, honors, pleasures, and feasts, so also must he live in the midst of ceremonies, that is, in the midst of dangers. Indeed, as infant boys need beyond all else to be cherished in the bosoms and by the hands of maidens to keep them from perishing, yet when they are grown up their salvation is endangered if they associate with maidens, so the inexperienced and perverse youth need to be restrained and trained by the iron bars of ceremonies lest their unchecked ardor rush headlong into vice after vice. On the other hand, it would be death for them always to be held in bondage to ceremonies, thinking that these justify them. They are rather to be taught that they have been so imprisoned in ceremonies, not that they should be made righteous or gain great merit by them, but that they might thus be kept from doing evil and might more easily be instructed to the righteousness of faith. Such instruction they would not endure if the impulsiveness of their youth were not restrained.

Hence ceremonies are to be given the same place in the life of a Christian as models and plans have among builders and artisans. They are prepared, not as a permanent structure, but because without them nothing could be built or made. When the structure is complete the models and plans are laid aside. You see, they are not despised, rather they are greatly sought after; but what we despise is the false estimate of them since no one holds them to be the real and permanent structure.

If any man were so flagrantly foolish as to care for nothing all his life long except the most costly, careful, and persistent preparation of plans and models and never to think of the structure itself, and were satisfied with his work in producing such plans and mere aids to work, and boasted of it, would not all men pity his insanity and think that something great might have been built with what he has wasted? Thus we do not despise ceremonies and works, but we set great store by them; but we despise the false estimate placed upon works in order that no one may think that they are true righteousness, as those hypocrites believe who spend and lose their whole lives in zeal for works and never reach that goal for the sake of which the works are to be done, who, as the Apostle says, "will listen to anybody and can never arrive at a knowledge of the truth" [II Tim. 3:7]. They seem to wish to build, they make their preparations, and yet they never build. Thus they remain caught in the form of religion and do not attain unto its power [II Tim. 3:5]. Meanwhile they are pleased with their efforts and even dare to judge all others whom they do not see shining with a like show of works. Yet with the gifts of God which they have spent and abused in vain they might, if they had been filled with faith, have accomplished great things to their own salvation and that of others.

Since human nature and natural reason, as it is called, are by nature superstitious and ready to imagine, when laws and works are prescribed, that righteousness must be obtained through laws and works; and further, since they are trained and confirmed in this opinion by the practice of all earthly lawgivers, it is impossible that they should of themselves escape from the slavery of works and come to a knowledge of the freedom of faith. Therefore there is need of the prayer that the Lord may give us and make us *theodidacti*, that is, those taught by God [John 6:45], and himself, as he has promised, write his law in our hearts; otherwise there is no hope for us. If he himself does not teach our hearts this wisdom hidden in mystery [I Cor. 2:7], nature can only condemn it and judge it to be heretical because nature is offended by it and regards it as foolishness. So we see that it happened in the old days in the case of the apostles and prophets, and so godless and blind popes and their flatterers do to me and to those who are like me. May God at last be merciful to them and to us and cause his face to shine upon us that we may know his way upon earth [Ps. 67:1–2], his salvation among all nations, God, who is blessed forever [II Cor. 11:31]. Amen.

TWO KINDS OF RIGHTEOUSNESS[1]

[This sermon, probably from the year 1519, is an indication of how the righteousness of God in Christ is received and related to the life of the Christian.]

Brethren, "have this mind among yourselves, which you have in Christ Jesus, who, though he was in the form of God, did not count equality with God a thing to be grasped" [Phil. 2:5–6].

There are two kinds of Christian righteousness, just as man's sin is of two kinds.

The first is alien righteousness, that is the righteousness of another, instilled from without. This is the righteousness of Christ by which he justifies through faith, as it is written in I Cor. 1 [:30]: "Whom God made our wisdom, our righteousness and sanctification and redemption." In John 11 [:25–26], Christ himself states: "I am the resurrection and the life; he who believes in me . . . shall never die." Later he adds in John 14 [:6], "I am the way, and the truth, and the life." This righteousness, then, is given to men in baptism and whenever they are truly repentant. Therefore a man can with confidence boast in Christ and say: "Mine are Christ's living, doing, and speaking, his suffering and dying, mine as much as if I had

1 Reprinted by permission of the publisher from *Luther's Works*, volume 31, *Career of the Reformer: I*, edited by Harold J. Grimm (Philadelphia: Muhlenberg Press, 1957), pp. 297–306. The translation is by Lowell J. Satre.

lived, done, spoken, suffered, and died as he did." Just as a
bridegroom possesses all that is his bride's and she all that is
his—for the two have all things in common because they are
one flesh [Gen. 2:24]—so Christ and the church are one spirit
[Eph. 5:29–32]. Thus the blessed God and Father of mercies
has, according to Peter, granted to us, very great and precious
gifts in Christ [II Pet. 1:4]. Paul writes in II Cor. 1 [:3]:
"Blessed be the God and Father of our Lord Jesus Christ, the
Father of mercies and God of all comfort, who has blessed us
in Christ with every spiritual blessing in the heavenly places."[2]

This inexpressible grace and blessing was long ago promised
to Abraham in Gen. 12 [:3]: "And in thy seed (that is, in
Christ) shall all the nations of the earth be blessed."[3] Isaiah 9
[:6] says: "For to us a child is born, to us a son is given." "To
us," it says, because he is entirely ours with all his benefits if
we believe in him, as we read in Rom. 8 [:32]: "He who did
not spare his own Son but gave him up for us all, will he not
also give us all things with him?" Therefore everything which
Christ has is ours, graciously bestowed on us unworthy men
out of God's sheer mercy, although we have rather deserved
wrath and condemnation, and hell also. Even Christ himself,
therefore, who says he came to do the most sacred will of his
Father [John 6:38], became obedient to him; and whatever
he did, he did it for us and desired it to be ours, saying, "I am
among you as one who serves" [Luke 22:27]. He also states,
"This is my body, which is given for you" [Luke 22:19]. Isaiah
43 [:24] says, "You have burdened me with your sins, you
have wearied me with your iniquities."

Through faith in Christ, therefore, Christ's righteousness becomes our righteousness and all that he has becomes ours;
rather, he himself becomes ours. Therefore the Apostle calls it
"the righteousness of God" in Rom. 1 [:17]: For in the gospel
"the righteousness of God is revealed . . . ; as it is written,
'The righteous shall live by his faith.'" Finally, in the same
epistle, chapter 3 [:28], such a faith is called "the righteousness of God": "We hold that a man is justified by faith." This

2 The section "who has blessed, etc." is not from II Corinthians,
as indicated by Luther, but from Eph. 1:3.

3 Gen. 12:3 has "in thee" instead of "in thy seed." The quotation above is actually from Gen. 22:18.

is an infinite righteousness, and one that swallows up all sins in a moment, for it is impossible that sin should exist in Christ. On the contrary, he who trusts in Christ exists in Christ; he is one with Christ, having the same righteousness as he. It is therefore impossible that sin should remain in him. This righteousness is primary; it is the basis, the cause, the source of all our own actual righteousness. For this is the righteousness given in place of the original righteousness lost in Adam. It accomplishes the same as that original righteousness would have accomplished; rather, it accomplishes more.

It is in this sense that we are to understand the prayer in Psalm 30 [Ps. 31:1]: "In thee, O Lord, do I seek refuge; let me never be put to shame; in thy righteousness deliver me!" It does not say "in my" but "in thy righteousness," that is, in the righteousness of Christ my God which becomes ours through faith and by the grace and mercy of God. In many passages of the Psalter, faith is called "the work of the Lord," "confession," "power of God," "mercy," "truth," "righteousness." All these are names for faith in Christ, rather, for the righteousness which is in Christ. The Apostle therefore dares to say in Gal. 2 [:20], "It is no longer I who live, but Christ who lives in me." He further states in Eph. 3 [:14–17]: "I bow my knees before the Father . . . that . . . he may grant . . . that Christ may dwell in your hearts through faith."

Therefore this alien righteousness, instilled in us without our works by grace alone—while the Father, to be sure, inwardly draws us to Christ—is set opposite original sin, likewise alien, which we acquire without our works by birth alone. Christ daily drives out the old Adam more and more in accordance with the extent to which faith and knowledge of Christ grow. For alien righteousness is not instilled all at once, but it begins, makes progress, and is finally perfected at the end through death.

The second kind of righteousness is our proper righteousness, not because we alone work it, but because we work with that first and alien righteousness. This is that manner of life spent profitably in good works, in the first place, in slaying the flesh and crucifying the desires with respect to the self, of which we read in Gal. 5 [:24]: "And those who belong to Christ Jesus have crucified the flesh with its passions and desires." In the second place, this righteousness consists in love to one's neighbor, and in the third place, in meekness and fear toward God. The Apostle is full of references to these, as is all the rest of Scripture. He briefly summarizes everything, however, in Titus 2 [:12]: "In this world let us live soberly (pertaining to crucifying one's own flesh), justly (referring to one's neighbor), and devoutly (relating to God)."

This righteousness is the product of the righteousness of the first type, actually its fruit and consequence, for we read in Gal. 5 [:22]: "But the fruit of the spirit [i.e., of a spiritual man, whose very existence depends on faith in Christ] is love, joy, peace, patience, kindness, goodness, faithfulness, gentleness, self-control." For because the works mentioned are works of men, it is obvious that in this passage a spiritual man is called "spirit." In John 3 [:6] we read: "That which is born of the flesh is flesh, and that which is born of the Spirit is spirit." This righteousness goes on to complete the first for it ever strives to do away with the old Adam and to destroy the body of sin. Therefore it hates itself and loves its neighbor; it does not seek its own good, but that of another, and in this its whole way of living consists. For in that it hates itself and does not seek its own, it crucifies the flesh. Because it seeks the good of another, it works love. Thus in each sphere it does God's will, living soberly with self, justly with neighbor, devoutly toward God.

This righteousness follows the example of Christ in this respect [I Pet. 2:21] and is transformed into his likeness (II Cor. 3:18). It is precisely this that Christ requires. Just as he himself did all things for us, not seeking his own good but ours only—and in this he was most obedient to God the Father—so he desires that we also should set the same example for our neighbors.

We read in Rom. 6 [:19] that this righteousness is set opposite our own actual sin: "For just as you once yielded your members to impurity and to greater and greater iniquity, so now yield your members to righteousness for sanctification." Therefore through the first righteousness arises the voice of the bridegroom who says to the soul, "I am yours," but through the second comes the voice of the bride who answers, "I am yours." Then the marriage is consummated; it becomes strong and complete in accordance with the Song of Solomon [2:16]: "My beloved is mine and I am his. Then the soul no longer seeks to be righteous in and for itself, but it has Christ as its righteousness and therefore seeks only the welfare of others. Therefore the Lord of the Synagogue threatens through the Prophet, "And I will make to cease from the cities of Judah and from the streets of Jerusalem the voice of mirth and the voice of gladness, the voice of the bridegroom and the voice of the bride" [Jer. 7:34].

This is what the text we are now considering says: "Let this mind be in you, which was also in Christ Jesus" [Phil. 2:5]. This means you should be as inclined and disposed toward one another as you see Christ was disposed toward you. How? Thus, surely, that "though he was in the form of God, [he] did not count equality with God a thing to be grasped, but emptied himself, taking the form of a servant" [Phil. 2:6–7]. The term "form of God" here does not mean the "essence of God" because Christ never emptied himself of this. Neither can the phrase "form of a servant" be said to mean "human essence." But the "form of God" is wisdom, power, righteousness, goodness—and freedom too; for Christ was a free, powerful, wise man, subject to none of the vices or sins to which all other men are subject. He was pre-eminent in such attributes as are particularly proper to the form of God. Yet he was not haughty in that form; he did not please himself [Rom. 15:3]; nor did he disdain and despise those who were enslaved and subjected to various evils.

He was not like the Pharisee who said, "God, I thank thee that I am not like other men" [Luke 18:11], for that man was delighted that others were wretched; at any rate he was unwilling that they should be like him. This is the type of robbery by which a man usurps things for himself—rather, he keeps what he has and does not clearly ascribe to God the things that are God's, nor does he serve others with them that he may become like other men. Men of this kind wish to be like God, sufficient in themselves, pleasing themselves, glorying in themselves, under obligation to no one, and so on. Not thus, however, did Christ think; not of this stamp was his wisdom. He relinquished that form to God the Father and emptied himself, unwilling to use his rank against us, unwilling to

be different from us. Moreover, for our sakes he became as
one of us and took the form of a servant, that is, he subjected
himself to all evils. And although he was free, as the Apostle
says of himself also [I Cor. 9:19], he made himself servant of
all [Mark 9:35], living as if all the evils which were ours were
actually his own.

Accordingly he took upon himself our sin and our punishment, and although it was for us that he was conquering those
things, he acted as though he were conquering them for himself. Although as far as his relationship to us was concerned,
he had the power to be our God and Lord, yet he did not
will it so, but rather desired to become our servant, as it is
written in Rom. 15 [:1, 3]: "We . . . ought . . . not to please
ourselves . . . For Christ did not please himself; but, as it is
written, 'The reproaches of those who reproached thee fell on
me' " [Ps. 69:9]. The quotation from the Psalmist has the same
meaning as the citation from Paul.

It follows that this passage, which many have understood
affirmatively, ought to be understood negatively as follows:
That Christ did not count himself equal to God means that he
did not wish to be equal to him as those do who presumptuously grasp for equality and say to God, "If thou wilt not
give me thy glory (as St. Bernard says), I shall seize it for
myself." The passage is not to be understood affirmatively as
follows: He did not think himself equal to God, that is, the
fact that he is equal to God, this he did not consider robbery.
For this interpretation is not based on a proper understanding
since it speaks of Christ the man. The Apostle means that each
individual Christian shall become the servant of another in accordance with the example of Christ. If one has wisdom, righteousness, or power with which one can excel others and boast
in the "form of God," so to speak, one should not keep all this
to himself, but surrender it to God and become altogether as if
he did not possess it [II Cor. 6:10], as one of those who lack
it.

Paul's meaning is that when each person has forgotten himself and emptied himself of God's gifts, he should conduct
himself as if his neighbor's weakness, sin, and foolishness were
his very own. He should not boast or get puffed up. Nor should
he despise or triumph over his neighbor as if he were his god

or equal to God. Since God's prerogatives ought to be left to God alone, it becomes robbery when a man in haughty foolhardiness ignores this fact. It is in this way, then, that one takes the form of a servant, and that command of the Apostle in Gal. 5 [:13] is fulfilled: "Through love be servants of one another." Through the figure of the members of the body Paul teaches in Rom. 12 [:4–5] and I Cor. 12 [:12–27] how the strong, honorable, healthy members do not glory over those that are weak, less honorable, and sick as if they were their masters and gods; but on the contrary they serve them the more, forgetting their own honor, health, and power. For thus no member of the body serves itself; nor does it seek its own welfare but that of the other. And the weaker, the sicker, the less honorable a member is, the more the other members serve it "that there may be no discord in the body, but that the members may have the same care for one another," to use Paul's words [I Cor. 12:25]. From this it is now evident how one must conduct himself with his neighbor in each situation.

And if we do not freely desire to put off that form of God and take on the form of a servant, let us be compelled to do so against our will. In this regard consider the story in Luke 7 [:36–50], where Simon the leper, pretending to be in the form of God and perching on his own righteousness, was arrogantly judging and despising Mary Magdalene, seeing in her the form of a servant. But see how Christ immediately stripped him of that form of righteousness and then clothed him with the form of sin by saying: "You gave me no kiss. . . . You did not anoint my head." How great were the sins that Simon did not see! Nor did he think himself disfigured by such a loathsome form as he had. His good works are not at all remembered.

Christ ignores the form of God in which Simon was superciliously pleasing himself; he does not recount that he was invited, dined, and honored by him. Simon the leper is now nothing but a sinner. He who seemed to himself so righteous sits divested of the glory of the form of God, humiliated in the form of a servant, willy-nilly. On the other hand, Christ honors Mary with the form of God and elevates her above Simon, saying: "She has anointed my feet and kissed them. She has wet my feet with her tears and wiped them with her hair." How great were the merits which neither she nor Simon saw.

Her faults are remembered no more. Christ ignored the form of servitude in her whom he has exalted with the form of sovereignty. Mary is nothing but righteous, elevated into the glory of the form of God, etc.

In like manner he will treat all of us whenever we, on the ground of our righteousness, wisdom, or power, are haughty or angry with those who are unrighteous, foolish, or less powerful than we. For when we act thus—and this is the greatest perversion—righteousness works against righteousness, wisdom against wisdom, power against power. For you are powerful, not that you may make the weak weaker by oppression, but that you may make them powerful by raising them up and defending them. You are wise, not in order to laugh at the foolish and thereby make them more foolish, but that you may undertake to teach them as you yourself would wish to be taught. You are righteous that you may vindicate and pardon the unrighteous, not that you may only condemn, disparage, judge, and punish. For this is Christ's example for us, as he says: "For God sent the Son into the world, not to condemn the world, but that the world might be saved through him" [John 3:17]. He further says in Luke 9 [:55–56]: "You do not know what manner of spirit you are of; for the Son of man came not to destroy men's lives but to save them."

But the carnal nature of man violently rebels, for it greatly delights in punishment, in boasting of its own righteousness, and in its neighbor's shame and embarrassment at his unrighteousness. Therefore it pleads its own case, and it rejoices that this is better than its neighbor's. But it opposes the case of its neighbor and wants it to appear mean. This perversity is wholly evil, contrary to love, which does not seek its own good, but that of another [I Cor. 13:5; Phil. 2:4]. It ought to be distressed that the condition of its neighbor is not better than its own. It ought to wish that its neighbor's condition were better than its own, and if its neighbor's condition is the better, it ought to rejoice no less than it rejoices when its own is the better. "For this is the law and the prophets" [Matt. 7:12].

But you say, "Is it not permissible to chasten evil man? Is it not proper to punish sin? Who is not obliged to defend righteousness? To do otherwise would give occasion for lawlessness."

I answer: A single solution to this problem cannot be given. Therefore one must distinguish among men. For men can be classified either as public or private individuals.

The things which have been said do not pertain at all to public individuals, that is, to those who have been placed in a responsible office by God. It is their necessary function to punish and judge evil men, to vindicate and defend the oppressed, because it is not they but God who does this. They are his servants in this very matter, as the Apostle shows at some length in Rom. 13 [:4]: "He does not bear the sword in vain, etc." But this must be understood as pertaining to the cases of other men, not to one's own. For no man acts in God's place for the sake of himself and his own things, but for the sake of others. If, however, a public official has a case of his own, let him ask for someone other than himself to be God's representative, for in that case he is not a judge, but one of the parties. But on these matters let others speak at other times, for it is too broad a subject to cover now.

Private individuals with their own cases are of three kinds. First, there are those who seek vengeance and judgment from the representatives of God, and of these there is now a very great number. Paul tolerates such people, but he does not approve of them when he says in I Cor. 6 [:12], " 'All things are lawful for me,' but not all things are helpful." Rather he says in the same chapter, "To have lawsuits at all with one another is defeat for you" [I Cor. 6:7]. But yet to avoid a greater evil he tolerates this lesser one lest they should vindicate themselves and one should use force on the other, returning evil for evil, demanding their own advantages. Nevertheless such will not enter the kingdom of heaven unless they have changed for the better by forsaking things that are merely lawful and pursuing those that are helpful. For that passion for one's own advantage must be destroyed.

In the second class are those who do not desire vengeance. On the other hand, in accordance with the Gospel [Matt. 5:40], to those who would take their coats, they are prepared to give their cloaks as well, and they do not resist any evil. These are sons of God, brothers of Christ, heirs of future blessings. In Scripture therefore they are called "fatherless," "widows," "desolate"; because they do not avenge themselves, God wishes to be called their "Father" and "Judge" [Ps. 68:5]. Far from avenging themselves, if those in authority should wish to seek revenge in their behalf, they either do not desire it or seek it, or they only permit it. Or, if they are among the most advanced, they forbid and prevent it, prepared rather to lose their other possessions also.

Suppose you say: "Such people are very rare, and who would be able to remain in this world were he to do this?" I answer: This is not a discovery of today, that few are saved and that the gate is narrow that leads to life and those who find it are few [Matt. 7:14]. But if none were doing this, how would the Scripture stand which calls the poor, the orphans, and the widows "the people of Christ?" Therefore those in this second class grieve more over the sin of their offenders than over the loss or offense to themselves. And they do this that they may recall those offenders from their sin rather than avenge the wrongs they themselves have suffered. Therefore they put off the form of their own righteousness and put on the form of those others, praying for their persecutors, blessing those who curse, doing good to evil-doers, prepared to pay the penalty and make satisfaction for their very enemies that they may be saved [Matt. 5:44]. This is the gospel and the example of Christ [Luke 23:34].

In the third class are those who in persuasion are like the second type just mentioned, but are not like them in practice. They are the ones who demand back their own property or seek punishment to be meted out, not because they seek their own advantage, but through the punishment and restoration of their own things they seek the betterment of the one who has stolen or offended. They discern that the offender cannot be improved without punishment. These are called "zealots" and the Scriptures praise them. But no one ought to attempt this unless he is mature and highly experienced in the second class just mentioned, lest he mistake wrath for zeal and be convicted of doing from anger and impatience that which he believes he is doing from love of justice. For anger is like zeal, and impatience is like love of justice so that they cannot be sufficiently distinguished except by the most spiritual. Christ exhibited such zeal when he made a whip and cast out the sellers and buyers from the temple, as related in John 2 [:14–17]. Paul did likewise when he said, "Shall I come to you with a rod, or with love in a spirit of gentleness?" [I Cor. 4:21].

II

A COMMENTARY ON ST. PAUL'S EPISTLE TO THE GALATIANS[1]

[While *Luther had lectured on Galatians in 1519 and 1523, he considered the lectures of 1531, which form the basis of the present text, among the few works of his worth saving. This was because of their theological significance. In these lectures he had again hammered out the meaning of justification with fresh power. While much of the material is polemical, Luther's fully developed thoughts on Gospel and Law clearly come to focus in this commentary. While Luther supplied an introduction to the material and approved the contents, the material itself comes from the notes of reliable individuals who attended the lectures.*]

[Introductory]

I have taken in hand, in the name of the Lord, yet once again to expound this Epistle of St. Paul to the Galatians: not because I do desire to teach new things, or such as ye have not heard before, especially since that, by the grace of God, Paul is now thoroughly known unto you: but for that (as I have often forewarned you) this we have to fear as the greatest and nearest danger, lest Satan take from us the pure

[1] The selections here reprinted are taken by permission of the publishers from *A Commentary on St. Paul's Epistle to the Galatians*, revised and edited on the basis of the "Middleton" edition by Philip S. Watson (London: James Clarke and Co., Ltd., 1953, 1956), pp. 21–28, 136–41, 158–66, 223–29, 268–72, 297–302, 501–18.

doctrine of faith, and bring into the Church again the doctrine of works and men's traditions. Wherefore it is very necessary, that this doctrine be kept in continual practice and public exercise both of reading and hearing. And although it be never so well known, never so exactly learned, yet the devil our adversary, who continually rangeth about seeking to devour us, is not dead; likewise our flesh and old man is yet alive; besides this, all kinds of temptations vex and oppress us on every side. Wherefore this doctrine can never be taught, urged, and repeated enough. If this doctrine be lost, then is also the whole knowledge of truth, life and salvation lost and gone. If this doctrine flourish, then all good things flourish, religion, the true service of God, the glory of God, the right knowledge of all things and states of life. Because therefore we would be occupied and not idle, we will there begin now where we made an end, according to the saying of the son of Sirach: 'When a man hath done what he can, he must begin again' [Ecclus. 18:6].

The Argument of the Epistle to the Galatians

First of all it behoveth that we speak of the argument of this Epistle: that is to say, what matter St. Paul here chiefly treateth of. The argument therefore is this.

St. Paul goeth about to establish the doctrine of faith, grace, forgiveness of sins, or Christian righteousness, to the end that we may have a perfect knowledge and difference between Christian righteousness and all other kinds of righteousness. For there be divers sorts of righteousness. There is a political or civil righteousness, which emperors, princes of the world, philosophers and lawyers deal withal. There is also a ceremonial righteousness, which the traditions of men do teach. This righteousness parents and schoolmasters may teach without danger, because they do not attribute unto it any power to satisfy for sin, to placate God, or to deserve grace: but they teach such ceremonies as are only necessary for the correction of manners, and certain observations concerning this life. Besides these, there is another righteousness called the righteousness of the law, or of the Ten Commandments, which Moses teacheth. This do we also teach after the doctrine of faith.

There is yet another righteousness which is above all these: to wit, the righteousness of faith, or Christian righteousness, the which we must diligently discern from the other afore-rehearsed: for they are quite contrary to this righteousness, both because they flow out of the laws of emperors, the traditions of the Pope, and the commandments of God, and also because they consist in our works, and may be wrought of us either by our pure natural strength (as the sophisters term it) or else by the gift of God. For these kinds of righteousness are also of the gift of God, like as other good things are which we do enjoy.

But this most excellent righteousness, of faith I mean (which God through Christ, without works, imputeth unto us), is neither political nor ceremonial, nor the righteousness of God's law, nor consisteth in our works, but is clean contrary: that is to say, a mere passive righteousness, as the other above are active. For in this we work nothing, we render nothing unto God, but only we receive and suffer another to work in us, that is to say, God. Therefore it seemeth good unto me to call this righteousness of faith or Christian righteousness, the passive righteousness.

This is a righteousness hidden in a mystery, which the world doth not know, yea, Christians themselves do not thoroughly understand it, and can hardly take hold of it in their temptations. Therefore it must be diligently taught and continually practised. And whoso doth not understand or apprehend this righteousness in afflictions and terrors of conscience, must needs be overthrown. For there is no comfort of conscience so firm and so sure, as this passive righteousness is.

But man's weakness and misery is so great, that in the terrors of conscience and danger of death, we behold nothing else but our works, our worthiness and the law: which when it sheweth unto us our sin, by and by our evil life past cometh to remembrance. Then the poor sinner with great anguish of spirit groaneth, and thus thinketh with himself: 'Alas! how desperately have I lived! Would to God I might live longer: then would I amend my life.' Thus man's reason cannot restrain itself from the sight and beholding of this active or working righteousness, that is to say, her own righteousness: nor lift up her eyes to the beholding of the passive or Christian righteousness, but resteth altogether in the active righteousness: so deeply is this evil rooted in us.

On the other side, Satan abusing the infirmity of our nature, doth increase and aggravate these cogitations in us. Then can it not be but that the poor conscience must be more grievously troubled, terrified and confounded. For it is impossible that the mind of man itself should conceive any comfort, or look up unto grace only, in the feeling and horror of sin, or constantly reject all disputing and reasoning about works. For this is far above man's strength and capacity, yea and above the law of God also. True it is, that of all things in the world, the law is most excellent: yet is it not able to quiet a troubled conscience, but increaseth terrors, and driveth it to desperation; for by the commandment sin is made exceeding sinful [Rom. 7:13].

Wherefore the afflicted and troubled conscience hath no remedy against desperation and eternal death, unless it take hold of the promise of grace freely offered in Christ, that is to say, this passive righteousness of faith, or Christian righteousness. Which if it can apprehend, then may it be at quiet and boldly say: I seek not the active or working righteousness, although I know that I ought to have it, and also to fulfil it. But be it so that I had it, and did fulfil it indeed, yet notwithstanding I cannot trust unto it, neither dare I set it against the judgment of God. Thus I abandon myself from all active righteousness, both of mine own and of God's law, and embrace only that passive righteousness, which is the righteousness of grace, mercy and forgiveness of sins. Briefly, [I rest only upon] the righteousness of Christ and of the Holy Ghost, which we do not, but suffer, and have not, but receive; God the Father freely giving it unto us through Jesus Christ.

Like as the earth engendereth not rain, nor is able by her own strength, labour and travail to procure the same, but receiveth it of the mere gift of God from above: so this heavenly righteousness is given us of God without our works or deservings. As much therefore as the earth of itself is able to do in getting and procuring to itself seasonable showers of rain to make it fruitful, even so much are we men able to do by our strength and works in winning this heavenly and eternal righteousness; and therefore we shall never be able to attain unto it, unless God himself by mere imputation and by his unspeakable gift do bestow it upon us. The greatest knowledge, then, and the greatest wisdom of Christians is, not to know the law, to be ignorant of works and of the whole active righteousness, especially when the conscience wrestleth with the judgment of God. Like as on the contrary, amongst those which are not of the number of God's people, the greatest point of wisdom is, to know and earnestly to urge the law, works, and the active righteousness.

But it is a thing very strange and unknown to the world, to teach Christians to learn to be ignorant of the law, and so to live before God, as if there were no law: notwithstanding, except thou be ignorant of the law, and be assuredly persuaded in thine heart that there is now no law nor wrath of God, but altogether grace and mercy for Christ's sake, thou canst not be saved; for by the law cometh the knowledge of sin [Rom. 3:20]. Contrariwise, works and the keeping of the law must be so straitly required in the world, as if there were no promise or grace; and that because of the stubborn, proud and hard-hearted, before whose eyes nothing must be set but the law, that they may be terrified and humbled. For the law is given to terrify and kill such, and to exercise the old man; and both the word of grace and of wrath must be rightly divided, according to the Apostle [II Tim. 2:15 f.].

Here is then required a wise and faithful disposer of the Word of God, which can so moderate the law, that it may be kept within his bounds. He that teacheth that men are justified before God by the observation of the law, passeth the bounds of the law, and confoundeth these two kinds of righteousness, active and passive, and is but an ill logician, for he doth not rightly divide. Contrariwise, he that setteth forth the law and works to the old man, and the promise of forgiveness of sins and God's mercy to the new man, divideth the Word well. For the flesh or the old man must be coupled with the law and works: the spirit or new man must be joined with the promise of God and his mercy. Wherefore when I see a man that is bruised enough already, oppressed with the law, terrified with sin, and thirsting for comfort, it is time that I should remove out of his sight the law and active righteousness, and that I should set before him by the Gospel the Christian and passive righteousness, which excluding Moses with his law, offereth the promise made in Christ, who came for the afflicted and for sinners. Here is man raised up again and conceiveth good hope, neither is he any longer under the law, but under grace [Rom. 6:14]. How not under the law? According to the new man, to whom the law doth not appertain. For the law hath his bounds unto Christ, as Paul saith afterwards: 'The end of the law is Christ' [Gal. 3:24; Rom. 10:4]; who being come, Moses ceaseth with his law, circumcision, the sacrifices, the sabbaths, yea and all the prophets.

This is our divinity, whereby we teach how to put a difference between these two kinds of righteousness, active and passive: to the end that manners and faith, works and grace, policy and religion should not be confounded, or taken the one for the other. Both are necessary, but both must be kept within their bounds: Christian righteousness appertaineth to the new man, and the righteousness of the law appertaineth to the old man, which is born of flesh and blood. Upon this old man, as upon an ass, there must be laid a burden that may press him down, and he must not enjoy the freedom of the Spirit, or grace, except he first put upon him the new man by faith in Christ (which notwithstanding is not fully done in this life); then may he enjoy the kingdom and unspeakable gift of grace.

This I say to the end that no man should think we reject or forbid good works, as the Papists do most falsely slander us, neither understanding what they themselves say, nor what we teach. They know nothing but the righteousness of the law, and yet they will judge of that doctrine which is far above the law, of which it is impossible that the carnal man should be able to judge. Therefore they must needs be offended, for they can see no higher than the law. Whatsoever then is above the law, is to them a great offence.

But we imagine as it were two worlds, the one heavenly and the other earthly. In these we place these two kinds of righteousness, being separate the one far from the other. The righteousness of the law is earthly and hath to do with earthly things, and by it we do good works. But as the earth bringeth not forth fruit except first it be watered and made fruitful from above (for the earth cannot judge, renew and rule the heaven, but contrariwise the heaven judgeth, reneweth, ruleth and maketh fruitful the earth, that it may do what the Lord hath commanded): even so by the righteousness of the law, in doing many things we do nothing, and in fulfilling of the law we fulfil it not, except first, without any merit or work of ours, we be made righteous by the Christian righteousness, which nothing appertaineth to the righteousness of the law, or to the earthly and active righteousness. But this righteousness is heavenly and passive: which we have not of ourselves, but receive it from heaven: which we work not, but apprehend it by faith; whereby we mount up above all laws and works. Wherefore like as we have borne (as St. Paul saith) the image of the earthly Adam, so let us bear the image of the heavenly [I Cor. 15:49], which is the new man in a new world, where is no law, no sin, no sting of conscience, no death, but perfect joy, righteousness, grace, peace, life, salvation and glory.

Why, do we then nothing? Do we work nothing for the obtaining of this righteousness? I answer: Nothing at all. For the nature of this righteousness is, to do nothing, to hear nothing, to know nothing whatsoever of the law or of works, but to know and to believe this only, that Christ is gone to the Father and is not now seen: that he sitteth in heaven at the right hand of his Father, not as a judge, but made unto us of God, wisdom, righteousness, holiness and redemption: briefly, that he is our high-priest intreating for us, and reigning over us and in us by grace. Here no sin is perceived, no terror or remorse of conscience is felt; for in this heavenly righteousness sin can have no place: for there is no law, and where no law is, there can be no transgression [Rom. 4:15].

Seeing then that sin hath here no place, there can be no anguish of conscience, no fear, no heaviness. Therefore St. John saith: 'He that is born of God cannot sin' [I John 3:9]. But if there be any fear or grief of conscience, it is a token that this righteousness is withdrawn, that grace is hidden, and that Christ is darkened and out of sight. But where Christ is truly seen indeed, there must needs be full and perfect joy in the Lord, with peace of conscience, which most certainly thus thinketh: Although I am a sinner by the law, as touching the righteousness of the law, yet I despair not, yet I die not, because Christ liveth, who is both my righteousness and my everlasting and heavenly life. In that righteousness and life I have no sin, no sting of conscience, no care of death. I am indeed a sinner as touching this present life and the righteousness thereof, as the child of Adam: where the law accuseth me, death reigneth over me, and at length would devour me. But I have another righteousness and life above this life, which is Christ the Son of God, who knoweth no sin nor death, but is righteousness and life eternal: by whom even this my body, being dead and brought into dust, shall be raised up again and delivered from the bondage of the law and sin, and shall be sanctified together with the spirit.

So both these continue whilst we here live. The flesh is accused, exercised with temptations, oppressed with heaviness and sorrow, bruised by the active righteousness of the law; but the spirit reigneth, rejoiceth and is saved by this passive and Christian righteousness, because it knoweth that it hath a Lord in heaven at the right hand of the Father, who hath abolished the law, sin, death, and hath trodden under his feet all evils, led them captive and triumphed over them in himself, Col. 2 [:15].

St. Paul therefore in this Epistle goeth about diligently to instruct us, to comfort us, to hold us in the perfect knowledge of this most Christian and excellent righteousness. For if the article of justification be once lost, then is all true Christian doctrine lost. And as many as are in the world that hold not this doctrine, are either Jews, Turks, Papists or heretics. For between the righteousness of the law and the righteousness of Christ, or between active and passive righteousness, there is no mean. He then that strayeth from this Christian righteousness, must needs fall into the active righteousness; that is to say, when he hath lost Christ, he must fall into the confidence of his own works.

This we see at this day in the fantastical spirits and authors of sects, which teach nothing, neither can teach anything aright, concerning this righteousness of grace. The words indeed they have taken out of our mouth and writings, and these only do they speak and write. But the thing itself they are not able to deliver and straitly to urge, because they neither do nor can understand it, since they cleave only to the righteousness of the law. Therefore they are and remain exactors of the law, having no power to ascend higher than that active righteousness. And so they remain the same as they were under the Pope, save that they invent new names and new works, and yet notwithstanding the thing remaineth the same: even as the Turks do other works than the Papists, and the Papists than the Jews, &c. But albeit that some do works more splendid, great, and difficult by far than others, notwithstanding the substance is the same, the quality only is different: that is to say, the works do differ in appearance and name only, and not in very deed, for they are works notwithstanding, and they which do them are and remain, not Christians, but hirelings, whether they be called Jews, Mahometists, Papists, &c.

Therefore do we so earnestly set forth and so often repeat this doctrine of faith or Christian righteousness, that by this means it may be kept in continual exercise, and may be plainly discerned from the active righteousness of the law. (For by this only doctrine the Church is built, and in this it consisteth.) Otherwise we shall never be able to hold the true divinity, but by and by we shall either become canonists, observers of ceremonies, observers of the law, or Papists, and Christ so darkened that none in the Church shall be either rightly taught or comforted. Wherefore, if we will be teachers and leaders of others, it behoveth us to have great care of these matters, and to mark well this distinction between the righteousness of the law and the righteousness of Christ. And this distinction is easy to be uttered in words, but in use and experience it is very hard, although it be never so diligently exercised and practised; for in the hour of death, or in other agonies of the conscience, these two sorts of righteousness do encounter more near together than thou wouldest wish or desire.

Wherefore I do admonish you, especially such as shall become instructors and guiders of consciences, and also every one apart, that ye exercise yourselves continually by study, by reading, by meditation of the Word and by prayer, that in the time of temptation ye may be able to instruct and comfort both your own consciences and others, and to bring them from the law to grace, from active and working righteousness to the passive and received righteousness, and, to conclude, from Moses to Christ. For the devil is wont, in affliction and in the conflict of conscience, by the law to make us afraid, and to lay against us the guilt of sin, our wicked life past, the wrath and judgment of God, hell and eternal death, that by this means he may drive us to desperation, make us bond-slaves to himself, and pluck us from Christ. Furthermore, he is wont to set against us those places of the Gospel, wherein Christ himself requireth works of us, and with plain words threateneth damnation to those who do them not. Now, if here we be not able to judge between these two kinds of righteousness, if we take not by faith hold of Christ sitting at the right hand of God, who maketh intercession unto the Father for us wretched sinners [Heb. 7:25], then are we under the law and not under grace, and Christ is no more a saviour, but a lawgiver. Then can there remain no more salvation, but a certain desperation and everlasting death must needs follow.

Let us then diligently learn to judge between these two kinds of righteousness, that we may know how far we ought to obey the law. Now we have said before, that the law in a Christian ought not to pass his bounds, but ought to have dominion only over the flesh, which is in subjection unto it, and remaineth under the same. When it is thus, the law is kept within his bounds. But if it shall presume to creep into thy conscience, and there seek to reign, see thou play the cunning logician, and make the true division. Give no more to the law than belongeth unto it, but say thou: O law, thou wouldest climb up into the kingdom of my conscience, and there reign and reprove it of sin, and wouldest take from me the joy of my heart, which I have by faith in Christ, and drive me to desperation, that I might be without all hope, and utterly perish. This thou dost besides thine office: keep thyself within thy bounds, and exercise thy power upon the flesh, but touch not my conscience; for I am baptized, and by the Gospel am called to the partaking of righteousness and of everlasting life, to the kingdom of Christ, wherein my conscience is at rest, where no law is, but altogether forgiveness of sins, peace, quietness, joy, health and everlasting life. Trouble me not in these matters, for I will not suffer thee, so intolerable a tyrant and cruel tormentor, to reign in my conscience, for it is the seat and temple of Christ the Son of God, who is the king of righteousness and peace, and my most sweet saviour and mediator: he shall keep my conscience joyful and quiet in the sound and pure doctrine of the Gospel, and in the knowledge of this passive and heavenly righteousness.

When I have this righteousness reigning in my heart, I descend from heaven as the rain making fruitful the earth: that is to say, I come forth into another kingdom, and I do good works, how and whensoever occasion is offered. If I be a minister of the Word, I preach, I comfort the broken-hearted, I administer the Sacraments. If I be an householder, I govern my house and my family, I bring up my children in the knowledge and fear of God. If I be a magistrate, the charge that is given me from above I diligently execute. If I be a servant, I do my master's business faithfully. To conclude: whosoever he be that is assuredly persuaded that Christ is his righteousness, doth not only cheerfully and gladly work well in his vocation, but also submitteth himself through love to the magistrates and to their laws, yea though they be severe, sharp and cruel, and (if necessity do so require) to all manner of burdens and dangers of this present life, because he knoweth that this is the will of God, and that this obedience pleaseth him.

Thus far as concerning the argument of this Epistle, whereof Paul intreateth, taking occasion of false teachers who had darkened this righteousness of faith among the Galatians, against whom he setteth himself in defending and commending his authority and office.

The True Rule of Christianity.

Contrary to these vain trifles and doting dreams (as we have also noted before) we teach faith, and give a true rule of Christianity in this sort: first, that a man must be taught by the law to know himself, that so he may learn to say with the prophet: 'All have sinned and have need of the glory of God' [Rom. 3:23]; also, 'There is not one righteous, no, not one: not one that understandeth, not one that seeketh after God: all have gone astray' [Rom. 3:10 ff.; Pss. 14:1 ff.; 53:1 ff.]; also: 'Against thee only have I sinned' [Ps. 51:4]. Thus we by a contrary way do drive men from the merit of congruence and worthiness. Now, when a man is humbled by the law, and brought to the knowledge of himself, then followeth true repentance (for true repentance beginneth at the fear and judgment of God), and he seeth himself to be so great a sinner that he can find no means how he may be delivered from his sin by his own strength, endeavour and works. Then he perceiveth well what Paul meaneth when he saith that man is the servant and bond-slave of sin [Rom. 7:14]; also that God hath shut up all under sin [Rom. 11:52; Gal. 3:22] and that the whole world is guilty before God [Rom. 3:19]. Then he seeth that all the divinity of the schoolmen touching the merit of congruence and worthiness, is nothing else but mere foolishness, and that by this means the whole Papacy falleth.

Here now he beginneth to sigh, and saith in this wise: Who then can give succour? For he being thus terrified with the law, utterly despaireth of his own strength: he looketh about, and sigheth for the help of a mediator and saviour. Here then cometh in good time the healthful word of the Gospel, and saith: 'Son, thy sins are forgiven thee' [Matt. 9:2]. Believe in Christ Jesus crucified for thy sins, &c. If thou feel thy sins and the burden thereof, look not upon them in thyself, but remember that they are translated and laid upon Christ, whose stripes have made thee whole [Isa. 53:5].

This is the beginning of health and salvation. By this means we are delivered from sin, justified and made inheritors of everlasting life; not for our own works and deserts, but for our faith, whereby we lay hold upon Christ. Wherefore we also do acknowledge a quality and a formal righteousness in the heart: not charity (as the sophisters do) but faith; and yet so notwithstanding, that the heart must behold and apprehend nothing but Christ the Saviour. And here it is necessary that you know the true definition of Christ. The schoolmen being utterly ignorant hereof, have made Christ a judge and a tormentor, devising this fond fancy concerning the merit of congruence and worthiness.

But Christ, according to his true definition, is no lawgiver, but a forgiver of sins and a saviour. This doth faith apprehend and undoubtedly believe, that he hath wrought works and merits of congruence and worthiness abundantly. For he might have satisfied for all the sins of the world by one only drop of his blood; but now he hath shed it plentifully, and hath satisfied abundantly. 'By his own blood hath he entered into the holy place once for all, and obtained eternal redemption,' Heb. 9 [:12]; and 'We are justified freely by his grace, through the redemption that is in Christ Jesus, whom God hath set forth to be a reconciliation unto us, through faith in his blood,' Rom. 3 [:24 f.]. Wherefore it is a great matter, by faith, to lay hold upon Christ bearing the sins of the world. And this faith alone is counted for righteousness, Rom. 3–4.

Here is to be noted, that these three things, faith, Christ, acceptation, or imputation, must be joined together. Faith taketh hold of Christ, and hath him present, and holdeth him inclosed, as the ring doth the precious stone. And whosoever shall be found having this confidence in Christ apprehended in the heart, him will God account for righteous. This is the mean, and this is the merit whereby we attain the remission of sins and righteousness. Because thou believest in me, saith the Lord, and thy faith layeth hold upon Christ, whom I have freely given unto thee that he might be thy mediator and high priest, therefore be thou justified and righteous. Wherefore God doth accept or account us as righteous, only for our faith in Christ.

And this acceptation, or imputation, is very necessary: first, because we are not yet perfectly righteous, but while we remain in this life, sin dwelleth still in our flesh; and this remnant of sin God purgeth in us. Moreover, we are sometimes left of the Holy Ghost, and fall into sins, as did Peter, David, and other holy men. Notwithstanding we have always recourse to this article: that our sins are covered, and that God will not lay them to our charge, Rom. 4. Not that sin is not in us (as the sophisters have taught, saying, that we must be always working well until we feel that there is no sin remaining in us): yea, sin is indeed always in us, and the godly do feel it, but it is covered, and is not imputed unto us of God for Christ's sake; whom because we do apprehend by faith, all our sins are now no sins. But where Christ and faith be not, there is no remission or covering of sins, but mere imputation of sins and condemnation. Thus will God glorify his Son, and will be glorified himself in us through him.

When we have thus taught faith in Christ, then do we teach also good works. Because thou hast laid hold upon Christ by faith, through whom thou art made righteous, begin now to work well. Love God and thy neighbour, call upon God, give thanks unto him, praise him, confess him. Do good to thy neighbour and serve him: fulfil thine office. These are good works indeed, which flow out of this faith and this cheerfulness conceived in the heart, for that we have remission of sins freely by Christ.

Now what cross or affliction soever do afterwards ensue, they are easily borne, and cheerfully suffered. For the yoke that Christ layeth upon us, is sweet, and his burden is light [Matt. 11:30]. When sin is pardoned, and the conscience delivered from the burden and sting of sin, then may a Christian bear all things easily: because he feeleth all things within sweet and comfortable, therefore he doeth and suffereth all things willingly. But when a man walketh in his own righteousness, whatsoever he doeth is grievous and tedious unto him, because he doeth it unwillingly.

We therefore do make this definition of a Christian, that a Christian is not he which hath no sin, or feeleth no sin, but he to whom God imputeth not his sin because of his faith in Christ. This doctrine bringeth strong consolation to afflicted consciences in serious and inward terrors. It is not without good cause, therefore, that we do so often repeat and beat into your minds the forgiveness of sins, and imputation of righteousness for Christ's sake: also that a Christian hath nothing to do with the law and sin, especially in the time of temptation. For inasmuch as he is a Christian, he is above the law and sin. For he hath Christ the Lord of the law present and inclosed in his heart (as we have said) even as a ring hath a jewel or precious stone inclosed in it. Therefore when the law accuseth and sin terrifieth him, he looketh upon Christ, and when he hath apprehended him by faith, he hath present with him the conqueror of the law, sin, death and the devil: who reigneth and ruleth over them, so that they cannot hurt him. Wherefore a Christian man, if ye define him rightly, is free from all laws, and is not subject unto any creature, either within or without: inasmuch as he is a Christian, I say, and not inasmuch as he is a man or a woman, that is to say, inasmuch as he hath his conscience adorned and beautified and enriched with this faith, with this great and inestimable treasure, or, as Paul saith, 'this unspeakable gift' [II Cor. 9:15], which cannot be magnified and praised enough, for it maketh us the children and heirs of God. And by this means a Christian is greater than the whole world. For he hath such a gift, such a treasure in his heart, that although it seemeth to be but little, yet notwithstanding the smallness thereof, is greater than heaven and earth, because Christ, which is this gift, is greater.

While this doctrine, pacifying and quieting the conscience, remaineth pure and uncorrupt, Christians are made judges over all kinds of doctrine, and are lords over the laws of the whole world. Then can they certainly judge that the Turk with his Alcoran is damned, because he goeth not the right way, that is, he acknowledgeth not himself to be a miserable and damnable sinner, nor apprehendeth Christ by faith, for whose sake he might be assured that his sins are pardoned. In like manner they boldly pronounce sentence against the Pope, that he is condemned with all his kingdom, because he so walketh and so teacheth (with all his religious rabble of sophisters and schoolmen), that by the merit of congruence we must come to grace, and that afterward by the merit of worthiness we are received into heaven. Here saith the Christian: this is not the right way to justify us, neither doth this way lead to heaven. For I cannot, saith he, by my works going before grace, deserve grace of congruence, nor by my works following grace, obtain eternal life of worthiness: but to him that believeth in Christ, sin is pardoned and righteousness imputed. This trust and this confidence maketh him the child of God and heir of his kingdom; for in hope he possesseth already everlasting life, assured unto him by promise. Through faith in Christ therefore all things are given unto us, grace, peace, forgiveness of sins, salvation and everlasting life, and not for the merit of congruence and worthiness.

Wherefore this doctrine of the schoolmen, with their ceremonies, masses, and infinite foundations of the papistical kingdom, are most abominable blasphemies against God, sacrileges and plain denials of Christ, as Peter hath foretold in these words: 'There shall be', saith he, 'false teachers among you, which shall privily bring in damnable heresies, denying the Lord that hath bought them,' etc., II Pet. 2 [:1]. As though he would say: The Lord hath redeemed and bought us with his blood, that he might justify and save us; this is the way of righteousness and salvation. But there shall come false teachers, which denying the Lord, shall blaspheme the way of truth, of righteousness and salvation; they shall find out new ways of falsehood and destruction, and many shall follow their damnable ways. Peter throughout this whole chapter most lively painteth out the Papacy, which neglecting and despising the Gospel and faith in Christ, hath taught the works and traditions of men: as the merit of congruence and worthiness, the difference of days, meats and persons, vows, invocation of saints, pilgrimages, purgatory, and such like. In these fantastical opinions the Papists are so misled, that it is impossible for them to understand one syllable of the Gospel, of faith, or of Christ.

And this the thing itself doth well declare. For they take that privilege unto themselves which belongeth unto Christ alone. He only delivereth from sins, he only giveth righteousness and everlasting life; and they most impudently and wickedly do vaunt that we are able to obtain these things apart from Christ by the merits of congruence and worthiness. This, saith Peter and the other Apostles, is to bring in damnable heresies and sects of perdition. For by these means they deny Christ, tread his blood under their feet, blaspheme the Holy Ghost, and despise the grace of God. Wherefore no man can sufficiently conceive how horrible the idolatry of the Papists is. As inestimable as the gift is which is offered unto us by Christ, even so and no less abominable are these profanations of the Papists. Wherefore they ought not to be lightly esteemed or forgotten, but diligently weighed and considered. And this maketh very much also for the amplifying of the grace of God and the benefit of Christ, as by the contrary. For the more we know the profanation of the papistical Mass, so much the more we abhor and detest the same, and embrace the true use of the Mass, which the Pope hath taken away, and hath made merchandise thereof, that being bought for money, it might profit others. For he saith that the massing priest, an apostate denying Christ and blaspheming the Holy Ghost, standing at the altar, doth a good work, not only for himself, but also for others, both quick and dead, and for the whole Church, and that only by the work wrought, and by no other means.

Wherefore even by this we may plainly see the inestimable patience of God, in that he hath not long ago destroyed the whole Papacy, and consumed it with fire and brimstone, as he did Sodom and Gomorrah. But now these jolly fellows go about, not only to cover, but highly to advance their impiety and filthiness. This we may in no case dissemble. We must therefore with all diligence set forth the article of justification, that as a most clear sun, it may bring to light the darkness of their hypocrisy, and discover their filthiness and shame. For this cause we do so often repeat and so earnestly set forth the righteousness of faith, that the adversaries may be confounded and this article established and confirmed in our hearts. And this is a most necessary thing: for if we once lose this sun, we fall again into our former darkness. And most horrible it is, that the Pope should ever be able to bring this to pass in the Church, that Christ should be denied, trodden under foot, spit upon, blasphemed, yea and that even by the Gospel and sacraments; which he hath so darkened, and turned into such an horrible abuse, that he hath made them to serve him against Christ, for the establishing and confirming of his detestable abominations. O deep darkness! O horrible wrath of God!

EVEN WE, I SAY, HAVE BELIEVED IN CHRIST JESUS, THAT WE MIGHT BE JUSTIFIED &C.

This is the true mean of becoming a Christian, even to be justified by faith in Jesus Christ, and not by the works of the law. Here we must stand, not upon the wicked gloss of the schoolmen, which say, that faith then justifieth, when charity and good works are joined withal. With this pestilent gloss the sophisters have darkened and corrupted this and other like sentences in Paul, wherein he manifestly attributeth justification to faith only in Christ. But when a man heareth that he ought to believe in Christ, and yet notwithstanding faith justifieth not except it be formed and furnished with charity, by and by he falleth from faith, and thus he thinketh: If faith without charity justifieth not, then is faith in vain and unprofitable, and charity alone justifieth; for except faith be formed and beautified with charity, it is nothing.

And to confirm this pernicious and pestilent gloss, the adversaries do allege this place, I Cor. 13 [:1 f.]: 'Though I speak with the tongues of men and angels, &c., and have no love, I am nothing.' And this place is their brazen wall. But they are men without understanding, and therefore they can see or understand nothing in Paul; and by this false interpretation, they have not only perverted the words of Paul, but have also denied Christ, and buried all his benefits. Wherefore we must avoid this gloss as a most deadly and devilish poison, and conclude with Paul, that we are justified, not by faith furnished with charity, but by faith only and alone. We must not attribute the power of justifying to that form [sc. charity] which maketh a man acceptable unto God, but we must attribute it to faith, which apprehendeth and possesseth in the heart Christ the Saviour himself. This faith justifieth without and before charity.

We grant that we must teach also good works and charity, but it must be done in time and place, that is to say, when the question is concerning works, and toucheth not this article of justification. But here the question is, by what means we are justified and attain eternal life. To this we answer with Paul, that by faith only in Christ we are pronounced righteous, and not by the works of the law or charity: not because we reject good works, as our adversaries accuse us, but for that we will not suffer ourselves to be turned aside from the principal point of this present matter as Satan most desireth. . . .

——— ——— ———

FOR I THROUGH THE LAW AM DEAD TO THE LAW, THAT I MIGHT LIVE UNTO GOD

These are marvellous words, and unknown kinds of speech, which man's reason can in no wise understand. And although they be but few, yet are they uttered with great zeal and vehemency of spirit, and as it were in great displeasure. As if he should say: Why do ye boast so much of the law, whereof in this case I will be ignorant? But if ye will needs have the law, I also have my law. Wherefore, as though he were moved through indignation of the Holy Ghost, he calleth grace itself the law, giving a new name to the effect and working of grace, in contempt of the law of Moses and the false apostles, which contended that the law was necessary to justification: and so he setteth the law against the law. And this is a sweet kind of speech, and full of consolation, when in the Scriptures, and specially in Paul, the law is set against the law, sin against sin, death against death, captivity against captivity, hell against hell, the altar against the altar, the lamb against the lamb, the passover against the passover.

In Romans 8 [:3] it is said: 'For sin he condemned sin'; in Psalm 68 [:18], Ephesians 4 [:8]: 'He hath led captivity captive'; in Hosea 13 [:14]: 'O death I will be thy death: O hell I will be thy destruction!' So he saith here, that through the law he is dead to the law. As if he said: the law of Moses accuseth and condemneth me; but against that accusing and condemning law, I have another law, which is grace and liberty. This law accuseth the accusing law, and condemneth the condemning law. So death killeth death: but this killing death is life itself. But it is called the death of death, by a vehement indignation of spirit against death. So righteousness taketh the name of sin, because it condemneth sin, and this condemning of sin is true righteousness.

And here Paul seemeth to be an heretic, yea of all heretics the greatest; and his heresy is strange and monstrous. For he saith that he being dead to the law, liveth to God. The false apostles taught this doctrine: Except thou live to the law, thou livest not to God; that is to say, unless thou live after the law, thou art dead before God. But Paul saith quite contrary: Except thou be dead to the law, thou canst not live to God. The doctrine of our adversaries at this day, is like to the doctrine of the false apostles of that time. If thou wilt live to God, say they, live to the law, or after the law. But contrariwise we say: If thou wilt live to God, thou must utterly die to the law. Man's reason and wisdom understandeth not this doctrine; therefore it teacheth always the contrary, that is: If thou wilt live unto God, thou must keep the law; for it is written, 'Do this and thou shalt live.' And this is a special principle amongst all the divines: He that liveth after the law, liveth unto God. Paul saith plainly the contrary: that is, we cannot live unto God, unless we be dead to the law. Wherefore we must mount up to this heavenly altitude, that we may be assured that we are far above the law, yea, that we are utterly dead unto the law. Now, if we be dead unto the law, then hath the law no power over us, like as it hath no power over Christ, who hath delivered us from the same, that through him we might live unto God. All these things tend to this end, to prove that we are not justified by the law, but by faith only in Jesus Christ.

And here Paul speaketh not of the ceremonial law; for he sacrificed in the Temple, circumcised Timothy, shaved his head at Cenchrea. These things had he not done, if he had been dead to the ceremonial law, but he speaketh of the whole law. Therefore the whole law, whether it be ceremonial or moral, to a Christian is utterly abrogate, for he is dead unto it. Not that the law is utterly taken away: nay, it remaineth, liveth, and reigneth still in the wicked. But a godly man is dead unto the law like as he is dead unto sin, the devil, death, and hell: which notwithstanding do still remain, and the world with all the wicked shall still abide in them. Wherefore when the sophister understandeth that the ceremonial law only is abolished, understand thou, that Paul and every Christian is dead to the whole law, and yet the law remaineth still.

As for example: Christ rising from death is free from the grave, and yet the grave remaineth still. Peter is delivered from the prison, the sick of the palsy from his bed, the young man from his coffin, the maiden from her couch, and yet the prison, the bed, the coffin, the couch do remain still. Even so, the law is abolished when I am not subject unto it, the law is dead when I am dead unto it, and yet remaineth still. But because I by another law am dead unto it, therefore it is dead also unto me: as the grave of Christ, the prison of Peter, the couch of the maiden, &c. do still remain; and yet Christ by his resurrection is dead unto the grave, Peter by his deliverance is freed from the prison, and the maid through life is delivered from the couch.

Wherefore these words: 'I am dead to the law,' are very effectual. For he saith not: I am free from the law for a time, or: I am lord over the law; but simply 'I am dead to the law,' that is to say, I have nothing to do with the law. Paul could have uttered nothing more effectual against the justification of the law, than to say: 'I am dead to the law,' that is, I care nothing at all for the law; therefore I am not justified by it.

Now, to die to the law, is, not to be bound to the law, but to be free from the law and not to know it. Therefore let him that will live to God, endeavour that he may be found without the law, and let him come out of the grave with Christ.

The soldiers were astonished when Christ was risen out of the grave; and they also which saw the maiden raised up from death to life, were amazed. So man's reason and wisdom is astonished and becometh foolish, when it heareth that we are not justified except we be dead to the law: for it is not able to reach into this mystery. But we know that when by faith we apprehend Christ himself in our conscience, we enter into a certain new law, which swalloweth up the old law that held us captive. As the grave in which Christ lay dead, after that he was risen again was void and empty, and Christ vanished away; so when I believe in Christ, I rise again with him, and die to my grave, that is to say, the law which held me captive: so that now the law is void, and I am escaped out of my prison and grave, that is to say, the law. Wherefore the law hath no right to accuse me, or to hold me any longer, for I am risen again.

It is necessary that men's consciences be diligently instructed, that they may understand the difference between the righteousness of the law and of grace. The righteousness of grace, or the liberty of conscience, doth in no wise pertain to the flesh. For the flesh may not be at liberty, but must remain in the grave, the prison, the couch: it must be in subjection to the law, and exercised by the Egyptians. But the Christian conscience must be dead to the law, that is to say, free from the law, and must have nothing at all to do with it. It is good to know this; for it helpeth very much to the comforting of poor afflicted consciences. Wherefore, when you see a man terrified and cast down with the sense and feeling of his sin, say unto him: Brother, thou dost not rightly distinguish; thou placest the law in thy conscience, which should be placed in the flesh. Awake, arise up, and remember that thou must believe in Christ the conqueror of the law and sin. With this faith thou shalt mount up above and beyond the law, into that heaven of grace where is no law nor sin. And albeit the law and sins do still remain, yet they pertain nothing to thee; for thou art dead to the law and sins.

These things are easily said: but blessed is he which knoweth how to lay sure hold on them in distress of conscience, that is, which can say when sin overweighteth him, and the law accuseth and terrifieth him: What is this to me, O law, that thou accusest me, and sayest that I have committed many sins? Indeed I grant that I have committed many sins, yea and yet still do commit sins daily without number. This toucheth me nothing: I am now deaf and cannot hear thee. Therefore thou talkest to me in vain, for I am dead unto thee. But if thou wilt needs dispute with me as touching my sins, get thee to my flesh and members my servants: teach them, exercise and crucify them, but trouble not me, not Conscience, I say, which am a lady and a queen, and have nothing to do with thee: for I am dead to thee, and now I live to Christ, with whom I am under another law, to wit the law of grace, which ruleth over sin and the law. By what means? By faith in Christ, as Paul declareth hereafter.

But this seemeth a strange and wonderful definition, that to live to the law is to die to God; and to die to the law, is to live to God. These two propositions are clean contrary to reason, and therefore no crafty sophister or law-worker can understand them. But learn thou the true understanding thereof. He that liveth to the law, that is, seeketh to be justified by the works of the law, is and remaineth a sinner: therefore he is dead and condemned. For the law cannot justify and save him, but accuseth, terrifieth, and killeth him. Therefore to live unto the law is to die unto God: and contrariwise, to die to the law is to live unto God. Wherefore if thou wilt live unto God, thou must die to the law: but if thou wilt live to the law, thou shalt die to God. Now, to live unto God, is to be justified by grace or by faith for Christ's sake, without the law and works.

This is then the proper and true definition of a Christian: that he is the child of grace and remission of sins, which is under no law, but is above the law, sin, death and hell. And even as Christ is free from the grave, and Peter from the prison, so is a Christian free from the law. And such a respect there is between the justified conscience and the law, as is between Christ raised up from the grave, and the grave; and as is between Peter delivered from the prison, and the prison. And like as Christ by his death and resurrection is dead to the grave, so that it hath now no power over him, nor is able any longer to hold him, but the stone being rolled away, the seals broken, and the keepers astonished, he riseth again, and goeth away without any let; and as Peter by his deliverance is dead to the prison, and goeth whither he will; even so the conscience by grace is delivered from the law. 'So is every one that is born of the Spirit' [John 3:8]. But the flesh knoweth not from whence this cometh, nor whither it goeth, for it cannot judge but after the law. But on the contrary, the Spirit saith: Let the law accuse me, let sin and death terrify me never so much, yet I do not therefore despair; for I have a law against the law, sin against sin, and death against death.

Therefore when I feel the remorse and sting of conscience for sin, I behold that brazen serpent Christ hanging upon the Cross. There I find another sin against my sin which accuseth and devoureth me. Now, this other sin (namely in the flesh of Christ) which taketh away the sin of the whole world, is almighty, it condemneth and swalloweth up my sin. So my sin, that it should not accuse and condemn me, is condemned by sin, that is, by Christ crucified: 'who is made sin for us, that we might be made the righteousness of God through him' [II Cor. 5:21]. In like manner I find death in my flesh, which afflicteth and killeth me: but I have in me a contrary death, which is the death of my death; and this death crucifieth and swalloweth up my death.

These things be not done by the law or works, but by Christ crucified; upon whose shoulders lie all the evils and miseries of mankind, the law, sin, death, the devil and hell: and all these do die in him, for by his death he hath killed them. But we must receive this benefit of Christ with a sure faith. For like as neither the law nor any work thereof is offered unto us, but Christ alone: so nothing is required of us but faith alone, whereby we apprehend Christ, and believe that our sins and our death are condemned and abolished in the sin and death of Christ.

Thus have we always most certain and sure arguments which necessarily conclude that justification cometh by faith alone. For how should the law and works avail to justification, seeing that Paul is so earnest both against the law and works, and saith plainly that we must be dead to the law, if we will live to God? But if we be dead to the law, and the law be dead to us, then hath it nothing to do with us. How then should it avail anything at all to our justification? Wherefore we must needs say, that we be pronounced righteous by grace alone, or by faith alone in Christ, without the law and works.

This the blind sophisters do not understand, and therefore they dream that faith justifieth not, except it do the works of charity. By this means faith which believeth in Christ, becometh unprofitable and of none effect; for the virtue of justifying is taken from it, except it be furnished with charity. But now let us set apart the law and charity until another time, and let us rest upon the principal point of this present matter; which is this, that Jesus Christ the Son of God died upon the cross, did bear in his body my sin, the law, death, the devil and hell. These invincible enemies and tyrants do oppress, vex and trouble me, and therefore I am careful how I may be delivered out of their hands, justified and saved. Here I find neither law, work, nor charity, which is able to deliver me from their tyranny. There is none but Christ only and alone, which taketh away the law, killeth my sin, destroyeth my death in his body, and by this means spoileth hell, judgeth and crucifieth the devil, and throweth him down into hell. To be brief, all the enemies which did before torment and oppress me, Christ Jesus hath brought to nought: he hath spoiled them and made a show of them openly, triumphing by himself over them [Col. 2:15], in such sort, that they now rule and reign no more over me, but are constrained to serve me.

By this we may plainly see, that there is nothing here for us to do: only it belongeth unto us, to hear that these things have been wrought and done in this sort, and by sure and confident faith to apprehend the same. And this is the true formed [and furnished] faith indeed. Now, when I have thus apprehended Christ by faith, and through him am dead to the law, justified from sin, delivered from death, the devil and hell, then I do good works, I love God, I give thanks to him, I exercise charity towards my neighbour. But this charity or works following, do neither form nor adorn my faith, but my faith formeth and adorneth charity. This is our divinity; which seemeth strange and marvellous, or rather foolish, to carnal reason: to wit, that I am not only blind and deaf to the law, yea delivered and freed from the law; but also wholly dead unto the same.

This sentence of Paul: 'through the law I am dead to the law,' is full of consolation. Which if it may enter into a man in due season, and take sure hold in his heart with good understanding, it may so work, that it will make him able to stand against all dangers of death, and all terrors of conscience and sin, although they assail him, accuse him, and would drive him to desperation never so much. True it is, that every man is tempted: if not in his life, yet at his death. There, when the law accuseth him and sheweth unto him his sins, his conscience by and by saith: Thou hast sinned. If then thou take good hold of that which Paul here teacheth, thou wilt answer: I grant I have sinned. Then will God punish thee. Nay, he will not do so. Why, doth not the law of God so say? I have nothing to do with that law. Why so? Because I have another law which striketh this law dumb, that is to say, liberty. What liberty is that? The liberty of Christ, for by Christ I am utterly freed from the law. Therefore that law which is and remaineth a law to the wicked, is to me liberty, and bindeth that law which would condemn me; and by this means that law which would bind me and hold me captive, is now fast bound itself, and holden captive by grace and liberty, which is now my law; which saith to that accusing law: Thou shalt not hold this man bound and captive, or make him guilty, for he is mine; but I will hold thee captive, and bind thy hands that thou shalt not hurt him, for he liveth now unto Christ, and is dead unto thee.

This to do, is to dash out the teeth of the law, to wrest his sting and all his weapons from him, and to spoil him of all his force. And yet the same law notwithstanding continueth and remaineth still to the wicked and unbelievers: and to us also that be weak, so far forth as we lack faith, it continueth yet still in its force; here it hath its edge and teeth. But if I do believe in Christ, although sin drive me never so much to despair, yet staying upon this liberty which I have in Christ, I confess that I have sinned: but my sin which is a condemned sin, is in Christ which is a condemning sin. Now this condemning sin is stronger than that which is condemned: for it is justifying grace, righteousness, life and salvation. Thus when I feel the terror of death, I say: Thou hast nothing to do with me, O death; for I have another death which killeth thee my death, and that death which killeth is stronger than that which is killed.

Thus a faithful man by faith only in Christ, may raise up himself, and conceive such sure and sound consolation, that he shall not need to fear the devil, sin, death, or any evils. And although the devil set upon him with all might and main, and go about with all the terrors of the world to oppress him, yet he conceiveth good hope even in the midst thereof, and thus he saith: Sir Devil, I fear not thy threatenings and terrors, for there is one whose name is Jesus Christ, in whom I believe; he hath abolished the law, condemned sin, vanquished death, and destroyed hell; and he is thy tormentor, O Satan, for he hath bound thee and holdeth thee captive, to the end that thou shouldest no more hurt me, or any that believeth in him. This faith the devil cannot overcome, but is overcome of it. 'For this,' saith St. John, 'is the victory that overcometh the world, even our faith. Who is it that overcometh the world, but he which believeth that Jesus is the Son of God?' [I John 5:4 f.].

Paul therefore, through a vehement zeal and indignation of spirit, calleth grace itself the law, which notwithstanding is an exceeding and inestimable liberty of grace which we have in Christ Jesus. Moreover he giveth this opprobrious name unto the law for our consolation, to let us understand that there is now a new name given unto it, for that it is not now alive any more, but dead and condemned. And here (which is a pleasant sight to behold) he bringeth forth the law, and setteth it before us as a thief and a robber which is already condemned and adjudged to death. For he describeth it as it were a prisoner having both hands and feet fast bound, and all his power taken away, so that it cannot exercise his tyranny, that is to say, it cannot accuse and condemn any more; and with this most pleasant sight, he maketh it contemptible to the conscience; so that now he which believeth in Christ, dare boldly and with a certain holy pride triumph over the law after this manner: I am a sinner; if thou canst do anything against me, O law, now do thy worst. So far off is it then, that the law is now terrible unto him which doth believe.

Since Christ is risen from death, why should he now fear the grave? Since Peter is delivered from the prison, why should he now fear it? When the maiden was at the point of death, then might she indeed fear the bed: but now being raised up, why should she fear it? In like manner, why should a Christian which verily possesseth Christ by faith, fear the law? True it is, that he feeleth the terrors of the law, but he is not overcome of them; but staying upon the liberty which he hath in Christ, he saith: I hear thee murmuring, O law, that thou wouldest accuse me and condemn me; but this troubleth me nothing at all; thou art to me as the empty grave was unto Christ; for I see that thou art fast bound hand and foot; and this hath my law done. What law is that? Liberty, which is called the law, not because it bindeth me, but because it bindeth my law. The law of the Ten Commandments did bind me. But against that law I have another law, even the law of grace; which notwithstanding is to me no law, neither doth it bind me, but setteth me at liberty. And this is a law against that accusing and condemning law; which law it so bindeth, that it hath no power to bind me any more. So against my death which bindeth me, I have another death, that is to say, life, which quickeneth me in Christ; and this death looseth and freeth me from the bonds of my death, and with the same bonds bindeth my death. So death which bound me is now fast bound; which killed me, is now killed itself by death—that is to say, by very life itself.

Thus Christ, with most sweet names, is called my law, my sin, my death, against the law, against sin, against death: whereas in very deed he is nothing else but mere liberty, righteousness, life and everlasting salvation. And for this cause he is made the law of the law, the sin of sin, the death of death, that he might redeem from the curse of the law, justify me and quicken me. So then, while Christ is the law, he is also liberty, while he is sin, he is righteousness, and while he is death, he is life. For in that he suffered the law to accuse him, sin to condemn him, and death to devour him, he abolished the law, he condemned sin, he destroyed death, he justified and saved me. So is Christ the poison of the law, sin and death, and the remedy for the obtaining of liberty, righteousness and everlasting life.

This manner of speech which Paul here useth, and is proper unto him alone, is very pleasant and full of consolation. Likewise in the seventh chapter to the Romans, he setteth the law of the spirit against the law of the members. And because this is a strange and marvellous manner of speaking, therefore it entereth more easily into the mind and sticketh faster in the memory. Moreover, when he saith: 'I through the law am dead to the law,' it soundeth more sweetly than if he should say: I through liberty am dead to the law. For he setteth before us, as it were, a certain picture, as if the law were fighting against the law. As though he should say: O law, if thou canst accuse me, terrify me, and bind me, I will set above and against thee another law, that is to say, another tyrant and tormentor, which shall accuse thee, bind thee and oppress thee. Indeed thou art my tormentor, but I have another tormentor, even Christ, which shall torment thee to death; and when thou art thus bound, tormented and suppressed, then am I at liberty. Likewise if the devil scourge me, I have a stronger devil, which shall in turn scourge him and overcome him. So then grace is a law, not to me, for it bindeth me not, but to my law; which this law so bindeth, that it cannot hurt me any more.

Thus Paul goeth about to draw us wholly from the beholding of the law, sin, death, and all other evils, and to bring us unto Christ, that there we might behold this joyful conflict: to wit, the law fighting against the law, that it may be to me liberty; sin against sin, that it may be to me righteousness; death against death, that I may obtain life; Christ fighting against the devil, that I may be the child of God; and destroying hell, that I may enjoy the kingdom of heaven.

THAT I MIGHT LIVE UNTO GOD

That is to say, that I might be alive in the sight of God. Ye see then that there is no life unless ye be without the law, yea unless ye be utterly dead unto the law, I mean in conscience. Notwithstanding, in the mean season (as I have often said) so long as the body liveth, the flesh must be exercised with laws, and vexed with exactions and penalties of laws. But the inward man, not subject to the law, but delivered and freed from it, is a lively, just and holy person, not of himself or in his own substance, but in Christ, because he believeth in him, as followeth.

Christian righteousness consisteth in faith of the heart, and
God's imputation.

It is not without cause that he addeth this sentence out of
the fifteenth chapter of Genesis: 'and it was imputed to him
for righteousness.' For Christian righteousness consisteth in two
things; that is to say, in faith of the heart, and in God's imputation. Faith is indeed a formal righteousness, and yet this
righteousness is not enough; for after faith there remain yet
certain remnants of sin in our flesh. This sacrifice of faith began
in Abraham, but at the last it was finished in death. Wherefore
the other part of righteousness must needs be added also to
perfect the same in us: that is to say, God's imputation. For
faith giveth not enough to God formally, because it is imperfect, yea rather our faith is but a little spark of faith, which
beginneth only to render unto God his true divinity. We have
received the first fruits of the Spirit, but not yet the tenths;
neither is reason utterly killed in this life. Which may appear
by our concupiscence, wrath, impatiency, and other fruits of
the flesh and of infidelity yet remaining in us. Yea, the holiest
that live, have not yet a full and continual joy in God, but have
their sundry passions, sometimes sad, sometimes merry, as
the Scriptures witness of the prophets and Apostles. But such
faults are not laid to their charge because of their faith in
Christ, for otherwise no man should be saved. We conclude
therefore upon these words: 'It was imputed to him for righteousness', that righteousness indeed beginneth through faith,
and by the same we have the first fruits of the Spirit; but because faith is weak, it is not made perfect without God's imputation. Wherefore faith beginneth righteousness, but imputation maketh it perfect unto the day of Christ.

The popist sophisters and schoolmen dispute also of imputation when they speak of the good acceptation of the work: but
besides and clean contrary to the Scripture; for they wrest it
only to works. They do not consider the uncleanness and
inward poison lurking in the heart, as incredulity, doubting,
contemning, and hating of God, which most pernicious and
perilous beasts are the fountain and cause of all mischief. They
consider no more but outward and gross faults and unrighteousness, which are little rivers proceeding and issuing out of

those fountains. Therefore they attribute acceptation to good works; that is to say, that God doth accept our works, not of duty indeed, but of congruence. Contrariwise we, excluding all works, do go to the very head of this beast which is called Reason, which is the fountain and headspring of all mischiefs. For reason feareth not God, it loveth not God, it trusteth not in God, but proudly contemneth him. It is not moved either with his threatenings or his promises. It is not delighted with his words or works, but it murmureth against him, it is angry with him, judgeth and hateth him: to be short, 'it is an enemy to God,' Rom. 8 [:7], not giving him his glory. This pestilent beast (reason I say) being once slain, all outward and gross sins should be nothing.

Wherefore we must first and before all things go about by faith, to kill infidelity, the contempt and hating of God, murmuring against his judgment, his wrath, and all his words and works; for then do we kill reason, which can be killed by none other means but by faith, which in believing God, giveth unto him his glory, notwithstanding that he speaketh those things which seem both foolish, absurd, and impossible to reason; notwithstanding also, that God setteth forth himself otherwise than reason is able either to judge or conceive, that is to say, after this manner: I will accept and pronounce thee as righteous, not for the keeping of the law, not for thy works and thy merits, but for thy faith in Jesus Christ mine only begotten Son, who was born, suffered, was crucified, and died for thy sins; and that sin which remaineth in thee, I will not impute unto thee. If reason then be not killed, and all kinds of religion and service of God under heaven that are invented by men to get righteousness before God, be not condemned, the righteousness of faith can take no place.

When reason heareth this, by and by it is offended; it rageth and uttereth all her malice against God, saying: Are then good works nothing? Have I then laboured and borne the burden and heat of the day in vain? Hereof rise those uproars of nations, kings and princes, against the Lord and his Christ [Ps. 2:2]. For the world neither will nor can suffer that her wisdom, righteousness, religions, and worshippings should be reproved and condemned. The Pope, with all his popish rabblement, will not seem to err, much less will he suffer himself to be condemned.

Wherefore let those which give themselves to the study of the holy Scripture, learn out of this saying: 'Abraham believed God, and it was counted to him for righteousness,' to set forth truly and rightly this true Christian righteousness after this manner: that it is a faith and confidence in the Son of God, or a confidence of the heart in God through Jesus Christ; and let them add this clause as a difference: Which faith and confidence is accounted righteousness for Christ's sake. For these two things (as I said before) work Christian righteousness: namely, faith in the heart, which is a gift of God and assuredly believeth in Christ; and also that God accounteth this imperfect faith for perfect righteousness, for Christ's sake, in whom I have begun to believe. Because of this faith in Christ, God seeth not my doubting of his goodwill towards me, my distrust, heaviness of spirit, and other sins which are yet in me. For as long as I live in the flesh, sin is truly in me. But because I am covered under the shadow of Christ's wings, as is the chicken under the wing of the hen, and dwell without all fear under that most ample and large heaven of the forgiveness of sins, which is spread over me, God covereth and pardoneth the remnant of sin in me: that is to say, because of that faith wherewith I began to lay hold upon Christ, he accepteth my imperfect righteousness even for perfect righteousness, and counteth my sin for no sin, which notwithstanding is sin indeed.

So we shroud ourselves under the covering of Christ's flesh, who is our 'cloudy pillar for the day, and our pillar of fire for the night' [Exod. 13:21], lest God should see our sin. And although we see it, and for the same do feel the terrors of conscience, yet flying unto Christ our mediator and reconciler (through whom we are made perfect), we are sure and safe: for as all things are in him, so through him we have all things, who also doth supply whatsoever is wanting in us. When we believe this, God winketh at the remnants of sin yet sticking in our flesh, and so covereth them, as if they were no sin. Because, saith he, thou believest in my Son, although thou have many sins, yet notwithstanding they shall be forgiven thee, until thou be clean delivered from them by death.

130 COMMENTARY ON GALATIANS

Let Christians learn with all diligence to understand this article of Christian righteousness, which the sophisters neither do nor can understand. But let them not think that they can learn it thoroughly in one lesson. Wherefore let them read Paul, and read him again, both often and with great diligence, and let them compare the first with the last; yea let them compare Paul wholly and fully with himself: then shall they find it to be true, that Christian righteousness consisteth in these two things: namely, in faith which giveth glory unto God, and in God's imputations. For faith is weak (as I have said) and therefore God's imputation must needs be joined withal: that is to say, that God will not lay to our charge the remnant of sin, that he will not punish it, nor condemn us for it; but will cover it and will freely forgive it, as though it were nothing at all; not for our sake, neither for our worthiness and works, but for Jesus Christ's sake in whom we believe.

Thus a Christian man is both righteous and a sinner, holy and profane, an enemy of God and yet a child of God. These contraries no sophisters will admit, for they know not the true manner of justification. And this was the cause why they constrained men to work well so long, until they should feel in themselves no sin at all. Whereby they gave occasion to many (which, striving with all their endeavour to be perfectly righteous, could not attain thereunto) to become stark mad; yea an infinite number also of those which were the authors of this devilish opinion, at the hour of death were driven unto desperation. Which thing had happened unto me also, if Christ had not mercifully looked upon me, and delivered me out of this error.

Contrariwise, we teach and comfort the afflicted sinner after this manner: Brother, it is not possible for thee to become so righteous in this life, that thou shouldest feel no sin at all, that thy body should be clear like the sun, without spot or blemish; but thou hast as yet wrinkles and spots, and yet art thou holy notwithstanding. But thou wilt say: How can I be holy, when I have and feel sin in me? I answer: In that thou dost feel and acknowledge thy sin, it is a good token; give thanks unto God and despair not. It is one step of health, when the sick man doth acknowledge and confess his infirmity. But how shall I be delivered from sin? Run to Christ the physician, which healeth them that are broken in heart, and saveth sinners. Follow not the judgment of reason, which telleth thee, that he is angry with sinners; but kill reason and believe in Christ. If thou believe, thou art righteous, because thou givest glory unto God, that he is almighty, merciful, true, etc. Thou justifiest and praisest God: to be brief, thou yieldest unto him his divinity, and whatsoever else belongeth unto him. And the sin which remaineth in thee, is not laid to thy charge, but is pardoned for Christ's sake in whom thou believest, who is perfectly just; whose righteousness is thy righteousness, and thy sin is his sin.

Here we see that every Christian is a true priest: for first he offereth up and killeth his own reason, and the wisdom of the flesh; then he giveth glory unto God, that he is righteous, true, patient, pitiful, and merciful. And this is that daily sacrifice of the New Testament which must be offered evening and morning. The evening sacrifice is to kill reason; the morning sacrifice is to glorify God. Thus a Christian daily and continually is occupied in this double sacrifice and in the exercise thereof. And no man is able to set forth sufficiently the excellence and dignity of this Christian sacrifice.

Christian righteousness, therefore, as I have said, is the imputation of God for righteousness or unto righteousness, because of our faith in Christ, or for Christ's sake. When the popish schoolmen hear this strange and wonderful definition, which is unknown to reason, they laugh at it. For they imagine that righteousness is a certain quality poured into the soul, and afterwards spread into all the parts of man. They cannot put away the imaginations of reason, which teacheth that a right judgment, and a good will, or a good intent is true righteousness. This unspeakable gift therefore excelleth all reason, that God doth account and acknowledge him for righteous without any works, which embraceth his Son by faith alone, who was sent into the world, was born, suffered, and was crucified &c. for us.

This matter, as touching the words, is easy (to wit, that righteousness is not essentially in us, as the Papists reason out of Aristotle, but without us in the grace of God only and in his imputation; and that there is no essential substance of righteousness in us besides that weak faith or firstfruits of faith, whereby we have begun to apprehend Christ, and yet sin in the meantime remaineth verily in us); but in very deed it is no small or light matter, but very weighty and of great importance. For Christ which is given unto us, and whom we apprehend by faith, hath done no small thing for us, but (as Paul said before): 'He hath loved us and given himself in very deed for us: he was made accursed for us,' &c. [Gal. 2:20; 3:13]. And this is no vain speculation, that Christ was delivered for my sins, and was made accursed for me, that I might be delivered from everlasting death. Therefore to apprehend that Son by faith, and with the heart to believe in him given unto us and for us of God, causeth that God doth account that faith, although it be imperfect, for perfect righteousness. And here we are altogether in another world, far from reason, where we dispute not what we ought to do, or with what works we may deserve grace and forgiveness of sins; but we are in a matter of most high and heavenly divinity, where we do hear this Gospel or glad tidings, that Christ died for us, and that we, believing this, are counted righteous, though sins notwithstanding do remain in us, and that great sins.

So Christ also defineth the righteousness of faith. 'The Father himself', saith he, 'loveth you' [John 16:27]. Wherefore doth he love you? Not because ye were Pharisees, unreprovable in the righteousness of the law, circumcised, doing good works, fasting, &c.; but because 'I have chosen you out of the world' [John 15:19], and ye have done nothing, but that 'ye have loved me and believed that I came out from the Father.' This object 'I' being sent from the Father into the world, pleased you. And because you have apprehended and embraced this object, therefore the Father loveth you, and therefore ye please him. And yet notwithstanding in another place he calleth them evil, and commandeth them to ask forgiveness of their sins. These two things are quite contrary: to wit, that a Christian is righteous and beloved of God, and yet notwithstanding he is a sinner. For God cannot deny his own nature: that is, he must needs hate sin and sinners; and this he doth of necessity, for otherwise he should be unrighteous and love sin. How then can these two contradictories stand together: I am a sinner, and most worthy of God's wrath and indignation;

and yet the Father loveth me? Here nothing cometh between, but only Christ the mediator. The Father, saith he, doth not therefore love you because ye are worthy of love, but because ye have loved me, and have believed that I came out from him.

Thus a Christian man abideth in pure humility, feeling sin in him effectually, and confessing himself to be worthy of wrath, the judgment of God, and everlasting death for the same, that he may be humbled in this life: and yet notwithstanding he continueth still in a pure and holy pride, in the which he turneth unto Christ, and through him he lifteth up himself against this feeling of God's wrath and judgment, and believeth that not only the remnants of sin are not imputed unto him, but that also he is loved of the Father, not for his own sake, but for Christ's sake, whom the Father loveth.

Hereby now we may see, how faith justifieth without works, and yet notwithstanding, how imputation of righteousness is also necessary. Sins do remain in us, which God utterly hateth. Therefore it is necessary that we should have imputation of righteousness, which we obtain through Christ and for Christ's sake, who is given unto us and received of us by faith. In the meantime, as long as we live here, we are carried and nourished in the bosom of the mercy and long-sufferance of God, until the body of sin be abolished, and we raised up as new creatures in that great day. Then shall there be new heavens and a new earth, in which righteousness shall dwell. In the meanwhile under this heaven sin and wicked men do dwell, and the godly also have sin dwelling in them. For this cause Paul in Rom. 7 [:23] complaineth of sin which remaineth in the saints; yet notwithstanding he saith afterwards in Rom. 8 [:1] that there is no damnation to them which are in Christ Jesu. Now, how shall these things, so contrary and repugnant, be reconciled together, that sin in us is no sin, that he which is damnable shall not be condemned, that he which is rejected shall not be rejected, that he which is worthy of the wrath of God and everlasting death shall not be punished? The only reconciler hereof is the mediator between God and man, even the man Jesus Christ, as Paul saith: 'there is no condemnation to them which are in Christ Jesu.'

———   ———   ———

CHRIST REDEEMED US FROM THE CURSE OF THE LAW,
HAVING BEEN MADE A CURSE FOR US (FOR IT IS WRIT-
TEN: 'CURSED IS EVERYONE THAT HANGETH ON A TREE')
&C. [DEUT. 21:23].

Here again Jerome and the popish sophisters which follow
him, are much troubled, and miserably rack this most comfortable place, seeking, as they would seem, with a godly
zeal to turn away this reproach from Christ, that he should
be called a curse or execration. They shift off this sentence
after this manner: that Paul spake not here in good earnest;
and therefore they most wickedly affirm, that the Scripture in
Paul agreeth not with itself. And this they prove after this
manner: the sentence (say they) of Moses which Paul here
allegeth, speaketh not of Christ. Moreover this general clause
'every one', which Paul allegeth, is not added in Moses. Again,
Paul omitteth the words 'of God,' which are in Moses. To conclude: it is evident enough that Moses speaketh of a thief or a
malefactor, which by his evil deeds hath deserved the gallows,
as the Scripture plainly witnesseth in Deuteronomy 21. Therefore they ask this question, how this sentence may be applied
to Christ, that he is accursed of God and hanged upon a tree,
seeing that he is no malefactor or thief, but righteous and
holy? This may peradventure move the simple and ignorant,
thinking that the sophisters do speak it not only wittily, but
also very godly, and thereby do defend the honour and glory
of Christ, and give warning to all Christians to beware that
they think not so wickedly of Christ, that he should be made
a curse, &c. Let us see therefore what the meaning and purpose of Paul is.

But here again we must make a distinction, as the words of
Paul do plainly shew. For he saith not that Christ was made
a curse for himself, but 'for us'. Therefore all the weight of the
matter standeth in this word 'for us'. For Christ is innocent as
concerning his own person, and therefore he ought not to have
been hanged upon a tree: but because according to the law of
Moses every thief and malefactor ought to be hanged, therefore Christ also according to the law of Moses ought to be
hanged, for he sustained the person of a sinner and a thief,
and not of one, but of all sinners and thieves. For we are sin-

ners and thieves, and therefore guilty of death and everlasting damnation. But Christ took all our sins upon him, and for them died upon the cross: therefore it behoved that he should become a transgressor, and (as Isaiah saith, chap. 53) 'to be reckoned among transgressors.'

And this, no doubt, all the prophets did foresee in spirit, that Christ should become the greatest transgressor, murderer, adulterer, thief, rebel, blasphemer, &c. that ever was or could be in all the world. For he being made a sacrifice for the sins of the whole world, is not now an innocent person and without sins, is not now the Son of God born of the Virgin Mary; but a sinner, which hath and carrieth the sin of Paul, who was a blasphemer, an oppressor and a persecutor; of Peter, which denied Christ; of David, which was an adulterer, a murderer, and caused the Gentiles to blaspheme the name of the Lord: and briefly, which hath and beareth all the sins of all men in his body, that he might make satisfaction for them with his own blood. Therefore this general sentence of Moses comprehendeth him also (albeit in his own person he was innocent), because it found him among sinners and transgressors: like as the magistrate taketh him for a thief, and punisheth him, whom he findeth among other thieves, though he never committed anything worthy of death. Now Christ was not only found amongst sinners, but of his own accord and by the will of his Father he would also be a companion of sinners, taking upon him the flesh and blood of those which were sinners, transgressors, and plunged into all kinds of sin. When the law therefore found him among thieves, it condemned and killed him as a thief.

The popish sophisters do spoil us of this knowledge of Christ and most heavenly comfort (namely, that Christ was made a curse for us, that he might deliver us from the curse of the law), when they separate him from sins and sinners, and only set him out unto us as an example to be followed. By this means they make Christ not only unprofitable unto us, but also a judge and a tyrant, which is angry with our sins and condemneth sinners. But we must as well wrap Christ, and know him to be wrapped, in our sins, our malediction, our death, and all our evils, as he is wrapped in our flesh and blood.

But some man will say: it is very absurd and slanderous to call the Son of God a cursed sinner. I answer: if thou wilt deny him to be a sinner and accursed, deny also that he suffered, was crucified and died. For it is no less absurd to say, that the Son of God (as our faith confesseth and pleadeth) was crucified and suffered the pains of sin and death, than to say that he is a sinner and accursed. But if it be not absurd to confess and believe that Christ was crucified between two thieves, then it is not absurd to say also that he was accursed and of all sinners the greatest. These words of Paul are not spoken in vain: 'Christ was made a curse for us;' 'God made Christ which knew no sin, to become sin for us, that we in him might be made the righteousness of God,' II Cor. 5 [:21].

After the same manner John the Baptist calleth him 'the Lamb of God' &c. [John 1:29]. He verily is innocent, because he is the unspotted and undefiled Lamb of God. But because he beareth the sins of the world, his innocence is burdened with the sins and guilt of the whole world. Whatsoever sins I, thou, and we all have done, or shall do hereafter, they are Christ's own sins as verily as if he himself had done them. To be brief: our sins must needs become Christ's own sin, or else we shall perish for ever. This true knowledge of Christ, which Paul and the prophets have most plainly delivered unto us, the wicked sophisters have darkened and defaced.

Isaiah speaketh thus of Christ: 'God', saith he, 'laid the iniquity of us all upon him,' Isa. 53 [:6]. We must not make these words less than they are, but leave them in their own proper signification. For God dallieth not in the words of the prophet, but speaketh earnestly and of great love: to wit, that Christ this Lamb of God should bear the iniquities of us all. But what is it to bear? The sophisters answer: to be punished. Very well. But wherefore is Christ punished? Is it not because he hath sin and beareth sin? Now, that Christ hath sin, the Holy Ghost witnesseth in Psalm 40 [:12]: 'My sins have taken such hold of me that I am not able to look up, yea they are more in number than the hairs of my head;' also Psalm 41 [:4], and 69 [:5]. In these Psalms the Holy Ghost speaketh in the person of Christ, and in plain words witnesseth that he had sins. For this testimony is not the voice of an innocent, but of a suffering Christ, which took upon him to bear the person of all sinners, and therefore was made guilty of the sins of the whole world.

Wherefore, Christ was not only crucified and died, but sin also (through the love of the Divine Majesty) was laid upon him. When sin was laid upon him, then cometh the law and saith: Every sinner must die. Therefore O Christ, if thou wilt answer, become guilty, and suffer punishment for sinners, thou must also bear sin and malediction. Paul therefore doth very well allege this general law out of Moses as concerning Christ: 'Everyone that hangeth upon the tree is the accursed of God.' Christ hath hanged upon the tree, therefore Christ is the accursed of God.

And this is a singular consolation for all the godly, so to clothe Christ with our sins, and to wrap him in my sins, thy sins, and the sins of the whole world, and so to behold him bearing all our iniquities. For the beholding of him after this manner shall easily vanquish all the fantastical opinions of the sophisters concerning the justification of works. For they do imagine (as I have said) a certain faith formed [and adorned] with charity. By this (they say) sins are taken away, and men are justified [before God]. And what is this else (I pray you) but to unwrap Christ, and to strip him quite out of our sins, to make him innocent, and to charge and overwhelm ourselves with our own sins, and to look upon them, not in Christ, but in ourselves? Yea what is this else but to take Christ clean away, and to make him utterly unprofitable unto us? For if it be so that we put away sin by the works of the law and charity, then Christ taketh them not away. For if he be the Lamb of God ordained from everlasting to take away the sins of the world; and moreover, if he be so wrapped of his own accord in our sins, that he became accursed for us, it must needs follow that we cannot be justified and take away sins by charity. For God hath laid our sins, not upon us, but upon his Son, Christ, that he bearing the punishment thereof might be our peace, and that by his stripes we might be healed [Isa. 53:5]. Therefore they cannot be taken away by us. To this all the Scripture beareth witness; and we also do confess the same in the articles of the Christian belief, when we say: 'I believe in Jesus Christ the Son of God, which suffered, was crucified and died for us.'

Hereby it appeareth that the doctrine of the Gospel (which of all other is most sweet and full of singular consolation) speaketh nothing of our works or of the works of the law, but of the unspeakable and inestimable mercy and love of God towards us unworthy and lost men: to wit, that our most merciful Father, seeing us to be oppressed and overwhelmed with the curse of the law, and so to be holden under the same that we could never be delivered from it by our own power, sent his only Son into the world and laid upon him all the sins of all men, saying: Be thou Peter that denier; Paul that persecutor, blasphemer and cruel oppressor; David that adulterer; that sinner which did eat the apple in Paradise; that thief which hanged upon the cross; and briefly, be thou the person which hath committed the sins of all men; see therefore that thou pay and satisfy for them. Here now cometh the law and saith: I find him a sinner, and that such a one as hath taken upon him the sins of all men, and I see no sins else but in him; therefore let him die upon the cross. And so he setteth upon him and killeth him. By this means the whole world is purged and cleansed from all sins, and so delivered from death and all evils. Now sin and death being abolished by this one man, God would see nothing else in the whole world, especially if it did believe, but a mere cleansing and righteousness. And if any remnants of sin should remain, yet for the great glory that is in Christ, God would not perceive them.

Thus we must magnify the article of Christian righteousness against the righteousness of the law and works, albeit no eloquence is able sufficiently to conceive, much less to set forth the inestimable greatness thereof. Wherefore the argument that Paul handleth in this place, of all other is most mighty against the righteousness of the law. For it containeth this invincible opposition: that is, if the sins of the whole world be in that one man Jesus Christ, then are they not in the world. But if they be not in him, then are they yet in the world. Also, if Christ be made guilty of all the sins which we all have committed, then are we delivered utterly from all sins, but not by ourselves, nor by our own works or merits, but by him. But if he be innocent and bear not our sins, then do we bear them, and in them we shall die and be damned. 'But thanks be to

God who hath given us the victory by our Lord Jesus Christ.
Amen [I Cor. 15:57]. . . .'

――――   ――――   ――――

Of the Double Use of the Law.

Here you must understand that there is a double use of the
law. One is civil: for God hath ordained civil laws, yea all laws
to punish transgressions. Every law then is given to restrain
sin. If it restrain sin, doth it therefore make men righteous? No,
nothing less. For in that I do not kill, I do not commit adultery,
I do not steal, or in that I abstain from other sins, I do it not
willingly or for the love of virtue, but I fear the prison, the
sword and the hangman. These do bridle and restrain me that
I sin not, as bonds and chains do restrain a lion or a bear, that
he tear and devour not every thing that he meeteth; therefore
the restraining from sin is not righteousness, but rather a signification of unrighteousness. For as a mad or a wild beast is
bound, lest he should destroy everything that he meeteth: even
so the law doth bridle a mad and a furious man, that he sin not
after his own lust. This restraint sheweth plainly enough, that
they which have need thereof (as all they have which are
without Christ) are not righteous, but rather wicked and mad
men, whom it is necessary by the bonds and prison of the law
so to bridle, that they sin not. Therefore the law justifieth not.

The first use, then, of laws is to bridle the wicked. For the
devil reigneth throughout the whole world, and enforceth men
to all kinds of horrible wickedness. Therefore God hath ordained magistrates, parents, teachers, laws, bonds and all civil
ordinances, that, if they can do no more, yet at the least they
may bind the devil's hands, that he rage not in his bondslaves
after his own lust. Like as therefore they that are possessed,
in whom the devil mightily reigneth, are kept in bonds and
chains lest they should hurt other: even so in the world, which
is possessed of the devil and carried headlong into all kinds of
wickedness, the magistrate is present with his bonds and
chains; that is to say, with his laws, binding his hands and
feet, that he run not headlong into all mischief. And, if he
suffer not himself to be bridled after this sort, then he loseth
his head. This civil restraint is very necessary, and appointed

of God, as well for public peace as for the preservation of all things, but specially lest the course of the Gospel should be hindered by the tumults and seditions of outrageous men. But Paul intreateth not here of this civil use [and office] of the law. It is indeed very necessary, but it justifieth not. For as a possessed [or a mad] man is not therefore free [from the snares of the devil] or well in his mind, because he hath his hands and his feet bound [and can do no hurt]: even so the world, although it be bridled by the law from outward wickedness and mischief, yet it is not therefore righteous, but still continueth wicked; yea this restraint sheweth plainly that the world is wicked and outrageous, stirred up [to all kinds of wickedness] by his prince the devil; for otherwise it need not be bridled by laws that it should not sin.

Another use of the law is theological or spiritual, which is (as Paul saith) 'to increase transgressions'; that is to say, to reveal unto a man his sin, his blindness, his misery, his impiety, ignorance, hatred and contempt of God, death, hell, the judgment and deserved wrath of God. Of this use the Apostle intreateth notably in the seventh to the Romans. This is altogether unknown to hypocrites, to the sophisters and schooldivines, and to all that walk in the opinion of the righteousness of the law, or of their own righteousness. But to the end that God might bridle and beat down this monster and this mad beast (I mean the presumption of righteousness and religion), which naturally maketh men proud, and puffeth them up in such sort that they think themselves thereby to please God highly: it behoved him to send some Hercules which might set upon this monster with all force and courage, to overthrow him and utterly to destroy him; that is to say, he was constrained to give a law in mount Sinai, with so great majesty and so terrible a shew, that the whole multitude was shaken with terror [Exod. 19-20].

This, as it is the proper and the principal use of the law, so it is very profitable and also most necessary. For if any be not a murderer, an adulterer, a thief, and outwardly refrain from sin, as the Pharisee did which is mentioned in the Gospel [Luke 18:11], he would swear (because he is possessed with the devil) that he is righteous; and therefore he conceiveth an opinion of righteousness, and presumeth of his good works and merits. Such a one God cannot otherwise mollify and humble, that he may acknowledge his misery and damnation, but by the law. For that is the hammer of death, the thundering of hell and the lightning of God's wrath, that beateth to powder the obstinate and senseless hypocrites. Wherefore this is the proper and absolute use of the law, by lightning, by tempest and by the sound of the trumpet (as in mount Sinai) to terrify, and by thundering to beat down and rend in pieces that beast which is called the opinion of righteousness. Therefore saith God by Jeremy the prophet: 'My word is a hammer, breaking rocks' [Jer. 23:29]. For as long as the opinion of righteousness abideth in man, so long there abideth also in him incomprehensible pride, presumption, security, hatred of God, contempt of his grace and mercy, ignorance of the promises and of Christ. The preaching of free remission of sins for Christ's sake, cannot enter into the heart of such a one, neither can he feel any taste or savour thereof. For that mighty rock and adamant wall, to wit, the opinion of righteousness, wherewith the heart is environed, doth resist it.

As therefore the opinion of righteousness is a great and an horrible monster, a rebellious, obstinate and stiff-necked beast: so, for the destroying and overthrowing thereof, God hath need of a mighty hammer; that is to say, the law: which then is in his proper use and office, when it accuseth and revealeth sin after this sort: Behold, thou hast transgressed all the commandments of God, &c.!—and so it striketh a terror into the conscience, so that it feeleth God to be offended and angry indeed, and itself to be guilty of eternal death. Here the heart feeleth the intolerable burden of the law, and is beaten down even to desperation, so that now, being oppressed with great anguish and terror, he desireth death, or else seeketh to destroy himself. Wherefore the law is that hammer, that fire, that mighty strong wind, and that terrible earthquake rending the mountains and breaking the rocks, that is to say, the proud and obstinate hypocrites. Elijah, not being able to abide these terrors of the law, which by these things are signified, covered his face with his mantle [I Kings 19:11 ff.]. Notwithstanding, when the tempest ceased, of which he was a beholder, there came a soft and gracious wind, in which the Lord was. But it behoved that the tempest of fire, of wind, and the earthquake should pass, before the Lord should reveal himself in that gracious wind.

This terrible shew and majesty wherein God gave his law in mount Sinai, did represent the use of the law. There was in the people of Israel which came out of Egypt, a singular holiness. They gloried and said: 'We are the people of God. We will do all those things which the Lord our God hath commanded' [Exod. 19:8]. Moreover, Moses did sanctify the people, and bade them wash their garments, refrain from their wives, and prepare themselves against the third day. There was not one of them but he was full of holiness. The third day Moses bringeth the people out of their tents to the mountain into the sight of the Lord, that they might hear his voice. What followed then? When the children of Israel did behold the horrible sight of the mount smoking and burning, the black clouds, and the lightnings flashing up and down in this thick darkness, and heard the sound of the trumpet blowing long and waxing louder and louder; and moreover when they heard the thunderings and the lightnings, they were afraid, and standing afar off they said unto Moses: 'We will do all things willingly, so that the Lord speak not unto us, lest that we die, and this great fire consume us. Teach thou us, and we will hearken unto thee' [Exod. 20:19; Deut. 5:24 ff.]. I pray you, what did their purifying, their white garments, their refraining from their wives, and their holiness profit them? Nothing at all. There was not one of them that could abide this presence of the Lord in his majesty and glory: but all being amazed and shaken with terror, fled back as if they had been driven by the devil. For God is a consuming fire, in whose sight no flesh is able to stand.

The law of God therefore hath properly and peculiarly that office which it had then in mount Sinai, when it was first given and first heard of them that were washed, righteous, purified and chaste: and yet notwithstanding it brought that holy people into such a knowledge of their own misery, that they were thrown down even to death and desperation. No purity nor holiness could help them; but there was in them such a feeling of their own uncleanness, unworthiness and sin, and of the judgment and wrath of God, that they fled from the sight of the Lord, and could not abide to hear his voice. 'What flesh

was there ever,' said they, 'that heard the voice of the living
God, and yet lived?' This day have we seen that when God
talketh with man, man cannot abide it.' They speak now far
otherwise than they did a little before, when they said: 'We
are the holy people of God, whom the Lord hath chosen for
his own peculiar people before all the nations upon earth. We
will do all things which the Lord hath spoken.' So it happeneth
at length to all justiciaries, who being drunken with the opinion of their own righteousness, do think, when they are out
of temptation, that they are beloved of God, and that God re-
gardeth their vows, their fastings, their prayers, and their will-
works, and that for the same he must give unto them a singular
crown in heaven. But when that thundering, lightning, fire,
and that hammer which breaketh in pieces the rocks, that is
to say, the law of God, cometh suddenly upon them, revealing
unto them their sin, the wrath and judgment of God, then the
selfsame thing happeneth unto them which happened to the
Jews standing at the foot of mount Sinai.

Here I admonish all such as love godliness, and specially
such as shall become teachers of others hereafter, that they
diligently learn out of Paul to understand the true and proper
use of the law: which I fear after our time will again be trodden under foot and utterly abolished. For even now while we
are yet living, and employ all our diligence to set forth the
office and use both of the law and the Gospel, there be very
few, yea even among those which will be accounted Christians, and make a profession of the Gospel with us, that understand these things rightly and as they should do. What
think ye then shall come to pass when we are dead and gone?
I speak nothing of the Anabaptists, of the new Arians and such
other vain spirits, who are no less ignorant of these matters
than are the Papists, although they talk never so much to the
contrary. For they are revolted from the pure doctrine of the
Gospel, to laws and traditions, and therefore they teach not
Christ. They brag and they swear that they seek nothing else
but the glory of God and the salvation of their brethren, and
that they teach the Word of God purely: but in very deed
they corrupt it and wrest it to another sense, so that they
make it to sound according to their own imagination. Therefore under the name of Christ they teach their own dreams,

and under the name of the Gospel, nothing else but ceremonies and laws. They are like therefore unto themselves, and so they still continue: that is to say, monks, workers of the law, and teachers of ceremonies, saving that they devise new names and new works.

It is no small matter then to understand rightly what the law is, and what is the true use and office thereof. And forasmuch as we teach these things both diligently and faithfully, we do thereby plainly testify that we reject not the law and works, as our adversaries do falsely accuse us: but we do altogether stablish the law, and require works thereof, and we say that the law is good and profitable, but in his own proper use: which is, first to bridle civil transgressions, and then to reveal and to increase spiritual transgressions. Wherefore the law is also a light, which sheweth and revealeth, not the grace of God, not righteousness and life; but sin, death, the wrath and judgment of God. For, as in the mount Sinai the thundering, lightning, the thick and dark cloud, the hill smoking and flaming, and all that terrible shew did not rejoice nor quicken the children of Israel, but terrified and astonished them, and shewed how unable they were, with all their purity and holiness, to abide the presence of God speaking to them out of the cloud: even so the law, when it is in his true sense, doth nothing else but reveal sin, engender wrath, accuse and terrify men, so that it bringeth them to the very brink of desperation. This is the proper use of the law, and here it hath an end, and it ought to go no further.

Contrariwise, the Gospel is a light which lighteneth, quickeneth, comforteth and raiseth up fearful minds. For it sheweth that God for Christ's sake is merciful unto sinners, yea and to such as are most unworthy, if they believe that by his death they are delivered from the curse, that is to say, from sin and everlasting death; and that through his victory the blessing is freely given unto them, that is to say, grace, forgiveness of sins, righteousness and everlasting life. Thus, putting a difference between the law and the Gospel, we give to them both their own proper use and office. Of this difference between the law and the Gospel there is nothing to be found in the books of the monks, canonists, school-divines; no, nor in the books of the ancient fathers. Augustine did somewhat understand this difference, and shewed it. Jerome and others knew it not. Briefly, there was wonderful silence many years as touching this difference in all schools and churches; and this brought men's consciences into great danger. For unless the Gospel be plainly discerned from the law, the true Christian doctrine cannot be kept sound and uncorrupt. Contrariwise, if this difference be well known, then is also the true manner of justification known, and then it is an easy matter to discern faith from works, Christ from Moses and all politic laws. For all things without Christ are the ministry of death for the punishing of the wicked.

FOR THE FLESH LUSTETH AGAINST THE SPIRIT, AND THE SPIRIT AGAINST THE FLESH

When Paul saith that the flesh lusteth against the spirit, and the spirit against the flesh, he admonisheth us that we shall feel the concupiscence of the flesh, that is to say, not only carnal lust, but also pride, wrath, heaviness, impatience, incredulity, and such-like. Notwithstanding he would have us so to feel them, that we consent not unto them, nor accomplish them: that is, that we neither think, speak, nor do those things which the flesh provoketh us unto. As, if it move us to anger, yet we should be angry in such wise as we are taught in the fourth Psalm, that we sin not. As if Paul would thus say: I know that the flesh will provoke you unto wrath, envy, doubting, incredulity, and such-like: but resist it by the Spirit, that ye sin not. But if ye forsake the guiding of the Spirit, and follow the flesh, ye shall fulfil the lust of the flesh, and ye shall die, as Paul saith in the eighth to the Romans. So this saying of the Apostle is to be understood, not of fleshly lusts only, but of the whole kingdom of sin.

AND THESE ARE CONTRARY ONE TO THE OTHER, SO THAT YE CANNOT DO THE THINGS THAT YE WOULD

These two captains or leaders, saith he, the flesh and the spirit, are one against another in your body, so that ye cannot do what ye would. And this place witnesseth plainly that Paul writeth these things to the saints, that is, to the Church believing in Christ, baptized, justified, renewed, and having full forgiveness of sins. Yet notwithstanding he saith that she hath flesh rebelling against the spirit. After the same manner he speaketh of himself in the seventh to the Romans: 'I (saith he) am carnal and sold under sin;' and again: 'I see another law in my members rebelling against the law of my mind,' &c.; also: 'O wretched man that I am,' &c.

Here, not only the schoolmen, but also some of the old fathers are much troubled, seeking how they may excuse Paul. For it seemeth unto them absurd and unseemly to say, that that elect vessel of Christ should have sin. But we credit Paul's own words, wherein he plainly confesseth that he is sold under sin, that he is led captive of sin, that he hath a law in his members rebelling against him, and that in the flesh he serveth the law of sin. Here again they answer, that the Apostle speaketh in the person of the ungodly. But the ungodly do not complain of the rebellion of their flesh, of any battle or conflict, or of the captivity and bondage of sin: for sin mightily reigneth in them. This is therefore the very complaint of Paul and of all the saints. Wherefore they have done very wickedly which have excused Paul and other saints to have no sin. For by this persuasion (which proceedeth of ignorance of the doctrine of faith) they have robbed the Church of a singular consolation: they have abolished the forgiveness of sins, and made Christ of none effect.

Wherefore when Paul saith: 'I see another law in my members,' &c., he denieth not that he hath flesh, and the vices of the flesh in him. It is likely therefore that he felt sometimes the motions of carnal lust. But yet (I have no doubt) these motions were well suppressed in him by the great and grievous [afflictions and] temptations both of mind and body, wherewith he was in a manner continually exercised and vexed, as his epistles do declare; or if he at any time being merry and strong, felt the lust of the flesh, wrath, impatiency, and suchlike, yet he resisted them by the Spirit, and suffered not those motions to bear rule in him. Therefore let us in no wise suffer such comfortable places (whereby Paul describeth the battle of the flesh against the spirit in his own body) to be corrupted with such foolish glosses. The schoolmen, the monks, and such other, never felt any spiritual temptations, and therefore they fought only for the repressing and overcoming of fleshly lust and lechery, and being proud of that victory which they never yet obtained, they thought themselves far better and more holy than married men. I will not say, that under this holy pretence they nourished and maintained all kinds of horrible sins, as dissension, pride, hatred, disdain, and despising of their neighbours, trust in their own righteousness, presumption, contempt of godliness and of the Word of God, infidelity, blasphemy, and such-like. Against these sins they never fought, nay rather they took them to be no sins at all: they put righteousness in the keeping of their foolish and wicked vows, and unrighteousness in the neglecting and contemning of the same.

But this must be our ground and anchor-hold, that Christ is our only perfect righteousness. If we have nothing whereunto we may trust, yet these three things, as Paul saith, faith, hope and love do remain. Therefore we must always believe and always hope; we must always take hold of Christ as the head and fountain of our righteousness. He that believeth in him shall not be ashamed. Moreover, we must labour to be outwardly righteous also: that is to say, not to consent to the flesh, which always enticeth us to some evil; but to resist it by the spirit. We must not be overcome with impatiency for the unthankfulness and contempt of the people, which abuseth the Christian liberty; but through the Spirit we must overcome this and all other temptations. Look then how much we strive against the flesh by the spirit, so much are we outwardly righteous. Albeit this righteousness doth not commend us before God.

Let no man therefore despair if he feel the flesh oftentimes to stir up new battles against the spirit, or if he cannot by and by subdue the flesh, and make it obedient unto the spirit. I also do wish myself to have a more valiant and constant heart, which might be able, not only boldly to contemn the threatenings of tyrants, the heresies, offences and tumults which the fantastical spirits stir up; but also might by and by shake off the vexations and anguish of spirit, and briefly, might not fear the sharpness of death, but receive and embrace it as a most friendly guest. But I find another law in my members, rebelling against the law of my mind, &c. Some other do wrestle with inferior temptations, as poverty, reproach, impatiency and such-like.

Let no man marvel therefore or be dismayed, when he feeleth in his body this battle of the flesh against the spirit: but let him pluck up his heart and comfort himself with these words of Paul:

'The flesh lusteth against the spirit,' &c., and: 'These are contrary one to another, so that ye do not those things that ye would.' For by these sentences he comforteth them that be tempted. As if he should say: It is impossible for you to follow the guiding of the Spirit in all things without any feeling or hindrance of the flesh; nay, the flesh will resist: and so resist and hinder you that ye cannot do those things that gladly ye would. Here, it shall be enough if ye resist the flesh and fulfil not the lust thereof: that is to say, if ye follow the spirit and not the flesh, which easily is overthrown by impatiency, coveteth to revenge, biteth, grudgeth, hateth God, is angry with him, despaireth, &c. Therefore when a man feeleth this battle of the flesh, let him not be discouraged therewith, but let him resist in the Spirit, and say: I am a sinner, and I feel sin in me, for I have not yet put off the flesh, in which sin dwelleth so long as it liveth; but I will obey the spirit and not the flesh: that is, I will by faith and hope lay hold upon Christ, and by his word I will raise up myself, and being so raised up, I will not fulfil the lust of the flesh.

It is very profitable for the godly to know this, and to bear it well in mind; for it wonderfully comforteth them when they are tempted. When I was a monk I thought by and by that I was utterly cast away, if at any time I felt the concupiscence of the flesh: that is to say, if I felt any evil motion, fleshly lust, wrath, hatred, or envy against any brother. I assayed many ways, I went to confession daily, &c., but it profited me not; for the concupiscence of my flesh did always return, so that I could not rest, but was continually vexed with these thoughts: This or that sin thou hast committed; thou art infected with envy, with impatiency, and such other sins; therefore thou art entered into this holy order in vain, and all thy good works are unprofitable. If then I had rightly understood these sentences of Paul: 'The flesh lusteth contrary to the spirit, and the spirit contrary to the flesh,' &c. and 'these two are one against another, so that ye cannot do the things that ye would do,' I should not have so miserably tormented myself, but should have thought and said to myself, as now commonly I do: Martin, thou shalt not utterly be without sin, for thou hast yet flesh; thou shalt therefore feel the battle thereof, according to that saying of Paul: 'The flesh resisteth the spirit.' Despair not therefore, but resist it strongly, and fulfil not the lust thereof. Thus doing thou art not under the law.

I remember that Staupitius was wont to say: 'I have vowed unto God above a thousand times, that I would become a better man; but I never performed that which I vowed. Hereafter I will make no such vow: for I have now learned by experience, that I am not able to perform it. Unless therefore God be favourable and merciful unto me for Christ's sake, and grant unto me a blessed and a happy hour when I shall depart out of this miserable life, I shall not be able with all my vows and all my good deeds, to stand before him.' This was not only a true, but also a godly and a holy desperation: and this must they all confess both with mouth and heart, which will be saved. For the godly trust not to their own righteousness, but say with David: 'Enter not into judgment with they servant, for in thy sight shall none that liveth be justified' [Ps. 143:2], and: 'If thou, O Lord, shouldst straitly mark iniquities, Lord who shall stand?' [Ps. 130:3]. They look unto Christ their reconciler, who gave his life for their sins. Moreover, they know that the remnant of sin which is in their flesh, is not laid to their charge, but freely pardoned. Notwithstanding in the meanwhile they fight in the Spirit against the flesh, lest they should fulfil the lust thereof. And although they feel the flesh to rage and rebel against the spirit, and themselves also do fall sometimes into sin through infirmity, yet are they not discouraged, nor think therefore that their state and kind of life, and the works which are done according to their calling, displease God: but they raise up themselves by faith.

The faithful therefore receive great consolation by this doctrine of Paul, in that they know themselves to have partly the flesh, and partly the spirit, but yet so notwithstanding that the spirit ruleth and the flesh is subdued, that righteousness reigneth and sin serveth. He that knoweth not this doctrine, and thinketh that the faithful ought to be without all fault, and yet seeth the contrary in himself, must needs at the length be swallowed up by the spirit of heaviness, and fall into desperation. But whoso knoweth this doctrine well and useth it rightly, to him the things that are evil turn unto good. For when the flesh provoketh him to sin, by occasion thereof he is stirred up and forced to seek forgiveness of sins by Christ, and to embrace the righteousness of faith, which else he would not so greatly esteem, nor seek for the same with so great desire. Therefore it profiteth us very much to feel sometimes the wickedness of our nature and corruption of our flesh, that even by this means we may be waked and stirred up to faith and to call upon Christ. And by this occasion a Christian becometh a mighty workman and a wonderful creator, which of heaviness can make joy, of terror comfort, of sin righteousness, and of death life, when he by this means repressing and bridling the flesh, maketh it subject to the Spirit.

Wherefore let not them which feel the concupiscence of the flesh, despair of their salvation. Let them feel it and all the force thereof, so that they consent not to it. Let the passions of lust, wrath and such other vices shake them, so that they do not overthrow them. Let sin assail them, so that they do not accomplish it. Yea the more godly a man is, the more doth he feel that battle. And hereof come those lamentable complaints of the saints in the Psalms and in all the holy Scripture. Of this battle the hermits, the monks, and the schoolmen, and all that seek righteousness and salvation by works, know nothing at all.

But here may some man say, that it is a dangerous matter to teach that a man is not condemned, if by and by he overcome not the motions and passions of the flesh which he feeleth. For when this doctrine is taught amongst the common people, it maketh them careless, negligent and slothful. This is it which I said a little before, that if we teach faith, then carnal men neglect and reject works: if works be required, then is faith and consolation of conscience lost. Here no man can be compelled, neither can there be any certain rule prescribed. But let every man diligently try himself to what passion of the flesh he is most subject, and when he findeth that, let him not be careless, nor flatter himself: but let him watch and wrestle in Spirit against it, that if he cannot altogether bridle it, yet at the least he do not fulfil the lust thereof.

This battle of the flesh against the spirit, all the saints have had and felt: and the selfsame do we also feel and prove. He that searcheth his own conscience, if he be not an hypocrite, shall well perceive that to be true in himself which Paul here saith: that the flesh lusteth against the spirit. All the faithful therefore do feel and confess that their flesh resisteth against the spirit, and that these two are so contrary the one to the other in themselves, that, do what they can, they are not able to perform that which they would do. Therefore the flesh hindereth us that we cannot keep the commandments of God, that we cannot love our neighbours as ourselves, much less can we love God with all our heart, &c. Therefore it is impossible for us to become righteous by the works of the law. Indeed there is a good will in us, and so must there be (for it is the Spirit itself which resisteth the flesh), which would gladly do good, fulfil the law, love God and his neighbour, and suchlike, but the flesh obeyeth not this good will, but resisteth it: and yet God imputeth not unto us this sin, for he is merciful to those that believe, for Christ's sake.

But it followeth not therefore that thou shouldest make a light matter of sin, because God doth not impute it. True it is that he doth not impute it: but to whom, and for what cause? Not to them that are hard-hearted and secure, but to such as repent and lay hold by faith upon Christ the mercy-seat, for whose sake, as all their sins are forgiven them, even so the remnants of sin which are in them, be not imputed unto them. They make not their sin less than it is, but amplify it and set it out as it is indeed; for they know that it cannot be put away by satisfactions, works, or righteousness, but only by the death of Christ. And yet notwithstanding, the greatness and enormity of their sin doth not cause them to despair, but they assure themselves that the same shall not be imputed unto them [or laid unto their charge], for Christ's sake.

This I say, lest any man should think that after faith is received, there is little account to be made of sin. Sin is truly sin, whether a man commit it before he hath received the knowledge of Christ or after. And God always hateth sin: yea all sin is damnable as touching the fact itself. But in that it is not damnable to him that believeth, it cometh of Christ the reconciler, who by his death hath expiated sin. But to him that believeth not in Christ, not only all his sins are damnable, but even his good works also are sin; according to that saying: 'Whatsoever is not of faith is sin' [Rom. 14:23]. Therefore the error of the schoolmen is most pernicious, which do distinguish sins according to the fact, and not according to the person. He that believeth hath as great sin as the unbeliever. But to him that believeth, it is forgiven and not imputed: to the unbeliever it is not pardoned but imputed. To the believer it is venial: to the unbeliever it is mortal [and damnable]: not for any difference of sins, or because the sin of the believer is less, and the sin of the unbeliever greater: but for the difference of the persons. For the believer assureth himself by faith that his sin is forgiven him, forasmuch as Christ hath given himself for it. Therefore although he have sin in him and daily sinneth, yet he continueth godly: but contrariwise, the unbeliever continueth wicked. And this is the true wisdom and consolation of the godly, that although they have and commit sins, yet they know that for Christ's sake they are not imputed unto them.

This I say for the comfort of the godly. For they only feel indeed that they have and do commit sins, that is to say, they feel they do not love God so fervently as they should do; that they do not trust him so heartily as they would, but rather they oftentimes doubt whether God have a care of them or no; they are impatient, and are angry with God in adversity. Hereof (as I have said) proceed the sorrowful complaints of the saints in the Scriptures, and especially in the Psalms. And Paul himself complaineth that he is 'sold under sin' [Rom. 7:14]; and here he saith that the flesh resisteth and rebelleth against the spirit. But because they mortify the deeds of the flesh by the spirit (as he saith in another place; and also in the end of this chapter: 'They crucify the flesh with the desires and lusts thereof'), therefore these sins do not hurt them nor condemn them. But if they obey the flesh in fulfilling the lusts thereof, then do they lose faith and the Holy Ghost. And if they do not abhor their sin and return unto Christ (who hath given the keys to his Church, to receive and raise up those that be fallen, that so they may recover faith and the Holy Ghost), they die in their sins. Wherefore we speak not of them which dream that they have faith, and yet continue still in their sins. These men have their judgment already: They that live after the flesh shall die [Rom. 8:13], also: 'The works of the flesh are manifest, which are, adultery, fornication, &c., whereof I tell you before, as also I have told you that they which do such things, shall not inherit the kingdom of God.'

Hereby we may see who be very saints indeed. They be not stocks and stones (as the monks and schoolmen dream) so that they are never moved with anything, never feel any lust or desires of the flesh: but, as Paul saith, their flesh lusteth against the Spirit, and therefore they have sin and can sin. And the thirty-second Psalm witnesseth, that the saints do confess their unrighteousness, and pray that the wickedness of their sin may be forgiven, where it saith: 'I said, I will confess against myself my wickedness unto the Lord, and thou forgavest the iniquity of my sin. For this shall everyone that is godly, make his prayer unto thee,' &c. Moreover the whole Church, which indeed is holy, prayeth that her sins may be forgiven her, and believeth the forgiveness of sins. And in Psalm 143, David prayeth: 'O Lord enter not into judgment with thy servant, for in thy sight shall none that liveth be justified.' And in Psalm 130: 'If thou, O Lord, shouldest straitly mark iniquities, Lord who shall stand? But with thee is mercy,' &c. Thus do the chiefest saints [and children of God] speak and pray: as David, Paul, &c. All the faithful therefore do speak and pray the same thing, and with the same spirit. The popish sophisters read not the Scriptures, or if they read them they have a veil before their eyes: and therefore as they cannot judge rightly of anything, so can they not judge rightly either of sin or of holiness.

IF YE BE LED BY THE SPIRIT YE ARE NOT UNDER THE LAW

Paul cannot forget his doctrine of faith, but still repeateth it and beateth it into their heads; yea even when he treateth of good works. Here some man may object: How can it be that we should not be under the law? And yet thou notwithstanding, O Paul, teachest us that we have flesh which lusteth against the spirit, and fighteth against us, tormenteth and bringeth us into bondage. And indeed we feel sin, and cannot be delivered from the feeling thereof, though we would never so fain. And what is this else but to be under the law? But saith he: Let this nothing trouble you; only do your endeavour that ye may be led by the Spirit, that is to say, shew yourselves willing to follow and obey that will which resisteth the flesh, and doth not accomplish the lusts thereof (for this is to be led and to be drawn by the Spirit); then are ye not under the law. So Paul speaketh of himself in Rom. 7: 'In my mind I serve the law of God;' that is to say, in the Spirit I am not subject to any sin: but yet in my flesh I serve the law of sin. The faithful then are not under the law, that is to say, in Spirit: for the law cannot accuse them, nor pronounce sentence of death against them, although they feel sin, and confess themselves to be sinners: for the power and strength of the law is taken from it by Christ, 'who was made under the law, that he might redeem them which were under the law' [Gal. 4:4]. Therefore the law cannot accuse that for sin in the faithful, which is sin indeed and committed against the law.

So great then is the power of the dominion of the Spirit, that the law cannot accuse the godly, though they commit that which is sin indeed. For Christ is our righteousness, whom we apprehend by faith: he is without all sin, and therefore the law cannot accuse him. As long as we cleave fast unto him, we are led by the Spirit, and are free from the law. And so the Apostle, even when he teacheth good works, forgetteth not his doctrine concerning justification; but always sheweth that it is impossible for us to be justified by works. For the remnants of sin cleave fast in our flesh, and therefore so long as our flesh liveth, it ceaseth not to lust contrary to the Spirit. Notwithstanding there cometh no danger unto us thereby, because we be free from the law, so that we walk in the Spirit.

And with these words: 'If ye be led by the Spirit, ye are not under the law,' thou mayest greatly comfort thyself and others that be grievously tempted. For it oftentimes cometh to pass, that a man is so vehemently assailed with wrath, hatred, impatiency, carnal desire, heaviness of spirit, or some other lust of the flesh, that he cannot shake them off, though he would never so fain. What should he do in this case? Should he despair? No, [God forbid]; but let him say thus with himself:

Thy flesh fighteth and rageth against the Spirit. Let it rage as long as it listeth: only see thou that in any case thou consent not to it, to fulfil the lust thereof, but walk wisely and follow the leading of the Spirit. In so doing thou art free from the law. It accuseth and terrifieth thee (I grant) but altogether in vain. In this conflict therefore of the flesh against the Spirit, there is nothing better, than to have the Word of God before thine eyes, and therein to seek the comfort of the Spirit.

And let not him that suffereth this temptation, be dismayed, in that the devil can so aggravate sin, that during the conflict he thinketh himself to be utterly overthrown, and feeleth nothing else but the wrath of God and desperation. Here in any wise let him not follow his own feeling [and the judgment of reason], but let him take sure hold of this saying of Paul: 'If ye be led by the Spirit,' that is to wit, if ye raise up and comfort yourselves through faith in Christ, 'ye be not under the law.' So shall he have a strong buckler wherewith he may beat back all the fiery darts which the wicked fiend assaileth him withal. How much soever then the flesh doth boil and rage, yet cannot her motions and rages hurt and condemn him, forasmuch as he, following the guiding of the Spirit, doth not consent unto the flesh, nor fulfil the lusts thereof. Therefore when the motions of the flesh do rage, the only remedy is to take to us the sword of the Spirit, that is to say, the Word of salvation (which is, that God would not the death of a sinner, but that he convert and live), and to fight against them: which if we do, let us not doubt but we shall obtain the victory, although so long as the battle endureth, we feel the plain contrary. But set the Word out of sight, and there is no counsel nor help remaining. Of this that I say, I myself have good experience. I have suffered many and various passions, and the same also very vehement and great. But so soon as I have laid hold of any place of Scripture, and stayed myself upon it as upon my chief anchor-hold, straightways my temptations did vanish away: which without the Word it had been impossible for me to endure any little space, and much less to overcome them.

The sum or effect therefore of all that which Paul hath taught in this disputation or discourse concerning the conflict or battle between the flesh and the spirit, is this: that the saints or believers cannot perform that which the Spirit desireth. For the spirit would gladly be altogether pure, but the flesh being joined unto the spirit, will not suffer that. Notwithstanding they be saved by the remission of sins, which is in Christ Jesus. Moreover, because they walk in the Spirit and are led by the Spirit, they be not under the law, that is to say, the law cannot accuse and terrify them: yea, although it go about never so much so to do, yet shall it never be able to drive them to desperation.

MOREOVER THE WORKS OF THE FLESH BE MANIFEST, WHICH ARE, ETC.

This place is not unlike to this sentence of Christ: 'By their fruits ye shall know them. Do men gather grapes of thorns; or figs of brambles? So every good tree bringeth forth good fruit, and an evil tree bringeth forth evil fruit,' &c. [Matt. 7:16]. Paul teacheth the very same thing which Christ taught, that is to say, that works and fruits do sufficiently testify whether the trees be good or evil: whether men follow the guiding of the flesh or of the Spirit. As if he should say: Lest some of you might say for himself, that he understandeth me not now when I treat of the battle between the flesh and the Spirit, I will set before your eyes first the works of the flesh, whereof many are known even to the ungodly; and then also the fruit of the Spirit.

And this doth Paul because there were many hypocrites amongst the Galatians (as there are also at this day among us), which outwardly pretended to be godly men, and boasted much of the Spirit, and as touching the words they understood very well the doctrine of godliness: but they walked not according to the Spirit, but according to the flesh, and performed the works thereof. Whereby Paul manifestly convinceth them to be no such [holy] men indeed as they boasted themselves to be. And lest they should despise this his admonition, he pronounceth against them this dreadful sentence, that they should not be inheritors of the kingdom of heaven, to the end that being thus admonished, they might amend. Every age, even in the faithful hath his peculiar temptations: as fleshly lusts assail a man most of all in his youth, in his middle-age ambition and vain-glory, and in his old-age covetousness. There was never yet (as I have said already) any of the saints whom the flesh hath not often in his lifetime provoked to impatiency, anger, &c. Paul therefore speaking here of the saints, saith that the flesh lusteth in them against the Spirit, &c. Therefore they shall never be without the desires and battle of the flesh: notwithstanding they do not hurt them. But of this matter we must thus judge, that it is one thing to be provoked of the flesh, and yet not willingly to yield to the lusts and desires thereof, but to walk after the leading of the Spirit, and to resist the flesh: and another thing to assent unto the flesh, and without all fear or remorse to perform and fulfil the works thereof, and to continue therein, and yet notwithstanding to counterfeit holiness and to brag of the Spirit &c. The first he comforteth, when he saith that they be led by the Spirit and be not under the law. The other he threateneth with everlasting destruction.

Notwithstanding sometimes it happeneth that the saints also do fall and perform the desires of the flesh: as David fell horribly into adultery. Also he was the cause of the slaughter of many men, when he caused Uriah to be slain in the forefront of the battle: and thereby also he gave occasion to the enemies to glory and triumph over the people of God, to worship their idol, and to blaspheme the God of Israel. Peter also fell most grievously and horribly when he denied Christ. But although these sins were great and heinous, yet were they not committed upon any contempt of God or of a wilful and obstinate mind, but through infirmity and weakness. Again, when they were admonished, they did not obstinately continue in their sins, but repented. Such he willeth afterwards in the sixth chapter to be received, instructed, and restored, saying: 'If a man be fallen by occasion' &c. To those therefore which sin and fall through infirmity, pardon is not denied, so that they rise again and continue not in their sin: for of all things continuance in sin is the worst. But if they repent not, but still obstinately continue in their wickedness and perform the desires of the flesh, it is a certain token that there is deceit in their spirit.

No man therefore shall be without [lusts and] desires so long as he liveth in the flesh, and therefore no man shall be

free from temptations. Notwithstanding some are tempted one
way and some another, according to the difference of the persons. One man is assailed with more vehement and grievous
motions, as with bitterness and anguish of spirit, blasphemy,
distrust, and desperation: another with more gross temptations,
as with fleshly lusts, wrath, envy, hatred and such-like. But in
this case Paul requireth us that we walk in the Spirit, and resist
the flesh. But whoso obeyeth the flesh, and continueth without
fear or remorse in accomplishing the desires and lusts thereof,
let him know that he pertaineth not unto Christ; and although
he brag of the name of a Christian never so much, yet doth he
but deceive himself. For they which are of Christ, do crucify
their flesh with the affections and lusts thereof.

Who be rightly called saints, and be so indeed.

This place (as I have also forewarned you by the way)
containeth in it a singular consolation: for it teacheth us that
the saints live not without concupiscence and temptations of
the flesh, nor yet without sins. It warneth us therefore to take
heed that we do not as some did, of whom Gerson writeth,
which laboured to attain [to such perfection], that they might
be without all feeling of temptations or sins: that is to say, very
stocks and stones. The like imagination the monks and schoolmen had of their saints, as though they had been very senseless
blocks and without all affections. Assuredly Mary felt great
grief and sorrow of heart when she missed her son, Luke 2.
David in the Psalms complaineth that he is almost swallowed
up with excessive sorrow for the greatness of his temptations
and sins. Paul also complaineth that he hath battles without,
and terrors within [II Cor. 7:5], and that in his flesh he serveth
the law of sin. He saith that he is careful for all the churches
[II Cor. 11:28], and that God shewed great mercy towards
him, in that he delivered Epaphroditus being at the point of
death, to life again, lest he should have had sorrow upon sorrow [Phil. 2:27]. Therefore the saints of the Papists are like
to the Stoics, who imagined such wise men, as in the world
were never yet to be found. And by this foolish and wicked
persuasion, which proceedeth from the ignorance of this doc-

trine of Paul, the schoolmen brought both themselves and others without number into [horrible] desperation.

When I was a monk I did oftentimes most heartily wish, that I might once be so happy, as to see the conversation and life of some saint or holy man. But in the meantime I imagined such a saint as lived in the wilderness abstaining from meat and drink, and living only with roots of herbs and cold water: and this opinion of those monstrous saints, I had learned not only out of the books of the sophisters [and schoolmen], but also out of the books of the Fathers. For thus writeth St. Jerome in a certain place: 'As touching meats and drinks I say nothing, forasmuch as it is excess, that even such as are weak and feeble should use cold water, or eat any sodden thing,' &c. But now in the light of the Gospel we plainly see who they are whom Christ and his Apostles call saints: not they which live a single life, or [straitly observe days, meats, apparel, and such other things], or in outward appearance do other great and monstrous works (as we read of many in the *Lives of the Fathers*); but they which being called by the sound of the Gospel and baptized, do believe that they be sanctified and cleansed by the death and blood of Christ. So Paul everywhere, writing to the Christians, calleth them holy, the children and heirs of God, &c. Whosoever then do believe in Christ, whether they be men or women, bond or free, &c., are all saints: not by their own works, but by the works of God, which they receive by faith: as his Word, his Sacraments, the passion of Christ, his death, resurrection, victory, and the sending of the Holy Ghost. To conclude, they are saints through [such a holiness as they freely receive, not through such a holiness as they themselves have gotten by their own industry, good works and merits: that is to say,] a passive, not an active holiness.

So the ministers of the Word, the magistrates of commonweals, parents, children, masters, servants, &c. are true saints, if first and before all things they assure themselves that Christ is their wisdom, righteousness, sanctification, and redemption: secondly, if everyone do his duty in his vocation according to the rule of God's word, and obey not the flesh, but repress the lusts and desires thereof by the Spirit. Now, whereas all be not of like strength [to resist temptations], but many infirmities and offences are seen in the most part of men: this nothing hindereth their holiness, so that their sins proceed not of an obstinate wilfulness, but only of frailty and infirmity. For (as I have said before) the godly do feel the desires and lusts of the flesh, but they resist them to the end that they accomplish them not. Also if they at any time unadvisedly fall into sin, yet notwithstanding they obtain forgiveness thereof, if by faith in Christ they be raised up again: who would not that we should drive away, but seek out [and bring home] the [straying and] lost sheep, &c. 'Therefore God forbid that I should straightway judge those which are weak in faith and manners, to be profane or unholy, if I see that they love and reverence the Word of God, to come to the Supper of the Lord, &c. For these God hath received and counteth them righteous through the remission of sins: to him they stand or fall, &c. [Rom. 14:4].

After this manner Paul speaketh everywhere concerning the saints. And with great rejoicing I give thanks to God, for that he hath abundantly and above measure granted that unto me, which I so earnestly desired of him when I was a monk: for he hath given unto me the grace to see not one but many saints, yea an infinite number of true saints; not such as the sophisters have devised, but such as Christ himself and his Apostles do describe; of the which number I also, by the grace of God, am one. For I am baptized, and I do believe that Christ my Lord by his death hath redeemed and delivered me from all my sins, and hath given to me eternal righteousness and holiness. And let him be holden accursed, whosoever shall not give this honour unto Christ, to believe that by his death, his Word, his Sacraments, &c., he is justified and sanctified.

Wherefore rejecting this foolish and wicked opinion concerning the name of saints (which once we thought to pertain only to the saints which are in heaven, and in earth to the hermits and monks which did certain great and strange works): let us now learn by the holy Scriptures, that all they which faithfully believe in Christ are saints. The world hath in great admiration the holiness of Benedict, Gregory, Bernard, Francis, and such-like, because it heareth that they have done certain rare and (in outward appearance) excellent works. Doubtless Hilary, Cyril, Athanasius, Ambrose, Augustine and

others were saints also, which lived not so strait and severe a
life as they did, but were conversant amongst men, and did
eat common meats, drank wine, and used cleanly and comely
apparel, so that in a manner there was no difference between
them and other honest men as touching the common custom,
and the use of things necessary for this life; and yet are they to
be preferred far above the other. These men taught the [doc-
trine and] faith of Christ sincerely and purely, without any superstition: they resisted heretics, they purged the Church from
innumerable errors: their company and familiarity was comfortable to many, and specially to those which were afflicted
and heavy-hearted, whom they raised up and comforted by
the Word of God. For they did not withdraw themselves from
the company of men, but they executed their offices even where
most resort of people was. Contrariwise, the other not only
taught many things contrary to faith, but also were themselves
the authors and first inventors of many superstitions, errors,
[abominable ceremonies] and wicked worshippings. Therefore
except at the hour of death they laid hold of Christ, and re-
posed their whole trust in his death and victory, their strait
and painful life availed them nothing at all.

These things sufficiently declare who be the true saints indeed, and which is to be called a holy life: not the life of those
which lurk in caves and dens, which make their bodies lean
with fasting, which wear hair, and do other like things with
this persuasion and trust, that they shall have singular reward
in heaven above all other Christians; but of those which be
baptized and believe in Christ, which put off the old man
with his works, but not at once: for concupiscence remaineth
in them so long as they live: the feeling whereof doth hurt
them nothing at all, if they suffer it not to reign in them, but
subdue it to the Spirit.

This doctrine bringeth great consolation to godly minds, that
when they feel these darts of the flesh, wherewith Satan assaileth the spirit, they should not despair: as it happened to
many in the Papacy, which thought that they ought to feel no
concupiscence of the flesh; whereas notwithstanding Jerome,
Gregory, Benedict, Bernard, and others (whom the monks set
before them as a perfect example of chastity and of all Christian virtues) could never come so far as to feel no concupis-

cence [or lust] of the flesh. Yea, they felt it, and that very strongly. Which thing they acknowledge and plainly confess in divers places of their books. Therefore God did not only not impute unto them these light faults, but even those pernicious errors which some of them brought into the Church. Gregory was the author of the private mass, than which there never was any greater abomination in the Church of the New Testament. Others devised monkery, wicked worshippings and voluntary religions. Cyprian contended that they which had been baptized of heretics should be re-baptized.

Therefore we rightly confess in the articles of our belief, that we believe [there is] a Holy Church. For it is invisible, dwelling in Spirit in a place that none can attain unto, and therefore her holiness cannot be seen: for God doth so hide her and cover her with infirmities, with sins, with errors, with divers forms of the cross and offences, that according to the judgment of reason it is nowhere to be seen. They that are ignorant of this, when they see the infirmities and sins of those which are baptized, which have the Word and believe it, are by and by offended, and judge them not to pertain to the Church. And in the meanwhile they dream that the hermits and monks [and such other shavelings] are the Church; which honour God only with their lips, and worship Him in vain, because they follow not the Word of God, but the doctrines and commandments of men, and teach others to do the same. And because they do certain superstitious and monstrous works, which [carnal] reason magnifieth and highly esteemeth, therefore they judge them to be saints and to be the Church; and in so doing they change and turn this article of faith clean contrary: 'I believe [that there is] a holy Church' &c., and in the stead of this word 'I believe,' they put in 'I see.' These kinds of righteousness and holiness of man's own devising, are nothing else but spiritual sorceries wherewith the eyes and minds of men are blinded and led from the knowledge of true holiness.

But thus teach we, that the Church hath no spot nor wrinkle, but is holy, and yet through faith only in Christ Jesus: again, that she is holy in life [and conversation] by abstaining from the lusts of the flesh, and by exercise of spiritual fruits; but yet not in such sort that she is delivered from all evil desires, or purged from all wicked opinions and errors.

For the Church always confesseth her sins, and prayeth that her faults may be pardoned [Matt. 6:12]; also she believeth the forgiveness of sins. The saints therefore do sin, fall, and also err: but yet through ignorance. For they would not willingly deny Christ, forsake the Gospel, revoke their Baptism, &c., therefore they have remission of sins. And if through ignorance they err also in doctrine, yet is this pardoned; for in the end they acknowledge their error, and rest only upon the truth and the grace of God offered in Christ, as Jerome, Gregory, Bernard, and others did. Let Christians then endeavour to avoid the works of the flesh; but the desires [or lusts of the flesh] they cannot avoid.

It is very profitable therefore for the godly to feel the uncleanness of their flesh, lest they should be puffed up with some vain and wicked opinion of the righteousness of [their own] works, as though they were accepted before God for the same. The monks being puffed up with this opinion of righteousness, thought themselves to be so holy because of their holy kind of life, that they sold their righteousness and holiness to others, although they were convinced by the testimony of their own hearts, that they were unclean. So pernicious and pestilent a poison it is for a man to trust in his own righteousness, and to think himself to be clean. But the godly, because they feel the uncleanness of their own hearts, therefore they cannot trust to their own righteousness. This feeling so maketh them to stoop, and so humbleth them, that they cannot trust to their own good works, but are constrained to fly unto Christ their mercy-seat and only succour, who hath not a corrupt and sinful but a most pure and holy flesh, which he hath given for the life of the world. In him they find a sound and perfect righteousness. Thus they continue in humility; not counterfeit and monkish, but true and unfeigned, because of the uncleanness which yet remaineth in their flesh: for the which if God would straitly judge them, they should be found guilty of eternal death. But because they lift not up themselves proudly against God, but with a broken and contrite heart humbly acknowledging their sins, and resting wholly upon the benefit of the mediator Christ, they come forth into the presence of God, and pray that for his sake their sins may

be forgiven them; God spreadeth over them an infinite heaven
of grace, and doth not impute unto them their sins for Christ's
sake.

This I say, to the end that we may take heed of the pernicious errors of the sophisters touching the holiness of life,
wherein our minds are so wrapped, that without great difficulty we could not wind ourselves out of them. Wherefore,
do you endeavour with diligence, that ye may discern and
rightly judge between true righteousness and holiness, and that
which is hypocritical: then shall ye behold the kingdom of
Christ with other eyes than [carnal] reason doth, that is, with
spiritual eyes, and certainly judge those to be true saints indeed which are baptized and believe in Christ, and afterwards
in the same faith whereby they are justified, and their sins both
past and present are forgiven, do abstain from the desires of
the flesh. But from these desires they are not thoroughly
cleansed; for the flesh lusteth against the spirit. Notwithstanding these uncleannesses do still remain in them to this end,
that they may be humbled, and being so humbled, they may
feel the sweetness of the grace and benefit of Christ. So these
unclean remnants of sin do nothing at all hinder, but greatly
further the godly; for the more they feel their infirmities and
sins, so much the more they fly unto Christ the throne of grace,
and more heartily crave his aid and succour: to wit, that he
will adorn them with his righteousness, that he will increase
their faith, that he will endue them with his Spirit, by whose
[gracious leading and] guiding they may overcome the lusts of
the flesh, that they may not rule and reign over them, but may
be subject unto them. Thus true Christians do continually
wrestle with sin, and yet notwithstanding in wrestling they are
not overcome, but obtain the victory.

This have I said, that ye may understand, not by men's
dreams, but by the Word of God, who be true saints indeed.
We see then how greatly Christian doctrine helpeth to the
raising up and comforting of [weak] consciences; which
treateth not of cowls, shavings, rosaries, and such-like toys, but
of high and weighty matters, as how we may overcome the
flesh, sin, death, and the devil. This doctrine, as it is unknown
to the justiciaries [and such as trust in their own works,] so

is it impossible for them to instruct or bring into the right way one [poor] conscience wandering and going astray; or to pacify and comfort the same when it is in heaviness, terror, or desperation.

THE BONDAGE OF THE WILL[1]

[At many points, humanists and the reformers joined hands. Both repudiated the corruption of the Church and the subtleties of Scholastic theology. Moreover, the classical knowledge and technical proficiency of Renaissance scholarship provided the critical tools behind the Reformation. Erasmus' Greek text of the New Testament was a boon to Luther. From its more accurate text, Luther was able to recover theological meanings obscured if not perverted in the medieval period.

For many humanists, the similarity of concern ended there. Among that group was Erasmus, the humanist scholar known and acclaimed throughout Europe. Aware of the need for reform, Erasmus was sympathetic to much that Luther said. But in spite of initial courteous relations between the two, it became more and more apparent that a rift was inevitable. Temperamentally, Erasmus had a dislike for strife and confessed a preference for peace and concord to truth and turmoil. For Erasmus, Luther had obviously gone too far, and Roman Catholic pressure made it impossible for Erasmus to remain neutral. Moreover, the central humanist core of Erasmus' thought was more congenial to a mild Scholastic Roman Catholic position than to the conceptions of grace and man

[1] The selections here reprinted are taken by permission of the publisher from *The Bondage of the Will*, translated by J. I. Packer and A. R. Johnston (London: James Clarke and Co. Ltd., 1957; Westwood, N.J.: Fleming H. Revell Company, 1957), pp. 66–86, 104–7, 169–71, 205–12, 313–18.

*held by the Reformers. In fact, Erasmus preferred not to have
to be too precise and rigorous on such matters.*

Erasmus' book on The Freedom of the Will *was undoubtedly written under pressure. Luther's reply, after some delay,
was caustic and tightly reasoned from the standpoint of his
position. Luther, in fact, considered* The Bondage of the Will
*to be his best theological book, and the only one in that class
worthy of publication. While the terms of the debate are no
longer acceptable, the issues posed are still real in the life of
the Church. The limited selection here printed from* The
Bondage of the Will *should serve to show both the form of
the debate and something of the issue.* The Bondage of the
Will *first appeared in 1525.]*

REVIEW OF ERASMUS' PREFACE

(i) *Of the necessity of assertions in Christianity*

First, I would run through some of the points in your
Preface, where you make some attempt to prejudice our
cause and embellish your own. To start with, I observe that, as
elsewhere you censure me for being over-bold in making
assertions, so here in this book you say that *you find so little
satisfaction in assertions that you would readily take up the
Sceptics' position wherever the inviolable authority of Holy
Scripture and the Church's decisions permit; though you
gladly submit your judgment to these authorities in all that
they lay down, whether you follow it or not.* That is the outlook which appeals to you.

I assume (as in courtesy bound) that it is your charitable
mind and love of peace that prompts such sentiments. Were
anyone else to express them, perhaps I should fall on him in
my usual way! Nor ought I to allow even you, well-meaning
as you are, to go astray any longer with such an idea. To take
no pleasure in assertions is not the mark of a Christian heart;
indeed, one must delight in assertions to be a Christian at all.
(Now, lest we be misled by words, let me say here that by
'assertion' I mean staunchly holding your ground, stating your
position, confessing it, defending it and persevering in it un-

vanquished. I do not think that the term has any other meaning, either in classical authors or in present-day usage. And I am talking about the assertion of what has been delivered to us from above in the Sacred Scriptures. Outside that field, we do not need Erasmus or any other teacher to tell us that over matters which are doubtful, or unprofitable and unnecessary, assertions and contentions are not merely stupid, but positively impious; Paul condemns them often enough! But I do not think you are speaking here about those things, unless like a comic orator you were intending to take up one subject and then deal with another, as the man did over the turbot; or unless you are godless and crazy enough to maintain that the article concerning 'free-will' is doubtful, or unnecessary.)

Away, now, with Sceptics and Academics from the company of us Christians; let us have men who will assert, men twice as inflexible as very Stoics! Take the Apostle Paul—how often does he call for that 'full assurance' which is, simply, an assertion of conscience, of the highest degree of certainty and conviction. In Rom. 10 [:10] he calls it 'confession'—'with the mouth confession is made unto salvation'. Christ says, 'Whosoever confesseth me before men, him will I confess before my Father' [Matt. 10:32]. Peter commands us to give a reason for the hope that is in us [I Pet. 3:15]. And what need is there of a multitude of proofs? Nothing is more familiar or characteristic among Christians than assertion. Take away assertions, and you take away Christianity. Why, the Holy Spirit is given to Christians from heaven in order that He may glorify Christ and in them confess Him even unto death—and is this not assertion, to die for what you confess and assert? Again, the Spirit asserts to such purpose that He breaks in upon the whole world and convinces it of sin [cf. John 16:8], as if challenging it to battle. Paul tells Timothy to reprove, and to be instant out of season [II Tim. 4:2]; and what a clown I should think a man to be who did not really believe, nor unwaveringly assert, those things concerning which he reproved others! I think I should send him to Anticyra![2]

But I am the biggest fool of all for wasting time and words on something that is clearer to see than the sun. What Christian can endure the idea that we should deprecate assertions?

[2] A health resort for treating mental illness.

That would be denying all religion and piety in one breath—asserting that religion and piety and all dogmas are just nothing at all. Why then do you—you!—*assert* that *you find no satisfaction in assertions* and that you *prefer an undogmatic temper to any other?*

You would have it understood, no doubt, that you were not here referring at all to the confession of Christ and His doctrines. A correct reminder; and in deference to you I waive the right of which I normally avail myself and eschew all conjecture as to your real thoughts and motives. That I leave for another occasion, perhaps for other writers. Meanwhile, I advise you to correct your tongue and your pen, and refrain from using such expressions in future. Your heart may be upright and honest, but your words—which mirror the heart, they say—are neither. If you really think that the subject of 'free-will' is not necessary knowledge and does not relate to Christ, then your language is correct (for it expresses your meaning), but your thought is blasphemous; if you think this knowledge essential, then your language is blasphemous (for it seems to say the opposite) though your thought is correct. (And in that case all your great heap of complaints about useless assertions and contentions was out of place and beside the point.)

But what will you say about the words I quoted, in which you did not confine yourself to the specific matter of 'free-will', but spoke quite generally of all religious dogmas whatsoever? There you said that *you would take up the Sceptics' position if the inviolable authority of Holy Scripture and the Church's decisions permitted you to do so, so little do you like assertions.* What a Proteus the man is to talk about 'inviolable authority' and 'the Church's decisions'!—as if you had a vast respect for the Scriptures and the Church, when in the same breath you tell us that you wish you had liberty to be a sceptic! What Christian could talk like that? If you are speaking of doctrines that are unprofitable and uncertain, what news do you bring us? Does not everyone wish for liberty to be a sceptic in such matters? Does not every Christian in fact freely avail himself of such liberty, and censure those who become slavish devotees of any opinion? Or perhaps you think (as your words certainly suggest) that all Christians are people whose dogmas are useless things, for which it is absurd of them to quarrel and fight

with their assertions! But if you are referring to essential truths
—why, what more irreligious assertion could a man possibly
make than that he wants to be free to assert precisely *nothing*
about such things? The Christian will rather say this: 'So little
do I like sceptical principles, that, so far as the weakness of
my flesh permits, not merely shall I make it my invariable
rule steadfastly to adhere to the sacred text in all that it
teaches, and to assert that teaching, but I also want to be as
positive as I can about those non-essentials which Scripture
does not determine; for uncertainty is the most miserable thing
in the world.'

What, now, shall we say of your next clause—'*I gladly submit my judgment to these authorities in all that they lay down,
whether I follow it or not.*' What do you mean, Erasmus? Is
it not enough to have submitted your judgment to Scripture?
Do you submit it to the Church as well?—why, what can the
Church settle that Scripture did not settle first? And what
room do you leave for that liberty and authority to judge the
framers of these decisions of which Paul speaks in I Cor. 14
[:29], when he says: 'let the others judge'? Do you object to
there being a judge of the Church's decisions, when Paul lays
it down that there must be? What is this new-fangled religion
of yours, this novel sort of humility, that, by your own example, you would take from us power to judge men's decisions
and make us defer uncritically to human authority? Where
does God's written Word tell us to do that? And what Christian would so throw to the winds the commands of both Scripture and the Church as to say '*whether I follow or not*'? You
defer to them, and yet you do not at all care whether you
follow them or not? Woe to the Christian who doubts the
truth of what is commanded him and does not follow it!—for
how can he believe what he does not follow? Perhaps you are
going to tell us that by 'follow' here you mean 'hold with
absolute certainty, without doubting in the Sceptical manner.'
But if 'follow' means 'see and comprehend perfectly,' what is
there in any creature that any man could follow? And then it
would never be the case that one who could follow some things
could yet not follow other things; for he who followed one
thing (I mean, God) would follow everything, whereas he
who does not follow God never follows any part of His creation.

In a word, what you say comes to this: that you do not think it matters a scrap what anyone believes anywhere, so long as the world is at peace; you would be happy for anyone whose life, reputation, welfare or influence was at stake to emulate him who said 'if they affirm, I affirm; if they deny, so do I;' and you would encourage him to treat Christian doctrines as no better than the views of human philosophers—about which, of course, it is stupid to wrangle and fight and assert, since nothing results but bad feeling and breaches of outward peace. 'What is above us does not concern us'—that is your motto. So you intervene to stop our battles; you call a halt to both sides, and urge us not to fight any more over issues that are so stupid and sterile. That, I repeat, is the meaning of your words. And I think you know what I am driving at here, my dear Erasmus. But, as I said, let the words go; for the moment, I acquit your heart; but you must write no more in this strain. Fear the Spirit of God, who searches the reins and heart, and is not deceived by stupid speeches. I say this in order that from now on you may stop accusing our side of obstinacy and stubbornness. By so doing, you merely let us see that in your heart you cherish a Lucian, or some other hog of Epicurus' herd, who, because he is an atheist himself, finds in all who believe in God and confess Him a subject for secret amusement. Leave us free to make assertions, and to find in assertions our satisfaction and delight; and you may applaud your Sceptics and Academics—till Christ calls you too! The Holy Spirit is no Sceptic, and the things He has written in our hearts are not doubts or opinions, but assertions—surer and more certain than sense and life itself.

(ii) *Of the perspicuity of Scripture*

Now I come to another point, which is linked with this. You divide Christian doctrines into two classes, and make out that we need to know the one but not the other. '*Some*,' you say, '*are recondite, whereas others are quite plain.*' Surely at this point you are either playing tricks with someone else's words, or practising a literary effect! However, you quote in your support Paul's words in Rom. 11 [:33]: 'O the depth of the riches both of the wisdom and knowledge of God!'; and also Isa. 40:13: 'Who gave help to the Spirit of the Lord, or who hath been his counsellor?' It was all very easily said, either because you knew that you were writing, not just to Luther, but for the world at large, or else because you failed to consider that it was against *Luther* that you were writing! I hope you credit Luther with some little scholarship and judgment where the sacred text is concerned? If not, behold! I will wring the admission out of you! Here is my distinction (for I too am going to do a little lecturing—or chop a little logic, should I say?): God and His Scripture are two things, just as the Creator and His creation are two things. Now, nobody questions that there is a great deal hid in God of which we know nothing. Christ himself says of the last day: 'Of that day knoweth no man, but the Father' [Matt. 24:36]; and in Acts 1 [:7] he says: 'It is not for you to know the times and seasons'; and again, he says: 'I know whom I have chosen' [John 13:18]; and Paul says: 'The Lord knoweth them that are his' [II Tim. 2:19]; and the like. But the notion that in Scripture some things are recondite and all is not plain was spread by the godless Sophists (whom now you echo, Erasmus)—who have never yet cited a single item to prove their crazy view; nor can they. And Satan has used these unsubstantial spectres to scare men off reading the sacred text, and to destroy all sense of its value, so as to ensure that his own brand of poisonous philosophy reigns supreme in the church. I certainly grant that many *passages* in the Scriptures are obscure and hard to elucidate, but that is due, not to the exalted nature of their subject, but to our own linguistic and grammatical ignorance; and it does not in any way prevent our knowing all the *contents* of Scripture. For what solemn truth can the Scriptures still be concealing, now that the seals are broken, the stone rolled away from the door of the tomb, and that greatest of all mysteries brought to light—that Christ, God's Son, became man, that God is Three in One, that Christ suffered for us, and will reign for ever? And are not these things known, and sung in our streets? Take Christ from the Scriptures—and what more will you find in them? You see, then, that the entire content of the Scriptures has now been brought to light, even though some passages which contain unknown words remain obscure. Thus it is unintelligent, and ungodly too, when you know that the contents of Scripture are as clear as can be, to pronounce them obscure on account of those few obscure words. If words are obscure in one place, they are clear in another. What God has so plainly declared to the world is in some parts of Scripture stated in plain words, while in other parts it still lies hidden under obscure words. But when something stands in broad daylight, and a mass of evidence for it is in broad daylight also, it does not matter whether there is any evidence for it in the dark. Who will maintain that the town fountain does not stand in the light because the people down some alley cannot see it, while everyone in the square can see it?

There is nothing, then, in your remark about the 'Corycian cavern'; matters are not so in the Scriptures. The profoundest mysteries of the supreme Majesty are no more hidden away, but are now brought out of doors and displayed to public view. Christ has opened our understanding, that we might understand the Scriptures, and the Gospel is preached to every creature. 'Their sound is gone out into all lands' [Ps. 19:4]. 'All things that are written, are written for our instruction' [Rom. 15:4]. Again: 'All Scripture is given by inspiration of God, and is profitable for instruction' [II Tim. 3:16]. Come forward then, you, and all the Sophists with you, and cite a single mystery which is still obscure in the Scripture. I know that to many people a great deal remains obscure; but that is due, not to any lack of clarity in Scripture, but to their own blindness and dullness, in that they make no effort to see truth which, in itself, could not be plainer. As Paul said of the Jews in II Cor. 4: 'The veil remains on their heart' [II Cor. 3:15]; and again, 'If our gospel be hid, it is hid to them that are lost, whose heart the god of this world hath blinded' [II Cor. 4:3–4]. They are like men who cover their eyes, or go from daylight into darkness, and hide there, and then blame the sun, or the darkness of the day, for their inability to see. So let wretched men abjure that blasphemous perversity which would blame the darkness of their own hearts on to the plain Scriptures of God!

When you quote Paul's statement, 'his judgments are incomprehensible,' you seem to take the pronoun 'his' to refer to Scripture; whereas the judgments which Paul there affirms

to be incomprehensible are not those of Scripture, but those
of God. And Isaiah 40 does not say: 'who has known the mind
of Scripture?' but: 'who has known the mind of the Lord?'
(Paul, indeed, asserts that Christians do know the mind of the
Lord; but only with reference to those things that are given to
us by God, as he there says in I Cor. 2 [:12]. You see, then,
how sleepily you examined those passages, and how apt is
your citation of them—as apt as are almost all your citations for
'free-will'! So, too, the examples of obscurity which you allege
in that rather sarcastic passage are quite irrelevant—the distinction of persons in the Godhead, the union of the Divine
and human natures of Christ, and the unpardonable sin. *Here*,
you say, *are problems which have never been solved*. If you
mean this of the enquiries which the Sophists pursue when
they discuss these subjects, what has the inoffensive Scripture
done to you, that you should blame such criminal misuse of it
on to its own purity? Scripture makes the straightforward affirmation that the Trinity, the Incarnation and the unpardonable
sin are facts. There is nothing obscure or ambiguous about
that. You imagine that Scripture tells us *how* they are what
they are; but it does not, nor need we know. It is here that
the Sophists discuss their dreams; keep your criticism and
condemnation for them, but acquit the Scriptures! If, on the
other hand, you mean it of the facts themselves, I say again:
blame, not the Scriptures, but the Arians and those to whom
the Gospel is hid, who, by reason of the working of Satan, their
god, cannot see the plainest proofs of the Trinity in the Godhead and of the humanity of Christ.

In a word: The perspicuity of Scripture is twofold, just as
there is a double lack of light. The first is external, and relates
to the ministry of the Word; the second concerns the knowledge of the heart. If you speak of *internal* perspicuity, the
truth is that nobody who has not the Spirit of God sees a jot
of what is in the Scriptures. All men have their hearts darkened, so that, even when they can discuss and quote all that
is in Scripture, they do not understand or really know any of
it. They do not believe in God, nor do they believe that they
are God's creatures, nor anything else—as Ps. 13 puts it, 'The
fool hath said in his heart, there is no God' [Ps. 14:1]. The
Spirit is needed for the understanding of all Scripture and

every part of Scripture. If, on the other hand, you speak of *external* perspicuity, the position is that nothing whatsoever is left obscure or ambiguous, but all that is in the Scripture is through the Word brought forth into the clearest light and proclaimed to the whole world.

(iii) *Of the importance of knowing what power 'free-will' has*

Still more intolerable is your classifying 'free-will' among the *'useless doctrines that we can do without'*. In its stead you give us a list of what you consider to be sufficient for Christian piety—a draft, indeed, which a Jew, or a Gentile who knew nothing of Christ, could easily draw up; for you do not mention Christ in a single letter—as if you think that Christian piety is possible without Christ, so long as God, (*'who is kindness itself,'* you say) is whole-heartedly served.

What shall I say here, Erasmus? You ooze Lucian from every pore; you swill Epicurus by the gallon. If you do not think this topic a necessary concern for Christians, kindly withdraw from the lists; we have no common ground; I think it vital. If it is *'irreligious'*, *'idle'*, *'superfluous'*—your words—to know whether or not God foreknows anything contingently; whether our will is in any way active in matters relating to eternal salvation, or whether it is merely the passive subject of the work of grace; whether we do our good and evil deeds of mere necessity—whether, that is, we are not rather passive while they are wrought in us—then may I ask what *does* constitute godly, serious, useful knowledge? This is weak stuff, Erasmus; it is too much. It is hard to put it down to ignorance on your part, for you are no longer young, you have lived among Christians, and you have long studied the sacred writings; you leave me no room to make excuses for you or to think well of you. And yet the Papists pardon and put up with these outrageous statements, simply because you are writing against Luther! If Luther were not involved, and you wrote so, they would tear you limb from limb! Plato and Socrates may be good friends, but truth must be honoured above all. And, limited though your understanding of the Bible and the Christian life may be, even one who opposes Christians should know what they do and do not consider profitable and necessary. Here you are, a theologian, a teacher of Christians, now about to write for their guidance an outline of Christianity, and not merely do you vacillate, in your sceptical way, as to what is profitable and necessary for them; you go back on yourself, defy your own principles and make an *assertion*—an unheard-of assertion!—that here is something non-essential; when, in fact, if it is not really essential, and is not surely known, then neither God, Christ, the gospel, faith nor anything else even of Judaism, let alone Christianity, is left! God Immortal, Erasmus, how vulnerable you make yourself, how wide you lay yourself open to assault and obloquy! What could you write about 'free-will' that was good or correct, when you betray by these words of yours such utter ignorance of Scripture and of godliness? But I shall furl my sails; I will not here use my own words to deal with you (that I may do later); I shall stick to yours.

The outline of Christianity which you have drawn up contains, among other things, this: *'We should strive with all our might, resort to the healing balm of penitence, and try by all means to compass the mercy of God, without which man's will and endeavour is ineffective.'* And this: *'Nobody should despair of pardon from a God who by nature is kindness itself.'* These Christ-less, Spirit-less words of yours are chillier than very ice; indeed, they spoil the beauty of your eloquence. Perhaps they are reluctant admissions dragged out of you (poor fellow!) by fear of a tyrannical hierarchy, lest you should seem an utter atheist! Anyway, this is what your words assert: that there is strength within us; there is such a thing as striving with all one's strength; there is mercy in God; there are ways of compassing that mercy; there is a God who is by nature just, and kindness itself; and so on. But if one does not know what this 'strength' is—what men can do, and what is done to them—what this 'striving' is, what is the extent and limit of its effectiveness—then what should he do? What will you tell him to do? Let us see.

'It is irreligious, idle and superfluous' (you say) *'to want to know whether our will effects anything in matters pertaining to eternal salvation, or whether it is wholly passive under the work of grace.'* But here you speak to the contrary, saying that Christian piety consists in *'striving with all our might'*,

and that *'apart from the mercy of God our will is ineffective.'*
Here you plainly assert that the will is in some respect active
in matters pertaining to eternal salvation, for you represent it
as striving; and, again, you represent it as the object of Divine
action when you say that without God's mercy it is ineffective.
But you do not define the limits within which we should think
of the will as acting and as acted upon; you take pains to
engender ignorance as to what God's mercy and man's will
can effect by your very teaching as to what man's will and
God's mercy *do* effect! Thus that caution of yours sends you
round in circles; it has made you resolve to side with neither
party, to emerge from between Scylla and Charybdis un-
scathed—so that if the waves in the open sea upset and overwhelm you, you can then assert all that you now deny, and
deny all that you now assert!

I will set your theology before your eyes by a few analogies.
Suppose a would-be poet or speech-maker never thought to
ask what ability he had, what he could and could not do, and
what the subject he was tackling demanded of him—never
considered Horace's adage about 'What the shoulders can sustain, and what they will not bear'—but went straight to work,
thinking: 'I must strive to get it done; it is *idle* and *superfluous*
to ask whether I have enough learning and eloquence and
ability'—what would you think of him? And if someone who
wanted a rich crop from his land was not *idle* enough to perform the *superfluous* task of investigating the nature of the
soil (as Virgil in the Georgics so *idly* and *pointlessly* advises),
but rushed precipitately into action, thinking of nothing but
the work, and ploughed the seashore and cast his seed wherever there was room, whether in the sand or in the mud—what
would you think of him? And what if a man who purposed
war, and wanted a glorious victory, or carried responsibility
for some other piece of public service, was not so *idle* as to
reflect upon what was in his power, whether the treasury
could finance him, whether the soldiers were fit, whether there
was opportunity for action; but disregarded the historian's advice[3] ('Before acting, deliberate, and when you have deliber-
ated, act speedily'), and charged ahead with eyes shut and
ears stopped, shouting nothing but 'War! War!'—pressing on

[3] Sallust, *De coniuratione Cat.*, I.

with the work? Tell me, Erasmus, what would you think of
such poets, farmers, generals and statesmen? I will add a text
from the Gospel: 'If anyone, intending to build a tower, does
not first sit down and count the cost, whether he has sufficient
to finish it'—well, what is Christ's judgment on that man? [cf.
Luke 14:28].

In just this way, you prescribe for us nothing but things to
do, and yet you forbid us to examine, measure and take knowledge of the limits of our ability, as if this were an idle, superfluous and irreligious enquiry. In this, for all that horror of
imprudence and that ostentatious sobriety to which your vast
caution prompts you, we find you teaching imprudence at its
worst. The Sophists are fools and madmen, in fact, to pursue
their idle enquiries; yet they sin less than you, who actually
instruct men to cultivate madness and give themselves over
to folly. And your madness is greater still, in that you assure
us that this folly is the loveliest Christian piety, gravity, serious
godliness—and salvation! And if we do not do as you tell us,
you *assert* (you, the sworn foe of assertions!) that we are
irreligious, idle and empty!—and thus you admirably dodge
Scylla and escape Charybdis too! Confidence in your own
ability drives you along here; you think that by your eloquence
you can so dupe the public that nobody will realise what you
cherish in your heart and what you are trying to achieve by
these slippery writings of yours. But God is not mocked, and
it is not good policy to run against Him!

Furthermore: were it with reference to writing poetry, or
preparing for harvest, or military or public service, or building houses, that you taught us such folly, it would still be
outrageous, particularly in so great a man as yourself, yet it
could have been forgiven you—at any rate, by Christians, who
pay no regard to these temporal things. But when you tell
Christian people to let this folly guide them in their labours,
and charge them that in their pursuit of eternal salvation they
should not concern themselves to know what is in their power
and what is not—why, this is plainly the sin that is really unpardonable. For as long as they do not know the limits of their
ability, they will not know what they should do; and as long
as they do not know what they should do, they cannot repent

when they err; and impenitence is the unpardonable sin. This is where your moderate, sceptical theology leads us!

So it is not irreligious, idle, or superfluous, but in the highest degree wholesome and necessary, for a Christian to know whether or not his will has anything to do in matters pertaining to salvation. Indeed, let me tell you, this is the hinge on which our discussion turns, the crucial issue between us; our aim is, simply, to investigate what ability 'free-will' has, in what respect it is the subject of Divine action and how it stands related to the grace of God. If we know nothing of these things, we shall know nothing whatsoever of Christianity, and shall be in worse case than any people on earth! He who dissents from that statement should acknowledge that he is no Christian; and he who ridicules or derides it should realise that he is the Christian's chief foe. For if I am ignorant of the nature, extent and limits of what I can and must do with reference to God, I shall be equally ignorant and uncertain of the nature, extent and limits of what God can and will do in me—though God, in fact, works all in all [cf. I Cor. 12:6]. Now, if I am ignorant of God's works and power, I am ignorant of God himself; and if I do not know God, I cannot worship, praise, give thanks or serve Him, for I do not know how much I should attribute to myself and how much to Him. We need, therefore, to have in mind a clear-cut distinction between God's power and ours, and God's work and ours, if we would live a godly life.

So, you see, this point is a further item in any complete summary of Christianity. Self-knowledge, and the knowledge and glory of God, are bound up with it. Which means, my dear Erasmus, that it is simply intolerable of you to call the knowledge of it irreligious, idle, and vain. Your claims upon us are many, but the fear of God claims of us everything. Indeed, you yourself see that all good in us is to be ascribed to God, and assert as much in your outline of Christianity; and this assertion certainly involves a second, namely, that God's mercy alone works everything, and our will works nothing, but is rather the object of Divine working, else all will not be ascribed to God. And yet a little further on you deny that it is religious, godly, or wholesome, to assert or know these things! But an inconsistent thinker, unsure and inexperienced in the things of God, cannot help talking in this fashion.

(iv) *Of the necessitating foreknowledge of God*

Another item in the summary of Christianity is knowing whether God foresees anything contingently, or whether we do all things of necessity. This knowledge also you represent as something irreligious, idle, and vain, just as all the ungodly do—indeed, the devils and the damned also represent it as hateful and abhorrent! You are wise to keep clear of such questions as far as you can; but you are a very poor rhetorician and theologian if you venture to open your mouth and instruct us about 'free-will' without any reference to these matters. I will act as your whetstone; though I am no rhetorician myself, I will dare to tell an excellent rhetorician his business. Suppose that Quintilian, having chosen to write on Oratory, were to say, 'In my judgment, all that superfluous nonsense about invention, arrangement, elocution, memory and pronunciation, should be left out; it is enough to know that Oratory is the ability to speak well'—would you not laugh at such an author? Yet, in just the same way, you first choose to write on 'free-will' and then exclude from consideration the entire substance and all the constituent parts of the topic you are going to write about! For you cannot know what 'free-will' is without knowing what ability man's will has, and what God does, and whether He foreknows of necessity.

Surely your rhetoricians teach that he who would speak about a subject should first say whether it exists, then what it is, what its parts are, what is contrary to it, allied to it, like it, and so on? But you deprive poor 'free-will' of all these advantages, and settle no single question relating to it save the first, i.e. whether it exists (and we shall see how worthless your arguments on *that* point are)—so that a more incompetent book on 'free-will' (apart from the elegance of its language) I never saw! In fact, the Sophists argue on this subject better than you, innocent though they are of rhetorical skill; for, when they tackle 'free-will', they do try to settle all the questions concerning it (whether it exists, what it is, what it does, how it exists, etc.)—even though they too fail to achieve their object. In this book of mine, therefore, I shall harry you and all the Sophists till you tell me exactly what 'free-will' can and does do; and I hope so to harry you (Christ helping me) as to make you repent of ever publishing your Diatribe.

It is, then, fundamentally necessary and wholesome for Christians to know that God foreknows nothing contingently, but that He foresees, purposes, and does all things according to His own immutable, eternal and infallible will. This bombshell knocks 'free-will' flat, and utterly shatters it; so that those who want to assert it must either deny my bombshell, or pretend not to notice it, or find some other way of dodging it. Before I establish this point by my own arguments and Scriptural authority, I shall first state it with the aid of *your* words.

Surely it was you, my good Erasmus, who a moment ago asserted that *God is by nature just, and kindness itself?* If this is true, does it not follow that He is *immutably* just and kind? that, as His nature remains unchanged to all eternity, so do His justice and kindness? And what is said of His justice and kindness must be said also of His knowledge, His wisdom, His goodness, His will, and the other Divine attributes. But if it is religious, godly and wholesome, to affirm these things of God, as you do, what has come over you, that now you should contradict yourself by affirming that it is irreligious, idle and vain to say that God foreknows by necessity? You insist that we should learn the immutability of God's will, while forbidding us to know the immutability of His foreknowledge! Do you suppose that He does not will what He foreknows, or that He does not foreknow what He wills? If He wills what He foreknows, His will is eternal and changeless, because His nature is so. From which it follows, by resistless logic, that all we do, however it may appear to us to be done mutably and contingently, is in reality done necessarily and immutably in respect of God's will. For the will of God is effective and cannot be impeded, since power belongs to God's nature; and His wisdom is such that He cannot be deceived. Since, then His will is not impeded, what is done cannot but be done where, when, how, as far as, and by whom, He foresees and wills. If the will of God were such that, when the work had been done and while it yet remained in being, the will ceased (as is the case with the will of a man, who, when he has built, say, the house he wants, ceases to will just as really as he does in death), then it could truly be said that things happen con-

tingently and mutably. But the contrary is in fact true: the
work ceases to be and the will remains in being—so far beyond
the bounds of possibility is it that the production and continued existence of anything can be contingent. Lest we be
deceived over our terms, let me explain that *being done contingently* does not, in Latin, signify that the thing done is itself
contingent, but that it is done by a contingent and mutable
will—such as is *not* to be found in God! And a deed cannot
be called *contingent* unless we do it 'contingently', i.e. by
chance (as it were) and without premeditation; that is, when
our will or hand fastens on something presented to us as if by
chance, without our having previously thought or planned anything about it.

I could wish, indeed, that a better term was available for
our discussion than the accepted one, *necessity*, which cannot
accurately be used of either man's will or God's. Its meaning is
too harsh, and foreign to the subject; for it suggests some sort
of compulsion, and something that is against one's will, which
is no part of the view under debate. The will, whether it be
God's or man's, does what it does, good or bad, under no compulsion, but just as it wants or pleases, as if totally free. Yet
the will of God, which rules over our mutable will, is changeless and sure—as Boetius sings, 'Immovable Thyself, Thou
movement giv'st to all;' and our will, principally because of its
corruption, can do no good of itself. The reader's understanding, therefore, must supply what the word itself fails to convey, from his knowledge of the intended signification—the immutable will of God on the one hand, and the impotence of our
corrupt will on the other. Some have called it *necessity of immutability*, but the phrase is both grammatically and theologi-
cally defective.[4]

This is a point over which the Sophists have toiled for many
years now (and have been defeated at last, and forced to give
in): they maintained that *all things take place necessarily, but
by necessity of consequence* (as they put it), *and not by necessity of the thing consequent*. By this distinction they eluded
the force of their own admission—or, rather, *de*luded themselves! I shall not find it hard to show how unreal the distinc-

---

[4] This paragraph appears only in the Jena edition of Luther's
works (1567).

tion is. By *necessity of consequence*, they mean, roughly speaking, this: If God wills something, then it must needs be; but that which thus comes to be is something which of itself need not be; for only God exists necessarily, and everything else can cease to be, if God so wills. This is to say that God's action is necessary, if He wills it, but the thing done is not in itself necessary. But what do they establish by this play on words? This, I suppose—the thing done is not necessary; that is, it has no necessity in its own essential nature: which is just to say, that the thing done is not God Himself! Nonetheless, it remains true that each thing *does* happen necessarily, if God's action is necessary or there is a necessity of consequence, however true it may be that it does *not* happen necessarily, in the sense that it is not God and has no necessity of its own essential nature. If I come to exist of necessity, it does not much worry me that my existence and being are in themselves mutable; contingent and mutable as I am (and I am not God, the necessary Being), yet I still come to exist!

So their absurd formula, *all things take place by necessity of consequence, but not by necessity of the thing consequent,* amounts merely to this: everything takes place by necessity, but the things that take place are not God Himself. But what need was there to tell us that?—as though there were any fear of our claiming that things which happen are God, or possess a divine and necessarily existent nature! So our original proposition still stands and remains unshaken: all things take place by necessity. There is no obscurity or ambiguity about it. In Isaiah, it says 'My counsel shall stand, and my will shall be done' [46:10]; and any schoolboy knows the meaning of 'counsel', 'will', 'shall be done', 'shall stand'!

And why should these matters be thought so recondite for us Christians that it is irreligious, idle, and vain to study and know them, when they are on the lips of heathen poets and ordinary people so frequently? How often does Virgil, for one, mention Fate? 'All things stand fixed by law immutable.' Again, 'Fixed is the day of every man.' Again, 'If the Fates summon you.' Again, 'If thou shalt break the binding cord of Fate.'[5] The poet simply seeks to show that in the destruction

---

[5] Vergil, *Aeneid*, 2.324, 6.883, 7.314, 10.465.

of Troy and the beginning of the Roman empire Fate did
more than all the efforts of men. Indeed, he makes even his
immortal gods subject to Fate. Jupiter and Juno themselves
needs must yield to it. Hence the poets represented the three
Fates as immutable, implacable and irrevocable in their decrees. Those wise men knew, what experience of life proves,
that no man's purposes ever go forward as planned, but events
overtake all men contrary to their expectation. 'Could Troy
have stood by human arm, it should have stood by mine,' says
Virgil's Hector.[6] Hence that commonest of all remarks, which
is on everyone's lips—'God's will be done'; and: 'If God will,
we will do it'; and: 'God so willed,' 'such was the will of those
above.' 'Such was your will,' says Vergil. Whence we see that
the knowledge of predestination and of God's prescience has
been left in the world no less certainly than the notion of the
Godhead itself. But those who wished to seem wise argued
themselves out of it till their hearts grew dark and they became fools, as Rom. 1 [:21–22] says, and denied, or pretended
not to know, things which the poets, and the common people,
and even their own consciences held as being most familiar,
most certain, and most true.

(v) *Of the importance of knowing that God necessitates all things*

I would also point out, not only how true these things are
(I shall discuss that more fully from Scripture on a later page),
but also how godly, reverent and necessary it is to know them.
For where they are not known, there can be no faith, nor any
worship of God. To lack this knowledge is really to be ignorant
of God—and salvation is notoriously incompatible with such
ignorance. For if you hesitate to believe, or are too proud to
acknowledge, that God foreknows and wills all things, not
contingently, but necessarily and immutably, how can you believe, trust and rely on His promises? When He makes promises, you ought to be out of doubt that He knows, and can
and will perform, what He promises; otherwise, you will be
accounting Him neither true nor faithful, which is unbelief, and
the height of irreverence, and a denial of the most high God!

[6] *Aen.*, 2.291 f.

And how can you be thus sure and certain, unless you know that certainly, infallibly, immutably and necessarily, He knows, wills and will perform what He promises? Not only should we be sure that God wills, and will execute His will, necessarily and immutably; we should glory in the fact, as Paul does in Rom. 3 [:4]—'Let God be true, but every man a liar', and again, 'Not that the word of God has failed' [Rom. 9:6], and in another place, 'The foundation of God standeth sure, having this seal, the Lord knoweth them that are his' [II Tim. 2:19]. In Tit. 1 [:2] he says: 'Which God, that cannot lie, promised before the world began'. And Heb. 11 [:6] says: 'He that cometh, must believe that God is, and that he is a rewarder of them that hope in him'.

If, then, we are taught and believe that we ought to be ignorant of the necessary foreknowledge of God and the necessity of events, Christian faith is utterly destroyed, and the promises of God and the whole gospel fall to the ground completely; for the Christian's chief and only comfort in every adversity lies in knowing that God does not lie, but brings all things to pass immutably, and that His will cannot be resisted, altered or impeded.

Observe now, my good Erasmus, where that cautious, peace-loving theology of yours leads us! You call us back, and prohibit our endeavours to learn about God's foreknowledge and the necessity which lies on men and things, and advise us to leave behind, and avoid, and look down on such enquiries; and in so doing you teach us your own ill-advised principles—that we should seek after ignorance of God (which comes to us without our seeking, and indeed is born in us), and so should spurn faith, abandon God's promises, and discount all the consolations of the Spirit and convictions of our consciences. Epicurus himself would hardly give such advice! Moreover, not content with this, you call those who are concerned to acquire the knowledge in question godless, idle and empty, and those who care nothing for it you call godly, pious and sober. What do you imply by these words, but that Christians are idle, empty and godless fellows? and that Christianity is a trivial, empty, stupid and downright godless thing? So here again, in your desire to discourage us from anything rash, you allow yourself to be carried to the contrary extreme (as fools

do) and teach the very quintessence of godless, suicidal folly.
Do you see, now, that at this point your book is so godless,
blasphemous and sacrilegious, that its like cannot be found
anywhere?

I do not speak of your heart, as I said before; for I do not
think you are so abandoned that you honestly want to teach
these principles or see them applied. But I wanted to make
you realise what appalling sentiments the champion of a bad
cause finds himself constrained unguardedly to blurt out; and
also what it means to go against God's facts and God's Word
when we dissemble to oblige others, and defy conscience by
acting a part at their bidding. It is no game and no joke to
teach the holy Scriptures and godliness, for it is so very easy
to fall here in the way that James described: 'he that offends
in one point becomes guilty of all' [2:10]. For when we show
ourselves disposed to trifle even a little and cease to hold the
sacred Scriptures in sufficient reverence, we are soon involved
in impieties and overwhelmed with blasphemies—as you are
here, Erasmus. May the Lord pardon and have mercy on you!

I know, and join you in affirming, that the Sophists have
raised a host of questions on these topics, and mixed in with
them a great deal of unprofitable matter besides, much of
which you specify; indeed, I have attacked them more vigorously and fully than you. But you are ill-advised and over-
hasty to confuse and lump together the purity of sacred truth
with the profane and foolish questions of the ungodly. 'They
have defiled the gold with dung, and changed its good colour,'
as Jeremiah says [Lam. 4:1]. But the gold should not be
equated with the dung and thrown away with it, as you are
doing. The gold must be reclaimed from their hands, the pure
Scripture must be separated from their own rotten rubbish;
which is what I have always tried to do, so that divine truth
may be kept distinct from their nonsense. Nor should it disturb us that nothing has been established through their investi-
gations save that a great loss of unity and decline in affection
results when we aspire to be over-wise. Our question is not,
what have the Sophistical enquirers achieved? but, how may
we become good men and Christians? And you should not
blame on to Christian doctrine the evil doings of the godless;

all that is quite irrelevant, and you could well speak of it elsewhere and save paper.

━━━   ━━━   ━━━

(ix) *That a will which has no power without grace is not free*

What if I prove from the very words in which you assert
'free-will' that there is no such thing as 'free-will'? and show
that you unwittingly deny what you are trying with such vast
sagacity to affirm? Why, if I fail here, I promise you that all
I write against you in this book shall be withdrawn, and all
that your Diatribe advances and seeks to establish against me
shall be ratified!

You describe the power of 'free-will' as small, and wholly
ineffective apart from the grace of God. Agreed? Now then,
I ask you: if God's grace is wanting, if it is taken away from
that small power, what can it do? It is ineffective, you say,
and can do nothing good. So it will not do what God or His
grace wills. Why? Because we have now taken God's grace
away from it, and what the grace of God does not do is not
good. Hence it follows that 'free-will' without God's grace is
not free at all, but is the permanent prisoner and bondslave of
evil, since it cannot turn itself to good. This being so, I give
you full permission to enlarge the power of 'free-will' as much
as you like; make it angelic, make it divine, if you can!—but
when once you add this doleful postscript, that it is ineffective
apart from God's grace, straightway you rob it of all its power.
What is *ineffective* power but (in plain language) *no* power?
So to say that 'free-will' exists and has power, albeit ineffective
power, is, in the Sophists' phrase, a contradiction in terms. It
is like saying ' "free-will" is something which is not free'—as if
you said that fire is cold and earth hot. Fire certainly has power
to heat; but if hell-fire (even) was cold and chilling instead
of burning and scorching, I would not call it 'fire', let alone
'hot' (unless you meant to refer to an imaginary fire, or a
painted one). Note, however, that if we meant by 'the power
of free-will' the power which makes human beings fit subjects
to be caught up by the Spirit and touched by God's grace, as
creatures made for eternal life or eternal death, we should have
a proper definition. And I certainly acknowledge the existence

of *this* power, this fitness, or 'dispositional quality' and 'passive aptitude' (as the Sophists call it), which, as everyone knows, is not given to plants or animals. As the proverb says, God did not make heaven for geese!

It is a settled truth, then, even on the basis of your own testimony, that we do everything of necessity, and nothing by 'free-will'; for the power of 'free-will' is nil, and it does no good, nor can do, without grace. (Unless you intend 'efficacy' to be taken in a new sense, as implying completion, and are suggesting that 'free-will' can actually will and begin a thing, though it cannot complete it. This I do not believe; I shall say more on the point later.) It follows, therefore, that 'free-will' is obviously a term applicable only to the Divine Majesty; for only He can do, and does (as the Psalmist sings) 'whatever he wills in heaven and earth' [Ps. 135:6]. If 'free-will' is ascribed to men, it is ascribed with no more propriety than divinity itself would be—and no blasphemy could exceed that! So it befits theologians to refrain from using the term when they want to speak of human ability, and to leave it to be applied to God only. They would do well also to take the term out of men's mouths and speech, and to claim it for their God, as if it were His own holy and awful Name. If they must at all hazards assign some power to men, let them teach that it must be denoted by some other term than 'free-will'; especially since we know from our own observation that the mass of men are sadly deceived and misled by this phrase. The meaning which it conveys to their minds is far removed from anything that theologians believe and discuss. The term 'free-will' is too grandiose and comprehensive and fulsome. People think it means what the natural force of the phrase would require, namely, a power of freely turning in any direction, yielding to none and subject to none. If they knew that this was not so, and that the term signifies only a tiny spark of power, and that utterly ineffective in itself, since it is the devil's prisoner and slave, it would be a wonder if they did not stone us as mockers and deceivers, who say one thing and mean another —indeed, who have not yet decided what we do mean! For, as the wise man says, 'he who speaks sophistically is hateful' [? Pr. 6:17], especially if he does so in matters of religion, where eternal salvation is at stake.

Since, therefore, we have lost the meaning and the real reference of this glorious term, or, rather, have never grasped them (as was claimed by the Pelagians, who themselves mistook the phrase) why do we cling so tenaciously to an empty word, and endanger and delude faithful people in consequence? There is no more wisdom in so doing than there is in the modern foible of kings and potentates, who retain, or lay claim to, empty titles of kingdoms and countries, and flaunt them, while all the time they are really paupers, and anything but the possessors of those kingdoms and countries. We can tolerate their antics, for they fool nobody, but just feed themselves up—unprofitably enough—on their own vainglory. But this false idea of 'free-will' is a real threat to salvation, and a delusion fraught with the most perilous consequences.

Most people would be amused, or, more likely, infuriated if at this late hour a linguistic revolutionary threw overboard established usage, and tried in its place to introduce the practice of calling a beggar *wealthy*, not because he had any wealth, but because it was possible that a king might give him his—and talked in this way, not as a figure of speech, like sarcasm or irony, but with all apparent seriousness. Thus, he would call one who was sick unto death *perfectly healthy*, on the ground that another might give him his health. Or he would call an unlettered idiot *a learned man*, on the ground that another might give him his learning. It is no different to say, *man has 'free-will'*—merely on the ground that God might grant him His! By thus misusing language, anyone can boast that he has anything: for instance, that he is the lord of heaven and earth—if God would give him that distinction! But such talk is more appropriate to actors and confidence tricksters than to theologians! Our words should be correct, pure and sober—in Paul's phrase, 'sound speech, that cannot be condemned' [Tit. 2:8].

If we do not want to drop this term altogether—which would really be the safest and most Christian thing to do—we may still in good faith teach people to use it to credit man with 'free-will' in respect, not of what is above him, but of what is below him. That is to say, man should realise that in regard to his money and possessions he has a right to use them, to do or to leave undone, according to his own 'free-will'—

though that very 'free-will' is overruled by the free-will of God alone, according to His own pleasure. However, with regard to God, and in all that bears on salvation or damnation, he has no 'free-will', but is a captive, prisoner and bondslave, either to the will of God, or to the will of Satan.

———   ———   ———

(x) *Of God preached and not preached, and of His revealed and secret will*

As to why some are touched by the law and others not, so that some receive and others scorn the offer of grace, that is another question, which Ezekiel does not here discuss. He speaks of the published offer of God's mercy, not of the dreadful hidden will of God, Who, according to His own counsel, ordains such persons as He wills to receive and partake of the mercy preached and offered. This will is not to be inquired into, but to be reverently adored, as by far the most awesome secret of the Divine Majesty. He has kept it to Himself and forbidden us to know it; and it is much more worthy of reverence than an infinite number of Corycian caverns!

When, now the Diatribe reasons thus: *'Does the righteous Lord deplore the death of His people which He Himself works in them? This seems too ridiculous'*—I reply, as I have already said: we must discuss God, or the will of God, preached, revealed, offered to us, and worshipped by us, in one way, and God not preached, nor revealed, nor offered to us, nor worshipped by us, in another way. Wherever God hides Himself, and wills to be unknown to us, there we have no concern. Here that sentiment: 'what is above us does not concern us', really holds good. Lest any should think that this distinction is my own, I am following Paul, who writes to the Thessalonians of Antichrist that 'he should exalt himself above all that is God preached and worshipped' [II Thess. 2:4]; clearly intimating that a man can be exalted above God as He is preached and worshipped, that is, above the word and worship of God, by which He is known to us and has dealings with us. But above God not worshipped and not preached, that is, God as He is in His own nature and Majesty, nothing can be exalted, but all things are under His powerful hand.

Now, God in His own nature and majesty is to be left alone; in this regard, we have nothing to do with Him, nor does He wish us to deal with Him. We have to do with Him as clothed and displayed in His Word, by which He presents Himself to us. That is His glory and beauty, in which the Psalmist proclaims Him to be clothed [cf. Ps. 21:5]. I say that the righteous God does not deplore the death of His people which He Himself works in them, but He deplores the death which He finds in His people and desires to remove from them. God preached works to the end that sin and death may be taken away, and we may be saved. 'He sent His word and healed them' [Ps. 107:20]. But God hidden in Majesty neither deplores nor takes away death, but works life, and death, and all in all; nor has He set bounds to Himself by His Word, but has kept Himself free over all things.

The Diatribe is deceived by its own ignorance in that it makes no distinction between God preached and God hidden, that is, between the Word of God and God Himself. God does many things which He does not show us in His Word, and He wills many things which He does not in His Word show us that He wills. Thus, He does not will the death of a sinner—that is, in His Word; but He wills it by His inscrutable will. At present, however, we must keep in view His Word and leave alone His inscrutable will; for it is by His Word, and not by His inscrutable will, that we must be guided. In any case, who can direct himself according to a will that is inscrutable and incomprehensible? It is enough simply to know that there is in God an inscrutable will; what, why, and within what limits It wills, it is wholly unlawful to inquire, or wish to know, or be concerned about, or touch upon; we may only fear and adore!

So it is right to say: 'If God does not desire our death, it must be laid to the charge of our own will if we perish'; this, I repeat, is right if you spoke of God preached. For He desires that all men should be saved, in that He comes to all by the word of salvation, and the fault is in the will which does not receive Him; as He says in Matt. 23 [:37]: 'How often would I have gathered thy children together, and thou wouldst not!' But why the Majesty does not remove or change this fault of will in every man (for it is not in the power of man to do it),

or why He lays this fault to the charge of the will, when man
cannot avoid it, it is not lawful to ask; and though you should
ask much, you would never find out; as Paul says in Rom. 11:
'Who art thou that repliest against God?' [Rom. 9:20].

———   ———   ———

(v) *Of God's method of hardening man*

There follows upon this the business of hardening, which
proceeds thus: As we have said, the ungodly man, like Satan
his prince, is wholly turned to self and to his own. He does
not seek God, nor care for the things of God: he seeks his own
riches, and glory, and works, and wisdom, and power, and
sovereignty in everything, and wants to enjoy it in peace. If
anyone stands in his way, or wants to detract from any of
these things, he is moved with the same perverted desire that
leads him to seek them, and is outraged and furious with his
opponent. He can no more restrain his fury than he can stop
his self-seeking, and he can no more stop his self-seeking than
he can stop existing—for he is still a creature of God; though
a spoiled one.

This is precisely the rage which the world shows against the
gospel of God. By the gospel there comes that stronger One,
to vanquish him who keeps his palace in peace; and He condemns those desires of glory, wealth, wisdom, righteousness of
one's own, and all the things in which the world trusts. This
very galling of the ungodly, as God says and does to them
the reverse of what they wanted, is the hardening and embit-
tering of them. As of themselves they are turned away from
God by the very corruption of their nature, so their antipathy
greatly increases and they grow far worse as their course away
from God meets with opposition or reversal. Thus, when God
purposed to deprive ungodly Pharaoh of his kingdom, he
galled and hardened him, and brought bitterness to his heart,
by falling upon him through the word of Moses, who seemed
about to take away his kingdom and deliver the people from
under his dominion. He did not give Pharaoh the Spirit within,
but allowed his own ungodly corruption, under Satan's sway,
to blaze with anger, to swell with pride, to boil with rage and
to advance along the path of scornful recklessness.

Let none think, when God is said to harden or work evil in us (for hardening is working evil) that he does it by, as it were, creating fresh evil in us, as you might imagine an ill-disposed innkeeper, a bad man himself, pouring and mixing poison into a vessel that was not bad, while the vessel itself does nothing, but is merely the recipient, or passive vehicle, of the mixer's own ill-will. When men hear us say that God works both good and evil in us, and that we are subject to God's working by mere passive necessity, they seem to imagine a man who is in himself good, and not evil, having an evil work wrought in him by God; for they do not sufficiently bear in mind how incessantly active God is in all his creatures, allowing none of them to keep holiday. He who would understand these matters, however, should think thus: God works evil in us (that is, by means of us) not through God's own fault, but by reason of our own defect. We being evil by nature, and God being good, when He impels us to act by His own acting upon us according to the nature of His omnipotence, good though He is in Himself, He cannot but do evil by our evil instrumentality; although, according to His wisdom, He makes good use of this evil for His own glory and for our salvation.

Thus God, finding Satan's will evil, not creating it so (it became so by Satan's sinning and God's withdrawing), carries it along by His own operation and moves it where He wills; although Satan's will does not cease to be evil in virtue of this movement of God.

David spoke in this way of Shimei, in the second book of Kings: 'Let him curse, for God hath bidden him to curse David' [II Sam. 16:10]. How could God bid anyone to curse, an act so virulent and evil? There was nowhere any external precept to that effect. But David keeps in view the fact that God omnipotent speaks and it is done: that is, He works all things by His own eternal word. In this case, therefore, the Divine action and omnipotence impel Shimei's already evil will (which was hot against David before), and all his members with it; confronts him at an appropriate moment, when David deserves such blasphemy; and the good God Himself, by means of an evil blaspheming instrument, commands this blasphemy (that is, speaks and effects it through His word, which is just the impelling force of His acting).

(vi) *Of the hardening of Pharaoh*

Thus God hardens Pharaoh: He presents to the ungodly, evil will of Pharaoh His own word and work, which Pharaoh's will hates, by reason of its own inbred fault and natural corruption. God does not alter that will within by His Spirit, but goes on presenting and bringing pressure to bear; and Pharaoh, having in mind his own strength, wealth and power, trusts to them by this same fault of his nature. So it comes to pass that, being inflated and uplifted by the idea of his own greatness, and growing vaingloriously scornful of lowly Moses and of the unostentatious word of God, he becomes hardened; and then grows more and more irked and annoyed, the more Moses presses and threatens him. His evil will would not have been moved or hardened of itself, but as the omnipotent Agent makes it act (as He does the rest of His creatures) by means of His own inescapable movement, it needs must actively will something. As soon as God presents to it from without something that naturally irritates and offends it, Pharaoh cannot escape being hardened, even as he cannot escape the acting of Divine omnipotence and the perversion and villainy of his own will. So God's hardening of Pharaoh is wrought thus: God presents from without to his villainous heart that which by nature he hates; at the same time, He continues by omnipotent action to move within him the evil will which He finds there. Pharaoh, by reason of the villainy of his will, cannot but hate what opposes him, and trust to his own strength; and he grows so obstinate that he will not listen nor reflect, but is swept along in the grip of Satan like a raging madman.

If I have gained your assent to these things, I have won this point. I have shattered the figures and glosses of men, and taken the words of God in their simple sense; and now there is no necessity to make excuses for God, nor to accuse him of unrighteousness. When He says: 'I will harden the heart of Pharaoh', He uses the words in their simple meaning. It is as if he said: 'I will cause the heart of Pharaoh to be hardened'; or 'it shall be hardened by My operation and action'.

We have heard how it was to be done; thus: 'By my ordinary movement within I will so move his evil will that he shall go on in his present headstrong course of willing; I will not cease to move it, nor can I. From without, I will present to him My word and work; and his evil fury shall hurl itself against it; for he, being evil, cannot but will evil as I move him by the power of omnipotence.' Thus God with full certainty knew, and with full certainty declared, that Pharaoh should be hardened; for He knew with full certainty that Pharaoh's will could neither resist the movement of omnipotence, nor put away its own villainy, nor bow to Moses, the adversary set before him. While his will remained evil, Pharaoh must necessarily grow worse, more hardened and more proud; in his headstrong course, he would hurl himself against that which he would not have and which he despised, for he was confident of his power. So here you see that these very words confirm that 'free-will' can do nothing but evil, inasmuch as God, Who does not make mistakes through ignorance nor speak lies in iniquity, thus surely promises the hardening of Pharaoh; for well He knew that an evil will can only will evil, and that when good is presented as opposing it, it cannot but wax worse.

It now remains for someone to ask: Why then does God not cease from that movement of omnipotence by which the will of the ungodly is moved to go on being evil, and to grow worse? The answer is: this is to desire that for the sake of the ungodly God should cease to be God; for you are desiring that His power and activity should cease—that is, that He should cease to be good, lest the ungodly should grow worse!

Why then does He not alter those evil wills which He moves? This question touches on the secrets of His Majesty, where 'His judgments are past finding out' [cf. Rom. 11:33]. It is not for us to inquire into these mysteries, but to adore them. If flesh and blood take offence here, and grumble, well, let them grumble; they will achieve nothing; grumbling will not change God! And however many of the ungodly stumble and depart, the elect will remain [cf. John 6:60 ff.].

The same reply should be given to those who ask: Why did God let Adam fall, and why did He create us all tainted with the same sin, when He might have kept Adam safe, and might have created us of other material, or of seed that had first

been cleansed? God is He for Whose will no cause or ground
may be laid down as its rule and standard; for nothing is on
a level with it or above it, but it is itself the rule for all things.
If any rule or standard, or cause or ground, existed for it, it
could no longer be the will of God. What God wills is not
right because He ought, or was bound, so to will; on the contrary, what takes place must be right, because He so wills it.
Causes and grounds are laid down for the will of the creature,
but not for the will of the Creator—unless you set another
Creator over him!

By these arguments, the figure-mongering Diatribe and its
figure with it are, I think, adequately confuted. However, let
us go to the text itself to see what agreement there is between
it and the figure. It is the way of all who parry arguments
with figures to hold the text in sovereign contempt, and to
concern themselves merely with picking out a word, torturing
it with their figures, and nailing it to the cross of their own
chosen meaning, in utter disregard of the surrounding context, of what comes before and after, and of the author's aim
and intention. So it is here. Without stopping to see the point
and purpose of Moses' words, the Diatribe tears from the text
the phrase: 'I will harden', which it finds objectionable, and
makes of it what it pleases, without a thought as to how it
may be re-inserted and fitted back so as to square with the
body of the passage. This is the reason why those learned and
time-honoured friends of yours have found Scripture insuf-
ficiently clear. No wonder! The sun itself could not shine if
assailed by such devices as theirs!

I demonstrated above, that it is not right to say that Pharaoh
was hardened because a long-suffering God bore with him and
he was not punished at once; for in fact he was chastised with
all the plagues. That I here pass by. But now—if 'harden' means
'bear with Divine long-suffering and not punish at once', what
need was there for God to promise so often, at the time when
the signs were occurring, that he would harden the heart of
Pharaoh? For already, before those signs and that hardening
took place, God had in long-suffering borne with Pharaoh, and
omitted to punish him, while Pharaoh, puffed up with his success and his power, was inflicting great woe upon the children
of Israel! Do you see, now, that your figure completely misses

the point of this passage? It would apply indiscriminately to all who sin while Divine long-suffering bears with them. In this sense, we shall say that all men are hardened, for there is none that does not sin, and none would sin did not Divine long-suffering bear with him! This hardening of Pharaoh is therefore something distinct, over and above the general forbearance of Divine long-suffering.

Moses' concern is to proclaim, not so much the villainy of Pharaoh as the veracity and mercy of God, lest the children of Israel should distrust the promises of God whereby He undertook to set them free. Since this was a tremendous task, He forewarns them of its difficulty, so that, knowing that it was all foretold and would be duly carried out by the executive action of Him Who had promised, they might not be shaken in their faith. It is as if He had said: 'I will certainly deliver you, but you will find it hard to believe, because Pharaoh will so resist and delay the deliverance. But trust nevertheless; for by My operation all his delaying shall only result in My performing more and greater miracles to confirm you in your faith and to display My powers, so that henceforth you may have more faith in Me in all other matters.'

Christ acts in the same way when at the last supper He promises His disciples a kingdom. He foretells abundance of difficulties—His own death, and their many tribulations—so that, when it came to pass, they might from then on have much more faith.

Moses plainly shows us that this is the meaning when he says: 'But Pharaoh shall not let you go, that many wonders may be wrought in Egypt' [Exod. 3:19–20]; and again: 'For this cause have I raised thee up, for to show in thee my power; and that my name may be declared throughout all the earth' [9:16]. Here you see that Pharaoh was hardened to resist God and to delay redemption in order that occasion might be given for many signs and a display of the power of God, so that He might be declared and believed on throughout all the earth. What does this mean, but that all these things were said and done to strengthen faith and to comfort the weak, that henceforth they might without hesitation believe in God as true, faithful, mighty and merciful? It is as if He were speaking in the most soothing strains to little children, saying: 'Do not be terrified at Pharaoh's stubbornness, for I work that very stubbornness Myself, and I Who deliver you have it under My control. I shall simply make use of it to work many signs and to declare My majesty, so as to help your faith.'

This is why Moses generally repeats after each plague: 'And the heart of Pharaoh was hardened, so that he would not let the people go; as the Lord had spoken' [Exod. 7:13, 22; 8:15; 9:12]. What was the point of: 'As the Lord had spoken', but that the Lord might appear true, as having foretold that Pharaoh should be hardened? Had there been in Pharaoh any power to turn, or freedom of will that might have gone either way, God could not with such certainty have foretold his hardening. But as it is, He who neither deceives nor is deceived guarantees it; which means that it is completely certain, and necessary, that Pharaoh's hardening will come to pass. And it would not be so, were not that hardening wholly beyond the strength of man, and in the power of God alone, in the manner that I spoke of above: that is, God was certain that He would not suspend the ordinary operation of omnipotence in Pharaoh, or on Pharaoh's account—indeed, He could not omit it; and He was equally certain that the will of Pharaoh, being naturally evil and perverse, could not consent to the word and work of God which opposed it; hence, while by the omnipotence of God the energy of willing was preserved to Pharaoh within, and the word and work that opposed him was set before him without, nothing could happen in Pharaoh but the offending and hardening of his heart. If God had suspended the action of His omnipotence in Pharaoh when He set before him the word of Moses which opposed him, and if the will of Pharaoh might be supposed to have acted alone by its own power, then there could perhaps have been a place for debating which way it had power to turn. But as it is, since he is impelled and made to act by his own willing, no violence is done to his will; for it is not under unwilling constraint, but by an operation of God consonant with its nature it is impelled to will naturally, according to what it is (that is, evil). Therefore, it could not but turn upon one word, and thus become hardened. Thus we see that this passage makes most forcibly against 'free-will,' on this account that God, who promises, cannot lie; and, if He cannot lie, then Pharaoh cannot but be hardened.

—— —— ——

(xviii) *Of the comfort of knowing that salvation does not depend on 'free-will'*

I frankly confess that, for myself, even if it could be, I should not want 'free-will' to be given me, nor anything to be left in my own hands to enable me to endeavour after salvation; not merely because in face of so many dangers, and adversities, and assaults of devils, I could not stand my ground and hold fast my 'free-will' (for one devil is stronger than all men, and on these terms no man could be saved); but because, even were there no dangers, adversities, or devils, I should still be forced to labour with no guarantee of success, and to beat my fists at the air. If I lived and worked to all eternity, my conscience would never reach comfortable certainty as to how much it must do to satisfy God. Whatever work I had done, there would still be a nagging doubt as to whether it pleased God, or whether He required something more. The experience of all who seek righteousness by works proves that; and I learned it well enough myself over a period of many years, to my own great hurt. But now that God has taken my salvation out of the control of my own will, and put it under the control of His, and promised to save me, not according to my working or running, but according to His own grace and mercy, I have the comfortable certainty that He is faithful and will not lie to me, and that He is also great and powerful, so that no devils or opposition can break Him or pluck me from Him. 'No one,' He says, 'shall pluck them out of my hand, because my Father which gave them me is greater than all' [John 10:28–29]. Thus it is that, if not all, yet some, indeed many, are saved; whereas, by the power of 'free-will' none at all could be saved, but every one of us would perish.

Furthermore, I have the comfortable certainty that I please God, not by reason of the merit of my works, but by reason of His merciful favour promised to me; so that, if I work too little, or badly, He does not impute it to me, but with fatherly compassion pardons me and makes me better. This is the glorying of all the saints in their God.

(xix) *Of faith in the justice of God in His dealings with men*

You may be worried that it is hard to defend the mercy and equity of God in damning the undeserving, that is, ungodly persons, who, being born in ungodliness, can by no means avoid being ungodly, and staying so, and being damned, but are compelled by natural necessity to sin and perish; as Paul says: 'We were all the children of wrath, even as others' [Eph. 2:3], created such by God Himself from a seed that had been corrupted by the sin of the one man, Adam. But here God must be reverenced and held in awe, as being most merciful to those whom He justifies and saves in their own utter unworthiness; and we must show some measure of deference to His Divine wisdom by believing Him just when to us He seems unjust. If His justice were such as could be adjudged just by human reckoning, it clearly would not be Divine; it would in no way differ from human justice. But inasmuch as He is the one true God, wholly incomprehensible and inaccessible to man's understanding, it is reasonable, indeed inevitable, that His justice also should be incomprehensible; as Paul cries, saying: 'O the depth of the riches both of the wisdom and knowledge of God! How unsearchable are His judgments, and His ways past finding out!' [Rom. 11:33]. They would not, however, be 'unsearchable' if we could at every point grasp the grounds on which they are just. What is man compared with God? How much can our power achieve compared with His power? What is our strength compared with His strength? What is our knowledge compared with His wisdom? What is our substance compared with His substance? In a word, what is all that we are compared with all that He is? If, now, even nature teaches us to acknowledge that human power, strength, wisdom, knowledge and substance, and all that is ours, is as nothing compared with the Divine power, strength, wisdom, knowledge and substance, what perversity is it on our part to worry at the justice and the judgment of the only God, and to arrogate so much to our own judgment as to presume to comprehend, judge and evaluate God's judgment!

Why do we not in like manner say at this point: 'Our judgment is nothing compared with God's judgment'? Ask reason whether force of conviction does not compel her to acknowledge herself foolish and rash for not allowing God's judgment to be incomprehensible, when she confesses that all the other things of God are incomprehensible! In everything else, we allow God His Divine Majesty; in the single case of His judgment, we are ready to deny it! To think that we cannot for a little while *believe* that He is just, when He has actually promised us that when He reveals His glory we shall all clearly *see* that He both was and is just!

I will give a parallel case, in order to strengthen our faith in God's justice, and to reassure that 'evil eye' which holds Him under suspicion of injustice. Behold! God governs the external affairs of the world in such a way that, if you regard and follow the judgment of human reason, you are forced to say, either that there is no God, or that God is unjust; as the poet said: 'I am often tempted to think there are no gods.' See the great prosperity of the wicked, and by contrast the great adversity of the good. Proverbs, and experience, the parent of proverbs, bear record that the more abandoned men are, the more successful they are. 'The tabernacle of robbers prosper,' says Job [12:6], and Ps. 72 complains that sinners in the world are full of riches [Ps. 73:12]. Is it not, pray, universally held to be most unjust that bad men should prosper, and good men be afflicted? Yet that is the way of the world. Hereupon some of the greatest minds have fallen into denying the existence of God, and imagining that Chance governs all things at random. Such were the Epicureans, and Pliny. And Aristotle, wishing to set his 'prime Being' free from misery, holds that he sees nothing but himself; for Aristotle supposes that it would be very irksome to such a Being to behold so many evils and injustices! And the Prophets, who believed in God's existence, were still more tempted concerning the injustice of God. Jeremiah, Job, David, Asaph and others are cases in point. What do you suppose Demosthenes and Cicero thought, when, having done all they could, they received as their reward an unhappy death? Yet all this, which looks so much like injustice in God, and is traduced as such by arguments which no reason or light of nature can resist, is most easily cleared up by the light of the gospel and the knowledge of grace, which teaches us that though the wicked flourish in their bodies, yet they perish in their souls. And a summary explanation of this whole inexplicable problem is found in a single little word: *There is a life after this life; and all that is not punished and repaid here will be punished and repaid there; for this life is nothing more than a precursor, or, rather, a beginning, of the life that is to come.*

If, now, this problem, which was debated in every age but never solved, is swept away and settled so easily by the light of the gospel, which shines only in the Word and to faith, how do you think it will be when the light of the Word and faith shall cease, and the real facts, and the Majesty of God, shall be revealed as they are? Do you not think that the light of glory will be able with the greatest ease to solve problems that are insoluble in the light of the word and grace, now that the light of grace has so easily solved this problem, which was insoluble by the light of nature?

Keep in view three lights: the light of nature, the light of grace, and the light of glory (this is a common and a good distinction). By the light of nature, it is inexplicable that it should be just for the good to be afflicted and the bad to prosper; but the light of grace explains it. By the light of grace, it is inexplicable how God can damn him who by his own strength can do nothing but sin and become guilty. Both the light of nature and the light of grace here insist that the fault lies not in the wretchedness of man, but in the injustice of God; nor can they judge otherwise of a God who crowns the ungodly freely, without merit, and does not crown, but damns another, who is perhaps less, and certainly not more, ungodly. But the light of glory insists otherwise, and will one day reveal God, to whom alone belongs a judgment whose justice is incomprehensible, as a God Whose justice is most righteous and evident—provided only that in the meanwhile we *believe* it, as we are instructed and encouraged to do by the example of the light of grace explaining what was a puzzle of the same order to the light of nature.

I shall here end this book, ready though I am to pursue the matter further, if need be; but I think that abundant satisfaction has here been afforded for the godly man who is willing to yield to truth without stubborn resistance. For if we believe it to be true that God foreknows and foreordains all things; that He cannot be deceived or obstructed in His foreknowledge and predestination; and that nothing happens but at His will (which reason itself is compelled to grant); then, on reason's own testimony, there can be no 'free-will' in man, or angel, or in any creature.

So, if we believe that Satan is the prince of this world, ever ensnaring and opposing the kingdom of Christ with all his strength, and that he does not let his prisoners go unless he is driven out by the power of the Divine Spirit, it is again apparent that there can be no 'free-will'.

So, if we believe that original sin has ruined us to such an extent that even in the godly, who are led by the Spirit, it causes abundance of trouble by striving against good, it is clear that in a man who lacks the Spirit nothing is left that can turn itself to good, but only to evil.

Again, if the Jews, who followed after righteousness with all their powers, fell into unrighteousness instead, while the Gentiles, who followed after unrighteousness, attained to an un-hoped-for righteousness, by God's free gift, it is equally apparent from their very works and experience that man without grace can will nothing but evil.

And, finally, if we believe that Christ redeemed men by His blood, we are forced to confess that all of man was lost; otherwise, we make Christ either wholly superfluous, or else the redeemer of the least valuable part of man only; which is blasphemy, and sacrilege.

III

SERMONS ON THE CATECHISM, 1528[1]

[In the year 1528, Luther preached three series of sermons on the Catechism. These sermons were part of a regular pattern of presenting the "elements and fundamentals of Christian knowledge and life four times each year". Hence they are expository and typify the teaching role of preaching in the Reformation. The sermons here included are the last five of the third series of ten, beginning just after the exposition of the Ten Commandments. The entire series of ten form the basis for the Large and Small Catechisms.]

THE CREED

You have heard the first part of Christian doctrine, namely, the Ten Commandments. And I have carefully admonished you to exhort your household to learn them word for word, that they should then obey God and you as their masters, and that you too should obey God. For if you teach and urge your families, things will go forward. There has never yet been a [perfect] learned man; the more he has studied the more learned he has become.

[1] Reprinted by permission of the publisher from Luther's Works, volume 51, Sermons: 1, edited and translated by John W. Doberstein (Philadelphia: Muhlenberg Press, 1959), pp. 162–93.

Now we shall take up the second part. In former times you heard preaching on twelve articles of the Creed. If anybody wants to divide it up, he could find even more. You, however, should divide the Creed into the main parts indicated by the fact that there are three persons: God the Father, Son, and Holy Spirit; since I believe in God the Father, I believe in God the Son, and I believe in God the Holy Spirit, who are one God. Thus you can divide each separate article into its parts. The first article teaches creation, the second redemption, the third sanctification. The first, how we are created together with all creatures; the second, how we are redeemed; the third, how we are to become holy and pure and live and continue to be pure. The children and uneducated people should learn this in the simplest fashion: the Creed has three articles, the first concerning the Father, the second concerning the Son, the third concerning the Holy Spirit. What do you believe about the Father? Answer: He is the creator. About the Son? He is the redeemer. About the Holy Spirit? He is the sanctifier. For educated people one could divide the articles into as many parts as there are words in it. But now I want to teach the uneducated and the children.

[The First Article]

The first article teaches that God is the Father, the creator of heaven and earth. What is this? What do these words mean? The meaning is that I should believe that I am God's creature, that he has given to me body, soul, good eyes, reason, a good wife, children, fields, meadows, pigs, and cows, and besides this, he has given to me the four elements, water, fire, air, and earth. Thus this article teaches that you do not have your life of yourself, not even a hair. I would not even have a pig's ear, if God had not created it for me. Everything that exists is comprehended in that little word "creator." Here we could go on preaching at length about how the world, which also says, I believe in God, believes this. Therefore, everything you have, however small it may be, remember this when you say "creator," even if you set great store by it. Do not let us think that we have created ourselves, as the proud princes do.

At this time I speak only of these things, for the creator, the

Father almighty, has still more in store [than I enumerate here]. I believe that he has given to me my life, my five senses, reason, wife, and children. None of these do I have of myself. God is the "creator," that is, God has given everything, body and soul, including every member of the body. But if everything is the gift of God, then you owe it to him to serve him with all these things and praise and thank him, since he has given them and still preserves them. But, I ask you, how many are there in the world who understand this word "creator"? For nobody serves him. We sin against God with all our members, one after another, with wife, children, house, home.

Therefore, this first article might well humble and terrify us, since we do not believe it. Note that I am basing [everything] on the word "creator," that is, I believe that God has given to me body and soul, the five senses, clothing, food, shelter, wife, child, cattle, land. It follows from this that I should serve, obey, praise and thank him. A man who believes this article and looks at his cow says: This the Lord gave to me; and he says the same with regard to wife and children.

In short, the first article teaches creation, the second redemption, the third sanctification. The creation, it teaches, means that I believe that God has given to me body, life, reason, and all that I possess. These things I have not of myself, that I may not become proud. I cannot either give them to myself or keep them by myself. But why has he given them to you and what do you think he gave them to you for? In order to found monasteries? No, in order that you should praise him and thank him. There are many who say these words, "I believe in God the Father," but do not understand what these words mean.

"And in Jesus Christ"

You have heard that for the simple and the children we divide the Creed into three articles. The first part deals with the Father, the second with the Son, the third with the Holy Spirit. The first teaches creation, the second redemption, the third sanctification, in order that each may know what he is saying when he says the Creed. I have emphasized the word "creator" in order that, when you are asked, you may answer:

I believe that God is the creator, who has given to me my body and soul, all members, all physical goods, all possessions. Therefore I owe it to him to serve, thank, and praise him. This first article requires that you believe. This is most certainly true.

Now follows the second article. This too we want to treat for the children and I shall emphasize only the words "our Lord." If you are asked, What do you mean when you say, "I believe in Jesus Christ"? answer: I mean by this that I believe that Jesus Christ, the true Son of God, has become my Lord. How? By freeing me from death, sin, hell, and all evil. For before I had no king and lord; the devil was our lord and king; blindness, death, sin, the flesh, and the world were our lords whom we served. Now they have all been driven out and in their stead there has been given to us the Lord Christ, who is the Lord of righteousness, salvation, and all good. And this article you hear preached constantly, especially on Sundays, as for example, "Behold, your king is coming to you" [Matt. 21:5]. Therefore, you must believe in Jesus, that he has become your Lord, that is, that he has redeemed you from death and sin and received you into his bosom. Therefore I have rightly said that the first article teaches the creation and the second redemption. For after we had been created, the devil deceived us and became our Lord. But now Christ frees us from death, the devil, and sin and gives us righteousness, life, faith, power, salvation, and wisdom.

It is because of this article that we are called Christians, for those who acknowledge and call upon Christ are called Christians. But the words which follow, "conceived by the Holy Ghost, born of the Virgin Mary," etc., are points which emphasize and show what Christ became, what he did as our Lord in order to redeem us, what it cost him, what he risked. This is what happened: He was conceived by the Holy Spirit without any sin whatsoever in order that he might become my Lord and redeem me. He did it all in order to become my Lord, for he must be so holy that the devil could have no claim upon him. These points show what kind of a God he is and what he paid in order that I might come under his lordship, namely, his own body, with which he established his kingdom. The whole gospel is contained in this article, for the gospel is nothing else but the preaching of Christ, who was conceived, born, [raised again, ascended, and so on].

Therefore learn to understand these words "our Lord." I should believe and I do believe that Christ is my Lord, that is, the one who has redeemed me, for the second article says that he has conquered death and sin and liberated me from them. At first, when I was created, I had all kinds of goods, body, [soul, etc.]; but I served sin, death, and the devil. Then came Christ, who suffered death in order that I might be free from death and become his child and be led to righteousness and to life. Thus the word "Lord" here is equivalent to the word "Redeemer."

The other points show what it was by which he accomplished this and what a price he paid for it, namely, not with gold, silver, or an army of knights, but with his own self, that is, with his own body. He was conceived by the Holy Spirit, born of the Virgin Mary, and so on. I shall not say any more about this article because I do not want to overwhelm you. It is true Christian article, which neither the Jews nor the papists nor the sectarians believe. For he who believes that he will be saved by his own works and not through Christ [does not believe that Christ is his Lord]. This belongs to the regular preaching.

In these two parts we have heard what we have received from the Father and from the Son, namely, from the Father creation, from the Son redemption.

"I believe in the Holy Ghost"

The third article is about the Holy Spirit, who is one God with the Father and the Son. His office is to make holy or to vivify. Here again one must understand the words, "Holy Spirit," what "Holy Spirit" means, for there is the human spirit, evil spirits, and the Holy Spirit. Here he is called the "Holy Spirit." Why is he so called? Because he sanctifies. And therefore I believe in the Holy Spirit, because he has sanctified me and still sanctifies me. How does this happen? In this way: just as the Son accepts and receives his lordship through his death, so the Holy Spirit sanctifies through the following parts. In the first place he has led you into the holy, catholic church and placed you in the bosom of the church. But in that church he preserves [you] and through it he preaches and brings you [to Christ] through the Word. Christ gained his lordship through death; but how do I come to it? If [his] work remains hidden, then it is lost. So, in order that Christ's death and resurrection may not remain hidden, the Holy Spirit comes and preaches, that is, the Holy Spirit leads you to the Lord, who redeems you. So if I ask you: What does this article mean? answer: I believe that the Holy Spirit sanctifies me. So, as the Father is my creator and Christ is my Lord, so the Holy Spirit is my sanctifier. For he sanctifies me through the following works: through "the forgiveness of sins, the resurrection of the body, and the life everlasting."

The Christian church is your mother, who gives birth to you and bears you through the Word. And this is done by the Holy Spirit who bears witness concerning Christ. Under the papacy nobody preached that Christ is my Lord in the sense that I would be saved without my works. There it was an evil and human spirit that was preaching. That spirit preaches Christ, it is true, but along with it, preaches works, that through them a man is saved. The Holy Spirit, however, sanctifies by leading you into the holy church and proclaiming to you the Word which the Christian church proclaims.

"The communion of saints." This is of one piece with the preceding. Formerly it was not in the Creed. When you hear the word "church" understand that it means group [Haufe], as we say in German, the Wittenberg group or congregation [Gemeine], that is, a holy, Christian group, assembly, or, in German, the holy, common church, and it is a word which should not be called "communion" [Gemeinschaft], but rather "a congregation" [eine Gemeine]. Someone wanted to explain the first term, "catholic church" [and added the words] communio sanctorum, which in German means a congregation of saints, that is, a congregation made up only of saints. "Christian church" and "congregation of saints" are one and the same thing. In other words: I believe that there is a holy group and a congregation made up only of saints. And you too are in this church; the Holy Spirit leads you into it through the preaching of the gospel. Formerly you knew nothing of Christ, but the Christian church proclaimed Christ to you. That is,

I believe that there is a holy church [*sanctam Christianitatem*], which is a congregation in which there are nothing but saints. Through the Christian church, that is, through its ministry [*officium*], you were sanctified; for the Holy Spirit uses its ministry in order to sanctify you. Otherwise you would never know and hear Christ.

Then, in this Christian church, you have "the forgiveness of sins." This term includes baptism, consolation upon a deathbed, the sacrament of the altar, absolution, and all the comforting passages [of the gospel]. In this term are included all the ministrations through which the church forgives sins, especially where the gospel, not laws or traditions, is preached. Outside of this church and these sacraments and [ministrations] there is no sanctification. The clerics are outside the church, because they want to be saved through their works. Here we would need to preach about these individually.

The third point is that the Holy Spirit will sanctify you through "the resurrection of the flesh." As long as we live here [on earth] we continue to pray, "Forgive us our trespasses, as we forgive those who trespass against us"; but after death sin will have completely passed away and then the Holy Spirit will complete his work and then my sanctification will be complete. Therefore it will also be life and nothing but life.

This is a brief explanation of the third article, but for you it is obscure, because you do not listen to it. The third article, therefore, is that I believe in the Holy Spirit, that is, that the Holy Spirit will sanctify me and is sanctifying me. Therefore, from the Father I receive creation, from the Son redemption, from the Holy Spirit sanctification. How does he sanctify me? By causing me to believe that there is one, holy church through which he sanctifies me, through which the Holy Spirit speaks and causes the preachers to preach the gospel. The same he gives to you in your heart through the sacraments, that you may believe the Word and become a member of the church. He begins to sanctify now; when we have died, he will complete this sanctification through both "the resurrection of the body" and "the life everlasting." When we [Germans] hear the word "flesh," we immediately think that what is being spoken of is flesh in a meat market. What the Hebrews called "flesh," we call "body"; hence, I believe that our body will rise from death and thus live eternally. Then we will be interred and buried "in dishonor," as I Cor. 15 [:43] says, but will be raised "in glory."

These latter clauses show the ways in which he sanctifies me, for the Holy Spirit does not justify you outside of the church, as the fanatics, who creep into corners, think. Therefore immediately after the Holy Spirit is placed the Christian church, in which all his gifts are to be found. Through it he preaches, calls you and makes Christ known to you, and breathes into you the faith that, through the sacraments and God's Word, you will be made free from sin and thus be totally free on earth. When you die, remaining in the church, then he will raise you up and sanctify you wholly. The apostles called him the Holy Spirit because he makes everything holy and does everything in Christendom and through the church. On the other hand, an evil spirit does the opposite. The creation we have had long since and Christ has fulfilled his office; but the Holy Spirit is still at work, because the forgiveness of sins is still not fully accomplished. We are not yet freed from death, but will be after the resurrection of the flesh.

I believe in God, that he is my creator, in Jesus Christ, that he is my Lord, in the Holy Spirit, that he is my sanctifier. God has created me and given me life, soul, body, and all goods; Christ has brought me into his lordship through his body; and the Holy Spirit sanctifies me through his Word and the sacraments, which are in the church, and will sanctify us wholly on the last day. This teaching is different from that of the commandments. The commandments teach what we should do, but the Creed teaches what we have received from God. The Creed, therefore, gives that which you need. This is the Christian faith: to know what you must do and what has been given to you.

ON PRAYER AND THE FIRST THREE PETITIONS OF THE LORD'S PRAYER

You have heard the Ten Commandments explained in the most simple way as what you must do and not do, and the Creed as what you should expect and receive from God. The Father gives his gifts by creation, the Son by redemption, the Holy Spirit by sanctification, as you have heard.

Now we must also take up the Lord's Prayer. In the first place necessity itself requires that we not only admonish you to pray but also teach you to pray. You should pray and you should know that you are bound to pray by divine command. For the second commandment teaches that you shall not swear, curse, or conjure, but call upon the name of God in every time of need, pray, praise, and exalt him; hence that it is commanded that we pray. Let no one think: If I do not pray, someone else will. You have been commanded to give honor to God's Name, to call upon him, and pray to him, and this is just as much a command as the other commandments, "You shall not kill," and so on. But you say: My prayer is nothing, and we get into such habits that it is thought that we do not teach that men should pray. But this is true: the prayers in the *Hortulus animae*[2] and other prayer books were not prayers. This [i.e., the recitation of prayers] is suitable for young children, in order that they may learn and become accustomed to read and pray from a script. Therefore this is not praying, but droning and howling. But praying is rather what the second commandment says: Do not curse, swear, conjure, but call upon my name in every time of need. This is what God demands of you and it is not a matter of choice whether you do it or not; you must do it. Therefore, my beloved, I point it out to you, that you may know that prayer is

[2] *Hortulus animae* (*Garden of the Soul*), a widely used title of medieval prayer books.

required in the second commandment. And here you must repel such thoughts as: What does my prayer matter? This is just the same as if a son were to say to his father: What does it matter whether I am obedient or not? No, indeed, you must obey. That's why we are so barbarous; it is because we do not pray. We preach, however, that we should pray. By no means do I reject prayer, but only the abuse of prayer. It is true that Christ in Matt. 6 [:5] rejects useless and heathenish prayers, but elsewhere he commands that we should pray without ceasing. So you must not say that Christ has rejected prayer. He did reject prayers, but only those stupid prayers; on the contrary, he taught the true prayers.

Therefore, since it is commanded that we pray, do not despise prayer and take refuge behind your own unworthiness. Take an example from other commands. A work which I do is a work of obedience. Because my father, master, or prince has commanded it, I must do it, not because of my worthiness, but because it has been commanded. So it is also with prayer. So, when you pray for wife or children or parents or the magistrates, this is what you should think: This work I have been commanded to do and as an obedient person I must do it. On my account it would be nothing, but on account of the commandment it is a precious thing. So you should pray for the prince, the city, the burgomaster, and so on. Therefore I admonish you most faithfully, do not despise your prayers! But do not pray as the clerics do, who merely pray at a venture and think: I am not holy enough and fit enough to be heard. Or: If I were as holy as Peter and Paul I would pray too! You must rather say: The commandment which applied to St. Peter applies to me also, and Peter's prayer was no more holy than mine, for I have been given the same second commandment as he. Therefore my prayer is just as holy and precious as St. Peter's. Your prayer is not one cent less valuable than St. Peter's. And this is the reason: I will grant that he is holier as far as his person is concerned, but the commandment and obedience upon which St. Peter based his prayer I base my own also.

You have needs enough: You are lacking in faith, in love, in patience, in gentleness, in chastity; my wife, my children are sick. Then pray undauntedly and with sure confidence, because God has commanded you to pray. He did not command it in order to deceive you and make a fool, a monkey of you; he wants you to pray and to be confident that you will be heard; he wants you to open your bosom that he may give to you. So open up your coat and skirt wide and receive God's gifts for which you pray in your prayer. It would be a shame if he were to have to accept from you. The monks want to give something to God. Therefore, you should say: Lord, thou hast commanded that I should pray; if I do not pray and ask of thee what I need, I am damned. But do not pray the Lord's Prayer as the vulgar people do, as the vigils,[3] the seven canonical hours,[4] the *Deus in adjutorium*[5] are prayed. This is nothing, and if all the monasteries and foundations were put together in one heap, they still would not pray for so much as a drop of wine. But you must present your need to God, not the need of which you are not aware, but in order that you may learn to know yourself, where you are lacking, and to receive more and more the longer you hold open your sack.

Therefore, children right from the cradle on should begin to pray for the princes, for their brethren and companions. For here you hear the command and the promise: "Ask, and it will be given you; seek and you will find; knock, and it will be opened to you" [Matt. 7:7]. You have been commanded to pray and promised that what you pray for will be given, as in [Ps. 50:15], "Call upon me in the day of trouble; I will deliver you, and you shall glorify me"; and [Ps. 91:15], "When he calls to me, I will answer him." So, go on that and say: Now I know that my prayer is not to be despised; for if I despise it, I despise the command and the promise of God. But God does not despise prayer, but rather has commanded it and promised that he will hear it. Why then should I despise it? But we live like the wild beasts who do not pray.

Let this be said as an introduction and admonition to prayer, for all our protection lies in prayer. We are too weak to withstand the princes, the kings, the world, and the devil; they are much greater and more powerful than we. Therefore we

---

[3] Wakes for the dead.

[4] The daily prayers of the clergy, fixed by canon.

[5] Ps. 70:1, "O Lord, make haste to help me"; which occurs repeatedly in the breviary.

must resort to Christian weapons and say: "Hallowed be thy name." Then Christ says: So shall it be! If the prayer of devout people had not accomplished it, Münzer[6] would probably not have been put down and the princes would now be raging in a different way. It was two or three Christians who prayed in earnestness and faith: "Thy will be done!" And Christ said: So shall it be. But if you do not know and you ask what or how you should pray, then listen to Christ, who enumerates seven successive petitions. Therefore, you must not plead that you feel no need. Look behind yourself for what makes you angry and remiss. Here he has combined all the needs which cause us to cry out to him. Therefore it is not only commanded that we pray, but promised that we shall be heard. And then also what and how we are to pray is prescribed as in a table. Therefore there is no doubt that our prayer will please God. The first need which ought to impel us to pray and call upon the name of God is [expressed in the words]:

"Hallowed be thy name"

This manner of speaking is unfamiliar to us [i.e., not in good German idiom], and it is the equivalent of: O dear Father, may thy name be holy! But what does this mean? Is it not already holy? It is holy in its nature, but not in our use. God's name has been given to us. By what means? We have been baptized in his name, we have the Word which makes us God's children, we have his sacraments, which unite us with him. He has implanted his name, Word, and sacrament among us. Therefore it is of the highest necessity that we pray to our Father. I will gladly endure poverty and sickness if only the heavenly Father has his glory, and I will gladly suffer want if this were to be the result, namely, that the name of God, which is altogether holy in heaven, would also be precious and holy among us.

What, then, does it mean to hallow the name of God? This: when our teaching and life are Christian and godly. The purpose of the second commandment is to cause us not to curse, swear, and lead people astray, as the sectarians do, but rather

---

[6] Thomas Münzer, a religious radical who was beheaded in 1525 for his leading role in the Peasants' War.

to praise and call upon this name. Those who misuse the name of God for deceiving and lying profane and desecrate the name of God, just as it used to be said that churches were desecrated when a fight had taken place in them. God's name is hallowed, therefore, when one calls upon him, prays, praises, and magnifies him, preaches about the Lord, that he is merciful and helps us in peril and otherwise. Therefore the first petition in the Lord's Prayer is explained by the second commandment. In short, when one teaches and lives Christianly, that is, when one does not curse, swear, and so on.

This is the first need which ought to move us to prayer. For in the world there are so many sectarians, all of whom impose upon and deceive the people by using this name, preach the Word of God falsely and say that what they preach is the name and the Word of God. Therefore, in this petition you pray against all who preach, teach, and believe falsely, against the pope and all sectarians, against the tyrants who persecute the Word of God by violence, and against those who lie, deceive, revile, and curse against us, who so coolly listen [to the Word of God]. God's name is never sufficiently praised and preached. Therefore, [we pray]: Let thy name become holy, that is, that the whole world may not curse and swear by thy name, but rather pray and call upon thee according to the second commandment. In short, grant that we may teach and live Christianly.

This is purely Hebrew speech; we are not accustomed to the language; but we must preach about it in order that you may learn it and become accustomed to it. The first petition is that God's name be honored, that his name never be put to shame by us either in teaching or in life.

"Thy kingdom come"

The second need which drives us to prayer is that we pray that God's kingdom may come. This, too, is somewhat Hebraically expressed, but it is not so obscure as the first petition which means: Grant that the world may not lie and deceive by thy name, nor curse and conjure, which is shame and dishonor to thy name, but rather that we may proclaim and praise [thy name]. The second petition is: "thy kingdom come." You must learn to understand the word "kingdom," what is the Father's kingdom, God's kingdom, the kingdom of heaven. Just as the name of God is holy in itself and we still must pray that it may be holy among us, so the kingdom of God comes, whether we pray or not. But we should pray, in order that I too may be a part of those in whom the name of God is hallowed, that God's kingdom may come also to me and his will be done in me. Christ is the king of righteousness and life against the devil, sin, death, and all evil conscience. He has given us his holy Word, that it may be preached, in order that we might believe in him and live holy lives. Therefore we must pray that this may become effective and powerful, that the Word may go out into the world with power, that many may come into this kingdom and learn to believe and thus become partakers of redemption from death, sin, and hell. The first petition is that God's name be not blasphemed, but rather [honored]. The second is that this may also bear fruit, that his name be so hallowed that his kingdom will come in us and we become members of his kingdom. But God's kingdom comes to us in two ways: first, here, through the Word, and secondly, in that the future, eternal life is given to us. This is a strong petition when it is expressed in German: Dear Father, grant thy pure Word, that it may be purely preached throughout the world, and then grant grace and power that it may also be accepted and the people believe. The first concerns the Word and the second the fruit of the Word. For, if the Word is preached but not accepted, the kingdom of God does not come. It is an obscure prayer because it is so Hebraically expressed. These are the two greatest needs. Here on [earth] God's kingdom comes through the beginning of faith and there [in eternity] through the revelation of eternal life. These are the two greatest petitions of this prayer, both of which are comprehended [in Christ's saying:] "Seek first his kingdom" [Matt. 6:33]. Here we pray that his name and kingdom may remain with us.

"Thy will be done"

When you pray this petition you must look askance at a gang, which is called the devil and his mates, who would hinder the kingdom of God. For the father of a household should not only support his own but also defend them. And so it is here; even if we already prayed the first two greatest petitions, the devil nevertheless cannot endure that the Word should be preached and people accept it. Here he has his poisoned arrows: he has the opposing world and our flesh, which is lazy. The will of the pope, the emperor, the princes, the devil, and our flesh prevents the will of God from being done. What we pray is: Dear Father, defend us from the devil and his cohorts and from our lazy flesh which would hinder thy will, and grant grace that thy gospel may go forth unhindered. Thus we are shown in these three petitions our need with regard to God, but in such a way that it redounds to our benefit. God's name is not only hallowed in itself, but in me. Likewise, God's kingdom not only comes of itself and his will is done not only of itself, but rather in order that God's kingdom may come in me, that God's will may be done in me, and his name be hallowed in me. In German, the first [petitions would be:] O Lord, grant grace that the gospel may be purely preached; let thy name be hallowed in us through thy Word; let thy Word be proclaimed to us. The second [petition:] Grant grace that we may diligently accept it, that it bring power to us, and that the people may sincerely adhere to it. The third: Restrain, O Father, all tyrants, devils, all those who would hinder and oppose it and let only thy will be done. In this petition the Christians are our wall and destroy all the counsels of the adversaries. This prayer demolishes the devices of all the tyrants who say, This is the way we will do it: our will must be done! We will shoot down Wittenberg, we will destroy the heretics! But we say one little petition: Dear Father, thy will be done! That is, Say to them, that not their, but thy will be done! Then whatever our enemies counsel will not prevail. But our will too must be broken; otherwise God's name will not be hallowed in us and his kingdom will not come to us.

Today we see the whole world raging against the gospel, and even many among us do not have the gospel. Therefore the name of the Father is constantly being profaned. This should move us Christians. When you feel that your own flesh, your slothfulness, avarice, fornication, and passion is hindering you, then say: "Thy will be done!"

Let this be sufficient for this time on these first three petitions.

THE FOURTH, FIFTH, SIXTH AND SEVENTH PETITIONS

Thus far you have heard the first three petitions. This is Hebrew speech, to which we are not accustomed. The matters of which the petitions speak are hidden from reason. Christ therefore commanded that they be preached, because he knows that we do not know them. The first [petition is:] God's name is holy in itself, but we pray that it may be hallowed in us and in the whole world and that the Word and the honor of God may be kept holy against all fanatics and blasphemers of his name. This is done when his name and his honor is in our teaching and life. The second: His kingdom comes when his Word increases and is powerful among us. In short, when we have God's power, which begins here through the Word and then becomes an actuality when we are buried. The third: That all those be restrained who oppose the name and kingdom of God, for Satan assails all its members. Will of God, John 6 [:38-40].

The fourth: "Give us this day our daily bread." This is beginning to be understood, though there are few who do understand it. When you pray this petition turn your eyes to everything that can prevent our bread from coming and the crops from prospering. Therefore extend your thoughts to all the fields and do not see only the baker's oven. You pray, therefore, against the devil and the world, who can hinder the grain by tempest and war. We pray also for temporal peace against war, because in times of war we cannot have bread. Likewise, you pray for government, for sustenance and peace, without which you cannot eat: Grant, Lord, that the grain may prosper, that the princes may keep the peace, that war may not

break out, that we may give thanks to thee in peace. Therefore it would be proper to stamp the emperor's or the princes'
coat-of-arms upon bread as well as upon money or coins. Few
know that this is included in the Lord's Prayer. Though the
Lord gives bread in sufficient abundance even to the wicked
and godless, it is nevertheless fitting that we Christians should
know and acknowledge that it comes from God, that we realize that bread, hunger, and war are in God's hands. If he opens
his hand, we have bread and all things in abundance; if he
closes it, then it is the opposite. Therefore, do not think that
peace is an accidental thing; it is the gift of God.

This petition, therefore, is directed against everything that
hinders bread, including also base coinage. It is not well with
the man who has lost the common prayers. Beware of this,
but even more if it is against you. It is the greatest of losses
if you are cut off from the church and no longer a member
of it and besides, have the prayers of the church against you.
Therefore, he who hinders bread and injures the people, let
him be afraid of this petition. Thus it is a petition against tempest, war, false buyers and sellers; against all of these this
prayer cries out. Do not be afraid of the rich people; Duke
Hans gets enough to eat from them; but fear the groans and
tears of those who pray: "Give us this day our daily bread,"
i.e., defend us from famine and evil men, that they may not
deprive us of bread.

Bread cannot come to me if there is no peace, so that there
are just prices in the market, so that there is no bloodshed.
Defend us from skinners and usurers! [The explanation of]
"daily" and "this day" belongs in the sharp sermons.[7] The
Lord does indeed give bread, but he also wants us to pray,
in order that we acknowledge it as his gift. This again is a great
need, which pertains to the body.

"Forgive us our debts, as we also have forgiven our debtors"

In the fourth petition you pray against that need which
the poor body has for bread, which it cannot get along with-

[7] Sermons in which greed and anxiousness for the morrow are
attacked.

out. It includes every peril which may hinder bread from coming to us. Now comes our life, which we cannot lead without sinning. Here is the greatest need of all, and we pray: "Forgive us our debts." Not that he does not give it without our prayer, for he has given us baptism, and in his kingdom there is nothing but forgiveness of sins. But it is to be done in order that we may acknowledge it. For the flesh is anxious for the belly and has evil lusts and loves, hatred, anger, envy, and wicked whims, so that we sin daily in words, deeds, and thoughts, in what we do and fail to do. No one does what he should do. So we get stuck in the mire of being proud and thinking that we are thoroughly holy people. Therefore he says here: None of you is good. All of you, no matter how holy and great you are, must say: "Forgive us our debts." Therefore one must pray God to give us a conscience unafraid, which is assured that its sins are forgiven.

Anyone, therefore, who has a burdened and sorrowful conscience prays here for grace and forgiveness of sins, that is, for the strength of the name, the kingdom, and the will of God. This petition therefore serves those who are conscious of their sins. May everyone acknowledge the need which he feels! I do not do enough in my office of preaching. You, burgomaster, captain, prince, husband, wife, you do not do enough in your office either. I do not do enough for my neighbor. Therefore we must pray daily for forgiveness of sins.

"As we also have forgiven our debtors." God has promised the forgiveness of sins. Of that you must be certain and sure, in so far as you [also forgive your neighbor]. If you have someone whom you do not forgive, you pray in vain. Therefore let each one look to his neighbor, if he has been offended by him, and forgive him from the heart; then he will be certain that his sin too has been forgiven. Not that you are forgiven on account of your forgiveness, but freely, without your forgiveness, your sins are forgiven. He, however, enjoins it upon you as a sign, that you may be assured that, if you forgive, you too will be forgiven.

There you have them both, the promise and the sign, that your heart may rejoice, if you can produce the sign and forgive your enemy. You must seek the sign. If you do not find

it here, do you think you will find it in far-away St. James?[8]
What are all the letters of indulgence compared with this petition in the Lord's Prayer? Here is where indulgence should
be preached. Here God promises forgiveness of sins and
stamps the seal upon it. He does not say: Put five pennies in
the poor-box, but only: Forgive the other person. If he will
not accept it, let him go, as long as your heart is at peace.
This is the way to look at all prayers. Don't mutter like the
clerics, "Forgive us our sins," but pray with sure confidence,
for he has added this seal in order that you may be certain.

"And lead us not into temptation"

"Into evil enticement." This is very fine old German. We
say "trial," "temptation" [Anfechtung, Versuchung]. Here we
need to know what these words mean. Sins cling [to us]. The
first temptation is that of the flesh, which says: Go ahead and
have illicit intercourse with another's wife, daughter, maid!
That is Master Flesh [Junker Fleisch]. Or he says: I'm going
to sell the grain, beer, or goods as dearly as I can. This is
the temptation of the flesh. Here the greed of your flesh is
seeking its own advantage. Then you should pray: Guard us,
dear Lord, from temptation! Likewise, the flesh seeks to satisfy its lust in glutting, guzzling, and loafing.

Next is the world, which tempts you with envy, hatred, and
pride. Your neighbor irritates you to anger when you are making a bargain and all of a sudden there is impatience, the
nature of the world—up she goes, blow your top, and it's all
off! Then one conforms to the world. These are worldly temptations. Therefore pray: O Lord, bring it to pass that the flesh
and the world shall not seduce me! Both of them, the flesh
and the world, contribute much toward your feeling an in-
clination to spite and lechery and dislike for your neighbor.
Against all this pray: "Lead us not into temptation." Dear Father, let me not fall into this or other temptations.

The third companion and tempter is Master Devil [Junker
Teufel]. He tempts you by causing you to disregard God's
Word: Oh, I have to look after the beer and malt, I can't go

[8] St. James of Compostella, a famous shrine in Spain, much fre-
quented by pilgrims seeking indulgences.

to hear a sermon; or if you do come to church to hear the sermon you go to sleep, you don't take it in, you have no delight, no love, no reverence for the Word. Then pray that you may not despise it! Then, too, it is Satan's temptation when you are assailed by unbelief, diffidence, by fanatics, superstition, witchcraft, and the like. When you feel such temptations, go running to the Lord's Prayer! You have the promise that God will deliver you from the temptation of the flesh, the world, and the devil. Our whole life is nothing but temptation by these three, the flesh, the world, the devil. Therefore pray: Father, let not our flesh seduce us, let not the world deceive us, let not the devil cast us down. Thus these six petitions deal with very great matters and needs. Whatever needs are in the world, they are included in the Lord's Prayer. And all the prayers in the Psalms and all the prayers which could ever be devised are in the Lord's Prayer.

"But deliver us from evil"

In the Greek it is *ponēros*. We receive evil from everything which hurts us. Its whole meaning points to the devil. We can sum it up this way: Deliver us from the wicked devil, who hinders everything we have previously been talking about; from that wicked one, evil one, deliver us! Nevertheless, you must include in this "evil" everything on earth which is evil, such as sickness, poverty, death, whatever evil there is in the dominion of Satan, of which there is very much on earth. For who can count all the evils? A child becomes sick, and so forth. In short: Deliver us from the devil! Then the name of God will be hallowed, his kingdom come, and his will be done, and we shall be delivered from all things.

First, we are commanded to pray; second, the promise [is given]; third, there are so many and such great needs, which ought to drive us to prayer. And finally, a form and way to pray has been prescribed for us.

Prayer, then, requires first that one lay before God the needs or perils, all of which are included in the Lord's Prayer. The first three petitions deal with the most important matters of all. We do not pray the petitions like clods, who pay no heed to the magnitude of the things we pray for, who seek only food for the belly, gold, and so forth, not caring about how we may become good, how we may have the pure Word and live holy lives, not caring that the will of God is hindered by the devil, who throws himself athwart to prevent its being done. We pray, therefore, that he trample the devil under foot and subject us to himself. Likewise there is great need to pray for the bread we eat, for grain, cattle, and the like, and for all that we have, in order that we may know that all this comes to us from God. But we are always falling down and hence we have a bad conscience; therefore we pray: "Forgive us our trespasses." In these seven petitions are found all our anxieties, needs, and perils, which we ought to bring to God. They are great petitions, indeed, but God, who wills to do great things, is greater. Therefore, let us learn to pray well since God wants us to do this. Then we shall experience the power of God, through which he is able to give us great things, to make us good, to keep the Word, to give us a holy life and all else. He allows such manifold perils to come upon us in order that we may learn to pray and experience his help in our great evils. This is our great consolation.

There you have, then, the three parts, which you children and you other simple folk should learn. First, the Ten Commandments, what I should do and what I should not do. Second, what kind of a God our God is, what is his name and his nature. Third, how we are to get it [his help]. These three parts the holy apostles and fathers put together in order that they should be known by all in common. And yet there is nothing in the Creed about the sacraments, nothing about secular power, about the office of bishops, and so on. It should be an *institutio*, that is, an instruction for the children and simple Christians. What is to be taught beyond this simple instruction, this is the responsibility of the preachers, who rule Christendom, in order that they may defend and uphold the church. When you know these three parts, you still do not have an adequate defense; for you do not know the reasons why this or another article is true. A preacher, however, must be instructed in the Word of God in order that he may be able to defend the church. Therefore, we do not say that everything that Christianity must know is included in these three parts. But there is enough there for the sucklings until they grow up. There are others in the state who educate children, others go off to war. Some have food and drink, others bear arms. So it is here, when these three parts are preached, we have only taught the catechism. Later, when they are grown up, we will preach to them on how to fight. A mother does not immediately give wine, bread, and meat to her child, but milk.

Next we shall deal with the two sacraments. The catechism was the teaching by which one prepared the people for receiving the sacrament [of the altar].

ON BAPTISM

You have heard the three parts, which we call the catechism [*Kinderlehre*] or common Christian teaching, set forth as simply and plainly as I can. On the two following days we shall deal with the two sacraments, which also belong here. For every Christian ought also to know these two sacraments.

Baptism is recorded in the last chapter of Mark: "Go into all the world and preach the gospel to the whole creation. He who believes and is baptized will be saved; but he who does not believe will be condemned" [Mark 16:15-16]. Even if a person is baptized but is without faith, he is lost. But we shall at this time omit discussion of that which serves us in disputation and controversy with the adversaries. In connection with baptism the words themselves, which are recorded here, must be understood. These every person must know. In the first place, note the command of God, which is very stern when he says: "He who believes and is baptized will be saved; but he who does not believe will be condemned" [Mark 16:16]. This is a strict command; if a person wants to be saved, let him be baptized; otherwise he is in God's disfavor. Therefore, these words are in the first place a strict, earnest divine command. Hence you cannot hold the opinion that baptism is a human invention or any kind of command or thing, such as putting a wreath on one's head; it is God's command. Consequently, you must esteem baptism as something high, glorious, and excellent; for here there is a divine word and command, which institutes and confirms baptism. If in former times you considered it a splendid and precious thing when the establishment of an altar was confirmed by a letter of the pope, then esteem baptism a thousand times more since it is instituted and ordained by God. If you look upon baptism as being only water, then you will consider it to be a paltry and ordinary thing.

Therefore, if you are asked what baptism is, you should not answer, as the fanatics do, that it is a handful of water, which is no good, that the Spirit, the Spirit must do it; the bathhouse servant, the minister, that is, effects nothing; therefore the Spirit should be present. But you should say: Baptism is water comprehended and sanctified in God's commandment and Word, that is, a divine and holy water because of God's commandment. The fanatics, the scoundrels rip off God's Word. If I skin a cow, it isn't worth much; but if I take the meat with the hide, it is worth four guldens. Therefore say that baptism is a living, saving water on account of the Word of God which is in it. The Word of God, however, is greater than heaven and earth, sun, moon, and all angels. Don't look at the water, and see that it is wet, but rather that it has with it the Word of God. It is a holy, living, heavenly, blessed water because of the Word and command of God, which is holy. You cannot sufficiently extol it; who can ever sufficiently extol God's Word? And all this comes in baptism because God's Word is in baptism. This is the way I also speak of parents and neighbors. If I look at a father, seeing only that he has a nose, that he is flesh and blood, with bones, limbs, skin and hair, or likewise a mother, if I do not look upon her otherwise than that, I am not seeing her at all, but trampling her under foot. But when the fourth commandment is added, then I see them adorned with a glorious crown and golden chain, which is the Word of God. And that shows you why you should honor this flesh and blood of your parents for the sake of God's Word. This the fanatics do not consider, nor can they do it, because they abominate the Word. The round halo which is painted around the heads of saints is around the heads of parents too. The golden halo or diadem came from the heathen. Later it became a garland, then flowers were added, and now it has become the bishop's mitre.

This Word of power is painted around the heads of parents as a diadem, just as if the majesty and the Word of God were painted about their heads.

So it is with baptism. Certainly when the devil sees baptism and hears the Word sounding, to him it is like a bright sun and he will not stay there, and when a person is baptized for the sake of the Word of God, which is in it, there is a veritable oven glow. Do you think it was a joke that the heavens were opened at Christ's baptism? [Matt. 3:16]. Say, therefore, that baptism is water and God's Word comprehended in one. Take the Word away and it is the same water with which the maid waters the cow; but with the Word, it is a living, holy, divine water. He who considers the words: "will be saved" [Mark 16:16] will find it [salvation]; for with his words, "will be saved," Christ puts salvation into baptism. Therefore it is impossible that this should be simple water when through it salvation, forgiveness of sins, and redemption from death and the devil is given.

But nobody believes what an excellent thing is in these words. The fanatics laugh at us and say: You neo-papists teach the people to trust in water. But when I ask them: What do you say about these words, "He who believes and is baptized will be saved"? they flutter away. So you say to them: We do not teach that one should trust in water, but we do teach that the water, when it becomes one thing with God's Word, is baptism. The water does not do it because of itself, but rather because of the Word, which is connected with it. But if you take away the Word, then don't go telling us that baptism is useless water. Then it is a figment of the devil, who is seeking to sow bad seed among us. You hear your Savior say: If you believe and are baptized, then salvation follows, not because of the water, but because you believe the Word. It is not for nothing that I insist so emphatically that you say that baptism is natural, physical water connected with the Word of God. When these two come together, water and the Word of God, then it is a baptism.

But, you say, can water benefit me? No. What then? Baptism. But isn't it water? No; for it is water connected with the Word of God; therefore it must be something other than water. That's why we declare that the water amounts to nothing, but baptism does. Therefore baptism is water with the Word of God, and this is the essence and whole substance of baptism. When, therefore, water and God's Word are conjoined, it must necessarily be a holy and divine water, for as the Word is, so the water becomes also.

Furthermore, the benefit of baptism must also be learned. If baptism is water with the Word of God, what is its purpose, work, fruit, and benefit? It saves those who believe, as the words say. A child is baptized, not in order that it may become a prince; it is baptized in order that it may be saved, as the words say, that is, in order that it may be redeemed from sin, death, and the devil, that it may become a member of Christ, and that it may come into Christ's kingdom and Christ become its Lord. Accordingly, baptism is useful to the end that through it we may be saved. There you have the transcendent excellence of baptism. The first honor is that it is a divine water, and when you see a baptism remember that the heavens are opened. The fruit is that it saves, redeems you from sin, liberates you from the devil, and leads you to Christ. The fanatics insist that one must first become holy. But I am not contending with them now, but teaching the simple.

Thirdly, that we may know the person who should be baptized: Who should receive baptism? The one who believes is the person to whom the blessed, divine water is to be imparted. If you believe that through this water you will be saved, it becomes a fact. The first point, therefore, is that baptism is water connected with God's Word. The second is the fruit, and the third is that the person who believes is the one who is worthy of baptism. Here some excellent things might be said; but you simple people, note these three points! The little word "believe" leaves no room for either works or monks' cowls. It does not say: he who obeys his parents, but: he who believes.

Here we meet the question whether children who are baptized believe? He who is simple, let him dismiss these questions and refer them to me or answer this way: I know that infant baptism pleases God; I know that I was baptized as a child; I know that I have the Holy Spirit, for this I have the interpretation of the Scriptures themselves. If the baptism of children were nothing, then certainly there would not be a single person on earth who would truly speak a single word about Christ [i.e., a Christian]. But since Christ most certainly bestows the Holy Spirit [and thus confirms baptism], for Bernard, Bonaventura, Gerson, and John Huss had the Spirit, because this is God's work, believe therefore that infant baptism is true. How do you know this? I see the wonderful works of God, I see that he has sanctified many and given them the Holy Spirit. Therefore you tell [the adversaries] that children are truly baptized and say: I prove it by the works [of God]. It is known by its fruit; if there is fruit, there must be a tree. Furthermore, for me the Word of God weighs a thousand times more, etc. But this becomes a bit more learned.

Note well, therefore, that baptism is water with the Word of God, not water and my faith. My faith does not make the baptism but rather receives the baptism, no matter whether the person being baptized believes or not; for baptism is not dependent upon my faith but upon God's Word. If today a Jew were to be baptized, who was seeking only the sponsor's christening gift, and we baptized him nevertheless, the baptism would be genuine, for it is God's Word with water. And even though the Jew did not believe, the baptism would nevertheless not be false. Likewise, if I administer the sacrament to someone who cherishes anger or the like, he nevertheless receives the true body [and the true blood of Christ]. Therefore it is false to say that infants do not believe and therefore should not be baptized. You have already heard that they do believe, because the fruits follow, namely, the gifts of the Holy Spirit. The sacrament [of the Lord's Supper] does not rest upon faith but upon the Word of God, who instituted it, and so it is with baptism also. Even if the children did not believe which, however, is false, the baptism is not to be repeated. Therefore you should say: The baptism was genuine, but I, unfortunately, did not believe it.

These are crude spirits [i.e., the Anabaptists]. I am a learned man and a preacher and I go to the sacrament in the faith of others and in my own faith. Nevertheless, I don't stand on that, I stand on [His words]: "Take; this is my body" [Mark 14:22]. Upon these words I go, and I know that Christ invites me, for he said, "Come to me, all who labor and are heavy-laden, and I will give you rest" [Matt. 11:28]; and this will not deceive me. Thus I certainly have the sacrament. Accordingly, I apply this to baptism and pray that faith may be given to it [the child]. But I do not baptize it upon its faith or someone else's faith, but upon God's Word and command. In my faith I may lie, but he who instituted baptism cannot lie. Therefore say: The children must necessarily be baptized, and their baptism is true, because God grants grace to children who are baptized immediately after their birth, namely, an excelling grace. Otherwise, if baptism were false, it would not manifest this [grace]. Secondly, even if the children did not believe, they must nevertheless not be rebaptized. You fanatics, you say that the earlier baptism was not genuine. This we by no means concede, for baptism is definitive, water with the Word. Therefore Augustine says, "The Word comes to the element, and it becomes a sacrament."[9]

These two sacraments may be received also by an unbeliever. Thus the devil would secretly teach us to build upon our works, and in order to accomplish this more easily he makes a sham of faith and says: If you do not believe then you are not baptized. But it simply does not follow that, if I do not obey my parents, therefore I have no parents; if I do not obey the government, therefore, the government is nothing. So it does not follow here: that person has not received baptism in faith, therefore, the baptism is nothing or is not genuine. Indeed, the baptism was genuine precisely because you did not rightly receive it. The abuse confirms the baptism; it does not deny it. If all of you here were to be baptized today and there were hardly three among you who were holy, the baptism would still not be false, but rather the contrary; for our work and misuse neither make nor unmake God's work. A prince remains a prince, whether you are obedient or not. This the fanatics do not know, for they are blinded; that's why they look at the sacrament without the Word. There is rebellion concealed in this mind, because it always wants to separate God's Word from the person. It wants to tear down the Word; therefore it is a rebel, secretly.

[9] *Lectures or Tractates on the Gospel According to St. John.*

THE LORD'S SUPPER

In the first place, every one of you should know the words with which this sacrament was instituted—for one should not administer the sacrament to those who do not know these words and what they do and perform. Here we are not going to enter into controversy with the blasphemers of this sacrament. You must deal with this sacrament in the same way that you heard with regard to baptism, namely, that the chief point is God's Word and command, just as in the Lord's Prayer, the Creed, and the Ten Commandments. Even though you never believe or keep the Ten Commandments, the Ten Commandments nevertheless exist and remain, and so baptism and the sacrament of the altar also remain baptism and the sacrament of the altar. Even though you never obey your parents, they still remain your parents.

Therefore, the primary thing in the sacrament is the Word: "Jesus took bread, etc." [Matt. 26:26–28]. If you believe it, blessed are you; if not, Christ will still remain faithful. When we die and are snatched away, these errors will come. Nobody wants to look upon it as God's Word; if one does not have regard for it, then it is nothing. In the sacraments, the Ten Commandments, and the Creed, God's Word is the chief thing. Therefore, do not look only upon the water, the bread and wine, but rather connect with them the words, "Take, eat"; "Do this in remembrance of me," and "Drink of it, all of you." Learn these words; in them the sacrament is summed up; if you have lost these words, you have lost the sacrament. The fanatics rip these words out, and the same goes for the pope, because he has concealed them. The Word of God is the chief thing in the sacrament. He who does not know them [the words of institution], let him not come to the sacrament.

Secondly: What is the sacrament of the altar? As baptism is water and God's Word conjoined, so it is here. Here the bread is not the kind of bread the baker bakes, nor is the wine the kind the vintner sells; for he does not give you God's Word with it. But the minister binds God's Word to the bread and the Word is bound to the bread and likewise to the wine, for it is said, "The Word comes to the element, and it becomes a sacrament." In all his lifetime Augustine never said anything better. It is not the word of our prince or the emperor, but of God. Therefore, when you hear this word "is," then do not doubt. Thus the sacrament is bread and body, wine and blood, as the words say and to which they are connected. If, therefore, God speaks these words, then don't search any higher, but take off your hat; and if a hundred thousand devils, learned men, and spirits were to come and say, How can this be? you answer that one single word of God is worth more than all of these. A hundred thousand learned men are not as wise as one little hair of our God. In the first place, therefore, learn that the sacrament is not simply bread and wine, but the body and blood of Christ, as the words say. If you take away the words, you have only bread and wine. Hence the command of God is the greatest thing in the sacrament, as in the Lord's Prayer. Take hold only of the words; they tell you what the sacrament is. If a fornicator comes [to the table], he receives the true sacrament, because it does not lose power on account of his impiety and infidelity. Our unbelief does not alter God's Word. This I have often said. When a whore decks herself with gold, it is still gold. Misuse does not change God's Word. A robber abuses the light of day, the sun, and yet it remains the sun. Christ does not found his sacrament upon our use of it. What he says or ordains remains, no matter whether one uses it rightly or wrongly. The sacrament is body and blood, as the words say, whether it is received by one who is worthy or unworthy.

What is the use or fruit of the sacrament? Listen to this: "given for you"; "shed." I go to the sacrament in order to take and use Christ's body and blood, given and shed for me. When the minister intones, "This cup is the New Testament in my blood," to whom is it sung? Not to my dog, but to those who are gathered to take the sacrament. These words must be apprehended by faith. Therefore I use the sacrament for the forgiveness of my sins; I say: I will go and take the body and the blood; it is a sure sign that it was instituted for me and against my death. "Which is given for you." There is the benefit.

Now follows: Who are those who lay hold of this benefit? He who believes has baptism and he who does not believe does not have it. Likewise, he who believes that the body, which he receives, is given for him, has the fruit of this sacrament. Therefore, he who believes takes his rightful place at this sacrament. That's why I have said that these words are spoken, not to stones or a pillar, but to Christians. "For you." Who does "for you" mean? The door or the window, perhaps? No, those who today hear the words "for you." I am to believe it. If you believe, then you take the sacrament on the strength of these words "for you." Mark only those words! because the words "for you" make the devil more hostile to us. He says to us, My dear fellow, you must not believe this "for you." What is it to you? Drink at home and enjoy yourself! The sacrament doesn't concern you. It is this "you" that makes it our concern, just as in baptism: "He who believes and is baptized will be saved." So here it is: "for you." Therefore, note well and learn well these words! The benefit is: "given for you, shed for you." Why do you go to the sacrament? I go because it is a body and blood which is given and shed for me; that's why I go.

If the sacrament is rightly administered, one should preach, first, that the sacrament is the body and blood of the Lord under the bread and wine, as the words say. Secondly, the benefit: it effects the forgiveness of sins, as the words say, "which is shed for the remission of sins."

Beyond this I admonish you to prepare yourselves for it. Since it is the sacrament in which there is the forgiveness of sins, it is not to be despised. It is true that a large number of you come, and yet there are some among you who are so strong that they have not come once in five years. But you should go because you are the ones who need it most of all! And above all note these words, "for the remission of sins," as the pledge of the sacrament which assures us that we have the forgiveness of sins because it is proclaimed, not to a stone, but to you and to me. Otherwise the minister might as well keep silent. I remind you again of this small particle: "for you."

Remember to include yourself in this "for you." Therefore let each one see to it that he comes to the sacrament himself and his family, if they want to be Christians. When you stay away so much, now that you have liberty to go to the sacrament, we see the attitude with which you came to it under the pope, when you came only by coercion. As only a few do good works, so only a few go to the sacrament. Formerly we were forced to go because we were driven. But now that nobody compels us we neglect it. I do not compel you to come to the preaching. But God ought to move you to come; for he requires it of you that you should hear and learn his Word. If you don't want to obey him, [then don't]. So neither do I compel you to come to the sacrament. What does it matter to me and the chaplains if you don't want to listen and receive the sacrament? You have four doors here—go on out! But he who is above says: If you want to be a Christian, if you want to have forgiveness of sins and eternal life, then come here! There stands your God; he offers you his body and blood, broken and shed for you. If you want to despise God and neglect the forgiveness of sins, then stay away. So I do not compel you, but Christ pleads with you lovingly. If you despise this, then you see to it! We are saying what your God is offering to you. Accordingly, I beg you to hold to the sacrament, for your sakes, not ours. There are now few boys and girls and women who come. I know that you are not holier than Peter. It really grieves me that you are so cold in your attitude toward it. If you will not do it for God's sake and my sake, then do it for the sake of your own necessity, which is exceedingly great, namely, your sins and death. There is the temptation of adultery, of fornication, avarice, hatred, pride, envy, of unbelief and despair, and you do not consider how you are ever going to get out of them, and you grow altogether cold in that ungodliness. But listen to what Christ says here: "for you." He did not give it to you as a poison; he did not say: Take and eat, this shall be your poison, or that this food should harm us, but rather free us from sin, devil, and death. But that's the attitude we take; as if it were poison. Here you have medicine, not poison. When a person is sick he can soon find an apothecary, a doctor. But who seeks this physician, who has given his body? Do you still not see your sickness; don't you want forgiveness of sins? Why do you avoid it as if it were poison? It is true that it is poison to those who sin, as formerly the priests committed fornication. But in itself it is not a poison but an antidote, which means salvation, blessedness, life, forgiveness of sins. Certainly you will find that you are full of envy, inclined to all kinds of villainy, to greed and the like. You fear death, you sense your unbelief. This certainly is lack enough. Then say: The sacrament is not given to those who are sick as a poison but as a remedy. See to it, then, that you seek the sacrament for your betterment when you find yourself in an hour of peril of life, when the flesh drives you, the world entices you, and Satan assails you. And beyond this it is of even greater benefit, etc.

Therefore, do not be so cold toward it. We are not forcing you, but you ought to come of your own free will. It is my duty to instruct you as to the reason why you should come, namely, your need, not a command, for you feel the infirmity of your faith and your propensity to all evil. These perils should move you without any command whatsoever. It is not the pope, not the emperor, not the duke who compels me, but my own need compels me. Therefore, take a better attitude now toward the sacrament and also keep your children to it when they come to understanding. For this is how we know which are Christians and which are not. If you will not go, then let the young people come; for us so much depends upon them. If you do not do it, we shall take action against you. For even if you adults want to go to the devil, we shall nevertheless seek after your children.

The need [which drives us to the sacrament] is that sin, devil, and death are always present. The benefit is that we receive forgiveness of sins and the Holy Spirit. Here, not poison, but a remedy and salvation is given, in so far as you acknowledge that you need it. Don't say: I am not fit today, I will wait a while. This is a trick of the devil. What will you do if you are not fit when death comes? Who will make you fit then? Say rather: Neither preacher, prince, pope, nor emperor compels me, but my great need and, beyond this, the benefit.

First, the sacrament is Christ's body and blood in bread and wine comprehended in the Word. Secondly, the benefit is forgiveness of sins. This includes the need and the benefit. Thirdly, those who believe should come.

——— ——— ———

SERMON IN
CASTLE PLEISSENBURG,
LEIPZIG, 1539[1]

[*This is a sermon on the Church, a theme naturally appropriate to the occasion of the inauguration of the Reformation in Leipzig. Twenty years before, the famous Leipzig debate had taken place there. Now the city of Leipzig had joined the Reformation.*]

Because I cannot depend upon my head, owing to physical infirmity, to venture upon expounding the doctrine in its entirety, I shall adhere by God's grace to the text of the Gospel which is customarily dealt with in the churches on the morrow.

These words of the Lord Christ, "If a man loves me, he will keep my word, etc." [John 14:23], were occasioned by the fact that shortly before this the Lord Christ had expressed himself in almost the same way: "He who has my commandments and keeps them, he it is who loves me . . . and I will love him and manifest myself to him" [John 14:21]. For this reason the good Judas (not Iscariot) asked, "Lord, how is it that you will manifest yourself to us, and not to the world?" [John 14:22]. It is to this question that the Lord Christ is replying here. And here one sees the fleshly and Jewish notions which the apostles held; they were hoping for a worldly kingdom of the Lord Christ and they wanted to be the chief ones in that kingdom. Already they had disputed about who should

[1] Reprinted by permission of the publisher from *Luther's Works*, volume 51, Sermons: 1, edited and translated by John W. Doberstein (Philadelphia: Muhlenberg Press, 1959), pp. 303–12.

be the greatest in that kingdom [Mark 9:34] and had divided
it up into provinces. To this day the Jews have this same attitude and they hope for an earthly messiah.

Thus since the Lord Christ said here, "He who has my commandments and keeps them, him will I love and manifest myself to him" [John 14:21], Judas says: Are we to be the only
ones? Is it to be such a meager revelation and manifestation?
Will it not be manifest to the whole world, including the Jews
and the Gentiles? What is it going to be? Are we to be the only
ones to inherit you, and the Gentiles know nothing? This false
Jewish delusion was in the apostles and that is why this Gospel
here describes the kingdom of the Lord Christ and paints a
far different picture of it for the disciples. It is as if he were saying: No, the world has a different kingdom, my dear Judas;
that's why I say: If a man loves me, he will keep my word,
and I will be with him along with my Father and the Holy
Spirit and make our home with him. This home is God's dwelling, as Jerusalem was called the dwelling of God, which he
himself chose as his own: Here is my hearth, my house and
dwelling [Isa. 31:9]; just as today the churches are called
God's dwellings on account of the Word and sacraments. Here
I think that Christ is pronouncing a severe judgment, here he
is prophesying and forgetting the dwelling of Jerusalem, of
which all the prophets said: Here will I dwell forever. This
dwelling the Lord Christ pulls down and erects and builds a
new dwelling, a new Jerusalem, not made of stones and wood,
but rather: If a man loves me and keeps my Word, there shall
be my castle, my chamber, my dwelling.

In saying this Christ gave the answer to the argument concerning the true church; for to this day you hear our papists
boasting and saying: the church, the church! It is true that
Christ wants to have his home where the Father and the Holy
Spirit want to be and to dwell. The entire Trinity dwells in
the true church; what the true church does and directs is done
and directed by God. Now the new church is a different dwelling from that of Jerusalem; he tears down all the prophecies
concerning Jerusalem, as if Jerusalem were nothing in his eyes,
and he builds another dwelling, the Christian church. Here
we agree with the papists that there is one Christian church;
but Christ wants to be everywhere in the land. These are fine,

heart-warming words—that God wants to come down to us, God wants to come to us and we do not need to clamber up to him, he wants to be with us to the end of the world: Here dwells the Holy Spirit, effecting and creating everything in the Christian church.

But what is the dissension about between the papists and us? The answer is: about the true Christian church. Should one then be obedient to the Christian church? Yes, certainly, all believers owe this obedience; for St. Peter commands in the fourth chapter of his first Epistle: "Whoever speaks" should speak "as one who utters oracles of God" [I Pet. 4:11]. If anybody wants to preach, let him suppress his own words and let them prevail in worldly and domestic affairs; here in the church he should speak nothing but the Word of this rich Householder; otherwise it is not the true church. This is why it must always be said that it is God who is speaking. After all, this is the way it must be in this world; if a prince wants to rule, his voice must be heard in his country and his house. And if this happens in this miserable life, so much the more must we let God's Word resound in the church and in eternal life. All subjects and governments must be obedient to the Word of their Lord. This is called administration. Therefore a preacher conducts the household of God by virtue and on the strength of his commission and office, and he dare not say anything different from what God says and commands. And even though there may be a lot of talk which is not the Word of God, the church is not in all this talk, even though they begin to yell like mad. All they do is to shriek: church, church! Listen to the pope and the bishops!

But when they are asked: What is the Christian church? What does it say and do? they reply: The church looks to the pope, cardinals, and bishops. This is not true! Therefore we must look to Christ and listen to him as he describes the true Christian church in contrast to their phony shrieking. For one should and one must rather believe Christ and the apostles, that one must speak God's Word and do as St. Peter and here the Lord Christ says: He who keeps my Word, there is my dwelling, there is the Builder, my Word must remain in it; otherwise it shall not be my house. Our papists want to improve on this, and therefore they may be in peril. Christ says:

"We will make our home with him"; there the Holy Spirit will be at work. There must be a people that loves me and keeps my commandments. Quite bluntly, this is what he wants.

Here Christ is not speaking of how the church is built, as he spoke above concerning the dwelling. But when it has been built, then the Word must certainly be there, and a Christian should listen to nothing but God's Word. Elsewhere, in worldly affairs, he hears other things, how the wicked should be punished and the good protected, and about the economy. But here in the Christian church it should be a house in which only the Word of God resounds. Therefore let them shriek themselves crazy with their cry: church, church! Without the Word of God it is nothing. My dear Christians are steadfast confessors of the Word, in life and in death. They will not forsake this dwelling, so dearly do they love this Prince. Whether in favor or not, for this they will leave country and people, body and life. Thus we read of a Roman centurion, a martyr, who, when he was stripped of everything, said, "This I know; they cannot take away from me my Lord Christ." Therefore a Christian says: This Christ I must have, though it cost me everything else; what I cannot take with me can go; Christ alone is enough for me. Therefore all Christians should stand strong and steadfast upon the Word alone, as St. Peter says, "by the strength which God supplies" [I Pet. 4:11].

Behold, how it all happens in weakness. Look at baptism, it is water; where does the hallowing and the power come from? From the pope? No, it comes from God, who says, "He who believes and is baptized" [Mark 16:16]. For the pope puts trust in the consecrated water. Why, pope? Who gave you the power? The *ecclesia*, the church? Yes, indeed, where is it written? Nowhere! Therefore the consecrated water is Satan's goblin bath [*Kobelbad*], which cripples, blinds, and consecrates the people without the Word. But in the church one should teach and preach nothing besides or apart from the Word of God. For the pastor who does the baptizing says: It is not I who baptize you; I am only the instrument of the Father, Son, and Holy Spirit; this is not my work.

Likewise, the blessed sacrament is not administered by men, but rather by God's command; we only lend our hands to it. Do you think this is an insignificant meal, which feeds not only the soul but also the mortal body of a poor, condemned sinner for the forgiveness of sins in order that the body too may live? This is God's power, this Householder's power, not men's.

So also in the absolution, when a distressed sinner is pardoned. By what authority and command is he pardoned? Not by human command, but by God's command. Behold, here by God's power I deliver you from the kingdom of the devil and transfer you to the kingdom of God [Col. 1:13]. So it is too with our prayer, which gains all things from God, not through its own power, or because it is able to do this, but because it trusts in God's promise. In the world you see how hard it is to approach the Roman emperor and gain help; but a devout Christian can always come to God with a humble, believing prayer and be heard.

In short, the Word and the Holy Spirit, who prepares us for prayer, are in God's power. It is the Word which we believe —this is what makes our hearts so bold that we dare to call ourselves the children of the Father. Where does this come from? The answer is: From God, who teaches us to pray in the Lord's Prayer and puts into our hands the book of Psalms. For if we prayed without faith, this would be to curse twice over, as we learned in our nasty papistical holiness. But where there is a believing heart and that heart has before it the promise of God it quite simply and artlessly prays its "Our Father" and is heard. Outside of this church of God you may present your prayers and supplications to great lords and potentates to the best of your ability, but here you have no ability to pray except in Christ Jesus, in order that we may not boast that we are holy as they do in the papacy, who protest, of course, and say: Oh, it would be a presumption for anybody to call himself holy and fit; and yet they teach that man of himself has a "certain preparation" for prayer.

They also teach prayer according to this doctrine in their chants and say: I have prayed in despair as a poor sinner. Oh, stop that kind of praying! It would be better to drop such praying altogether if you despair. For despair ruins everything and if you go to baptism, prayer, and the sacrament without faith and in despair, you are actually mocking God. What you should quickly say, however, is this: I am certain that my dear God has so commanded and that he has assured me of the forgiveness of sins; therefore I will baptize, absolve, and pray. And immediately you will receive this treasure in your heart. It does not depend on our worthiness or unworthiness, for both of these can only make us despair. Therefore do not allow yourself by any means to be driven to despair. For it is a mockery of God when we do not believe the words, "Go and baptize" [Matt. 28:19], that is, baptize those who repent and are sorry for their sins. Here you hear that this is not human work, but the work of God the Father; he is the Householder who wills to dwell here. But if we despair, then we should stay away from the sacrament and from prayer, and first learn to say: All right, it makes no difference that I am unworthy, God is truthful nevertheless, and he has most certainly promised and assured us; I'll stake my life on this.

And this we did not know under the papacy. Indeed, I, Martin Luther, for a long time could not find my way out of this papistical dream, because they were constantly blathering to me about my worthiness and unworthiness. Therefore, you young people, learn to know the church rightly.

Concerning penitence or penance we teach that it consists in the acknowledgment of sins and genuine trust in God, who forgives them all for Christ's sake. The pope, on the contrary, does nothing but scold and devise intolerable burdens; and besides he knows nothing of grace and faith, much less does he teach what the Christian church really is.

But don't you forget the main point here, namely, that God wants to make his dwelling here. Therefore, when the hand is laid upon your head and the forgiveness of sins is proclaimed to you in the words: "I absolve you from all your sins in the name of Christ," you should take hold of this Word with a sure faith and be strengthened out of the mouth of the preacher. And this is what Christ and St. Peter are saying: He, the Lord, wants to dwell in this church; the Word alone must resound in it.

In short, the church is a dwelling, in order that God may be loved and heard. Not wood or stones, not dumb animals, it should be people, who know, love, and praise God. And that you may be able to trust God with certainty in all things, including cross and suffering, you should know that it is the true church, even though it be made up of scarcely two believing persons. That's why Christ says: He who loves me keeps my Word; there I will dwell, there you have my church.

So now you must guard yourselves against the pope's church, bedaubed and bedizened with gold and pearls; for here Christ teaches us the opposite. To love God and keep his Word is not the pope's long robe and crown, nor even his decretals. There is a great difference between what God commands and what men command. Look how the pope brazenly announces—we should invoke the saints and conduct ourselves according to his human precepts. Does God's Word command this too? I still do not see it. But this I know very well, that God's Word says: I, Christ, go to the Father, and he who believes in me will be saved. For I, I have suffered for him and I also give him the Holy Spirit from on high.

So the Lord Christ and the pope each have their own church, but with this mighty difference, which Christ himself, the best dialectitian [*der beste Dialecticus*], here describes, telling us what it is and where it is, namely, where his Word is purely preached. So where you hear this, there you may know that this is the true church. For where the Word of God is not present, there also are no true-believing confessors and martyrs. And if the Word of God were lacking, then we would have been deceived by Christ; then he really would have betrayed us!

Oh, if we could only stake it all on Christ and mock and laugh at the pope, since Christ clearly says here, not "he who has my Word," but "he who keeps it loves me" and is also my disciple. There are many of you who have the Word, true enough, but do not keep it, and in time of trouble and trial fall away altogether and deny Christ.

It would, of course, be desirable if we could always have both: the Word and our temporal crumbs, but the good venison, peace, is very scarce in the kingdom of heaven. It is therefore something which must be recognized as a great blessing of God when there is peace among temporal lords and mutual understanding. But if not, then let them all go—goods, fame, wife, and child—if only this treasure remain with us.

I fear, however, that unfortunately there will be among us many weathercocks, false brethren, and suchlike weeds; and yet I am not going to be a prophet, because I must prophesy nothing but evil, and who would presume to be able to fathom it all? It will turn out all right; now we have it, let us see to it that we hold on to it. But let us be valiant against Satan, who intends to sift us like wheat [cf. Luke 22:31]. For it may well be that you will have your bit of bread under a good government and then the devil will soon set a snare for you in your security and presumption, so that you will no longer trust and give place to the Word of God as much as you did before. That's why Christ says: My sheep not only hear me, they also obey and follow me [John 10:3–5]; they increase in faith daily through hearing the Word of God and the right and perfect use of the blessed sacraments. There is strengthening and comfort in this church. And it is also the true church, not cowls, tonsures, and long robes, of which the Word of God knows nothing, but rather wherever two or three are gathered together [Matt. 18:20], no matter whether it be on the ocean or in the depths of the earth, if only they have before them the Word of God and believe and trust in the same, there is most certainly the real, ancient, true, apostolic church.

But we were so blinded in the papacy that, even though St. Peter tells us that "we have the prophetic word made more sure" and that we "do well to pay attention to this as to a lamp shining in a dark place" [II Pet. 1:19], we still cannot see what a bright light we have in the gospel. Therefore we must note here once again the description of the Christian church which Christ gives us, namely, that it is a group of people who not only have his Word but also love and keep it and forsake everything for the sake of love.

From this then you can answer the screamers and spitters who have nothing in their gabs but "church! church!": Tell me, dear pope, what is the church? Answer: the pope and his cardinals. Oh, listen to that; you dunce, where is it written in God's Word that Father Pope and Brother Cardinal are the true church? Was it because that was what the fine parrot bird said to the black jackdaw?

But Christ tells you and me something far different. He says: My church is where my Word is preached purely and is unadulterated and kept. Therefore St. Paul warns that we should flee and avoid those who would lead us away from God's Word, for if anyone defiles God's temple, which we are, God will destroy him [I Cor. 3:17]. And St. Peter also says: Take heed, if you are going to preach, then you should preach nothing but God's Word [I Pet. 4:11], otherwise you will defile God's church.

Hence it is again to be diligently noted how Christ described his church for us; for this description is a strong thunderbolt against the miserable pope and his decretals by which he has made of the church of God a filthy privy.[2]

If anybody wants to teach human precepts, let him do so in secular and domestic affairs and leave the church alone. After all, the papists are really empty spewers and talkers, since Christ himself here says: He who hears my Word and keeps it, to him will I and my Father come and make our home with him. This is the end of Jerusalem and Moses; here there is to be a little band of Christ, [Heufflein Christi], who hear God's Word and keep the same and rely upon it in every misfortune. This is my church. This Lord we shall believe, even though the pope blow his top over it.

But in these words Christ was also answering the apostle Judas, who also allowed himself to imagine that Christ would become a great secular emperor and that they, the apostles, would become great lords in the nations when he should manifest himself. But how wrong he was! Here Christ tells them straight out that his kingdom is not of this world, but that they and all believers should be that kingdom of heaven in which God the Father, Son, and Holy Spirit himself dwells. He does not install angels, emperors, kings, princes, and lords in that church. He himself wants to be the householder and be the only one to speak and act; there I will dwell, he says, and with me all believers from everlasting to everlasting.

But Judas, the good man, still cannot understand this and therefore the Holy Spirit must come and teach it to him. Of this future and this ministry, dear Christians, you will hear tomorrow, God willing. If I cannot do it, then it will be done by others who can do it better than I, though they will not admit it. Let this today serve as an introduction or the morning sermon. May the Lord help us, I cannot go on further now.

[2] The original repeats this in Latin: *contra Papam, qui fecit ex Ecclesia cloacam*, and also includes an untranslatable play on words: *Decret* and *Secret* (privy).

THE PAGAN SERVITUDE
OF THE CHURCH[1]

[The Pagan Servitude of the Church, *more commonly
known as* The Babylonian Captivity of the Church, *belongs
to the series of pivotal writings of 1520. Chief among the back-
ground factors precipitating Luther's writing are undoubtedly
the withholding of the cup in the Mass from the laity and the
fact that he had been excommunicated. In that setting, Luther addresses himself to the total sacramental understanding
of the Roman Church and, in contrast, develops a Biblical
and Reformation conception of the sacraments and of the
Church. In reading this document, it is well to remember that
it was written on the eve of developments which led to the
organization of Reformation churches. It represents a theological viewpoint which made the Reformation necessary.*]

JESUS

Martin Luther, Augustinian, to his friend, Hermann
Tulich,[2] greetings.

As long as there are so very many outstanding masters
urging me on and making me work, I cannot help becoming
more of a scholar every·day. It is two years since I wrote on

[1] Reprinted by permission of the publisher from *The Reformation Writings of Martin Luther*, volume 1, *The Basis of the
Protestant Reformation*, translated and edited by Bertram Lee
Woolf (London: Lutterworth Press, 1953), pp. 208–329.
[2] Went to Wittenberg as a student at the same time as Luther
arrived as professor. Graduated B.A. in 1511, and D.D. in 1520.
Rector of Wittenberg 1525–26.

indulgences, but I now greatly regret having published that little book.[3] At that time I was still entangled in the gross superstitions of a masterful Rome, but I still thought that indulgences ought not to be wholly rejected, as they had received the approval of a very large number of people. My attitude was not strange, for otherwise I should have been alone in trying to move the mountain. Afterwards, thanks to Sylvester, and helped by those friars who strenuously defended indulgences, I saw that these were simply impositions on the part of the hypocrites of Rome to rob men of their money and their faith in God. I now wish I could prevail upon the booksellers, and persuade all my readers, to burn the whole of my booklets on indulgences, and, instead of all I have written on this subject, to adopt the following proposition:

Indulgences are Evils devised by the Toadies at Rome

Meantime Eck, Emser,[4] and their compeers began to read me a lesson on the primacy of the pope. Lest I should appear to be ungrateful to such learned men, I hereby confess that their works have benefited me greatly. Although I denied divine jurisdiction to the papacy, I admitted a human jurisdiction. But when I had heard and read the most ingenious argument put forward by these five gentlemen to establish their idol in a workmanlike manner, and as I am not entirely lacking in intelligence in such matters, I saw clearly that the papacy was to be understood as the kingdom of Babylon and the régime of Nimrod, the mighty hunter. Hence once again, and in order that my friends may be well on the right side, I beg both the booksellers and my readers to burn whatever I have published on this subject. Instead, let them adopt this proposition:

[3] *Resolutiones disputationum*, 1518.
[4] Jerome Emser (?1477–1527) once a Humanist professor in Erfurt, when Luther was a student; later, secretary to duke George of Saxony.

The Papacy provides Grand Hunting for the Bishop of Rome

This is proved by the arguments put forward by Eck, Emser, and the Leipzig lecturer on the Bible.[5]

They pretend to school me in regard to communion in both kinds,[6] and a few other subjects of the highest importance. Here again I had to be watchful that I overlooked nothing while listening to these eminent masters. A certain Italian friar of Cremona[7] has written a *Revocation of Martin Luther to the Holy See.* In this work he makes it sound as if I have revoked something, whereas he means that he recalls me; but that is the way Italians of to-day are writing Latin. Another friar, a German of Leipzig, who is a "Lecturer on the Whole Bible" and one known to you, has written again about the sacraments in both kinds,[8] and, as I hear, is about to produce some bigger books which will be marvels. The Italian has taken the precaution of writing anonymously, perhaps warned by the examples I made of Cajetan[9] and Sylvester. But the Leipzig Lecturer, as befits a vigorous and hefty German, uses a great many lines on his title-page to proclaim his name, his life, his sanctity, his knowledge, his fame, his honours, and almost his wooden shoes.[10] Without doubt, there is much for me to learn from this book, for he has dedicated it to the Son of God Himself; so intimate are these saintly men with the Christ who reigns on high. It seems to me that three magpies are now speaking, the first in good Latin, the second in better Greek, and the third in excellent Hebrew. Surely, my dear Hermann, I can do no other than prick up my ears. The discussion is being conducted in Leipzig by the Observants of the Holy Cross.

Heretofore, in my folly, I thought it would be a fine thing if a General Council were to decree that the sacraments should be administered to the laity in both kinds. But our

[5] Augustine Alveld.
[6] Consisting of both bread and wine.
[7] Isidoro Isolani, *Revocatio Martini Lutherii Augustini ad sanctam Sedem.*
[8] Augustine Alveld, *Tractatus de communione sub utraque specie.*
[9] Head of his Order and leader of the school of Thomists, he was regarded as the foremost theologian in Rome.
[10] The Observants wore sandals with wooden soles.

exceedingly learned friar corrects this view, and says that the offering of both kinds to the laity is neither commanded, nor advised, by Christ or the Apostles, but that it was left to the judgment of the church whether to do it, or leave it undone; and the church must be obeyed. That is his contention.

Perhaps you will ask, What extravagances are upsetting him? or Whom is he attacking? I myself have never condemned the use of one kind, and I have deferred to the judgment of the church whether it should decree the use of both kinds. This is just what he himself is trying to assert in order to attack me. My reply is that that way of conducting an argument is the same as that adopted by all those who write against me. They attack either what they themselves affirm, or some enemy of their own invention. This was the way of Sylvester, Eck, Emser, and of the people in Cologne and Louvain. The present friar would have been a renegade to their spirit if he had not written against me.

But this good man has been more fortunate than the rest; he set out to prove that the use of both kinds was neither decreed nor advised, but left to the decision of the church. Then he adduces Scripture, out of which he proves that the use of one kind by the laity was decreed by Christ. The result is, according to this Biblical exegete, that the use of one kind was both commanded, and yet, at the same time, not commanded by Christ. You understand of course that this new way of arguing is peculiar to the usage of the logicians of Leipzig. In his earlier booklet,[11] Emser professed he would be fair to me. Yet when convicted by me of base envy and dirty falsehoods, he confessed in his later book,[12] which was intended to confute me, that both writings were true, and that what he had written had been fair and also foul. A fine fellow for you— as you are aware!

But listen to this specious advocate of the use of one kind, who professes to follow the will of the church and also the commandment of Christ, and yet again, both the commandment of Christ and the absence of such commandment. With this dexterous twist, he proves that the one kind is to be given to the laity by the commandment of Christ, i.e., the will of

---

[11] De disputatione Lipsicensi, 1519.
[12] A venatione Luteriana Aegocerotis Assertio, 1519.

the church. He uses capital letters for this truth and calls it:
THE INFALLIBLE FOUNDATION. He then proceeds to handle
John 6 [:48–63] with incredible skill. In this passage, Christ
speaks of Himself as the bread of heaven and the bread of
life. But our scholar applies these words to the bread of the
altar, and goes further. Because Christ had said: "I am the
living bread", and not, "I am the living cup", he concludes
that this passage institutes, for the laity, the sacrament in one
kind. But he learnedly avoids touching the words that follow.
These say: "My flesh is truly food, and my blood is truly
drink"; and, again: "Unless you eat the flesh of the Son of
Man, and drink His blood". But when it entered the friar's
head that these words supported the use of both kinds, and
irrefutably discountenanced the use of only one kind, with
what felicity and learning did he explain it away! He said
that "Christ meant by these words simply that he who partook
of the one kind, partook under this kind of both the body and
the blood"! He puts this forth as the "infallible foundation"
of a structure well worthy of holy and heavenly "Observance".

But let us continue taking lessons from this man; he says
that, in John 6, Christ commands the use of one kind, and
yet prescribes it in such a way that He left it to the will of
the church; and that, moreover, in this chapter, Christ is
speaking only of the laity and not of the priests. Apparently
the bread of life from heaven is not meant for the latter, but
perhaps the bread of death from hell! What, also, of the case
of the deacons and subdeacons, who are neither laymen nor
priests? According to this distinguished writer, they ought to
use neither one kind only, nor both. You will now understand,
my dear Tulich, the new method of applying Scripture that
is found current among the Observants.

But you will also be shown that, in John 6, Christ was
speaking of the sacrament of the Eucharist, although He Himself teaches that He was speaking of faith in the Incarnate
Word when He said: "This is the work of God, that you should
believe in Him whom He sent" [John 6:29]. Truly we must
grant that the Leipzig professor of the Bible can prove anything he pleases from any passage of Scripture whatever. He
is a theologian of the breed of Anaxagoras, if not Aristotle;
nouns and verbs have the same meaning, even when replacing

one another, and they signify anything you like. Throughout his book, he so conjoins passages of Scripture that, if he wishes to prove that Christ is in the sacrament, he might well begin by saying: "The lesson is from the Book of Revelation of the blessed John the Apostle."[13] Everything he says would be as appropriate as this, and the wise fellow thinks that it will enhance the value of his own drivel to quote passages copiously.

I pass over other matters lest I drown you in the sludge of this foul drain. Finally, he adduces Paul, who says in I Corinthians 11 that he received from the Lord, and handed on to the Corinthians, the use of the bread and the cup. Here once more this distinguisher of kinds, as everywhere in his egregious application of Scripture, teaches that Paul, in this passage, permitted, but did not hand on, the use of both kinds. Do you ask where he found the proof? In his own head, just as he did with regard to John 6. For it does not become our lecturer to give reasons for what he says, as he is one of the kind who prove and teach everything on the basis of their own imagination. Accordingly, we are taught, in this connection, that the Apostle did not write that passage for the benefit of the whole church at Corinth, but only for the laity. Apparently, therefore, he gave no permission to the priests in that passage, but, we gather, deprived them of the whole of the sacrament. Then, by the new grammar, "I have received of the Lord" becomes the same as "It is permitted by the Lord"; and "I have handed on to you" means "I have permitted you". Please make a special note of this, because it would be a logical inference that not only the church but any passing poltroon would be in order in turning any and all of the commandments, institutions, and ordinances of Christ and the Apostles into "things permitted".

Therefore I regard this man as instigated by an angel of Satan, and I include those in collusion with him. They seek the worldly fame of being able to enter into a disputation with me. But their hope will be disappointed, and they will be despised by me to the extent that I shall never even mention them by name. I shall be content with this one reply to all their books. If they are worthy of being brought back to sanity by Christ, I pray He will do it, in His mercy. But if

[13] The title as given by Luther.

they are not worthy, my prayer is that they may never cease
writing such books, and that the enemies of the truth may
never deserve to read any others. It is a common and faithful saying:

> Strive I with the filthy, I know, not in vain,
> That, victor or vanquished, dark spots I retain.

Then, as I perceive they have abundance of leisure and
plenty of paper, I will see to it that they have ample cause
for writing. I will keep ahead of them just to such an extent
that, while they are celebrating a most glorious victory over
what they conceive to be one of my heresies, I shall be con-
structing a new one in the interim; for I, like them, desire that
these mighty leaders in battle should be decorated with many
honours. Thus, they complain that I commend the use of both
kinds in Holy Communion; and so, while they are happily engaged in a subject most worthy of themselves, I shall be on
ahead, trying to show that it is most impious to deny to the
laity the use of both kinds in Holy Communion. To do this the
more conveniently, I shall write in a preliminary way on *The
Pagan Servitude of the Church of Rome,* reserving more to a
future date when these most learned Romanists shall have refuted that book.

I shall adopt this method lest any religious-minded reader
comes my way and takes offence at the unclean things with
which I have dealt. He may rightly object that he finds nothing here hard to follow, or particularly new; or at all events
nothing of a scholarly nature. You know how impatient my
friends are with me for bothering myself with the paltry propositions of these persons. My friends say that the mere reading
of their writings suffices to confute them; they say that they
are looking for better things from me, things which Satan is
trying to obstruct through the agency of these men. At last,
I have resolved to follow their advice, and to leave to those
hornets the business of brawling and denigration.

I shall say nothing about the Italian friar of Cremona. He
is an untrained and simple fellow attempting to write a few
rhetorical pages to "revoke" me to the Holy See. I am not
aware of having ever withdrawn from it, nor has any one
shown that I have done so. His main concern in these silly

pages is to show that, on account of my vows, and for the sake of the empire which has been granted to us Germans, I ought to be moved elsewhere. The object of his writing does not by any means appear to have been to "revoke" me, but rather to extol the French people and the Roman pontiff. He has my permission to write this little book, such as it is, and testify to his own obsequiousness. Nothing here merits serious discussion, since he does not seem to be moved by ill-will; nor is the book worthy of a scholarly review, since, in his complete ignorance and inexperience, he only trifles with the whole subject.

The first thing for me to do is to deny that there are seven sacraments, and, for the present, to propound three: baptism, penance, and the Lord's Supper. All these have been taken for us into a miserable servitude by the Roman curia and the church has been robbed of all her liberty. If, however, I were to use the language of Scripture, I should say that there was only one sacrament, [Cf. I Tim. 3:16] but three sacramental signs of which I shall speak in detail in the proper place.

(1) *The Lord's Supper*

In regard to the sacrament of the Lord's Supper, which is the most important of all, I shall discuss in what way my ideas have progressed while meditating on the administration of this sacrament. For, at the time, when I published my tractate on the Eucharist,[14] I held to the common usage, quite undisturbed by what was right or wrong according to the pope. But now that I have been cited and attacked, and even forcibly thrust into the arena, I shall give free expression to my ideas, no matter whether the Papists all join together to mock or reproach me.

In the first place, John 6 is to be totally set on one side, on the ground that it does not utter a syllable about the sacrament. The sacrament was not yet instituted; and, a more important point, the chapter is plainly and obviously speaking about faith, as is shown by the warp and woof of the words and thoughts. For Jesus said: "My words are spirit and they

[14] *On the Holy Sacrament,* 1519.

are life", showing that He was speaking of spiritual eating, by doing which any partaker would live; whereas the Jews understood Him to mean eating His flesh, and so raised the dispute. No sort of eating gives life except eating in faith. This is the true eating, the spiritual. Accordingly, Augustine says: "Why do you make your teeth and stomach ready? Believe, and thou hast eaten." In itself, sacramental eating does not give life, for many eat unworthily. Therefore Jesus cannot be understood to have spoken of the sacrament in this passage.

This passage has often been wrongly thought to teach the sacrament, as, e.g., in the decretal *Dudum,* and many others. But it is one thing to use the Scriptures wrongly, and another to understand them properly. Otherwise, if Jesus had intended it to be a commandment to eat of the sacraments when He said: "Unless you eat my flesh and drink my blood, you will not have life", He would have condemned all infants, all the sick, all those kept back by any cause and prevented from partaking of the sacraments, no matter how firm their faith. Hence Augustine, in the second book of *Contra Julianum,* proves from Innocent[15] that even infants, who do not yet partake of the sacrament, eat the flesh and drink the blood of Christ; i.e., they communicate through the faith of the church. Let us then regard this proposition as proved, and that John 6 is not relevant here. Elsewhere,[16] I have written that the Bohemians had no assured support in this passage when they sought to prove the use of the sacrament in both kinds.

Thus there remain two records which deal, and that very clearly, with this subject, viz.: the gospel passages on the Lord's Supper, and St. Paul in I Corinthians 11. Let us consider them. For, as Matthew, Mark, and Luke all agree, Christ gave all His disciples both kinds. And that Paul gave both kinds is so certain that no one has had the effrontery to say anything to the contrary. A further fact is that, according to Matthew, Christ did not say of the bread: "All of you eat of this"; but he does say of the cup: "All of you drink of this"; and in Mark He does not say: "All of you ate", but "All of you drank from it". Each writer attaches the mark of univer-

---

[15] Pope Innocent I.
[16] *Verklärung etliche Artikel in dem Sermon von heiligen sacrament,* 1520.

sality to the cup, but not to the bread. It is as if the Spirit foresaw the coming division forbidding the communion of the cup to some, though Christ would have had it common to all. You may be sure the Romanists would let us feel their anger smartly if they found the word "all" applied to the bread and not to the cup. They would leave us no loophole; they would cry aloud, brand us as heretics, and damn us as schismatics. But now, when Scripture is on our side and against them, they refuse in their perversity to be bound by logic, even in those things which be of God; they change, change again, and tangle everything together.

Now, suppose I were to approach my lords the Romanists, and ask them whether the whole sacrament, under both kinds, at the Lord's Supper is to be given only to the priests, or also to the laity. If, as they wish, only to the priests, then logically neither kind is to be given to the laity on any excuse; for it is not to be lightly given to anyone to whom Christ did not give it when He first instituted the rite. Otherwise, if we allow an alteration in one institution of Christ's, all His ordinances are immediately brought to nought, and any one whatever is in a position to say that he is not bound by anything Christ ordained or instituted; for a single exception, especially in the Scriptures, disproves any universal law. But, if the cup was given to the laity also, the logical consequence is that no one can deny both kinds to the laity. If, nevertheless, the administration is denied to those who desire it, that is done impiously and against Christ's act, example, and institution.

This argument seems unassailable, and I confess that it has convinced me. I have neither heard of, nor discovered, anything opposed to it. Christ's word and example stand here as firmly as possible. When He says, "All ye drink of it", He is not giving a permission, but issuing a command. Everyone ought to drink of it, and that commandment ought not to be understood as addressed only to the priests. Hence, it is undoubtedly impious to deny it to the laity who ask for it; yes, even if an angel from heaven were to do so. To support the Romanists' view that it was entrusted to the free judgment of the church to administer which kind she preferred, they bring forward no reasons, and no proofs from Scripture. The question is more easily passed over than proved; but their contention avails nothing against an opponent who faces them with the words or the works of Christ. Such a person must be refuted with the Word of Christ, the very thing we Romanists lack.

If, however, in the Lord's Supper, either kind could be denied to the laity, so also might a part of the rites of baptism and penitence be withheld from them, equally, at the free dispensation of the church; because in each instance they have equal grounds and authority for so doing. Therefore, just as the rites of baptism and absolution are administered to the laity in their complete form, so also should the complete sacrament of the Supper, if asked for. I am greatly astonished that the Romanists insist that, under pain of mortal sin, the priests must never receive only one kind at mass. The reason given by them all, with one voice, is that the two kinds constitute a full and complete sacrament, and should not be sundered. I would like them to tell me why the two kinds are separated for the laity, whereas the undivided sacrament must be administered only to themselves. Do they not acknowledge, by their own practice, either that both kinds should be given to the laity, or that the true and genuine sacrament is not in fact given them under the one form? Or is it that, in the case of the priests, the sacrament in one kind is not complete, but is complete in the case of the laity? Why do they appeal at this point to the free choice of the church and the power of the pope? Yet no such appeal abolishes either the Word of God or the testimony of the truth.

Further, if the church has authority to withhold the wine from the laity, she can also withhold the bread; and, on the same basis, she could withhold the whole sacrament of the altar from the laity, and deprive the laity altogether of what Christ instituted. But, I deny that she has such authority. If, on the other hand, she is commanded to administer either the bread alone, or both kinds (according to the desire of the communicant), it is not in her choice to withhold the wine. No attack on this position can succeed. Either the church has authority over both kinds, and the same authority applies to each separately; or else it is not valid over both together, and neither is it valid over each separately. I am hoping to hear what answer the toadies of Rome will give to that.

The most important proof, and, to me, a fully cogent one,

is that Christ said: "This is my blood, shed for you and for
many for the remission of sins." Here you may see very plainly
that the blood was given to all, and that it was shed for the
sins of all. No one will dare to say that it was not shed for the
laity, for it is clear who was addressed, when Jesus was speaking of the cup. Did He not address all? He used the words
"for you". Good, let us grant these words referred to the priests.
Even so, the words Jesus added, viz., "and for many", cannot
also apply to them only. Besides all this, He said: "All ye
drink of it." I could easily make a little word-play here, and
jest with Christ's words, as does that trifler whom I have already mentioned. But those who rely on Scripture to refute
us, must be overcome by Scripture.

These considerations have kept me from condemning the
Bohemians, who, whether in the right or the wrong, have certainly the words and works of Christ on their side. We Romanists have neither the words nor the works, but only that inane
remark: "The church has so ordained." Yet it is not the church
which ordained these things, but those who tyrannize over the
church without the consent of the church, which is the people
of God.

My next question is: Why is it in any way necessary, why
is it religious, what value is it, to deny both kinds to the laity?
Why withhold the visible sign when all agree that they receive the content of the sacrament without that sign? If they
grant them the content, the more important part, why do they
not grant the sign, which is the less important? In every sacrament, the merely outward sign is incomparably less important
than the thing symbolized. What prevents the less important
from being administered when the more important is administered? It almost seems to me that matters have been allowed
to go thus far by the wrath of God, in order to give occasion
for a schism in the church; which would mean that, long ago,
we had lost the content of the sacrament while contending for
the outer sign; and that while striving for what is of minor
importance, we are hostile to the things of greatest value and
alone worth while. In the same way, some Romanists fight
for ceremonial but oppose love. Indeed, this monstrous state
of affairs arose at the time when, contrary to Christian love,
we began, in our folly, to pursue worldly wealth. God showed

it by that terrible sign, namely, that we preferred the outer signs rather than the things themselves. How perverse it would be if you were to concede that a candidate received faith in baptism, but you were to refuse him the sign of faith, i.e., water!

But, in the end, Paul is impregnable, and he stops the mouth of everyone when he says, in I Corinthians 11: "I have received of the Lord, that which I have handed on to you" [I Cor. 11:23]. He does not say: "I permitted you", as our mendacious friar asserts. Nor is it true that it was because of the contentions in the church at Corinth that Paul gave both kinds. Firstly, the document still shows that the contention was not about the two kinds, but about the mutual contempt and envy between the rich and the poor. The text says clearly: "One is hungry and another is drunken, and ye put to shame those that are poor." A further point on the same side is that Paul is not speaking of the time when he first administered the sacraments to them. He does not say: "I am receiving from the Lord", and "I am giving to you"; but "I received" and "I handed on"; this was when first he preached to them, and long before the rise of these disputes. He meant that he had handed on the use of both kinds, because "handed on" means "passed on the commandment", with the same meaning as when he uses the same word elsewhere. Not even a vestige remains here of the friar's "permission", which he raked up apart from Scripture, reason, or other foundation. His opponents do not ask what he dreamed of, but what verdict Scripture pronounces here. He cannot produce a letter of Scripture in support of his pretences, whereas they can produce mighty thunderbolts on behalf of their faith.

Come forward, then, all ye fair-speaking toadies of the pope; make ready, and rid yourselves of impiety, tyranny, treason against the Gospel, and the crime of slandering your brothers. You proclaim them to be heretics if they do not agree with the very fabrications of your own brains, or if they do not think them inherently right and proper even where contrary to Scripture—as is both patent and potent. If any are to be called heretics and schismatics, it is neither the Bohemians, nor the Greeks, who take their stand on the gospel; rather, you Romanists are heretics and impious schismatics, who presume on your figments alone, and fly contrary to plain passages in divine Scripture. Get rid of these things, my friends.

What could be more ridiculous and more worthy of our precious friar's intellect than to say that the Apostle wrote that passage, and gave that permission, not to the church universal, but to the church at Corinth, a local church? Whence does he derive this proof? From one and only one storeroom, viz., his own impious head. When the church universal accepted and read the epistle, and obeyed it completely, did it not also obey this passage? If we admit that any epistle of Paul's, or a single passage in them, does not pertain to the church universal, all Paul's authority is nullified. On that basis, the Corinthians might aver that what Paul had taught the Romans about faith did not apply to them. Could anything more blasphemous be imagined? Away with the idea that there is a single syllable in the whole of Paul which the whole church is not obliged to follow and obey. That was not the view of the Fathers, up to the perilous present. It was of our day that Paul spoke when he foretold that men would be blasphemers, and blind, and without understanding. This friar is one, if not the chief, of them.

However, for the sake of argument, let us proceed with this intolerable lunacy. If Paul gave permission to a particular church, then, from your Romanist point of view, the Greeks are in the right, and so are the Bohemians, for they too are particular churches. Hence, the situation is satisfactory, so long as they do not act contrary to Paul, who at least gave permission. Moreover, Paul could not permit anything contrary to what Christ had instituted. Accordingly, I hold it against you, O Rome, and all your hangers-on, that these words of Christ and Paul speak on behalf of the Greeks and the Bohemians. You cannot show by a tittle of evidence that power has been given you to change these things; and far less that you can accuse of heresy those who disregard your proud pretensions. You yourself deserve to be criminally accused of impiety and oppression.

Cyprian is strong enough, even when alone, to refute all the Romanists. He discusses the point at issue in his work, *On the Lapsed*, book V. He testifies that it was the custom in the church at Carthage to give both kinds to many of the laity, even children; and he provides many examples. Among other points, he reproves some of the people as follows: "The sacrilegious man is wrath with the priests when he is not forthwith given the body of the Lord though his hands are unwashed; or allowed to drink the blood of the Lord though with unclean lips." Would you find anything here, you miserable toady, at which to snarl? Would you declare that this holy martyr, a teacher in the church, and filled with the apostolic spirit, was a heretic and that he used that permission in a particular church?

In the same book, Cyprian recounts the story of something that happened in his presence, and that he himself witnessed. A deacon was administering the cup to a young girl, but she drew back shyly; whereupon he poured the blood of the Lord into her open mouth. Similarly, we read of St. Donatus at the time when his chalice had been broken; but this wretched toady of ours easily disposes of the incident by saying: "My record says the chalice was broken, but not that the blood was administered." No wonder. A man who can give his own meaning to Scripture can also read what he wishes into history. But that is no way to establish the authority of the church, or to confute heretics.

Enough! for I did not begin writing in order to reply to that man, who is not worth replying to, but in order to bring the truth of the matter into the open.

I conclude, therefore, that to deny both kinds to the laity is impious and oppressive; and it is not in the power of any angel, nor of any pope or council whatever to deny them. Neither does the ruling of the council of Constance disturb me. If its authority were valid, why not that of Basel, which decreed the contrary, and permitted the Bohemians to receive both kinds? This result was reached after a lengthy argument, as is proved by the extant records and documents of that council, which our servile ignoramus adduces to support his own fabrications. It is with similar sagacity that he discusses the whole subject.

The question of its substance and completeness is what constitutes the first shackling of this sacrament. Of that substance and completeness, the Roman dictatorship has deprived us. Granted that it is not sin against Christ to partake of the sacrament under one kind only, for Christ did not decree the use of either, but left the matter to each man's choice. He said: "This do ye, as oft as ye do it, in remembrance of me." It is sin to refuse to give both kinds to those who wish to exercise freedom of choice; and it is the priests, and not the laity, who must bear the guilt. The sacrament does not pertain to the priests alone, but to all; the priests are not lords but servants, and it is their duty to administer both kinds to those who so desire, and as often as they desire. If they deny and forcibly deprive the laity of this right, they are oppressive; the laity incur no guilt, whether they have to do without one or both; meanwhile they will be preserved from harm by their faith and by their desire for the whole sacrament. Similarly, because the priests are servants, they ought to administer baptism and absolution to one who makes the request as of right. If they do not so administer it, the seeker has full merit in his faith, whereas they will be accused before Christ as wicked servants. In former times, the desert Fathers for a long period did not receive the sacrament in any form.

Thus I am not arguing that force be used to seize both kinds, but I am seeking to instruct men's consciences, so that, when any one suffers under the tyranny of Rome, he may know that it is for his own sinful complicity that he has been deprived of his right in the sacrament. My desire is only that no one should be able to uphold the Roman dictatorship as rightly denying one kind to the laity. We ought rather to abhor it and refuse consent, although we should bear ourselves just as if we were prisoners among the Turks and not allowed to use either kind. This was my point when I said it would seem well that this servitude were abolished at a general council, and that our noble Christian liberty were restored to us, and that we were set free from the hands of the dictator at Rome. Each man should be allowed his free choice in seeking and using the sacrament, just as in the case of baptism and penance. At present, year by year, the tyrant exercises his despotism, and compels us to accept one kind only. That is the measure of the utter loss of the liberty which we received from Christ, and that is the due recompense for our impious ingratitude.

The second shackle imposed on this sacrament is less serious as regards our conscience, but far more perilous to discuss, and yet worse to condemn. Here I shall be called a Wycliffite and six hundred times a heretic. But what does it matter? Now that the Romish bishop has ceased to be a bishop and has become a dictator, I fear none of his decrees at all; for I know that he has no power to make a new article of faith, nor has a general council. Some time ago, when I was studying scholastic theology, I was greatly impressed by Dr. Pierre d'Ailly,[17] cardinal of Cambrai. He discussed the fourth book of the *Sententiae* very acutely, and said it was far more likely, and required the presupposition of fewer miracles, if one regarded the bread and wine on the altar as real bread and wine, and not their mere accidents—had not the church determined otherwise. Afterwards, when I saw what was the kind of church which had reached this conclusion, namely, the Thomist,[18] or Aristotelian church, I gained more courage. At last, after hesitating between conflicting opinions, I found peace in my conscience in accepting the earlier opinion, viz., that the true flesh and the true blood of Christ were in the true bread and true wine, and this not otherwise, nor less, than the Thomists regard them as under the accidents. I adopted this view, because I saw that the opinions of the Thomists, even though approved by pope and council, remained opinions still, and would not become articles of faith even if decreed by an angel from heaven. For what is ascribed without a basis of Scripture or a proven revelation, may be held as an opinion, but is not to be believed of necessity. This opinion of Thomas's, being without a basis in Scripture or reason, is so uncertain that it seemed to me as if he understood neither his philosophy nor his logic. Aristotle speaks of accidents and their subject very differently from St. Thomas. I feel we ought to be sorry for so great a man, not only for drawing his views from Aristotle in matters of faith, but also for attempting to found them upon

[17] Born in northern France 1350, became a student in Paris, 1372, and became Chancellor of that university, 1388. He was chairman of the council which condemned John Huss, June 28, 1415; and exercised much political influence. He died at Avignon, Aug. 9, 1420.
[18] Named after Thomas Aquinas, who died in A.D. 1274.

a man whom he did not understand, thus building an unfortunate superstructure on an unfortunate foundation.

I would therefore allow anyone to hold whichever opinion he prefers. The only thing I aim at for the present is to banish scruples of conscience, so that no one may fear being called a heretic if he believes that the bread and wine on the altar are real bread and wine. Let him understand that, without endangering his soul's salvation, he may believe and think and opine either the one or the other, because no particular view is a necessary article of the faith.

But I shall now pursue my own opinion further.

1. I shall not give an ear, nor pay any attention, to those who cry out that my opinion is Wycliffite or Hussite heresy, and contrary to the decree of the church. This kind of device is adopted only by those whom I have convicted many times of heresy in questions of the indulgences, of free will and God's grace, of good works and sins, etc. If Wycliffe was a heretic in one degree, they are such in ten degrees. It is a pleasure to be blamed and accused by heretics and perverse sophists, for to please them would be the worst sort of impiety.

2. Moreover, they can neither prove their own contentions, nor disprove the opposite, nor do other than say: "That is Wycliffite, Hussite, or heretical." They carry this feeble objection always on the tip of their tongues, but nothing else. If you ask for a scriptural proof, they reply: "That is our opinion, and the church (i.e., ourselves) has decreed it so." That shows the extent to which men of reprobate faith, unworthy to be believed, not only propound to us their own imaginations as articles of faith, but do so under the authority of the church.

There is very good reason, however, for my standpoint. Firstly, that the word of God does not need to be forced in any way by either men or angels. Rather, its plainest meanings are to be preserved; and, unless the context manifestly compels one to do otherwise, the words are not to be understood apart from their proper and literal sense, lest occasion be given to our adversaries to evade Scripture as a whole. This is why Origen was rightly repudiated long ago; he made allegories out of the trees and all else described in Paradise, and ignored the plain, literal sense. One might have inferred from what he said that God had not created trees. Similarly, in the second place, in regard to our special subject, the evangelists plainly record that Christ took bread and blessed it; the book of Acts and the apostle Paul call it bread; therefore we are intended to understand it means real bread; and so also true wine, and a true chalice. Even our opponents do not say that the chalice is changed. Since, therefore, it is not necessary to assume that divine power effected a transubstantiation, this must be regarded as a human invention, because it is not supported by Scripture or reason, as we shall see.

It gives a new and foolish twist to the words to hold that "bread" means the form, or the "accidents", of the bread; and "wine" the form, or the accidents, of the wine. Why then do they not take everything else to consist of forms and accidents? Even if all else were consistent with that idea, nevertheless the word of God ought not to be taken so lightly, nor deprived of its original meaning, with so little justification.

For over 1,200 years the church remained orthodox. On no occasion, and in no place, do the Fathers mention the word transubstantiation—monstrous whether as a locution or as an idea—until the specious philosophy of Aristotle took root in the church, and attained a rank growth in the last 300 years. During this time, many other perverse conclusions were arrived at. Examples are: "That the divine Being is not begotten, nor does it beget"; "That the soul is the form to which the human body corresponds as the substance"; and the like. These assertions are made without any reason or ground, as the cardinal of Cambrai himself acknowledges.

The Romanists may perhaps object that the danger of idolatry forbids that the bread and wine should be real. This is a very ridiculous objection, because the laity have never understood the hair-splitting philosophy of substance and its accidents; nor, if they were taught it, could they grasp it. Thus the danger remains the same whether it is the visible accidents that are retained or the invisible substance. For if they do not worship the accidents, but the Christ which they conceal, why should they worship the bread which they do not see?

Why could not Christ maintain His body within the substance of the bread as truly as within its accidents? Iron and fire are two substances which mingle together in red-hot iron in such a way that every part contains both iron and fire. Why cannot the glorified body of Christ be similarly found in every part of the substance of the bread?

What will they reply? Christ is believed to have been born from his mother's virgin womb. Let them aver, here also, that the flesh of the virgin was temporarily deprived of being, or, as they would more aptly have it put, "transubstantiated", in order that Christ, having been enfolded in the accidents, might come forth through the accidents. The same thing will have to be said of the shut door of the upper room and the closed mouth of the sepulchre, through which He went in and out without doing them injury. Out of this theory has arisen that Babel of a philosophy of a constant quantity distinct from substance, till the stage is reached when they themselves do not know which are the accidents and which the substance. No one has given a certain proof that heat, colour, cold, luminosity, weight, and shape, are accidents. Further, they have been forced to pretend that a new substance is created by God and added to the accidents on the altar. This has been required because Aristotle said: "The nature of accidents is to be in something." They have been led to an infinite number of monstrous ideas, from all of which they would be free if they would simply grant that the bread was truly there. And I rejoice to think that, at least among the ordinary people, simple faith in this sacrament still abides. Because they do not understand the dispute, they do not argue whether the accidents are there without the substance; rather, they believe, in simple faith, that the body and blood of Christ are truly contained there, and they leave the business of arguing what contains them to those who have time to spare.

Perhaps the Romanists will say: "Aristotle teaches that, in an affirmative sentence, the subject and the predicate ought to mean the same thing"; or, to quote this beast's own words in the *Metaphysics VI*, "An affirmative proposition requires the agreement of the extremes." It would then follow that when Christ said, "This is my body", the subject cannot stand for the bread, but for the body of Christ. What is our response when Aristotle, and the doctrines of men, are made the arbiters of these very sublime and divine things? Why not hiss these ingenious inquiries off the stage, and hold to the words of Christ in simple faith, satisfied not to understand what takes place, and content to know that the true body of Christ is there by virtue of the words of institution? We do not need to understand completely the mode of the divine operation.

But what do the Romanists say when Aristotle attributes a subject to all the categories of accidents, although he grants that the substance is the prime subject? According to him "this white", "this great", "this something", are all subjects because something is predicated of them. If this is true, then, since *transubstantiation* has to be propounded in order to avoid declaring the bread to be the body of Christ, I ask: Why not propound a *transaccidentation* and so avoid affirming that an accident is the body of Christ? The danger remains the same if one were to understand the "subject" to be "this white or this round object", and to be the body of Christ. On whatever grounds transubstantiation is taught, on the same grounds transaccidentation might be taught, the principle being that the two terms of a proposition refer to the same thing.

But if, by a *tour de force,* you rise above the accident, and do not wish to regard it as signified by the subject when you say, "This is my body"; why not, with equal ease, transcend the substance of the bread when you do not wish to regard it as the subject? Then to say, "This is my body", will be as true in the substance as in the accident, especially as this would be a miracle performed by God's almighty power, which can operate to the same degree, and in the same way, in the substance as in the accident.

But let us not carry on our dialectics too long; does it not seem that Christ used plain words in anticipation of these curious ideas? He did not say of the wine, "This substance is my blood", but "This is my blood". It was still clearer when He introduced the word "cup" and said, "This is the cup of the new testament in my blood." Does He not seem to have wished us to continue in simple faith, and believe only that His blood was in the cup? When I fail to understand how bread can be the body of Christ, I, for one, will take my understanding prisoner and bring it into obedience to Christ; and, holding fast with a simple mind to His words, I will firmly believe, not only that the body of Christ is in the bread, but that the bread is the body of Christ. My warrant is in the words which say, "He took bread and gave thanks and brake it, and said, Take, eat, this" (i.e., this bread which He had taken and broken) "is my body". Paul says: "The bread which we break, is it not participation in the body of Christ?" He does not say: "It is in the bread", but, "this bread is participation in the body of Christ." What if the philosophers do not grasp it? The Holy Spirit is greater than Aristotle. How can the Romanists maintain that their fine doctrine of transubstantiation is comprised in any system of philosophy at all, when they themselves confess that here all philosophy falls short? However that may be in Greek or Latin, the possessive adjective "this" is linked to "body" by identity of gender; in Hebrew, which has no neuter gender, "this" refers to the bread. The meaning in Hebrew is: "This (bread) is my body", when Jesus said: "This is my body". The idiom of the language and also common sense show that the subject indicated by Jesus was the bread, and not His body, i.e., when Jesus said, "This is my body", he meant, "this bread is my body".

Thus what is true in regard to Christ is also true in regard to the sacrament. It is not necessary for human nature to be transubstantiated before it can be the corporeal habitation of the divine, and before the divine can be contained under the accidents of human nature. Both natures are present in their entirety, and one can appropriately say: "This man is God"; or, "This God is man". Though philosophy cannot grasp it, yet faith can. The authority of the word of God goes beyond the capacity of our mind. Thus, in order that the true body and the true blood should be in the sacrament, the bread and wine have no need to be transubstantiated, and Christ contained under the accidents; but, while both remain the same, it would be true to say: "This bread is my body, this wine is my blood", and conversely. That is how I would construe the words of divine Scripture and, at the same time, maintain due reverence for them. I cannot bear their being forced by human quibbles, and twisted into other meanings. Nevertheless, in my view, other men must be allowed another opinion, e.g., that laid down in the decretal *Firmiter*.[19] But, as I have said, let them not press their opinions on us to be accepted as articles of faith.

The third shackle imposed upon this sacrament is by far

---

[19] *Decret. Greg., lib.* I, tit.; cap. 3.

the most wicked abuse of all. The result of it is that there is no belief more widely accepted in the church to-day, or one of greater force, than that the mass is a good work and a sacrifice. And this abuse has brought in its train innumerable other abuses; and these, when faith in the sacrament has completely died away, turn the holy sacrament into mere merchandise, a market, and a business run for profit. This is the origin of the special feasts, the confraternities, intercessions, merits, anniversaries, and memorial days. Things of this kind are bought and sold in the church, dealt in and bargained for; the whole income of priests and monks depending on it.

It is difficult, perhaps impossible, to do away with the abuse which I shall now discuss. It is a matter which has been confirmed by so many centuries of ancient custom, and has become so ingrained, that to alter or abolish it would require that the great majority of the books which are to-day regarded as authoritative, and almost the whole form of church life, should be changed and done away with. Entirely different rites and ceremonies would have to be introduced, or rather reintroduced. But the Saviour lives, and the word of God must be obeyed with greater care than any nice notions, human or angelic. I will discharge my office by bringing the facts to light, and teaching the truth as I have understood it; I shall do this neither under compulsion nor for the sake of money. In other matters, let each work out his own salvation. I mean to labour faithfully as one who must stand before Christ's judgment seat, and in such a way that no one will be able to blame me for his unbelief, or his ignorance of the truth.

Firstly, in order to be happy and assured, and to reach a true and unconstrained understanding of this sacrament, we must be careful to begin by setting aside all the later additions to the first, simple institution. Those additions have been made by men's devotion and through their zeal, and include such things as vestments, ornaments, chants, prayers, organs, candles, and the whole pageantry of things visible. Let us turn our eyes and devote our minds purely and simply to that alone which Christ Himself instituted. Let us confine ourselves to the very words by which Christ instituted and completed the sacrament, and commended it to us. For these words alone, and apart from everything else, contain the power, the nature, and the whole substance of the mass. All the rest are human productions, additions to the words of Christ, things without which the mass could still continue, and remain at its best.

These are the words with which Christ instituted this sacrament:

"As they were eating, Jesus took bread and blessed and brake, and gave to His disciples, and said: Take and eat; this is my body which is given for you. And taking the cup, He gave thanks, and gave to them, saying: All ye drink of it. This cup is the new testament in my blood which is poured out for you and for many for the remission of sins. This do in remembrance of me" [Matt. 26:26 ff.; Luke 22:19].

St. Paul hands these words down in I Corinthians 11, and explains them at greater length. We ought to rest on them, and stand upon them as firmly as upon a rock, if we do not wish to be carried about by every wind of doctrine, as we have been carried about till now by irreverent doctrine, man-made, and contrary to the truth. This passage omits nothing pertaining to the integrity, the usefulness and the fruitfulness of this sacrament; and nothing is introduced which is superfluous or not necessary for us to know. Anyone who passes these words by, and yet meditates on or teaches the mass, teaches a monstrous impiety. This is, in fact, done by those who make an *opus operatum*,[20] and a sacrifice of it.

The first point stands infallibly fast. The mass or sacrament is Christ's testament which He bequeathed to be distributed after His death, among those who believed on Him. For His words run: "This cup is the new testament in my blood." I say this truth stands firm, and is the unchanging foundation on which to build everything else we have to say. For you will see how we shall undermine all the sacrilege which men have imported into this sweetest of all sacraments. Christ, who is the Truth, truly said: "This is the new testament in my blood which is shed for you." I do not stress this without reason; the matter is not a small one, and is to be received in the depths of our heart.

[20] Luther's own words, "a finished work", is the usual translation in the German form.

Let us inquire, therefore, what a testament is, and, at the same time, it will also become clear to us what is the mass, what its use, its fruit, and its abuse.

Without question, a testament is a promise made by a man in view of his death. In it, he bequeaths his heritage, and appoints heirs. A testament, therefore: (a) anticipates the death of the testator; (b) embodies the promise of the heritage; and (c) appoints the heirs. That is how Paul discusses a testament at length in Romans 4, Galatians 3 and 4, and Hebrews 9. The words of Christ show the same quite plainly. Christ testifies of His own death when He says: "This is my blood which is given. This is my blood which is shed." He names and designates the bequest when He says, "In remission of sins." Similarly, He appoints the heirs when He says, "For you and for many", i.e., those who accept, and believe in, the promise of the testator. Faith here makes men heirs, as we shall see.

You will see, therefore, that what we call the mass is a promise made by God for the remission of our sins; a promise which was confirmed by the death of the Son of God. Now a promise and a testament only differ in so far as a testament contemplates the death of the promiser. The testator is the same as the promiser with his death in view, whereas a mere promiser is, so to speak, a testator who is not contemplating death. Now Christ's death was foreshadowed in all the promises of God from the beginning of the world. Indeed, whatever value the ancient promises had, depended on that new promise in Christ which lay in the future. Hence the very frequent use in Scripture of the words, "covenant", "compact", "testament of the Lord". Their meaning was that God would die at some future date; because, before a testament comes into effect, the testator's death must take place (Hebrews 9). But it was God who made the testament, and therefore He needs must die. But He Himself could not die unless He became man. Therefore the one comprehensive word, "testament", envisages both the incarnation and the death of Christ.

These things having been said, it becomes obvious what is the right and the wrong use of the mass, and what constitutes a worthy or an unworthy preparation for it. If, as I have argued, it is a promise, we cannot prepare ourselves for it by any works, by the use of force, or by any merits; but only by faith. For where there is the word of a promise-keeping God, there is needed the faith of a man who accepts it. It is plain that our salvation begins in our faith, and this clings to the word of the God of the promises. And God, apart from and before all that we can do, manifests His mercy, which is unearned and unmerited, and proffers His words of promise: "For He sent His word and healed them" [Ps. 107:20].

He does not first accept our works, and then save us. The word of God is prior to all else; faith follows it; then love succeeds faith, and gives rise to every good work. Love does not cause evil, for it is the fulfilling of the law. There is no way by which a man can commune with God, or treat with Him, except by faith; that is to say, no man by his works, but God by His promises, is the author of our salvation. All things depend on His authoritative word, and are upheld and maintained by it. He begot us by it that we might be, as it were, the first-fruits of His creative work.

Thus, when Adam came to be restored after the Fall, God gave him this promise, and said to the serpent: "I am putting enmity between you and the woman, between your seed and her seed. She shall bruise your head, and you shall lie in wait to bruise her heel" [Gen. 3:15]. According to this word of promise, Adam and his family were carried for a long time in God's bosom, and kept by faith in Him. He patiently waited for the woman who was to bruise the serpent's head as God had promised. He died in this faith and expectation, not knowing when or how she would come, but not doubting that she would come. For such a promise, being the truth of God, preserves, even in hell, those who believe and wait for it. After this there was another promise, made to Noah, and reaching to Abraham. Its sign was the rainbow of the covenant placed in the clouds. Noah and his posterity had faith in it, and found God beneficent. Afterwards, He promised Abraham that all the nations should have blessing in his seed. It was into Abraham's bosom that his posterity were received when they died. Then to Moses and the children of Israel, and especially to David, He plainly made the promise of Christ, and so revealed what the earlier promise had implied [Deut. 18:18; II Sam. 7:16].

Thus we come to the most perfect promise, that of the new

testament. The words used are plain: life and salvation are promised without price; they are given to those who believe in the promise. God plainly distinguishes this testament from the former by calling it the new testament. For the older testament, mediated through Moses, was not a promise of remission of sins, or of eternal life, but of temporal things, to wit, the land of Canaan. No one was renewed in spirit by this promise so as to lay hold on a heavenly heritage. For this reason, an unthinking beast had to be slain as a figure of Christ, and the testament was confirmed by its blood. Thus the blood corresponded to the testament, and the victim to the promise. Now Christ said: "The new testament in my blood"; not another's, but His own; and, by this blood, grace is promised through the spirit for the remission of sins, that we might receive the inheritance.

Therefore the mass, in essence, is solely and simply the words of Christ just quoted, viz., "Take and eat," etc.; as if He had said, "Lo! thou sinful and lost soul, out of the pure and free love with which I love thee, and in accordance with the will of the Father of mercies, I promise thee with these words, and apart from any deserts or undertakings of thine, to forgive all thy sins, and give thee eternal life. In order that thou mayest be most assured that this my promise is irrevocable, I will give my body and shed my blood to confirm it by my very death, and make both body and blood a sign and memorial of this promise. As often as thou partakest of them, remember me; praise and laud my love and bounty, and be thankful."

From all of which you will see that nothing else than faith is needed for a worthy observance of the mass, and the mass is truly founded on this promise. Faith believes Christ to be truthful in these words, and does not doubt that she has had these immeasurable blessings bestowed upon her. Given this faith, there immediately follows the most precious affection of the heart, enlarging and deepening the human soul, i.e., love as given by the Holy Spirit through faith in Christ. Thus the believer draws near to Christ, that loving and bounteous testator, and becomes a new and different man through and through. Who would not weep inward tears and in very joy surrender himself entirely to Christ, if he believed firmly and without doubt that this inestimable promise of Christ's belonged to him? How could he help loving so great a benefactor, who offered, promised, and presented to him, in his unworthiness and while deserving something quite different, this great wealth and also an eternal inheritance?

The one and only pity about it all is that there are many masses said, while none, or few of us, recognize, consider, and apprehend, the promises and riches they set before us. Of a truth, during mass, nothing else should be done with greater zeal, indeed with all our zeal, than to give all our attention to these words, these promises of Christ, for they truly constitute the mass itself. We should meditate on these words, ponder them, exercise and nourish our faith in them, make it grow and add to its strength, by daily commemoration of it. This is to fulfil Christ's command when He said, "This do in remembrance of me." Preachers ought to do the same thing in order to impress the promise faithfully on the people, to commend it and awaken their faith in it.

But, to-day, how many know that the mass is Christ's promise? I pass over those irreverent men who recount fables, teaching man-made traditions instead of these great promises. Even when they do teach these words of Christ, they teach them, not as a promise or a testament, nor in order to rouse faith by their means.

What we deplore, in the servitude of the church, is that the priests take every care nowadays lest any of the laity hear these words of Christ. It is as if they were too sacred to be uttered to the common people. For we priests have no more sense, as to the terms which we call the words of institution, than to arrogate them to ourselves alone. We say them privately, and in such a way that they do us no good; for we ourselves do not feel them as promises, nor regard them as a testament to nourish our faith. But I know not whether it is superstition or blasphemy for us to repeat the words after we have lost belief in them. Satan has taken advantage of this lamentable condition of ours to remove every trace of the real mass from the church. At the same time, he has taken care that every corner of the world is full of spurious masses, i.e., abuses and travesties of God's testament. He burdens the world more and more with sacrilege, that gravest of sins, and so increases its guilt; for what more sinful sacrilege could there be than to replace God's promises by perverse opinions, or to neglect them, or to extinguish all faith in them?

As we have said, God never has dealt, and never does deal, with mankind at any time otherwise than by the word of promise. Neither can we, on our part, ever have to do with God otherwise than through faith in His word and promise. He does not hold works in high esteem, nor does He need them. We use them in dealing with one another and with our own selves. But He does require that we should regard Him as faithful to His promises; we should pray without ceasing, and worship Him in faith, hope, and love. In this way, He is glorified in us, since it is not of us who run, but of Him who shows mercy, and who promises and gives, that we receive and possess all good things. Lo, this is the true worship and service of God which we ought to offer in the mass. But when the words of the promises are not handed on, how can faith be exercised? And, without faith, what of hope? What of love? and, without faith, hope, and love, what of service? Thus without any doubt, all the priests and monks to-day, together with the bishops and all their other superiors, are idolaters and in a state of peril on account of this ignorance, abuse, and mockery of the mass, i.e., sacrament, i.e., promise of God.

For anyone readily understands that these two, promise and faith, are necessarily yoked together. No one can believe if there is no promise. If there is no faith, a promise is useless, because faith is its counterpart and completion. From these considerations, any one can easily deduce that the mass, which is simply a promise, can only be attended and celebrated in faith. Without that faith, any ancillary thing by way of prayer, self-preparation, good works, outer signs, and genuflections, are far rather instigations to irreligion than religious exercises. It readily happens that those who have prepared themselves in this way think they have a right of access to the altar, whereas in reality they are more unfit than at any other time, or by any other means; and this on account of the unbelief which they bring with them. How many priests you may see everywhere and every day offering the sacrifice of the mass, who, if they have made some error in vestment, or have unwashed hands, or if they stumble in the prayers, or blunder in some small way, make themselves very miserable, as if guilty of a great crime! But, on the other hand, they are not in the least conscience-stricken if they do not reverence or believe the mass itself, i.e., the divine promise. Oh, the unworthy religion of our times, the most irreligious and thankless of all times! There is, therefore, no other worthy self-preparation and no other proper observance of the mass than by faith, the faith by which we believe in the mass, i.e., in the divine promise. Therefore, let him who desires to approach the altar, or to receive the sacrament, beware lest he appear empty before the face of the Lord our God. But he will be empty without faith in the mass, i.e., in this new testament. By what state of mind, other than this unbelief of his, could he sin more grievously against the divine truth? As far as it lies in his power, he is making God a liar and a promiser of vain things. The safest course, therefore, would be to attend mass in the same spirit as in hearing some other promise made by God, i.e., in such a way that, while you would not be ready to do or contribute much yourself, you would be ready to believe and accept all that was promised you there, i.e., the promises pronounced by the priest in discharging the office. If you do not come in this spirit, beware of drawing near at all, for you will undoubtedly draw near to the judgment seat.

Thus I was right in saying that the whole virtue of the mass consisted in the words of Christ, when He gave testimony to the remission of the sins of all who believed that His body had been given for them and His blood shed for them. On this account, nothing is more important for those who hear mass than to meditate on His words carefully, and in fullness of faith. Unless they do that, all else they do is in vain. Nevertheless it is true to say that God's way is almost always to add some sign as a mark or reminder of His promise, that thus we might serve Him the more faithfully, or that He might admonish us the more effectually. When He made the promise to Noah that the earth should not again be destroyed by flood He gave His bow, and placed it in the clouds, as the sign that He would be mindful of His covenant. After promising Abraham that his seed should gain the inheritance, He gave circumcision as the seal of justification by faith. Similarly, He gave Gideon at first a dry and then a wet fleece, in confirma-

tion of His promise of victory over the Midianites. Through
Isaiah, He offered Ahaz a sign of his victory over the kings of
Syria and Samaria, to confirm his faith in the promise of it. And
so we read of many other signs accompanying the promises of
God in the Scriptures.

Similarly in the mass, the greatest promise of all, He adds
a sign as a memorial of this great promise, His own body and
His own blood in the bread and wine, when He says: "This do
in remembrance of me." So, at baptism, He adds the sign of
immersion in the water to the words of the promise. From
these instances we learn that, in every promise, God presents
two things to us, a word and a sign, in order that we may
understand the word to be a testament, and the sign a sacrament. In the mass, the word of Christ is the testament, the
bread and wine are the sacrament. Since greater power resides
in a word than in a sign, so more power resides in a testament
than in a sacrament; for a man may have, and use, a word or
testament without a sign or sacrament. "Believe", says Augustine, "and thou hast eaten." But what is believed is nothing
less than the word of the promiser. Thus I am able daily, indeed hourly, to have the mass; for, as often as I wish, I can set
the words of Christ before me, and nourish and strengthen my
faith by them. This is the true spiritual eating and drinking.

You will not understand the nature or importance of the
things which our theologians have produced in the *Sentences*.[21]
(1) The crux and sum of the whole matter is that the testament, or word of promise, is not discussed by any of them;
consequently they abrogate faith and the whole virtue of the
mass. Then (2) they discuss only the second part of the mass,
the sign or sacrament. But they do it in such a way that, here
once more, they teach nothing about faith, but only about its
presuppositions; or about *opera operata*, participations, and
the fruits of the mass. At last (3) they come to the profundi-
ties, and talk trumpery stuff about transubstantiation, and
other metaphysical nonsense without end. Meantime they have
done away with the true knowledge and use of both the testament and the sacrifice, together with the whole of faith. In
addition, as the prophet declared, they have caused the people

[21] See Introduction, p. xvi.

of Christ to forget their God "days without number" [Jer. 2:32].

But you should let others recount the various benefits of hearing mass. Give it your attention that you may say and believe, with the prophet, that here is a table which has been made ready for you by God in the face of all who cause you anxiety, and at which your faith may feed and grow strong [Ps. 23:5]. Your faith feeds only on the word of the divine promise, for "man doth not live by bread alone, but by every word that proceedeth out of the mouth of God" [Matt. 4:4; Deut. 8:3]. Hence, at mass, you ought, first of all, to be a most minute observer of the words of the promise, as forming the richest banquet, with every variety of food and holy nourishment. You must esteem it greater than all else, trust in it above all else, cleave to it most firmly in spite of every sin, and unto death. If you do so, you will obtain not only those tiny drops and crumbs of fruits of the mass, which some have fabricated superstitiously, but the principal fountain of life itself. By this I mean faith in the very word, the source of all good; as it says in John 4 [John 7:38], "He that believeth in me, out of his belly shall flow living waters"; and again: "Whosoever drinketh of the water that I shall give him, there shall be in him a well of living water springing up into eternal life" [John 4:14].

Now there are two defects from which we commonly suffer, and which prevent our understanding the fruits of the mass. The first is that we are sinners; and our profound unworthiness makes us unfit for such great things. Secondly, even if we were worthy, these things are so highly exalted that our timorous nature would not dare either to seek or to hope for them. Forgiveness of sins and eternal life!—who would not be overawed by them, rather than dare to hope for them, if the great benefits issuing from them were given their due importance. By them, we may have God as our Father, and ourselves become sons and heirs of all God's riches. To outweigh this twofold defect of our nature, we must lay hold of the word of Christ, and look to Him more steadily than to our sense of weakness. For great are the works of the Lord; they are all full of His purposes, and He is able to give beyond what we ask or think. If they did not exceed our worth, our capacity, and indeed every talent of ours, they would not be divine. Christ also encourages us in the same way when He says: "Fear not, little flock, for it is the Father's good pleasure to give you the Kingdom" [Luke 12:32]. This incomprehensible wealth of God, showered upon us through Christ, causes us to love Him, in return, most ardently and above all else. We are drawn to Him with the fullest confidence, despising all things else, and being made ready to suffer all things for Him. Thus the sacrament is aptly called "a fount of love".

In this connection, consider an example from human affairs. Suppose a very rich nobleman were to bequeath 1,000 guilders to a beggar, or even a worthless and wicked fellow. The man would assuredly claim them boldly and take them without regard to his own worthlessness, or the magnitude of the bequest. If someone should accost him in the road, and remind him of his own worthlessness and the magnitude of the bequest, what do you think he would reply? Presumably: "What business is that of yours? I am receiving what I receive, not as my deserts, nor on account of any special claim on my part. I know I do not deserve it and that I am getting more than I have earned; in fact, I have earned the opposite. But by the generosity of my benefactor, I am making a perfectly valid claim through the processes of the law which deals with wills and bequests. If it was not an unworthy act on his part to make a bequest to a man as unworthy as me, why should I make my unworthiness a reason for not accepting it? Nay, unworthy of it though I am, the more thankfully should I accept this gracious gift of a stranger." Every one ought to fortify his conscience with such considerations against all doubts and fears, in order to hold this promise of Christ with an unwavering faith. Take great care that no one goes to mass trusting in confession, or prayer, or self-preparation; but lacking confidence in all these things, let him rather go in high confidence in the Christ who gives the promise. As already said at sufficient length, the word of the promise must reign unchallenged here in pure faith, which faith in itself constitutes the sole and sufficient preparation.

I have shown how God, in His great wrath, has permitted the perfidious teachers to hide from us the words of this testament, and thereby to eradicate faith as far as they could. It is easy to see now what would inevitably follow on blotting out faith, viz., the most ungodly superstition of works. For when faith dies, and the word of faith is dumb, works soon take its place, and the tradition of works. This substitution results in our soon being taken prisoner out of our own land, exiled to Babylon, and robbed of all our treasures. That is what has happened to the mass; it has been transformed, by the teaching of godless men, into a good work. They themselves call it an *opus operatum*. Through it, they presume themselves to be all-powerful with God. From that starting-point they have gone on to the last folly of falsely asserting that, because the mass avails by virtue of its *opus operatum*, it is no less beneficial to others even if it be hurtful to a celebrant priest who is a wicked man. That is the foundation of sand on which they base their "applications", "participations", sodalities, anniversaries, and an infinite number of other profitable, money-making schemes of that kind.

These spectres are so strong, numerous, and firmly ensconced, that you will scarcely be able to stand against them unless you exercise unceasing vigilance, and remember what the mass is, and what I have said about it. I have said that the mass is simply the divine promise or testament of Christ confirmed in the sacrament of His body and blood. That being so, you will understand that it is impossible for it ever to be an outward work; nor does anything happen in it, nor can any benefit be attained in it, except by faith alone. Faith is not a work, but it teaches us to do good works, and is their soul! Can any one be found so foolish as to regard a promise he has received, or a testament he has been given, as a good work of his own? What heir thinks he is doing good to his father when he receives the instruments of the bequest along with the bequest he has inherited? How then shall we describe our impious temerity when we act as if we were going to perform a good work for God in coming to receive the divine testimonies? This ignorance of the testament, and this servitude of the sacrament, are things that go beyond tears. When we ought to be grateful to accept, we come arrogantly to give the things that are to be accepted. With unheard-of perversity, we mock at the mercy of the Giver; for we give as a work what we should be accepting as a gift, till the Testator now no longer distrib-

utes the largesse of His own good things, but becomes the
recipient of ours. Alas for such sacrilege!

Who has ever been so lacking in sense as to consider baptism to be a good work? Has any candidate for baptism believed he was doing a good work which he was offering and
communicating to God for himself and others? If, therefore,
no good work is communicable to others in a sacrament and
testament of any kind, there cannot be one in the mass, for
the mass itself is simply a testament and a sacrament. Hence
it is plainly an impious error to offer or apply a mass for sins,
for satisfactions, for the benefit of the departed or any necessity of one's own or that of another. You will easily understand
this as the plainest truth, if you hold it firmly that the mass is
a divine promise which can benefit no one, be applied to no
one, intercede for no one, be communicated to no one, except
only to the believer himself by the sole virtue of his own faith.
Who can receive or accept, on another's behalf, the promises
of God, which require faith from each one individually? Can
I give the promises of God to another, even if he be an unbeliever? Or can I believe on behalf of another, or cause another to believe? But these powers are needed if I am to be
able to apply and communicate the mass to others, since the
mass contains only those two things: the divine promise and
the human faith, the latter accepting what the former promises. If this were not the case, I should be able to hear the
gospel for others, and believe for them; I could be baptized
for someone else; I could communicate in the sacrament of
the altar for another, and, to go through the list of their sacraments, I could marry a wife for another, be ordained for another, be confirmed for another, and receive extreme unction
for another.

But if this can be done, why did not Abraham believe on
behalf of all the Jews? Why was faith in the same promise as
was believed in by Abraham, demanded of every Jew individually? Therefore, this truth is irrefragable: each one stands
for himself where the divine promise is concerned. His own
faith is required. Each must respond for himself, and bear his
own burden, as Mark says in chapter 16 [:16]: "Every one
who believes and has been baptized will be saved; but he who
does not believe, will be condemned." So also each one can

take mass only for his own good, through his own faith; and he can communicate for no one else at all. So also, the priest cannot administer the sacrament to any one in another's stead, but administers the same sacrament to each one individually. In consecrating and administering, the priests are our servants. We do not offer a good work through them or actively communicate; rather, through them we receive the promises and the sign, and we communicate passively; and that has remained the case to this day as far as the laity are concerned. For the laity are not said to do good, but to receive it. But the priests have gone astray in their impieties, and have made a good work of their own out of the fact that they communicate, and administer, the sacrament and testament of God, in which the good shall be received by the laity.

But, you will say: What is this? Surely your contentions will overturn the practices and purposes of all the churches and monasteries, and destroy those by which they have waxed rich for many centuries, since they have been founded on masses at anniversaries, intercessions, "applications", "communications". You will deprive them of their largest incomes. My answer is: That is the very thing which led me to write that the church has been taken prisoner. For this sacred testament of God has been forced into the service of impious greed for gain by the opinions and traditions of irreligious men. They have passed over God's word; they have laid before us the thoughts of their own hearts, and led the world astray. To point to the numbers or the eminence of those whom I assert to be in error carries no weight with me. The truth is mightier than all else. If you were able to refute Christ who taught that the mass was a testament and a sacrament, I would admit them to be in the right. Further, if you could show that to receive the benefit of a will and testament, or to receive the sacrament of promise, is to do a good work, then I would be ready and willing to condemn my own teachings. Since you can do neither, why do you hesitate to treat with contempt the mob who are going from bad to worse? Give God the glory and confess His truth. His truth is, in particular, that to-day all those priests have perverted views who regard the mass as a good work which will help them and others out of their difficulties even in matters of life or death. This is to say things

unheard-of hitherto and repellent now. But examine the mass
as it is to-day, and you will know that I have spoken the truth.
The misfortune is that we have now gained a sense of security
which prevents our realizing that the wrath of God is being
visited upon us.

But I gladly agree that the prayers, which we pour out
before God as soon as we assemble to partake of the mass, are
good works and appropriate acts. In them, we confess to one
another, utter our own desires, pray for the common weal, and
for each other. It is thus that James taught us to pray for each
other that we might be saved [Jas. 5:16]; and that Paul commanded, in I Timothy 2 [:1 ff.], that there should be "supplications, prayers, intercessions for all men; for kings and all that
are in high places." Yet the prayers are not the mass, but the
works of the mass, if the prayers of the heart and the mouth
can be properly called works, since they issue from the faith
received or increased in the sacrament. For the mass, or otherwise God's promise, is not fulfilled by praying, but only by
believing; and it is as believers that we pray and do every good
work. Yet what priest sacrifices the mass in such a way that
his object is only to offer the prayers? All of them imagine that
they are offering Christ Himself to God the Father, as a fully
sufficient sacrifice; and that they are doing a good work on
behalf of all whom they wish to help. They trust in the efficacy
of the mass, and they do not ascribe its efficacy to prayer. The
error has gradually increased in this way until they ascribe to
the sacrament what belongs to the prayer, and they bring to
God what they ought to receive from Him as a gift.

We must therefore make a clear distinction between testament and sacrament on the one hand; and, on the other, the
prayers which we offer at the same time. Not only so, but we
ought also to bear in mind that the prayers are of no avail
either for him who offers them, or for those on whose behalf
they are offered, unless the testament be first received in faith.
It is faith which prays, and its voice alone which is heard, as
James teaches in his first chapter [Jas. 1:6]. Thus, prayer is
something quite different from the mass. Prayer can be extended to comprehend as many people as I choose; the mass
covers none other than him who exercises his own faith, and
then only in so far as he exercises it. Nor can the mass be

given to God or to other men; rather God bestows it on men
through the agency of the priest; and men receive it through
faith alone, apart from all works or merits. There will be few
persons so foolish as to assert that a poor man does a good
work if he comes in his poverty to receive a gift from the hand
of a rich man. But the mass is, as I have said, the gift of the
divine promise, offered to all men by the hand of the priest.

It follows that the mass is not a work in which others can
share, but an object of faith, as I have already explained; and
it is meant for nourishing and strengthening the personal faith
of the individual.

But there is another misconception to be done away with
which is much more serious and more specious, viz., the common belief that the mass is a sacrifice offered to God. This
belief seems to be expressed in the words of the canon which
speak of "these gifts, these offerings, these holy sacrifices"; and,
later, "this oblation". Moreover, the request is very definite
that the sacrifice will be accepted as was Abel's sacrifice, etc.
Then, too, Christ is said to be the victim on the altar. In support of these false views, there are many sayings of the holy
Fathers, and the whole custom of the church as observed
throughout the world.

We must resolutely oppose them all with the words and
example of Christ, in spite of the fact that they are so strongly
entrenched. For if we do not hold firmly that the mass is the
promise, or testament, of Christ, as His words plainly show,
we shall lose the whole gospel, and all its comfort. We must
not allow anything to prevail contrary to these words, not even
if an angel from heaven were to teach otherwise. Those words
contain nothing about a good work or a sacrifice. Moreover,
Christ's example is on our side. At the Last Supper, when
Christ initiated this sacrament, and instituted this testament,
He did not offer Himself to God, or perform any "good work"
for others. He took His seat at the table, He offered the same
testament to each, one by one, and gave the same sign. Now
the closer our mass resembles that first mass of all, which
Christ celebrated at the Last Supper, the more Christian it will
be. But the mass which Christ celebrated was extremely simple, without any display of vestments, genuflections, chants,

and other ceremonies. If it was necessary to offer Himself as a sacrifice, then He did not institute it completely.

Not that any one ought to speak evil of the universal church, because it has embellished and amplified the mass with many other rites and ceremonies. But the point is that no one should be deceived by the outward splendour of the ceremonies, and hindered by the impressive pomp. This would be to pass over the simple form of the mass and, in fact, practise a kind of transubstantiation; for it would be a case of passing over the simple substance of the mass, and of clinging to the various elements accidental to its outward appearance. Everything additional to the words and the example of Christ is an "accident" of the mass. Nothing of this must we regard otherwise than we are accustomed to regard the "monstrances" and the altar cloths, within which the host itself is contained. Hence, as it is a self-contradiction to speak of distributing a testament, or accepting a promise on the one hand, and on the other, of offering a sacrifice, so it is a self-contradiction to call a mass a sacrifice; for a mass is something we receive, but a sacrifice is something we offer. But one and the same thing cannot be both received and offered at the same time, nor can it at once be given and accepted by the same person, any more than a prayer can be the same thing as that which we pray for; nor is it the same to pray and to receive the thing prayed for.

What then are we to say of the Canon, and of the patristic authorities? I answer, in the first place, that even if we had no objection to raise, it would be safer to deny everything rather than to grant that the mass is either a good work or a sacrifice. For we must not deny Christ's word and destroy both faith and mass at the same time. Nay, in order to retain the mass, we shall declare that we have been taught by the apostle, in I Corinthians 11 [:20 f.], how the Christian believers, when they assembled for mass, used to bring food and drink with them. These they called "the collections", and they used to distribute them among all who were in need, after the example of the apostles in Acts 4 [:34 f.]. A portion of this food was taken and consecrated as the bread and wine of the sacrament. Just because all this was consecrated by word and prayer in accordance with the Hebrew custom, namely, by being "lifted up", as we read in the Pentateuch, therefore the terminology and the custom of "lifting up" or offering remained in use long after an end had come to the custom of bringing and collecting together what was to be sacrificed and "lifted up". Thus, according to Isaiah 37 [:4], Hezekiah commanded Isaiah to lift up his prayer before God's face on behalf of the remnant. In the Psalms, we read: "Lift up your hands in the Sanctuary"; and again, "Unto thee will I lift up my hands". I Timothy 2 [:8] says: "Lifting up pure hands in every place." That is why the words "sacrifice" and "offering" ought to be used, not in reference to the sacrament or testament as such, but to the collections themselves. This is also the source whence comes the word "collect" which is still used of the prayers at mass.

For the same reason, the priest consecrates the bread and wine, and immediately elevates them. But this does not show that he is offering something to God, for no word he uses reminds one of a sacrifice or an offering. Rather, this is either a survival of the Hebrew custom according to which the gift, which had been received with thanksgiving, was brought back to God, and then "lifted up"; or, on the other hand, it may be an exhortation to stimulate our faith in this testament. The priest has expounded and described it in the words of Christ in order to exhibit the sign of the testament at the same time. In this case, the offering of the bread really corresponds to the demonstrative adjective "this", in the words: "This is my body"; and the priest, in a way, uses this sign as an allocution to those of us who are standing round him. Similarly, the offering of the cup properly corresponds to the demonstrative adjective in the words: "This cup of the new testament". For the purpose of the rite of elevation is that the priest should arouse faith in our hearts. But I wish that, at the same time as he "elevates" the sign or sacrament openly before our eyes, he would pronounce, in an audible and clear voice, the words of the testament; and that he would do it in the vernacular, whatever that may be, in order that faith may be the more effectively awakened. For why should it be permissible to celebrate mass in Greek, Latin, and Hebrew, but not in German or any other language?

Therefore let the priests who offer the sacrifice of the mass in these corrupt and most perilous times, take care, firstly, that the words of the greater and lesser canons of the mass, to-

gether with the collects, which all too plainly re-echo the sense
of sacrifice, do not refer to the sacrament but either just to
the bread and wine which the words consecrate, or to their
own prayers. Indeed, the bread and wine were formerly offered in order to receive the blessing, and so become sanctified
by the word and by prayer. After the blessing and consecration, they are no longer offerings, but gifts received from God.
Throughout the rite, let the priest bear in mind that the gospel
is superior to all the canons and collects, which are but man-
made; and the gospel offers no warrant for calling the mass a
sacrifice, as you have heard.

Further, when a priest is celebrating mass publicly, his intention should be only to "communicate" himself and let others
"communicate" through the mass. At the same time, he may
offer prayers for himself and others, but he must take care
lest he presume to offer the mass. But if a priest is saying a
private mass, he must conceive his act as one of communicating himself. For a private mass differs in no way from, and
operates to no greater extent than, the simple communion
which every layman receives from the hand of the priest. The
difference is in the prayers, and in the fact that he himself
consecrates the elements and then administers them to himself. In the matter of the mass and the sacraments, we are all
equals, whether priests or laity.

If a priest be requested by others to celebrate "votive"
masses, let him not dare to accept payment for them, or presume to offer any votive sacrifice. Let him be careful to confine
himself entirely to prayers, whether for the living or the dead.
Let his thought be: "Lo! I am to go and take the sacrament
for myself alone; but while I am taking it, I will pray for so
and so." In this way the money he receives will be, not for the
mass, but for the prayers, and to buy himself food and clothing. Do not be disturbed if the whole world is of the contrary
opinion and practice. Thou hast the utmost certainty in the
gospel. Trust in it, and thou canst well afford to despise man-
made beliefs and opinions. But if thou rejectest my words,
and goest to offer a mass, and not the prayers only, bear in
mind that I have warned thee faithfully, and I shall be held
guiltless on the Day of Judgment. Thou thyself wilt bear the
penalty of thine own sins. I have said what I was under com-

pulsion to say to thee as brother to brother for the sake of thy salvation. Observe it and it will be to thy advantage; neglect it, and it will be to thy hurt. If man would condemn what I have said, I would reply in Paul's words: "But evil men and impostors shall wax worse and worse, deceiving and being deceived" [II Tim. 3:13].

All the above enables any one to understand the frequently quoted saying of Gregory's: "The mass said by a wicked priest is not less effective than that said by a good one; nor was one said by Saint Peter any better than one said by Judas the traitor, if they indeed say masses." With this saying as a cloak, many have sought to hide their godlessness; and, in so doing, they have drawn a distinction between *opus operatum* and *opus operans*, in order to be free to live an evil life themselves, and yet to do good to others.

What Gregory says is true, but they take him wrongly. It is quite certainly true that ungodly priests give and receive the testament and sacrament no less completely than do the most godly; and no one doubts that even ungodly priests preach the gospel. But the mass is a part of the gospel, nay the sum and substance of the gospel; for the whole gospel is simply the good news of the forgiveness of sins. And whatever can be said about forgiveness of sins and the mercy of God, in the broadest and richest sense, is comprehended, in brief, in the word of the testament. For this reason, popular sermons ought to be nothing else than expositions of the mass, or explanations of the divine promise contained in this testament. This is the way to teach faith and to edify the church. But those who to-day expound the mass, play and make mockery with allegorical human ceremonies.

Hence, just as an ungodly priest may baptize, i.e., apply the word of promise and the sign of water to the candidate for baptism, so also may he administer the promise of this sacrament to the partaker, and also himself partake—as did also Judas the traitor at the last supper of the Lord. Nevertheless it remains the same sacrament and testament, which does its own work in the believer, but a "strange work" in the unbeliever. But in the case of offering a sacrifice there is a complete difference. For it is not the mass, but the prayers, which are offered to God; and so it is obvious that the prayers offered by an ungodly priest are without avail; but, as Gregory likewise said, when an unworthy person is the intercessor, the heart of the judge is only turned to greater sternness. Those two things, mass and prayer, or sacrament and work, or testament and sacrifice, must not be confused. The first comes from God to us through the intermediation of the priest, and demands faith. The second issues from our faith, ascends to God through the priest, and requires One who hears. The former descends; the latter ascends. The former, therefore, does not necessarily require a worthy and religious-minded minister; but the latter does require such an one, because God does not listen to sinners, although He knows how to give good gifts even through evil men. But He accepts no wicked man's works. He showed this to Cain, and, as we read in Proverbs 15 [:8], "The sacrifice of the wicked is an abomination to the Lord"; and Romans 14 [:23], "Whatsoever is not of faith is sin."

Let us bring this first section to a close, but with the reservation that I shall have more to say if an enemy should arise. The conclusion we draw is, that, of all for whom the mass has been provided, only those partake of it worthily whose consciences make them sad, humble, disturbed, confused, and uncertain. The word of the divine promise in this sacrament offers forgiveness of sin; therefore let each come forward undisquieted, whoever he may be, even though troubled by remorse, or suffering from temptation. This testament of Christ's is the only antidote for sins past, present, or future. But you must cling to Him with unwavering faith. You must believe that what the words of the testament declare is granted to you freely. If you do not believe this, then never, nowhere, by no good works, and by no kinds of efforts, can you gain peace of conscience. For faith alone means peace of conscience, and unbelief nought but distress of mind.

(2) The Sacrament of Baptism

Blessed be the God and Father of our Lord Jesus Christ who of His rich mercy has preserved at least this one sacrament in His church unspoiled and unspotted by man-made ordinances, and made it free to all races and classes of men;

nor has He allowed it to be suppressed by foul money-grubbing and ungodly monsters of superstition. His purpose was that little-children, who were incapable of greed and superstition, might be sanctified by it and initiated into simple faith in His word. To-day baptism is indeed of the highest advantage for them. For if this sacrament were administered only to grown-up people and older folk, I do not believe it could retain its power and beauty in the teeth of the overwhelming greed and superstition which have overthrown all religion among us. There is no doubt that carnal cunning would have devised its preparations and dignities, and then its reservations, restrictions, and what other traps there may be for catching money, until the font would have been sold for as high a price as parchment itself.

But Satan, though unable to do away with the virtue of baptizing little children, has shown his power by putting an end to it among adults. To-day there is scarcely any one who calls to mind his own baptism, still less takes pride in it; because so many other ways have been found of getting sins forgiven and entering heaven. Jerome's dangerous saying, whether because it is ill-phrased or wrongly understood, has given occasion to these views. He speaks of penitence as the second plank after shipwreck, as if baptism were not a sign of penitence. Hence those who have fallen into sin lose faith in the first plank, or the ship, as though it were lost; and they begin to trust and cling to the second plank, i.e., penitence. That situation has given rise to the innumerable impositions of vows, orders, works, satisfactions, pilgrimages, indulgences, and monastic sects; together with that torrent of books, questions, opinions, and man-made ordinances, for which the whole world has hardly room. The result is that the oppressiveness of this state of things reduces the church to an incomparably worse condition than was ever known to Jews or any other race under heaven.

The part of the pontiffs should have been to remove these things, and to strive with zeal to recall Christians to the integrity proper to baptized persons. These might then understand what manner of people they were, and how Christians ought to live. But, at the present time, the one endeavour of the popes is to remove the people as far away as possible from their baptism, plunge them all into an ocean of dictatorship, and cause the people of Christ, as the prophet said, to forget Him for ever [Jer. 2:32]. Oh! unhappy are all they who bear the name of bishops nowadays; for not only do they not know what a bishop should be like, but they are not even aware what bishops ought to know or do. They fulfil what Isaiah 56 [:10 f.] says: "His watchmen are blind; they are all ignorant; they are shepherds without knowledge; all have turned to their own way, each one to his gain."

1. The first point about baptism is the divine promise, which says: "He that believeth and is baptized shall be saved" [Mark 16:16]. This promise is far superior to all the outer show of works, vows, orders, and whatever else men have introduced. Our entire salvation depends on this promise, and we must be watchful to keep our faith in it knowing without any dubiety of mind that, once we have been baptized, we are saved. Unless faith is present, or comes to life in baptism, the ceremony is of no avail; indeed it is a stumbling-block not only at the moment we receive baptism but for all our life thereafter. For that kind of unbelief is equivalent to accusing God of promises that cannot be trusted, and that is the greatest of all sins. When we first try to exercise faith in God's baptismal promises we shall immediately find how difficult it is to believe. Human nature in its infirmity and its consciousness of sin, finds it a most difficult thing to believe in the possibility of salvation. Yet, without believing it, men cannot be saved; and this just because they do not believe in the divine promise of salvation.

The people ought to have been taught this message, and this promise should have been assiduously repeated; baptism ought to have been constantly brought to mind, and faith should have been constantly aroused and cultivated. Once the divine promise has been accepted by us, its truth lasts till death; and similarly our faith in it must never falter, but must grow ever stronger until death, in abiding remembrance of the promise made to us in our baptism. Therefore, when we regain our faith, or repent of our sins, we are only returning to the strength and faith of baptism from which we fell when sin made us deserters. For the truth of this promise, once made, abides for ever, ready with outstretched arms to receive us when we return. And that, if I mistake not, is what they mean who say, but not clearly, that baptism is the prime sacrament, the foundation of them all, and without it none of the others can be received.

Hence it is no small benefit to a penitent first of all to remember his baptism. Let him recall the divine promise which he has abandoned, and confess it to the Lord. Let him rejoice to be still within the fortress of salvation, for it is still the case that he has been baptized; and let him abhor the impious ingratitude shown when he fell away from the faith and truth of his baptism. His heart will be wonderfully strengthened and inspired with the hope of mercy, if he will but keep in mind the divine promise which has been made to him. It is impossible for that promise to play false. Hitherto it has remained unbroken and unchanged, nor can it be changed by any sin. That is Paul's message in II Timothy 2 [:13]: "If we do not believe, he remaineth faithful; he cannot deny himself." This truth of God will preserve the penitent, so that if all else fail, this, if we believe in it, will not fail. In it, he possesses something which he can hold against a scornful enemy, something he can oppose to the sins which assault his conscience, something which is proof against the terrors of death and judgment. Finally, he has a solace in every temptation, in the unique truth, which he utters when he says: "God is faithful in His promises, and I received His sign when I was baptized. If God is for me who can be against me?"

When the children of Israel turned in penitence, they remembered, first of all, their exodus from Egypt; and in remembering this they returned to the God who had led them out. Moses constantly impressed this memory and this leadership on them, and David did the same. But how much more ought we to be mindful of our exodus from our Egypt, and, with that in mind, to return to Him who led us out through the baptism of rebirth which we are commanded to remember for this very purpose! This can be done most appropriately in the sacrament of bread and wine. Formerly the three sacraments of penitence, baptism, and the Lord's Supper, were celebrated with the same end; and they supplemented one another. Thus we read of a holy virgin, who, as often as she suffered temptation, made her baptism her sole defence; she said briefly, "I am a Christian." The enemy immediately perceived the power of baptism and of a faith which clings to the truth of a promise-keeping God, and fled from her.

In this way, you will see how rich a Christian is, i.e., one who has been baptized. Even if he wished, he could not lose his salvation however often he sinned, save only if he refused to believe. No sins have it in their power to damn him, but only unbelief. If his faith relies on the divine promise made at baptism, all things else are embraced by that same faith, nay by the truth of God; because He cannot deny Himself, if you confess Him and continue to cling to His promise. But "contrition" and "confession of sin" followed by "satisfaction", and all the other devices thought out by men, will desert you suddenly and leave you in distress, if you forget this divine truth and batten upon those things. Whatever is done apart from faith in the truth of God, is vanity of vanities and vexation of spirit.

Similarly, you will see how dangerous, indeed false, it is to imagine that penitence is a plank to which you can cling after shipwreck; and how pernicious is the error of supposing that the power of baptism is annulled by sin, and that even this ship is dashed in pieces. Nay, that one ship remains, solid and indestructible, and its timbers will never be broken to pieces. All who voyage in it are travelling to the haven of salvation, namely, the divine truth promised in the sacraments. True, it often happens that many people foolishly leap out of the ship into the sea, and perish. These are they who abandon faith in the promise and plunge themselves in sin. But the ship itself survives and, being seaworthy, continues on its course. If any one, by some gracious gift, is able to return to the ship, he is carried into life not by some plank, but by the well-found ship itself. One who returns to the abiding and enduring promise of God through faith is such a man. On this account, Peter, in II Peter 1 [:9], rebukes those who sin, because they are forgetful of the time when they were cleansed from their former sins; doubtless reproving them for their ingratitude after accepting baptism, and for their disloyal impiety.

What is the use then of writing so much about baptism, and yet not teaching this faith in its promises? All the sacraments were instituted to feed our faith, but ungodly men never deal with faith sufficiently, but declare that no man can be certain of the forgiveness of his sins or of sacramental grace. By this sacrilegious doctrine they deprive the whole world of understanding. They lay hold of, nay totally deny, the sacrament of baptism on which stands the first glory of our consciousness as Christians. Meanwhile they talk in extravagant terms to the miserable people about "contritions", anxious "confessions", "circumstances", "satisfactions", "works", and other such absurdities without end. Let us be cautious, then, or rather scornful, in reading the "Master of the Sentences" in his fourth book, and all those who copy him. At best they only write about the material and form of the sacraments, that is they deal only with the dead letter of the sacraments; but their spirit, life, and use, or the truth of the divine promise and of our faith—this they leave altogether untouched.

Be very cautious, then, lest you be deceived by the outward show of works, and the deceitfulness of man-made ordinances, and lest you are thereby led to do wrong both to the divine truth and your own faith. If you desire to be saved, you must start from faith in the sacraments—anterior to any works. The works will follow the faith, unless your faith be too feeble. In fact, faith is the most excellent and most difficult of all "works". You would be sustained by it alone, if you were prevented from doing any others. For faith is the work, not of man, but of God alone, as Paul teaches. God does the other works through us and by us; in the case of faith, He works in us and without our co-operation.

These considerations show clearly the difference, as regards the rite of baptism, between the ministry which man renders, and the initiative which comes from God. For the man baptizes; and yet does not baptize. He baptizes in as far as he performs the rite: he submerges the candidate. Yet, in one sense, he does not baptize, but only acts on God's behalf, and not on his own responsibility. Hence we ought to understand baptism at human hands just as if Christ Himself, nay God Himself, baptized us with His own hands. The baptism which we receive through human hands is Christ's and God's, just as everything else that we receive through human hands is God's. Be careful, therefore, in regard to baptism, to ascribe only the external rite to man, but the internal operation to

God. You may rightly ascribe both to God, and regard the officiating person as the instrument acting for God, through whom the Lord, sitting in heaven, submerges you in the water with His own hands, and promises you forgiveness of your sins by a human voice speaking to you through the lips of His servant on earth.

The words themselves bear this out: "I baptize you in the name of the Father, and the Son, and the Holy Spirit, Amen." The minister does not say: "I baptize you in my name"; he says, as it were: "This which I am doing, I am not doing by my own authority, but in the stead and in the name of God; and what you receive is just the same as if the Lord Himself had given it visibly. The One who effects the work, and the one through whose agency it is done, are different; but the work of the two is the same; nay, I but minister on behalf of Him who is the sole Author." What is meant, in my view, is that the words, "in the name", refer to the person of the Author in such a way that it is not merely the case that the name of the Lord is only uttered or invoked during the rite; rather, the rite itself, far from being an act of the minister's, is done in the name and the stead of another. In Matthew 24 [:5], Christ speaks in the same mode: "Many shall come in my name"; and Romans 1 [:5] says: "Through whom we have received grace and apostleship, for the sake of obedience to the faith among all peoples, for His name's sake."

I am glad to adopt this point of view because it gives a very complete support to our confidence and a real incentive to faith, to know that we are not baptized by human hands, but by the Holy Trinity itself through the agency of the man who performs the rite in Their name. This puts an end to that tiresome dispute about the words employed, and which are called the "form" of the baptism. The formula of the Greek Church is: "May a servant of Christ be baptized"; and that of the Latin: "I baptize." Others again, sticking rigidly to their pedantry, condemn the use of the words, "I baptize thee in the name of Jesus Christ", although it is certain that the Apostles used that form in baptizing, as we read in the Acts of the Apostles [Acts 10:48]. They refuse to regard any as valid except: "baptize in the name of the Father, and of the Son, and of the Holy Spirit, Amen." The Romanists urge their point of view in vain; they bring no proofs, but only assert their own fabrications. The truth is that no matter in what words baptism is administered, as long as it is not in a human name but in the Lord's name, it surely saves. Indeed, I have no doubt that any one who receives it in the name of the Lord, even if the ungodly minister were not to give it in His name, would be truly baptized in the Lord's name. For the virtue of baptism lies not so much in the faith or practice of the administrator, as in that of the recipient. An instance is even recorded where an actor was baptized for a joke. Pointless disputes about questions of this kind are raised for us by those who lay no emphasis on faith, but all on works and the proper rites; whereas we lay all the stress on faith alone, and none on a mere rite; and this makes us free in spirit from all these scrupulosities and distinctions.

2. The second point in regard to baptism is that it is a sign or sacrament: an immersion in water, whence the name. For the Greek word *baptizō* means "immerse", or "plunge", and the word *baptisma* means "immersion". I have already said that the divine promises were accompanied by signs to set forth what the words mean; or, as the moderns say, the sacrament has an effective significance. Let us consider what that means.

A great majority maintain that there is a certain spiritual virtue hidden in the word and the water, which operates in the soul of the recipient by the grace of God. Others, however, contend that there is no virtue in the sacraments themselves, but that grace is given by God alone, who is present by covenant at the sacraments which He has instituted. Yet all agree that the sacraments are effective signs of grace. They are moved to this conclusion by the single argument that they see no other reason why the sacraments of the New Law should take precedence over those of the Old Law if they are only signs. Hence they have been driven to attribute to the sacraments of the New Law something which makes them beneficial even to those who are in mortal sin. Neither faith nor grace are needed, it being enough if there is no obstacle imposed, i.e., no actual intention to sin anew.

Such contentions, however, are lacking in both reverence and faith; they are contrary to faith and to the nature of the sacraments, and therefore should be carefully avoided and shunned. For it is wrong to hold that the sacraments of the New Law differ from those of the Old Law in point of their effective significance. Both have the same meaning; for the God who now saves by baptism and the Supper, saved Abel by his sacrifice, Noah by the rainbow, Abraham by circumcision, and the others by their own signs. With regard to the meaning of the sacraments, there is no difference between those of the Old Covenant and those of the New, except that you may describe as belonging to the Old Law everything which God did among the patriarchs and their fathers at the time of the Law. For the signs which were given to the patriarchs and fathers should be widely distinguished from the legal form in which Moses instituted his law, such as the priestly customs regarding vestments, vessels, foods, houses, and the like. For these are very different, not only from the sacraments of the new law, but also from the signs which were given by God from time to time to the fathers who lived under the law; e.g., the fleece to Gideon [Judges 6:36 ff.], the sacrifice in Noah's case, and that which Isaiah offered Ahaz in Isaiah 7 [:10 ff.]. Each of these was accompanied by a promise of some kind, and this demanded faith in God.

Thus the legal formulas differ from both the old and the new signs in that the legal forms are not accompanied by any word of promise which calls for faith. They are not signs of justification because they are not sacraments of faith, which alone justifies, but merely sacraments of works. Their entire force and nature consisted in the rite, not in faith. He who performed them fulfilled them, even when he performed them without faith. But our signs, and those given to the fathers, are accompanied by a word of promise demanding faith, the fulfilment being impossible by any other work. They are signs, or sacraments, of justification because they are sacraments of a justificatory faith, and not of works. The whole of their effectiveness lies in faith, and not in anything that is done. He who believes in them, fulfils them, even if nothing is done. This is the root of the saying: "Not the sacrament, but the sacramental faith, is what justifies." Accordingly, it was not circumcision that justified Abraham and his seed, although the apostle calls it the seal of the righteousness of faith [Rom.

4:11]; rather, faith in the promise to which circumcision was attached, gave righteousness and implemented what the circumcision signified. For faith was the spiritual circumcision of the heart which was figured by the literal circumcision of the flesh. What justified Abel was by no means his sacrifice, but his faith; for by this he gave himself up to God, and of this his sacrifice was only the outward figure.

Thus, baptism justifies nobody, and gives advantage to nobody; rather, faith in the word of the promise to which baptism was conjoined, is what justifies, and so completes, that which the baptism signified. Faith is the submersion of the old self and the emersion of the new self. Hence the new sacraments cannot differ from the old; both alike have the divine promises, and the spirit of faith is the same. But they differ incomparably from the old imagery by the word of promise which is the sole, but very effective, means of distinguishing them. So also at the present time, the showy display of vestments, the holy places, or the meals, together with the innumerable ceremonies, doubtless imply things that are to receive an impressive fulfilment in the realm of the spirit; yet, because they contain no word of a divine promise, they cannot be compared with the signs of baptism and the Supper. Neither do they confer righteousness, nor are they of any other advantage of that kind; because their purpose is fulfilled in the very use, or practice, of them, apart from faith. The apostle speaks of them accordingly in Colossians 2 [:22]: "All which things are to perish in the using after the precepts and doctrines of men." The sacraments are not fulfilled by the ritual, but only when they are believed.

Therefore it cannot be true that there resides in the sacraments a power capable of giving justification, or that they are the "signs" of efficacious grace. All such things are said to the detriment of faith, and in ignorance of the divine promises. They must be called efficacious, however, in the sense that, when faith is indubitably present, they most assuredly and effectively impart grace. That this is not the sense in which the Romanists say they are efficacious is proved by the assertion that sacraments do good to all, even to wicked and unbelieving men, provided these latter impose no obstacle to them. But this contention is as much as to say that unbelief itself is not the most obstinate and hostile of all obstacles to grace. In this way, the Romanists have put precepts in place of the sacraments, and works in place of faith. Now, if a sacrament were to give me grace just because I receive that sacrament, then surely I should obtain the grace, not by faith, but by my works. I should not gain the promise in the sacrament, but only the sign instituted and commanded by God. Thus you can see quite clearly that the sacraments have been completely misunderstood by the theologians who follow the *Sentences*. They offer no reason for either the sacramental faith or the sacramental promises. They stick to the sign, and to the use of the sign, thus seducing us from faith to works, and from the word to the sign. As I have said, they have not only taken the sacraments into servitude, but as far as possible abolished them.

Therefore, let us open our eyes, and learn to pay more attention to the word than to the sign, to faith than to works or ritual. We know that, wherever we meet a divine promise, there faith is required of us; and moreover that both are necessary, for neither is efficacious without the other. Belief is impossible without a promise to believe in, and a promise is void when it is not believed. But if both react on each other as they should, they bring about the true and indubitable efficacy of the sacraments. Therefore it is futile to look for an efficacious sacrament apart from promise and faith; it is, indeed, to fall into condemnation. Christ said: "He that believeth and is baptized shall be saved; but he that disbelieveth shall be condemned" [Mark 16:16]. Here He points out that, in the sacrament, faith is necessary to such a degree that it can save even apart from the sacrament; that is why He did not add, after "He who disbelieveth", the words *"and is not baptized"*.

There are two things which baptism signifies, namely, death and resurrection, i.e., the fulfilling and completion of justification. For, when the minister submerges the child in the water, that signifies death; but, when he again lifts it out, that signifies life. That is how Paul explains it in Romans 6 [:4]: "We were buried therefore with him through baptism into death; that, as Christ was raised from the dead through the glory of the Father, so we also might walk in newness of life." We call this death and resurrection a new creation, a regeneration, a spiritual birth; and it ought not to be understood, allegorically, of the death of sin and the life of grace, as is the custom of many, but of a real death and a real resurrection. For the significance of baptism is not a matter of our imagination. Sin is not dead, nor is grace fully received, till the sinful body which we inhabit in this life is no more, as the apostle says in the same passage. For, while we are in the flesh, the desires of the flesh are active, and often stirred up. When we begin to have faith, at the same time we begin to die to this world and to live to God in the future life. Thus, faith is verily both death and resurrection; and this is that spiritual baptism into which we are submerged and from which we rise.

It is permissible to regard baptism as a washing away of sin, but this meaning is too slight and mild to express the full meaning of baptism, which is, rather, symbolical of death and resurrection. For this reason I would that those who are to be baptized were wholly submerged in the water, as the term implies and the mystery signifies; not that I consider it necessary to do so, but that I consider it to be a beautiful act to give the sign of baptism as fully and completely as possible. It represents something complete and full, and without doubt it was so instituted by Christ in the form of total immersion. A sinner requires, not so much to be washed, as to die. This is in order that he should be reborn and made another creature, and that the rite may correspond with the death and resurrection of Christ. Then through baptism the sinner would, as it were, also die and rise again. Though you may say that Christ was washed clean of His mortality when He died and rose again, yet the expression is less forceful than if you were to say that He was totally transformed and renewed. Thus there is more vigour in our form of words if we say that to us our baptism means to die utterly and in every way, and to rise to eternal life, than merely that we are washed from our sins.

Here again you will see that the sacrament of baptism, even as a sign, is not a momentary action, but something permanent. While the rite itself is quite transitory, yet the purpose which it signifies lasts till death; indeed till the resurrection at the last day. That which baptism signifies, operates as long as we live, i.e., every day we die, and every day we rise again. We die, I say, not merely mentally and spiritually, in that we renounce

the sins and vanities of the world; but, rather, we begin in
fact to leave this mortal body and to lay hold on the future
life. In this way, we experience what they call a "real" and
bodily transition from this world to the Father.

We must beware of those who have weakened and diminished the force of baptism, and, while declaring it true that
grace is infused into us, yet maintain that, through our sin,
this grace gradually disappears. Then we are compelled to go
to heaven by some other route—as if our baptism had now
become quite inoperative. You must not adopt that view. You
must understand baptism to mean something by which ever-
more you die and live; and, therefore, whether you use the
confessional, or any other means of grace, you must still return
to the very power that baptism exercises, and begin again to
do what you were baptized for, and what your baptism signified. But baptism never does lose its efficacy—not so long as
you refuse to despair of reaching salvation. It is true that you
may wander awhile from the sign, but that does not make the
sign impotent. Although you only receive the sacrament of
baptism once, you are continually baptized anew by faith, always dying and yet ever living. When you were baptized, your
whole body was submerged and then came forth again out of
the water. Similarly, the essence of the rite was that grace
permeated your whole life, in both body and soul; and that it
will bring you forth, at the last day, clothed in the white robe
of immortality. It follows that we never lose the sign of baptism nor its force; indeed we are continually being rebaptized,
until we attain to the completion of the sign at the last day.

You will perceive, therefore, that whatever kind of life we
live, if it serves for the mortification of the flesh and the vivifi-
cation of the spirit, it is relevant to our baptism. The sooner we
depart this life, the more quickly we bring our baptism to its
completion; and the worse our sufferings, the more fully we
conform to our baptism. Similarly, the church was soundest
when martyrs suffered death every day, and were accounted
as sheep for the slaughter. At that time, the virtue of baptism
was in full force in the church, whereas to-day we are actually
unaware of that force, overwhelmed as we are by works and
man-made doctrines. All our experience of life should be baptismal in character, viz., the fulfilment of the sign or sacrament

of baptism. We have been freed from all else that we might devote ourselves to baptism alone, that is to say, death and resurrection.

Our splendid freedom, and our proper understanding of baptism, are in shackles to-day, and the blame can be laid at the door of the autocratic pontiff of Rome. As chief shepherd, it ought to be quite emphatically his first duty to preach this doctrine and defend this freedom; as Paul says, I Corinthians 4 [:1]: "Let a man so account of us, as of ministers of Christ, and stewards of the mysteries or sacraments of God." But the pontiff's only concern is with oppressing us with his decrees and laws, and in ensnaring and keeping us captive under his absolute authority. Without discussing the impious and indefensible fact that the pope omits teaching these mysteries, I ask most earnestly, By what right does he impose laws upon us? Who gave him power to deprive us of this liberty of ours which was given to us in our baptism? As I have already said, there is no greater duty set before us in the whole of our life than to be baptized, and so to die and live by our faith in Christ. This is the sole thing that should be taught, especially by the chief shepherd. But, to-day, faith is passed over in silence; the church is smothered by endless regulations about rites and ceremonies; the virtue and the knowledge of baptism have vanished; faith in Christ is obstructed.

Therefore I declare that neither pope, nor bishop, nor any one else, has the right to impose so much as a single syllable of obligation upon a Christian man without his own consent. Whatever is done otherwise is done autocratically. Therefore the prayers, fastings, donations, and whatever else the pope ordains and demands in the whole body of his decrees, which are as numerous as they are iniquitous, he has no right to demand and ordain; and he sins against the liberty of the church in so doing. The churchmen of to-day are most energetic guardians of "ecclesiastical liberty", in the sense of their freedom to use and possess the stones, timber, lands, and rents; for "ecclesiastical" has come to mean the same as "spiritual". By this same false terminology, they not only put the true liberty of the church into bonds but utterly destroy it. They have done worse than the Turks, and contrary to the apostle when he said: "Be ye not the servants of men" [I Cor. 7:23].

But it is indeed to become servants of men when we are made subject to their statutes and tyrannical laws.

The disciples of the pope help on this impious and sinful despotism when they twist and debase in their own support Christ's words: "He that heareth you, heareth me" [Luke 10:16]. For they puff out their cheeks, and cry up this passage on behalf of their usages. Yet Christ spoke these words to the apostles when they were going forth to preach the gospel and He meant them to refer to the gospel only; but the Romanists leave out the gospel and apply the words only to their own fabrications. It says again, in John 10 [:27]: "My sheep hear my voice, and the voice of another they do not hear." The Romanists, therefore, leave out the gospel so that the popes may sound forth their own voice as if it were the voice of Christ Himself; nevertheless, it is their own voice which they sound, and yet they expect to get a hearing. But the apostle said that he had not been sent to baptize but to preach the gospel [I Cor. 1:17]. Therefore no one is subject to the papal traditions, nor is he required to obey the pope except when he is teaching the gospel and proclaiming Christ; and the pope ought not to teach anything except faith, and this is the freest of all things. Christ said: "He that heareth you, heareth me"; why then does not the pope hear others? It was not to Peter only that Christ said: "He that heareth you". In fine, where true faith abides, there of necessity must be also the word of faith. Why does not the pope, who is no believer, sometimes hear a servant of his who does believe, and who preaches faith? The pontiffs are nought but blind.

Other Romanists are even more shameless in their deductions from the passage in Matthew 16 [:19]: "Whatsoever ye shall bind", etc. They claim that here the pope is given authority to decree laws, whereas, in that passage, Christ was dealing with those sins which were to be retained, and those to be forgiven; He was not giving authority to take the whole church into captivity and oppress it by any laws. But this dictator of ours takes and falsifies everything with his lies, and forcibly twists and deforms the word of God. Yet, I must acknowledge that even this absolutism, accursed though it be, ought to be borne with by Christians, as is the case with every other act of violence in this world. Christ said: "Whosoever shall smite thee

on thy right cheek, turn to him the other also" [Matt. 5:39].
But my complaint against those ungodly priests is that they
can, and do, perform these deeds legally; and also they pretend, while doing so, to be seeking the welfare of Christendom
with this Babylon of theirs; and they try to persuade everyone
to believe this pretence. If they, on their part, do these things,
and we, on our part, suffer their violence, both sides being
aware of its wicked and oppressive nature, then we should
rightly count it among the things which contribute to the mortifying of this life, and the fulfilling of our baptism. In that
case, our conscience might remain unhurt, and even rejoice
in the wrongs we had suffered. But as it is, they wish to deprive
us of our consciousness of liberty in such a way that we believe
that what they do is well done; and that it is not permissible
to censure it, or complain that what they do is evil. Just because they are wolves, they pretend to work like shepherds;
and just because they are Antichrist, they wish to be honoured
as Christ.

It is solely on behalf of this liberty that I cry aloud; and I
do so with good conscience, and in the faith that it is not possible for either men or angels rightfully to impose even a single law upon Christians except with their consent; for we are
free from all things. Yet, whatever the impositions may be,
they are to be borne in such a way that we preserve liberty of
conscience; the conscience that knows and affirms unhesitat-
ingly that an injury is being done to it, even though it glories
in bearing that injury. In this way we take precautions not to
justify the tyranny, even though we do not murmur against it.
"For who is it", asks St. Peter, "that will harm you if ye be
followers of that which is good?" [I Pet. 3:13]. "All things
work together for good for the chosen" [Rom. 8:28]. Yet but
few are aware of this glorious aspect of baptism, or know how
happy is this practice of Christian freedom; the majority cannot know them on account of papal oppression. I hereby dis-
entangle myself, and redeem my conscience, by laying this
charge against the pope and all the Romanists, and say: If
they do not abrogate their laws and traditions, restore proper
liberty to the churches of Christ, and cause that liberty to be
taught, then they are guilty of all the souls which perish in this
miserable servitude; and that the papacy is identical with the

kingdom of Babylon and the real Antichrist. For who else is the
"man of sin" and the "son of perdition" [II Thess. 2:3] than
he who, by his doctrines and statutes, increases sin and multi-
plies the loss of souls in Christendom, while himself enthroned
in the church as if he were God? All of this has been done to
excess for many generations by papal absolutism. It has ex-
tinguished faith, beclouded the sacraments, suppressed the
gospel, decreed laws which are not merely impious and sacrilegious but even barbarous and ignorant; and it has multiplied
them without limit.

Consider, then, the wretchedness of our servitude. "How
doth the city sit solitary that was full of people, and the mis-
tress of the gentiles is become as a widow, the princess of
provinces is laid under tribute! There is none to comfort her,
even her friends spurn her", etc. [Lam. 1:1 f.]. There are to-
day as many ordinances, as many rites, as many sects, as many
votaries, as many anxieties and works, as there are Christians
busied with them; and the result is that Christian people forget
they have been baptized. Because of the multitude of locusts,
caterpillars, and cankerworms, I say, no one is able to remember that he has been baptized or what benefits follow on baptism. We ought, when baptized, to have been like little children, who are not preoccupied with any cares or any works,
but entirely free, redeemed, and safe merely through the glory
of their baptism.

As against what I have been saying, it may be objected
that, when infants are baptized, they cannot receive the promises of God; are incapable of accepting the baptismal faith;
and that, therefore, either faith is not a requisite, or else it is
useless to baptize infants. On this matter I agree with everyone
in saying that infants are helped by vicarious faith: the faith
of those who present them for baptism. The word of God,
whenever uttered, is powerful enough to change the hearts
even of the ungodly, and these are not less unresponsive and
incapable than any infant. Further, all things are possible in
response to the prayers of a believing church when it presents
the infant, and this is changed, cleansed, and renewed, by their
infused faith. Nor should I doubt that an irreligious adult could
be transformed by any of the sacraments, if he were presented and prayed for by such a church; just as we read in the

Gospel that the paralytic was healed by vicarious faith [Matt. 9:2 ff.; Mark 2:1 ff.]. For these reasons, I would readily admit that the sacraments of the new law are efficacious in giving grace, not only to those who offer no resistance, but even to those who resist most obstinately. What cannot the faith of the church and the prayer of believers remove, seeing it is believed that Stephen converted the apostle Paul by this power? In that case, however, the sacraments accomplish what they do, not of themselves, but by virtue of faith, without which they are without any effect, as I have said.

The question has been raised whether a child yet unborn could be baptized, if a hand or a foot were projecting from the womb. On this point, I am uncertain what to say, and I confess my ignorance. Nor do I know whether it is satisfactory to assume, as the Romanists do, that the whole soul is in every part of the body; for it is not the soul, but the body that receives the outer baptism of water. But neither do I agree with those who say, quite insistently, that it is impossible for one not yet born to be reborn. Therefore I leave this question to the further teaching of the Spirit; meanwhile, let each one follow his own judgment.

But there is one point I should like to add, of which I wish I could persuade the world, namely, that all vows whatsoever should be abolished or ignored, no matter whether "spiritual" vows, or those about pilgrimages, or other works; and that we should remain in that most spiritual and active freedom which is given us by baptism. No one can say how much this excessively widespread delusion about vows detracts from the due value of our baptism, and darkens our knowledge of Christian freedom; to say nothing, for the time being, about the utterly innumerable and immeasurable dangers which are increased every day by the passion for vows, and by the unthinkable lightheartedness in which they are undertaken. Oh! you most ungodly priests and unfaithful pastors slumbering in security and wanton in greed, without any sympathy for the most serious and perilous "affliction of Joseph"! [Amos 6:6].

A general edict would be needed in this case, abolishing all vows, especially those of a life-long character, and recalling everyone to his baptismal vows; either this, or else all should be earnestly advised not to take a vow temerariously. None should be invited to take them. It would be better if difficulties and delays were put in the way of taking vows. For the vows we took at our baptism were ample, more than we are able to keep. We shall have enough on our hands if we give ourselves to this duty alone. As matters stand, we compass sea and land to convert many, to fill the world with priests, monks and nuns, and to incarcerate them all under vows in perpetuity. On this point, there are some who assert and argue that a work done within the ambit of a vow is more valuable than a work outside, and takes precedence of it; and in heaven will be preferred to the others, and receive no one knows what reward. Oh! blind Pharisees who measure righteousness and sanctity by size, or number, or some such standard; although, in God's sight, it is measured solely by faith. In His sight, there is no difference between works except that of the measure of faith which they express. Ungodly men are very facile in the use of language, employing their own inventions to deck out man-made views and works, and to draw the unthinking masses on. These can usually be led on by the outer show of works, to the great detriment of faith, the oblivion of baptism, and the hurt of Christian freedom. Since a vow is a kind of law or obligation, it follows of necessity that, when vows are multiplied, laws and works are multiplied; whereas faith is blotted out, and our baptismal freedom is made captive. Others, not content with these alluring evils, add that the entry into a religious order is a kind of new baptism, and baptism may afterwards be repeated as often as the purpose of the "spiritual" life itself is again renewed. In this way, these votaries must take credit to themselves alone for their righteousness, holiness, and glory; and leave nothing at all whereby those who have only been baptized may bear comparison with themselves. To-day, the Roman pontiff, the fount and source of all superstitions, has used pompously-worded bulls and indulgences to confirm, approve, and embellish these ways of life; while no one thinks baptism worthy even of being remembered. And, as I have said, the Romanists drive the guileless people of Christ, by this specious outer show, into whatever giddy dangers are chosen for them, until the latter lose all gratitude for their baptism, and begin to think they are becoming better Christians by their works than others by their faith. Therefore God, on

His part, shows Himself froward with the froward; and punishes the ingratitude and pride of those given to vows; and so orders it that they do not fulfil their own vows, not even by the most strenuous labours, and although the votaries remain swamped under by them. Meanwhile they remain unaware of the grace given by faith and by baptism. And, because their spirit is unworthy in God's sight, He ordains that they persist in their hypocrisy to the end of time, yet never reaching righteousness. Thus they fulfil what Isaiah said, "The land is full of idols" [Isaiah 2:8].

Of course, I should not prohibit or discourage any one who, of his own choice, wished to make some vow in private, for I am far from despising or condemning vows as such; but I am altogether against the kind of votive life which is publicly established and instituted. To have a private liberty to make vows at one's own peril is enough. But I regard it as pernicious, both to the church and to ordinary people, to urge and commend a system of living publicly under the obligation of discharging a vow. I do this, first, because it is in no small degree repugnant to the Christian life; because a vow is a kind of ceremonial law, a mere human tradition, and arrogation of rights, from which the church has been delivered by baptism. Secondly, because the votive life is not commended in the Scriptures; particularly the vows of perpetual celibacy, obedience, and poverty. Now whatever cannot be supported by Scriptural example is fraught with danger; it should never be urged on any one, much less set up for the public in general as a recognized mode of life. On the other hand, it must be permitted to any one to venture on it at his own peril. For certain special works are wrought by the Spirit in a few, but such works should not be cited as examples, or as a mode of life for all.

But I fear very much that these ways of living under a vow, as among the monastics, are of the sort which the apostle foretold: "They shall teach lies in hypocrisy, forbidding to marry, and commanding to abstain from meats which God hath created to be received with thanksgiving" [I Tim. 4:2 f.]. Nor let any one face me with St. Bernard, St. Francis, St. Dominic, and others who have founded orders, or augmented them. God is terrible and marvellous in His counsels in regard to the sons of men. He could preserve Daniel, Ananias, Azarias, and Misael, one and all, when they were engaged in administering the kingdom of Babylon (and when they were surrounded by paganism); therefore, He is able to sanctify those whose way of life is full of peril, or to control them by some strange work of His Spirit, while yet not desiring this to be a precedent for others. Further, it is certain that not one of them was saved by his vows and his religiosity, but only by faith, through which indeed all are saved. Pretentious lives, lived under vows, are more hostile to faith than anything else can be.

However, on matters like these, everyone is fully entitled to his own opinion. But let me continue the discussion I have already begun. I now wish to speak up for the liberty of the church and the glory of baptism. I feel that, for the general good, I ought to give the counsel which I learnt under the guidance of the Spirit. With this in mind, I would suggest to those in high places in the church, firstly, that they should do away with all vows and religious orders; or at least not speak of them with approval or praise. If they are unwilling to do this, I would urge all who wish to be more certain of being saved to refrain from taking any vows, especially those of great and life-long consequence, particularly in the case of youths in their teens and early twenties. My first reason, as I have said, is that this kind of life finds no testimony or support in Scripture, but has been made to look imposing solely by the works of monks and priests. However numerous, sacred, and arduous they may be, these works, in God's sight, are in no way whatever superior to the works of a farmer labouring in the field, or of a woman looking after her home. Rather, all are measured by Him by faith alone; as it says in Jeremiah 5 [:3], "O Lord, thine eyes have respect unto faith", and Ecclesiasticus 32 [:27], "In all thy works believe with faith in thy heart, for this is to keep the commandments of God." Indeed, it occurs quite frequently that the common work of a serving man or a maid is more acceptable than all the fastings and other works of monks and priests where faith is lacking. That is in fact our present situation; vows only tend to the increase of pride and presumption. It would almost seem, indeed, that nowhere is there less of faith, or of the true church, than among the priests, monks, and bishops; and that, in fact, these

persons are gentiles or hypocrites although they consider themselves the church, or the heart of the church, and spiritual
men and rulers of the church, when really they are far from it.
These are in fact "the people of the captivity", who hold in
captivity the gifts given freely to us in baptism, while the few
poor "people of the land" appear contemptible in their eyes,
as also do those who are married.

From the foregoing, we may deduce two major errors of
the pope of Rome:

Firstly, that he grants dispensations from sworn vows, and
does it as if he alone among all Christians had authority, such
is human temerity and audacity. Surely, if he is able to grant
dispensations, then any Christian whatever may grant them,
either to his neighbour or even to himself. If, however, the
ordinary Christian has no power of dispensation, the pope has
no right to it. Whence does he derive "authority"? From the
possession of the keys? But the keys belong to all, and have to
do only with the question of sin, Matthew 18 [:15 f.]. Since
the Romanists themselves admit that vows come within the
divine law, why then does the pope cheat and ruin wretched
men by granting dispensations in matters falling within the
divine laws where there are dispensations? On the basis of the
section in the decretals entitled "Of vows and their redemption",[22] he babbles away and claims that he has the power to
alter vows. Formerly the Mosaic law taught that the firstling
of an ass might be exchanged for a lamb; and the pope uses
this permission as an analogy—as if the firstling of an ass were
the same thing as a vow which requires to be fulfilled. Again,
if the Lord in His own law decreed that a lamb should be
exchanged for an ass, it scarcely follows that the pope, who is
a man, has the same power of dealing with a law which not
he, but God had made. It was not the pope who made this
decretal, but, since it is so exceptionally crazy and impious, it
must have been an ass masquerading as the pope.

Secondly, he greatly errs in decreeing that a marriage
should be terminated if one of the parties enters a monastery
without the consent of the other, and before the marriage has
been consummated. By all that is holy, I ask which of the

22 *Decret. Greg., lib.* III, tit. 24, cap. 7.

devils gave the pope this portentous power? God commanded men to keep faith, and to guard the truth towards each other; and, further, that a man should do good with what is his own, for God hates robbery for burnt offering, as He says through the mouth of Isaiah [Isaiah 61:8]. Now, in marriage, each of the parties owes fidelity to the other by their compact, and no longer is either his own. Neither has any right or power to break faith, and what either does alone, against the will of the other, is a kind of robbery. And, further, why should it not be permitted, by the same ruling, that a man heavily in debt should enter, and be welcomed, into a religious order, and be freed from his debts, and be at liberty to break faith? O blind, blind men! Which is greater, fidelity commanded by God, or vows worked out and assumed by men? You, O pope, are a pastor of souls; and you, who teach these doctrines, are Doctors of Sacred Theology. Then why do you teach them? It is because you have extolled the votive life to appear superior to marriage, but not faithfulness, which is such as to exalt all things. Rather, you exalt works, which are as nothing in God's sight, or are all of equal worth as far as merit is concerned.

For myself, therefore, I am sure that neither men nor angels can grant dispensation in regard to vows rightly so called. On this point I am, for myself, not fully persuaded that all the vows that are made nowadays belong to the category of a vow. An example of this is that astonishingly ridiculous piece of folly wherein parents vow on behalf of a child, perhaps a baby and still unborn, that it should enter a religious order, or observe perpetual chastity. It is quite certain that this cannot be classed as a vow. Rather it seems to be a kind of mockery of God, since the parents' vows in no way lie within their province to perform. As to the religious orders, candidates themselves take three vows, which the more I study the less I understand; and I am puzzled to know the origin of the custom of taking these vows. Still less by far do I understand in what year of one's age it is possible to take vows, properly so called, and of a valid kind. It is a good thing that all agree that no vows are valid if taken before the age of puberty. Yet the Romanists deceive a large number of children on this point, who know nothing of the age of puberty, or of what they are vowing. Those who are receiving them leave the age of puberty out of account; nevertheless when these children make their profession, they are kept captive just as if their consent had been given in riper years; then they become the prey of uneasy consciences—it is all as if an invalid vow became valid at last by the passage of time.

To me it seems foolish for one group of people to fix a date when the vows of others will become operative, or to do this at a time when the votaries cannot prescribe for themselves. Nor do I see why a vow should be valid if taken after the eighteenth birthday, but not after the tenth or twelfth. It is not enough to say that, at eighteen, a person is aware of his sensual impulses. What about it if he scarcely feels them at twenty or thirty, or if they are stronger at thirty than twenty? And why not fix a date in respect of the vows of poverty and obedience? What age will you set for the feelings of greed and pride, seeing that even very spiritually-minded persons are scarcely aware of possessing these motives? It follows that there is no special age at which any vow becomes valid and binding, unless and until we shall have become spiritually-minded; but then, however, we should have no need of vows. It is obvious therefore that this is an uncertain and very dangerous matter; and it would be a counsel of safety to keep these lofty ways of life free of vows, and leave them to the Spirit only, as used to be done. They should never be transformed into ways of life to which one is bound for ever.

For the time being, however, I have said enough about baptism and the liberty pertaining to it. In due time, perhaps, I shall discuss the matter of vows at greater length, and in very truth there is an urgent need of discussing them.

(3) The Sacrament of Penance

In the third section we are to discuss the sacrament of penance. I have already expounded at length my views on this subject in tracts and discussions which have been published but which have given considerable offence to many.[23] In the present instance, and for the sake of unveiling the tryanny which is as aggressive here as in the case of the sacra-

---

[23] Ablass und Gnade; Sermo de Poenitentia, WA I, 317–24; Freiheit des Sermons, WA I, 380–93; etc.

ment of the bread, I must briefly repeat what I have said. On account of the many opportunities afforded by these two sacraments for money-making and self-seeking, the greed of the shepherds has raged with unbelievable activity against Christ's sheep. As we have already seen in discussing vows, baptism has largely lost its place among adults, with the result that papal greed has further opportunities of indulgence.

The first and principal evil connected with the sacrament of penance is that the sacrament itself has been made so utterly void that not a vestige of it remains. Like the other two sacraments I have already discussed, this also consists, on the one hand, of the words of the divine promise, and, on the other, of our faith. But the Romanists have undermined both. In conformity with their arrogance, they have adapted the words of promise in which Christ said, in Matthew 16 [:19], "Whatsoever thou shalt bind", etc.; in 18 [:18], "Whatsoever ye shall have bound", etc.; and in John 20 [:23], "Whose soever sins ye remit, they are remitted unto them", etc. These words evoke the faith of penitents, and make them fit to receive forgiveness of sins. But in none of their books, teachings, or sermons, do the Romanists explain that these words of Scripture contain promises made to Christians; nor do they explain what things are to be believed, and what great comfort may be gained by doing so. Rather, their only object has been to extend their own dictatorship by force and violence as far, as widely, and as deeply as possible. At length, some have begun to command the angels in heaven; they give themselves airs, in their incredibly rampant impiety, as if they had received in these words the right of ruling in heaven and earth, and of possessing the power of "binding" even in heaven. They say nothing about saving faith required of the people, but are garrulous about the absolute powers of the popes. Christ, however, said nothing at all about power, but spoke only of faith.

For Christ established in His church neither emperors, nor potentates, nor despots, but ministers—as we learn when the apostle says: "Let a man account of us as ministers of Christ and dispensers of God's mysteries" [I Cor. 4:1]. When Christ says: "Whosoever believes and is baptized, shall be saved" [Mark 16:16], this is to evoke the faith of those about to be baptized, so that they might have the assurance, based on this promise, that, if they were baptized as believers, they would receive salvation. And, in founding this ceremony, He imparted no power whatever. The only thing instituted was the service rendered by those who perform the act of baptizing. Similarly, in the place where it says: "Whatsoever thou shalt bind", etc. [Matt. 16:19], Christ is calling out the faith of the penitent, by giving a certitude based on the words of the promise, that, if he be forgiven as a believer here below, his forgiveness holds good in heaven. This passage makes no mention at all of conferring power, but only deals with the service performed by the administrator promising the words of forgiveness. It is very remarkable that, by some chance, these blind and overbearing men have not arrogated to themselves an oppressive authority out of the baptismal promise. But if they have not done so there, why have they presumed to do it in the case of the penitential promise? Both are equally cases of ministry, the promises being alike, and the sacraments of the same sort. If baptism is not the right of Peter alone, then it is a wicked imposition to arrogate the power of the keys to the pope alone.

Similarly, when Christ says: "Take, this is my body which is given for you. This is the cup in my blood", etc. [I Cor. 11:24 f.], the eating calls forth the faith of the partakers, so that, when their conscience has been confirmed by faith in these words, they may have the certitude, as they eat, that their sins are forgiven. Nor is there anything said here about power, the administration being alone mentioned. Whereas the baptismal promise is still held valid so far as infants are concerned, the promise connected with the bread and the cup has been annulled to minister to their avarice; instead of faith we find works; and, for the testament, a sacrifice. The penitential promise has been transformed into a most outrageous instrument of tyranny, and a power of control has been established greater than any in the temporal sphere.

Not content with this, our Babylon has so nearly put an end to faith that it barefacedly denies the latter to be necessary in this sacrament. With an antichristian impiety, it even defines as heretical any assertion that faith is necessary. What more could be done by the arbitrary use of power than they have already done? Truly, "by the rivers of Babylon we sat and wept when we remembered thee, O Zion. We hanged our

harps upon the willows in the midst thereof" [Ps. 137:1 f.].
May the Lord curse the sterile willows growing by the rivers
which belong to men like that. Amen.

Promise and faith having thus been blotted out or subverted, let us see what the Romanists have put in their place.
They have divided penance into three parts: contrition, confession, and satisfaction; but they have done it in such a manner as to set aside what was good in them in detail, and have set
up in each part the form of oppression which they preferred.

In the first place, they teach contrition in such a way that
it not only takes precedence of faith in the promises, but is
held far superior. Indeed, they never mention faith. They stick
closely to works, and to those examples of it in Scripture which
tell of many who obtained rewards on account of their heartfelt contrition and humility; but they do not advert to the faith
which effected that contrition and remorse of heart; as it is
written of Nineveh in Jonah 3 [:5], "And the people of Nineveh
believed in the Lord and proclaimed a fast." Being more au-
dacious and more wicked than the Ninevites, these men have
invented a kind of semicontrition which, by virtue of the keys
(which they do not understand), becomes contrition proper.
This they present to the ungodly and the unbelieving, and
thereby entirely abnegate the true contrition. O the unbearable
wrath of God in that these things are taught in the very church
of Christ! Faith and its works having been destroyed, we feel
secure when we adopt man-made doctrines and opinions, and
so we simply perish. For a contrite heart is a matter of very
great importance, but it is only found in connection with an
ardent faith in God's promises of reward and punishment.
This faith, divining the unchangeableness of the truth of God,
disturbs and reproves the conscience, and so renders it contrite;
but, at the same time, it exalts and comforts that conscience,
and so keeps it contrite. Wherever faith is found, the certainty
of punishment causes contrition, and the trustworthiness of the
promises is the means of consolation; and through this faith a
man merits forgiveness of sin. Hence, faith takes precedence
of all else as a thing needing to be taught and called forth.
Once faith is present, contrition and divine comfort follow naturally and inevitably.

Therefore, although the Romanists are partly right in teach-

ing that you will become contrite if you enumerate and examine your sins; yet that is a hazardous and perverse method
of teaching. For they should previously teach the prime elements in, and causes of, contrition: the unchangeable character
of the divine verities, whether of warning or promise. This
teaching should be given in the way that will induce faith, so
that they may understand the importance of having their
minds centred on the divine truth; then they will be made
humble and yet lifted up. This is far better than to meditate
on one's seething sins, which, if considered before taking God's
truth into account, will rather refresh and increase the desire
for sin than produce contrition. I shall not discuss at the present juncture that insurmountable and chaotic heap of labours
which they impose upon us, when they formulate a special
contrition for each and every sin; for this is to ask the impossible. Besides, we can only know the minor part of our sins; and,
further, even our good works are found to be sins according to
Psalm 143 [:2]: "Enter not into judgment with thy servant;
for in thy sight shall no man living be justified." It is enough
if we sorrow for those sins which are actually gnawing our
consciences, and which can be easily recognized in the mirror
of our memory. Anyone in this mood is undoubtedly prepared
to feel sorrow and fear for all his sins; and he will sorrow and
be afraid whenever they recur to his mind in the future. Therefore beware of confiding in your own contrition, or of attribut-
ing the forgiveness of your sins to your own remorse. God does
not esteem you on account of these feelings, but on account
of the faith by which you have believed in His admonitions
and His promises, and which causes its own kind of remorse.
From all that I have said, it follows that none of the virtue of
penitence is due to the diligence with which we have recol-
lected and enumerated our sins, but only to God's fidelity and
to our faith. All the rest are works and fruits which are produced afterwards spontaneously. These do not reform a man's
character; rather, they are the things a man does after he has
been regenerated by faith in God's faithfulness. So it is that "a
smoke went up in his wrath, and because he was wroth he
shook the mountains and kindled them", as it says in Psalm
18 [:8]. Fear of His warnings comes first, and this burns up

the wicked; but faith, which accepts the warnings, sends up contrition like a cloud of smoke, etc.

Contrition, however, has suffered less from unbridled power and greed than from ungodliness and pestilential doctrines, to which, indeed, it has fallen a total prey. Confession and satisfaction, on the other hand, have been made into an egregious factory of money and power.

First, in regard to confession:

Without doubt, confession of sins is necessary, and in accordance with the divine commandments. In Matthew 3 [:6], we read that they "were baptized by John in the Jordan confessing their sins"; and I John 1 [:9 f.], "If we confess our sins, he is faithful and just to forgive us our sins. If we say that we have not sinned, we make him a liar, and his word is not in us." If it was not permissible for the saints to deny their sins, how much more obligatory is it for those guilty of great and open sins to confess them. Most conclusively of all, the institution of confession is proved by Matthew 18 [:15 ff.], where Christ teaches that a brother who is doing wrong should be reproved, brought before the church, and accused; and then excommunicated if he will not listen. But he can be said "to hear" when, heeding the correction, he acknowledges and confesses his sin.

As for secret confession as practised to-day, though it cannot be proved from Scripture, yet it seems a highly satisfactory practice to me; it is useful and even necessary. I would not wish it to cease; rather I rejoice that it exists in the church of Christ, for it is a singular medicine for afflicted consciences. If we lay bare to a brother what lies on our conscience, and in confidence unveil that which we have kept hidden, we receive, through the mouth of a brother, a comfort which God has spoken. When we accept this in faith, it gives us peace by the mercy of God through the words spoken to us by a brother. What I reject is solely that this kind of confession should be transformed into a means of oppression and extortion on the part of the pontiffs. For they "reserve" to themselves even the secret sins, and order them to be made known to confessors nominated by themselves, of course to the torment of consciences. They not merely play at being pontiffs, but utterly scorn the true duties of a pontiff, which are to preach the gos-

pel and to care for the poor. Nay, the impious despots reserve
to themselves those trespasses which are mostly of little moment; while the greater, sure enough, they leave everywhere to
the common run of priests. Of the former class are the ridiculous kind fabricated in the bull, *"Coena domini"*. Indeed, as
if in order that their wicked perversity might become the more
obvious, not only do they not reserve, but even teach and approve, things which are adverse to the worship of God, to the
faith, and to the chief commandments. One might specify such
things as running about on pilgrimages, the perverse worship
of saints, the mendacious legends of saints, various beliefs in
works and in the practice of ceremonies; by all of which, faith
in God is lessened, while idolatry is fostered, as is the case
nowadays. The result is that, now, all our pontiffs are of the
kind that Jeroboam formerly instituted in Dan and Beersheba.
They were to serve the golden calves, but they knew nothing
of God's laws, of faith, or of anything that pertained to shepherding Christ's sheep. But, by practising what they themselves invented, they oppressed the people by fear and violence.

Now, I urge that these "reservations", that have been imposed upon us by force, should be borne patiently, just as
Christ commanded us to bear all forms of oppression, and
taught us to obey such despots. Nevertheless I deny, and I refuse to credit, that Romanists have any right to make these
reservations, or that they can prove a single jot or tittle of
them; whereas I myself can prove the opposite. In the first
place, in Matthew 18, when speaking of known transgressions,
Christ taught us that we had gained the soul of our brother if
he listened when corrected; and that he was not to be haled before the church unless he refused to hear us. It must therefore
be all the more relevant to secret sins, that they would be forgiven if voluntarily confessed by one brother to another. It follows that it is unnecessary for this kind of sin to be brought
before the church: the prelate or priest as they pretentiously
interpret the term. We have Christ's authority in this passage,
as also in another, where He says, to the same effect: "Whatsoever ye shall bind on earth shall be bound in heaven and
whatsoever ye shall loose on earth shall be loosed in heaven"
[Matt. 18:18]. This is said to Christians individually and col-
lectively. He said the same thing again when He declared:

"Again I say unto you, that if two of you shall agree on earth as touching anything that they shall ask, it shall be done for them of my Father which is in heaven" [Matt. 18:19]. Similarly, in the case of the brother who lays bare his secret sins before his fellow and seeks forgiveness, he is assuredly at one in the truth with his brother on earth, and that truth is Christ. Christ speaks even more plainly on this point, confirming what has been said, when He declares: "Of a truth I say unto you, where two or three are gathered together in my name, there am I in the midst of them."

In view of the foregoing, there is no doubt in my mind that a man's secret sins are forgiven him when he makes a voluntary confession before a brother in private, and, on reproof, he asks for pardon and mends his ways. No matter how much any pope may rage against these contentions, the fact is that Christ manifestly gave the power of pronouncing forgiveness to anyone who had faith in Him. As a minor argument in support, it may be said that, if it were valid to "reserve" any secret sins in such a way that, unless they were forgiven, the transgressor were not saved, then the good works and superstitious acts of worship noted above would prove the greatest hindrance to attaining salvation, in spite of their being inculcated by the popes at the present day. Because if the very weighty matters are not a hindrance, surely there is far less reason for foolishly reserving the smaller matters. Such are the astonishing things which the ignorance and blindness of the shepherds bring about in the church. Therefore, I would admonish those princes in Babylon, and bishops in Bethaven [Hos. 4:15; 10:5], firstly, to refrain from making reserved cases of any kind; and, secondly, to give free permission for any brother or sister to hear confessions of secret sins. The result would be that one who has done wrong might lay bare his sin to whomsoever he chooses, and beg absolution, comfort, and Christ's very word from the mouth of his neighbour. For the only object of the Romanists, in their temerity, is to entrap the consciences of the weak-willed, to confirm their own powers of oppression, and to gain satisfaction for their greed out of the sins and failures of their brethren. Thus they stain their hand with the blood of men, with souls, and children are devoured by their parents.

Ephraim shall devour Juda, and Syria Israel, and not be satisfied, as Isaiah says [Isaiah 9:20 f.].

To these evils they have added the "circumstances", in detail; the "mothers", "daughters", "sisters", "sisters-in-law", "branches" and "fruits", worked out, if you please, by these most perspicacious men who have nothing else to do, into a kind of family tree of sins, with consanguinities and relationships; such is the fertility of irreligion and ignorance. No matter what good-for-nothing may have invented it, this kind of conception passes into the public law, like much else. The shepherds watch over the church of Christ in such a way that, whatever new superstitions or works may have entered the heads of these stupid devotees, they are immediately published, and even decked out with indulgences, or fortified by bulls. That shows how remote they are from prohibiting these things, and guarding faith and liberty for the people of God. For what is there in common between liberty and a despotic Babylon?

I would urge, no matter what the "circumstances", that they should be altogether passed over. Among Christian people there is only one "circumstance": it is, that a brother has sinned. No other person can be compared in importance with a Christian brother; nor will any reference to places, seasons, days, or any other rank superstition, do anything else than magnify things which matter nothing, to the hurt of those which matter everything. It is impossible for anything to be of greater weight and importance than the glory of Christian fellowship. But they tie us down to places and days and persons till the name of "brother" loses its value, and we serve, not in freedom, but in bondage, we to whom days, places, persons, and whatever else is external, are all on the same level.

In regard to "satisfaction", how unworthily the Romanists have dealt with it! I have discussed it in detail in dealing with indulgences. They have abused it to an extraordinary extent, to the ruin of Christians in body and soul. In the first place, they have expounded it in such a manner that the people in general have not the slightest understanding of the true satisfaction, although it means the renovation of life. Moreover, they are so insistent on satisfaction, and construe it as necessary in such a way, that they leave no room for faith in Christ.

With consciences pitilessly tortured by scruples on this point, one person runs to Rome, another here, and yet another there; this man to Chartreuse, that to some other place; one flays himself with rods, while another is mortifying his body with vigils and fasting. Under the same delusion, all are crying: "Lo! here is Christ, and lo! there", and thinking that the kingdom of Christ, though it is within us, will come with observation. These monstrous things we owe to thee, O thou whose seat is in Rome, together with thy soul-destroying laws and rituals. By these enormities, thou hast brought the world into such disorder that men think they can propitiate God for their sins by means of their works, whereas He is propitiated only by faith in the contrite heart. But thou dost not only silence faith by means of this restlessness, but even suppress it. Thy insatiable horse-leech then has some to whom it may cry, "Give, give", and to whom it may now sell sins.

Some Romanists have gone further, and have contrived machinations for driving souls to despair. They have decreed that if the satisfactions enjoined for any sins have not been duly fulfilled, all those sins must be confessed afresh. But there is no limit to the temerity of men who were bred to imprison their victims ten times over. Further, what is the proportion of those imbued with the idea that they are among the saved, and have made atonement for their sins if they have mumbled the words of the prayers enjoined by the priest, although, meanwhile, it never struck them to amend their mode of life? Their belief is that their lives were changed at the time of their contrition and repentance, the only further condition being that they should make satisfaction for the sins they have committed. How can they think otherwise when they have not been taught anything else? Not a thought is given to the mortification of the flesh. No value is attached to the example of Christ who, when He forgave the woman taken in adultery, said: "Go and sin no more" [John 8:11], thus imposing the cross, which meant mortifying the flesh. Considerable excuse has been given for perverted notions by the custom of pronouncing absolution to sinners before they have completed their "satisfaction". Hence it comes about that they are more concerned about fulfilling their "satisfaction", which is a lasting thing, than they are about contrition, which they believe was over and done with when they confessed. In the early church, on the other hand, absolution was posterior, and was only given when satisfaction had been completed. Thus it arose that, once the works had been completed, the penitents were exercised more fully in the faith and newness of life.

But, in regard to these matters, it must suffice to repeat what I have said in greater detail in connection with the subject of indulgences. In any case I have said enough for the time being about these three sacraments, which are both discussed, and yet not discussed, in so many noxious books on the Sentences and the laws. It remains to say a few words on the rest of the sacraments, lest I should needlessly appear to have rejected them.

(4) Confirmation

It is difficult to understand what the Romanists had in mind when they made the sacrament of confirmation out of the laying on of hands. We read that Christ touched the children in that way, and by it the apostles imparted the Holy Spirit, ordained presbyters, and cured the sick [Mark 10:16; Acts 8:17, 19:6, 6:6]; as the apostle wrote to Timothy: "Lay hands hastily on no man" [I Tim. 5:22]. Why have they not made a "confirmation" out of the sacrament of the Lord's Supper? It is written in Acts 9 [:19], "And he took food and was strengthened"; and, in Psalm 104 [:15], "And bread strengtheneth man's heart." On this reasoning, confirmation would include three sacraments—the Supper, ordination, and confirmation itself. But this argument suggests that anything whatever that the apostles did was a sacrament; but, in that case, why did the Romanists not make a sacrament of preaching?

I am not saying this because I condemn the seven sacraments as usages, but because I deny that it can be proved from Scripture that these usages are sacraments. O would that there were in the church the kind of laying on of hands that obtained in the time of the apostles, whether we preferred to call it confirmation or healing! But nothing of this remains nowadays, except what the Romanists have devised to embellish the duties of bishops, lest they be entirely without function in the church. For, after the bishops had ceased themselves to administer those sacraments which, together with preaching the gospel, would have been truly work of value, but which they regarded as inferior; and after they had handed these functions to assistants (probably because what the divine Majesty had instituted must be contemptible to men!), it was only right that something new should be introduced, that would be easy and not so very vexatious to these high and mighty supermen; and also that we should never treat the innovation as if it were something common, and commit it to subordinates. The argument is that what has been set up by the wisdom of men ought to be reverenced by men. The ministry any priest exercises, and the office he fills, should correspond in quality to that of the man himself. A bishop who neither preaches nor practises the cure of souls is nothing at all but an idol, in spite of the name and appearance of a bishop. This, however, is a digression; our present inquiry has to do with the nature of the *sacraments of divine institution, and we find no reason for enumerating confirmation among them.* What is required above all else for constituting a sacrament is that it should be accompanied by a divine promise, and this, of itself, calls for our faith. But nowhere do we read that Christ gave a promise in regard to confirmation, although He placed His hands on many people. Among other relevant passages, we read in Mark 16 [:18], "They shall lay hands on the sick and they shall recover." But no one has turned this into a sacrament, because it is impossible.

For these reasons, it is enough to regard confirmation as a rite, or ceremony, of the church, like the other ceremonies of the consecration of water, and similar things. If in all other cases physical objects may be sanctified by preaching and prayer, surely there is greater reason for thinking that a man may be sanctified by them. Nevertheless, since sermons and prayers for these purposes are not mentioned in Scripture as accompanied by a divine promise, they cannot be called sacraments in which we must have faith; nor are they helpful in promoting salvation from sin. On the other hand, by their very nature, sacraments save those who believe the divine promises always attaching to them.

(5) *Marriage*

There is no Scriptural warrant whatsoever for regarding marriage as a sacrament; and indeed the Romanists have used the same traditions, both to extol it as a sacrament, and to make it naught but a mockery. Let us look into this matter.

We have maintained that a word of divine promise is associated with every sacrament, and anyone who receives the sacrament must also believe in that word of promise, for it is impossible that the sign should in itself be the sacrament. But nowhere in Scripture do we read that anyone would receive the grace of God by getting married; nor does the rite of matrimony contain any hint that that ceremony is of divine institution. Nowhere do we read that it was instituted by God in order to symbolize something, although we grant that all things done in the sight of men can be understood as metaphors and allegories of things invisible. Yet metaphors and allegories are not sacraments, and it is of sacraments that we are speaking.

There has been such a thing as marriage itself ever since the beginning of the world, and it also exists amongst unbelievers to the present day. Therefore no grounds exist on which the Romanists can validly call it a sacrament of the new law, and a function solely of the church. The marriages of our ancestors were no less sacred than our own, nor less real among unbelievers than believers. Yet no one calls marriage of unbelievers a sacrament. Also, there are irreligious marriages even amongst believers, worse than among any pagans. Why then should it be called a sacrament in such a case, and yet not among pagans? Or are we talking the same sort of nonsense about marriage as about baptism and the church, and saying it is only a sacrament within the church? Is it the case that some people speak as if they were demented, and declare that temporal power exists only in the church? Yet this is so childish and laughable as to expose our ignorance and foolhardiness to the ridicule of unbelievers.

The Romanists will reply that the apostle says in Ephesians 5 [:31 f.], "The twain shall become one flesh; this is a great sacrament." Do you mean to contradict this plain statement of the apostle? My reply would be that to put forth this argu-

ment shows great negligence, and very careless and thought-
less reading. Nowhere in Holy Scripture does the noun, "sacrament", bear the meaning which is customary in the church,
but rather the opposite. In every instance, it means, not "a sign
of something sacred", but the sacred, secret, and recondite
thing itself. Thus in I Corinthians 4 [:1], Paul says: "Let a
man so account of us, as of ministers of Christ, and stewards
of the mysteries of God", that is the sacraments. Where the
Vulgate uses *sacramentum*, the Greek text reads *mysterion*, a
word which the translator sometimes translates, and sometimes
transliterates. Thus in the present case, the Greek says: "The
twain shall become one flesh. This is a great mystery." That
explains how it came about that they understood it as a sacrament of the new dispensation, and this they would have been
far from doing if they had read *mysterion*, as it is in Greek.

So also in I Timothy 3 [:16], Paul calls Christ Himself a
sacrament, when he says: He was evidently a great sacrament
(i.e., *mysterion*), for He was manifested in the flesh, justified
in the spirit, seen of angels, preached among the nations, believed on in the world, received up in glory. Why have the
Romanists not made an eighth sacrament out of this, when
Paul's authority is so plainly there? Although they restrained
themselves in this instance, when they had abundant opportunity to contrive sacraments, why are they so extravagant in
the others? Plainly, they have been betrayed by their ignorance
both of the facts and of the vocabulary; going simply by the
sound of the words, they have founded their own opinions on
them. Once they had arbitrarily taken "sacrament" to mean
"sign", they immediately, and without further criticism or
closer examination, set down the word "sign" every time they
read "sacrament" in Holy Scripture. In this manner also, they
have brought verbal meanings, human customs and such like,
into the sacred writings, transforming the proper meaning into
what they themselves have fabricated, turning anything into
anything else. Thus it comes about that they are always making a vague use of terms like "good works", "evil works", "sin",
"grace", "justification", "virtue", and almost all the main terms
and subjects. For they employ the whole of these arbitrarily,
on the basis of writings which are merely human, to the detriment of God's truth and our salvation.

According to Paul, sacrament, or mystery, is the very wisdom of the Spirit, and this is hidden in the mystery, as he says in I Corinthians 2 [:7 ff.]: "This wisdom is Christ, and, for the reason just given, He is unknown to the rulers of this world; and therefore they crucified Him. To them, He is still foolishness, a scandal, a stumbling-block, and a sign to be controverted." "Stewards of the mysteries" is the name given by Paul to those preachers who preach Christ and proclaim Him as the power and the wisdom of God, and this in such a way that, unless you believe, you will not understand [I Cor. 4:1]. Thus a sacrament is a *mysterion*, a secret thing described by words, but seized by faith in the heart. That is what is said in the passage under discussion: "The twain shall be one flesh, this is a great sacrament" (Greek—*mysterion*). The Romanists think this was said of matrimony, whereas Paul himself is using these words about Christ and the church, as he himself goes on to explain clearly when he says: "But I speak of Christ and of the church" [Eph. 5:32]. You see, then, the nature of the agreement between the Romanists and Paul? Paul says that he is speaking of the great sacrament in Christ and the church; they, however, preach it in terms of male and female. If it were permissible to handle Scripture in this unbridled fashion, there would be no room for surprise whatever sacrament they found in it, nor even if they found a hundred.

We conclude that Christ and the church are a "mystery", or something at once hidden and of great importance, a thing which can, and should, be spoken of metaphorically, and of which matrimony is a sort of material allegory; but matrimony ought not to be called a sacrament on this account. The heavens are meant to represent the apostles in Psalm 19 [:1 ff.] and the sun is metaphorically Christ, and the seas the people; but this does not mean that they are sacraments. There is no mention of either a divine institution, or a promise, which together would constitute a sacrament. Therefore Paul, in Ephesians 5 [:23 ff.], either quotes Genesis 2 [:24] for the words about marriage, and applies them on his own initiative to Christ; or else, according to prevailing opinion, he teaches that the spiritual marriage of Christ is contained here, when he says: "Even as Christ cherisheth the church, because we are members of His body, of His flesh, and of His bones. For this

cause shall a man leave his father and mother, and shall cleave
to his wife; and the twain shall become one flesh. This mystery
is great, but I speak in regard of Christ and of the church"
[Eph. 5:29 ff.]. You see that Paul means this whole passage to
have been spoken by him about Christ, and he takes pains to
warn the reader to understand that the sacrament is not in the
marriage but in Christ and the Church.[24]

Granted, therefore, that matrimony is a figure for Christ
and the church, yet it is not a sacrament of divine institution;
it was introduced into the church by men who were misled by
their ignorance both of the subject and the record. But, if this
fact is not a hindrance to faith, it ought to be borne with in a
charitable spirit, just as many other human devices due to
weakness and ignorance in the church are to be tolerated so
long as they do not stand in the way of faith and the Holy
Scriptures. But at the present moment we are arguing on behalf of the certainty and purity of faith and the Scriptures.

[24] At this point, a passage from some other writing of Luther's
has been interpolated. It clearly breaks the context, and is out of
position here. A footnote in W., VI, p. 552, says it appears to have
been introduced here by mistake. I have therefore followed the
example of modern scholars in relegating the interpolation to a
footnote as follows:

"Of course, I agree that there was a sacrament of penance in
the Old Law, and that it was so from the beginning of the world.
But the new promise for penitence and the gift of the keys are
peculiar to the New Law. Instead of circumcision, we now have
baptism, and, similarly, instead of sacrifice, or other signs of repentance, we have the keys. I have already said that the same God
gave different promises and different signs at different times, in
regard to the forgiveness of sins and the salvation of men; yet all
received the same grace. Thus, in II Cor. 4 Paul says: 'Having
the same spirit of faith, we also believe, and therefore also we
speak.' And in I Cor. 10: 'Our fathers did all eat the same spiritual meat and did all drink of the same spiritual drink; for they
drank of a spiritual rock that followed them; and the rock was
Christ.' Similarly, Heb. 11: 'And these all, being dead, received
not the promise, God having provided some better thing concerning us, that apart from us they should not be made perfect. For
Christ is yesterday, to-day, and forever, Himself the head of His
Church from the beginning even to the end of the world.' Thus
the signs vary, but the faith is the same in every case, because
without faith it is impossible to please God, yet it is that by which
Abel pleased Him. Heb. 11."—B.L.W.

Our faith would be exposed to scoffing if we affirmed that something was contained in the Holy Scriptures or in the articles of our faith, which was later proved not to be there. Then we should be found unversed in our own special province, causing difficulties to our enemies and to the weak; but most of all we should detract from the authority of the Holy Scriptures. For there is a very great difference between what has been handed down about God in the Holy Scriptures, on the one hand; and, on the other, that which has been introduced into the church by men of no matter what sanctity or learning. Thus far about matrimony as a rite.

What then shall we say about those impious, man-made laws in which this divinely instituted way of life has become enmeshed, and which have sometimes exalted, and, at others, debased it? Merciful God! what a dreadful thing it is to examine the temerity of the Romanizing oppressors who divorce couples, or enforce marriages, just according to their own sweet will. I ask in all earnestness: Has the human race been handed over to the good pleasure of these men to be made sport of, to be subjected to any sort of misuse, and for the sake of whatever filthy lucre they can make out of it?

A greatly esteemed book entitled the *Summa Angelica*[25] enjoys a wide circulation, but it consists of a jumbled collection, a kind of bilge-water, of the offscourings of all that men have handed down. It would more appropriately be called the *Summa worse than Diabolical*. It contains numberless horrible things by which confessors think they receive instruction, whereas they are led into most pernicious confusion. It enumerates eighteen impediments to marriage; but, if you will examine them with the unbiassed mind and the uncensored view given by faith, you will see that a number of them are foretold by the apostle when he said: "They shall give heed to the spirits of devils, who shall speak lies in hypocrisy, forbidding to marry" [I Tim. 4:1 ff.]. Is not the invention of so many impediments, and the setting of so many traps, the rea-

---

[25] The *Summa Angelica* of Angelus de Clavassio Chiavasso in Liguria (died 1495), published 1486, one of the favourite handbooks of casuistry, in which all possible cases of conscience were treated in alphabetical order. It was among the papal books burned by Luther.

son that people do not marry; or if they are married, the reason why the marriage is annulled? Who gave this power to man? It may be that they were religious men, zealous and devout, yet by what right does another man's saintliness put limits on my own liberty? Let any one who is so minded be a saint and a zealot to any extent he likes, but let him not harm any one else in doing it, or steal my freedom.

Yet I rejoice that these men have got their due in these disgraceful regulations. By their means the Romanists of to-day have become market-stall holders. What is it they sell? It is male and female pudenda, goods most worthy of these merchants whose avarice and irreligion are worse than the most sordid obscenity imaginable. For there is no impediment to marriage nowadays which they cannot legitimize for money. These man-made regulations seem to have come into existence for no other reason than raking in money and netting in souls, to serve these greedy and rapacious hunters. It is all done in order that the "Abomination" might stand in the church of God, and publicly sell to men the pudenda of both sexes; or, in Scriptural language, their "shame and nakedness" [Lev. 18:6 ff.], of which they had already robbed them by the effect of these laws. O traffic worthy of our pontiffs who, being given up unto a reprobate mind, carry on that traffic with extreme baseness and utter lack of decency, instead of exercising the ministry of the gospel, which their greed and ambition make them despise!

You will probably ask me what I can say or do. If I were to enter into detail, I should go on without end. Everything is in such confusion that you do not know where to begin, in which direction to turn, or where to stop. But this I know, that the body politic cannot be felicitously governed merely by rules and regulations. If the administrator be sagacious, he will conduct the government more happily when guided by circumstances rather than by legal decrees. If he be not so wise, his legal methods will only result in harm, since he will not know how to use them, nor how to temper them to the case in hand. Hence, in public affairs, it is more important to make sure that good and wise men are in control than that certain laws are promulgated. Men of this kind will themselves be the best of laws, will be alert to every kind of problem, and will resolve them equitably. If knowledge of the divine laws accompanies native sagacity, it is obvious that written laws will be superfluous and noxious. Above all else, remember that Christian love has no need of any laws at all.

Similarly, with regard to those impediments to marriage in respect of which the pope claims power to grant dispensations, but which are not mentioned in Scripture, I would urge it upon every priest and friar with all the power I possess, to declare, without more ado, that all those marriages are valid, the only objection being that they have been contracted merely against one or other of the ecclesiastical or pontifical canons. Let them arm themselves with the divine law which says: "What God hath joined together, let no man put asunder" [Matt. 19:6]. The union of man and wife is in accordance with divine law, and this holds good no matter how it may contradict any regulations made by men; and these same regulations ought therefore to be disregarded without any hesitation. If a man ought to leave his father and mother, and cleave to his wife, so much the more ought he to trample upon frivolous and wicked human regulations, in order to cleave to his wife. And if the pope, or bishop, or official, should dissolve a marriage contracted contrary to one of these man-made laws, then he is an Antichrist; he does violence to nature, and is guilty of contempt of the divine Majesty; for the text still remains true that: "What God hath joined together let no man put asunder."

Remember, also, that no man has a right to promulgate such laws, that Christ has given Christians a freedom which rises above all human laws, especially when the divine law intervenes. Similarly, it says in Mark 2 [:28, 27], "The Son of Man is also lord of the Sabbath, for man was not made for the Sabbath, but the Sabbath for man." Further, Paul condemned such laws in advance when he foretold that there would be those who prohibited marriage [I Tim. 4:3]. Therefore, as far as the Scriptures permit, there should be an end to the validity of those impediments which arise from spiritual or legal affinities, or from consanguinities. The Scriptures forbid only the second degree of consanguinity, as in Leviticus 18 [:6 ff.]. Here twelve persons are within the prohibited degrees, viz.: mother, step-mother, full sister, half-sister by either parent, granddaughter, father's sister, mother's sister, daughter-in-law, brother's wife, wife's sister, step-daughter, uncle's wife. Thus only the first grade of affinity and the second of consanguinity are prohibited, and not even these in every respect, as is clear on close examination. The daughter and granddaughter of a brother or sister are not mentioned as prohibited, although they fall in the second grade. Therefore, if at any time a marriage has been contracted outside these grades, than which none other has at any time been prohibited by the divine laws, then it should never be dissolved on the ground that it is contrary to any laws of human origin. Marriage itself, as a divine institution, is incomparably superior to any laws, so that it ought not to be broken for the sake of laws, but laws for its sake.

In the same way, the nonsense about compaternity, commaternity, confraternity, consorority, and confiliety, ought to be completely blotted out, and the marriage contracted. These spiritual affinities are due purely to superstition. If neither the one who administers the baptism, nor the godparent at the baptism, is permitted to marry the one who has been baptized, then why is any Christian man permitted to marry any Christian woman? Does a fuller relationship arise from the rite or the sign of the sacrament, than from the sacrament itself? Is not a Christian man the brother of a Christian sister? Is not a baptized man spiritual brother to a baptized woman? What silly stuff they talk! If any husband teaches the gospel to his wife, and instructs her in faith in Christ, whereby he in very truth becomes her spiritual father—then ought she no longer to remain his wife? Would Paul not have been allowed to marry one of the Corinthian girls, all of whom he claims to have begotten in Christ? [I Cor. 4:15]. See how Christian liberty has been oppressed by the blindness of human superstition!

Even more trifling are the legal affinities, and yet the Romanists have made these superior to the divine right of marriage. Nor would I grant that there is any impediment in what they call "disparity of religion". This means that a Christian man is not permitted to marry an unbaptized woman, either as such, or only on condition that she be converted to the faith. Was it God or man who set up this prohibition? Who has given men the authority of prohibiting this kind of marriage? It was a spirit "speaking lies in hypocrisy", as Paul says [I Tim. 4:2]. It would be to the point to say of them: "The wicked have related fables to me, not according to thy law" [Ps. 119:85]. Patritius, a pagan, married the Christian Monica, the mother of St. Augustine; why should not a similar marriage be allowed nowadays? The same obstinate, if not sinful, harshness is seen in the "impediment of crime", e.g., if a man marries either a woman with whom he had previously committed adultery, or the widow of a man whose death he had contrived in order that he might marry her. I beg you, in all earnestness, to tell me whence comes this harshness of man towards men, such as God has nowhere demanded? Or do they pretend not to know that David, a man held in the highest reverence, married Bathsheba, Uriah's wife, after both the above crimes had been committed? I mean her previous adultery, and the murder of her husband. If the divine law operates in this way, why do men act despotically against their fellow servants?

What Romanists call the "impediment of a tie" is also recognized: whereby a man is engaged to one woman, but has sexual relations with another woman. In such a case their ruling is that his engagement to the first is ended. This I simply do not understand. My view is that a man who has betrothed himself to a woman is no longer his own, and though he has had sexual relations with the second, he belongs to the first by the divine commandment, even though he has had no sexual relations with her. He cannot give away the self he does not possess; rather, he has deceived the first, and in fact committed adultery with the second. The reason the Romanists see it differently is that they give more weight to the carnal union than to the divine command according to which the man has "plighted his troth" already, and ought to keep it for ever. For you can only give what is your own. God forbid that anyone should circumvent his brother in any matter that ought to be kept in good faith above and beyond all human traditions whatever. I do not believe that he could live with the second with a good conscience, and therefore I think that this impediment ought to be completely done away with. For if the vow of one of the religious orders takes away one's self-disposal, why not also a troth plighted and received? This is indeed one of the precepts and fruits of the spirit according to Galatians 5 [:22], whereas these vows derive from the human will. Moreover, if a married woman can claim her husband back, in spite of the fact that he has taken a monastic vow, why is it not allowed that an engaged woman should claim her betrothed back, even though he has had sexual connections with another woman? Rather, as I have already said, anyone who has plighted his troth to a woman cannot rightly take a monastic vow. His duty is to marry her, because it is his duty to keep faith. This precept comes from God, and therefore cannot be superseded by any human decree. In a case like this, he is under a far greater obligation to keep faith with the first woman, because he could only plight his faith with the second with a lie in his heart, and therefore it would not be plighted. What he has done, in God's sight, is to deceive her. For these reasons, the "impediment of error" operates here, and makes marriage with the second woman null and void.

The "impediment of ordination" is also a purely man-made regulation, especially when the Romanists blatantly say that it overrides a marriage which has already been solemnized; for they always exalt their own rules as superior to the divine ordinances. I am not criticizing ordination to the priesthood as known to-day, but I see that Paul commands that "the bishop be the husband of one wife" [I Tim. 3:2]. Therefore it is not possible to annul the marriage of a deacon, priest, bishop, or anyone who is ordained; although, of course, it must be admitted that Paul knew nothing of the kinds of priests and ordinations that pertain to-day. Perish then those accursed man-made regulations which seem only to have entered the church to multiply the dangers, the sins, and the evils there! Between a priest and his wife, therefore, there exists a valid and inseparable marriage, as is proved by the divine commands. What of it, then, if men who fear not God prohibit, and even annul, such a marriage entirely on their own authority? Nevertheless, what men have prohibited God permits, and His laws take precedence when at variance with human regulations.

The "impediment of public propriety", by which marriage contracts can be annulled, is a similar fiction. I am angered by the irreligious audacity which so speedily separates those whom God has joined, that you can recognize the Antichrist who attacks everything Christ said or taught. In the case of an engaged couple, if one of them should die before their marriage, what reason is there why the survivor should not marry one of the deceased's relatives who comes within the fourth degree of consanguinity? To forbid this is not a case of the vindication of public propriety, but ignorance of it. The people of Israel possessed the best laws, because they were divinely instituted, and yet there was none of this kind of vindication of public propriety. On the contrary, God commanded the next of kin to marry a woman left a widow. Otherwise, the question might be asked: Ought the people who possess the liberty of Christians to be burdened with more onerous laws than the people in bondage to the Mosaic law? To sum up my discussion of what should be called fictions rather than impediments: there appears to me at present to be no impediment which can annul a legal contract of marriage, except sexual impotence, ignorance of a marriage already existing, or a vow of chastity. Concerning such a vow, my uncertainty up to now is such that I do not know at what age it ought to be regarded as valid, as I have already said with reference to the sacrament of baptism. Matrimony, therefore, is an example sufficient in itself to show up the nature of the present unhappy and hopeless state of confusion. It also shows that any and all of the practices of the church are impeded, and entangled, and endangered, on account of the pestilential, unlearned, and irreligious, man-made ordinances. There is no hope of a cure unless the whole of the laws made by men, no matter what their standing, are repealed once for all. When we have recovered the freedom of the gospel, we should judge and rule in accordance with it in every respect. Amen.

Now it is needful to discuss sexual impotence, for, by so doing, it may be easier to give advice to those whose minds are labouring and in peril. But I would preface this with the remark that what I have said above about impediments applies to marriages already solemnized; and none of these should be annulled on account of such impediments as I have discussed. But in regard to a marriage which has yet to be solemnized, I will briefly repeat what I have already said.

When if youthful passion makes the case urgent, or if there are other needs that the pope would meet by granting a dispensation, then any Christian can grant one to his brother, or he can grant one to himself. This opinion means that he is given permission to carry his wife off in the teeth of any oppressive laws whatsoever. Why should I be deprived of my freedom by someone else's ignorance or superstition? Or, if the pope would grant a dispensation for a fee, why should not I grant one to myself or my brother for the good of my salvation? Is it the pope who decrees laws? Let him decree them for himself, but leave my freedom to me, or I will take it without his knowing.

On the question of impotence:

Let us examine such a case as this. A woman is married to an impotent man, but cannot, or perhaps will not, prove in court her husband's impotence, because of the numerous items of evidence, and the notoriety, which would be occasioned by a legal process. Still she wishes to have a child, and is unable to remain continent. In addition, suppose I had advised her to seek a divorce in order to marry another, as she was content, in her conscience, to do, and after ample experience on the part of herself and her husband, that he was impotent; if, then, however, her husband would not agree to her proposal, I myself would give the further advice,[26] that, with her husband's consent (although now really he is not her husband, but only a man who lives in the same house) she should have coition with another man, say her husband's brother, but keeping this "marriage" secret, and ascribing the children to the putative father, as they call such a one. As to the question whether such a woman is "saved" or in a state of salvation, I would reply, Yes, because in this case a mistake due to ignorance of the man's impotence created a false situation which impedes the marriage proper; the harshness of the law does not allow divorce; yet by the divine law the woman is free, and so cannot be forced to remain continent. Therefore the husband ought to concede this right to her, allowing her coition with another, since she is his wife in a formal and unreal sense only.

Further, if the man will not consent, and if he does not

[26] In the confessional, was doubtless meant by Luther.

wish to be separated, then, rather than let her burn or commit adultery, I would counsel her to contract matrimony with someone else, and flee to some distant and unknown region. What other counsel can be given to one constantly struggling with the dangers of her own natural emotions? I know, of course, that some will be disturbed because it would be unfair for the children of a secret marriage of this kind to be the heirs of the putative father. But, on the one hand, if it were done with the husband's consent, there would be no unfairness. If, on the other hand, he were ignorant of it, or had refused his consent, then let an unfettered, and therefore Christian, reasonableness, if not charity itself, judge the case and say which of the two was the more harmful to the other. The wife alienates her husband's estate, but the husband deceives the wife, and is defrauding her totally in body and life. Does not the man commit the greater sin by wasting the body and life of his wife, than the woman in alienating a quantity of temporal property? So either let him agree to a divorce, or else let him bear with children not his own. The fault is his in having deceived an innocent girl, and defrauded her of the full use of both her life and her body, besides giving her an almost unbearable cause for committing adultery. Let these two cases be weighed in a just balance. According to any legal code, forsooth, fraud ought to recoil on the fraudulent, and any one doing harm should make it good. In what respect does a husband, such as we are discussing, differ from a man who keeps another's wife in prison along with her husband? Would not such a bully be compelled to support the wife and children as well as the husband, or else set them free? And this should happen in the case under discussion. Hence, in my judgment, the man ought to be compelled either to accept divorce, or support his putative child as his own heir. Without doubt that is the judgment which charity calls for. In that case, the impotent man, because not really a husband, should support his wife's issue in the same spirit as if his wife were ill, or suffered some other indisposition, and he had to nurse her at great cost. For it is by his own fault, and not his wife's, that she labours under this wrong. I have set out my views to the best of my ability for the sake of giving instruction to those whose consciences are disquieted, for my desire is to bring what little comfort I can to my afflicted brethren who are in this kind of captivity.

In regard to divorce, it is still a subject for debate whether it should be allowed. For my part, I have such a hatred of divorce that I prefer bigamy to divorce, yet I do not venture an opinion whether bigamy should be allowed. Christ's own command, as chief pastor, is given in Matthew 5 [:32], "Every one that putteth away his wife, saving for the cause of fornication, maketh her an adulteress; and whosoever shall marry her when she is put away committeth adultery." Hence, Christ permitted divorce, but only in case of fornication. It follows that the pope is in error where he grants divorce for other causes. No one, therefore, should think his case sound if he has been granted a divorce by a papal dispensation, for that shows presumptuousness rather than authority. But I marvel even more that the Romanists do not allow the re-marriage of a man separated from his wife by divorce, but compel him to remain single. Christ permitted divorce in case of fornication, and compelled no one to remain single; and Paul preferred us to marry rather than to burn, and seemed quite prepared to grant that a man may marry another woman in place of the one he has repudiated [I Cor. 7:9]. But this is a subject that ought to be fully discussed, and a decision reached, so that it would be possible to give counsel to those who, though surrounded by an infinite number of dangers, are forced to remain unmarried to-day through no fault of their own; cases where wives or husbands have run away and deserted their partners, to return perhaps ten years later, or even never. This kind of thing distresses and depresses me, for there are instances day by day, whether due to some special piece of wickedness of Satan's, or to our neglect of God's word.

For my own part, and speaking entirely for myself in this matter, I cannot make any rules and regulations; yet I wish that passage in I Corinthians 7 [:15] were applied, which reads: "If the unbelieving departeth, let him depart; the brother or the sister is not in bondage in such cases." Here the apostle rules that the unbeliever who deserts his wife should be divorced, and he pronounces the believer free to marry another. Surely the same principle should hold good if a believer (i.e., nominally a believer, but in fact an unbeliever) deserts his wife, especially if he never intends to return. At least I can see no difference between the two cases. On the other hand, I believe that if, in the apostle's time, an unbeliever had returned, and had either become a believer, or promised to live together with his believing wife, he would not have been given that permission; rather, he would have been given permission to marry someone else. As I have said, however, in these matters I am not enunciating any principles, although there is nothing which I desire more to see settled; for there is nothing that disquiets me more to-day, and many others with me. Nevertheless, I would not have the matter settled by the mere fiat of the pope or the bishops. Rather, if two learned and good men were to agree, in Christ's name and in Christ's spirit, and issue a pronouncement, I myself would prefer their verdict even to that of a council. For the kinds of council which usually assemble nowadays are more notable for their numbers and power than for their learning and sanctity. So I hang up my harp, until I can discuss the subject with another and wiser man than myself.

(6) *Ordination*

This was unknown as a sacrament to the church of Christ's time, the doctrine having been devised by the church of the popes. A promise of grace is nowhere given, nor does the whole of the New Testament contain a passage with any allusion to it. It is ridiculous to assert that what can nowhere be proved to have been instituted by God is nevertheless a sacrament. My point is, not that I wish to condemn a rite which has been celebrated ever since the church was founded, but that I refuse to place a man-made fiction among things divine; I refuse to construe anything as if it were of divine institution when it has not been divinely ordained. Otherwise we shall appear ridiculous to a hostile critic; and we ought to try, as far as we ourselves are concerned, to have everything assured, unassailable, plainly confirmed by Scripture, before it is put forward as an article of the faith. But in the present "sacrament" we cannot satisfy these requirements with a single tittle of evidence.

The church has no power to initiate and institute divine

promises of grace, as is the case when the Romanists pretentiously claim that anything instituted by the church has no
less authority than what has been ordained by God, since the
church is governed by the Holy Spirit. For the church was
born by virtue of her faith in the word of promise, and by
that promise she is both fed and maintained. In other words,
she was instituted by God's promises, and not God's promise
by her. For the word of God is beyond comparison superior
to the church. She is a created thing, and, being such, has no
power to institute, to ordain, or to make; but only to be instituted, to be ordained, and to be brought into being. No
man can beget his own parents or settle the author of his own
being.

Of course, the church has the power of distinguishing the
word of God from the word of man. This is borne out by
Augustine, who confesses that, moved by the authority of the
church, he believed in the gospel, because it proclaimed that
this was the gospel. But this does not make it superior to the
gospel, for by the same argument the church would be superior to the God in whom it believes, since the church's message is that He is God. Rather, as Augustine says elsewhere,
the mind is so laid hold of by the truth itself, that, by virtue
of that truth, it is able to reach certainty in any judgment.
Nevertheless, the mind is unable to judge the truth as such,
although it is compelled to say, when entirely confident, This
is true. For example, the mind declares with infallible assurance that three and seven make ten, and yet it cannot adduce
any reason why that is true, although it cannot deny its truth.
The fact is that, rather than being itself the judge, the mind has
been taken captive, and has accepted a verdict pronounced by
the Truth herself sitting on the tribunal. Similarly by the il-
lumination of the spirit, when doctrines come up for decision
and approval, the church possesses a "sense" whose presence
is certain, though it cannot be proved. Just as no philosopher
attempts to appraise the conceptions of common sense, but is
rather judged by them, so, among ourselves, there is a spirit
of which we are aware, which judges all things, but is judged
by none [I Cor. 2:15], as the apostle says. But I digress.

For these reasons we can be sure that, because it belongs
to God alone to do so, the church has no power to promise

grace, and, by the same sign, none to institute a sacrament. Even if she possessed these powers in the highest degree, it would by no means follow that ordination was a sacrament. For when these decrees were passed, it was customary for only a few bishops and doctors, and no others, to be present; and who knows if they constituted a church possessing the spirit? It was possible they did not constitute a church, and that they all erred. Councils have often erred, especially that of Constance,[27] which was the most wicked of them all. There is reliable proof only of what has received the assent of the church universal, and not merely that of Rome. On this basis, I would go as far as to say that ordination is an ecclesiastical ceremony, like many others which have been introduced by the Church Fathers, e.g., consecration of vases, houses, vestments, water, salt, candles, herbs, wine, and the like. No one suggests that any of these cases constitutes a sacrament; nor is a promise attached to any of them. Hence, neither anointing a man's hands, shaving his poll, nor anything else of the sort, can be made into a sacrament, for they convey no promise; they are merely rites employed solely to prepare men for certain duties, as in the case of vases or implements.

The question may be asked: What, then, have you to say about Dionysius (Areopagiticus),[28] who enumerates six sacraments, and includes ordination among them in his *Ecclesiastica Hierarchia?* My answer is, that I know this is the only ancient writer who argues on behalf of seven sacraments, although, by omitting to speak of matrimony, he gives only six. Apart from him, among the rest of the Fathers there is no mention of these as sacraments. On no occasion when they speak of these subjects do they regard them as sacraments, for the innovation of sacraments is a modern phenomenon. And, if I may dare to say so, it is by no means to my liking to assign much importance to this particular Dionysius; whoever he may have been, he shows hardly any signs of solid learning. I would ask: On whose authority or by what logic does he prove the statements about angels which he has jumbled together in the *Coelesti Hierarchia*—a book over which

[27] It condemned John Huss and Jerome of Prague.
[28] Really the pseudonym of a fifth-century writer of *The Celestial Hierarchy, The Ecclesiastical Hierarchy,* etc.

inquisitive and superstitious minds have pored? If read and judged without prejudice, all the fruits of his meditations seem very much like dreams. In the *Theologia Mystica*—rightly so-called—of which certain pretentious, but very unscholarly, theologians make so much, Dionysius is very pernicious, being more of a Platonist than a Christian. In sum, I myself do not want any believer to give the least weight to these books. So far indeed from learning about Christ in them, you will be led to lose what you know. I am speaking from experience. Rather, let us listen to Paul, that we may learn of "Jesus Christ and Him crucified" [I Cor. 2:2]. "He is the way, the truth, and the life" [John 14:6]. He is the ladder by which we may come to the Father; as He Himself said: "No one cometh unto the Father, but by me."

Similarly, in the *Ecclesiastica Hierarchia,* Dionysius only describes a number of rites of the church; he plays with his allegories, but this does not make them realities. The same sort of thing has been done amongst us by someone who has written a book called *Rationale Divinorum.* This business of allegorizing is only for men who have nothing else to do. I am sure that I myself would not find it difficult to trump up allegories round any thing in creation. Did not Bonaventura use allegory to convert the liberal arts into theology? Then Gerson turned the smaller *Donatus* into a mystical theology. It would not give me much trouble to write a better *Hierarchy* than that of Dionysius; but he knew nothing of pope, cardinals, and archbishops, and so he put a bishop at the head of the church. And whose ingenuity is so slight that he could not try his hand at allegorizing? In my view, no theologian should waste time on allegories until he has become expert in the proper and simple sense of Scripture. Otherwise, as in Origen's case, he will endanger his theological thinking.

Therefore, nothing ought without more ado to be held as a sacrament merely because Dionysius so describes it; or else why not make a sacrament of the procession which he describes in the same passage, and which is practised to the present day? Why not as many sacraments as rites and ceremonies which have grown up in the church? On this same weak basis, the Romanists have attributed to the sacrament of ordination a certain fictitious "character", which is said to be indelibly impressed upon an ordinand. I would ask whence do such ideas arise, and on whose authority and for what reason have they become established? Not that we are unwilling for the Romanists to be free to invent, to say, or to assert, whatever they like; but we also insist on our own freedom, lest they arrogate to themselves the right of making articles of the faith out of their own ideas, as they have hitherto presumed to do. It is sufficient that, for the sake of concord, we should accommodate ourselves to their ceremonies and idiosyncrasies; but we refuse to be compelled to accept them as necessary for salvation, which they are not. Let them do away with the element of compulsion in their arbitrary demands, and we will yield free obedience to their wishes in order that we may live in peace towards each other. For it is mean, iniquitous, and servile for a Christian man, with his freedom, to be subjected to any regulations except the heavenly and divine.

At this point, the Romanists adduce their strongest argument, in that, at the Last Supper, Christ said: "This do ye in remembrance of me." Look, they say at this point: "Christ ordained His disciples as priests." From this, also, they infer, among other things, that the elements in both kinds are only to be given to the priests. After that, they deduce from it anything at will, with the effect that, once they have arrogated to themselves the right of making free decisions, they assert what they like on the basis of Christ's word no matter what the occasion. But is that what is meant by expounding the word of God? Answer me, I beg you. Christ promised nothing on this occasion, but only commanded that this was to be done in memory of Him. Why do they not argue that He ordained as priests those on whom He laid the office of the word and of baptism when He said: "Go ye into all the world and preach the gospel to every creature, baptizing them in the name", etc?

It is the very duty of priests to preach and baptize. Further, since it is the primary, and, they say, the indispensable duty of the priests to-day to read the canonical hours, why have the Romanists not discovered a sacrament of ordination in those passages where Christ gives a command to pray? There are many such occasions, but especially one in the garden, where He says: "Pray, lest ye enter into temptation" [Matt.

26:41]. They may object that this is no commandment to pray, and that it is enough to read the canonical hours. If so, nowhere can it be proved from Scripture that praying is a duty of the priests. By the same mark, the sacerdotal kind of praying is not of God, as indeed it is not.

Not one of the ancient Fathers asserts that priests were ordained when those words were used. What then is the origin of this new piece of intelligence? Perhaps they sought by this means to establish a seed-bed of unappeasable discord, through which clergy and laity were to be more widely separated than heaven and earth; yet this has proved to be unbelievably hurtful to baptismal grace, and to the confusion of fellowship based on the gospel. Here is the root of the terrible domination of the clergy over the laity. In virtue of a physical anointing, when their hands are consecrated, and in virtue of their tonsure and vestments, the clergy claim to be superior to the Christian laity, who, nevertheless, have been baptized with the Holy Spirit. The clergy can almost be said also to regard the laity as lower animals, who have been included in the church along with themselves.

Thus it arises that they make bold to command and demand, to threaten and urge and oppress, as they please. In sum, the sacrament of ordination is the prettiest of devices for giving a firm foundation to all the ominous things hitherto done in the church, or yet to be done. This is the point at which Christian fellowship perishes, where pastors become wolves, servants become tyrants, and men of the church become worse than men of the world.

Now we, who have been baptized, are all uniformly priests in virtue of that very fact. The only addition received by the priests is the office of preaching, and even this with our consent. If the Romanists had to grant this point, they would have to admit that they had no right to lord it over us, except in so far as we, of our own free will, allowed them to do so. Thus it says in I Peter 2 [:9], "Ye are an elect race, a royal priesthood, and a priestly kingdom." It follows that all of us who are Christian are also priests. Those whom we call priests are really ministers of the word and chosen by us; they fulfil their entire office in our name. The priesthood is simply the ministry of the word. So in I Corinthians 4 [:1] it says: "Let a man so account of us as of ministers of Christ and stewards of the mysteries of God."

That being the case, it follows (i) that any one who has been called by the church to preach the Word, but does not preach it, is in no way a priest; and (ii) that the sacrament of ordination cannot be other than the rite by which the church chooses its preacher. That is how Malachi 2 [:7] defines a priest: "The priest's lips should keep knowledge, and they should seek the law at his mouth; for he is the messenger of the Lord of Hosts." Be assured that anyone who is not a messenger of the Lord of Hosts, or any one who is called to do something other than be such a messenger is, if I may say so, by no means a priest. Accordingly, Hosea 4 [:6] says: "Because thou hast rejected knowledge, I will also reject thee, that thou shalt be no priest to me." Moreover, the reason they are called pastors is that their duty is to find pasture for, or, to teach, their flock. From this, it follows that those men who are ordained merely to read the canonical hours and to celebrate mass may be papal priests, but they are not Christian priests; for not only do they not preach, but they are not even appointed to preach. Indeed, our contention is that a priesthood of this kind has another status than that of the office of preaching. Thus, they are the priests of the Hours and the Missals, merely a kind of living idols which bear the name of the priesthood; they are exactly the kind of priests whom Jeroboam ordained at Bethaven [I Kings 12:31; Hosea 10:5], and whom he had taken from the lowest dregs of the people, and not from the tribe of Levi.

Lo! how far the glory of the church has departed! The whole world is full of priests, bishops, cardinals, and clergy, not one of whom, as far as his official responsibilities go, is a preacher, unless, apart from the sacrament of ordination, he is called upon to preach by virtue of some other requirement different from that of his ordination. He considers that he fulfils the requirements of his ordination completely by mumbling through the "vain repetition" of the prayers which he has to read, and by celebrating the masses. But in repeating the "hours" he never prays, or if he prays, he does so to himself. And the mass, by an extreme perversity, is offered as if it were a sacrifice, whereas it is just the celebration of a sacrament. Thus it is plain that ordination, which is used as a sacrament to conse-crate this type of man, and make a cleric of him, is really and truly, purely and simply, a man-made ceremonial. Those who compacted it knew nothing of the church in its essence; noth-ing of the priesthood; of preaching the word; or of the sac-raments. The result is that this sacrament and those priests stand on the same level. In addition to these errors and stu-pidities, is that closer incarceration by which they separate themselves more widely still from other Christians, now re-garded as profane; like the Galli, who were the priests of Cyb-ele, they unman themselves by assuming the burden of a very spurious celibacy.

Nor was it enough to satisfy this piece of hypocrisy and the operation of this error, that bigamy should be prohibited, i.e., that no man should have two wives at the same time, as was forbidden in the law, and as is the common meaning of bigamy. The Romanists have interpreted bigamy to mean marrying two virgins in succession, or one widow. Indeed, so very sacred is the sanctity of this most sacrosanct sacrament, that it is im-possible for a man to be ordained if he has married a virgin and while she still remains alive as his wife. In order to attain the very summit of sanctity, a man is prohibited access to the priesthood if he has married a girl who was not a virgin, though he may have done so in ignorance, and by an unfor-tunate mischance. But he may have had vile commerce with six hundred prostitutes, and seduced countless matrons and vir-gins, and kept many mistresses, yet nothing of this would be an impediment, and prevent his becoming a bishop, or a car-dinal, or a pope. As a consequence, it has become needful to expound the apostle's saying, "husband of one wife" [I Tim. 3:2], as "prelate of one church". Out of this arises the principle of "incompatible benefices". But the pope, who magnani-mously grants dispensations, may allow three, twenty, or a hundred wives, i.e., churches, to count as one, after he has been bribed with money, or induced by some favour; I should say, of course, moved by godly generosity, and constrained by concern for the churches.

O pontiffs worthy of this venerable sacrament of ordination! O prince, not of the church universal, but of the synagogues of Satan and of Darkness itself! Now is the time to cry out with

Isaiah: "O ye scornful men, that rule my people which is in Jerusalem" [Isaiah 28:14]; and with Amos 6 [:1]: "Woe to you that are at ease in Zion, and are secure in the mountain of Samaria, notable men, heads of the people, going in state into the house of Israel." O! the disgrace which these monstrous priesthoods bring upon the Church of God! Where can you find priests who know the gospel, not to mention preach it? Why then do they boast of being priests? Why do they wish to be regarded as holier, and better, and more powerful, than other Christians who pass as laymen? As for reading the "hours", what ordinary person, or, as the apostle says, what man that speaketh with tongues, is not equal to that? The prayers of the hours are suitable for monks, hermits, and private persons, although laymen. The function of the priest is to preach; if he does not preach, he is no more a priest than the picture of a man is a man. Or does it make a man a bishop if he ordains this kind of clapper-tongued priest, or consecrates churches and bells, or confirms children? Never! These are things that any deacon or layman might do. What makes a priest or a bishop is the ministry of the Word.

Do not accept my standpoint if you wish to live at ease. Be off with you, young men. Refuse to accept this kind of ordination; refuse, unless you want to preach the gospel, and unless you can believe that you will become superior to a layman by the sacrament of ordination. Reading the "hours" is of no consequence. And, again, to offer mass is only to receive the sacrament. What function, then, is left for you as a priest which is not equally appropriate for a layman? Tonsure and vestments? It is a poor sort of priest that is made up of tonsure and vestments! Or is it the oil that anointed your fingers? But every Christian whatsoever has been anointed with the oil of the Holy Spirit, and sanctified in body and soul. Formerly laymen used to administer the sacraments as often as priests do now. Yet the superstitious of our day regard it as a great offence if a layman touch the bare chalice, or even the cover of it. Nor is a nun, though a consecrated virgin, allowed to wash the altar cloth or the sacred linen. O my God! this shows how far the sacrosanct sanctity of this sacrament has gone! I expect the time will come when the laity will not be allowed even to touch the altar—except with money in their hand. I almost burst with indignation when I think of the wicked impositions of these most brazen monsters, who, with their tricks and puerile traps, make sport of the Christian religion, and bring its liberty and glory into ruin.

Therefore every one who knows that he is a Christian should be fully assured that all of us alike are priests, and that we all have the same authority in regard to the word and the sacraments, although no one has the right to administer them without the consent of the members of his church, or by the call of the majority (because, when something is common to all, no single person is empowered to arrogate it to himself, but should await the call of the church). Moreover, the sacrament of ordination, if it has any validity at all, is only the rite through which someone is called to the ministry of the church, since the priesthood is simply the ministry of the word; the word, I say; not the law, but the gospel. The diaconate, on the other hand, is not a ministry for reading the gospel, or the epistle, as the present custom is, but for distributing the church's bounty to the poor, in order that the priests might be relieved of the burden of temporal matters, and be more at liberty for prayer and the word. It was on this plan, as we read in Acts 6 [:1 ff.], that deacons were installed; and therefore a man who neither knows nor preaches the gospel is not a priest or a bishop, but only a kind of nuisance in the church. Under the false title of priest or bishop, or dressed in sheep's clothing, he does violence to the gospel and acts as a wolf in the church.

Therefore, unless those priests or bishops, with whom the church abounds to-day, work out their own salvation in another way, and unless they recognize that they are neither priests nor bishops, let them bemoan the fact that they bear the name. They are ignorant of the duties and unable to fulfil them. Let them deplore their pitiable lot, appropriate to their hypocrisy, with prayers and tears. Otherwise, of a truth, they will be the sons of eternal perdition. It was only speaking the truth about them when Isaiah said: "Therefore my people are gone into captivity, for lack of knowledge; and their honourable men are famished, and their multitude are parched with thirst. Therefore hell hath enlarged her desire, and opened her mouth without measure: and their glory, and their multitude, and their pomp, and he that rejoiceth among them descend into it" [Isaiah 5:13 f.]. What a dreadful prophecy of our times when Christians are being swallowed up in such an abyss!

According to what Scripture teaches us, what we call priesthood is a form of service. I quite fail to see the reason why a man, who has once become a priest, cannot again become a layman, since he only differs from the laity by his ministry. Further, it has not hitherto been impossible for him to be deposed from the ministry, seeing that this punishment is actually imposed from time to time on priests found in fault; they may be either suspended temporarily, or deprived permanently of office. The fiction of the "indelible character" has long been ridiculous. I agree that the pope imparts this character to the man, though it was unknown to Christ; and that thereby the man is consecrated for ever as the servant and prisoner, not of Christ but of the pope, as is the case nowadays. Further, unless I am mistaken, if at any time this fictitious sacrament should decay and disappear, the papacy itself would scarcely continue and retain its "characters". A joyful liberty would come back to us, in which we should understand that we are all equal by any law whatever; and, when the oppressive yoke had been cast aside, we should know that he who is a Christian possesses Christ; that he who possesses Christ possesses all things that are Christ's, and is able to do all things. This is a subject on which I shall have more to say, and with more emphasis, when I perceive that the above has displeased my friends the papists.

(7) The Sacrament of Extreme Unction

The theologians of the present day have made two additions, well worthy of themselves, to the ceremony of anointing the sick. In the first place, they call it a sacrament; and in the second, they make it the last. Thus we have nowadays a sacrament of extreme unction which is only to be administered to those who are on the brink of death. As the theologians are very acute in argument, perhaps they relate it to the first unction of baptism, and the two subsequent unctions of confirmation and ordination. This time, they have something to

throw in my face; it is that, on the authority of the apostle
James, here are both promise and sign: things by which, as I
have hitherto contended, a sacrament is constituted. The
apostle says: "Is any among you sick? let him call for the elders
of the church; and let them pray over him, anointing him with
oil in the name of the Lord: and the prayer of faith shall save
him that is sick, and the Lord shall raise him up; and if he
have committed sins, it shall be forgiven him" [Jas. 5:14 f.].
Behold, they say, the promise of forgiveness of sins, and the
sign of the oil.

My reply is: If nonsense is spoken anywhere, this is the very
place. I pass over the fact that many have maintained, with
much probability, that this epistle was not written by the
apostle James, and is not worthy of the spirit of an apostle.
Nevertheless, no matter who may have been the author, it has
the authority due to custom. Yet, even if it were by the apostle
James, I would say that no apostle was licensed to institute a
sacrament on his own authority, or, to give a divine promise
with an accompanying sign. This pertains to Christ alone. That
is why Paul says that it was from the Lord that he received the
sacrament of the eucharist [I Cor. 11:23]; and that he had
not been sent to baptize, but to preach the gospel [I Cor.
1:17]. Nowhere in the gospels is there any mention of this sacrament of Extreme Unction. But, allowing that to pass, let us
look at the actual words of the apostle, or whoever was the
author, and we shall see, at once, that those who have multiplied the sacraments have paid no real attention to his words.

Firstly, if they hold that what the apostle said in the present instance is true, and ought to be kept, by what authority
have they changed and restricted it? Why do they make an
extreme unction, to be administered only once, out of what the
apostle intended to be of general application? It was not the
apostle's intention that it should be extreme, or that it should
be given only to those at the point of death. Rather he says,
purely and simply: "Is any among you sick?"; he does not say:
"Is any among you at the point of death?" I shall ignore the
sapient remarks on this subject in Dionysius's *Ecclesiastica
Hierarchia;* the apostle's words are plain; Dionysius and the
Romanists alike rely on them—but without obeying them. It
appears, therefore, that, without any other authority than their

own choice, they have wrongly interpreted the words of the apostle, and transformed them into the sacrament of Extreme Unction. This has been to the harm of the other sick persons whom they have deprived, on their own authority, of the benefit of the anointing as appointed by the apostle.

Here is a nicer point: the promise of the apostle expressly says: "The prayer of faith shall cure the sick, and the Lord will grant him recovery", etc. [Jas. 5:13–15]. You will have noticed that, in this passage, the apostle commands anointing and prayer in order that the sick man may be made well and recover, i.e., not die; and the anointing, therefore, is not that of extreme unction. This point is also proved in that, to the present day, while the Romanists are administering the last unction, prayers are said asking for the sick man's recovery. But the Romanists maintain, in spite of those prayers, that the unction is only to be administered to the dying, i.e., not in order that such a person may get well and recover. If this were not a serious matter, who could help laughing at this pretty, neat, and sensible comment on the apostle's words? Do we not here plainly detect that stupid sophistry which, both in this passage as well as in many others, affirms what Scripture denies, and denies what it affirms? Shall we pass a vote of thanks to these egregious masters of ours? Surely I was right in saying that nowhere else have they spoken such utter folly as in dealing with this passage!

Furthermore, if Extreme Unction is a sacrament, there should be no doubt that it is (as they say) an efficacious sign of what it signifies and promises. Now, it promises the health and recovery of the sick man, as the words plainly say: "The prayer of faith shall cure the sick, and the Lord will heal him" [Jas. 5:15]. But every one knows that this promise is seldom, or never, fulfilled. Scarcely one in a thousand is restored, and then no one thinks it is by the sacrament, but by the help of nature or medicine. Indeed, they attribute to the sacrament the opposite effect. What, then, is our conclusion? It is that either the apostle did not speak the truth when he made this promise, or else that this unction of theirs is not a sacrament. A sacramental promise is certain, whereas this is usually fallacious.

But let us again take cognizance of the care and insight of

these theologians; we may note that they mean it to be "extreme unction" just in order that the promise shall not hold good, or, lest the sacrament be a sacrament. For if it is extreme, it does not heal, but increases the infirmity. If it healed, it would not be extreme. Thus, it comes about, according to the exegesis of these masters, that James is to be understood to have contradicted himself: he instituted a sacrament to avoid instituting a sacrament! and the Romanists wanted to have the unction just in order that it should be untrue that the sick were healed by it, as James decreed! If this is not talking nonsense, then what is?

A remark of the apostle Paul is apposite here, when he says, I Timothy 1 [:7], "Desiring to be teachers of the law, though they understand neither what they say, nor whereof they confidently affirm", since they read and follow everything uncritically. With the same carelessness, they have also deduced auricular confession from the apostle's words: "Confess your sins to one another" [Jas. 5:16]. But they do not keep the apostle's command that the elders of the church should be brought in, and that they should pray over the sick [Jas. 5:14]. To-day, they will hardy send even one of the minor ranks of priests, although it was the apostle's will that many persons should be present, and this not to administer the unction, but to pray. That is why he said: "The prayer of faith will heal the sick", etc. [Jas. 5:15]; although I am uncertain whether he meant "priests" to be understood when he said *presbyteroi*, or elderly men, nor does it follow that a priest or minister is an elderly man. Therefore we may suppose that the apostle's intention was that the older and graver members of the church should visit the sick. They would be doing a work of mercy, and, by praying in faith, would heal the sick. This is an interpretation of the apostolic injunction which cannot be denied, for the church was formerly governed by the older members without any being ordained and consecrated; and they were elected for this purpose on account of their years and long experience of affairs.

From this standpoint, I take it that this early unction is the same as that when Mark 6 [:13], speaking of the apostles, says: "And they anointed with oil many that were sick and healed them." This appears to have been a rite, now long obsolete, in the first church, by which they worked miracles on the sick. In the same way, the last chapter of Mark's gospel tells how Christ gave power to believers to pick up serpents, lay their hands on the sick, etc. [Mark 16:17 f.]. It is surprising that the Romanists did not make sacraments out of this passage, for the essential power and promise here are very like that which James speaks of. The fictitious "Extreme Unction" of these Romanists is not a sacrament, but a piece of James's advice which anyone who wishes may follow. As I have said, it is based on Mark 6, and so handed down. Moreover, since the glory of the church is seen where there is weakness, and since death is gain, I do not believe that this counsel was given for the sake of sick persons in general; rather, it was meant for those who were bearing their illness too impatiently, and with an immature faith; from whom, therefore, the Lord had departed. In such cases, the miraculous power of faith would show up more conspicuously.

James purposely and carefully made provision for the view I am propounding, for he did not ascribe the promise of healing and of the forgiveness of sins to the unction, but to the prayer of faith. His words are: "And the prayer of faith shall heal the sick, and the Lord shall cure him; and if he have committed sins, it shall be forgiven him" [Jas. 5:15]. A sacrament, so it is said, does not require the administrant to pray or to have faith; for an ungodly man may administer baptism, and need not pray in order to consecrate. It depends for its validity entirely on being instituted by God, and on what He then promised; and it requires faith on the part of the recipient. But in Extreme Unction as practised in our day, there is no prayer of faith. No one prays in faith over the sick, confidently expecting their restoration. Yet James describes that kind of faith in this passage, and he had already spoken of it in Chapter 1: "But let him ask in faith, nothing doubting" [Jas. 1:6]. Christ also had said: "All things whatsoever ye pray for, believe that ye have received them, and ye shall have them" [Mark 11:24].

There is no doubt at all that if, at the present day, this kind of prayer were offered over the sick, i.e., by the older and graver men, men saintlike and full of faith, as many as we desired would be healed. Nothing is impossible for faith. Yet we neglect this faith although, on apostolic authority, it is most necessary. Further, we interpret "elders", i.e., men outstanding on account of age and faith, to mean any sort of ordinary priest; and we go on to convert the unrestricted anointing, i.e., the unction meant to be administered at any time, into an Extreme Unction. Not only do we not pray for healing to be granted, as promised by the apostle, but actually render the promise void by doing the very contrary. Nevertheless, we take pride in thinking that our present sacrament, though really a figment, is founded on, and proved by, this passage from the apostle; although, in fact, it is further apart from it than two octaves on the organ. What theologians!

But, let it be understood that I am not condemning the present practice of the "sacrament" of Extreme Unction; but I do firmly deny that Extreme Unction was prescribed by the apostle James. His anointing was in no way congruent with our "sacrament", either in form, or usage, or effectiveness, or purpose. Rather, we should class Extreme Unction among those "sacraments" which we ourselves have instituted, such as the blessing and sprinkling of salt, or holy water. We cannot deny that any creature whatever may be sanctified by the word and by prayer, a fact taught us by the apostle Paul [I Tim. 4:5]. Similarly, we cannot deny that forgiveness and peace are given through Extreme Unction. This, however, does not take place because it is a sacrament divinely instituted, but because he who receives it, receives it believing that forgiveness and peace are now his. The receiver's faith makes no error, however much the administrant may go astray. Even if the latter were baptizing or absolving in jest, i.e., not absolving at all as far as he himself was concerned, yet, in fact, he does absolve and baptize in as far as the man seeking baptism and forgiveness has faith. How much more truly will he who administers extreme unction give peace, even though the rite itself does not give peace, because it is no sacrament. The faith of the anointed man can receive even what the administrant either cannot give, or does not want to give. It is enough if the anointed man hears the word and believes; for whatever we believe we shall receive; in fact, we do receive, no matter what the minister does and leaves undone; whether he feigns or jests. For Christ's pronouncement holds good: "All things are possible to him that believes" [Mark 9:23]; and, again: "As thou hast believed, so be it done unto thee" [Matt. 8:13]. Yet none of our sophisticators mention faith when discussing the sacraments, but strive only to talk what is, in fact, mere nonsense about the virtues of the sacraments as such, "ever learning but never coming to the knowledge of the truth" [II Tim. 3:7].

By being made the extreme or *last* unction, it has had the advantage that it has been less abused than any other sacrament, and that the benefit it confers has been less subject to the Romanists' insufferable conduct and greed. This one mercy has been left to the dying: to receive the unction without charge, without even confessing, or communicating. If unction had continued in daily use, and especially for curing the sick, even if not for the forgiveness of sins, one could not imagine what stretches of territory the popes would have possessed by now. Merely by abuse of the sacrament of penitence, the power of the keys, and the sacrament of ordination, they have far outvied emperors and princes. But now, fortunately, they so despise the prayer of faith that they never undertake the cure of the sick; rather, out of the old rite they have trumped up another sacrament.

I know that what I have said so far about these four sacraments used by the Romanists will be quite enough to displease those persons who think that the number and the employment of the sacraments derive, not from Scripture, but from papal authority. Their view is that these particular sacraments were bestowed by the papacy. In fact, however, they originated in the universities; and it cannot be contested that every one of the papal "sacraments" comes from that source. Nor would the papal oppressiveness have attained its present intensity if Rome had not accepted many things from the universities; for among the famous bishoprics, there is scarcely one which has had so few scholars enthroned as in the case of Rome. Hitherto the Roman pontiffs have been pre-eminent, indeed unrivalled, in violence, craftiness, and superstition. Those who occupied that throne a thousand years ago were very different from their successors, who have become so mighty in the interim; so much so that one cannot help saying that, either the early popes were not true pontiffs of Rome, or else those of the present day are not true pontiffs.

There are several other rites which it would have seemed possible to class among the sacraments, particularly all those to which a divine promise has been attached, such as prayer, the word, and the cross. There are many passages in which Christ promised that those who prayed would be heard; especially in Luke 11 [:5 ff.], where many parables admonish us to pray. Concerning the word, we read: "Blessed are they who hear the word of God, and keep it" [Luke 11:28]. And none can tell how often He promised help and blessedness to all the troubled, the suffering, and the humble. In particular, it is true that no one can count all God's promises, seeing that the whole of Scripture is concerned to rouse faith in us, now urging us with commandments 'or retributions, and again encouraging us with promises and consolations. In fact, the whole of Scripture consists of either precepts or promises. The precepts make demands which humble the haughty, whereas the promises lift up the lowly by forgiving their sins.

It seemed most proper, however, to give the name of sacrament to those ordinances which consisted of promises conjoined with signs. The others, to which no signs are attached, are promises pure and simple. It follows that, strictly speaking, there are but two sacraments in the church of God: baptism and the Lord's Supper, since we find in these alone a sign divinely instituted, and here alone the promise of the forgiveness of sins. I added the sacrament of penance to these two; but it lacks a visible sign, and was not divinely instituted; and, as I said, it is simply a means of reaffirming our baptism. Not even the Scholastics can claim that their definition of a sacrament covers penance, because they, too, require a sacrament to have a visible sign which impresses on the senses the nature of the operation which is taking place invisibly. Since neither penance nor absolution have any such sign, they are compelled by their own definition either to deny that penance is a sacrament, and so to reduce their number; or else to propose another definition of a sacrament.

I have shown that baptism applies to the whole of our life, and that it suffices for whatever sacrament we require in the course of our journey through life. On the other hand, the Supper is really the sacrament for mortal men, and for those departing this life. In it, we commemorate Christ's departure from the present world, so that we may become like Him. Thus we apply these two sacraments in such a way as to apportion baptism to cover the beginning and the whole course of our life, while the Supper has in view our life's end in death. But let a Christian use both while he inhabits this mortal frame, until his baptism having reached its fullness and his strength its summit, he then passes out of this world as one born into a new and everlasting life, where he will eat with Christ in the kingdom of His Father. This is in harmony with His promise at the Last Supper, when He said: "Verily I say unto you, I will not drink henceforth of the fruit of the vine, until it is fulfilled in the Kingdom of God" [Matt. 26:29; Mark 14:25; Luke 22:18]. Thus it seems clear that He instituted the sacrament of the Supper with a view to our entry into the future life. Then both sacraments will have fulfilled their purpose, and baptism and Supper will be no more.

Here I come to the end of my Prelude. I place it freely and gladly at the disposal of all those religious-minded people who desire to have an unbiassed understanding of the Scriptures and the proper use of the sacraments. To know what God has given us, as it says in I Corinthians 2 [:12], and to know how the gifts ought to be used, are matters of no mean importance. For, if we have learned to judge spiritually, we shall not make the mistake of relying on things that are wrong. Contemporary theologians have never explained these two sacraments to our understanding, even if they have not actually tried to hide them. If I, for my part, have not explained them, at least I have managed not to hide them; and I have given to others an opportunity of thinking them out to better conclusions. At any rate, I have tried to bring them both out into the light. But none of us can do everything. In confidence and without reserve, I proffer what I have written and fling it at the ungodly and those who, arrogantly and insistently, teach us their own ideas instead of the divine. I am indifferent to their coarseness, but I wish that they would come to the right understanding. I do not despise their efforts, but I differentiate their efforts so far from what is really and truly Christian.

I have heard a rumour that once more a bull and other maledictions are being prepared against me by the papal authorities, by which I shall be pressed to recant, lest I be de-

clared a heretic. If the rumour is true, then I want this little
book to be part of the recantation that I shall make, lest these
arrogant despots complain of having spent their breath in vain.
I will publish a sequel shortly, and in such kind, please Christ,
as the popes of Rome have neither seen nor heard hitherto.
I will give ample testimony of my obedience. In the name of
Jesus Christ, our Lord, Amen.

> Why, impious Herod, shouldst thou fear
> Because the Christ is come so near?
> He who doth heavenly kingdoms grant
> Thine earthly realm can never want.[29]

[29] From Coelius Sedulius, c. A.D. 450.
The translation is according to *The English Hymnary*.

IV

SECULAR AUTHORITY: TO WHAT EXTENT IT SHOULD BE OBEYED[1]

[*Luther attacked the secular power of the Roman Church on many occasions. But* Secular Authority *is one of his less polemical works on the general subject of "secular authority" and provides us with a general over-all theory. The nature of secular authority is defined, the attitude of Christians to it delineated, and the responsibility of Christian princes defined. The work was published in 1523.*]

LETTER OF DEDICATION

To the Illustrious, High-born Prince and Lord, John, Duke of Saxony, Landgrave of Thuringia, Margrave of Meissen, My Gracious Lord.

Grace and peace in Christ. Again, illustrious, high-born prince, gracious lord, necessity is laid upon me, and the entreaties of many, and above all your grace's wishes impel me, to write concerning the secular authorities and the sword they bear; how it should be used in a Christian manner and in how

[1] Reprinted by permission of the Muhlenburg Press from *Works of Martin Luther*, volume III (Philadelphia: A. J. Holman Co. and the Castle Press, 1930), pp. 228–73. This text was translated by J. J. Schindel.

far men are bound to obey it. For men are perplexed by the word of Christ in Matthew 5 [:25, 39, 40], "Thou shalt not resist evil, but agree with thine adversary; and if any man take away thy coat, let him have thy cloak also," and Romans 12 [:19], "Vengeance is mine, I will repay, saith the Lord." These very texts Prince Volusian of old quoted against Saint Augustine, and charged Christianity with permitting the wicked to do evil and with being incompatible with the power of the sword.

The sophists[2] in the universities also were perplexed by these texts, because they could not reconcile the two spheres. In order not to make heathen of the princes, they taught that these sayings of Christ are not precepts but counsels of perfection. Thus Christ had to become a liar and be in error, in order that the princes might continue in honor. For they could not exalt the princes without putting down Christ,—wretched blind sophists that they are. And thus their poisonous error has spread through the whole world, so that every one regards these teachings of Christ as counsels of perfection, and not as precepts binding on all Christians alike. It has gone so far that they have permitted the imperfect duty of the sword and of secular authority not only to the perfect class of bishops, but even to the pope, whose rank is the most perfect of all; nay, they have ascribed it to no one on earth so completely as to him. So thoroughly has the devil taken possession of the sophists and of the universities, that they themselves do not know what and how they speak or teach.

I hope, however, to instruct the princes and the secular authorities in such a way that they shall remain Christians and that Christ shall remain Lord, yet so that Christ's commandments need not for their sake be changed into counsels.

This will I do as a dutiful service to your princely grace, for the profiting of every one who may need it, and to the praise and glory of Christ our Lord. I commend your princely grace with all your kin to the grace of God. May He mercifully have you in His keeping. Amen.

Your Princely Grace's obedient servant,
Martin Luther.

Wittenberg, New Year's Day, 1523.

[2] The Scholastic theologians.

THE TREATISE

Formerly I addressed a booklet to the German nobility, setting forth their Christian office and functions. But how they have carried out my suggestions is very plain to see. Hence I must change my tactics and write them, this time, what they should omit and not do. I fear this writing will have just as little effect on them as the former one had,—they will by all means remain princes and by no means become Christians. For God Almighty has made our rulers mad. They actually think they have the power to do and command their subjects to do, whatever they please. And the subjects are led astray and believe they are bound to obey them in everything. It has gone so far that the rulers have ordered the people to put away books, and to believe and keep what they prescribe. In this way they presumptuously set themselves in God's place, lord it over men's conscience and faith, and put the Holy Spirit to school according to their mad brains. They let it be known, at the same time, that they are not to be contradicted, but called gracious lords into the bargain.

They issue public proclamations, saying that this is the emperor's command and they desire to be Christian and obedient princes, as though they were in earnest about it and one did not see the knave behind the mask. If the emperor took a castle or a city from them or commanded some other injustice, we should see how quickly they would find themselves obliged to resist the emperor and disobey him.

But when it comes to fleecing the poor and to doing what they please with God's Word, it must be called obedience to the imperial command. Such people were formerly called knaves, now they must be addressed as Christian and loyal princes. Yet they will not permit any one to appear before them for a hearing or to defend himself, no matter how humbly he may petition. If the emperor or any one else should do the same to them they would regard it as most intolerable. These are the princes who rule the empire in German lands to-day; hence also there must needs be such prosperity in all lands, as we see.

Because the raving of such fools tends to the suppression of Christian faith, the denying of the divine Word, and the blaspheming of the divine Majesty, I can and will no longer look upon my ungracious lords and angry nobles, but must resist them at least with words. And since I have not been in terror of their idol, the pope, who threatens to deprive me of soul and of heaven, I must show that I am not in terror of his scales and bubbles which threaten to deprive me of body and of earth. God grant that they may have to rage until grey habits[3] perish, and that we die not of their threatenings. Amen.

I. We must firmly establish secular law and the sword, that no one may doubt that it is in the world by God's will and ordinance. The passages which establish this are the following: Romans 13 [:1 f.], "Let every soul be subject to power and authority, for there is no power but from God. The power that is everywhere is ordained of God. He then who resists the power resists God's ordinance. But he who resists God's ordinance shall bring himself under condemnation." Likewise, I Peter 2 [:13–14], "Be subject to every kind of human ordinance, whether to the king as supreme, or to the governors, as to those sent of Him for the punishing of the evil and for the reward of the good."

This penal law existed from the beginning of the world. For when Cain slew his brother he was in such great terror of being in turn killed that God specially forbade it and suspended the sword for his sake,—and no one was to slay him [Gen. 4:14 f.]. He would not have had this fear if he had not seen and heard from Adam that murderers should be slain. Moreover God re-established and confirmed it after the Flood in unmistakable terms when He said, "Whoso sheds man's blood, his blood shall be shed again by man" [Gen. 9:6]. This cannot be understood as a plague and punishment of God upon murderers; for many murderers who repent or are pardoned continue to live, and die by other means than the sword. But it is said of the right of the sword, that a murderer is guilty of death and should in justice be slain by the sword. Though

3 The Franciscans.

justice be hindered or the sword be tardy, so that the murderer dies a natural death, the Scripture is not on that account
false when it says, "Whoso sheddeth man's blood, by man
shall his blood be shed." For it is men's fault or merit that this
law commanded of God is not carried out; even as other commandments of God are broken.

Afterward it was also confirmed by the law of Moses, Exodus 21 [:14], "If a man presumptuously kill thou shalt take
him from My altar that he may die." And again, in the same
place, "A life for a life, an eye for an eye, a tooth for a tooth,
a foot for a foot, a hand for a hand, a wound for a wound, a
bruise for a bruise" [Ex. 21:23 ff.]. Christ also confirms it when
He says to Peter in the garden, "He that taketh the sword
shall perish by the sword" [Matt. 26:52], which is to be interpreted like Genesis 9 [:6], "Whoso sheddeth man's blood,"
etc. Doubtless Christ refers in these words to that passage and
incorporates and confirms it in them. John Baptist teaches the
same. When the soldiers asked him what they should do, he
answered, "Do injustice or violence to no one, and be content
with your wages" [Luke 3:14]. If the sword were not divinely
appointed he should have commanded them to cease being
soldiers, since he was to perfect the people and direct them
in a proper Christian way. Hence it is sufficiently clear and
certain that it is God's will that the sword and secular law be
used for the punishment of the wicked and the protection of
the upright [I Pet. 2:14].

II. There seems to be a powerful argument on the other
side. Christ says, Matthew 5 [:38 f.], "Ye have heard that it
was said to them of old: An eye for an eye, a tooth for a
tooth. But I say unto you, That a man shall not resist evil,
but if any one strikes thee upon the right cheek, turn to him
the other also; and whoever will go to law with thee to take
thy coat, let him have the cloak also, and whoever forces thee
a mile, with him go two miles." Likewise Paul, Romans
12 [:19], "Dearly beloved, defend not yourselves, but give
place to God's wrath, for it is written, Vengeance is mine, I
will repay saith the Lord." Likewise Matthew 5 [:44], "Love
your enemies, do good to them that hate you." And I Peter
3 [:9], "Let no one repay evil with evil, nor railing with rail-

ing," etc. These and the like passages truly would make it appear as though in the New Testament there should be no secular sword among Christians.

Hence the sophists also say that Christ has abolished Moses' law; of such commandments they make counsels for the perfect, and divide Christian teaching and Christians into two classes. One part they call the perfect, and assign to it such counsels. To the other, the imperfect, they assign the commandments [Matt. 5:19]. This they do out of sheer perversity and caprice, without any scriptural basis. They do not see that in the same passage Christ lays such stress on His teaching that He is unwilling to have the least word of it set aside, and condemns to hell those who do not love their enemies [Matt. 5:25 ff.]. Therefore we must interpret these passages differently, so that Christ's words may apply to all alike whether they be "perfect" or "imperfect." For perfection and imperfection consist not in works and do not establish a distinct external order among Christians; but they exist in the heart, in faith and love, so that they who believe and love the most are the perfect ones, whether outwardly they be male or female, prince or peasant, monk or layman. For love and faith produce no sects or outward differences.

III. We must divide all the children of Adam into two classes; the first belong to the kingdom of God, the second to the kingdom of the world. Those belonging to the kingdom of God are all true believers in Christ and are subject to Christ. For Christ is the King and Lord in the kingdom of God, as the second Psalm and all the Scriptures say [Ps. 2:6]. For this reason He came into the world, that He might begin God's kingdom and establish it in the world. Therefore He says before Pilate, "My kingdom is not of the world, but whoever is of the truth hears My voice" [John 18:36 f.]; and continually in the Gospel He refers to the kingdom of God and says, "Amend your ways, the kingdom of God is at hand" [Matt. 3:2]. Likewise, "Seek first the kingdom of God and His righteousness" [Matt. 6:33]. He also calls the Gospel, a Gospel of the kingdom, for the reason that it teaches, governs, and contains God's kingdom.

Now observe, these people need no secular sword or law.

And if all the world were composed of real Christians, that is, true believers, no prince, king, lord, sword, or law would be needed. For what were the use of them, since Christians have in their hearts the Holy Spirit, who instructs them and causes them to wrong no one, to love every one, willingly and cheerfully to suffer injustice and even death from every one. Where every wrong is suffered and every right is done, no quarrel, strife, trial, judge, penalty, law or sword is needed. Therefore, it is not possible for the secular sword and law to find any work to do among Christians, since of themselves they do much more than its laws and doctrines can demand. Just as Paul says in I Timothy 1 [:9], "The law is not given for the righteous, but for the unrighteous."

Why is this? Because the righteous does of himself all and more than all that all the laws demand. But the unrighteous do nothing that the law demands, therefore they need the law to instruct, constrain, and compel them to do what is good. A good tree does not need any teaching or law to bear good fruit, its nature causes it to bear according to its kind without any law and teaching [Matt. 7:18]. A man would be a fool to make a book of laws and statutes telling an apple tree how to bear apples and not thorns, when it is able by its own nature to do this better than man with all his books can define and direct. Just so, by the Spirit and by faith all Christians are throughout inclined to do well and keep the law, much more than any one can teach them with all the laws, and need so far as they are concerned no commandments nor law.

You ask, Why then did God give to all men so many commandments, and why did Christ teach in the Gospel so many things to be done? Concerning this I have written much in the Postil[4] and elsewhere. To put it as briefly as possible here, Paul says that the law is given for the sake of the unrighteous, that is, that those who are not Christians may through the law be externally restrained from evil deeds, as we shall hear later [I Tim. 1:9]. Since, however, no one is by nature Christian or pious, but every one sinful and evil, God places the restraints of the law upon them all, so that they may not dare give rein to their desires and commit outward, wicked deeds.

4 Sermons on the Church Year.

In addition, St. Paul gives the law another function in Romans 7 [:7] and Galatians 3 [:19, 24]. It is to teach men to recognize sin, that they may be made humble unto grace and unto faith in Christ. Christ also does this here, when He teaches in Matthew 5 [:39] that we should not resist evil, and thereby glorifies the law and teaches how a real Christian ought to be and must be disposed, as we shall hear further on.

IV. All who are not Christians belong to the kingdom of the world and are under the law. Since few believe and still fewer live a Christian life, do not resist the evil, and themselves do no evil, God has provided for non-Christians a different government outside the Christian estate and God's kingdom, and has subjected them to the sword, so that, even though they would do so, they cannot practice their wickedness, and that, if they do, they may not do it without fear nor in peace and prosperity. Even so a wild, savage beast is fastened with chains and bands, so that it cannot bite and tear as is its wont, although it gladly would do so; whereas a tame and gentle beast does not require this, but without any chains and bands is nevertheless harmless. If it were not so, seeing that the whole world is evil and that among thousands there is scarcely one true Christian, men would devour one another, and no one could preserve wife and child, support himself and serve God; and thus the world would be reduced to chaos. For this reason God has ordained the two governments; the spiritual, which by the Holy Spirit under Christ makes Christians and pious people, and the secular, which restrains the unchristian and wicked so that they must needs keep the peace outwardly, even against their will. So Paul interprets the secular sword, Romans 13 [:3], and says it is not a terror to good works, but to the evil. And Peter says it is for the punishment of evil doers [I Pet. 2:14].

If any one attempted to rule the world by the Gospel, and put aside all secular law and the secular sword, on the plea that all are baptised and Christian, and that according to the Gospel, there is to be among them neither law nor sword, nor necessity for either, pray, what would happen? He would loose the bands and chains of the wild and savage beasts, and let them tear and mangle every one, and at the same time say they were quite tame and gentle creatures; but I would have the proof in my wounds. Just so would the wicked under the name of Christian abuse this freedom of the Gospel, carry on their knavery, and say that they were Christians subject neither to law nor sword, as some are already raving and ranting.

To such an one we must say, It is indeed true that Christians, so far as they themselves are concerned, are subject to neither law nor sword and need neither; but first take heed and fill the world with real Christians before ruling it in a Christian and evangelical manner. This you will never accomplish; for the world and the masses are and always will be unchristian, although they are all baptized and are nominally Christian. Christians, however, are few and far between, as the saying is. Therefore it is out of the question that there should be a common Christian government over the whole world, nay even over one land or company of people, since the wicked always outnumber the good. Hence a man who would venture to govern an entire country or the world with the Gospel would be like a shepherd who should place in one fold wolves, lions, eagles, and sheep together and let them freely mingle with one another and say, Help yourselves, and be good and peaceful among yourselves; the fold is open, there is plenty of food; have no fear of dogs and clubs. The sheep, forsooth, would keep the peace and would allow themselves to be fed and governed in peace, but they would not live long; nor would any beast keep from molesting another.

For this reason these two kingdoms must be sharply distinguished, and both be permitted to remain; the one to produce piety, the other to bring about external peace and prevent evil deeds; neither is sufficient in the world without the other. For no one can become pious before God by means of the secular government, without Christ's spiritual rule. Hence Christ's rule does not extend over all, but Christians are always in the minority and are in the midst of non-Christians. Where there is only secular rule or law, there, of necessity, is sheer hypocrisy, though the commandments be God's very own. Without the Holy Spirit in the heart no one becomes really pious, he may do as fine works as he will. Where, on the other hand, the spiritual government rules alone over land and people, there evil is given free rein and the door is opened for every kind of knavery; for the natural world cannot receive or comprehend spiritual things.

You see the purpose of Christ's words which we quoted above from Matthew 5 [:39]. They mean that Christians shall not go to law nor use the secular sword among themselves. In reality He says it only to His dear Christians. They alone also accept it and act accordingly, nor do they make counsels of it, as the sophists do, but are so inclined in their heart, through the Spirit, that they do evil to no one and willingly endure evil at every one's hands. If the whole world were Christian, all these words would apply to it and it would keep them. Since, however, it is unchristian the words do not apply to it, nor does it keep them, but is under another rule in which those who are not Christians are under external constraint and are forced to keep the peace and do what is good.

For this reason Christ did not wield the sword nor give it a place in His kingdom; for He is a King over Christians and rules by His Holy Spirit alone, without law. And although He acknowledged the sword, He nevertheless did not use it; for it is of no use in His kingdom, in which are none but the pious. Hence David of old dared not build the temple, because he had shed much blood and had borne the sword; not that he had done wrong thereby, but because he could not be a type of Christ, who without the sword was to have a kingdom of peace [II Sam. 7:5 ff.]. It must be built by Solomon [I Kings 5:17 ff.], whose name means "Frederick" or "peaceful," who had a peaceful kingdom, by which the truly peaceful kingdom of Christ, the real Frederick and Solomon, could be represented. In like manner, during the entire building of the temple not the sound of a tool was heard, as the text says [I Kings 6:7]; all for this reason, that Christ, without constraint and force, without law and the sword, was to have a people who serve Him freely.

This is what the prophets mean in Psalm 110 [:3], "Thy people shall be willing"; and in Isaiah 11 [:9], "They shall not hurt nor destroy in all my holy mountain"; and in Isaiah 2 [:4], "They shall beat their swords into plowshares and their spears into pruning hooks, and no one shall lift up the sword against another, neither shall they busy themselves in war anymore," etc. Whoever would apply these and similar passages wherever Christ's name is professed, would entirely pervert the Scriptures; for they are spoken only of true Christians, who really do this among themselves.

V. But perhaps you will say, Since Christians do not need the secular sword and the law, why does Paul say to all Christians, in Romans 13 [:1], "Let all souls be subject to power and authority"? And St. Peter says, "Be subject to every human ordinance," etc., as quoted above [I Pet. 2:13]. I answer, as I have said, that Christians, among themselves and by and for themselves, need no law or sword, since it is neither necessary nor profitable for them. Since, however, a true Christian lives and labors on earth not for himself but for his neighbor, therefore the whole spirit of his life impels him to do even that which he need not do, but which is profitable and necessary for his neighbor. Because the sword is a very great benefit and necessary to the whole world, to preserve peace, to punish sin and to prevent evil, he submits most willingly to the rule of the sword, pays tax, honors those in authority, serves, helps, and does all he can to further the government, that it may be sustained and held in honor and fear. Although he needs none of these things for himself and it is not necessary for him to do them, yet he considers what is for the good and profit of others, as Paul teaches in Ephesians 5 [:21].

He serves the State as he performs all other works of love, which he himself does not need. He visits the sick, not that he may be made well; feeds no one because he himself needs food: so he also serves the State not because he needs it, but because others need it,—that they may be protected and that the wicked may not become worse. He loses nothing by this, and such service in no way harms him, and yet it is of great profit to the world. If he did not do it, he would be acting not as a Christian but contrary even to love, and would also be setting a bad example to others, who like him would not submit to authority, though they were not Christians. In this way the Gospel would be brought into disrepute, as though it taught rebellion and made self-willed people, unwilling to benefit or serve any one, when in reality it makes a Christian the servant of every one. Thus in Matthew 17 [:27], Christ gave the tribute money that He might not offend them, although He did not need to do it.

Thus you observe in the words of Christ quoted above from Matthew 5 [:39] that He indeed teaches that Christians among themselves should have no secular sword nor law. He does not, however, forbid one to serve and obey those who have the secular sword and the law; much rather, since you have no need of them and are not to have them, are you to serve those who have not progressed so far as you and still need them. Although you do not need to have your enemy punished, your weak neighbor does. You should help him, that he may have peace and that his enemy may be curbed; which is not possible unless power and authority are honored and feared. Christ does not say, "Thou shalt not serve the State or be subject to it," but "Thou shalt not resist evil." As though He said, "Take heed that you bear everything, so that you may not need the State to help and serve you and be of profit to you, but that you may on the other hand, help, serve, and be of profit and use to it. I would have you to be far too exalted and noble to have any need of it, but it should have need of you."

VI. You ask whether a Christian, also, may bear the secular sword and punish the wicked, since Christ's words, "Thou shalt not resist the evil," are so clear and definite that the sophists have had to make a counsel of them. I answer, You have now heard two propositions. The one is, that the sword can have no place among Christians, therefore you cannot bear it among and against Christians, who do not need it. The question, therefore, must be directed to the other side, to the non-Christians, whether as a Christian you may there bear it. Here the other proposition applies, that you are under obligation to serve and further the sword by whatever means you can, with body, soul, honor or goods. For it is nothing that you need, but something quite useful and profitable for the whole world and for your neighbor. Therefore, should you see that there is a lack of hangmen, beadles, judges, lords, or princes, and find that you are qualified, you should offer your services and seek the place, that necessary government may by no means be despised and become inefficient or perish. For the world cannot and dare not dispense with it.

The reason you should do this is, that in this case you would enter entirely into the service and work of others, which benefited neither yourself nor your property nor your character, but only your neighbor and others; and you would do it not to avenge yourself or to recompense evil for evil, but for the good of your neighbor and for the maintenance of the safety and peace of others. As concerns yourself, you would abide by the Gospel and govern yourself according to Christ's word, gladly turning the other cheek and letting the mantle go with the coat, when the matter concerned you and your cause [Matt. 5:39, 40]. In this way, then, things are well balanced, and you satisfy at the same time God's kingdom inwardly and the kingdom of the world outwardly, at the same time suffer evil and injustice and yet punish evil and injustice, at the same time do not resist evil and yet resist it. For in the one case you consider yourself and what is yours, in the other you consider your neighbor and what is his. In what concerns you and yours, you govern yourself by the Gospel and suffer injustice for yourself as a true Christian; in what concerns others and belongs to them, you govern yourself according to love and suffer no injustice for your neighbor's sake; this the Gospel does not forbid, but rather commands in another place.

In this way all the saints wielded the sword from the beginning of the world: Adam and his descendants; Abraham when he rescued Lot, his brother's son, and smote the four kings, though he was a thoroughly evangelical man [Gen. 14:15]; Samuel, the holy prophet, slew King Agag [I Sam. 15:33], and Elijah the prophets of Baal [I Kings 18:40]. So did Moses, Joshua, the children of Israel, Samson, David, and all the kings and princes in the Old Testament. In the same way did Daniel and his associates, Ananias, Asarias and Misael, in Babylon; in the same manner did Joseph in Egypt, and so on.

Should any one advance the argument, that the Old Testament is abolished and avails no more, and that therefore such examples cannot be set before Christians, I answer, That is not correct. For St. Paul says in I Corinthians 10 [:3 f.], "They did all eat the same spiritual meat as we, and did drink the same spiritual drink from the rock, which is Christ"; that is, they have had the same spirit and faith in Christ as we and were Christians as well as we are. Therefore, wherein they did right, all Christians do right, from the beginning of the world unto the end. For time and external circumstances matter not among Christians. Neither is it true that the Old Testament was abolished in such a way that it need not be kept, or that it would be wrong for any one to keep it in full, as St. Jerome and many more erred in thinking. It is indeed abolished in the sense that we are free to keep it or not to keep it, and it is no longer necessary to keep it on penalty of one's soul, as was formerly the case.

For Paul says in I Corinthians 7 [:19] and Galatians 6 [:15], that neither uncircumcision nor circumcision avails anything, but a new creature in Christ; that is, it is not sin to be uncircumcised, as the Jews thought, nor is it sin to be circumcised, as the heathen thought, but either is right and permissible for him who does not think he will be saved by so doing. This is true also of all other parts of the Old Testament; it is not wrong to omit them nor wrong to do them, but all is permissible and good, to do and to leave undone. Nay, if they were necessary or profitable to one's fellow-man for his salvation, it would be necessary to keep them all; for every one is under obligation to do what is for his neighbor's good, whether it be Old or New Testament, Jewish or heathen, as Paul teaches in I Corinthians 12 [:13], for love pervades all and transcends all, considers only what is for the profit of others, and does not ask whether it is old or new. Hence, the precedents for the use of the sword also are matters of freedom, and you may follow them or not, but where you see that your neighbor needs it, there love constrains you so that you must needs do what otherwise would be optional and unnecessary for you to do or to leave undone. Only do not suppose that you will grow pious or be saved thereby, as the Jews presumed to be saved by their works, but leave this to faith, which without works makes you a new creature.

To prove our position also by the New Testament, the testimony of John Baptist in Luke 3 [:14] cannot be shaken on this point. It was his work to point to Christ, to witness for Him, and to teach about Him; and the teaching of the man who was to prepare a people for Christ and lead them to Him, has of necessity to be purely New Testament and evangelical. And he endorses the work of the soldiers and says they should be content with their wages. If it had been an unchristian thing to bear the sword, he ought to have censured them for it and told them to abandon both wages and sword, or he would not have taught them the Christian estate correctly. So also, when St. Peter in Acts 10 [:34 ff.] preached Christ to Cornelius, he did not tell him to abandon his work, which he would have had to do if it had prevented Cornelius from being a Christian. Moreover, before he was baptized, the Holy Ghost came upon him [Acts 10:44]. St. Luke also lauds him as a pious man previous to Peter's sermon, and does not find fault with him because he was a captain of soldiers and under a heathen emperor. What the Holy Ghost permitted to remain and did not censure in Cornelius' case, it is meet that we too should permit and not censure.

A similar case is that of the Ethiopian captain, the eunuch, in Acts 8 [:30 ff.], whom Philip the evangelist converted and baptized and permitted to remain in his work and to return home again, although without bearing the sword he could not possibly have been so high an official under the queen in Ethiopia. It was the same with the governor in Cyprus, Sergius Paulus, in Acts 13 [:12], whom St. Paul converted, and yet permitted to remain governor among heathen and over heathen. Many holy martyrs did the same, who were obedient to heathen Roman emperors, and went under them into battle, and doubtless also slew people, for the sake of preserving peace; as is written of St. Maurice, St. Achacius, St. Gereon, and many others under the emperor Julian.

Beyond these, we have the clear, definite statement of St. Paul in Romans 13 [:1], where he says, "The powers that be are ordained of God"; and again, "The power does not bear the sword in vain; but is the minister of God for thy good, an avenger unto him that doeth evil" [Rom. 13:4]. Be not so wicked, my friend, as to say, A Christian may not do that which is God's peculiar work, ordinance and creation. Else you must also say, A Christian must not eat, drink or be married, for these are also God's work and ordinance. If it is God's work and creation, it is good, and so good that every one

can use it in a Christian and saving way, as Paul says in I
Timothy 4 [:4], "Every creature of God is good, and nothing
to be rejected by the believing and those who know the truth."
Among "every creature of God" you must reckon not simply
food and drink, clothes and shoes, but also government, citizen-
ship, protection and administration of justice.

In short, since St. Paul here says the power is God's servant
[Rom. 13:1], we must admit that it is to be exercised not only
by the heathen, but by all men. What else does it mean when
it is said it is God's servant except that the power is by its very
nature such that one may serve God by it? Now, it should be
quite unchristian to say that there is any service of God in
which a Christian ought not and dare not take part, when such
a service belongs to no one so much as to Christians. It would
indeed be good and profitable if all princes were real and good
Christians, for the sword and the government, as a special service of God, belong of right to Christians, more than to all other
men on earth. Therefore you should cherish the sword or the
government, even as the state of matrimony, or husbandry, or
any other handiwork which God has instituted. As a man can
serve God in the state of matrimony, in husbandry, or at a
trade, for the benefit of his fellow-man, and must serve Him if
necessity demand; just so he can also serve God in the State
and should serve Him there, if the necessities of his neighbor
demand it; for the State is God's servant and workman to
punish the evil and protect the good. Still it may also be
omitted if there is no need for it, just as men are free not to
marry and not to farm if there should be no need of marrying
and farming.

You ask, Why did not Christ and the apostles bear the
sword? Tell me, Why did He not also take a wife, or become
a cobbler or a tailor? If an occupation or office is not good
because Christ Himself did not occupy it, what would become
of all occupations and offices, with the exception of the ministry which alone He exercised? Christ fulfilled His own office
and vocation, but thereby did not reject any other. It was not
meet that He should bear the sword, for He was to bear only
that office by which His kingdom is governed and which properly serves His kingdom. Now it does not concern His kingdom
that He should be a married man, a cobbler, a tailor, a farmer,

a prince, a hangman or a beadle, neither is the sword or secular law of any concern, but only God's Word and Spirit, by which His people are inwardly governed. This office which He exercised then, and still exercises, always bestows God's Word and Spirit; and in this office the apostles and all spiritual rulers must needs follow Him. For they are kept so busily employed with the spiritual sword, the Word of God, in fulfilling this their calling, that they must indeed neglect the worldly sword, and leave it to those who do not have to preach; although it is not contrary to their calling to use it, as I have said. For every one must attend to his own calling and work.

Therefore, even though Christ did not bear the sword nor prescribe it, it is sufficient that He did not forbid or abolish it, but rather endorsed it; just as it is sufficient that He did not abolish the state of matrimony, but endorsed it, though He Himself took no wife and gave no commandment concerning it. He had to identify Himself throughout with the occupation and work which properly and entirely served the furtherance of His kingdom, so that no occasion and binding example might be made of it, to teach and believe that the kingdom of God cannot exist without matrimony and the sword and such externals (since Christ's examples are binding), when it is only by God's Word and Spirit that it does exist. This was and had to be Christ's peculiar work as the supreme King in this kingdom. Since, however, not all Christians have this same office, though innately it belongs to them, it is meet that they should have some other, external one, by which God may also be served.

From all this we see what is the true meaning of Christ's words in Matthew 5 [:39], "Resist not evil," etc. It is this, that a Christian should be so disposed that he will suffer every evil and injustice, not avenge himself nor bring suit in court, and in nothing make use of secular power and law for himself. For others, however, he may and should seek vengeance, justice, protection and help, and do what he can toward this. Likewise, the State should, either of itself or through the instigation of others, help and protect him without complaint, application or instigation on his part. When the State does not do this, he ought to permit himself to be robbed and despoiled, and not resist the evil, as Christ's words say.

Be quite certain, also, that this teaching of Christ is not a counsel of perfection, as our sophists blasphemously and falsely say, but a universal, strict command for all Christians. Then you will learn that all those who avenge themselves or go to law and wrangle in the courts over their property and honor are nothing but heathen masquerading under the name of Christians. It cannot be otherwise, I tell you. Do not look to the multitude and to the common practice, for, have no doubt, there are few Christians on earth; and God's Word is something very different from the common practice.

You see that Christ does not abolish the law when He says, "You have heard that it was said to them of old: An eye for an eye; but I say unto you that ye resist not evil," etc. [Matt. 5:38]. But He expounds the meaning of the law as it is to be understood, as though He would say, You Jews consider it right and good before God if you recover by law what belongs to you, and you rely on what Moses said, An eye for an eye, etc. I say unto you, however, that Moses gave such a law for the wicked, who do not belong to God's kingdom, that they might not avenge themselves or do worse things, but be compelled by such outward law to desist from evil-doing, in order that by outward law and rule they might be kept under authority. But you should so conduct yourselves as not to need or invoke such a law. Although the secular authority must have such a law by which to judge unbelievers, and although you yourselves might use it to judge others, still you should not invoke or use it for yourselves and in your own affairs. You have the kingdom of heaven; therefore you should leave the kingdom of earth to any one who wants to take it.

You see, then, Christ's words do not mean that He abolishes Moses' law, or prohibits secular power, but He excepts His own. They are not to use them for themselves, but to leave them to unbelievers, whom indeed they may serve with the law. For unbelievers are not Christians; and no one can be compelled to be a Christian. But that Christ's words apply only to His own is evident, since He afterward says they should love their enemies and be perfect like their heavenly Father [Matt. 5:44, 48]. He, however, who loves his enemies lets the law alone and does not use it to demand an eye for an eye. Neither does he oppose the non-Christians who do not love their enemies and wish to use the law; nay, he lends his help that these laws may restrain the wicked from doing worse.

In this way, I take it, the word of Christ is reconciled with the passages which establish the sword, so that this is the meaning: No Christian shall wield or invoke the sword for himself and for his cause; but for another he can and ought to wield and invoke it, so that wickedness may be hindered and godliness defended. Even as the Lord says, in the same passage, A Christian shall not swear, but let his word be Yea, yea; Nay, nay,—that is, for himself and of his own choice and desire, he should not swear [Matt. 5:34 ff.]. When, however, need, welfare and salvation, or God's honor demand, he should swear; thus he uses the forbidden oath to serve another, just as he uses the forbidden sword in another's service; as Christ and Paul often swore to make their teaching and testimony valuable and credible to others, as men do and have a right to do in covenants and compacts, of which Psalm 63 [:11] says, "They shall be praised who swear by His name."

But you ask further, whether the beadles, hangmen, jurists, advocates, and their ilk, can also be Christians and in a state of salvation. I answer: If the State and its sword are a divine service, as was proved above, that which the State needs in order to wield the sword must also be a divine service. There must be those who arrest, accuse, slay and destroy the wicked, and protect, acquit, defend and save the good. Therefore, when such duties are performed, not with the intention of seeking one's own ends, but only of helping to maintain the laws and the State, so that the wicked may be restrained, there is no peril in them and they may be followed like any other pursuit and be used as one's means of support. For, as was said, love of neighbor seeks not its own, considers not how great or how small, but how profitable and how needful for neighbor or community the works are [I Cor. 13:5].

You ask, Why may I not use the sword for myself and for my own cause, with the intention by so doing not of seeking my own interest, but the punishment of evil? I answer, Such a miracle is not impossible, but quite unusual and hazardous. Where there is such affluence of the Spirit it may be done, for so we read of Samson in Judges 15 [:11], that he said, "I have done unto them as they did unto me"; yet, on the contrary,

Proverbs 24 [:29] says, "Say not, I will do unto him as he has done unto me"; and Proverbs 20 [:22], "Say not thou, I will recompense evil." For Samson was called of God to harass the Philistines and deliver the children of Israel. Though he used them as an occasion to advance his own cause, still he did not do so to avenge himself or to seek his own interests, but to serve others and to punish the Philistines. No one but a real Christian and one who is full of the Spirit will follow this example. If reason also should follow this example, it would indeed pretend not to be seeking its own, but this would be untrue. It cannot be done without grace. Therefore, first become like Samson, and then you can also do as Samson did.

PART TWO

How Far Secular Authority Extends

We come now to the main part of this treatise. For as we have learned that there must be temporal authority on earth, and how it is to be employed in a Christian and salutary way, we must now learn how far its arm extends and how far its hand reaches, lest it extend too far and encroach upon God's kingdom and rule. And it is very necessary to know this, since where it is given too wide a scope, intolerable and terrible injury follows; and, on the other hand, it cannot be too much restricted without working injury. In the latter case the punishment is too light; in the former, too severe. It is more tolerable, however, to err on the latter side and punish too little; since it always is better to let a knave live than to kill a good man, for the world will still have knaves, and must have them, but of good men there are few.

In the first place, it must be noted that the two classes of Adam's children, the one in God's kingdom under Christ, the other in the kingdom of the world under the State, have two kinds of laws, as was said above. Every kingdom must have its own laws and regulations, and without law no kingdom or government can exist, as daily experience sufficiently proves. Worldly government has laws which extend no farther than to life and property and what is external upon earth. For over the soul God can and will let no one rule but Himself. Therefore, where temporal power presumes to prescribe laws for the soul, it encroaches upon God's government and only misleads and destroys the souls. We desire to make this so clear that every one shall grasp it, and that our junkers, the princes and bishops, may see what fools they are when they seek to coerce the people with their laws and commandments into believing one thing or another.

When a man-made law is imposed upon the soul, in order to make it believe this or that, as that man prescribes, there is certainly no word of God for it. If there is no word of God for it, it is uncertain whether God will have it so, for we cannot be certain that what He does not command pleases Him. Nay, we are sure that it does not please Him, for He desires that our faith be grounded simply and entirely on His divine Word, as He says in Matthew 16 [:18], "On this rock will I build my church"; and in John 10 [:27, 5], "My sheep hear my voice and know me; but the voice of strangers they hear not, but flee from them." It follows from this that the secular power forces souls to eternal death with such an outrageous law, for it compels them to believe as right and certainly pleasing to God what is nevertheless uncertain, nay, what is certainly displeasing to Him, since there is no clear word of God for it. For whoever believes that to be right which is wrong or uncertain denies the truth, which is God Himself, and believes in lies and errors and counts that right which is wrong.

Hence it is the height of folly when they command that one shall believe the Church, the fathers, the councils, though there be no word of God for it. The devil's apostles command such things, not the Church; for the Church commands nothing unless it is sure it is God's Word, as St. Peter says, "If any man speak let him speak as the oracles of God" [I Pet. 4:11]. It will be a very long time, however, before they prove that the statements of the councils are God's Word. Still more foolish is it when they assert that kings and princes and the mass of men believe thus and so. If you please, we are not baptized unto kings, princes, or even unto the mass of men, but unto Christ and unto God himself; neither are we called kings, princes or common folk, but Christians. No one shall and can command the soul, unless he can show it the way to heaven; but this no man can do, only God. Therefore in matters which concern the salvation of souls nothing but God's Word shall be taught and accepted.

Again, consummate fools though they are, they must confess that they have no power over souls. For no human being can kill a soul or make it alive, conduct it to heaven or hell. And if they will not believe us in this, Christ indeed will certify strongly enough to it, since He says in Matthew 10 [:28], "Fear not them which kill the body and after that have power to do naught; but rather fear Him Who after He has killed the body has power to condemn to hell." I consider that here it is sufficiently clear that the soul is taken out of all human hands and is placed under the power of God alone. Now tell me, how much wit is there in the head of him who imposes commandments where he has no power at all? Who would not regard one as insane if he commanded the moon to shine when he desired it? How fitting it would be if the Leipzigers would impose laws on us Wittenbergers, or again, if we in Wittenberg would lay laws on those in Leipzig. They would certainly send the law-makers a thank-offering of hellebore to clear the brain and cure the snuffles. Nevertheless, our emperors and wise princes continue to permit pope, bishops and sophists to lead them on, one blind man leading the other, to command their subjects to believe, without God's Word, whatever they please, and still would be known as Christian princes. God help us!

Besides, we can understand how any authority shall and may act only where it can see, know, judge, change and convert. For what kind of judge would he be who should blindly judge matters which he neither heard nor saw? Tell me, how can a man see, know, judge, condemn and change hearts? This is reserved for God alone, as Psalm 7 [:9] says, "God trieth the heart and reins"; likewise, "The Lord shall judge the people" [Ps. 7:8]; and Acts 15 [:8], "God knoweth the hearts"; and, Jeremiah 17 [:9 f.], "Wicked and unsearchable is the human heart; who can know it? I the Lord, who search the heart and reins." A court ought and must be quite certain and clear about everything, if it is to pass sentence. But the thoughts and intents of the heart can be known to no one but God; there-

fore it is useless and impossible to command or compel any
one by force to believe one thing or another. It must be taken
hold of in a different way; force cannot accomplish it. And I
am surprised at the great fools, since they themselves all say,
De occultis non judicat ecclesia,—the Church does not judge
secret things. If the spiritual rule of the Church governs only
public matters, how dare the senseless secular power judge
and control such a secret, spiritual, hidden matter as faith?

Furthermore, every man is responsible for his own faith,
and he must see to it for himself that he believes rightly. As
little as another can go to hell or heaven for me, so little can he
believe or disbelieve for me; and as little as he can open or shut
heaven or hell for me, so little can he drive me to faith or unbelief. Since, then, belief or unbelief is a matter of every one's
conscience, and since this is no lessening of the secular power,
the latter should be content and attend to its own affairs and
permit men to believe one thing or another, as they are able
and willing, and constrain no one by force. For faith is a free
work, to which no one can be forced. Nay, it is a divine work,
done in the Spirit, certainly not a matter which outward authority should compel or create. Hence arises the well-known
saying, found also in Augustine, "No one can or ought be constrained to believe."

Besides, the blind, wretched folk do not see how utterly
hopeless and impossible a thing they are attempting. For no
matter how much they fret and fume, they cannot do more
than make the people obey them by word and deed; the heart
they cannot constrain, though they wear themselves out trying.
For the proverb is true, "Thoughts are free." Why then would
they constrain people to believe from the heart, when they see
that it is impossible? In this way they compel weak consciences
to lie, to deny, and to say what they do not believe in their
hearts, and they load themselves down with dreadful alien
sins. For all the lies and false confessions which such weak
consciences utter fall back upon him who compels them. It
were far better, if their subjects erred, simply to let them err,
than that they should constrain them to lie and to say what is
not in their hearts; neither is it right to defend evil with what
is worse.

Would you like to know why God ordains that the temporal

princes must offend so frightfully? I will tell you. God has given them over to a perverse mind and will make an end of them, as well as of the spiritual nobles [Rom. 1:28, Jer. 30:11, Amos 9:8]. For my ungracious lords, the pope and the bishops, should be bishops and preach God's Word; this they leave undone and are become temporal princes, and govern with laws which concern only life and property. How thoroughly they have turned things upside down! Inwardly they ought to be ruling souls by God's Word; hence outwardly they rule castles, cities, land and people and torture souls with unspeakable outrages. Similarly, the temporal lords should rule land and people outwardly; this they do not do. All they can do is to flay and scrape, put tax on tax, tribute on tribute, let loose now a bear, now a wolf. Besides this, there is no justice, fidelity or truth to be found among them; what they do would be beneath robbers and knaves, and their temporal rule has sunk quite as low as that of the spiritual tyrants. Hence God also perverts their minds, that they rush on in their senselessness and would establish a spiritual rule over souls, as the others would establish a temporal rule, in order that they may contentedly burden themselves with alien sins, and with God's and all men's hate, until they go under with bishops, priests and monks, one knave with the other. Then they lay all the blame on the Gospel, and instead of doing penance, blaspheme God and say that our preaching has brought about what their perverse wickedness has merited and still unceasingly merits, as the Romans did when they were destroyed. Here then you have God's decree regarding the high and mighty. But they are not to believe it, lest this severe decree of God be hindered by their repentance.

You reply, But Paul said in Romans 13 [:1], "Every soul shall be subject to power and authority," and Peter says, "We should be subject to every ordinance of man" [I Pet. 2:13]. I answer, That is just what I want! These sayings are in my favor. St. Paul speaks of authority and power. Now, you have just heard that no one but God can have authority over souls. Hence Paul cannot be speaking of any obedience except where there can be corresponding authority. From this it follows that he does not speak of faith, and does not say that secular authority should have the right to command faith, but he is

speaking of external goods, and that these are to be set in order
and controlled on earth. This his words also clearly indicate,
when he prescribes the limits to both authority and obedience,
and says, "Render to every one his dues, tribute to whom tribute is due, custom to whom custom; honor to whom honor;
fear to whom fear" [Rom. 13:7]. You see, temporal obedience
and power apply only externally to tribute, custom, honor and
fear. Likewise when he says, "The power is not a terror to
good, but to evil works" [Rom. 13:4], he again limits the
power, so that it is to have the mastery not over faith or the
Word of God, but over evil works.

This is what St. Peter also desires, when he says, "Ordinance of man" [I Pet. 2:13]. Human ordinance cannot possibly extend its authority to heaven and over souls, but belongs only to earth, to the external intercourse of men with
each other, where men can see, know, judge, sentence, punish
and acquit. Christ Himself made this nice distinction and
summed it all up briefly when He said, "Give unto Cæsar the
things that are Cæsar's, and unto God the things that are
God's" [Matt. 22:21]. If, then, imperial power extended to
God's kingdom and power, and were not something by itself,
He would not thus have made it a separate thing. For, as was
said, the soul is not under Cæsar's power; he can neither teach
nor guide it, neither kill it nor make it alive, neither bind it nor
loose it, neither judge it nor condemn it, neither hold it nor
release it, which he must do had he power to command it and
impose laws upon it; but over life, goods and honor he indeed
has this right, for such things are under his authority.

David, too, stated this long ago in one of his short sayings
when he says in Psalm 115 [:16], "The heavens hath he given
to the Lord of heaven; but the earth hath he given to the
children of men." That is, over what is on earth and belongs to
the temporal, earthly kingdom, man has authority from God,
but that which belongs to the heavenly eternal kingdom is entirely under the heavenly Lord. Nor does Moses forget this
when he says in Genesis 1 [:26], "God said, Let us make man
to rule over the beasts of the earth, over the fish in the waters,
over the birds in the air." There only external rule is ascribed
to men. And, in short, this is the meaning, as St. Peter says,
Acts 5 [:29], "We must obey God rather than men." Thereby

he clearly sets a limit to worldly government, for if we had
to do all that worldly government demands it would be to no
purpose to say, "We must obey God rather than men."

If then your prince or temporal lord commands you to hold
with the pope, to believe this or that, or commands you to
give up certain books, you should say, It does not befit Lucifer
to sit by the side of God. Dear Lord, I owe you obedience with
life and goods; command me within the limits of your power
on earth, and I will obey. But if you command me to believe,
and to put away books, I will not obey; for in this case you
are a tyrant and overreach yourself, and command where you
have neither right nor power, etc. Should he take your property
for this, and punish such disobedience, blessed are you. Thank
God that you are worthy to suffer for the sake of the divine
Word, and let him rave, fool that he is [I Pet. 4:14, 16; Acts
5:41]. He will meet his judge. For I tell you, if you do not
resist him but give him his way, and let him take your faith
or your books, you have really denied God.

Let me illustrate. In Meissen, Bavaria, in the Mark, and
other places, the tyrants have issued an order that the New
Testaments be delivered to the courts everywhere. In this case
their subjects ought not deliver a page or a letter, at risk of
their salvation. For whoever does so, delivers Christ into
Herod's hands, since they act as murderers of Christ, like
Herod. But if their houses are ordered searched and books or
goods taken by force, they should suffer it to be done. Outrage
is not to be resisted, but endured, yet they should not sanction
it, nor serve or obey or follow by moving foot or finger. For
such tyrants act as worldly princes should act,—"worldly"
princes they are; but the world is God's enemy. Therefore they
must also do what is opposed to God, and in accord with the
world, that they may by no means lose all honor, but remain
worldly princes. Hence do not wonder that they rage and mock
at the Gospel; they must live up to their name and title.

You must know that from the beginning of the world a wise
prince is a rare bird indeed; still more so a pious prince. They
are usually the greatest fools or the worst knaves on earth;
therefore one must constantly expect the worst from them and
look for little good from them, especially in divine matters,
which concern the salvation of souls. They are God's jailers

and hangmen, and His divine wrath needs them to punish the wicked and preserve outward peace. Our God is a great Lord, and therefore must have such noble, honorable and rich hangmen and beadles, and desires that they shall have riches, honor and fear, in full and plenty, from every one. It pleases His divine will that we call His hangmen gracious lords, fall at their feet and be subject to them in all humility, so long as they do not ply their trade too far and desire to become shepherds instead of hangmen. If a prince becomes wise, pious or a Christian, it is one of the great wonders, and one of the most precious tokens of divine grace upon that land. For the usual course is according to the saying in Isaiah 3 [:4], "I will give children to be their princes and babes shall rule over them," and in Hosea 13 [:11], "I will give thee a king in my anger and take him away in my wrath." The world is too wicked, and does not deserve to have many wise and pious princes. Frogs need storks.

Again you say, Temporal power does not force men to believe, but simply prevents them from being misled by false doctrine; otherwise how could heretics be prevented from preaching? I answer, This the bishops should do, to whom, and not to the princes, such duty is entrusted. Heresy can never be prevented by force. That must be taken hold of in a different way, and must be opposed and dealt with otherwise than with the sword. Here God's Word must strive; if that does not accomplish the end it will remain unaccomplished through secular power, though it fill the world with blood. Heresy is a spiritual matter, which no iron can strike, no fire burn, no water drown. God's Word alone avails here, as Paul says, II Corinthians 10 [:4 f.], "Our weapons are not carnal, but mighty through God to destroy every counsel and high thing that exalteth itself against the knowledge of God, and to bring into captivity every thought to the obedience of Christ."

Moreover, faith and heresy are never so strong as when men oppose them by sheer force, without God's Word. For men count it certain that such force is for a wrong cause and is directed against the right, since it proceeds without God's Word, and does not know how to further its cause except by force, just as the brute beasts do. For even in secular affairs force can be used only after the wrong has been legally condemned. How much less possible is it to act with force, without justice and God's Word, in these high, spiritual matters! See, therefore, what fine, shrewd nobles they are. They would drive out heresy, and set about it in such a way that they only strengthen the opposition, make themselves suspected, and justify the heretics. Friend, would you drive out heresy, then you must find a plan to tear it first of all from the heart and altogether to turn men's wills away from it; force will not accomplish this, but only strengthen the heresy. What avails it to strengthen heresy in the heart and to weaken only its outward expression, and to force the tongue to lie? God's Word, however, enlightens the hearts; and so all heresies and errors perish of themselves from the heart.

Such overpowering of heresy the prophet Isaiah proclaimed in his eleventh chapter when he said, "He shall smite the earth with the rod of His mouth, and slay the wicked with the breath of His lips" [Isa. 11:4]. You see, if the wicked is to be smitten and converted, it is accomplished by the mouth. In short, such princes and tyrants do not know that to fight against heresy is to fight against the devil, who fills men's hearts with error, as Paul says in Ephesians 6 [:12], "We fight not with flesh and blood, but with spiritual wickedness, with the rulers of the darkness of this world." Therefore, as long as the devil is not repelled and driven from the heart, it matters as little to him that I destroy his vessels with fire or sword, as it would if I fought lightning with a straw. Job bore abundant witness to this, when in his forty-first chapter he said that the devil esteemeth iron as straw and fears no power on earth [Job 41:27]. We learn it also from experience, for although all the Jews and heretics were burned, yet no one has been or will be convinced and converted thereby.

Nevertheless such a world as this deserves such princes, none of whom do their duty. The bishops are to leave the Word of God alone and not rule souls by it, but command the worldly princes to rule them with the sword. The worldly princes, in their turn, are to permit usury, theft, adultery, murder, and other evil works, and themselves do them; and then allow the bishops to punish with the ban. Thus they turn things topsy-turvy, and rule souls with iron and the body with bans, so that worldly princes rule in a spiritual, and spiritual

princes in a worldly way. What else does the devil have to do
on earth than thus to play the fool and hold carnival with his
folk? These are our Christian princes, who defend the faith
and devour the Turk. Fine fellows, to be sure, whom we may
well trust to accomplish something by such refined wisdom,
namely, break their necks and plunge land and people into
suffering and want.

I would, however, in all fidelity advise the blinded folk to
take heed to the short saying in Psalm 107 [:40], *"Effundit
contemptum super principes."*[5] I swear unto you by God that,
if through your fault this little text becomes effective against
you, you are lost, though every one of you be as mighty as
the Turk; and your snorting and raving will help you nothing.
A large part has already come true. For there are very few
princes that are not reckoned fools or knaves. That is because
they show themselves to be such; the common man is learning
to think, and the prince's scourge, which God calls *contemptum*, is gathering force among the mob and with the common man. I fear there is no way to stop it, unless the princes
conduct themselves in a princely manner and begin again to
rule reasonably and thoroughly. Men ought not, men cannot,
men will not suffer your tyranny and presumption much
longer. Dear princes and lords, be wise and guide yourselves
accordingly. God will no longer tolerate it. The world is no
longer what it was when you hunted and drove the people
like so much game. Therefore drop your outrage and force,
and remember to deal justly and let God's Word have its
course, as it will and must and shall, nor will you prevent it.
If there is heresy abroad, let it be overcome, as is proper, with
God's Word. But if you will keep on brandishing the sword,
take heed lest there come one who shall bid you sheath it, and
that not in God's name.

But should you ask, Since there is to be no secular sword
among Christians, how are they to be ruled outwardly? There
certainly must be authority also among Christians. I answer,
Among Christians there shall and can be no authority; but all
are alike subject to one another, as Paul says in Romans 12
[:10], "Each shall count the other his superior," and Peter in

[5] "He poureth contempt upon princes."

I Peter 5 [:5], "All of you be subject one to another." This is also what Christ means in Luke 14 [:10], "When you are bidden to a wedding sit down in the lowest room." There is no superior among Christians, but Christ Himself and Christ alone. And what kind of authority can there be where all are equal and have the same right, power, possession, and honor, and no one desires to be the other's superior, but each the other's inferior? One could not establish authority where there are such people, even if one would, since their character and nature will not permit them to have superiors, for no one is willing or able to be the superior. But where there are no such people, there are no real Christians.

What, then, are the priests and bishops? I answer, Their government is not one of authority or power, but a service and an office; for they are neither higher nor better than other Christians. Therefore they should not impose any law or decree on others without their will and consent; their rule consists in nothing else than in dealing with God's Word, leading Christians by it and overcoming heresy by its means. For, as was said, Christians can be ruled by nothing but by God's Word. For Christians must be ruled in faith, not by outward works. Faith, however, can come through no word of man, but only through the Word of God, as Paul says in Romans 10 [:17], "Faith cometh by hearing, and hearing by the Word of God." Those who do not believe are not Christians, do not belong to Christ's kingdom, but to the worldly kingdom, and are constrained and ruled by the sword and by outward rule. Christians do of themselves, without constraint, every good thing, and find God's Word alone sufficient for them. Of this, however, I have written frequently and at length elsewhere.

PART THREE

Now that we know the limits of secular authority, it is time also to inquire how a prince should use it; for the sake of those who fain would be Christian princes and lords, and desire to enter the life beyond, of whom there are very few.

For Christ Himself describes the nature of temporal princes in Luke 22 [:25], when he says, "The worldly princes exercise lordship, and they that are chief exercise authority." For if they are born princes or chosen to office, they think only that it is their right to be served and to rule with power. He who would be a Christian prince certainly must lay aside the intention to rule and to use force. For cursed and condemned is every kind of life lived and sought for selfish profit and good; cursed are all works not done in love. But they are done in love when they are directed with all one's heart, not toward selfish pleasure, profit, honor, ease and salvation, but toward the profit, honor and salvation of others.

I will say nothing here of secular affairs and of the laws of government, for that is a large subject and there are too many law-books already; although, if a prince himself is not wiser than his jurists, and does not know more than is in the law-books, he will surely rule according to the saying in Proverbs 28 [:16], "A prince that wanteth understanding will oppress many with injustice." No matter how good and equitable the laws are, they all make exceptions of cases of necessity, in which they cannot be enforced. Therefore a prince must have the law in hand as firmly as the sword, and decide in his own mind when and where the law must be applied strictly or with moderation, so that reason may always control all law and be the highest law and rule over all laws. A housefather who, although he appoints a definite time and amount of work and food for his servants and children, must yet reserve the power to change or omit such regulations if his servants happen to be sick, imprisoned, detained, deceived, or otherwise hindered, and not deal as severely with the sick as with the well. I say this in order that man may not think it sufficient and an excellent thing if they follow the written law or the legal advisers; more than that is required.

What should a prince do, if he is not sufficiently wise, and must follow the directions of jurists and law-books? I answer, For this reason I said that the position of a prince is a perilous one, and if he is not wise enough to master both the law and his advisers, the saying of Solomon is fulfilled, "Woe to the land whose king is a child" [Eccl. 10:16]. Solomon recognized this; therefore he despaired of all law, even of that which

Moses, through God, had prescribed for him and of all his princes and counselors, and turned to God Himself and prayed to Him for a wise heart to rule the people [I Kings 3:9]. A prince must follow this example and proceed with fear; he must depend neither upon dead books nor upon living heads, but cling solely to God, pray without ceasing to Him, and ask for a right understanding, above all books and masters, wisely to rule his subjects. Therefore I know of no law to prescribe for a prince, but will simply instruct him what the attitude of his heart and mind ought to be with respect to all laws, counsels, decisions and actions, so that if he govern himself thereby God will surely grant him the power to carry out all laws, counsels, and actions in a proper and godly way.

I. He must consider his subjects and rightly dispose his heart toward them in this matter. He does this if he applies his whole mind to making himself useful and serviceable to them, and does not think, "Land and people are mine; I will do as I please"; but thus, "I belong to land and people; I must do what is profitable and good for them. My concern must be, not how I may rule and be haughty, but how they may be protected and defended by a good peace." And he should picture Christ to himself, and say, "Behold, Christ the chief Ruler came and served me, sought not to have power, profit and honor from me, but only considered my need, and did all He could that I might have power, profit and honor from Him and through Him. I will do the same, not seek mine own advantage in my subjects, but their advantage, and thus serve them by my office, protect them, give them audience and support, that they, and not I, may have the benefit and profit by it." Thus a prince should in his heart empty himself of his power and authority, and interest himself in the need of his subjects, dealing with it as though it were his own need. Thus Christ did unto us; and these are the proper works of Christian love.

You say, Who then would be a prince? For that would make the position of a prince the worst on earth, full of trouble, labor and sorrow. Where would there be room for the princely pleasures, such as dancing, hunting, racing, gaming, and similar worldly enjoyments? I answer, We are not prescribing now how a temporal prince shall live, but how a temporal prince shall be a Christian, in order that he also may reach heaven. Who does not know that a prince is a rare bird in heaven? I do not speak because I have any hope that princes will give heed, but because there might possibly be one of them who would fain be a Christian and would like to know what he ought to do. For I am sure that God's Word will neither turn nor bend to princes; but the princes must bend themselves according to it. It is enough for me to point out that it is not impossible for a prince to be a Christian, though it is a rare thing and surrounded with difficulties. If they would so manage that their dancing, hunting and racing were done without injury to their subjects, and if they would otherwise conduct their office in love toward them, God would not be so hard as to begrudge them their dancing, hunting and racing. But it would follow of itself that, if they served and cared for their subjects as their office requires, full many a fine dance, hunt, race and game would have to be abandoned.

II. He must beware of the high and mighty and of his counselors, and so conduct himself toward them that he despise none, and trust none enough to leave everything to him. For God cannot tolerate either. He once spake by an ass; therefore no man is to be despised, no matter how humble he be [Num. 22:28]. On the other hand, He permitted the highest angel to fall from heaven [Rev. 12:9]; therefore no man is to be trusted, no matter how wise, holy and great he is, but one must give a hearing to all and wait to see through which one of them God will speak and act. For the greatest harm done at court is when a prince enslaves his mind to the high and mighty and to the flatterers, and does not look into things himself; since, when a prince fails and plays the fool, not only one person is affected, but land and people must bear the result of such foolishness. Therefore a prince should bestow only so much trust and power upon his rulers that he will still keep the reins of government in his own hand. He must keep his eyes open and give attention, and, like Jehoshaphat, ride through the land and observe everywhere how the government and the law is administered [II Chron. 19:4 ff.]. In this way he will learn for himself that one must not implicitly trust any man.

For you have no right to think that another will interest himself in you and in your land so deeply as you yourself, unless he be filled with the Spirit and be a good Christian. The natural man does not do it. Since, however, you do not know whether he is a Christian or how long he will remain one, you cannot safely depend on him.

Beware especially of those who say, "Gracious lord, why does your grace not trust me more? Who is so willing to serve your grace,?" etc. Such an one is certainly not guileless, but desires to be lord in the country and make a jackanapes of you. If he were a true and pious Christian he would be quite willing that you should entrust him with nothing, and would praise you for keeping so careful a watch on him; for he acts in accordance with God's will and therefore he is willing, and can bear it, to have his acts brought to the light by you or any one else, as Christ says in John 3 [:21], "He that doeth well cometh to the light, that his deeds may be made manifest, for they are wrought in God." The former, however, would blind your eyes, and act under cover of darkness, as Christ also says in the same place, "Every one that doeth evil hateth the light, lest his deeds should be punished" [John 3:20]. Therefore, beware of him. And if he complain of it, say, "Friend, I do thee no wrong; God is not willing that I trust myself or any other man; find fault with Him, then, because He will have it so, or that He has not made you more than human; although, even if you were an angel, since Lucifer indeed was not to be trusted, I would not trust you completely, for we should trust God alone."

Let no prince think that he shall fare better than David, who is an example to all princes. He had so wise a counselor, named Ahithophel, that the text says, "The counsel which Ahithophel counselled availed as if a man had inquired at the oracle of God" [II Sam. 16:23]. Nevertheless he fell, and sank so low that he sought to betray, kill and destroy David his own lord [II Sam. 17:1 ff.]. Then David had to learn that no man is to be trusted. Why do you suppose God permitted such a horrible example to occur, and to be recorded, if not in order to warn the princes and lords against the most perilous misfortune that may befall them, so that they might trust no one. For it is most deplorable when flatterers reign at court, or when the prince depends on others, puts himself in their hands, and lets every one do as he will.

You say, perchance, If no one is to be trusted, how will one rule land and people? I answer, You should entrust and take the venture, but you should not trust and depend save on God alone. You must certainly entrust the offices to some one and take a chance with him; but you should not trust him otherwise than as one who may fail you and whom you must watch with unfailing vigilance; as a driver has confidence in the horses and wagon he drives, yet does not let them go their own way, but holds reins and lash in his hand and does not sleep. Remember the old proverbs, which are the sure fruits of experience: "A careful master makes a good horse," and "The master's footsteps make a fruitful field,"—that is, if the master does not look after things himself, but depends upon counselors and servants, things never go right. God also will have it so, and causes it to happen, in order that the lords may be driven of necessity to fulfil their office themselves, as everyone must fulfil his calling and every creature do its work; otherwise the lords will become fatted pigs and a worthless lot, of no profit to any one but themselves.

III. He must take heed that he deal justly with evil doers. Here he must be very wise and prudent to mete out punishment without injuring others. I know no better example of this than David again. He had a captain, Joab by name, who played two wicked pranks in that he treacherously murdered two loyal captains [II Sam. 3:27; 20:10], whereby he justly merited death twice over; yet David did not put him to death during his lifetime, but commanded his son Solomon without fail to do so, because he could not punish him without great injury and disturbance [I Kings 2:5 f.]. A prince must punish the wicked in such a way that he does not step on the dish while picking up the spoon, and for the sake of one man's head plunge land and people into want and fill the land with widows and orphans. Therefore he must not obey the counselors and fire-eaters who incite and provoke him to begin war and say, "What, must we suffer such insults and injustice?" He is a poor Christian indeed who for the sake of a single castle would make an armed camp of the whole land. In brief, here one must hold by the proverb, "He cannot rule who cannot wink at faults." Let this, therefore, be his rule: Where wrong cannot be punished without greater wrong, there let him waive his rights, however just. He must not regard his own injury, but the wrong which others must suffer as a consequence of the penalty he imposes. For what have the many women and children done that they should be made widows and orphans in order that you may avenge yourself on an idle tongue or a wicked hand which has injured you?

You ask, But shall not a prince go to war, nor his subjects follow him into battle? I answer, That is a far-reaching question, but let me answer it very briefly. To act here as a Christian, I say, a prince should not wage war against his overlord—the king, emperor or other liege—but should let him who takes take. For one must not resist the government with force, but only with knowledge of the truth; if it is influenced by it, well; if not, you are innocent, and suffer wrong for God's sake. But if your opponent is your equal, your inferior, or of a foreign government, you should first offer him justice and peace, as Moses taught the children of Israel. If he is unwilling, then use your best strategy and defend yourself by force against force, as Moses well describes it all in Deuteronomy 20 [:10 ff.]. In doing this you must not consider your own interests and how you may remain lord, but your subjects, to whom you owe help and protection, that all may be done in love. For, since your entire land is in peril, you must make the venture, so that with God's help all may not be lost; and if you cannot prevent some from becoming widows and orphans, as a consequence of this, you must nevertheless prevent it that all go to ruin and there be nothing left but widows and orphans.

In this matter subjects are in duty bound to follow and risk life and property for the cause. For in such a case one must risk his property and himself for the sake of the other. And in such a war it is a Christian act and an act of love confidently to kill, rob, and pillage the enemy, and to do everything that can injure him until one has conquered him according to the methods of war. Only, one must beware of sin, not violate wives and virgins, and when victory comes, offer mercy and peace to those who surrender and humble themselves. Therefore in such a case let the saying hold true, "God helps those

who help themselves." So Abraham did when he smote the
four kings, as Genesis 14 [:14 ff.] tells us, when he certainly
caused great slaughter and showed little mercy until he conquered them. Such happenings must be considered as sent of
God, that He may now and then cleanse the land and drive
out the knaves.

But when a prince is in the wrong, are his people bound to
follow him then too? I answer, No, for it is no one's duty to do
wrong; we ought to obey God Who desires the right, rather
than men [Acts 5:29]. How is it, when the subjects do not
know whether the prince is in the right or not? I answer, As
long as they cannot know, nor find out by any possible means,
they may obey without peril to their souls. For in such a case
one must apply the law of Moses, when he writes in Exodus
21 [:13], that a murderer who has unknowingly and involun-
tarily killed a man shall be delivered by fleeing to a city of
refuge and by the judgment of the congregation [Num.
35:12]. For whichever side is defeated, whether it be in the
right or in the wrong, must accept it as a punishment from
God; but whichever side wars and wins, in such ignorance,
must regard their battle as though one fell from the roof and
killed another, and leave the matter to God. For it is the same
to God whether He deprives you of goods and life by a just
lord or by an unjust. You are His creature, and He can do with
you as He will—if only your conscience is clear. God Himself
thus excuses Abimelech in Genesis 20 [:6], when he took Abraham's wife, not because he had done right, but because he
had not known that she was Abraham's wife.

IV. We come to what really should be foremost, and of
which we spoke above. A prince must act also in a Christian
way toward his God, that is, he must subject himself to Him
in entire confidence and pray for wisdom to rule well, as Solomon did [I Kings 3:9]. But of faith and trust in God I have
written so much elsewhere that it is not necessary to say more
here. Therefore we will close by saying briefly that a prince's
duty is fourfold: First, that toward God consists in true confidence and in sincere prayer; second, that toward his subjects
consists in love and Christian service; third, that toward his
counselors and rulers consists in an open mind and unfettered

judgment; fourth, that toward evil doers consists in proper zeal and firmness. Then his state is right, outwardly and inwardly, pleasing to God and to the people. But he must expect much envy and sorrow,—the cross will soon rest on the shoulders of such a ruler.

Finally, in addition, I must make answer to those who dispute about restitution, that is, about the returning of goods unlawfully acquired. This is a common task of the temporal sword, and much has been written concerning it, and there has been much hairsplitting in the discussion of it. I will put it all in a few words, and dispose at one and the same time of all these laws and the quibbles that follow. No more definite law can be found on this subject than the law of love. In the first place, when such a case is brought before you, in which one is to make restitution to another, the matter is soon settled if they are both Christians; for neither will withhold what belongs to the other, nor will either of them demand that it be returned. If only one is a Christian, namely, the one to whom restitution is to be made, it is again easy to settle, for he does not care whether it never be returned. The same is true if the one who is to make restitution is a Christian; he will do so. But whether one is a Christian or not a Christian, you must decide the restitution as follows. If the debtor is poor and unable to make restitution, and the other party is not poor, then you should let the law of love prevail and acquit the debtor. For, according to the law of love, the other party, too, owes it to him to relinquish the debt, and if necessary to give him something besides. But if the debtor is not poor, then let him restore as much as he can, all, half, a third, or a fourth of it, provided that you leave him enough to assure a house, food and clothing for himself, his wife and children; for this you would owe him if you could give it, much less ought you to take it away now, since you do not need it and he cannot do without it.

But if neither is a Christian, or if either is unwilling to be judged by the law of love, you may ask them to call in another judge, and announce to them that they are acting against God and the law of nature, even though they may obtain absolute justice through human law. For nature, like love, teaches that I should do as I would be done by [Matt. 7:12]. Therefore I cannot strip any one else, even if I have the very best right to do so, if I myself am not willing to be stripped of my goods, but as I would that another should relinquish his right to me in such an instance, even so should I also relinquish my rights. Thus one should deal with all property unlawfully held, whether in public or private, that love and the law of nature may always prevail. For when you judge according to love, you will easily decide and adjust matters without any law-books. But when you ignore love and natural law, you will never succeed in pleasing God, though you have devoured all the law-books and jurists; they will only cause you to err, the more you depend on them. A good and just decision must not and cannot be given out of books, but must come from a free mind, as though there were not a single book. Such a free decision, however, is given by love and by the law of nature, of which the reason is full; but out of the books come rigid and vague judgments. Of this I will give you an example.

An incident of this sort is told of Duke Charles of Burgundy. A certain nobleman took an enemy prisoner, whereupon the prisoner's wife came to redeem her husband. The nobleman promised to give her back her husband provided she would lie with him. The woman was virtuous, yet desired to set her husband free; so she goes and asks her husband whether she shall do this thing in order to set him free. The husband desired to be set free and to save his life, and gives his wife permission. After the nobleman had lain with the wife, he had the husband beheaded the next day and gave him to her a corpse. She laid the whole case before Duke Charles, who summoned the nobleman and commanded him to marry the woman. When the wedding day was over, he had the man beheaded, put the woman in possession of his property, and raised her again to honor. Thus he punished the crime in a princely way.

You see, such a decision no pope, nor jurist, and no law-book could have given him; but it sprang from untrammeled reason, above the law in the books, and is so excellent that every one must approve of it and find the justice of it written in his own heart. St. Augustine in his Sermon of the Lord on the Mount writes in the same fashion. Therefore we should keep written laws subject to reason, whence indeed they have welled as from the spring of justice, and not make the spring dependent on its rivulets, nor take reason captive to the letter.

AN APPEAL TO THE RULING CLASS OF GERMAN NATIONALITY AS TO THE AMELIORATION OF THE STATE OF CHRISTENDOM[1]

[*In this work of 1520, which preceded* The Pagan Servitude of the Church *and* The Freedom of a Christian, *Luther calls upon the ruling class to reform the Church, since the Church will not reform itself. The abuses mentioned in this work were attacked by humanists and reformers alike and indeed many of them were later rejected by the Roman Church also. It should be noted that this document antedates the establishment of Reformation churches and is essentially a call to reform.*]

JESUS

Dedicated by Dr. Martin Luther to his dear friend, the honourable and worthy gentleman, Nicholas von Amsdorf, Licentiate in Holy Scripture, and Canon in Wittenberg.

The Salutation

May the grace and peace of God be yours, my honourable, worthy, and dear friend.

The time for silence is over, and the time for speech has

[1] Reprinted by permission of the publisher from *The Reformation Writings of Martin Luther*, volume 1, *The Basis of the Protestant Reformation*, translated and edited by Bertram Lee Woolf (London: Lutterworth Press, 1953), pp. 109–200.

come, as Ecclesiastes [3:7] says. In accordance with our project, I have put together a few paragraphs on the amelioration of the condition of Christendom. I intend the writing for the consideration of Christians belonging to the ruling classes in Germany. I hope that God will grant help to His church through the laity, since the clergy, who should be the more appropriate persons, have grown quite indifferent. I am sending to your worthy self all I have written. Please examine, and, where desirable, modify it. I know that I shall not escape the criticism that I presume too much, in that I, an unimportant and inferior person, dare to address such a high and responsible class of society on very special and important subjects. I am acting, I confess, as if there were no other in the world than Doctor Luther to play the part of a Christian, and give advice to people of culture and education. But I shall not apologize, no matter who demands it. Perhaps I owe God and the world another act of folly. For what it is worth, this pamphlet is an attempt to pay that debt as well as I can, even if I become for once a Court-fool. No one needs to buy me a fool's cap nor shave me my poll.[2] The question is, Which of us is to put the bells on the other? I must act according to the proverb, "A Monk must be in it whatever the world is doing, even if he has to be painted in."[3] A fool often says wise things and frequently sages speak very foolishly. St. Paul said: "If any wishes to be wise, he must become a fool" [I Cor. 3:18]. Moreover, since I am not only a fool, but also sworn in as a Doctor of Holy Scripture, I am glad that I have the opportunity to fulfil my oath even in the guise of a fool. I beg you to make my apologies to those of average understanding, for I make no pretence of attempting to win the favour and goodwill of the super-intelligent. I have often tried hard to do it, but never again will I attempt it, nor worry about it. God help us not to seek our own glory but His alone. Amen.

Wittenberg, The Augustinian Monastery, on the eve of John the Baptist's day, A.D. 1520.

[2] I.e., a monk's tonsure was the equivalent of a jester's cap and bells.
[3] As a figure or the back-cloth at a play.

The Appeal

Doctor Martin Luther to His Most Illustrious, Most Mighty and Imperial Majesty, and to the Christians of the German Ruling Class.

Grace and power from God to his Illustrious Majesty, and to you, most gracious and honourable Gentlemen.

It is not due to sheer impertinence or wantonness that I, a lone and simple man, have taken it upon myself to address your worships. All classes in Christendom, particularly in Germany, are now oppressed by distress and affliction, and this has stirred not only me but everyman to cry out anxiously for help. It has compelled me to beg and pray that God will endow someone with His Spirit to bring aid to this unhappy nation. Proposals have often been made at councils, but have been cunningly deferred by the guile of certain men, and matters have gone from bad to worse. Their artifices and wickedness I intend with God's help to lay bare in order that, once shown up, they may never again present such hindrances or be so harmful. God has given us a young man of noble ancestry to be our head[4] and so has raised high hopes in many hearts. In these circumstances, it is fitting for us to do all we can to make good use of the present time and of God's gracious gift to us.

The first and most urgent thing just now is that we should each prepare our own selves in all seriousness. We must not begin by assuming we possess much strength or wisdom, even if we had all the authority in the world. For God cannot and will not suffer a goodly enterprise to be begun if we trust in our own strength and wisdom. God will surely abase such pride, as is said in Psalm 33 [:16], "No king stands by the multitude of his host, and no lord by the greatness of his strength." For this reason, I fear, it came to pass in former times that the good princes, emperors Frederick I and II, and many other German emperors, were shamelessly trodden under foot and oppressed by the popes whom all the world feared. Perhaps they relied more on their own strength than on God, and therefore had to fall. And what else, in our day,

[4] The emperor, Charles V.

has raised the bloodthirsty Julius II[5] so high, if it were not, as I fear, that France, Germany, and Venice depended on themselves? The children of Benjamin slew 42,000 Israelites because they relied on their own strength.[6]

Lest we have the same experience under our noble emperor, Charles, we must be clear that we are not dealing permanently with men in this matter, but with the princes of hell who would fill the world with war and bloodshed, and yet avoid letting themselves be caught by the flood. We must go to work now, not depending on physical power, but in humble trust in God, seeking help from Him in earnest prayer, with nothing else in mind than the misery and distress of all Christendom suffering over and above what sinful men have deserved. Otherwise our efforts may well begin with good prospects, but, when we get deeply involved, the evil spirit will cause such confusion as to make the whole world swim in blood, and then nothing will be accomplished. Therefore, in this matter let us act wisely, and as those who fear God. The greater the power we employ, the greater the disaster we suffer, unless we act humbly and in the fear of God. If hitherto the popes and Romanists have been able, with the devil's help, to bring kings into conflict with each other, they will be able to do it again now, if we set forth without God's help, and armed only with our own strength and shrewdness.

I. THE THREE WALLS

The Romanists have very cleverly surrounded themselves with three walls, which have protected them till now in such a way that no one could reform them. As a result, the whole of Christendom has suffered woeful corruption. In the first place, when under the threat of secular force, they have stood firm and declared that secular force had no jurisdiction over them; rather the opposite was the case, and the spiritual was superior to the secular. In the second place, when the Holy

[5] Julius II, Pope, 1503–13.
[6] Judges 20:21 says 22,000.

Scriptures have been used to reprove them, they have responded that no one except the pope was competent to expound Scripture. In the third place, when threatened with a council, they have pretended that no one but the pope could summon a council. In this way, they have adroitly nullified these three means of correction, and avoided punishment. Thus they still remain in secure possession of these three walls, and practise all the villainy and wickedness we see to-day. When they have been compelled to hold a council, they have made it nugatory by compelling the princes to swear in advance that the present position shall remain undisturbed. In addition they have given the pope full authority over all the decisions of a council, till it is a matter of indifference whether there be many councils or none, for they only deceive us with make-believes and sham-fights. So terribly fearful are they for their skins, if a truly free council were held. Further, the Romanists have overawed kings and princes till the latter believe it would be impious not to obey them in spite of all the deceitful and cunning dodges of theirs.

May God now help us, and give us one of those trumpets with which the walls of Jericho were overthrown; that we may blow away these walls of paper and straw, and set free the Christian, corrective measures to punish sin, and to bring the devil's deceits and wiles to the light of day. In this way, may we be reformed through suffering and again receive God's blessing.

i. Let us begin by attacking the first wall.

To call popes, bishops, priests, monks, and nuns, the religious class, but princes, lords, artizans, and farm-workers the secular class, is a specious device invented by certain time-servers; but no one ought to be frightened by it, and for good reason. For all Christians whatsoever really and truly belong to the religious class, and there is no difference among them except in so far as they do different work. That is St. Paul's meaning, in I Corinthians 12 [:12 f.], when he says: "We are all one body, yet each member hath his own work for serving others." This applies to us all, because we have one baptism, one gospel, one faith, and are all equally Christian. For baptism, gospel, and faith alone make men religious, and create a

Christian people. When a pope or bishop anoints, grants tonsures, ordains, consecrates, dresses differently from laymen, he may make a hypocrite of a man, or an anointed image, but never a Christian or a spiritually-minded man. The fact is that our baptism consecrates us all without exception, and makes us all priests. As St. Peter says, I Pet. 2 [:9], "You are a royal priesthood and a realm of priests", and Revelation, "Thou hast made us priests and kings by Thy blood" [Rev. 5:9 f.]. If we ourselves as Christians did not receive a higher consecration than that given by pope or bishop, then no one would be made priest even by consecration at the hands of pope or bishop; nor would anyone be authorized to celebrate Eucharist, or preach, or pronounce absolution.

When a bishop consecrates, he simply acts on behalf of the entire congregation, all of whom have the same authority. They may select one of their number and command him to exercise this authority on behalf of the others. It would be similar if ten brothers, king's sons and equal heirs, were to choose one of themselves to rule the kingdom for them. All would be kings and of equal authority, although one was appointed to rule. To put it more plainly, suppose a small group of earnest Christian laymen were taken prisoner and settled in the middle of a desert without any episcopally ordained priest among them; and they then agreed to choose one of themselves, whether married or not, and endow him with the office of baptizing, administering the sacrament, pronouncing absolution, and preaching; that man would be as truly a priest as if he had been ordained by all the bishops and the popes. It follows that, if needs be, anyone may baptize or pronounce absolution, an impossible situation if we were not all priests. The fact that baptism, and the Christian status which it confers, possess such great grace and authority, is what the Romanists have overridden by their canon law, and kept us in ignorance thereof. But, in former days, Christians used to choose their bishops and priests from their own members, and these were afterwards confirmed by other bishops without any of the pomp of present custom. St. Augustine, Ambrose, and Cyprian each became bishops in this way.

Those who exercise secular authority have been baptized like the rest of us, and have the same faith and the same gospel; therefore we must admit that they are priests and bishops. They discharge their office as an office of the Christian community, and for the benefit of that community. Every one who has been baptized may claim that he has already been consecrated priest, bishop, or pope, even though it is not seemly for any particular person arbitrarily to exercise the office. Just because we are all priests of equal standing, no one must push himself forward and, without the consent and choice of the rest, presume to do that for which we all have equal authority. Only by the consent and command of the community should any individual person claim for himself what belongs equally to all. If it should happen that anyone abuses an office for which he has been chosen, and is dismissed for that reason, he would resume his former status. It follows that the status of a priest among Christians is merely that of an office-bearer; while he holds the office he exercises it; if he be deposed he resumes his status in the community and becomes like the rest. Certainly a priest is no longer a priest after being unfrocked. Yet the Romanists have devised the claim to *characteres indelebiles*, and assert that a priest, even if deposed, is different from a mere layman. They even hold the illusion that a priest can never be anything else than a priest, and therefore never a layman again. All these are human inventions and regulations.

Hence we deduce that there is, at bottom, really no other difference between laymen, priests, princes, bishops, or, in Romanist terminology, between religious and secular, than that of office or occupation, and not that of Christian status. All have spiritual status, and all are truly priests, bishops, and popes. But Christians do not all follow the same occupation. Similarly, priests and monks do not all work at the same task. This is supported by Romans 12 [:4 f.] and I Corinthians 12 [:12 f.], and by I Peter 2 [:9], as I showed above. In these passages, St. Paul and St. Peter say that we are all one body, and belong to Jesus Christ who is the head, and we are all members of one another. Christ has not two bodies, nor two kinds of body, one secular and the other religious. He has one head and one body.

Therefore those now called "the religious", i.e., priests, bishops, and popes, possess no further or greater dignity than other Christians, except that their duty is to expound the word of God and administer the sacraments—that being their office. In the same way, the secular authorities "hold the sword and the rod", their function being to punish evil-doers and protect the law-abiding. A shoemaker, a smith, a farmer, each has his manual occupation and work; and yet, at the same time, all are eligible to act as priests and bishops. Every one of them in his occupation or handicraft ought to be useful to his fellows, and serve them in such a way that the various trades are all directed to the best advantage of the community, and promote the well-being of body and soul, just as all the organs of the body serve each other.

Now let us consider whether it is Christian to affirm and declare that secular authorities do not exercise jurisdiction over religious office-bearers, and should not inflict penalties on them. That is as much as to say that the hand ought to do nothing to help when the eye suffers severely. Would it not be unnatural, or indeed unchristian, for one organ not to help another and not ward off what is destroying it? Rather, the more precious an organ is, the more ought the other to help. Therefore, I maintain, that since the secular authorities are ordained by God to punish evil-doers and to protect the law-abiding, so we ought to leave them free to do their work without let or hindrance everywhere in Christian countries, and without partiality, whether for pope, bishops, pastors, monks, nuns, or anyone else. If, to prevent the exercise of secular authority, it were enough to say that the civil administration was, from the Christian standpoint, a lower function than that of preacher or confessor or the religious status, then surely tailors, shoemakers, stonemasons, carpenters, cooks, menservants, farmers, and all secular craftsmen, being lower still, should be forbidden to make shoes, clothes, houses, things to eat and drink, or pay rents and tributes to the pope, bishops, priests, and monks. But if these laymen are to be allowed to do their work undisturbed, what is the purpose of Romanist writers who make laws by which they exempt themselves from the secular Christian authorities? It is simply that they may do evil unpunished, and fulfil what St. Peter said, "There shall arise false teachers among you, moving among you with false and imaginary sayings, selling you a bad bargain."

Hence secular Christian authorities should exercise their

office freely and unhindered and without fear, whether it be pope, bishop, or priest with whom they are dealing; if a man is guilty let him pay the penalty. What canon law says to the contrary is Romish presumptuousness and pure invention. For this is what St. Paul says to all Christians, "Let every soul (I hold that includes the pope's) be subject to the higher powers, for they bear not the sword in vain. They serve God alone, punishing the evil and praising the good" [Rom. 13]. And St. Peter [I Pet. 2:13, 15], "Be subject unto every ordinance of man for God's sake, whose will is that it should be so." He has also proclaimed that such men would come, and would contemn secular authority; and this has, in fact, come about through canon law.

That in my view overturns the first wall—of paper. The reason is that the social corpus of Christendom includes secular government as one of its component functions. This government is spiritual in status, although it discharges a secular duty. It should operate, freely and unhindered, upon all members of the entire corpus, should punish and compel where guilt deserves or necessity requires, in spite of pope, bishops, and priests; and whether they denounce or excommunicate to their hearts' desire. That is why guilty priests, before being handed over to the secular arm, are previously deprived of the dignities of their office. This would not be right unless the secular "sword" already possessed authority over them by divine ordinance. Moreover, it is intolerable that in canon law, the freedom, person, and goods of the clergy should be given this exemption, as if laymen were not exactly as spiritual, and as good Christians, as they, or did not equally belong to the church. Why should your person, life, possessions, and honour be exempt, whereas mine are not, although we are equally Christian, with the same baptism, guilt, and spirit and all else? If a priest is killed, a country is placed under interdict; why not also if a farmer is killed? Whence comes such a great difference between two men equally Christian? Simply from human law and fabrications.

It cannot have been a man of goodwill who devised such distinctions, and made some sins exempt and immune. For it is our duty to strive as much as we can against the Evil One and his works and to drive him away, for so Christ and His apostles

bade us. How comes it then that we are told to hold our peace
and be silent when the pope or his supporters design impious
words or deeds? Are we, on account of certain men, to neglect
divine commands and God's truth which we swore at our baptism to defend with life and limb? Of a truth we shall be held
responsible for the souls of all who are abandoned and led
astray thereby. Surely, it must be the archdevil himself who
propounded that canon law which declares, "Even if the pope
were so wicked that he led men in multitudes to the devil,
nevertheless he could not be deposed." This is the accursed
and impious foundation on which they build at Rome, maintaining that we should sooner let all the world go to the devil
than oppose their villainy. If a certain person were not to be
penalised on the ground that he was superior to the rest, then
no Christian may penalise his fellows, since Christ bade us one
and all to serve the meanest and humblest.

There is no longer any defence against punishment where
sin exists. St. Gregory himself wrote[7] that, while we are all
equal, guilt makes one man subject to others. All this shows
plainly how the Romanists deal with Christian people, robbing them of their freedom without any warrant from Scripture, but by sheer wantonness. But God and the apostles made
them subject to the secular "sword". Well may we fear that
Antichrist has been at work, or is completing his preparations.

ii

The second wall is more loosely built and less indefensible.
The Romanists profess to be the only interpreters of Scripture,
even though they never learn anything contained in it their
lives long. They claim authority for themselves alone, juggle
with words shamelessly before our eyes, saying that the pope
cannot err as to the faith, whether he be bad or good; although
they cannot quote a single letter of Scripture to support
their claim. Thus it comes about that so many heretical, unchristian, and even unnatural laws are contained in the canon
law—matters of which there is no need for discussion at the
present juncture. Just because the Romanists profess to believe

[7] Pope Gregory the Great (590–604), in the Regula pastoralis, II,
6 (Migne, Patrol. Ser. Lat., 77, 34).

that the Holy Spirit has not abandoned them, no matter if they are as ignorant and bad as they could be, they presume to assert whatever they please. In such a case, what is the need or the value of Holy Scripture? Let it be burned, and let us be content with the ignorant gentlemen at Rome who "possess the Holy Spirit within", who, however, in fact, dwells in pious souls only. Had I not read it, I should have thought it incredible that the devil should have produced such ineptitudes at Rome, and have gained adherents to them. But lest we fight them with mere words, let us adduce Scripture. St. Paul says, I Corinthians 14 [:30], "If something superior be revealed to any one sitting there and listening to another speaking God's word, the first speaker must be silent and give place." What would be the virtue of this commandment if only the speaker, or the person in the highest position, were to be believed? Christ Himself says, John 6 [:45], "that all Christians shall be taught by God". Then if the pope and his adherents were bad men, and not true Christians, i.e., not taught by God to have a true understanding; and if, on the other hand, a humble person should have the true understanding, why ever should we not follow him? Has not the pope made many errors? Who could enlighten Christian people if the pope erred, unless someone else, who had the support of Scripture, were more to be believed than he?

Therefore it is a wicked, base invention, for which they cannot adduce a tittle of evidence in support, to aver that it is the function of the pope alone to interpret Scripture, or to confirm any particular interpretation. And if they claim that St. Peter received authority when he was given the keys—well, it is plain enough that the keys were not given to St. Peter only, but to the whole Christian community. Moreover the keys have no reference to doctrine or policy, but only to refusing or being willing to forgive sin. Whatever else the Romanists claim in virtue of the keys is an idle invention. But Christ's word to Peter, "I have prayed for thee that thy faith fail not" [Luke 22:32], cannot be stretched to apply to the pope, seeing that the majority of the popes have had no faith, as they themselves are obliged to confess. Therefore, Christ did not pray for Peter only, but for all apostles and Christians. As He said in John 17 [:9, 20], "Father, I pray for those whom Thou hast given me, and not only for them, but for all those who believe on me through their word." Surely these words are plain enough.

Think it over for yourself. You must acknowledge that there are good Christians among us who have the true faith, spirit, understanding, word, and mind of Christ. Why ever should one reject their opinion and judgment, and accept those of the pope, who has neither that faith nor that spirit? That would be to repudiate the whole faith and the Christian church itself. Moreover, it can never be the pope alone who is in the right, if the creed is correct in the article, "I believe in one, holy, Christian church"; or should the confession take the form: "I believe in the pope of Rome"? But this would be to concentrate the Christian church entirely in one man, and that would be in every way an impious, pernicious, error.

In addition, as I have already said, each and all of us are priests because we all have the one faith, the one gospel, one and the same sacrament; why then should we not be entitled to taste or test, and to judge what is right or wrong in the faith? How otherwise does St. Paul's dictum stand, I Corinthians 2 [:15], "He that is spiritual judges all things and is judged by none", and II Corinthians 4 [:13], "We all have the one spirit of faith"? Why then should we not distinguish what accords or does not accord with the faith quite as well as an unbelieving pope? These and many other passages should give us courage and set us free. We ought not to allow the spirit of liberty—to use St. Paul's term—to be frightened away by pronouncements confabricated by the popes. We ought to march boldly forward, and test everything the Romanists do or leave undone. We ought to apply that understanding of the Scriptures which we possess as believers, and constrain the Romanists to follow, not their own interpretation, but that which is in fact the better. In former days, Abraham had to listen to Sarah [Gen. 21:12], who was more completely subject to him than we are to anyone in the world. Similarly, Balaam's ass was more perspicacious than the prophet himself [Num. 22:28]. Since God once spoke through an ass, why should He not come in our day and speak through a man of faith and even contradict the pope? Moreover, St. Paul upbraided St. Peter as a wrongdoer [Gal. 2:11]. Hence it is the duty of every Christian to accept the implications of the faith, understand and defend it, and denounce everything false.

iii

The third wall falls without more ado when the first two are demolished; for, even if the pope acts contrary to Scripture, we ourselves are bound to abide by Scripture. We must punish him and constrain him, according to the passage, "If thy brother sin against thee, go and tell it him between thee and him alone; but if he hear thee not, take with thee one or two more; and if he hear them not, tell it to the church; and if he hear not the church, let him be unto thee as a Gentile" [Matt. 18:15–17]. This passage commands each member to exercise concern for his fellow; much more is it our duty when the wrongdoer is one who rules over us all alike, and who causes much harm and offence to the rest by his conduct. And if I am to lay a charge against him before the church, then I must call it together.

Romanists have no Scriptural basis for their contention that the pope alone has the right to summon or sanction a council. This is their own ruling, and only valid as long as it is not harmful to Christian well-being or contrary to God's laws. If, however, the pope is in the wrong, this ruling becomes invalid, because it is harmful to Christian well-being not to punish him through a council.

Accordingly, we read in Acts 15 [:6] that it was not St. Peter, but all the apostles and elders, who called the Apostolic Council. If that had been the sole right of St. Peter, it would not have been a Christian council, but an heretical *conciliabulum*. Further, the bishop of Rome neither called nor sanctioned the council of Nicea, the most celebrated of all, but the emperor, Constantine. After him, many other emperors did the same, and these councils were the most Christian of all. But if the pope had really had the sole authority, then they would necessarily all have been heretical. Moreover, when I examine decisions of those councils which the pope himself called, I find they did nothing of special importance.

Therefore, when need requires it, and the pope is acting harmfully to Christian well-being, let anyone who is a true member of the Christian community as a whole take steps as early as possible to bring about a genuinely free council. No one is so able to do this as the secular authorities, especially since they are also fellow Christians, fellow priests, similarly religious, and of similar authority in all respects. They should exercise their office and do their work without let or hindrance where it is necessary or advantageous to do so, for God has given them authority over every one. Surely it would be an unnatural proceeding, if fire were to break out in a town, if everyone should stand still and let it burn on and on, simply because no one had the mayor's authority, or perhaps because it began at the mayor's residence. In such a case, is it not the duty of each citizen to stir up the rest, and call upon them for help? Much more ought it to be the case in the spiritual city of Christ, were a fire of offence to break out, whether in the pope's régime or anywhere else. The same argument would hold, if an enemy were to attack a town; that man who called his fellow citizens together at the earliest moment would deserve honour and gratitude. Why then should not honour be accorded to one who makes our infernal enemies known, rouses Christian people, and calls them together?

It is empty talk when the Romanists boast of possessing an authority such as cannot properly be contested. No one in Christendom has authority to do evil, or to forbid evil from being resisted. The church has no authority except to promote the greater good. Hence, if the pope should exercise his authority to prevent a free council, and so hinder the reform of the church, we ought to pay no regard to him and his authority. If he should excommunicate and fulminate, that ought to be despised as the proceedings of a foolish man. Trusting in God's protection, we ought to excommunicate him in return, and manage as best we can; for this authority of his would be presumptuous and empty. He does not possess it, and he would fall an easy victim to a passage of Scripture; for Paul says to the Corinthians, "For God gave us authority, not to cast down Christendom, but to build it up" [II Cor. 10:8]. Who would pretend to ignore this text? Only the power of the devil and the Antichrist attempting to arrest whatever serves the reform of Christendom. Wherefore, we must resist that power with life and limb, and might and main.

Even if some supernatural sign should be given, and appear to support the pope against the secular authority; e.g., if a plague were to strike someone down, as they boast has happened sometimes, we ought only to regard it as caused by the devil on account of our lack of faith in God. It is what Christ proclaimed, "False Christs and false prophets will come in my name, and will do signs and wonders, so as to lead astray, if possible, even the elect" [Matt. 24:24]. St. Paul says to the Thessalonians [II Thess. 2:9] that the Antichrist shall, through Satan, be mighty in false, miraculous signs.

Therefore, let us firmly maintain that no Christian authority is valid when exercised contrary to Christ. St. Paul says, "We can do nothing against Christ, but only for Christ" [II Cor. 13:8]. But if an authority does anything against Christ, it is due to the power of the Antichrist and of the devil, even if that authority makes it rain and hail miracles and plagues. Miracles and plagues prove nothing, especially in these latter days of evil, for specious miracles of this kind are foretold everywhere in Scripture. Therefore, we must hold to God's Word with firm faith. The devil will soon abandon his miracles.

And now, I hope that I have laid these false and deceptive terrors, though the Romanists have long used them to make us diffident and of a fearful conscience. It is obvious to all that they, like us, are subject to the authority of the state, that they have no warrant to expound Scripture arbitrarily and without special knowledge. They are not empowered to prohibit a council or, according to their pleasure, to determine its decisions in advance, to bind it and to rob it of freedom. But if they do so, I hope I have shown that of a truth they belong to the community of Antichrist and the devil, and have nothing in common with Christ except the name.

II. SUBJECTS TO BE DISCUSSED BY THE COUNCILS

Now let us consider the subjects which might properly be discussed in the councils, or with which popes, cardinals, bishops, and all scholars might well busy themselves day and night if they held Christ or His church dear. Otherwise, Christians at large, and those who exercise authority in the state, ought to do so despite the Romanists' excommunications or fulminations. For one undeserved excommunication is better than ten justifiable absolutions; and one undeserved absolution is worse than ten justifiable excommunications. Therefore let us wake up, my dear fellow countrymen, and fear God rather than men, lest we suffer like all those poor folk who have gone astray so pitiably through the shameless and impious régime of Rome. Under this régime, the devil prospers more and more every day; and, if such a thing were possible, this impious régime must become worse as a consequence, although I still cannot conceive nor believe how.

1. In the first place, it is painful and shocking to see that the head of Christendom, proclaiming himself the Vicar of Christ and the successor of St. Peter, lives in such a worldly and ostentatious style that no king or emperor can reach and rival him.[8] He claims the titles of "Most Holy" and "Most Spiritual", but there is more worldliness in him than in the world itself. He wears a triple crown, whereas the mightiest kings wear only one. If that is like the lowly Christ or St. Peter, it is to me a new sort of likeness. The Romanists bleat that it would be heretical to speak against it; they refuse to consider how unchristian and ungodly such conduct is. In my view, however, if the pope were to pray before God with fear, he would have to lay aside his triple crown, for our God tolerates no haughtiness. Of course, his duty ought to be nothing less than to weep and pray day by day for all Christian people, and to show an example of deep humility.

No matter how his inclinations may lead him, such pomp is evil; and for the sake of his soul's salvation, the pope ought to lay it aside, if only because St. Paul says, "Abstain from all demeanour which is evil" [I Thess. 5:22], and again, "We ought to bring forth what is good, not only in God's sight, but also before all men" [Rom. 12:17]. An ordinary bishop's crown ought to suffice the pope. He should be above others

[8] The reigning pope was the Medici, Leo X, under whom the papacy reached its greatest splendour.

in wisdom and holiness, and leave the crown of pride to the Antichrist, as his predecessors did centuries ago. The Romanists declare he is the Lord of the earth. That is false; for Christ, whose vicegerent and steward he boasts of being, said before Pilate, "My kingdom is not of this world" [John 18:36]. No vicegerent can have a rulership greater than his lord. Nor is the pope vicegerent on behalf of the Risen Christ, but of the Crucified Christ, for Paul says, "For I determined not to know anything among you save Christ and him crucified" [I Cor. 2:2]; and, "You ought so to think of yourselves as you see in Christ, who emptied himself, and took on the mien of a servant" [Phil. 2:5–7], and again, "We preach Christ, the crucified" [I Cor. 1:23]. But now they create the pope the vicegerent of the Risen Christ in heaven; and some popes have let the devil rule in them so fully that they have claimed that the pope is above the angels in heaven and has them at his command; which surely is the work of Antichrist himself.

2. What Christian purpose is served by the ecclesiastics called cardinals? I will tell you. In Italy and Germany there are many wealthy monasteries, institutions, benefices, and parishes. No better way has been devised of bringing them into Rome's possession than by creating cardinals and giving them bishoprics, monasteries, and prelacies as their property, thus destroying the service of God. The consequence is that Italy is now almost devastated; monasteries are in disorder, bishoprics despoiled, the revenues of prelacies and all the churches drawn to Rome, cities devastated, land and people ruined, because no longer are services held or sermons preached. Why so? Because the cardinals must have their revenues. The Turk himself could not have ruined Italy in like manner nor put an end to divine worship to such an extent.

Now that Italy is drained dry, they are coming into the German countries, and beginning with calculated restraint. But let us watch, for the German countries will soon become like Italy. Already we have a few cardinals. They think the drunken Germans will not understand what the game is, till there is not a single bishopric, monastery, parish or benefice, not a cent or farthing, left for them. The Antichrist must take the treasures of the world, as it is written [I John 2:15–18]. This is what happens: they take a heavy toll of the bishoprics, monasteries, and benefices. While they do not yet dare entirely to despoil the country, as they have done in Italy, meantime they use such unction and adroitness that they clump ten or twenty prelacies together. They then wrest annual tribute from each, amounting in total to a considerable sum. The priory at Wurzburg pays 1,000 guilders, that at Bamberg also makes a contribution, besides Mayence, Trèves, and others. In this way 1,000 or 10,000 guilders may be collected in order that a cardinal shall live in Rome in princely style.

Having reached this stage, they proceed to create thirty or forty cardinals in a single day, give to one the convent on the Mönchberg, near Bamberg, plus the bishopric of Wurzburg, with a few wealthy parishes tacked on, until churches and cities are laid waste; and then they proceed to justify it all by saying, "We are Christ's agents and the shepherds of Christ's sheep. The silly drunken Germans must put up with it."

My way would be to create fewer cardinals, or else let the pope support them at his own expense. Twelve of them would be more than enough, each with 1,000 guilders income. How has it come about that we Germans have to tolerate such robbery, such confiscations of our property? If the kingdom of France has resisted it, why do we Germans let the Romanists make fools and apes of us in this way? It would be more tolerable if they only stole our possessions in this fashion; but they devastate the church by it, rob Christ's sheep of their devout pastors, and debase the service of God and the Word of God. Even if there were not a single cardinal, the church would still not decline. As things are, they do nothing to serve Christendom; they only bargain and quarrel about bishoprics and prelacies just as any thief might do.

3. If ninety-nine per cent. of the papal court were abolished and only one per cent. were left, it would still be large enough to deal with questions of Christian faith. At present there is a crawling mass of reptiles, all claiming to pay allegiance to the pope, but Babylon never saw the like of these miscreants. The pope has more than 3,000 secretaries alone, and no one can count the others he employs, as the posts are so numerous. It is hardly possible to number all those that lie in wait for

the institutions and benefices of Germany, like wolves for the sheep. I fear that Germany to-day is giving far more to the pope in Rome than she used to give formerly to the emperors. Some have estimated that more than 300,000 guilders go annually from Germany to Rome, quite uselessly and to no purpose, while we get nothing in return except contempt and scorn. It is not at all astonishing if princes, aristocracy, towns, institutions, country, and people grow poor. We ought to marvel that we still have anything left to eat.

Now that we have come to close quarters, let us pause a while and consider whether the Germans are quite such simpletons as not to grasp or understand the Romish game. For the moment, I shall say nothing by way of deploring the fact that God's commandments and Christian justice are despised in Rome. The state of Christendom, especially in Rome, is not so happy that we should risk calling such exalted matters into question at the present time. Nor am I objecting that natural or secular right and reason are of no avail. The root of the trouble goes altogether deeper. My complaint is that the Romanists do not observe the very canon law which they themselves have devised, though this in itself is simply a piece of tyranny, avarice, and worldly pomp rather than law—as I shall proceed to show.

Many years ago, German emperors and princes granted the pope permission to take the "annates" of all the benefices in Germany, i.e., the half of the first year's income of every single benefice. The permission was granted in order that the pope might gather together sufficient treasure to enable him to make war against Turks and infidels, and to defend Christendom, so that the burden of fighting the war should not press too heavily upon the ruling class, but that the priesthood should also contribute something. The popes have made such use of the praiseworthy and straightforward intentions of the German people that they have taken these revenues now for more than a hundred years, until, to-day, they have converted them into an obligatory tax and impost—due as of right. Not only have they accumulated nothing, but they have used the money to found many posts and offices in Rome, and to pay their yearly salaries as out of a fixed rent. If it is now proposed to make war against the Turks, they despatch emissaries to collect money—indulgences being often sent out also with the same pretext of fighting the Turks. Their opinion is that Germans will always be gullible fools, and go on paying the money to satisfy their indescribable greed; and this in spite of the facts now evident to us all, namely, that not a farthing of the annates or the indulgence money or the like contribution will be used against the Turks, but all will go into the bottomless bag. They lie and deceive; they make agreements with us, of which they do not intend to keep a single letter. Yet all is done ostensibly for the sake of the holy name of Christ and St. Peter.

The German nation, including their bishops and princes, should remember that they too are Christian. They should protect the populace whom it is their duty to rule; they should defend them by means of their temporal and spiritual possessions against these ravening wolves who come dressed in sheep's clothing as shepherds and rulers. Further, since the annates are so shamefully misused, and agreements are not kept, the German bishops and princes ought not to allow their country and people to be so pitiably harassed and impoverished without any regard for justice. Rather, by an imperial decree, or a national law, they ought to suspend payment of the annates, or abolish them entirely. Since the pope and his adherents do not keep agreements, they have no right to the annates; rather, the bishops and princes are under an obligation to punish or prevent this theft and robbery, as the law demands.

They ought to stand by the pope if he is willing to receive help to deal with abuses of this character, for perhaps he is not strong enough to deal with them alone; or, should he prefer to defend and maintain these abuses, they should resist and repel him as a wolf and a tyrant, seeing that he has no authority to do or to defend anything evil. Moreover, if it is desirable to accumulate a war chest against the Turks, we ought then to have wit enough to see that the German people are more able to guard it than the pope, since the German people are numerous enough to wage the war themselves if the funds are there. The case of the annates is similar to that of many another Romish pretence.

Further, the year has been so divided between the pope and the ruling bishops and chapters, that the pope appoints

incumbents to those benefices which fall vacant in six months
in the year, i.e., during the alternate months; the ruling bishops
and chapters being left to make appointment to those which
fall vacant in the other six months. The result of this device is
that almost all the benefices fall into the hands of Rome, especially the wealthiest livings and dignities. Those which fall
to Rome in this way are never relinquished by her, even
though afterwards they do not become vacant in the papal
months. Hence the chapters receive far too few. This is pure
robbery, and the intention clearly is that nothing should escape. This spoliation must now be brought to an end. It is
high time to abolish the pope's months, and to reclaim everything which has accrued to Rome in this way. On that account, therefore, princes and peers ought to take steps for the
restitution of the stolen property, for punishing the thieves,
and cancelling the privileges of those who have abused them.
If it is legally valid that the pope, immediately on election,
should make rules and regulations in his chancellery to do
what he has no moral right to do, i.e., steal our canonries
and livings, it should be much more valid for the emperor
Charles, immediately on his coronation, to issue rules and
regulations forbidding throughout Germany that any further
benefices and livings should accrue to Rome by the papal
months; and that those which have fallen to Rome should be
set free again and liberated from the Roman thief; he has an
official right to do so by virtue of his authority as a ruler.

But the Romish pontiff, Avarice and Robbery, has not had
patience to await the time when all benefices would fall to
him by the device of the papal months. Rather, urged by his
insatiable appetite, and in order to snatch them all for himself
at the earliest moment, he has devised a plan whereby, in
addition to the annates and months, the benefices and livings
should fall to Rome in three ways:

(i) If anyone possessing a "free" living should die in Rome
or on the way there, that living becomes the property in perpetuity of the Romish—I might say thievish—papacy, and yet
he is not to be called a thief, although no one has ever heard
or read of more barefaced robbery.

(ii) Similarly, if anyone on the staff of the pope or the car-

dinals possesses or takes over a benefice, or if anyone has previously possessed a benefice and later enters the service of the
pope and the cardinals, that benefice falls to the pope. But who
can count the staff of the pope and the cardinals, even when
the pope only goes out riding for pleasure? He is accompanied
by three or four thousand on mules, as much as any emperor
or king. Did Christ and St. Peter go on foot, in order that their
Vicar might have the more pomp and pride to display? But
His Avarice has developed further cunning devices, and
brought it about that many outside Rome are said to belong
to the papal staff, just as if they lived in Rome. Thus in every
place whatsoever, the roguish little term, "papal staff", may
bring all benefices to the Roman pontiff, and pin them there
for ever. Are those not vexatious and impious little devices?
If we inquire into it, we shall find that Mayence, Magdeburg,
and Halberstadt will go comfortably to Rome, and then the
cardinals will cost a pretty penny. Soon, all German bishops
will be made cardinals so as to make a clean job of it.

(iii) The third device is to initiate a dispute at Rome about
some benefice; this seems the commonest way of getting livings into Rome's hands. If no dispute has already arisen, there
are innumerable sycophants who will raise a dispute about
nothing of moment, and make a grab at livings anywhere. The
consequence is that many a faithful priest has either to lose
his living or buy appeasement for a time. When a dispute has
been fastened on a benefice in this way rightly or wrongly, it
will eventually belong to Rome in perpetuity. Who could be
astonished if God were to rain down sulphur and hell-fire from
the sky, or plunge Rome into the abyss, as He once did with
Sodom and Gomorrah? What value is the pope to Christendom, if he only uses his power for defending and practising
such arch-wickedness? O my noble princes and lords, how long
will you let these ravening wolves range at will over your land
and people?

But even these devices are insufficient to satisfy their greed,
for time drags too slowly for them to engulf all the bishoprics.
So our good friend Avarice has invented the theory that while
it is true that the bishoprics bear provincial names, yet in origin
they are indigenous to Rome. No bishop, therefore, can be

confirmed in his episcopate unless he pays up heavily for his pallium,[9] and swears a solemn oath binding himself to the personal service of the pope. That is why no bishop dare take any action against the pope. And that was their objective when the Romanists imposed the oath, and explains why the very richest bishoprics fall into debt and ruin. I am told that Mayence pays 20,000 guilders. That is typically Romish, as it seems to me. Some time ago, the canon law decreed that the pallium should be a free gift, that the papal tax should be reduced, disputes made less frequent, chapter and bishop given freedom of action; but this law brought in no money, so they turned the ruling topsy-turvy. All power was taken from bishops and chapters. They sit there like figure-heads and as if without office, authority, or function. The chief transgressors in Rome control everything, almost down to the sextons and bellringers in each church. Every dispute is called to Rome, and everyone who gets the pope's licence does as he likes.

What has happened this very year? The bishop of Strassburg was planning to put his chapter into seemly order, and introduce certain improvements into the divine services. With this in view, he put forward various propositions which were in themselves both religious and Christian. But the dear pope and the saintly see of Rome took this ordinance, reverent and religious though it was, smashed it to bits, and damned it, all at the request of the local priests. What an example of shepherding Christ's sheep! Priests ought to be supported against their own bishops and to be defended in disobeying ungodly regulations! I do not expect even the Antichrist to exhibit contempt of God like that. But that is the pope for you! Is it after your heart? Why does he act like this? Alas, because, if one church were to be reformed, the movement might spread and, perhaps reach Rome! Rather than that, no two priests should be left in agreement, and the custom must be kept up of sowing discord among princes and kings, flooding the world with Christian blood, lest unity among Christian people should enable them to compel the Holy Roman See to reform.

The foregoing gives an idea as to how they deal with livings

[9] The short woollen cape which is the emblem of the rank, and which must be bought in Rome.

that fall vacant, and come free. However, too few vacancies occur for their shameful greed. Hence they take measures in advance in regard to benefices still having incumbents. Steps must be taken as if they had already become vacant, although they are not vacant; to this end, several artifices are resorted to:

(a) My Lord Greed lies in wait where fat prebends or bishoprics are held by an aged, ailing incumbent, or by one accused of some trumped-up disqualification. The Holy See presents such a man with a *coadjutor*, i.e., an "assistant", whether wanted or not. It is done for the sake of the coadjutor, because he is on the pope's staff, or has paid for it, or has otherwise earned a reward for some service which the Romanists have forced on him. That ends the free choice of the local chapter or the patron of the living; all goes to Rome.

(b) Then comes the little word "*Commend*".[10] This means that the pope gives a cardinal, or another of his supporters, a rich abbey or church in charge, just as if I were to put you in charge of a hundred guilders. This does not mean giving or bestowing the abbey, or destroying it, or abolishing divine service, but only to give it in charge. Nor is the nominee obliged to preserve it or build it up; rather, he is to drive out the incumbent, take possession of the properties and income, or install some apostate monk, a truant from his monastery. This man gets paid five or six guilders per annum, but sits in the church during the day, selling sketches and little images to the pilgrims; there is no more chanting or scripture-reading in that church. But if that were described as destroying the abbey or abolishing divine services, the pope would have to be called one who destroys abbeys and does away with divine services, and he certainly does much of this sort of thing. But in Rome this would be thought an impolite way of talking, and so taking an abbey in charge is called a *commend*, i.e., an *order*.

(c) There are certain benefices called *incompatibilia*, which according to the regulations of canon law cannot both

---

[10] To receive an office *in commendam* did not imply any duties, but only a right to the entire income of a living or abbey, when a vacancy occurred.

be in one man's charge, e.g., two parishes, two bishoprics, and so on. At this point, however, the Holy Roman See and Avarice wriggles itself out of the reach of canon law by making glosses[11] called *unio* or *incorporatio*. This means that the pope makes one body of many *incompatibilia*, till they belong to each other as members of one organism, and so are now treated as a single parish. They are no longer incompatibles now, and yet it is all done according to canon law. In fact, canon law is never binding except on those who refuse to buy these glosses from the pope and his *datarius*.[12]

The *unio*, i.e., combination, is of the same character, in that it means coupling up many of these livings like a bundle of sticks, and, because there is now one bundle, they call it one living. Accordingly, there is at present a court follower in Rome who is in sole possession of 22 parishes and 7 priories together with 44 canonries. A clever "gloss" leads to all these results, and at the same time shows the practice is not against canon law. Let each one work it out for himself what the cardinals and other prelates possess. The Germans are now to have their purses emptied and their pride deflated in this same way!

One of the "glosses" is also called *administratio*. The term is applied to a case where a man possesses, in addition to his bishopric, also an abbacy or a dignity together with all the property pertaining to it, simply because he bears the title of *administrator*. For it suffices Rome if the precious titles are recognized, regardless of whether the duties are done; it is just as if I were to announce that a procuress should be called mayoress, but continue to behave as she does now. Peter prophesied this kind of Romish régime when he said, "False teachers will come, and in covetousness shall they, with feigned words, make merchandise of you to get their profits" [II Pet. 2:3].

The worthy pontiff, Avarice of Rome, has also thought out

---

[11] At first an explanatory note, usually brief, bringing out the meaning or application of a difficult or doubtful passage; it was the earliest form of commentary. Afterwards the glosses were much expanded and often became part of the text and of equal authority.

[12] The head, usually a cardinal, of a papal office (*Dataria*) registering and issuing certain documents with an appended phrase, *Datum ad Petrum*.

a certain device whereby a living or a benefice is sold or disposed of on condition that the seller or disposer retains the reversion and promise of it, in such a way that, if the new owner dies, the living reverts gratis to him who had sold it, disposed of it, or surrendered it. Thus they have converted livings into heritable property. Nobody can come to possess them except the man to whom the seller is willing to dispose of them, or to whom they are bequeathed under his will. There are many who confer the bare title of a benefice, but on the understanding that, as incumbent, he draws not a single farthing. It is also an established custom to bestow a benefice on another, while reserving a certain amount of the yearly income—a practice formerly called simony. There is much more of this sort of thing—beyond the telling. The Romanists traffic in livings more disgracefully than the Gentiles under the cross trafficked with Christ's garments.

But the whole of the above is almost ancient history at Rome, and has become a custom. Yet Avarice has devised one thing more, perhaps the last, for I hope it will choke him. The pope possesses a refined device called *pectoralis reservatio,* i.e., his mental reservation, *et properius motus,* i.e., and his own free will and power. This is how it works. A certain candidate comes to Rome seeking a specified benefice. It is duly assigned under seal to him in the customary manner. Then comes another applicant who either offers to purchase the same benefice, or makes his claim in consideration of services rendered to the pope in a way which we shall not recount. The pope thereupon annuls the appointment already made, and gives it to the second applicant. If anyone were to protest that this transaction was an injustice, the Most Holy Father has to offer some explanation, lest he be accused of having flagrantly violated the law. He therefore declares that he had made reservations in his heart and conscience about that particular benefice, and had retained his control of it undiminished—and this, though in fact he had never given it another thought, or heard another word about it. Such an instance shows that the pope has discovered a worthy little "gloss", by using which he can tell lies and play tricks without incurring censure, and can deceive and fool everybody publicly without a blush. Yet all the time he claims to be the head of the Christian Church, although he is a barefaced liar letting the Evil One dominate him.

This arbitrary and deceptive "mental reservation" on the part of the pope creates a state of affairs in Rome that beggars description. You can find there a buying and selling, a bartering and a bargaining, a lying and trickery, robbery and stealing, pomp, procuration, knavery, and all sorts of stratagems bringing God into contempt, till it would be impossible for the Antichrist to govern more wickedly. There is nothing in Venice, Antwerp, or Cairo to compare with the fair which traffics in Rome. In those cities, right and reason enjoy some respect; but here things go on in a way that pleases the devil himself. This kind of morality flows like a tide into all the world. Such people rightly fear a reformation, or an unfettered council. They would rather set kings and princes at odds than that these should unite and bring a council together. No one could bear to have villainies of this kind come to the light of day.

Finally, the pope has built a market-house for the convenience of all this refined traffic, viz.: the house of the *datarius* in Rome. This is where all those resort who deal in this way in benefices and livings. From him they must buy these "glosses" and transactions, and get power to practise their archvillainy. In former days, Rome was still gracious enough to sell or suppress justice for a moderate price. But to-day, she has put her prices so high that she lets no one act the villain before he has paid a huge sum. If that is not more like a den of iniquity than any other den one can imagine, then I do not know what a den of iniquity is.

But, if you bring money to this ecclesiastical market, you can buy any of the goods I have described. Here any one can pay and then legally charge interest on loans of any sort. You can get a legal right to goods you have stolen or seized. Here vows are annulled; here monks receive liberty to leave their orders; here marriage is for sale to the clergy; here bastards can become legitimate, and any form of dishonour and shame can achieve dignity; all kinds of iniquity and evil are knighted and ennobled. Here a marriage is permitted which is within the forbidden degrees, or which is otherwise objectionable. O what a jugglery and extortion go on here! until it would seem that all the laws of the canon were only given to produce gilded nooses, from which a man must free himself if he would become a Christian. Indeed, here the devil becomes a saint and a god: what cannot be done anywhere else in heaven or earth, can be done in this house. They call the process *compositiones*. Yes, compositions, really confusions. O how light a tax is the Rhine-toll compared with the exactions of this sacred house!

Let no one imagine I am overdrawing the picture. Everything is public, and people in Rome have to acknowledge that it is terrible beyond the power to describe. I have not yet touched, nor do I intend to touch, upon the hellish dregs of the personal vices; I am dealing only with commonplace things, and yet I have not space to name them all. The bishops and priests, and especially the university doctors, whose salaries are given for the purpose, ought to have done their duty and, with one accord, written and declaimed against these things; but they have done the very opposite.

I must come to an end and have done with this section. Because the whole immeasurable greed which I have recounted is not satisfied with all this wealth, enough probably for three mighty kings, the business is now to be transferred, and sold to Fugger of Augsburg.[13] Henceforward bishoprics and livings for sale or exchange or in demand, and dealings in the spiritualities, have arrived at their true destination, now that the bargaining for spiritual or secular properties has become united into a single business. But I would like to hear of a man who is clever enough to discover what Avarice of Rome might do which has not already been done. Then perhaps Fugger would transfer and sell to someone else these two lines of business which are now to be combined into one. In my view, we have reached the limit.

For to describe what they have stolen in all countries, and are still stealing, and extorting, by indulgences, bulls, letters of confession,[14] butter letters,[15] and other *confessionalia*[16]—to describe all this is work for the odd-job man, and is like playing

---

[13] The Fuggers were bankers to the Roman curia.
[14] Allowing choice of confessor and of items to confess.
[15] Allowing certain foods on fast days.
[16] Letters given, for a fee, to excuse a person from various burdensome duties, etc.

pitch and toss with a devil in hell. Not that it brings in little profit: it is enough to supply ample revenues for a mighty king; but it is not to be compared with the swelling flood of treasure described above. For the time being, I shall hold my tongue, and not say where the Indulgence-money has gone. Later I shall inquire about it. The Campofiore[17] and Belvedere[18] and a few more places probably know something about it.

This wicked régime is not only barefaced robbery, trickery, and tyranny appropriate to the nether regions, but also a destruction of the body and soul of Christendom. Therefore we ought to make every effort to protect Christendom from this hurt and damage. If we are willing to make war on the Turks, let us begin here where they are most iniquitous. If we are right in hanging thieves and beheading robbers, why should we leave Avarice of Rome unpunished? Here is the greatest thief and robber that has ever come or is likely to come on earth, and the scandal is perpetrated in the holy names of Christ and St. Peter. Who can go on tolerating it or keeping silence? Almost all he possesses has been got by theft and robbery. Everything recorded in the histories tells the same story. The pope has never bought properties so great that his income from his ecclesiastical offices should amount to ten hundred thousand ducats, apart from the mines of treasure as already described, and his landed estates. Neither is it that which Christ and St. Peter bequeathed to him, nor that which any one has given or loaned to him; nor has it been acquired by prescription or ancient right. Tell me where he got it? On this point watch what they are seeking for and aiming at when they send out legates to gather funds against the Turks.

[17] Costly restorations done here by Eugenius IV (1431–47).
[18] Part of the Vatican housing many works of art, ancient and modern.

III.   TWENTY-SEVEN PROPOSALS FOR IMPROVING THE STATE OF CHRISTENDOM

Although I am really of too little consequence to make proposals for the improvement of such a terrible state of affairs, I will go on, although foolishly, to the end, and declare, as far as I understand the case, what might well be done and should be done, either by the secular arm or an ecumenical council.

1. Firstly, I suggest that every prince, peer, and city should strictly forbid their subjects to pay the annates to Rome, and should do away with them entirely. For the pope has broken the agreement about the annates, and so stolen them, to the hurt and shame of the whole German people. He bestows them on his friends, sells them for large sums, and endows certain offices with them. Hence he has lost the right to them, and deserves to be punished. The secular arm is now under obligation to protect the innocent and prevent injustice, as St. Paul teaches, and St. Peter, and, also, the canon law in Case 16, Question 7, *de filiis*. Hence one says to the pope and his adherents, *"Tu ora"*, Thou shalt pray; but to the emperor and his minister, *"Tu protege"*, Thou shalt protect; and to the ordinary man, *"Tu labora"*, Thou shalt work. Not as if praying and protecting and working were not each man's duty, for he who fulfils his own task, prays, protects, and labours; but to each should be assigned a special function.

2. With his Romish practices, viz., commends, coadjutors, reservations, *gratiae expectativae*,[19] "papal months", incorporations, unions, pensions, palliums, rules in chancery, and similar villainies, the pope is engulfing all foundations of German origin, without authority or justice, and bestowing and selling them in Rome to strangers who do nothing for Germany in

---

[19] A kind of *post obit:* the promise of a living not yet vacant, often made without regard to rights of third parties.

return. It follows that the proper incumbents are robbed of their rights, and the bishops become figureheads and targets for ridicule. This means acting contrary to Canon Law, common sense, and reason. The final issue will be that the livings and benefices will be sold only to coarse ignoramuses and scoundrels in Rome, for greed alone. Merit and wisdom will avail nothing even to devout and learned men, with the result that the poorer classes of Germany will have to do without kindly and scholarly prelates, and will perish eternally. This is sufficient reason for the Christian ruling classes to set their faces against the pope as a common foe, who is wreaking destruction in Christendom; and to do so for the sake of saving the poor, who cannot avoid perishing under this tyranny. They should decree, command, and ordain that not another benefice shall in future be transferred to Rome, and that by no device whatever shall a single further appointment be obtained there. Rather, the benefices shall be rescued and kept from this tyrannical power; the proper incumbents should have their rights and offices restored, so that those benefices, which belong to Germany, may be brought into the best possible order. If a legate should arrive from Rome, he should be given stern orders to keep off, or jump into the Rhine or the nearest stretch of water, and give the Romish ban, complete with seals and epistles, a cold douche. They would then take note in Rome that Germans are not silly and besotted all the time, but that they are really converted Christians, and such that they will no longer tolerate the holy name of Christ to be scoffed at and scorned, thus permitting rogues to live and souls to perish. Rather they reverence God's honour more than man's power.

3. An imperial law should be decreed, whereby no bishop should go to Rome for his pallium, or for the confirmation of any other dignity, from now onwards. Instead of this, the ordinance of Nicea, the holiest and most celebrated of all the councils, should be re-established. This regulation declares that a bishop shall be confirmed by the two nearest bishops, or by the archbishop. If the pope intends to abolish the statute of this and all other councils, what is the value of having councils? Moreover, who has given him authority to despise and nullify councils? All the more reason for us to depose all bish-

ops, archbishops, and primates, and make plain pastors of
them, with the pope as their sole superior, as in fact he is. For
he leaves no regular authority or office to the bishops, archbishops, and primates. He appropriates everything for himself,
and allows them to retain only the name and the empty title.
By using his "exemption", the abbot of a cloister, and the prelates, are made no longer subject to the regular authority of
the bishop. This results in lack of system and order in Christendom, with the inevitable consequence, already to be seen, that
penalties are lax, and one is free to do all manner of evil. Of a
truth, I fear it is possible to call the pope "the man of sin".
Who is to blame if, throughout Christendom, there is neither
discipline, nor punishment, nor rule, nor order? None other
than the pope who, by the arbitrary power he has assumed,
extends to them his patronage while depriving them of power;
and, by gift or purchase, freeing from their authority those
whom they should control.

Lest the pope complain of loss of authority, it should be
decreed that if primates and archbishops are not equal to dealing with a problem, or if a dispute should arise between them,
the issue must be referred to the pope, if and when it is of
sufficient importance. That is what used to be done in earlier
times, and was substantiated by the very famous council at
Nicea. His Holiness ought not to be burdened with small matters that can be dealt with by others. He should be able to
give himself to prayer, to study, and to concern for Christendom; indeed, he claims to do so, just as did the Apostles (Acts
6), who said: "It is not fit that we should forsake the Word
of God and serve tables. But we will continue in preaching
and prayer, and set others over such work" [Acts 6:2, 4]. At
Rome preaching and prayer are simply despised. All is a matter of serving of tables, i.e., subordination to secular profit.
The régimes of the Apostles and the pope harmonize together
about as well as Christ and Lucifer, heaven and hell, or night
and day; and yet he is called the Vicar of Christ and Successor
of the Apostles.

4. It should be decreed that no secular matter is to be referred to Rome. All such issues should be left to the secular
arm, as the Romanists themselves affirm in their canon laws,

which, however, they do not observe. It should be the pope's part, as the man most learned of all in the Scriptures, and as actually and not merely nominally the holiest of all, to regulate whatever concerns the faith and holy life of Christians. He should hold the primates and archbishops to this duty, join them in handling these matters, and bearing these cares. So St. Paul teaches, I Corinthians 6 [:7], and severely reproves them for their concern about secular affairs. For it does intolerable hurt in every country that these cases should be tried in Rome. It makes them more expensive; the judges themselves are ignorant of the customs, laws, and manners of other lands, and so, frequently, force cases to fit with their own.

Besides the above, the gross malpractices of the judges in the ecclesiastical courts ought to be forbidden. They ought to be concerned only with matters of faith and good morals; whereas money, property, life, and honour should be left for the secular judges to deal with. Therefore the secular arm ought not to allow sentences of excommunication or exile, except where matters of faith or good conduct are concerned.

Nevertheless it should be permissible for cases concerning livings and benefices to be tried before bishops, archbishops, and primates. Therefore to settle disputes and quarrels, the primate of Germany should, where possible, hold a general consistory, with auditors and chancellors who, as in Rome, should be the heads of the *signaturae gratiae* and *justitiae;*[20] and these consistories should be the Courts of Appeal to which cases in Germany should be regularly brought and referred. These courts ought not to be maintained, as in Rome, by unspecified presents and gifts, a custom leading to the selling of justice and injustice, as necessarily takes place now in Rome. Since the pope pays them no salary, they have to contrive their own income out of the presents they receive. The result is that nothing in Rome depends on the rights and wrongs of a case, but only whether there is money in it or not. Instead of this financial bribery, the courts might be maintained from the annates, or some other method devised by more eminent and experienced persons than I. My own purpose is to stir up, and give food for thought to, those who can and will help the

---

[20] The two departments through which the pope administered the matters that he claimed as his prerogatives.

German people to regain their Christian faith, and to liberate themselves from the wretched, pagan, and unchristian régime of the pope.

5. Not another reservation should hold good, and not another living should be taken possession of by Rome, even if the incumbent die, or a dispute arise about it, or the incumbent is a cardinal, or one of the pope's staff. A court follower must be strictly forbidden, and prevented from beginning, litigation against the holder of any benefice, or citing and disturbing any dutiful priests, or driving them to some compromise. If, as a consequence, Rome pronounces excommunication or exercises spiritual pressure, it should be ignored just as it would be if a thief excommunicated someone who would not let him steal. Indeed, the Romanists ought to be severely punished for blasphemous misuse of excommunication and of God's name in support of their robberies. They devise threats, which are lies, in order to compel us to tolerate and even praise this blasphemy of the divine name and misuse of Christian power, and to make us take part in their wickedness in God's sight. Far from giving them support, our duty before God is to repudiate them. In Romans 1 [:32], St. Paul condemns their like as worthy of death. But they not only do such things, but also encourage and legalize them. In particular, the mendacious "mental reservation" is intolerable, because it brings the Christian religion blasphemously and publicly into shame and contempt, when its head acts with unconcealed mendacity, and unashamedly deceives and fools everyone with his favours for the sake of accursed money.

6. The reserved cases, which the pope alone can absolve, should be abolished. Not only are the people cheated of much money by them, but the ravenous tyrants ensnare and confuse tender consciences with intolerable harm to their faith in God. Particularly is this true of the ridiculous and childish cases which the bull, *coena domini*,[21] blows up like bladders. They do not deserve to be called "common sins", still less are they

---

[21] A bull issued at Rome each Maundy Thursday against heretics and those offences which only the pope can absolve.

sins so great that even the pope cannot absolve them. Examples from the list are: preventing a pilgrim from going to Rome; or providing the Turks with arms; or counterfeiting papal briefs. They fool us with these insulting, silly, and clumsy devices; yet Sodom and Gomorrah, and all the sins that are or may be done against God's commandments—these are not "reserved cases". What God never ordained, but Romanists themselves invented—these forsooth are "reserved cases". The reason is that no one must be prevented from bringing money to Rome, where, safe from the Turks, the Romanists live in luxury, and keep the rest of the world in chains with wanton and useless bulls and briefs.

Really every priest ought to know, and a public decree should declare, that no private and undenounced trespass constitutes a reserved case; and that every priest is empowered to pronounce absolution, no matter what the sin, or whatever it may be called. If it is private, neither abbot, bishop, nor pope has power to "reserve" it to himself; if they presume to do so, their action is null and void. Rather they ought to be punished for it, as interfering without authority in the judgment which God pronounces, and, without cause, binding and burdening the tender consciences of the uninformed. But where the sins are of a public character and widespread, especially those committed against God's commandments, there are perhaps grounds for making "reserved cases"; but they should not be numerous, and not be "reserved" arbitrarily and without cause; for Christ did not provide tyrants but pastors in His church, as St. Peter says [I Pet. 5:3].

7. The Holy See of Rome should abolish the *officia*[22] and lessen the creeping and crawling swarms of hirelings in the city. The object of this abolition is that the papal staff should be supported out of the pope's own income, and his court not outvie in magnificence and extravagance that of any king. Regard should be paid to the fact that such a state of affairs has never been of any service to the Christian faith, but has been a very great hindrance to study and prayer, until the court officials now know scarcely anything about Christian faith. This

[22] Posts and positions on sale.

was proved plainly at the last council which was held recently at Rome.[23]

Among many childish and frivolous clauses, they introduced one which declared the human soul immortal, and that a priest was to say prayers once every month or lose his benefice. How can the affairs of Christendom and questions of faith be settled by men who, having been made stupid and blind by much avarice, wealth, and worldly splendour, only now for the first time pronounce the soul immortal? It is no small shame, but one that affects all Christendom, when they treat the faith so disgracefully in Rome. If their wealth and splendour were less, they might be more diligent in study and prayer, and become worthy and capable of dealing with questions of faith. This they were in former days, but then they were content to be bishops, and did not pretend to outvie kings in their wealth and splendour.

8. The far-reaching and fearful oaths, which bishops are wrongfully compelled to swear to the pope, should be abolished. They keep the bishops bound like domestic servants. The decree stands with its arbitrary authority and its great stupidity in the worthless and unscholarly chapter entitled *Significasti*.[24] Is it not enough that their numerous foolish laws should burden us in body, soul, and property, to the weakening of faith and the ruin of the Christian estate? But now they make a prisoner of the bishop with his office and duties, including his very investiture. Formerly, this last was performed by the German emperor, and still is carried out by the king in France and other countries. On this point, the Romanists struggled and disputed hotly with the emperors, until at last they had the barefaced effrontery to seize the right and retain it to the present day. They must think the German Christians are, to a greater extent than any others, the household fools of the pope and the papacy, for doing and suffering what no one elsewhere will suffer or do. Since, therefore, this example of oppression and robbery hinders the bishop from exercising his proper authority and is harmful to needy souls, then an

[23] The fifth Lateran Council, A.D. 1512–17.
[24] *Decret. Greg.*, lib. I, tit. 6, cap. 4. It deals with the oath of obedience sworn by bishops.

obligation falls on the emperor and the ruling classes supporting him, to repel and punish it as a piece of tyranny.

9. The pope should exercise no authority over the emperor, except the right to anoint and crown him at the altar as a bishop crowns a king. Never again should his iniquitous Arrogance be permitted to make the emperor kiss the pope's feet, or sit at them, or, as it is said, hold the stirrup and bridle of his mule when he mounts to go riding. Still less should he do homage to the pope, and swear faithfulness to him as his liege lord, as the popes shamelessly presume to demand as if by right. The chapter entitled *Solite*,[25] which raises the power of the pope above that of the emperor, is not worth a farthing; nor are any that are based on it or recognize its authority. For what it actually does is to wrest the meaning of the holy Word of God from its proper interpretation to fit their own ambitions, as I have shown in a Latin treatise.[26]

This ultra-excessive, arrogant, and frivolous presumption of the pope's is a device of the devil's to be used betimes as a cover for introducing the Antichrist, and raising the pope above God, as many have already done and are doing. It is not fitting for the pope to arrogate to himself superiority over the secular authorities, except in his spiritual functions such as preaching and pronouncing absolution. In other respects, he is inferior, as Paul teaches, Romans 13, and Peter, I Peter 2 [:13], too, as I have already said. He is not the Vicar of the Christ in heaven, but only of the Christ who lived on earth. Christ in heaven, in His work as king, needs no vicar. For, seated on His Throne, He can see, know, and perform all things. He is omnipotent. But He needs a vicar as a servant, the form in which He Himself walked on earth where He laboured, preached, suffered, and died. But the Romanists turn things inside out, take from Christ the status of heavenly regent, and confer it on the pope, while allowing the idea of servant to fall into oblivion. The pope seems almost the Counter-Christ, called in Scripture the Antichrist, for the whole of his system, his efforts, and his pretensions are contrary to Christ, and directed solely to blotting

[25] *Decret. Greg.*, lib. I, tit. 33, cap. 6.
[26] *Resolutio Lutheriana super propositione XIII de potestate papae* (1520).

out and destroying whatever Christ has informed with His spirit, and whatever work He has done.

Further, it is ridiculous and childish for the pope to use stupid and perverse statements in the Decretal *Pastoralis* and claim that he is the legal heir of the empire if the throne becomes vacant. Who gave it to him? Did Christ when He said, "The princes of the Gentiles are lords, but ye shall not be so"? [Luke 22:25 f.]. Or did the pope inherit it from St. Peter? It annoys me that we have to read and learn these shameless, gross, and silly untruths in the canon law, and, besides, receive them as Christian doctrine although they are infernal lies. Further, the "Donation of Constantine" is an unheard-of falsification of the same class.[27] It must have been by virtue of a special plague sent by God that so many knowledgeable people let themselves be talked into believing these falsehoods. They are so gross and clumsy that, methinks, a tipsy boor could have told lies more plausibly and with greater slickness. How is it possible to combine and harmonize the ruling of an empire with preaching, praying, studying, and attending on the poor? Of all the offices, these are most characteristic of a pope. They were imposed by Christ so urgently, that he forbade his disciples to carry cloak or money, since any one who was responsible for a single family could scarcely attend to such responsibilities. Yet the pope wants to administer an empire while yet remaining pope. That is what those rogues have conceived who would like to use the pope's name to dominate the world, and would gladly restore the ruins of the Roman empire, through the pope and the name of Christ, to its former condition.

10. The pope should withdraw from temporal affairs, take his finger out of the pie, and lay no claim to the throne of

[27] In 1440, Lorenzo (Laurentius) Valla had proved this document to be a forgery in a work which Ulrich von Hutten republished in Germany in 1517, and which probably came into Luther's hands, to his immense indignation, in the spring of 1520. The "Donation" is a document of the eighth century, and pretends to be written by the Emperor Constantine, conveying to the pope the title to Rome, parts of Italy, and the "Islands of the Sea". On it the medieval popes based their claim to temporal power. Luther published an annotated edition of it in 1537.

the kingdom of Naples and Sicily. He has no more right to it than I have, and yet wants to be its overlord. It is robbery by violence, like almost every other of his possessions. Therefore, the emperor ought not to confirm him in such tenures, and, in cases where he has already done so, withdraw his support. Instead, let him point the pope to the Bible and the prayer books. The pope should let temporal lords rule land and people, while he himself preaches and prays.

The same principle should also apply to Bologna, Imola, Vicenza, Ravenna, and everywhere else in the provinces of Ancona, Romagna, and other parts of Italy, which the pope has seized by force and keeps without justification, meddling in these matters contrary to all the commandments of Christ and St. Paul. For this is what St. Paul says, "No one entangleth himself in the affairs of this life who should attend on the divine order of chivalry" [II Tim. 2:4]. Now the pope should be the head and the leader of this order of chivalry, yet he intervenes more in worldly affairs than any emperor or king; and so we must help him to renounce all this, and attend to his own order of chivalry. Christ Himself, whose Vicar he claims to be, never was desirous of dealing with the temporal régime. When a certain man asked Him to decide a question regarding his brother, He said, "Who made me a judge over you?" [Luke 12:14]. But the pope intrudes uninvited, seizes everything as if by divine right, until he himself no longer really knows what Christ was, though pretending to be His Vicar.

11. No one should ever again kiss the pope's feet. It is unchristian, indeed antichristian, that a pitiable and sinful man should let his feet be kissed by another who may be a hundred times better than himself. If it is intended to pay tribute to his authority, why does the pope not do it to others as a tribute to their sanctity? Compare them with one another, Christ and the pope; Christ washed' and dried His disciples' feet, but the disciples never washed His. The pope, presuming to be higher than Christ, reverses the relation, and with much condescension allows his feet to be kissed. But it would be proper for him, if any one were to ask permission, to refuse at all costs to allow it. Paul and Barnabas at Lystra would not let themselves be worshipped as gods, but declared, "We also are men like you"

[Acts 14:11–16]. But the lickspittles have brought matters to such a pass that they have made an idol for us. The result is that now no one fears God so much as he does the pope; no one does God equal reverence. This fact does not trouble the Romanists, and they will not permit the papal splendour to be diminished by the breadth of a hair. If they were Christian, and held God in greater honour than themselves, the pope would never be content to see God's honour despised and his own exalted. Nor would he allow any one to do him honour until he saw that God's honour was again exalted, and raised above his own.[28]

[Another example of the same overweening and scandalous arrogance is the hateful way in which the pope takes exercise in the open air, and is not content with horseback or a carriage although he is strong and well enough. But he prefers to be carried by bearers like an idol and with unheard-of magnificence. Dear readers, how does such satanic pride harmonize with Christ, who went on foot as did all His apostles? Has there ever been a king who travelled with the worldliness and pomp of him who claims to be chief of all those who ought to despise and flee from worldly glory: the Christians? Not that that disturbs us very much as far as he himself is concerned, but surely we are in danger of God's wrath, if we belaud this kind of arrogance and do not show our indignation. It is enough for the pope himself to indulge in foolish pomp and show of this kind, but it would be inexcusable for us to agree with it and approve it.

Further, what Christian will be happy at heart on watching the pope when he takes communion? He remains seated and looks like a milord; the sacrament is passed to him on a golden staff by a cardinal who bows to him on bended knee. It is as if the holy sacrament were not really worthy of the pope, for, although he is a poor and unclean sinner, he does not stand and do honour in the presence of God. That is how all other Christians, who are much holier than the Most Holy Father the pope, receive it—with every mark of reverence. Would it be astonishing if God sent an epidemic, because we tolerated such dishonour being done to Him, and because we praised it

[28] The three following paragraphs were lacking in Luther's earliest edition.

in our prelates, and ourselves participated in this accursed arrogance by our silence and adulation?

Similar things are seen when the pope carries the sacrament round in procession. He must be carried, but the sacrament is put in front of him like a jug of wine at table. In short, Christ counts for nothing in Rome, but the pope counts for everything. Yet the Romanists would urge upon us and threaten us to approve of their antichristian offences, and join in praise and respect them, contrary to God and all Christian teaching. May God grant His aid to a free council to instruct the pope that he, too, is human, and not greater than God, as he now regards himself.]

12. Pilgrimages to Rome should be disallowed. No person actuated merely by curiosity or his own religious feelings should be permitted to make a pilgrimage. Rather, he must be previously recognized by his minister, city council, or liege lord as having sufficient good reasons for making the pilgrimage. I do not say this because pilgrimages are wrong, but because they are ill-advised just now; for what one sees in Rome is not exemplary, but scandalous. The Romanists themselves have coined the saying, "The nearer Rome, the worse the Christians", and they bring about contempt of God and God's commandments. Another saying runs, "The first time one goes to Rome, one has to look for a rogue; the second time, one finds him; the third time, one brings him back." But they have become so slick by now that the three journeys are made at the same time, and indeed, in Rome they have coined us the catch-phrase, "It would be better not to have seen or known Rome."

Even if this were not true, there is a more cogent reason, namely, these pilgrimages seduce untrained minds into a false idea and a misapprehension of the divine commandments; simple folk hold that pilgrimages are works of rare merit, which is untrue. They are works of little merit, and, if frequently repeated, they are evil and seductive; God never gave such a commandment. But He has commanded that a man should cherish his wife and children, and perform the duties proper to the married state, besides serving and helping his neighbours. This is what happens when a man undertakes a pilgrimage to Rome, which no one has laid on him: it costs him 50 or 100 guilders more or less, while his wife and child, or his neighbour, suffer from distress at home. And yet the silly fellow thinks that his disobedience to, and contempt for, God's commandments will all be atoned for by the pilgrimage, which he undertook on his own responsibility, although it was pure, self-willed, or Satanic seduction. The popes have given this movement a fillip by their deceitful, trumped up, foolish "Golden Years", which stir up the people, blind them to God's commandments, and seduce them into delusive enterprises. In this way, the popes have caused exactly what they should have forbidden. But it brings money in, and fortifies a fictitious authority; therefore it must go on no matter whether it be contrary to the will of God or the salvation of souls.

In order to eradicate this false and seductive faith from untrained Christian minds, and to re-establish a right conception of meritorious works, all pilgrimages ought to be stopped. They are without value; no commandment enjoins them, and canonical obedience does not require them; nay, they give very frequent occasions for sin and for despising God's commandments. They give rise to a large mendicant class, who perpetrate innumerable villainies on these pilgrimages, and learn the habit of begging even when they are not in distress.

This gives rise to vagabondage and further abuses which I will not stay to recount. If any man to-day wants to go on pilgrimages or esteems them highly, let him first go to his pastor or his liege lord and tell him. If it turns out that his purpose is to do a good work, then let the pastor or the liege boldly trample the vow and the work underfoot as a satanic delusion, and tell the man to apply the money and effort required for the pilgrimage to fulfilling God's commandments, and to doing works a thousand times better than a pilgrimage, namely, meet the needs of his family and his poor neighbours. But if his object is only to satisfy his curiosity and go sightseeing in country and city, let him have his way. If, however, he vowed the pilgrimage during an illness, the vow must be annulled, and set aside. In contradistinction, the divine commandments must be stressed, with the idea that henceforward he will deem it sufficient to keep his baptismal vow to obey God's commandments. Nevertheless, for this once, and in order to satisfy his conscience, he may be allowed to fulfil his foolish vow. Men do not desire to walk in the straight path of God's commandments common to all; each finds new ways, and vows new vows for himself, as if he had already completed his obedience to all God's other commandments.

13. We now come to the great multitudes who swear many vows, but keep few. Do not be angry, my dear readers; I mean nothing wrong. For it is the truth, at once sweet and bitter, that no more mendicant houses should be built. God knows, there are already far too many of them. Would to God they were all dissolved, or all combined into two or three Orders. There is no merit, and there will never be any merit, in simply walking about over the face of the earth. I would therefore counsel that ten, or as many as may be necessary, should be joined together into one house and made into a single institution. Let this be endowed sufficiently so as to require no mendicancy. There is far more need for concern in what the multitudes of ordinary folk need for their salvation, than in the rules laid down for the mendicant orders by St. Francis, St. Dominic, St. Augustine, or any one else, especially as their purpose has not been fulfilled.

These Orders must also abandon preaching and hearing confessions, unless they are called upon and desired to do so by the bishops, pastors, churches, or the civil authorities. Their preaching and hearing confession has only led to mutual hatred and envy between priests and monks, and this has become a great offence and obstacle to the common people. Hence it is proper, and very desirable, that it should cease because it can be dispensed with. It appears unlikely that the Holy Roman papacy has increased this army inadvertently, but rather that the priests and bishops who are weary of his tyranny should not by any chance become too strong for him, and begin a reformation, a thing which His Holiness could not bear.

At the same time, the numerous sects and differences within the one Order should be abolished. These have often arisen for minor reasons, and been maintained for less; they are struggling with each other with indescribable hate and envy. The outcome is that the Christian faith, which intrinsically contains no such differences, is swept away by both parties. The effect of all this is the view that the essence and meaning of a true Christian life can be found among outer laws, works, and customs; but this can only cause hypocrisy, and lead to decay of the spirit, as everyone can see for himself.

The pope must be forbidden to institute, or set his seal on, any more of these Orders. Indeed, he must be ordered to dissolve some, or force them to reduce their numbers. For faith in Christ, which is alone the supreme good, and which exists apart from any of the Orders, suffers no small danger. The many different works and customs may easily lead men rather to rely on these works and customs than to care for faith. Without wise prelates in the cloisters caring more for preaching and practising the Christian faith than for the rules of their order, it cannot but be that the Order will do harm to simple folk, and lead them astray, since they only pay attention to works.

But to-day, almost everywhere, the prelates who possessed the faith and who founded the Orders, have passed away. In olden days among the children of Israel, when the Patriarchs had gone who had known God's works and marvellous deeds, their descendants, lacking knowledge of the divine works and faith, immediately began to establish idolatry and their own human works. In the same way, at the present time unhappily, the Orders, now lacking knowledge of the divine works and faith, only torment themselves pitiably, worrying and labouring about their own rules, laws, and customs, without ever reaching a true understanding of what constitutes a religious and virtuous life. This the Apostle foretold when he said (II Timothy 3 [5–7]): "They have a form of godliness, but there is nothing to support it; ever learning, but never able to come to the knowledge of true godliness." It is better to do without a cloister unless, at its head, is a spiritually-minded prelate versed in the Christian faith. For one who is not so minded cannot rule without doing hurt and harm, and the more so in proportion as he appears saintly and concerned with a godly life as far as his outer conduct goes.

In my view, it is necessary to decree, especially in these dangerous times of ours, that monasteries and priories should return to the way in which they were regulated by the apostles and for a long time afterwards. In those days, each votary was free to stay just as long as he pleased. For monasteries and priories were only Christian schools to teach Scripture and morals according to the Christian way. They trained students how to lead the churches, and how to preach. Thus we read that St. Agnes went to school, and we still see it done in certain nunneries, like those at Quedlimburg and elsewhere. In truth, all monasteries and priories ought to be so free, that the brethren might serve God fully, and not under constraint.

Later on, however, they were restricted by vows, and turned into permanent prisoners, until, to-day, greater respect is paid to these vows than to those made at baptism. But day by day, more and more, do we see, hear, read, and learn what sort of fruit they bear. I fear that my opinion will be regarded as altogether foolish, but I shall not worry about that. My view accords with my conscience, no matter who rejects it. I am well acquainted with the ways in which those vows are kept, especially that of continence. This vow is very widespread throughout these cloisters, yet Christ never commanded it. Indeed, both He Himself and St. Paul said that to keep it was given only to few. Would that help were brought to everyone, and would that Christian souls were not taken prisoner by arbitrary customs and rules of human devising!

14. We know also how the priesthood has declined. Many a poor priest is responsible for wife and child, and has a troubled conscience; yet no one lends a hand, although it would be a very kindly act to help them. The pope and the bishop may let these abuses go on untouched, even though ruin ensue, if ruin it must be. So I will obey my conscience, and speak my mind freely, in spite of hurting the pope, the bishops, or anyone else. What I say is that, according to what Christ and the Apostles instituted, each single town should have a pastor or bishop. Paul says this clearly in Titus 1, and also that that pastor shall not be compelled to live without a lawful wife. He may have one, as St. Paul writes in I Timothy 3 [:2, 4] and Titus 1 [:6] and say: "A bishop shall be a man without reproach and the husband of only one wife, having his children in subjection with all gravity, etc." According to St. Paul, a bishop and a pastor are identical, and

this is also St. Jerome's testimony. The Scriptures know nothing of the present-day kind of bishops who, by ordinances of the Christian church, have authority over several pastors.

Thus the Apostle teaches us plainly that the method to be followed among Christians is that each separate town should choose from its church a scholarly and devout citizen, and lay upon him the duties of a pastor; his maintenance being cared for by the church. He should be quite free to marry, or not. At his side, he should have several priests or deacons, either married or not, as he prefers, to help him in ministering to the church and the people at large with sermons and the sacraments. This is the custom retained to our own day in the Greek church. There, after apostolic times, when there was much persecution and many disputes with heretics, many of the holy Fathers voluntarily refrained from marriage, in order to devote themselves more fully to study, and to be prepared instantly, either to defend the faith, or to die.

At that point the papacy interfered entirely on its own initiative, and turned this practice into a universal rule; they forbade ordained persons to marry. The devil must have ordered it, for St. Paul declared in I Timothy 4 [:1–4], "Teachers will come with doctrines of devils, forbidding to marry." Unfortunately a more lamentable state of affairs has ensued than can be recounted; moreover, it has caused the Greek church to separate off, and multiplied boundless quarrels, sins, shame, and scandal, as always happens with what the devil initiates and incites.

What ought we to do about it? My advice is, Break the bonds, let each follow his own preference whether to marry or not to marry. But then there will have to be quite a different arrangement and order of things in regard to salaries; also the whole of the canon law must be razed to the ground; nor must many benefices become Rome's. I fear that avarice is one reason for the rule of celibacy, lamentable and incontinent though that condition is; with the result that every man wants to be a priest, or wishes his son to study with that in view. But continence is not the life he thinks of, for that can be practised without joining the priesthood. Rather the purpose is to receive temporal support without work or worry, contrary to God's commandment, Genesis 3 [:19], "In the sweat of thy face shalt thou eat bread", a commandment which the Romanists have coloured to mean that reciting the liturgy and the administration of the sacraments are their work.

I am not referring just now to the pope, bishops, canons, and monks: offices which God did not institute. They have put burdens on themselves, and must carry them. My purpose is to speak of the ministry, which God did institute, and which was intended to train a church by sermons and sacraments, with pastors living among the people and keeping house as other people do. Such men should be granted permission by a Christian council to marry, in order to avoid temptation and sin. For, if God has not forbidden them, no man should or may do so, not even an angel of heaven, not to mention the pope. Anything to the contrary in the canon law is pure fabrication and idle chatter.

Furthermore, my advice to anyone taking Holy Orders or adopting any other vocation, is on no account to swear to the bishop to remain continent. Rather, point out to him that he has no authority to demand such a vow, and that it is an act of impious tyranny to demand it. If any prefers or is compelled to say, as some do, *"Quantum fragilitas humana permittet"*,[29] let him frankly give it the negative sense of *"non promitto castitatem"*;[30] for *"fragilitas humana non permittit caste vivere"*;[31] but only *"angelica fortitudo et celestis virtus"*,[32] in order that his conscience may not be burdened by any vows.

I do not wish either to encourage or discourage those, who have as yet no wife, on the question whether they should marry or remain single. I leave that to be pronounced by an ecumenical, Christian council, and also by the conscience of the man's better self. But I will not conceal my own real view from the many who are distressed, nor will I withhold from them words of comfort. I mean those who have fallen into disgrace with a woman, and have a child, and who suffer grievously in conscience because she is called a priest's prosti-

[29] "As far as human nature allows."
[30] "I do not promise continence."
[31] "Human frailty does not allow continent living."
[32] "The strength of angels and the heroism of heaven."

tute and the children scorned as "priest-brats". My claim to
be a court-fool gives me that right.

There is many a duteous priest, otherwise blameless, who,
because of his frailty, has fallen into dishonour with a woman.
Both are so minded in the depth of their hearts that, if they
could only do it with good conscience, they would gladly live
faithfully and permanently together in a regular, conjugal
union. But, even though they both have to suffer public disrepute, they are certainly espoused in God's sight. I will even
add that if the two people are so minded and if, on that basis,
they enter into a common life, they should keep their consciences undaunted. Let him take and keep her as if she were
his lawful wife, and in other respects live in a regular way
with her as a married man. Let him disregard the pope's pleasure or displeasure, and the transgression of canon or man-made
law. The salvation of your soul is of greater importance than
tyrannical, oppressive, and wanton laws, unnecessary for salvation, and not commanded by God. You must do as did the
Children of Israel, who stole the wages they had earned from
the Egyptians; or do like a servant who steals his earnings
from his wicked master. So, too, you should steal from the
pope your conjugal wife and child.

Let him who has faith enough to make the venture, boldly
follow my word; I shall not lead him astray. I have not the
power of a pope, but I have the power of a Christian to help
and advise my neighbour to escape from his sins and temptations; and that not without rhyme or reason. Not every pastor
can live without a woman, not just on account of the weakness of the flesh, but much more on account of keeping his
house. If, then, he employs a woman, and the pope will permit him to do this, but will not allow him to have her in
marriage, that means nothing else than leaving a man and a
woman alone together, and yet forbidding them to yield to
temptation. It is like bringing fire and straw together, and trying to forbid blaze or smoke.

The pope in making such a rule has no more power than
if he were to forbid eating, or drinking, or the performance
of other natural functions, or growing fat. Hence it is no one's
duty to obey this rule. On the other hand, the pope is responsible for all the sins which have thereby been committed,

for all the souls which have consequently been lost, and for all the consciences which have been confused and tortured. The fact is that he ought to have been chased out of the world long ago, as a man who has throttled so many miserable people with this Satanic halter of his. But I hope that God will be more merciful to multitudes when they die than the pope was to them in their lifetime. Nothing good has ever issued, or will ever issue, from the papacy and its rules.

In spite of being contrary to the pope's ruling, and even if the married state be entered into in spite of the pope's specific ruling, that ruling is null and void, and retains no validity. For God's commandment, which ordains that no one shall separate man and wife, far overrides the pope's ruling. Nor may God's commandment be broken or deferred for the sake of the papal ordinances. Nevertheless, many hare-brained jurists have sided with the pope, devised impediments to marriage, and so have prevented, or destroyed, or confused the conjugal state. God's commandment has consequently been entirely defeated. Is there any need for me to enlarge on this? In the entire canon law, there are not two lines which can teach anything to a devout Christian; and, unfortunately, there are so many erroneous and dangerous regulations, that nothing better could be done than to make a bonfire of them.

If you should object that the marriage of the clergy would be scandalous unless the pope had previously given a dispensation, I would reply that the scandal in it is the fault of the Roman papacy for setting up such a ruling without any right, and against God. In God's sight, and according to Holy Scripture, there is no offence. Moreover, in a case where the pope, with his greed and his oppressive regulations, can grant a dispensation on payment of a fee, in that very instance any Christian whatever may grant a dispensation just for the sake of God and the salvation of souls. For Christ has set us free from all man-made laws, especially when they operate contrary to God and the soul's good, as St. Paul teaches in Galatians 5 [:1] and I Corinthians 9 [:4 f.].

15. Nor would I forget the sad condition of the monasteries. The evil spirit, who to-day confuses all classes by man-made laws and makes life intolerable, has taken possession of cer-

tain abbots, abbesses, and prelates. The result is that they so govern the brothers and sisters that they consign them the more speedily to hell; meanwhile, the poor things lead a lamentable existence here on earth, as do all martyrs to the devil. To go into detail, the papists reserve to their own dispensation all, or at least some, of the deadly sins which are committed in private, and from which no friar is allowed to absolve his fellow under his vow of obedience and on penalty of excommunication. Nowhere are people angels all the time, but only men of flesh and blood; and they would rather risk threats and excommunication than confess their secret sins to the prelates and appointed confessors. Over and above this, they take the sacraments, and do so with such consciences that they become *irregulares*,[33] and fall into many other miseries. O blind shepherds, O fatuous prelates, O ravening wolves!

What I say on this point is: It is right for the prelate to punish open and notorious sins; these alone and no others may he reserve to himself, and make exceptional cases of them. But he should have no authority to deal with secret sins, not even the most scandalous. If a prelate claims jurisdiction over these, then he is acting as a tyrant, acting without justification, and invading the judgment of God. Hence I give this counsel to those same poor creatures, whether friars or nuns. If your Superior will not allow you to confess your secret sins to someone of your own choice, nevertheless take them and bewail them to the brother or sister whom you prefer. Receive your absolution and comfort; go away, follow your bent, and do your duty. Only remain firm in the faith that you have been absolved, and that nothing further is necessary. Do not let yourself be troubled or led astray by threats of excommunication, or of being *"irregulares"*, or anything of this kind. These apply only to public or known sins such as no one wants to confess; they do not apply to you. What are you thinking of, you blind prelates, trying to exclude secret sins by a fence of threats? Leave untouched what you cannot openly deal with; let the judgment and mercy of God work among those who belong to your care. God has not delivered them so com-

---

[33] A term applied to monks and nuns guilty of offences of three classes: especially those of the body, of neglecting the sacrament, and of 23 specified cases.

pletely into your hands that He has let them go from His own. Indeed you have but the smaller share in those under your rule. Let your statutes be statutes, but do not exalt them into heavenly decrees, nor give them the force of divine justice.

16. Further, masses on anniversaries, or at celebrations, and for the dead, ought to be either entirely abolished, or at least reduced in number. It is plain to see that they become merely subjects for contempt, things with which God will be greatly angered, seeing that they will be celebrated only for money, and as an excuse for eating and drinking to excess. How can it be to God's good pleasure when, alas, the vigils and masses are dreadfully gabbled, in a way which is neither reading nor praying? Even when they are treated as prayers, it is not from a loving devotion, or for God's sake, but for the sake of pay, or to carry out a bounden duty. Yet it is impossible for any work to please God, or to serve any purpose with Him, unless offered out of unconstrained love. Therefore, it is always a Christian act to abolish or reduce everything which we see abused, and which provokes God rather than reconciles Him. It would seem to be far preferable, and surely more pleasing to God, as well as much better in itself, that a Chapter, a church, or a cloister, should combine all their annual masses and vigils into a single celebration. On an appointed day, let them hold a real vigil and mass, in earnestness of heart, in devotion and faith, on behalf of all their benefactors; this, rather than observing thousands upon thousands of them every year, with a special mass for each benefactor, but celebrated without any devotion or faith. O beloved Christians, God is not concerned with how often, but with how truly we pray. He even condemns long and frequent prayers, Matthew 6 [:7], and says they will only earn the more punishment. But the greediness of priests who cannot trust God gives rise to the familiar state of affairs, as it leads to fear of death from starvation otherwise.

17. Certain of the penances or penalties of canon law ought to be abolished, especially the *interdict* which is undoubtedly a device of the Evil One. Is it not a trick of Satan to wipe

away one sin by causing many sins of a worse character? For
it is a greater sin to silence God's Word and to abolish serving
Him, than to strangle twenty popes at once, not to mention
merely killing one priest or keeping back church property.
That is another example of the gentle virtues taught in the
canon law. The reason that this law is called "spiritual" is
that it derives from the spirit—not, however, the Holy Spirit,
but the Evil Spirit.

Excommunication must never be employed as a penalty except where the Scriptures prescribe its use, i.e., against those
who believe amiss, or who live in open sin; but it should not
be used for the sake of temporal advantages. But, to-day, the
opposite is the case; everyone lives and believes as he will,
most of all those who harass and plunder other people with
interdicts; and every one of the bans is pronounced purely for
the sake of temporal property, all of it owing to the holy
Canon Law of Unrighteousness, with which I have already
dealt at greater length in a sermon.[34]

The remaining punishments and penances, suspensions, ir-
regularities, aggravations, re-aggravations, depositions, lightnings, thunders, cursings and damnings, and whatever else
there is of that kind, ought to be buried thirty feet deep un-
derground, till neither their name nor their memory continued
on earth. The Evil One, freed from fetters by the canon law,
has brought these dreadful plagues and sufferings into the
heavenly kingdom of holy Christendom, and has effected
nothing thereby except to destroy men's souls or hinder their
faith. Christ's word could well be applied to it when He said,
Matthew 23 [:13]: "Woe unto you scribes, you have seized
authority to teach, and you close the Kingdom of Heaven to
men. You do not enter yourselves and you prevent those who
are entering."

18. All festival days should be abolished, and Sunday alone
retained. But, if it is preferred to keep the festivals of Our
Lady and of the greater saints, they should all be transferred
to Sundays, or observed only at morning Mass, after which
the whole day should be a working day. The reason for the

[34] *Sermon von dem Bann.*

proposed change is the present misuse of festival days in drinking, gaming, idleness, and all sorts of sins. In this way, we incur the wrath of God more on holy days than on the rest. Thus all is turned upside down till "holy days" are not holy, whereas "working days" are "holy". Not only is no service done to God and His saints, but great irreverence is shown on the numerous "holy" days. Yet certain senseless prelates believe that if, in accordance with their blind feelings of devotion, they observe a festival of St. Ottilia or St. Barbara, they have done a good work; although they would be doing a much better work if, in honour of a certain saint, they turned a holy day into a working day.

In addition, the ordinary man suffers two material injuries over and above this spiritual injury, namely, he neglects his work, and he spends more money than otherwise. He also weakens his body, and makes himself less skilful. We see this happen daily, but no one thinks of reforming it. In a case like this, no one ought to ask whether the pope ordained these festivals, or whether a dispensation or permission is required in advance. Each community, council, and administration has authority to abolish and prevent, apart from the knowledge or consent of pope or bishop, anything contrary to God, and hurtful to man in body and soul. Persons of the ruling class are also under an obligation to prevent it, on danger to their soul's salvation, even against the will of pope or bishop, who themselves indeed ought to be the first to prevent it.

Especially ought we to root out the anniversaries which celebrate the consecrating of a church. They have become nothing less than occasions for frequenting taverns, fairs, and gaming places, to the increase of irreverence towards God and the dereliction of the soul. It is useless to repeat the argument that it had a good beginning, and it is a good thing to do. God suspended His own law, which He had sent down from heaven, when it was turned into an abuse; and every day He changes what He has ordained, and destroys what He has made, on account of the same sort of abuses. In Psalm 18 [:26] it is written of Him, "Thou showest Thyself perverse with the perverse."

19. The grades or degrees within which marriage is for-

bidden should be altered, such as those affecting godparents, or third and fourth degrees of kinship. Here the pope, in his scandalous traffic, grants a dispensation for a fee, where every individual pastor should be able to grant dispensations without fee, and for the eternal good of the people concerned. Would God that every pastor might do or permit gratis everything that Rome must be paid for. This would untie the monetary strangle-hold of the canon law; e.g., indulgences, letters of indulgence, butter letters, mass letters, and whatever dispensations and deceptions are otherwise to be had in Rome, by which the people, poor things, are tricked and eased of their money. For, if the pope has the right to sell gilded nooses and spiritual snares (I should have said canonical wares) for money, then, of a truth, a pastor has much more right to tear them apart and tread them underfoot for God's sake. In fact, he has no right, nor has the pope, to sell them like goods at a fair.

In this connection, it should be said that the question of fasting ought to be a matter of free choice, and the foods which may be eaten left unrestricted, as the gospel has ordained. For the people at Rome themselves scoff at fasts, and leave us in the provinces to use as food oil with which they would not grease their shoes. But they sell us permission to eat butter and other things, in spite of the holy apostle who says that the gospel gives us complete freedom to do everything. But with their canon law, the Romanists have bound and robbed us in order that we should have to buy ourselves off again. Meanwhile they have made our consciences so pallid and timid, that it is not felt commendable to preach about this liberty any longer, because the ordinary people soon become greatly alarmed. They think that eating butter is a greater sin than lying, swearing, or committing fornication. All the same, what men have decreed is man-made, no matter where it is said to originate; and no good ever comes out of it.

20. The extra-parochial chapels and churches, away from inhabited parts, should be pulled down. I mean those which have recently become the goal of pilgrimages, e.g., Wilsnack, Sternberg, Trèves, the Grimmenthal, and now Regensburg and many others. Oh, what a heavy and pitiful reckoning inevita-

bly awaits the bishops who agree to these tricks of the devil's own, and get profit out of them! They ought to be the first to stop them. But they regard it as something divine and holy, and do not see that the devil is behind it to increase avarice, to establish a hollow and fictitious faith, to weaken parish churches, to multiply taverns and spread immorality, to waste money and labour to no purpose, and lead humble folk about by the nose. If they had read Scripture as well as they have read the damnable canon law, they would know how to provide a remedy.

It is useless to argue that miracles are seen in these places, for the Evil Spirit can also work miracles, as Christ declared (Matthew 24 [:24]). If they got to work in all seriousness and forbade things of this kind, the miracles would soon cease. On the other hand, if they were of God, no prohibition would prevent their taking place. If there were no other indication that this custom were not of God, it would be enough in itself that the people go there rowdily and without common sense, in crowds like cattle, which unseemliness would be impossible if it were of God. And as God never commanded anything of the sort, there is neither "obedience" nor merit in doing it. Therefore, the thing to do is to step in boldly and stop the people. For what has not been commanded, but is more concerned for itself than for what God has commanded, is of a truth inspired by the very devil. It also results in harm to the parish churches, in that they are held in less respect. To put it in a nutshell: these things are indications of great unbelief among the people; for, if their faith were as it should be, they would find everything needful in their own churches which it is ordained they should attend.

But what is it my duty to say? Each bishop is only thinking how he can start one of these pilgrimages in his own province, not caring whether the people believe and live as they should; the rulers are like the people, one blind man leads another. Nay, in places where the pilgrimages are poorly attended, a movement is set on foot to canonize saints, but not for the sake of honouring the saints who would be reverenced without canonization; rather it is to draw crowds and cause money to flow. At this point, the pope and bishops lend their aid, indulgences pour in for which there is always enough money.

But as to God's commandments, no one is concerned about them, nor follows them, nor has money for them. The pity is that we are so blind that we do not leave the devil alone to play his tricks in his own way; rather, we support him and multiply them. I wish people would leave the saints in peace, and not mislead humble folk. What spirit was it that gave the pope authority to canonize saints? Who tells him whether they are holy or not? Are there not sins enough already on earth without tempting God, interfering when He judges, and setting up the blessed saints as decoys for bringing in money?

In my view, therefore, the saints should be allowed to canonize themselves. Nay, only God should canonize them. Let every one of us stay each in his own parish, where he will discover more useful work than in all the making of pilgrimages, even if they were all combined into one. Here, at home, you will find baptism, sacrament, preaching, and your neighbour; these are more important to you than all the saints in heaven, for all of them have been sanctified by God's Word and by the sacraments. While we continue to despise these great matters, God is just in judging us with His wrath and in allowing the devil to lead us hither and thither, to institute pilgrimages, build chapels and churches, to set about canonizing saints, and other foolish things. Thus we, although having the right faith, fall into new misbeliefs. This is what the devil brought about in olden times when he misled the children of Israel from the temple at Jerusalem to innumerable other places. It was all done in God's name, and with every appearance of sanctity; all the prophets preached against it, and were martyred for doing so. But, nowadays, no one preaches against it, perhaps for fear that bishop, pope, priest, and monk will suffer martyrdom! In pursuance of this practice of canonization, Antonius of Florence, and certain others, are shortly to be sainted and canonized. Hitherto they have only served the glory of God and passed as good examples; but now their sanctity is to be vaunted, and so made to bring in money.

Even if the canonization of a saint were proper in the early days, it is never so to-day; just as many another thing was proper in early days, but now hurtful and scandalous; e.g., feast days, relics treasured in churches, and "ornaments". For it is plain that the objective in canonizing saints is not the glory of God, nor the reform of Christians, but money and notoriety. A church wants something special, more than the rest are or have, and it would be sorry if another possessed a similar thing, or if what made it outstanding became common property. Spiritual treasures have been so completely misused, and made to serve the increase of temporal goods in these wicked, modern days, that everything which can be called by the name of God is made to serve Avarice. Further, any such special possession only leads to schisms, sects, and to pride, if one church is different from the others; and this, again, is accompanied by mutual contempt and self-exaltation. Yet all the things that are good in God's sight are common to all and equally at their disposal, for they are only meant to serve the whole. But the pope likes things as they are, and he would be sorry to see all Christians equal and united.

It is relevant here to say that we should abolish, ignore, or else make common to all churches, the licences, the bulls, and whatever else the pope may have for sale in Rome at the place where he fleeces people. For if he sells or gives rights to livings, if he grants privileges, indulgences, graces, advantages, faculties, to Wittenberg, Halle, Venice, and especially to his own city of Rome, why does he not give them to the churches in general? Is it not his duty to do, without fee and for God's sake, everything in his power for all Christian people, even to the extent of shedding his blood for them? Why is it that he gives or sells to one church, but not to another? Or must it be the case, in the eyes of His Holiness, that accursed gold makes a very great difference between Christians, who, nevertheless, have the same baptism, gospel, Christ, God, and all else? Are the Romanists trying to blind us while yet we have eyes to see, and fool us while yet our reason is unspoiled, till we do obeisance to this greed, and villainy, and jugglery? A pastor only acts as a pastor if you have money, but not otherwise; and yet the popes are not ashamed to forward these villainies with their bulls here, there, and elsewhere.

So my view is, if this tomfoolery is not abolished, that all duteous Christian men and women should open their eyes, and not allow themselves to be led astray by the Romish bulls, seals, and make-believes. Let each stay at home in his own church. Let each be content with the baptism, gospel, faith,

Christ, and God he knows. These are everywhere the same. Let the pope remain a blind leader of the blind. Neither angel nor pope can give you as much as God gives you in your own church. Nay, the pope seduces you away from the gifts of God which you receive unpaid for, to his own "gifts" which you must buy; he gives you lead instead of gold, hides instead of meat, the string instead of the purse, wax instead of honey, words instead of goods, the letter instead of the spirit, as you may see with your own eyes but refuse to notice. If you were to think of going to heaven riding on his parchment and wax, your chariot would break only too soon, and you would tumble into hell; but in God's name, No! Be content with the one sure norm; what you have to buy from the pope is neither good nor godly. What comes from God is not only freely given, but all the world suffers and lies under condemnation for not wishing to receive it, although it is free: I mean the gospel and the works of God. We have deserved it from God that we should have been thus led astray, because we have neglected His holy Word and the grace given at our baptism. It is all as St. Paul says, "God will send a great error unto all those who have believed not the truth given for their salvation, that they should believe and follow a lie and villainy" [II Thess. 2:11 f.], as they deserve.

21. Probably one of our greatest needs is to abolish all mendicancy everywhere in Christendom. No one living among Christians ought to go begging. It would be an easy law to make, if only we dared, and were in earnest that every town should support its own poor. No outside beggars should be allowed in, whatever they called themselves, whether pilgrims, friars, or mendicant orders. Every town could provide for its own poor, or, if it were too small, the surrounding villages could be urged to contribute. In any case, they are compelled to-day to provide for the same number of vagabonds and wicked rogues under the name of the mendicant Orders. By this means it would be possible to learn who were really poor and who not.

An overseer or guardian would be required. He would know all the poor, and would inform the town council or the pastor what they needed, or what the best arrangements would be.

In my view, nowhere else is there so much wickedness and deception as in mendicancy, and yet all of it could be easily done away with. In addition, much woe falls on the common people on account of this open and general mendicancy. I have calculated that each of the five or six mendicant Orders[85] makes a visitation of one and the same place more than six or seven times every year. Besides this there are the common beggars, and those who beg alms in the name of a patron saint, and then the professional pilgrims. This reckons up to sixty times a year that the town is laid under tribute, besides what goes to the secular authorities in rates, taxes, and assessments; all this the Roman papacy steals in offering its bargains, and then consumes to no purpose. To me it is one of the greatest of God's miracles that, in spite of all, we can still live and keep ourselves.

But certain people think that, if my proposals were adopted, the poor would not fare properly, and that fewer great stone houses and cloisters would be built, and fewer so well adorned. All this I can well believe. Nor is any of it necessary. He who has chosen poverty, ought not to be rich; but if a man chooses wealth, let him put his hand to the plough and get his wealth for himself out of the earth. It is sufficient if the poor are decently provided for, in such a way that they do not die of hunger or cold. It is not seemly that one man should live in idleness on the labours of his fellows, or possess wealth and luxury through the hardships which others suffer, as is the prevailing, perverse custom. St. Paul says, "If a man will not work, neither shall he eat" [II Thess. 3:10]. God has commanded no one to live at another man's expense, except preachers and administrating priests for the sake of their spiritual labours. As St. Paul says in I Corinthians 9 [:14], and as Christ said to the Apostles, "Every labourer is worthy of his hire."

22. I am also concerned to think that the numerous masses, which have been endowed in benefices and cloisters, are both of very little use, and greatly incur the wrath of God. For that reason, it would be wise to endow no more of them, but to

[85] Franciscans, Dominicans, Augustinians, Carmelites, and Servites.

abolish many of those that are already endowed. For it is obvious that they are only held to be sacrifices and good works in spite of the fact that, like baptism and penance, they are sacraments which are of value, not to others, but only to him who receives them. Yet, nowadays, it has become prevalent to say masses for the living and the dead. Every hope is based on these masses; that is why so many masses have been endowed, and why the state of affairs which we are familiar with, has arisen. My proposal is perhaps too bold and unprecedented, especially for those who fear to lose their trade and livelihood, if masses of this kind were to come to an end. Unfortunately, it is now many years since it became a trade at which one worked for the sake of a temporal livelihood. Therefore, my advice to a man in future would be to become a shepherd, or else learn a handicraft, rather than become a priest or a monk, unless he were well aware in advance what it means to celebrate mass.

What I have said here does not apply to the ancient monasteries and cathedral chapters, which were undoubtedly founded for the sake of noblemen's children. According to German custom, only some of a nobleman's issue can become landowners or rulers, and it was intended that the rest should enter these monasteries, and there be free to serve God, to study, to become scholarly people, and to help others to do so. But my present subject is the recent monasteries, founded only for repeating the liturgy and saying mass. Their example is pressing itself on the older institutions and imposing similar repetitions of liturgy and mass, until even these institutions serve little or no useful purpose. But by God's grace, they finally, and deservedly, come to the drudgery of being mere choral singers and pipe-organ players, and to the saying of cold and unattractive masses,—all of them means by which the temporal endowment-incomes are earned and spent. Surely the pope, the bishops, and the doctors ought to go into these things and report on them. But it is precisely they who are responsible for most of it. They always let it proceed if it brings in money. Always one blind man leads another. That is what is done by Avarice and canon law.

Further, it ought no longer to be permitted that one person should hold more than one canonry or one living. Each should be content with a moderate position, and leave something for his neighbour. This would put an end to the excuses of those who say that, in order to support their station properly, they require more than one office. But it would be possible to interpret the term "properly" so broadly, that a whole country would not suffice to support it. Covetousness and hidden unbelief, in a case like this, go, of a truth, hand in hand, so that what pretends to be the requirements for "proper support" is simply the pretences of greed and unbelief.

23. The "fraternities",[36] indulgences, letters of indulgence, butter-briefs, mass briefs, dispensations and the like, ought all to be drowned and destroyed as containing nothing good. If the pope can grant you a dispensation to eat butter, or from hearing mass, he should allow a pastor the power to grant it; indeed he had no right to deprive him of the power. I am also including (with the pope) the "fraternities" which grant indulgences, say masses, and prescribe good works. My dear friend, when you were baptized, you entered into fellowship with Christ, with all the angels and saints, and with all Christians on earth. Hold fast to it and do what it demands, and you have all the necessary fraternities. Let the other things be as attractive as they may, they are still only counters as compared with coins. But if a "fraternity" were such that it subscribed funds to feed the poor, or otherwise gave help to someone, that "fraternity" would be sound, and would find its indulgences and merits in heaven. At present, however, their privileges only lead to gluttony and drunkenness.

The first thing is to chase out of Germany the papal legates with the "faculties" which they sell to us at a high figure, although the traffic is nought but trickery. As things are, they take the money, and make unrighteousness righteous, dissolve vows, oaths, and agreements, thereby destroying and teaching us to destroy faithfulness and faith, which men have promised one another; and they plead that the pope has authority to do all these things. This means that the Evil One speaks through

[36] Associations of laymen for purposes of prayer and organizing good works.

them; also, that they are selling impious doctrine, and taking our money to teach us to sin and to lead us to hell.

If there were no other insidious device making it clear that the pope was the true Antichrist, this particular example would prove it. Do you hear that, O pope, you who are not most holy, but most sinful? Would that God in heaven immediately destroyed your throne, and sent it into the abyss of hell! Who is it that gave you power to exalt yourself above your God? to relax and break His commandments, and to teach Christians, especially those of Germany, whom all the books of history esteem for their noble, steadfast, and faithful character, to be inconstant, perjured traitors, and faithless profligates? God's commandment is that we should keep our vows and our honour even with our enemies. Yet you interfere and pretend to relax this commandment; and you claim, in your heretical and antichristian decretals, that you have power to do so. Satan, the Evil One, uses you as his mouthpiece and scribe to lie as he never lied before. You even force the meaning of Scripture and twist it to suit yourself. Oh Christ, my Lord! look down; let Thy final day come and destroy this nest of devils at Rome. There sits the man of whom St. Paul said, "The Man of Sin and the son of perdition shall exalt himself over thee, and sit in thy church setting himself up as God" [II Thess. 2:3 ff.]. To exercise papal power as the pope does, what else is it than to teach and multiply sin and wickedness, to lead souls into perdition under God's name and prerogative?

In the days of old, the children of Israel had unknowingly been deceived into swearing an oath with the Gibeonites their enemies, but they had to keep it [Joshua 9:6 ff.]. King Zedekiah broke his oath with the king of Babylon, and so he and the whole of his people were miserably defeated [II Kings 24:20 and 25:4 ff.]. Among our own selves, a hundred years ago, Wladislaus, that splendid king of Poland and Hungary, was slain with a large number of his people, because he allowed himself to be misled by the papal legate and cardinal, to break the propitious and advantageous treaty which he had sworn with the Turks.[87] Sigismund, the religious-minded em-

[87] The Turkish treaty was made in 1443 and broken at the instance of Cardinal Julian Cesarine the following year. The king perished at Varna November 10, 1444.

peror, had no success after the council at Constance, when he allowed those rogues to break the safe-conduct which had been given to John Huss and Jerome of Prague.[38] Out of this arose all sorts of trouble between Bohemia and ourselves. And in living memory, God spare us, how much Christian blood has been poured out for the sake of the treaty sworn between Emperor Maximilian and King Louis of France, which Pope Julius instigated, and then broke? How could I possibly recount all the woe which the popes have caused, with presumption like the devil, in breaking oaths and vows made between powerful princes, to suit their own fancy and to the advantage of their own pocket? I hope that the Last Day is at hand; things surely cannot possibly grow worse than what the conduct of the papacy has brought to pass. It has suppressed God's commandments, replacing them with its own. If that is not the Antichrist, let some one else say what it is. But more of this another time and more incisively.

24. It is high time that we took up the Hussite question and dealt with it seriously. We ought to make an earnest effort to get the Hussites to join us, and for us to unite ourselves with them.[39] It would put an end to defamation, hatred, and envy on both sides. In accord with my present boldness, I will be the first to propound an opinion, but I will defer to any one with a better grasp of the situation.

(a) In the first place we must confess the truth faithfully, and stop our self-justification. We must grant the point to the Hussites, that John Huss and Jerome of Prague were burnt at Constance, despite the Christian safe-conduct vouched to them by the pope and the emperor. This was done contrary

[38] Not to Jerome, though he too was burned at Constance, in 1416. John Huss had a safe conduct from Sigismund, but this was overridden, and Huss was burned at Constance in 1415.

[39] The Hussites represented a popular religious movement in Bohemia which became quite vigorous owing to widespread indignation at the burning of John Huss in Constance, July 6, 1415. The more moderate, the Calistines or Utraquists, demanded preaching in the vernacular, communion in both kinds, reform of the clergy, and prohibition of property and secular jurisdiction to the clergy. The extreme party, Taborites, would prohibit the use of images and the worship of saints, condemn purgatory, etc.

to God's commandment, and gave the Hussites every cause for embitterment. Of course they ought to have been perfect Christians, and to that extent their duty was to have endured this deep wrong of ours, and this disobedience to God; nevertheless, it was no part of their duty to approve it, or acknowledge it as right. Indeed to-day they ought rather to sacrifice life and limb than agree that it was right to break a Christian safe-conduct vouchsafed by the pope and the emperor, and to act faithlessly against it. While, then, the impatience of the Hussites was a fault, the pope and those who side with him are far more responsible for all the misery, all the wrong-doing, and all loss of life which have ensued since the Council of Constance.

I have no desire to justify at this stage John Huss's propositions or defend his error, although to my way of thinking he wrote nothing erroneous. I do not find it difficult to believe that they who dealt in that faithless way with a Christian safe-conduct, and broke God's commandment, did not pronounce a fair verdict or a righteous condemnation. They were certainly possessed rather by the Evil One than by the Holy Spirit. Nobody can doubt that the Holy Spirit does not work contrary to God's decrees; and nobody is so ignorant as not to know that to break a safe-conduct and a pledge is contrary to God's commandments, even though the promises were given to the devil himself, not to mention a heretic. It is also public knowledge that such a safe-conduct was given to John Huss and the Bohemians, and was not respected. He was burned in spite of it. I am not to be understood as meaning that John Huss was a saint or a martyr, as certain of his fellow-countrymen maintain. But I do declare my belief that he suffered a wrong, and that his books and his teaching were wrongly condemned. The terrible judgments of God are given in secret, and are such that no other than Himself has a right to reveal and publish abroad. My point is: John Huss may have been a heretic as bad as could be found; nevertheless he was unjustly banned, and was burned contrary to God's will. No one should bring pressure and compel the Bohemians to assent to the act, or we shall reach no agreement. What must unite us is, not an obstinate opinion, but the plain truth. It does not help matters to say, as was done at the time, that a safe-conduct need not be respected if given to a heretic. That would be the equivalent of the self-contradiction of saying that one ought *not* to keep a commandment of God's if one *is* to keep a commandment of God's. The devil has made the Romanists insane and foolish, or they would have understood what it is they were saying and doing. God has commanded that oaths should be respected even though the world fall. How much more when it is only a question of letting a heretic go free. Heretics ought to be persuaded by argument, and not by fire; and this was the way of the early Fathers. If it were wise policy to suppress heretics by burning them, then the executioners would be the most learned teachers on earth. We should have no need to study books any longer, for he who could overthrow his fellow by violence would have the right to burn him at the stake.

(*b*) In the second place, the emperor and princes ought to send the Bohemians an embassy of religious-minded and perspicacious bishops and scholars, but never a cardinal, or papal legate, or inquisitor. These officials are much too unschooled in Christian affairs. Nor do they seek the soul's good, but, like all papal play-actors, only their own power, or advantage, or glory. These persons were also the principal figures in the calamitous business at Constance. But those who constitute the embassy which we ought to send, should inquire among the Bohemians as to the nature of their faith, and whether it would be possible to unite all their sects into a whole. This is where the pope, for the good of his soul, ought long ago to have asserted his authority. Following the statutes of the most Christian Council at Nicea, he ought to have allowed them to choose for themselves an archbishop of Prague, and should have let him be confirmed by the bishop of Olmutz in Moravia, or the bishop of Grau in Hungary, or the bishop of Magdeburg in Germany. It would suffice if he had been confirmed by one or two of these, as was the custom in St. Cyprian's time. The pope has nothing he can say against that; should he oppose it, he would be acting like a wolf and a tyrant. No one should follow him, and excommunication by him should be met by counterexcommunication.

If it is preferred to follow this course only after informing the pope, out of respect for the papacy, let it be done that way. But we must see to it that the Hussites are not required to pay a farthing, and the pope must demand no pledges of them even as little as a hair, and must not tyrannize over them, nor bind them with oaths and vows. This is what he does with all other bishops, contrary to God and the right. If he refuses to be satisfied with the honour of being asked for his consent, then let him simply keep his vows, rights, regulations, and tyrannies to himself. Let the election stand on its own feet, and may the blood of all those who remain in danger cry out against him. No one ought to consent to what is wrong. It is a sufficient mark of respect for a tyrant if we offer him an honour. If no other course is open, remember that the choice and consent of the common people is as good as any confirmation a tyrant can give. Nevertheless, I hope that a popular vote will not be necessary. Surely it will happen ere long that some of the Romanists and the religious-minded bishops and scholars will become aware of the papal tyranny, and repudiate it.

Nor is it my view that the Hussites be compelled to abandon taking the sacraments in both kinds, for that practice is neither unchristian nor heretical. Let them be free to follow that custom if they prefer it. But let the new bishop see to it that no dissension arises in regard to the custom. He should teach them in a kindly spirit, and show that neither practice is wrong. Similarly, there ought to be no quarrel if the priests dress, or live, differently from laymen. The same principle holds good if they are unwilling to observe the canon law of Rome. Pressure should not be brought to bear on them. It should be their prime concern that they live sincerely by faith, and in accord with Holy Scripture. For there can well be both the Christian faith and the Christian status apart from the intolerable papal laws; indeed that faith and status cannot very well exist unless the Romish rules are diminished or abolished. When we were baptized, we were set free, subject only to God's Word. Why should any man use human words and make us prisoner? As St. Paul says: "Ye are bought with a price; become not bondservants of men" [I Cor. 6:20; Gal. 5:1], namely, of those who rule according to man-made laws.

If I knew that the Beghards[40] held nothing more erroneous about the sacrament of the altar than the belief that the ele-

[40] A name here given by Luther to the "Bohemian Brethren", a sect of the Hussites.

ments remained truly natural bread and wine, while yet the
true body and blood of Christ were present under them, then
I myself would not condemn them; I would consent to their
being recognized by the bishop of Prague. There is no article
of faith which declares that bread and wine are not present in
the sacrament in their own essence and nature, which delusion
St. Thomas Aquinas and the pope maintain. But it is an article
of faith that the natural body and blood of Christ are truly
present in the natural bread and wine. Hence the preference
held by either side ought to be patiently tolerated till the two
reach agreement, because there is nothing dangerous in believing either that the bread is there, or is not there. It is our
duty to tolerate all varieties of those manners and customs
which do not endanger the faith. But if the Hussites held a
different creed from us I should prefer to leave them outside
the Church, although they ought then to receive instruction
in the truth.

Any further errors and dissensions which might be brought
to light in Bohemia should be borne with until the archbishop
had been reinstalled, and had had time to bring the people
together again, with one self-consistent doctrine. They will certainly not unite again if we use violence or threats, or act impatiently. Patience and gentleness are needed here. Christ had
to associate with His disciples, and bear their unbelief for a
long time before they reached the faith that He would rise
again from the dead. If only a good bishop and a proper régime
were restored to Bohemia, without any Romish depotism, I
am confident that there would soon be an improvement.

The temporal possessions, once belonging to the church,
should not be demanded back again very strictly. Since we
are Christian, and each of us under obligation to help our
neighbour, we are empowered, for the sake of harmony, to
give or surrender the properties to them as in God's sight and
man's. For Christ says: "If two of you agree on earth, there
am I in your midst" [Matt. 18:19]. Would to God that we, on
both sides, helped in that direction; that each gave the other
his hand in brotherly lowliness; and that we did not stubbornly
insist on our authority or our rights! Love is greater and more
needful than the papacy at Rome, which is without love;
whereas love can do without the papacy. Having said this, I

have done all I could to the purpose. If the pope or those around him interfere, they will have to give an account for having preferred their own advantage rather than their neighbour's, contrary to the love of God. The pope ought to be willing to surrender his papacy, all his property and glory, if in so doing he could effect the salvation of one soul. But to-day, he would rather see the world perish than abandon a jot or tittle of his authority; nevertheless he retains the title of "His Holiness". There I leave this subject.

25. The universities need a sound and thorough reformation. I must say so no matter who takes offence. Everything that the papacy has instituted or ordered is directed solely towards the multiplication of sin and error. Unless they are completely altered from what they have been hitherto, the universities will fit exactly what is said in the Book of Maccabees: "Places for the exercise for youth, and for the Greekish fashion" [II Macc. 4:9, 12]. Loose living is practised there; little is taught of the Holy Scripture or the Christian faith; the blind pagan teacher, Aristotle, is of more consequence than Christ. In my view, Aristotle's writings on *Physics, Metaphysics, On the Soul,* and *Ethics,* hitherto regarded as the most important, should be set aside along with all others that boast they treat of natural objects, for in fact they have nothing to teach about things natural or spiritual. Remember too that no one, up to now, has understood his teaching, but much precious time and mental energy have been uselessly devoted to wasteful work, study, and effort. I venture to say that a potter has more understanding of the things of nature than is written down in those books. It pains me to the heart that this damnable, arrogant, pagan rascal has seduced and fooled so many of the best Christians with his misleading writings. God has made him a plague to us on account of our sins.

In his book, *On the Soul,* which is one of his best, the wretched fellow teaches that the soul dies with the body; and many have tried, in vain, to defend him. It is as if we did not possess the Holy Scriptures where we find a superabundance of teaching on the whole subject, of which Aristotle has not the faintest inkling. Yet this defunct pagan has attained supremacy; impeded, and almost suppressed, the Scriptures of the living God. When I think of this lamentable state of affairs, I cannot avoid believing that the Evil One introduced the study of Aristotle.

On the same principles, his book on *Ethics* is worse than any other book, being the direct opposite of God's grace, and the Christian virtues; yet it is accounted among the best of his works. Oh! away with such books from any Christian hands. Let no one accuse me of overstating the case, or object that I do not understand. My dear sir, I know well enough what I am saying. Aristotle is as familiar to me as to you and your like. I have read him and studied him with more understanding than did St. Thomas Aquinas or Duns Scotus. Without pride, I can make that claim, and if needs be, prove it. It makes no difference that for centuries so many of the best minds have devoted their labours to him. Such objections do not affect me as at one time they used to do. For it is plain as the day that the longer the lapse of time, the greater the errors which abound in the world and the universities.

I would gladly grant the retention of Aristotle's books on *Logic, Rhetoric,* and *Poetics;* or that they should be abridged and read in a useful form to train young men to speak and preach well. But the comments and notes should be set aside, and, just as Cicero's *Rhetoric* is read without notes and comments, so also Aristotle's *Logic* should be read in its simple form, and without the lengthy comments. But to-day no man learns from it how to speak or preach; the whole thing has become a mere subject of argumentation and a weariness to the flesh.

Then there are the languages: Latin, Greek, and Hebrew, the mathematical disciplines, and history. But this is a subject which I commend to men of greater knowledge than I possess; it will right itself if a reformation is undertaken seriously; much depends on that. For Christian youth, and those of our upper classes, with whom abides the future of Christianity, will be taught and trained in the universities. In my view, no work more worthy of the pope and the emperor could be carried out than a true reformation of the universities. On the other hand, nothing could be more wicked, or serve the devil better, than unreformed universities.

I leave the medical men to reform their own faculties, but

I claim to speak for the jurists and theologians. In regard to the former, I aver that it would be well if the canon law, in particular the Decretals, were completely blotted out, from the first letter to the last. There is a superabundance of material at our disposal in the Biblical writings, telling what our conduct should be in all circumstances. The pursuit of the other studies only prevents that of the Holy Scriptures; and, moreover, for the most part, the former are tainted with greed and pride. Even if there were much of value in the canon law, it would still be wise to let it perish, because the pope claims to have all the canon laws ensconced in the chambers of his heart. Henceforth, therefore, to study it is a mere waste of time and a self-deception. To-day, the canon law does not consist of what is written in books, but in the arbitrary choices preferred by the pope and his lickspittles. Even if your case is most firmly established according to the written canon law, the pope still retains his *"scrinium pectoris"* superior to it, and by which he will settle what is legal, and rule the world. Often a villain, or even the devil himself, controls that chamber, although the popes proudly claim that the Holy Spirit rules it. That is their way with the humble folk who belong to Christ; they impose many rules, but keep none; they compel other people to observe them, or to buy themselves off for gold.

Since, then, the pope and those about him have rescinded the entire canon law, refusing to respect it themselves, and observing only their own wanton will in despite of the whole world, we ought to follow them, and ourselves reject these books. We shall never be able to know the papal, arbitrary will through and through, which is the present-day substitute for the canon law, alas! But let that law perish, in the name of God, for it has been exalted in the devil's name. Let there be no more *doctores decretorum*,[41] but only *doctores scrinii*, i.e., papal play-actors. It is said that no finer secular administration exists anywhere than among the Turks, and they possess neither the canonical nor the temporal law, but only the Qoran. But we must confess that no more scandalous administration exists than our own with its spiritual and temporal laws,

[41] Doctors of Canon Law.

till no class of the people now lives in obedience to natural reason, to say nothing of Holy Scripture.

The temporal law! God help us, what a rank growth that has become. Although it is much better, wiser, and more proper than the "spiritual law", in which nothing is good except the name, nevertheless there is far too much temporal law. Surely there would be quite enough law if there were but wise rulers side by side with the Holy Scriptures. As St. Paul says in I Corinthians 6 [:1 ff.], "Is there no one among you who is able to judge his neighbour's cause that you must go to law before the unrighteous?" In my opinion, appeal should be made to common law and established custom rather than to the general law decreed by the emperor; and only in case of necessity should the imperial law be invoked. And just as every land has its own manners and customs, so, would to God, that each had its own laws, and these few and brief. That is what obtained before the imperial laws were introduced, many lands being still without the latter. Rambling and far-fetched laws only burden the people, and are a hindrance rather than a help in settling their cases. But I hope that this subject will be considered and examined by others better fitted than I to discuss it.

Our worthy theologians have ceased from worrying and working; and so they leave the Bible alone and read the *Sententiae*. I should have thought that theological students would have begun with the study of the *Sententiae*, and left the Bible to the doctors, but it is done the other way round. The Bible comes first and is studied till they reach the Bachelor's degree; the *Sententiae* comes last and remains even after reaching the doctorate. A very sacred obligation is attached here. A man who is not a priest may read the Bible, but a priest must read the *Sententiae*. It looks to me as if a married man might be a doctor in the Bible, but not by any means in the *Sententiae*. How can we expect to enjoy well-being when we act so perversely, and degrade God's holy Word like this? Moreover, the pope uses very stern language, and commands that his laws are to be read and used in the schools and law courts; but he says little of the gospel. His command is obeyed; with the result that the gospel lies in the dust in the schools and courts, while the pope's scandalous laws are alone in force.

If we bear the name and title of Doctors of Holy Scripture, the very name should make it compulsory for us to teach Holy Scripture alone; this high-sounding and proud title, however, is too exalted, and no man should boast it, or be accorded the degree of Doctor of Holy Scripture. It would only be tolerable if his duties bore out his title. As it is, however, the *Sententiae* hold the field; and more of pagan and man-made opinions are to be found among theologians than of the sacred certainties of scriptural doctrine. What then are we to do about it? I have no other suggestion to make on this point than to offer humble prayer to God that He give us real Doctors of Theology. The pope, the emperor, the universities create Doctors of the Arts, of Medicine, and of Law; but be assured that no one can make a Doctor of Holy Scripture, except the Holy Spirit from heaven; as Christ said in John 6 [:45], "They shall all be taught of God Himself." Now the Holy Spirit asks no questions about red or brown birettas[42] and other adornments, nor whether a candidate is young or old, layman or priest, monk or secular, celibate or married; nay, in olden times, the spirit spoke through a she-ass against the prophet who rode on it. Would to God that we were worthy of being given these doctors, no matter whether they were priests or laymen, married or celibate. But to-day they try to force the Holy Spirit to enter the popes, the bishops, and the doctors, although there is no gleam or glimpse to show that He has actually entered them.

The number of books on theology must also be reduced, only the best being retained. For neither many books nor much reading make a man learned; but a good book, often read, no matter how short, will give Scriptural scholarship plus religious-mindedness. Even the writings of any one of the holy Fathers or, indeed, all of them, should only be read for a while, and in order that they might lead us to the Bible. To-day, however, we read them alone, and get no further; we never enter on the Bible. Thus we are like those who look at the sign-posts, but never set out on the journey. The intention of the early Fathers in their writing was to introduce us to the Bible; but we use them only to find a way of avoiding it.

[42] Doctors' caps.

Nevertheless, the Bible is our vineyard, and there we should all labour and toil.

Above all, the most important and most usual teaching, in both the universities and the lower schools, ought to be concerned with the Holy Scriptures; beginning with the gospels for the young boys. Would to God also that each town had a girls' school where, day by day, the girls might have a lesson on the gospel, whether in German or Latin. Of course, as we read in the accounts of St. Agnes and other saints in olden times, it was with that praiseworthy and Christian purpose that the schools, monasteries, and nunneries were founded. Those were the days of holy virgins and martyrs, and all was well in the Christian community. But now they only use prayers and hymns in those places. Would it not be reasonable for every Christian person on reaching his ninth or tenth year to know the holy gospel in its entirety, since his name and standing as a Christian are based on it? A woman who spins or sews, teaches her craft to her daughter in her early years. To-day, however, great and learned prelates and bishops themselves do not know the gospel.

Oh! how unwisely we deal with our poor young folk, whom we are commanded to train and instruct [Prov. 22:6]! But we shall have to give a serious account of our stewardship, and explain why we have not set the Word of God before them. Their lot is that of which Jeremiah speaks in Lamentations 2, "Mine eyes do fail with tears, my bowels are troubled, my liver is poured upon the earth, for the destruction of the daughter of my people, because the young children and the sucklings swoon in the streets of the city. They say to their mothers, Where is corn and wine? When they swooned as the wounded in the streets of the city, when their soul is poured out into their mothers' bosom" [Lam. 2:11]. We fail to notice the present pitiful distress of the young people. Though they live in the midst of a Christian world, they faint and perish in misery because they lack the gospel in which we should be training and exercising them all the time.

Moreover, even if the universities diligently studied the Holy Scriptures, we should not, as now, send everyone there for the mere sake of having many students, or because everyone wants a doctor in the family. Only the cleverest should be sent, and after having received a good education in the lower schools. The prince and the local town council ought to see to this, and send only those who are well qualified. But I would not advise anyone to send his son to a place where the Holy Scriptures do not come first. Every institution, where the Word of God is not taught regularly, must fail. That is why we observe the kind of people who are now and will continue to be in the universities. It is nobody's fault except that of the pope, the bishops, and the prelates, who have been charged with the care of the young people. For the universities ought to give students a thorough training in the Bible. Some of them might become bishops and pastors, and stand in the forefront against heretics, and the devil, and the whole world. But that is nowhere to be found. I greatly fear that the universities are but wide-open gates leading to hell, as they are not diligent in training and impressing the Holy Scripture on the young students.

[26.[43] I am well aware that the crew in Rome will object and cry aloud that the pope took the Holy Roman empire from the Greek emperor, and transferred it to the German people.[44] In exchange for this honour and favour, he deserves, and should have received, our willing submission, and thanks, and every other expression of gratitude. For this reason, they will perhaps attempt to scatter to the winds every effort to reform them, and let nothing happen except things like making a present of the Roman empire. From this starting-point, they have till now persecuted and oppressed many an excellent emperor so arbitrarily and arrogantly that it is distressing to talk of. And they have used the same adroitness in making themselves the overlords of every secular authority and government, contrary to the holy gospel. I must therefore say a word on that subject.

It is unquestionable that the real Roman empire perished and ended long ago. This empire and its destruction were pre-

[43] This section does not occur in Luther's first edition.
[44] The whole of the following argument depends on the crowning of Charlemagne in Rome by Pope Leo III on Christmas Day, A.D. 800, thereby founding the Holy Roman Empire of the German People and making a basis for the claim to papal supremacy.

dicted in the writings of Moses in Numbers 24, and of Daniel. Thus Balaam clearly prophesied in Numbers 24 when he said, "The Romans shall come and destroy the Jews, and afterwards they themselves shall perish."[45] That took place at the hands of the Goths, but was confirmed when the Turkish empire arose a thousand years ago. In the course of time, Asia and Africa, and afterwards France and Spain, and finally Venice, fell away, and nothing remained to Rome of its former power.

When the pope could no longer force the Greeks and the emperor to suit his arbitrary preferences, he invented the device of robbing him of his empire and title, and transferring them to the Germans who, at that time, were warlike and of good repute. In so doing, the Romanists wished to make the power of the Roman empire subject to themselves, and then give it away in the form of feudal states. All happened according to plan. It was taken from the emperor at Constantinople, and its name and title ascribed to us Germans. Thereby we became the pope's feudatories, and there is now a second Roman empire, one built by the popes, but on German foundations. For the other, the first, as I have said, had perished long before.

Thus the Roman pontiff has his way. Rome has been seized, the German emperor driven out and bound under oath not to reside in Rome. He is to be Roman emperor, and yet not live in Rome. Meanwhile he is to be dependent on, and live by, the good pleasure of the pope and his entourage. The result is that we possess the title, and they the land and the towns. All the time, they have misused us in our simplicity to the advantage of their arrogant and despotic ways. They call us "senseless Germans" for letting ourselves be deceived and fooled just as it suited them.

So be it. For God, the Lord, it is a small thing to toss empires and principalities to and fro. He makes so free with them that sometimes He gives a kingdom to an arrant knave, and takes it from one of a religious mind. Sometimes He does this through the treachery of wicked and faithless men, sometimes by the laws of inheritance. This is what we read of the kingdom of Persia, and of Greece, and almost all empires. It says in Daniel

[45] Num. 24:24, an interpretation rather than a quotation.

2 [:21] and 4 [:19 ff.], "He who dwelleth in heaven ruleth over all things, and it is He alone who overthroweth kingdoms, tosseth them to and fro, and setteth them up." Since no one can regard it as a great matter that a kingdom has been given to him, especially if he be a Christian, we Germans have no cause for pride if a new Roman empire is apportioned to us. For in God's eyes it is but a poor gift, such as He has often given to the most unworthy, as it says in Daniel 4 [:35], "All who dwell on earth are as nothing in His eyes, and in all the empires of men, He has power to give them to whom He will."

In spite of the fact, however, that the pope has used violence and injustice in robbing the true emperor of the Roman empire, or of the title of Roman Emperor, and transferred it to us Germans, it is certain, all the same, that God made use of the pope's wickedness in this matter, in giving such an empire to the German people. After the fall of the first Roman empire, He set up another, that which now exists. While we gave no occasion for the wickedness of the popes in this transaction, neither did we understand their deceitful purposes and intentions. Nevertheless, we have unhappily paid far too dearly for this empire, through pontifical cunning and unscrupulousness, at the cost of immeasurable bloodshed, with the suppression of our freedom, the loss and theft of our property, especially of our churches and canonries, and the suffering of unspeakable fraud and contempt. We have the title of empire, but the pope has our goods, our honour, our bodies, lives, souls, and all we possess. That is the way to cheat the Germans, and, because they are Germans, to go on cheating them.[46] The popes had this in mind when they wanted to become emperors; when they could not accomplish this, they set themselves above the emperors.

Since, therefore, by the providence of God and the efforts of evil men, the empire has been given us through no fault of ours, I do not believe that we ought to abandon it; but, rather, to administer it properly in the fear of God, as long as it may please Him. For, as I have said, He does not look to see whence an empire arose; His will is that it should be rightly administered. Though the popes took it improperly

[46] An untranslatable pun: *Szo sol die Deutschen teuschen und mit teuschen teuschenn.*

from others, we did not receive it improperly. It has been given us by God's will through the hands of wicked men. We rely on Him more than on the false intentions which the popes had at the time when their object was to become emperors, and more than emperors themselves, while merely tricking us with the name, and scorning us.

The king of Babylon seized his kingdom by robbery and violence. Nevertheless, God wished it to be ruled by saintly princes, viz., Daniel, Hananiah, Azariah, and Meshach [Dan. 3:20 and 5:29]. Much more is it His will that the present empire should be ruled by Christian German princes, no matter whether the pope stole it, or got it by robbery, or established it afresh. It was all done by God's will, and it came to pass before we understood it.

For these reasons, the pope and his entourage have no room to boast that they have conferred great benefit on the German people by giving this Roman empire to them. Firstly, because they did not grant it to us for our benefit. Rather, they took advantage of our simplicity when they did so, in order to give support for their arrogance towards the true Roman emperor in Constantinople. The pope took it from him contrary to God and the right, and without authority. Secondly, because the pope's objective was not to give the empire to us, but to keep it for himself, to claim all our power, freedom, property, our bodies and souls; and with us, if God had not prevented it, all the world besides. He has said so himself plainly in the Decretals and tried to carry it out, with many a trick on several German emperors. How beautifully have we Germans been taught our German! While we supposed we were to become masters, we have become serfs of the most cunning tyrant. We have come into possession of the name, the titles, and the coat of arms of empire; but the treasures, the powers, the rights, and liberties of it remain the pope's. So the pope eats the nut while we play with the empty shell.

May God help us, after having received the empire from Him, as I have said, to rule it as we have been commissioned. We must give substance to the name, the title, and the coat of arms, and retrieve our freedom. We must let the Romanists see for once what it is that we have received from God through them. So be it, and be it so! Let the pope give us the Roman empire and all it means, but let our country be free from his intolerable taxes and frauds. Give us back our freedom, our power, our honour, our bodies and souls; and let us be an empire as an empire ought to be, and let there be an end of his word and claims!

If he will not do so, then why does he make moonshine with false pretences and conjuring tricks? Has there not been enough after so many centuries, of insulting a noble people, and leading it about by the nose all the time? It does not follow that the pope should be superior to the emperor by virtue of crowning or instituting him. For, at God's command, the prophet, St. Samuel, anointed and crowned Saul and David king, but still remained their subject [I Sam. 10:1; 16:13]. The prophet, Nathan, anointed king Solomon, and was not made superior to him thereby. Again, Elisha let one of his servants anoint Jehu king of Israel, but yet remained in subjection to him [II Kings 9:1 ff.]. Nowhere else in all the world, except in the case of the pope, does he who crowns and consecrates a king become his superior.

Even in his own case, the crowning is done by three cardinals, lower in rank than he; nevertheless he remains above them. Why then, in spite of his own example, in spite of the customs of all the world and the teaching of Scripture, does he set himself above the secular authority and the empire, simply on the basis that he crowns and consecrates the emperor? It is enough for the pope to be his superior in divine affairs, i.e., in preaching, teaching, and dispensing the sacraments. In these respects, a bishop or pastor is superior to the rest, as St. Ambrose was superior to the emperor Theodosius in the confessional, and as the prophet Nathan was over David, and Samuel over Saul. Therefore, let the German emperor be a genuine and a free emperor, and let not his authority and government suffer destruction by the purblind claim of the papal dissembler, pretending to be superior to temporal power and to be ruler in all things.]

27. And now I have spoken at sufficient length about the transgressions of the clergy, though you may and will find more of them if you look in the right place. We shall now devote a section to the consideration of temporal failings.

In the first place, there is urgent need of a general order and decree on behalf of the German people against the overflowing abundance and the great expensiveness of the clothing worn by so many nobles and rich folk. To us, as to other people, God has given enough wool, fur, flax, and everything that would provide proper, suitable, and worthy garments for each class. We do not need to waste such huge sums for silk, and velvet, and articles of gold, and other imports from abroad. I believe that, even if the pope did not rob us Germans with his intolerable, fraudulent practices, we should still have had too many of these native robbers, the silk and velvet merchants. As things stand, we see that each wants to keep up with the others, to the awakening and increase of pride and envy among us, as we have deserved. All this and much else that brings misery would cease if the desire for display would let us be thankful and content with the good things which God has supplied to us.

In the same way, the spice traffic ought to be reduced, for it is another of the great channels by which money is conveyed out of Germany. By the grace of God, more things to eat and drink are indigenous to our own country than to any other, and are just as precious and wholesome. Perhaps I am now bringing forward foolish and impossible suggestions which would endanger the principal trade of the merchants. But I am expressing my own views. Unless things improve in the community, let him bring about improvements who can do so. I do not see many goodly habits which have ever been introduced into the country by commerce. In olden days, God caused the children of Israel to dwell far from the sea, and did not allow them to engage in much commerce.

But the greatest misfortune suffered by the German people is certainly the traffic in annuities. If nothing of this kind existed, much of the silk and velvet, many of the articles of gold, spices and all sorts of ornaments, would remain unbought. The trade has not yet been in existence for many centuries, but it has already brought misery and ruin on almost all the princes, monasteries, towns, nobles, and their heirs. If it should continue for another century, it would be impossible for Germany to keep a single penny, and we should be compelled to adopt cannibalism! It is a device of the devil; and the pope, in approving it, has brought woe upon the whole world. Therefore, I hereby beg and pray that everyone will open his eyes and look at the ruin of himself, his children, and his heirs. It does not stand outside at the door, but already haunts the house. Let the emperor, the princes, the lords, and the towns do their part to see that this trade be condemned as soon as possible and henceforth forbidden, no matter whether the pope and all his law or illegality are against the action; nor if benefices and monasteries are founded thereon. It is better to have one benefice in a town founded on proper freeholds or taxes, than a hundred on the annuity system; indeed, one benefice founded on the annuity system is worse and more oppressive than twenty on freeholds. Nay, the annuities are nothing else than a sign and a symbol that, for its many sins, the world has been sold to the devil; therefore, both temporal and spiritual resources must alike fail us. And we take no notice.

At this point, I would say that we must surely bridle the Fuggers and similar trading companies. How can it happen in a godly and righteous manner, and in a single lifetime, that great wealth, worthy of a king, should be accumulated into a single pile? I am no man for figures. But I do not understand how a hundred guilders can make twenty profit in a single year, or even one guilder make another. Nothing like this takes place by cultivating the soil, or by raising cattle, where the increase does not depend on human wits, but on God's blessing. I commend that observation to men of affairs. As a theologian, I have no further reproof to utter on this subject than as regards its wicked and scandalous appearance, about which St. Paul says, "Abstain from every form and appearance of evil" [I Thess. 5:22]. But I do know that it would be much more godly to increase farming and decrease commerce; and that more of those are on the right side, who till the earth as the Bible says, and seek their livelihood in this way. All this was said to us and all others in the case of Adam, "Cursed be the ground wherein thou labourest; thorns also and thistles shall it bring forth to thee, and in the sweat of thy face shalt thou eat bread" [Gen. 3:17 ff.]. There is still much land untilled, and not farmed.

The next thing is the abuse of eating and drinking, a matter which gains us no good repute abroad, but is thought a special failing of ours. Preaching never makes any impression on it, so firmly is it rooted and so well has it gained the upper hand. The waste of money would be its least evil; but it often entails the vices of murder, adultery, robbery, blasphemy, and every form of immorality. Here is something for the secular government to prevent; otherwise what Christ said will happen, "The last day will come like a secret snare, when they will drink and eat, marry and court, build and plant, buy and sell" [Luke 21:34]. To-day it has come to such a pass, that I verily hope the Last Day is at hand, although it is expected by very few at present.

Finally, is it not a lamentable thing that we Christians should openly tolerate in our midst common houses of ill-fame, though we all took the oath of chastity at our baptism? I am well aware of the frequent reply, that it is a custom not confined to any one people, that it would be difficult to stop, and that it is better to have such houses than that married women, or maidens, or others held in greater respect, should be dishonoured. Nevertheless, ought not the secular but Christian government to consider that that is not the way to get rid of a heathen custom? If the children of Israel could exist without such an abomination, surely Christians ought to be much better able to do so! Nay, how do many cities, market towns, villages, and hamlets manage without such houses? Why should it not be the same in the great cities?

In this, and in other matters which I have discussed earlier, I have tried to show how many good works the secular government can perform, and what ought to be the duty of every administration. Everyone might learn from this what a fearful responsibility it is to sit on high and to act as a ruler. What use would it be if some ruler-in-chief were, in himself, as holy as St. Peter, but not also diligent in planning to help those under him in these respects? His very authority would cry out against him. For it is the part of those in authority to see to the good of their subjects. But, if the administrators would concern themselves with bringing young people together in marriage, the hope of marriage would give great help to each to endure, and to resist temptation. But what happens now when a young man is attracted into the ministry? I fear that not

one in a hundred has any other reason than the need of a livelihood, plus doubt about being able to support himself as a
married man. Hence they first lead very disorderly lives, and
sow their wild oats, and are sated; but experience shows they
tend to sow them within. I think it is a true proverb which
says, "Most of the monks and priests are doubters." So things
go on, as we see.

But, on account of avoiding the many sins which gnaw their
way within us so disgustingly, I will give the faithful advice
that neither youths nor maidens should take the vows of continence or the "spiritual" life before they are thirty. It requires
a special gift, as St. Paul says [I Cor. 7:7]. Therefore, unless
specially drawn to it by God, delay your becoming a cleric, or
taking the vows. Further: I say that if you trust God so little
that you doubt whether you could support yourself and a wife,
and if that doubt is your only reason for entering the clerical
status, then I beg you for the good of your soul not to become
a cleric, but rather a farmer; or else make some other choice.
Where a simple faith in God is needed in regard to earning
your temporal support, there must be ten times as much faith
required to sustain the life of a cleric. If you have no confidence
that God will provide for you in the world, how are you to
trust Him to sustain you as a cleric? Alas, unbelief and distrust
destroy everything, and lead into all sorts of misery, as we see
among all classes. Much could be said of this misery. Young
people have no one to take care of them. Each follows the
custom, and the government is of as much value to them as
if it were not there, although the care of the young ought to
be the prime concern of the pope, the bishops, the ruling
classes, and the councils. They want to exercise authority far
and wide, and yet they are of no use. Oh, what rarities will
lords and rulers be in heaven on this account, even though
they build a hundred churches to God and raise to life again
all the saints and the dead!

I have said enough for the present. In my little book, *On
Good Works*, I have sufficiently discussed what the secular authorities and the nobles ought to do. There is room for better
conduct in the way they live and rule, yet there is no comparison between the temporal and the spiritual abuses, as I
have shown there. I am aware that I have spoken strongly,

and suggested much that will be felt impossible, and attacked many subjects too severely. But what am I to do? I cannot but speak. If I were able, I would also act. I would rather that the world were wroth with me than that God were. No man can do more than take away my life. Many times heretofore I have proposed peace with my enemies. But as it seems to me, God has used them to compel me to raise my voice even more insistently; and because they are not satisfied, I must speak, shout, shriek, and write till they have had enough. Oh well! I have still a little song[47] about Rome and about them. Their ears are itching for me to sing it to them, and pitch the notes in the treble clef. Do you grasp my meaning, oh worthy Rome?

I have offered to stand and be cross-examined for what I have written, but without avail. Nevertheless, I know that if my cause is just, though of necessity condemned on earth, it must be justified in heaven. For the whole Bible shows that the cause of Christians and Christianity shall be judged by God alone; it has never yet been judged on earth by men, but has always been too great and strong for my enemies. My great concern and primary fear are that my case may remain uncondemned; that would show me it was not yet pleasing to God. Therefore, let them but come boldly forward, whether pope, bishop, priest, monk, or scholar; they are the right people to pursue the truth. They should have done so all the time. God grant to us a Christian mind, and, in particular, God grant a truly religious courage to the ruling class of the German people, to do the best they can for the church that is so much to be pitied.

Amen.

Wittenberg. A.D. 1520.

[47] A reference to the *Pagan Servitude,* which he began to write almost immediately and which he called a "prelude," a musical term.

V

APPENDIX

THE NINETY-FIVE THESES[1]

[*The* Ninety-five Theses, *to use the popular term for the* Disputation on the Power and Efficacy of Indulgences, *are more widely associated with Luther in common parlance than anything else which he wrote. But neither a casual nor careful reading suffices to understand them. They deal with the problem of indulgences in a manner which demands a good deal of orientation. This is one of the reasons for placing them so late in this volume, even though, from a chronological standpoint, they should come first. They were posted on the Castle church door at Wittenberg on either October 31 or November 1, 1517. The second reason for placing them in an Appendix at the end of the selections is that they are more adequately understood from the standpoint of Luther's mature faith than as a beginning vantage point for understanding it. Scholars may disagree on the question of the extent to which Luther's fundamental insights were already operative in the formulation of the* Theses *for debate. Certainly a full-blown understanding of faith is not expressly evident in the limited subject matter of the* Theses. *In fact, the* Theses *are significant because they precipitated a controversy concerning abuses which led to theological ideas demanding a more radical reformation of the Church than initially intended.*]

[1] Reprinted by permission of the publishers from *The Reformation Writings of Martin Luther*, volume 1, *The Basis of the Protestant Reformation*, translated and edited by Bertram Lee Woolf (London: Lutterworth Press, 1953), pp. 32–42.

Out of love and concern for the truth, and with the object of eliciting it, the following heads will be the subject of a public discussion at Wittenberg under the presidency of the reverend father, Martin Luther, Augustinian, Master of Arts and Sacred Theology, and duly appointed Lecturer on these subjects in that place. He requests that whoever cannot be present personally to debate the matter orally will do so in absence in writing.

1. When our Lord and Master, Jesus Christ, said "Repent",[2] He called for the entire life of believers to be one of penitence.

2. The word cannot be properly understood as referring to the sacrament of penance, i.e., confession and satisfaction, as administered by the clergy.

3. Yet its meaning is not restricted to penitence in one's heart; for such penitence is null unless it produces outward signs in various mortifications of the flesh.

4. As long as hatred of self abides (i.e., true inward penitence) the penalty of sin abides, viz., until we enter the kingdom of heaven.

5. The pope has neither the will nor the power to remit any penalties beyond those imposed either at his own discretion or by canon law.

6. The pope himself cannot remit guilt, but only declare and confirm that it has been remitted by God; or, at most, he can remit it in cases reserved to his discretion. Except for these cases, the guilt remains untouched.

[2] This quotation from Matt. 4:17 was known throughout Europe in its Latin form: *poenitentiam agite*. Unfortunately, the phrase was capable of two meanings: repent; and, do penance.

7. God never remits guilt to anyone without, at the same time, making him humbly submissive to the priest, His representative.

8. The penitential canons apply only to men who are still alive, and, according to the canons themselves, none applies to the dead.

9. Accordingly, the Holy Spirit, acting in the person of the pope, manifests grace to us, by the fact that the papal regulations always cease to apply at death, or in any hard case.

10. It is a wrongful act, due to ignorance, when priests retain the canonical penalties on the dead in purgatory.

11. When canonical penalties were changed and made to apply to purgatory, surely it would seem that tares were sown while the bishops were asleep.

12. In former days, the canonical penalties were imposed, not after, but before absolution was pronounced; and were intended to be tests of true contrition.

13. Death puts an end to all the claims of the church; even the dying are already dead to the canon laws, and are no longer bound by them.

14. Defective piety or love in a dying person is necessarily accompanied by great fear, which is greatest where the piety or love is least.

15. This fear or horror is sufficient in itself, whatever else might be said, to constitute the pain of purgatory, since it approaches very closely to the horror of despair.

16. There seems to be the same difference between hell, purgatory, and heaven as between despair, uncertainty, and assurance.

17. Of a truth, the pains of souls in purgatory ought to be abated, and charity ought to be proportionately increased.

18. Moreover, it does not seem proved, on any grounds of reason or Scripture, that these souls are outside the state of merit, or unable to grow in grace;

19. Nor does it seem proved to be always the case that they are certain and assured of salvation, even if we are very certain of it ourselves.

20. Therefore the pope, in speaking of the plenary remission of all penalties, does not mean "all" in the strict sense, but only those imposed by himself.

21. Hence those who preach indulgences are in error when they say that a man is absolved and saved from every penalty by the pope's indulgences;

22. Indeed, he cannot remit to souls in purgatory any penalty which canon law declares should be suffered in the present life.

23. If plenary remission could be granted to anyone at all, it would be only in the cases of the most perfect, i.e., to very few.

24. It must therefore be the case that the major part of the people are deceived by that indiscriminate and high-sounding promise of relief from penalty.

25. The same power as the pope exercises in general over purgatory is exercised in particular by every single bishop in his bishopric and priest in his parish.

26. The pope does excellently when he grants remission to the souls in purgatory on account of intercessions made on their behalf, and not by the power of the keys (which he cannot exercise for them).

27. There is no divine authority for preaching that the soul flies out of purgatory immediately the money clinks in the bottom of the chest.

28. It is certainly possible that when the money clinks in the bottom of the chest avarice and greed increase; but when the church offers intercession, all depends on the will of God.

29. Who knows whether all souls in purgatory wish to be redeemed in view of what is said of St. Severinus[3] and St. Paschal?[4]

30. No one is sure of the reality of his own contrition, much less of receiving plenary forgiveness.

31. One who *bona fide* buys indulgences is as rare as a *bona fide* penitent man, i.e., very rare indeed.

32. All those who believe themselves certain of their own salvation by means of letters of indulgence, will be eternally damned, together with their teachers.

33. We should be most carefully on our guard against those who say that the papal indulgences are an inestimable divine gift, and that a man is reconciled to God by them.

34. For the grace conveyed by these indulgences relates simply to the penalties of the sacramental "satisfactions" decreed merely by man.

35. It is not in accordance with Christian doctrine to preach and teach that those who buy off souls, or purchase confessional licences, have no need to repent of their own sins.

[3] Pope, 638–40, successor to Honorius I.
[4] Paschal I, pope 817–24. The legend is that he and Severinus were willing to endure the pains of purgatory for the benefit of the faithful.

36. Any Christian whatsoever, who is truly repentant, enjoys plenary remission from penalty and guilt, and this is given him without letters of indulgence.

37. Any true Christian whatsoever, living or dead, participates in all the benefits of Christ and the Church; and this participation is granted to him by God without letters of indulgence.

38. Yet the pope's remission and dispensation are in no way to be despised, for, as already said, they proclaim the divine remission.

39. It is very difficult, even for the most learned theologians, to extol to the people the great bounty contained in the indulgences, while, at the same time, praising contrition as a virtue.

40. A truly contrite sinner seeks out, and loves to pay, the penalties of his sins; whereas the very multitude of indulgences dulls men's consciences, and tends to make them hate the penalties.

41. Papal indulgences should only be preached with caution, lest people gain a wrong understanding, and think that they are preferable to other good works: those of love.

42. Christians should be taught that the pope does not at all intend that the purchase of indulgences should be understood as at all comparable with works of mercy.

43. Christians should be taught that one who gives to the poor, or lends to the needy, does a better action than if he purchases indulgences;

44. Because, by works of love, love grows and a man becomes a better man; whereas, by indulgences, he does not become a better man, but only escapes certain penalties.

45. Christians should be taught that he who sees a needy person, but passes him by although he gives money for indulgences, gains no benefit from the pope's pardon, but only incurs the wrath of God.

46. Christians should be taught that, unless they have more than they need, they are bound to retain what is necessary for the upkeep of their home, and should in no way squander it on indulgences.

47. Christians should be taught that they purchase indulgences voluntarily, and are not under obligation to do so.

48. Christians should be taught that, in granting indulgences, the pope has more need, and more desire, for devout prayer on his own behalf than for ready money.

49. Christians should be taught that the pope's indulgences are useful only if one does not rely on them, but most harmful if one loses the fear of God through them.

50. Christians should be taught that, if the pope knew the exactions of the indulgence-preachers, he would rather the church of St. Peter were reduced to ashes than be built with the skin, flesh, and bones of his sheep.

51. Christians should be taught that the pope would be willing, as he ought if necessity should arise, to sell the church of St. Peter, and give, too, his own money to many of those from whom the pardon-merchants conjure money.

52. It is vain to rely on salvation by letters of indulgence, even if the commissary, or indeed the pope himself, were to pledge his own soul for their validity.

53. Those are enemies of Christ and the pope who forbid the word of God to be preached at all in some churches, in order that indulgences may be preached in others.

54. The word of God suffers injury if, in the same sermon, an equal or longer time is devoted to indulgences than to that word.

55. The pope cannot help taking the view that if indulgences (very small matters) are celebrated by one bell, one pageant, or one ceremony, the gospel (a very great matter) should be preached to the accompaniment of a hundred bells, a hundred processions, a hundred ceremonies.

56. The treasures of the church, out of which the pope dispenses indulgences, are not sufficiently spoken of or known among the people of Christ.

57. That these treasures are not temporal is clear from the fact that many of the merchants do not grant them freely, but only collect them;

58. Nor are they the merits of Christ and the saints, because, even apart from the pope, these merits are always working grace in the inner man, and working the cross, death, and hell in the outer man.

59. St. Laurence said that the poor were the treasures of the church, but he used the term in accordance with the custom of his own time.

60. We do not speak rashly in saying that the treasures of the church are the keys of the church, and are bestowed by the merits of Christ;

61. For it is clear that the power of the pope suffices, by itself, for the remission of penalties and reserved cases.

62. The true treasure of the church is the Holy Gospel of the glory and the grace of God.

63. It is right to regard this treasure as most odious, for it makes the first to be the last.

64. On the other hand, the treasure of indulgences is most acceptable, for it makes the last to be the first.

65. Therefore the treasures of the gospel are nets which, in former times, they used to fish for men of wealth.

66. The treasures of the indulgences are the nets to-day which they use to fish for men of wealth.

67. The indulgences, which the merchants extol as the greatest of favours, are seen to be, in fact, a favourite means for money-getting;

68. Nevertheless, they are not to be compared with the grace of God and the compassion shown in the Cross.

69. Bishops and curates, in duty bound, must receive the commissaries of the papal indulgences with all reverence;

70. But they are under a much greater obligation to watch closely and attend carefully lest these men preach their own fancies instead of what the pope commissioned.

71. Let him be anathema and accursed who denies the apostolic character of the indulgences;

72. On the other hand, let him be blessed who is on his guard against the wantonness and licence of the pardon-merchants' words.

73. In the same way, the pope rightly excommunicates those who make any plans to the detriment of the trade in indulgences.

74. It is much more in keeping with his views to excommunicate those who use the pretext of indulgences to plot anything to the detriment of holy love and truth.

75. It is foolish to think that papal indulgences have so much power that they can absolve a man even if he has done the impossible and violated the mother of God.

76. We assert the contrary, and say that the pope's pardons are not able to remove the least venial of sins as far as their guilt is concerned.

77. When it is said that not even St. Peter, if he were now pope, could grant a greater grace, it is blasphemy against St. Peter and the pope.

78. We assert the contrary, and say that he, and any pope whatever, possesses greater graces, viz., the gospel, spiritual powers, gifts of healing, etc., as is declared in I Corinthians 12 [:28].

79. It is blasphemy to say that the insignia of the cross with the papal arms are of equal value to the cross on which Christ died.

80. The bishops, curates, and theologians, who permit assertions of that kind to be made to the people without let or hindrance, will have to answer for it.

81. This unbridled preaching of indulgences makes it difficult for learned men to guard the respect due to the pope against false accusations, or at least from the keen criticisms of the laity;

82. They ask, e.g.: Why does not the pope liberate everyone from purgatory for the sake of love (a most holy thing) and because of the supreme necessity of their souls? This would be morally the best of all reasons. Meanwhile he redeems innumerable souls for money, a most perishable thing, with which to build St. Peter's church, a very minor purpose.

83. Again: Why should funeral and anniversary masses for the dead continue to be said? And why does not the pope

repay, or permit to be repaid, the benefactions instituted for these purposes, since it is wrong to pray for those souls who are now redeemed?

84. Again: Surely this is a new sort of compassion, on the part of God and the pope, when an impious man, an enemy of God, is allowed to pay money to redeem a devout soul, a friend of God; while yet that devout and beloved soul is not allowed to be redeemed without payment, for love's sake, and just because of its need of redemption.

85. Again: Why are the penitential canon laws, which in fact, if not in practice, have long been obsolete and dead in themselves,—why are they, to-day, still used in imposing fines in money, through the granting of indulgences, as if all the penitential canons were fully operative?

86. Again: Since the pope's income to-day is larger than that of the wealthiest of wealthy men, why does he not build this one church of St. Peter with his own money, rather than with the money of indigent believers?

87. Again: What does the pope remit or dispense to people who, by their perfect penitence, have a right to plenary remission or dispensation?

88. Again: Surely greater good could be done to the church if the pope were to bestow these remissions and dispensations, not once, as now, but a hundred times a day, for the benefit of any believer whatever.

89. What the pope seeks by indulgences is not money, but rather the salvation of souls; why then does he not suspend the letters and indulgences formerly conceded, and still as efficacious as ever?

90. These questions are serious matters of conscience to the laity. To suppress them by force alone, and not to refute them by giving reasons, is to expose the church and the pope to the ridicule of their enemies, and to make Christian people unhappy.

91. If, therefore, indulgences were preached in accordance with the spirit and mind of the pope, all these difficulties would be easily overcome, and, indeed, cease to exist.

92. Away, then, with those prophets who say to Christ's people, "Peace, peace," where there is no peace.

93. Hail, hail to all those prophets who say to Christ's people, "The cross, the cross," where there is no cross.

94. Christians should be exhorted to be zealous to follow Christ, their Head, through penalties, deaths, and hells;

95. And let them thus be more confident of entering heaven through many tribulations rather than through a false assurance of peace.

THESES FOR THE
HEIDELBERG DISPUTATION[1]

[*As an Augustinian, Luther attended the meeting in Heidelberg of the general chapter of the Augustinians of Germany in April 1518. At this meeting, Johann Staupitz, the German vicar of the order, asked Luther and some of his associates to participate in a discussion of the newer evangelical ideas, but to avoid the more controversial and debatable points. For this purpose, Luther drew up* Theses *in accord with the usual custom. The* Theses *exhibit a good deal of the theological direction which Luther developed. But essentially they do not attack the heart of the Roman Church nor exhibit ideas which necessarily demand a different conception of the Church. For this reason, these* Theses, *along with the* Ninety-five Theses, *have been placed in an Appendix.*]

[1] The theological theses here presented were translated by my colleague, Karlfried Froehlich, from the Latin in WA I, 353–4. Twelve philosophical theses, as well as the proofs for both sets of theses, are not included in this selection.

1. The law of God, although the soundest doctrine of life, is not able to bring man to righteousness but rather stands in the way.

2. Much less can the works of men, often "repeated" as it were with the help of natural precept, do so.

3. The works of men may always be attractive and seemingly good. It appears nevertheless that they are mortal sins.

4. The works of God may always appear to be unattractive and seemingly bad. They are nevertheless truly immortal merits.

5. It is not that the works of men (we are talking about the seemingly good ones) are deadly, in the sense that they are crimes.

6. It is not that the works of God (we are talking of those performed through man) are merits, in the sense that they are not sins.

7. The works of righteous people would be deadly, if they were not feared to be deadly by these righteous people themselves in pious fear of God.

8. The works of men are all the more deadly when they are done without fear, and with pure and evil assurance.

9. To say, as it were, that works without Christ are dead, but not deadly, seems to be a dangerous surrender of the fear of God.

10. Indeed, it is very difficult to see how a work would be dead and nevertheless not a harmful and deadly sin.

11. Presumption cannot be avoided, nor can there be true hope, unless the condemning judgment is feared in every work.

12. Sins are truly venial in the sight of God, when they are feared by men to be deadly.

13. "Free Will" after the fall is nothing but a word, and as long as it is doing what is within it, it is committing deadly sin.

14. "Free Will" after the fall has the potentiality toward good as an unrealizable capacity only; towards evil, however, always a realizable one.[2]

15. Nor was free will able to remain as a realizable potentiality in the state of innocence. Even there it was an unrealizable possibility, not to speak of making any progress toward the good.

16. A man who thinks that he wants to attain righteousness by doing what is in him is adding sin to sin, so that he becomes doubly guilty.

17. To say this does not mean to give cause for-despair but rather for humility, and for stirring up the eagerness to seek the grace of Christ.

18. It is certain that a man must completely despair of himself in order to become fit to obtain the grace of Christ.

19. The one who beholds what is invisible of God, through the perception of what is made [cf. Rom. 1:20], is not rightly called a theologian.

20. But rather the one who perceives what is visible of God, God's 'backside' [Ex. 33:23], by beholding the sufferings and the cross.

[2] The contrast here, and in the next thesis, is between "subiectiva potentia" and "activa potentia".

21. The 'theologian of glory' calls the bad good and the good bad. The 'theologian of the cross' says what a thing is.

22. That wisdom which beholds the invisible things of God as perceived from works,—puffs up, blinds, and hardens man altogether.

23. The law also brings about the wrath of God,—it kills, reviles, makes guilty, judges, condemns all that is not in Christ.

24. Nevertheless, this wisdom is not bad nor is the law to be fled. But without a theology of the cross, man misuses the best things in the worst way.

25. The one who does much 'work' is not the righteous one, but the one who, without 'work', has much faith in Christ.

26. The law says: "Do this!", and it never is done. Grace says: "Believe in this one!", and forthwith everything is done.

27. The work of Christ shall rightly be called an active work, and ours that which is worked, so the one which is worked is well-pleasing unto God, thanks to the active work.

28. The love of God does not find its object but rather creates it. Human love starts with the object.

SELECTED BIBLIOGRAPHY
FOR FURTHER READING ON LUTHER

Biography

Bainton, Roland H., *Here I Stand*, Nashville: Abingdon-Cokesbury Press, 1950; New York: New American Library, 1955 (Paperback).

Boehmer, Heinrich, *Road to Reformation*, trs. by John W. Doberstein and Theodore G. Tappert, Philadelphia: Muhlenberg Press, 1946; New York: Meridian, 1957 (Paperback).

Rupp, Gordon, *Luther's Progress to the Diet of Worms*, Chicago: Wilcox and Follett Co., 1951.

Thiel, Rudolf, *Luther*, trs. by Gustav K. Wiencke, Philadelphia: Muhlenberg Press, 1955.

Luther in Context

Bornkamm, Heinrich, *Luther's World of Thought*, trs. by Martin H. Bertram, St. Louis: Concordia Publishing House, 1958.

Fife, Robert H., *The Revolt of Martin Luther*, New York: Columbia University, 1957.

Schwiebert, E. G., *Luther and His Times*, St. Louis: Concordia Publishing House, 1950.

Reformation Period

Grimm, Harold J., *The Reformation Era*, New York: The Macmillan Co., 1954.

Harbison, E. Harris, *The Age of Reformation*, Ithaca, N. Y.: Cornell University Press, 1955.

Holborn, Hajo, *A History of Modern Germany, The Reformation*, New York: Alfred A. Knopf, 1959.

Lindsay, T. M., *Luther and the Reformation*, Grand Rapids, Michigan: Zondervan, 1955.

The New Cambridge Modern History, II, The Reformation, Cambridge at the University Press, 1958.

Theological Views

Pauck, Wilhelm, *The Heritage of the Reformation*, Glencoe, Illinois: Free Press, 1950, 1960.

Rupp, Gordon, *The Righteousness of God*, London: Hodder and Stoughton, 1953.

Watson, Philip S., *Let God Be God*, Philadelphia: Muhlenberg Press, 1950.

Special Problems

Bizer, Ernst, *Fides ex Auditu, Eine Untersuchung über die Entdeckung der Gerechtigkeit Gottes durch Martin Luther*, Neukirchen Kreis Moers, 1958.

Cranz, F. Edward, *An Essay on the Development of Luther's Thought on Justice, Law, and Society*, Cambridge, Mass.: Harvard University Press, 1959.

Erikson, Erik H., *Young Man Luther; A Study in Psychoanalysis and History*, New York: W. W. Norton and Co., 1958.

Forell, George W., *Faith Active in Love*, New York: The American Press, 1954.

Gyllenkrok, Axel, *Rechtfertigung und Heiligung in der frühen evangelischen Theologie Luthers*, Uppsala und Wiesbaden, 1952.

Lazareth, William H., *Luther on the Christian Home*, Philadelphia: Muhlenberg Press, 1960.

Pelikan, Jaroslav, *Luther's Works, Companion Volume, Luther the Expositor*, St. Louis: Concordia Publishing House, 1959.

Prenter, Regin, *Spiritus Creator*, trs. by John M. Jensen, Philadelphia: Muhlenberg Press, 1953.

Sasse, Hermann, *This Is My Body; Luther's Contention for the Real Presence in the Sacrament of the Altar*, Minneapolis: Augsburg Publishing House, 1959.

Vajta, Vilmos, *Luther on Worship*, trs. and condensed by U. S. Leupold, Philadelphia: Muhlenberg Press, 1958.

Wingren, Gustaf, *Luther on Vocation*, trs. by Carl C. Rasmussen, Philadelphia: Muhlenberg Press, 1957.

General Essays
Martin Luther Lectures, Decorah, Iowa: Luther College Press.
  Volume I—*Luther Today*, 1957
        II—*More About Luther*, 1958
        III—*The Mature Luther*, 1959
        IV—*Luther and Culture*, 1960

INDEX

INDEX OF SUBJECTS

Repentance (*cont'd*)
proceeds from law of God,
72–73
Reservation, 319, 320, 321, 429,
432, 436, 437
Reserved cases, 436–37
Resolutio, 439 n.
Restitution, 400
Resurrection, 29, 35, 38, 118,
212–14
Revelation, book of, 254
Revocation by Isolani, 251
Rhine-toll, 430
Righteousness, xxv, xxix, 16, 17,
20–21, 24, 54, 86–96, 113,
114, 116, 119, 123, 125,
129, 130, 131, 133, 138,
144, 147, 150, 151, 154,
501, 502
active, 101, 102, 103, 104,
106, 107, 108
ceremonial, 100
Christ's, 86–89, 210
Christian, 100, 104, 105, 106,
107, 109, 110, 130, 131
civil, 100
formal, 127
God's, xv
God's gift, 11, 12
heavenly, 108
imputed, 101
of faith, 101, 115, 150
of the law, 100
passive, 101, 102, 104, 105,
106, 108
by works, 199
Romagna, 441
Roman Catholic, xiii, xxv, xxxii,
166, 403
Roman Church, 363, 500
Roman court, 7
Roman emperor, 477–78
Roman empire, 184, 477–78,
479–80
Romanists, 34, 323, 328, 330,
406, 409, 412, 416, 418–19,
420, 421, 449, 459, 467,
479
Romans, epistle to, 19–34

Romans, lecture on, xvii, xviii
Rome, xvi, 34, 323, 421, 429,
430, 431, 443, 444, 459
Rosaries, 164
Rules and regulations, 331
Ruling class, 405, 433

Sacrament, sacraments, xv, xxiii,
xxvi, xxxi, xxxii, xxxiii, 109,
159, 213–14, 218, 227, 228,
232–33, 234–39, 243–45,
253, 254, 256 n., 271–72,
285, 300, 301, 307, 324,
326, 340, 343, 356–57, 414
sacramental, 249
and sign, 260–61, 279, 298–
301
seven, 256, 324
three, 256, 324
two, 357–58
use of both kinds, 255–59, 261
Sacramentum, 327
Sacrifices, 104
Saint, saints, xxix, 37–40, 133,
146, 150, 151, 152, 153,
155, 158, 159, 160, 161,
163, 164, 200, 212–13, 496
St. Peter's, xx, 498
Salvation, 18, 23, 27, 31, 60–
61, 108, 110, 113, 114, 123,
125, 199, 210, 238, 274,
295, 344, 381, 492, 493,
495
Sanctification, 159, 160, 204,
209, 211–15
Satan, 99, 161, 172, 174, 192,
194, 203. *See also* Devil
Satisfaction, xviii, xx, 151, 295,
322, 323, 324, 490, 493
Saxony, 8 n.
Sceptics, 167, 168, 169, 171
Schismatics, 261
Scholastics, xvi, 357
Scholastic theology, 166
theologians, xi, xiii
Schoolmen, 110, 113, 115, 127,
131, 140, 144, 146, 150,
152, 153, 159
Schools, monastic, 446–47

INDEX OF SCRIPTURAL REFERENCES

OLD TESTAMENT